(Continued on back endsheets)

South Slavic Writers Before World War II

Dictionary of Literary Biography® • Volume One Hundred Forty-Seven

South Slavic Writers Before World War II

Edited by
Vasa D. Mihailovich
University of North Carolina at Chapel Hill

A Bruccoli Clark Layman Book

An International Thomson Publishing Company

I(T)P
NEW YORK • LONDON • BONN • BOSTON • DETROIT • MADRID
MELBOURNE • MEXICO CITY • PARIS • SINGAPORE • TOKYO
TORONTO • WASHINGTON • ALBANY NY • BELMONT CA • CINCINNATI OH

Contents

Authors by Nationality

Bulgarian

Elisaveta Bagryana
Khristo Botev
Elin Pelin
Aleko Konstantinov
Pencho Slaveykov

Ivan Vazov
Peyo Yavorov
Yordan Yovkov

Croatian

Marin Držić
Ivan Gundulić
Jure Kaštelan
Ante Kovačić
Silvije Strahimir Kranjčević
Miroslav Krleža
Ranko Marinković

Antun Gustav Matoš
Ivan Mažuranić
Vladimir Nazor
Vjenceslav Novak
August Šenoa
Augustin ("Tin") Ujević
Ivo Vojnović

Macedonian

Kočo Racin

Serbian

Ivo Andrić
Miloš Crnjanski
Jovan Dučić
Vuk Stefanović Karadžić
Laza K. Lazarević
Desanka Maksimović
Momčilo Nastasijević

Petar II Petrović Njegoš
Branislav Nušić
Dositej Obradović
Rastko Petrović
Milan Rakić
Borisav ("Bora") Stanković

Slovene

Ivan Cankar
Edvard Kocbek
Srečko Kosovel
Francè Prešeren

Ivan Tavčar
Prežihov Voranc
Oton Župančič

Plan of the Series

The advisory board, the editors, and the publisher of the *Dictionary of Literary Biography* are joined in endorsing Mark Twain's declaration. The literature of a nation provides an inexhaustible resource of permanent worth. We intend to make literature and its creators better understood and more accessible to students and the reading public, while satisfying the standards of teachers and scholars.

To meet these requirements, *literary biography* has been construed in terms of the author's achievement. The most important thing about a writer is his writing. Accordingly, the entries in *DLB* are career biographies, tracing the development of the author's canon and the evolution of his reputation.

The purpose of *DLB* is not only to provide reliable information in a convenient format but also to place the figures in the larger perspective of literary history and to offer appraisals of their accomplishments by qualified scholars.

The publication plan for *DLB* resulted from two years of preparation. The project was proposed to Bruccoli Clark by Frederick C. Ruffner, president of the Gale Research Company, in November 1975. After specimen entries were prepared and typeset, an advisory board was formed to refine the entry format and develop the series rationale. In meetings held during 1976, the publisher, series editors, and advisory board approved the scheme for a comprehensive biographical dictionary of persons who contributed to North American literature. Editorial work on the first volume began in January 1977, and it was published in 1978. In order to make *DLB* more than a reference tool and to compile volumes that individually have claim to status as literary history, it was decided to organize vol-

umes by topic, period, or genre. Each of these freestanding volumes provides a biographical-bibliographical guide and overview for a particular area of literature. We are convinced that this organization — as opposed to a single alphabet method — constitutes a valuable innovation in the presentation of reference material. The volume plan necessarily requires many decisions for the placement and treatment of authors who might properly be included in two or three volumes. In some instances a major figure will be included in separate volumes, but with different entries emphasizing the aspect of his career appropriate to each volume. Ernest Hemingway, for example, is represented in *American Writers in Paris, 1920–1939* by an entry focusing on his expatriate apprenticeship; he is also in *American Novelists, 1910–1945* with an entry surveying his entire career. Each volume includes a cumulative index of the subject authors and articles. Comprehensive indexes to the entire series are planned.

With volume ten in 1982 it was decided to enlarge the scope of *DLB*. By the end of 1986 twenty-one volumes treating British literature had been published, and volumes for Commonwealth and Modern European literature were in progress. The series has been further augmented by the *DLB Yearbooks* (since 1981) which update published entries and add new entries to keep the *DLB* current with contemporary activity. There have also been *DLB Documentary Series* volumes which provide biographical and critical source materials for figures whose work is judged to have particular interest for students. One of these companion volumes is entirely devoted to Tennessee Williams.

We define literature as the *intellectual commerce of a nation:* not merely as belles lettres but as that ample and complex process by which ideas are generated, shaped, and transmitted. *DLB* entries are not limited to "creative writers" but extend to other figures who in their time and in their way influenced the mind of a people. Thus the series encompasses historians, journalists, publishers, and screenwriters. By this means readers of *DLB* may be aided to perceive literature not as cult scripture in the keeping of intellectual high priests but firmly positioned at the center of a nation's life.

DLB includes the major writers appropriate to each volume and those standing in the ranks immediately behind them. Scholarly and critical counsel has been sought in deciding which minor figures to include and how full their entries should be. Wherever possible, useful references are made to figures who do not warrant separate entries.

Each *DLB* volume has a volume editor responsible for planning the volume, selecting the figures for inclusion, and assigning the entries. Volume editors are also responsible for preparing, where appropriate, appendices surveying the major periodicals and literary and intellectual movements for their volumes, as well as lists of further readings. Work on the series as a whole is coordinated at the Bruccoli Clark Layman editorial center in Columbia, South Carolina, where the editorial staff is responsible for accuracy of the published volumes.

One feature that distinguishes *DLB* is the illustration policy – its concern with the iconography of literature. Just as an author is influenced by his surroundings, so is the reader's understanding of the author enhanced by a knowledge of his environment. Therefore *DLB* volumes include not only drawings, paintings, and photographs of authors, often depicting them at various stages in their careers, but also illustrations of their families and places where they lived. Title pages are regularly reproduced in facsimile along with dust jackets for modern authors. The dust jackets are a special feature of *DLB* because they often document better than anything else the way in which an author's work was perceived in its own time. Specimens of the writers' manuscripts are included when feasible.

Samuel Johnson rightly decreed that "The chief glory of every people arises from its authors." The purpose of the *Dictionary of Literary Biography* is to compile literary history in the surest way available to us – by accurate and comprehensive treatment of the lives and work of those who contributed to it.

The *DLB* Advisory Board

Introduction

Dictionary of Literary Biography volume 147, *South Slavic Writers Before World War II,* covers five literatures – Bulgarian, Croatian, Macedonian, Serbian, and Slovenian – all of which have existed on the Balkan peninsula for more than a thousand years. The southern Slavs, consisting of Serbs, Bulgarians, Croats, Slovenes, and Macedonians, belong to the Slavic race in eastern Europe. Because of the lack of documentation, much of their earliest history is shrouded in guesswork and reconstruction, resulting in broad suppositions. What is generally known is that they migrated to the Balkans from an area east of the Carpathian Mountains between the third and the seventh centuries. Their initial minor tribal differences became increasingly pronounced; consequently, the Slovenes organized their first state in the eighth century, the Bulgarians and the Serbs in the ninth, and the Croats in the tenth. Most of these states were short lived and often fell prey to more powerful states, with the Bulgarians and the Serbs maintaining their independence the longest. By the fifteenth century, however, all southern Slavs were subjected either to the Turkish or Austrian dominations that lasted several centuries. The struggle for renewed independence was long and bloody; by the nineteenth century the Serbs had regained their independence, to be followed in the next several decades by other South Slavic kin.

The writers presented here are chosen as the best representatives of their respective literatures. In a sense this selection can serve indirectly as a history of each of these literatures in all genres. The alphabetical listing, though artificial, is preferred for several reasons: to avoid any impression of partiality – within the Balkan framework always a thorny potentiality; to show that these literatures can be treated individually or as a group; and, with the demise of Yugoslavia, to lay to rest this artificial political term that is no longer valid – even though the term *South Slav* means Yugoslav. At the same time the grouping of South Slav writers in one volume shows that, despite different historical, political, religious, social, and cultural conditions, they have followed similar paths, undergone almost identical influences, and showed remarkable kinship at various stages of development. Among the traits common to all of these literatures, one can point to their

similar beginnings during the conversion to Christianity in the ninth century; to significant oral literature, including traces of prehistoric pagan motifs; and to an almost simultaneous following of Western literary trends during different periods.

The Bulgarians occupy the easternmost part of the Balkan Peninsula, bordered clockwise by the Black Sea, Turkey, Greece, Macedonia, Serbia, and Romania. Their history is somewhat different from that of the rest of the South Slavs in that the original Bulgars came behind the Huns from Asia and an area between the Urals and the Volga, and they were heavily mixed with various Asiatic tribes, such as Huns, Avars, and even the Khazars. After they went to the Balkans and mixed with other Slavic tribes already there, they were assimilated by the Slavs in language, religion, culture, customs, and local institutions. By the time they accepted Christianity in the ninth century, they had been completely Slavicized.

Bulgarian literature, like most South Slav literatures, emerged after the Bulgarians had accepted Christianity from Byzantium. There must have been oral literature before that time in the form of folk songs and tales, but there are no traces of them except for pagan motifs in later works, either because there were no ways of recording them in a written form or, if there were, because they were not preserved.

The first literary works came into being almost entirely because of the needs of the fledgling church. Thus the church not only gave the impetus for literature but remained its main promoter for a long time. The first works, inspired by the missionaries Cyril (826 or 827–869) and Methodius (815–885), were closely connected with liturgy and were translated from the Greek. Cyril and Methodius devised an alphabet called Cyrillic, which was based on a Slavic dialect around Salonika and which later became the liturgical language of the Orthodox Slavs – Old Church Slavonic – that is still in use.

In the next five centuries Bulgarian literature remained church oriented, producing liturgical works, lives of saints and rulers, apocrypha, chronicles, and translations of Greek texts, mostly scripture. Even during the Turkish occupation for more than four centuries, a severely limited literary life continued, almost exclusively in monasteries, where chronicles were written and translations were made. The thoroughness of the Turkish occupation, however, made impossible any contact with the rest of Europe, precluded any public cultural life, and severely retarded literature for centuries.

The first signs of revival became noticeable during the late eighteenth and the first half of the nineteenth centuries, when Sofroni Vrachanski (1739–1813) wrote the first autobiography in Bulgarian literature and Petar Beron (1800–1871) introduced the ideas of the Enlightenment through tales, fables, and parables. By then the writers were using the vernacular Bulgarian, a dialect that had evolved into a full-fledged South Slavic language, leaving the Old Church Slavonic for church use only. Petko Slaveykov (1827–1895) was the first Bulgarian writer of stature. In 1842 the first Bulgarian verse was published in a periodical, *Lyuboslovie* (The Literature Lover), in Smyrna, Turkey. The first novel, *Neshtastna familia* (The Unfortunate Family) by Vasil Drumev (1840–1901), appeared in 1860, and the first play, *Raina Knyaginya* (Princess Raina) by Dobri Voinikov (1833–1878), was staged in 1866. During the second half of the nineteenth century all Bulgarians were preoccupied with national revival, and most leading writers, including Khristo Botev (1847–1876), Lyuben Karavelov (1834–1879), and Ivan Vazov (1850–1921), devoted much of their talents to writing works that inspired the nation in the struggle for liberation from the Turks. Vazov's epic novel *Pod igoto* (Under the Yoke, 1888) is an apotheosis of this struggle. The collection and publication of oral literature in the form of folk songs, tales, and legends was also used for this purpose. Moreover, the entire literature was imbued with the spirit of Romanticism.

Realism was somewhat late in coming, but upon its arrival in the last decades of the nineteenth century it contributed to the most prolific period in Bulgarian literature. The main concerns of the realists were the conditions and changes of village life and the problems arising from the growing urban communities. The main representatives of this trend were Vazov and Aleko Konstantinov (1863–1897). Alongside the realists were the neo-Romanticists as well as the nascent modernists. This fruitful period carried over into the twentieth century. Under the influence of symbolist and naturalist writing from France, the Bulgarian modernists developed into a strong force that included the aforementioned literary currents along with expressionism and futurism. The leading symbolist poets were Teodor Trayanov (1882–1945) and Dimcho Debe-

lyanov (1887–1916). The writings of Stoyan Mikhailovski (1856–1927), Georgi Stamatov (1869–1942), Peyo Yavorov (1878–1914), and Pencho Slaveykov (1866–1912) gave expression to the disillusionment with modern life that sometimes bordered on nihilism. The writers in the circle *Misŭl* (Thought), led by Yavorov and Slaveykov, were especially vocal in their rebellion against traditions and in their efforts to open literature to wider international influences. Many of these writers perished in World War I.

Literature during the interim between the two world wars was characterized by further disillusionment and social unrest, attracting many writers to the leftist and Communist causes. However, few of these writers possessed adequate talent and, consequently, produced few works of lasting value. Some of these writers and most of the others who were not Marxists were affiliated with the journal *Zlatorog*. They included Yordan Yovkov (1880–1937) and Elisaveta Bagryana (1893–1991), while another outstanding writer, Elin Pelin (1877–1949), shied away from all groups. However, the interwar period, despite producing some good works by Yovkov, Bagryana, and Elin Pelin, could not measure up to the frenzied activity before World War I.

The Croats migrated with other Slavic tribes to the Balkan Peninsula in the early centuries of the millennium. They occupied a crescentlike territory in the western Balkans, centering around what is now Zagreb and spreading into the Slavonia, a Pannonian region north of the Sava river, parts of Bosnia and Herzegovina, and along the Adriatic coast.

Croatian literature also goes back to the conversion to Christianity by Cyril and Methodius in the ninth century. These missionaries and their followers introduced church-related writings in Old Church Slavonic but written in Glagolitic, an alphabet originally devised by Cyril and Methodius that was later influenced by the local tongue, thus creating a link with other South Slav literatures. The first preserved text written in this alphabet is *Bašćanska ploča* (The Baska Tablet, circa 1100) from the island of Krk. During the short-lived independence from the ninth century to the end of the eleventh, the Croats managed to create literature adequate for church needs — prayers, homilies, apocrypha, and hagiographies. In addition, there were translations of Greek tales and legends, such as the saga of Troy and the romance of Alexander the Great. The vernacular, as well as folk literature, penetrated more and more the Old Church Slavonic, so that what was a common language gradually acquired its own characteristics. Most of the works of that period have been lost.

The independent Croatian state lasted only until 1102; afterward the Croats lived under Hungarian or Austrian rule until 1918. However, literature continued to be written during the ensuing centuries. The first known piece of poetry is contained in *Misal Kneza Novaka* (The Missal of Prince Novak, 1368), also written in Glagolitic. All these works, church-related or in the vernacular, though limited in subject matter and scope, represent the necessary preparation for and transition to the blossoming of literature in cultural centers along the Adriatic coast from the second half of the fifteenth century to about 1835. The Adriatic coast escaped the Turkish occupation and was able to develop in every respect, especially in the Republic of Dubrovnik, which experienced a remarkable flowering in the sixteenth and seventeenth centuries. Culturally, this area was under the direct influence of Italian humanism and Renaissance and Petrarchan poetry. Many poets were educated in Italy and even wrote for the most part or exclusively in Latin, although some wrote bilingually. More important, even though the general tenor and spirit of their works were unmistakably under the Italian influence, the Croatian poets of Dalmatia were able, mainly under the inspiration of folk literature, to give their works a native color, not only in the language and settings but also in their understanding of the function and purpose of literature. Among the many writers from this area and period most outstanding are Marko Marulić (1450–1520), Petar Hektorović (1487–1572), Marin Držić (1508–1567), and Ivan Gundulić (1589–1638).

As the Republic of Dubrovnik began to decline, so did its literature. The center of Croatian culture began moving northward and inland. Although the conditions there were much less favorable due to the unsettled political and social conditions, incessant fighting against the Turks and new writers gradually emerged, thus assuring continuity in Croatian literature.

The Counter-Reformation and the growth of centers such as Zagreb enabled writers to assert themselves. These efforts were led at first by didactic writers, such as Andrija Kačić Miošić (1704–1760) and Matija Reljković (1732–1798), but later, around the middle of the nineteenth century, more accomplished writers became predominant, ushering in the modern period in Croatian literature.

This century saw the rise of the Illyrian movement, which had as its main idea the unification of all South Slavs into one state. Its leader, Ljudevit Gaj (1809–1872), advocated a reform of the standard literary language similar to that of the Serbian language reformer Vuk Karadžić (1787–1864). During this period Croatian romanticism, influenced by European models, became the leading literary mode, represented by several outstanding writers such as Stanko Vraz (1810–1851), Ivan Mažuranić (1814–1890), Petar Preradović (1818–1872), and August Šenoa (1838–1881).

As in other South Slav literatures, romanticism gave way to realism in the second half of the century. The change from rural to urban society prompted writers, led by Ante Kovačić (1854–1889), Josip Kozarac (1858–1906), and Vjenceslav Novak (1859–1905), to address the burning issues of the times. At the turn of the century, as a reaction to realism, a strong movement called Moderna (borrowing from Hermann Bahr) emerged. As its name implies, Moderna brought a new, invigorating, and cosmopolitan spirit into Croatian literature. It was led by Milan Marjanović (1879–1955) and Antun Gustav Matoš (1873–1914). Several outstanding writers, all connected with Moderna in one way or another, made their appearance: Silvije Strahimir Kranjčević (1865–1908), Ivo Vojnović (1857–1929), Vladimir Nazor (1876–1949), Milan Begović (1876–1948), and others. Several of these writers continued to be active after World War I. The bustling interwar period was personified by the towering figure of Miroslav Krleža (1893–1981), a prolific Marxist writer who, placing freedom of the arts above his leftist leanings, led the avant-garde movement and set the tone for decades. Among other outstanding writers at this time were Antun Branko Šimić (1898–1925), Augustin ("Tin") Ujević (1891–1955), and Nikola Šop (1904–1982).

The story of Macedonian literature is one of the most interesting in the annals of world literature. Originating approximately at the same time as other South Slav literatures, it was subjected to the historical vicissitudes of the Macedonian people, much more so than for any other South Slav nation. Nestled between the Serbs, Bulgarians, and Greeks, the Macedonians have had difficulties asserting themselves; the similarity of their language to both Bulgarian and Serbian and identical religious denominations leading to sectional rivalries have not made it any easier. After centuries of Turkish occupation, they were able to establish for the first time their own republic within the state of Yugoslavia only after World War II.

Like the Serbs and Bulgarians, the Macedonians contributed to the first awakenings of literature in the ninth century after the conversion to Christianity. The religious figures and cultural pioneers, led by Saint Klement (830–916), were instrumental in establishing the foundation of South Slavic culture, producing the first literary works in the process. However, the aforementioned rivalry among the Serbs, Bulgarians, and Greeks over their territory, along with centuries-old Turkish occupation, prevented the Macedonians from acquiring their independence before 1944 and from developing their literature until late in the nineteenth century. Even then, writers were under constant pressure to accept foreign supremacies that forbade the use of their language. Nevertheless, they were able to write poetry, fiction, and drama, although they could only publish them abroad. There are no writers of stature in the period before World War II except Kosta Kočo Racin (1908–1943), who published his magnum opus, *Beli mugri* (1939; translated as *White Dawns,* 1974), in Zagreb. Perhaps the most important literature during all these centuries was in the form of a large body of oral songs and tales, which had been collected all along but have been published only recently. The flowering of Macedonian literature came only after the official standards of the Macedonian language were created in 1944, when for the first time Macedonian writers were allowed to publish freely in their own language.

The Serbs migrated to the Balkan Peninsula with other South Slavs. They were able to establish their state in the ninth century, and they retained their independence well into the fifteenth century, although they lost most of it after the fateful battle with the Turks at Kosovo in 1389. At one time their empire covered a great deal of the Balkans. The Serbs occupy the central part of the peninsula, although they can be found in other areas as well. Because of the Turkish occupation, Serbia was reduced to a small territory, which forced many Serbs to migrate centuries ago westward and northward to other parts, such as Croatia and Vojvodina, where they were prized by the Austrians for their defense against the Turks. In the nineteenth century they gradually became the first South Slavs to regain their independence. They were also instrumental in helping others gain theirs, albeit in the common state of Yugoslavia. Their religion is Eastern Orthodox, like that of the Bulgarians and Macedonians, and their language is almost identical with Croatian. It was called Serbian until 1918, and it is increasingly called that now.

Serbian literature also had its beginnings shortly after the conversion of the Serbs to Christianity in the ninth century. The national identity at that time centered on the church, which was closely affiliated with the Byzantine church and culture. When the brothers Cyril and Methodius devised a new alphabet and adapted it to a Slavic dialect, they and their followers not only initiated the creation of the material necessary for church services but also inspired other kinds of literature: church songs, hagiographies, encomiums, translations of medieval narratives such as *The Trojan War* and *Alexander the Great,* and folk songs. There were also folk poems imitating chansons de geste sung by the singers accompanying the First Crusade (1096–1097) passing through Serbian lands. The first truly artistic work is the illuminated *Miroslavljevo jevandjelje* (Miroslav's Gospel, twelfth century). From the twelfth through the fifteenth centuries the prosperous and enlightened Serbian kings, especially the founder of Serbian church and culture Saint Sava (1174–1236), fostered literature, resulting in several excellent biographies of kings and church leaders. This thriving period came to an end with the Serbian defeat by the Turks at Kosovo. After that, the only literature possible was in oral form, producing many exquisite heroic poems extolling the glorious past and keeping the national spirit and hope for the future alive during the several centuries of Turkish occupation. These epic poems were held in high esteem by, among others, Sir Walter Scott, Johann Wolfgang von Goethe, Aleksandr Pushkin, and Adam Mickiewicz, who translated them into their languages.

The revival of Serbian literature did not begin until the eighteenth century; it gathered momentum in the nineteenth, coinciding with the gradual restoration of national independence. It was primarily the work of the Serbs who had moved north to Vojvodina to escape the stifling Turkish occupation and had exposed themselves to the influences of Western ideas. The two pioneering figures, Dositej Obradović (1740?–1811) and Vuk Karadžić (1787–1864), are widely considered to be the fathers of modern Serbian literature. Obradović who traveled widely abroad, brought the spirit of rationalism and the Enlightenment to Serbian literature, and Karadžić devised a reform of the written Serbian language, compiled the first dictionary, wrote the first grammar, and collected and published folk songs and other oral literature.

From then on, Serbian literature made steady progress and to some extent made up for the lost centuries. It was fortunate that at the outset perhaps the best Serbian poet, Petar Petrović Njegoš (1813–1851), the prince-bishop of Montenegro, wrote several seminal works, most notably the epic play in verse *Gorski vijenac* (The Mountain Wreath, 1847), and set high standards that are yet unsurpassed. In some ways he initiated the Serbian Romantic movement around the middle of the nineteenth century, while other notable writers, including Branko Radičević (1824–1853), Jovan Jovanović Zmaj (1833–1904), Djura Jakšić (1832–1878), and Laza Kostić (1841–1910), also made valuable contributions to Romantic literature.

This movement, dominated by poetry, was short-lived, however, and it gave way in the second half of the nineteenth century to realism under the strong influence of realist writers from France and Russia. Realist writers, such as Milovan Glišić (1847–1908), Laza K. Lazarević (1851–1890), Janko Veselinović (1861–1905), Stevan Sremac (1855–1906), and others, reflected in their works the profound and rapid changes of their society. They excelled in short fiction, especially in the so-called village short story, while poetry and the novel were neglected.

At the turn of the century modernist European tendencies made their way into Serbian literature. The two poets most responsible for this development were Jovan Dučić (1871–1943) and Milan Rakić (1876–1938), both pupils of the French symbolists and Parnassians. They turned Serbian poetry away from traditional patriotic and love themes toward more subjective and complex concerns while approaching literature from the position of "art for art's sake." Modernist tendencies became even more pronounced after World War I, when a new generation of writers, disillusioned by the horrors of war, embraced the tenets of expressionism and other isms. Moreover, writers such as Ivo Andrić (1892–1975), Miloš Crnjanski (1893–1977), Rastko Petrović (1898–1949), and Momčilo Nastasijević (1894–1938) infused their works with a level of sophistication, maturity, and erudition unseen before.

In the interwar period Serbian writers truly opened themselves to the world, which was reflected in the universality of their art. The so-called modernists were joined by other groups – traditional realists, social activists, a Serbian branch of surrealism, folklorists, and strong loners. The period is characterized by bustling activity and a plethora of literary works, though few of outstanding quality. They were to come after World War II.

The Slovenes occupy the westernmost part of the Balkans and are in many ways more tuned to the Western world, especially Austria and Germany, than are their South Slavic brethren. They were the first South Slavs to establish their own state, in the eighth century, but it was short-lived. After they had lost their independence to Austria,

they did not recover it until 1918, and even then only as a part of Yugoslavia. In one way they were fortunate – they escaped Turkish domination. Like the Croats, they are predominantly Roman Catholic. They are the most homogenous of all South Slavs, along with the Bulgarians, and their language is somewhat less comprehensible to other South Slavs. They have miraculously survived culturally more than a thousand years of foreign domination.

The beginnings of Slovene literature were also connected with the Slovenes' acceptance of Christianity, although the first attempts at writing were most likely prompted by Irish monks rather than Cyril and Methodius. The first written works, created for religious purposes, were in Latin, but Cyril and Methodius offered the Slovenes translations of the Scriptures in their own tongue. Of those writings, only a few have been preserved: the so-called *Brižinski spomenici* (Freising Texts, tenth century) – named after the Bavarian city of Freisingen, where they were preserved and discovered – and some manuscripts of prayers and legal documents from the fourteenth and fifteenth centuries. Aside from those few preserved manuscripts, there was no Slovene literature to speak of until the sixteenth century.

The first Slovene book was printed in 1550 during the Protestant Reformation by the leader of the Slovene Protestant church, Primož Trubar (1508–1586), who helped create a Slovene literary language for that purpose. His efforts resulted in extensive literary activity: Adam Bohorič (circa 1520–circa 1600) wrote the grammar in Latin, Juri Dalmatin (circa 1547–1589) translated the Bible, and more than fifty books were printed. This pioneering activity came to an end with the defeat of the Reformation. The ensuing Counter-Reformation did relatively little for Slovene literature because the leading intelligentsia used German. The revival started in the second half of the eighteenth century, spurred by the Enlightenment policies of the Austrian government. Books – mostly of a didactic nature and about history, and even poetry – were again published in large numbers, along with literary journals. The revival was complete with the arrival of strong literary figures, led by Anton Linhart (1756–1795), Valentin Vodnik (1758–1819), and Franče Prešeren (1800–1849). They were aided by an influential linguist, Jernej Kopitar (1780–1844), who wrote the first scholarly Slovene grammar. The work of the greatest Slovene poet, Prešeren, gave Slovene literature a reputation equal to that of other South Slav literatures. His *Sonetni venec* (A Wreath of Sonnets, 1834) and the epic poem *Krst pri Savici* (1836; translated as "The Baptism on the Savica," 1985) belong to the best works in all of South Slav literature. Prešeren was also the main force behind the Romantic movement in Slovenia.

Romanticism gave way to realism in the second half of the nineteenth century. Writers found inspiration in history and in folk narratives and turned their attention to the realistic portrayal of everyday life. The contribution of the leading realists – Fran Levstik (1831–1887), Josip Stritar (1836–1923), Josip Jurčič (1844–1881), Janko Kersnik (1852–1897), Anton Aškerc (1856–1912), and Ivan Tavčar (1851–1923) – made it possible for later writers to raise Slovene literature to the European level, thanks primarily to the greatest Slovene writer of the twentieth century, Ivan Cankar (1876–1918). His short stories, novels, and plays not only gave substance to the rising modernist movement but also set new standards of excellence and pertinence. Other important modernists were Dragotin Kette (1876–1899), Josip Murn Aleksandrov (1879–1901), and Oton Župančič (1878–1949).

In the interwar period Slovene writers showed attitudes and concerns similar to those of other South Slavs by following European trends, depicting the conditions in the new state, and showing strong leftist leanings. Several new faces were complemented by a large volume of literary works. Writers such as Srečko Kosovel (1904–1926), Prežihov Voranc (1893–1950), and Ciril Kosmač (1910–1980) produced poetry and fiction of lasting value. They also prepared the ground for greater achievements after World War II.

As stated, the South Slav writers have been arranged alphabetically in order to avoid potential nationalistic bias. The selection of the authors is based on their generally recognized reputations as recorded in literary histories. The inclusion or exclusion of some authors may be debatable, but those represented in this volume have all left their marks on their respective literatures and have exerted strong influence on other writers. Although slightly more than half of the contributors are natives of South Slavic countries, the fact that they have spent most of their adult lives abroad has given them fresh vistas in analyzing the writers without neglecting the approaches they acquired in the old countries. As is customary with the *DLB* series, they have concentrated on the lives and works of their subjects rather than engaging in abstract discussions. Special attention has been given to the bibliographic material because in many instances the writers under discussion are presented here for the first time to the English-speaking world. Following the established practice of the series, the first editions are listed chronologically under Books, and translations, if any, are listed after original works, or under Editions in English – but not individual poems, stories, and other short pieces; those interested in a complete list of translations into English should consult the all-encompassing bibliographies compiled by Vasa D. Mihailovich and M. Matejić (Columbus, Ohio: Slavica, 1984) and supplements. In some instances works in lesser genres are listed under Other and Periodical Publications. Secondary sources, where available, are listed under Letters, Bibliographies, and Biographies as well as under References. The latter has concentrated on the most important sources to avoid cluttering; those published in English have been listed exhaustively, while those in the respective languages, which are often inaccessible to outside readers, have been restricted for practical reasons to the most outstanding ones. Finally, a Papers section is listed whenever known; the war conditions in the Balkans in the early 1990s, however, sometimes make it difficult to ascertain where papers are deposited.

The editor is grateful to the contributors for their labor of love, without which the volume would have been very difficult to complete. Similarly, gratitude is expressed to the publishers for their understanding and highly professional work, especially in obtaining necessary information and illustrations under rather difficult conditions due to the war.

It is hoped that this volume will help in filling the gap in informing the general public in the English-speaking world about South Slav literatures, which until now have been known outside their respective countries only to a small circle of specialists. It is also hoped that the volume will lead to additional endeavors toward the same goal, so that eventually the achievements of these writers will receive their well-deserved due in the family of world literature.

– Vasa D. Mihailovich

PRONUNCIATION GUIDE

a	*fa*ther or m*o*ther
e	w*e*ll or s*e*t
i	s*ee*k or s*i*ck
o	g*o* or b*a*ll
u	bl*ue* or t*oo* or p*u*t
j	*y*ell or bo*y*
lj	mi*lli*on or bri*lli*ant
nj	ca*ny*on or *n*ew

dj, ǵ	resi*due*
c	ca*ts*
ć, ḱ	*tu*ne
č	chur*ch*
š	*sh*e
ž	plea*s*ure
dž	*Ge*or*ge*
h	Ba*ch*
ŭ	*ea*rth

All other letters are pronounced the same way as in English. Some of the examples above are approximations because sometimes there are no exact equivalents in English.

Acknowledgments

This book was produced by Bruccoli Clark Layman, Inc. Karen L. Rood, senior editor for the *Dictionary of Literary Biography* series, and Darren Harris-Fain were the in-house editors.

Production coordinator is George F. Dodge. Photography editors are Bruce Andrew Bowlin and Josephine A. Bruccoli. Photographic copy work was performed by Joseph M. Bruccoli. Layout and graphics supervisor is Penney L. Haughton. Copy-editing supervisor is Bill Adams. Typesetting supervisor is Kathleen M. Flanagan. Julie E. Frick is editorial associate. The production staff includes Phyllis A. Avant, Ann M. Cheschi, Melody W. Clegg, Patricia Coate, Brigitte B. de Guzman, Denise W. Edwards, Joyce Fowler, Laurel M. Gladden, Mendy Gladden, Stephanie C. Hatchell, Leslie Haynsworth, Rebecca Mayo, Kathy Lawler Merlette, Jeff Miller, Pamela D. Norton, Delores I. Plastow, Patricia F. Salisbury, William L. Thomas, Jr., and Robert Trogden.

Walter W. Ross and Robert S. McConnell did library research. They were assisted by the following librarians at the Thomas Cooper Library of the University of South Carolina: Linda Holderfield and the interlibrary-loan staff; reference-department head Virginia Weathers; reference librarians Marilee Birchfield, Stefanie Buck, Cathy Eckman, Rebecca Feind, Jill Holman, Karen Joseph, Jean Rhyne, Kwamine Washington, and Connie Widney; circulation-department head Caroline ("Tucky") Taylor; and acquisitions-searching supervisor David Haggard.

The editors would like to express their gratitude to Professors Lyubomira Parpulova-Gribble and Peter Scherber for their unselfish assistance in giving advice and supplying illustrations.

Dictionary of Literary Biography® • Volume One Hundred Forty-Seven

South Slavic Writers Before World War II

Dictionary of Literary Biography

Ivo Andrić

(9 October 1892 – 13 March 1975)

E. Celia Hawkesworth
University of London

BOOKS: *Ex Ponto* (Zagreb: Književni jug, 1918);
Nemiri (Zagreb: Sv. Kugli, 1920);
Put Alije Djerzeleza (Belgrade: Cvijanović, 1920);
Pripovetke I (Belgrade: Srpska književna zadruga, 1924);
Pripovetke (Belgrade: Srpska književna zadruga, 1931);
Pripovetke II (Belgrade: Srpska književna zadruga, 1936);
Na Drini ćuprija (Belgrade: Prosveta, 1945);
Travnička hronika (Belgrade: Državni izdavački zavod Jugoslavije, 1945);
Gospodjica (Sarajevo: Svjetlost, 1945);
Pripovjetke (Zagreb: Matica hrvatska, 1948);
Prokleta avlija (Novi Sad: Matica srpska, 1954);
Kuća na osami (Belgrade: Prosveta, 1976).

Editions: *Sabrana dela,* 17 volumes, edited by Vera Stojić, Petar Džadžić, Muharem Pervić, and Radovan Vučković (Belgrade: Prosveta / Sarajevo: Svjetlost / Zagreb: Mladost, 1982) — comprises volume 1: *Na Drini ćuprija;* volume 2: *Travnička hronika;* volume 3: *Gospodjica;* volume 4: *Prokleta avlija;* volume 5: *Nemirna godina;* volume 6: *Žedj;* volume 7: *Jelena, žena koje nema;* volume 8: *Znakovi;* volume 9: *Deca;* volume 10: *Staze, lica, predeli;* volume 11: *Ex Ponto, Nemiri, Lirika;* volume 12: *Istorija i legenda;* volume 13: *Umetnik i njegovo delo;* volume 14: *Znakovi pored puta;* volume 15: *Kuća na osami;* volume 16: *Omerpaša Latas;* volume 17: *Sveske.*

Editions in English: "The Žepa Bridge," translated by L. Vidaković, *Slavonic Review,* 14 (1926): 398–405;

Ivo Andrić in 1920

"Gjerzelez at the Inn," translated by N. B. Jopson, *Slavonic and East European Review,* 14 (July 1935): 13–19;

"Gjerzelez at the Gypsy Fair," translated by Jopson, *Slavonic and East European Review,* 14 (April 1936): 556–563;

Bosnian Story, translated by Kenneth Johnstone (London: Lincolns Prager, 1948); published as *Bosnian Chronicle,* translated by Joseph Hitrec (New York: Knopf, 1963); published as *The Days of the Consuls,* translated by Celia Hawkesworth (London & Boston: Forest Books, 1992);

The Bridge on the Drina, translated by Lovett Edwards (New York: Macmillan, 1959; London: Allen & Unwin, 1959);

Devil's Yard, translated by Johnstone (New York: Grove Press, 1962; London: Calder, 1964); published as *The Damned Yard,* translated by Hawkesworth (London & Boston: Forest Books, 1992);

The Vizier's Elephant: Three Novellas, translated by Drenka Willen (New York: Harcourt, Brace & World, 1962);

The Woman from Sarajevo, translated by Hitrec (New York: Knopf, 1965; London: Calder & Boyars, 1966);

"The Story of a Bridge," "Miracle at Olovo," and "Neighbors," translated by Michael Scammell in *Death of a Simple Giant and Other Modern Yugoslav Stories,* edited by Branko Alan Lenski (New York: Vanguard, 1965);

"The Climbers" and "The Bridge on the Žepa," in *Yugoslav Short Stories,* translated by Svetozar Koljević (London & New York: Oxford University Press, The World's Classics, 1966);

The Pasha's Concubine and Other Tales, translated by Hitrec (New York: Knopf, 1968);

The Development of Spiritual Life in Bosnia under the Influence of Turkish Rule, translated by Ž. B. Juričić and John F. Loud (Durham, N.C.: Duke University Press, 1991) – comprises Andrić's Ph.D. dissertation (1924).

Conversation with Goya and Signs by the Roadside, translated by Hawkesworth and Andrew Harvey (London: Menard Press, 1992).

Ivo Andrić's international importance as a major twentieth-century European writer was acknowledged in 1961, when he was awarded the Nobel Prize for Literature. While most of his works are set in his native Bosnia in specific historical settings, they are both timeless and universal: Bosnia is a microcosm of human society, highlighting its potential for national, cultural, and religious misunderstanding and conflict. All Andrić's works are shaped by a wise, balanced, humane philosophy which does not shrink from recognizing brutality in human interaction but is directed toward harmony as a constant, if unattainable, impulse of humanity. Andrić's dominant symbol of the bridge stands for this fundamental need to overcome divisions and obstacles, to connect a vision of harmony with fragmented, brutal, hate-ridden reality.

Ivo Andrić, the only child of Catholic parents, was born on 9 October 1892 in Travnik, the old center of Ottoman administration in Bosnia. When his father, Ivan Antun Andrić, died in 1894, Ivo's mother, Katarina Andrić, took him to her sister-in-law in Višegrad, a small town with a well-known bridge spanning the river Drina. He spent his formative years in Višegrad and attended elementary school there. In "Staze" (Paths, 1940) he describes the profound effect of the surroundings in which he grew up in a short passage of reflective prose, which came to be one of his favorite genres:

> It was on these paths, which the wind sweeps and the rain washes, which the sun infects and disinfects, where you meet only exhausted livestock and silent people with hard faces, it was on these paths that I founded my dream about the riches and beauty of the world. It was here that, uneducated, weak and empty-handed, I was happy with an intoxicating happiness, happy because of all that was not here, which could not be and never would be.... And on all the roads and highways I passed along in later life, I lived only from that meagre happiness, from my Višegrad thoughts about the riches and beauty of the created world. For, beneath all the roads of the world, there always ran, visible and sensible only to me, the sharp Višegrad path, from the day I left it until today. It was on it that I measured my step and adapted my stride. It never left me, all my life.

Višegrad – with its mixed Catholic, Orthodox, Muslim, and Jewish community among the rugged hills of Bosnia – is the setting for many of Andrić's works. This background provided his choice of themes and point of departure throughout his writing career. The four years he spent in elementary school there were the happiest of his formal education and evidently helped foster in him the fascination with books and the life of the imagination that was to stay with him always. His home was humble, and, like all the poor houses of Bosnia, it would have contained no books except possibly one or two reference works or church calendars. Even secondary school offered little or no literature, and during his school years in Sarajevo there were only three or four stationery shops which also

Andrić during an Allied air raid on Belgrade in 1944

stocked a few books. Andrić has described how he used to spend hours as a schoolboy in front of the window of one of these shops – for him the only window into the world – and at night he would go home and dream about it: "Then it was no longer an ordinary shop window, with books in it, but . . . a part of some constellation towards which I was drawn with intense longing, but also with the painful realisation that it was inaccessible to me." He would visit this window every day, wondering what was hidden behind the names of the writers and titles and making up his own meanings for them. Andrić describes this experience as the beginning of his writing – not on paper but in his mind and thoughts. He attended the high school in Sarajevo from 1902 until 1912, when he registered at the University of Zagreb. The following year he transferred to Vienna, where he began to show signs of the tuberculosis which had killed his father and his three uncles. He requested permission to leave Vienna on health grounds and to continue his studies in Russia. It is likely that he was motivated also by a political protest by fellow Slav students in Vienna encouraging Slavs to boycott German-speaking centers and to move to Slav universities. Early in 1914 Andrić transferred to Kraków. While he was there,

in the first months of 1914 Andrić began to contribute reviews, poems, and notices of art exhibitions to several Zagreb periodicals. Early in June an anthology of *Hrvatska mlada lirika* (New Croatian Lyric Verse) appeared in Zagreb, including six poems by Andrić. The poems, and others that he published at this time, are typical of the age, imbued with a neoromantic melancholy that contrasts with the active political commitment of his generation.

Andrić had vigorously allied himself to the Young Bosnia Movement, dedicated to violent revolutionary action and a belief that a revolution in the spiritual and intellectual life of individuals had to precede radical social and political change. In 1911 a group of radical schoolboys and students in Sarajevo had founded the "Croato-Serb or Serbo-Croat or Yugoslav Progressive Youth Organisation," with the nineteen-year-old Andrić as its first president. Among the first to join the new society was Gavrilo Princip, who was to fire the shots that killed Archduke Francis Ferdinand in Sarajevo in 1914.

On 28 June 1914 a friend in Kraków told Andrić the news of the assassination. Leaving his few belongings with his landlady, Andrić went straight to the station and took a train to Zagreb. In July he set off to spend the summer vacation with a friend in Split on the Dalmatian coast. The police took an obvious interest in his movements, and by the time war was declared Andrić was fully expecting to be arrested: most of his friends were already in prison. On 29 July he was finally arrested and imprisoned. In the middle of August he was transferred to Maribor, in Slovenia, where he stayed until March 1915. The case against him was eventually dropped through lack of evidence, but he spent the next two years interned in Bosnia.

The image of the prison recurs in Andrić's work, contributing to the underlying theme that the essential condition of human society is constraint. His two first volumes of reflective prose grew out of this experience: *Ex Ponto* (1918) and *Nemiri* (Anxieties, 1920). They are youthful works that Andrić refused to have republished in his lifetime, but their form – a combination of aphoristic short statements and longer reflective passages – continued to appeal to him. They may also be seen as including the germ of many ideas and themes developed in his later works.

During these years of solitary reflection Andrić realized that he should express his commitment to broad political, moral, and social issues indirectly through his writing. From then on his writing took two main directions: although he continued to write verse throughout his life, it was prose that became his main medium, and he definitively turned away from European models and trends to focus on his own immediate heritage.

Andrić's first prose work was the short story *Put Alije Djerzeleza* (The Journey of Ali Djerzelez, 1920). The protagonist is the hero of many heroic ballads popular among the Muslim community in Bosnia throughout the period of Turkish rule. The story offers a key to understanding Andrić's work from two points of view: it is rooted in the oral tradition which represents the rich and vital "literary" heritage of the Serbo-Croat language and the culture expressed through it, and it explores the nature of legend, the perennial human need for heroes and storytelling.

Following the amnesty of 1917, Andrić went to Zagreb, where he entered fully into the intellectual life of the time. He was seriously ill and spent long spells in the hospital, but with the end of the war he shared in the euphoria of the creation of the new kingdom of Serbs, Croats, and Slovenes, describing the idea of national unity in a 1918 article ("Let the Intruders Remain Silent") as "the legacy of our finest generations and the fruit of heavy sacrifice." In 1919, recuperating from his illness on the Dalmatian island of Brač, Andrić wrote to a friend

and former teacher, now a government minister in Belgrade, asking him to help him find permanent employment. He was immediately offered a post and in October 1919 left Zagreb for Belgrade.

Andrić arrived as an established writer, whose first book was sold out after enthusiastic reviews, and entered into the literary life of Belgrade, where he was immediately welcomed and accepted. The role of public figure did not appeal to him, however, and he withdrew increasingly into himself, taking less and less part in the literary gatherings and debates of the capital's literary circles. In 1920 he entered the diplomatic service, a career ideally suited to his temperament. It may be seen almost as an image of Andrić's involvement in the outside world: it was not Andrić as an individual who appeared in public, but Andrić the writer with a deep sense of obligation to his country and its culture, the representative of that culture – just as he was his country's representative abroad.

Andrić was posted to several European cities in the course of his career: Rome, Bucharest, Trieste, Graz, Marseilles, Madrid, Geneva, and finally Berlin from 1937 to 1939. While he drew on this rich experience indirectly, it seems that the chief contribution of his travels was the distance it gave him from his native land, which remained the constant preoccupation of his literary work.

The large number of notebooks Andrić filled with short pieces of reflective prose suggests that he had a marked temperamental preference for the short statement rather than the broad canvas. The main focus of his writing was the short story. Between 1920 and 1941 he published thirty-three stories, and this form continued to be his favored medium after 1945, although he also published three novels and left a fourth unfinished.

There is a sense in which the main elements of Andrić's fundamental philosophical outlook and his ideas about art were formed by the time he began to write: there is a remarkable coherence in his opus as a whole. Consequently it is artificial to impose a chronological organization on his work, particularly the short stories. It is, however, possible to arrange them in broad thematic groups. This was the procedure adopted, with Andrić's participation, when the collected works were published. The analogy with the oral tradition is inescapable: since the time of the first major collections in the mid nineteenth century the songs have been grouped according to rough historical period and theme. Each individual song stands on its own, but each also reinforces the meaning of the others.

If one can make a general statement about the stories published between the two world wars, then the first observation would be that their main focus is Bosnia: it provides the setting for twenty-five of them. In this period of twenty years, Andrić lived in eight major European cities, but only four of the stories he wrote then are set in Europe. Yet Andrić was far from being a provincial writer — concerned with a narrow, exotic, and unknown corner of the Balkans — as he was sometimes portrayed in the 1960s in the English-speaking world. On the contrary, he was a highly sophisticated observer of humanity in the most varied circumstances, whose journeys served to convince him that the essential categories of human experience are constant. But he believed that in art such observations must be embedded in concrete instances.

In his one extended statement on the nature of art, "Razgovor sa Gojom" (1935; translated as "Conversation with Goya," 1992), Andrić suggests that all human activity is conditioned by two fundamental impulses: attack and defense. This idea offers a clue for an interpretation of the Bosnian stories of the interwar period: several of them are dominated by archetypal victims or aggressors. "Mustafa Madžar" (Mustafa the Hungarian, 1923) portrays a soldier with a reputation for bravery, whose mental health is undermined by his exposure to violence and who gradually declines into a dangerous and unpredictable psychopath. "Mara milosnica" (1926; translated as "The Pasha's Concubine," 1968) describes various forms of victimization to which women may be exposed. "Anikina vremena" (Anika's Times, 1931), on the other hand, is concerned with the power women may wield by exploiting their sexuality. All of these characters, and similar ones from this period, represent categories of human behavior which underlie less extreme experience and form the material of myth.

It would seem appropriate at this stage to consider one of the central ideas of the essay "Razgovor sa Gojom" because of the light it casts on the stories under consideration. This is Andrić's notion, expressed also in his speech of acceptance of the Nobel Prize, that the "true history" of mankind is contained in legend and fairy tales.

In the passage in "Razgovor sa Gojom" in which Andrić refers to the fundamental dynamics of human interaction as attack and defense, he stresses the distorting nature of the artistic process: in daily life these impulses are diluted by many tiny actions which are neutral in themselves, but the artist must depict a concentration of such movements in their essential nature in order for them to be expressive

Title page for Andrić's Na Drini ćuprija (translated as The Bridge on the Drina), a novel about the life of a community

and convincing. These stories may thus be seen as distorted accounts of individual aspects of human experience, which in reality form part of a more complex totality. Andrić has isolated these categories to see them clearly as nuclei of experience around which other layers are built up until the form of the original core is no longer recognizable, although it continues to be reproduced in the shape of the outer layers.

Another central idea in the essay is the notion that intellectual and spiritual experience is somehow exiled in the world of matter. The story "Smrt u Sinanovoj tekiji" (Death in Sinan's Tekke, 1924) describes the death of a wise dervish, witnessed by devoted followers who cannot imagine the nature of his last words to his God: far from a peaceful offering up of his soul, they are a wry acknowledgment that "it is harder and more bitter than I believed to be enslaved by the laws of Your earth."

The "otherworldly" nature of intellectual and spiritual activity is eloquently expressed in the image of the arch of the little stone bridge over the

Žepa in the story of that name, "Most na Žepi" (1925; translated as "The Žepa Bridge," 1926): "Seen from the side, the bold sweep of its arch looked always separate and alone, and took the traveller by surprise, like an unusual idea which had gone astray and been trapped among the wild limestone mountains." In this story the Grand Vizier who has the bridge built, a native of the Bosnian village by the Žepa River, is betrayed and falls from power. A spell in prison under sentence of death helps him reassess his life. He decides against inscribing his bridge even with the minimal motto In Silence Lies Safety. Words can be used for good or ill; it was by words that he was himself betrayed. Better then to leave the bridge to stand for itself. In the same way Andrić, shunning abstraction, builds his meaning into concrete form in his stories; like fairy tales and legends, they cannot be paraphrased, but they convey truth.

Andrić's *Pripovetke* (Short Stories), his first collections, published in 1924, 1931, and 1936, were awarded prizes. At the same time he received several distinctions for his diplomatic work. As tension mounted in Europe toward the end of the 1930s, Andrić had less and less time for literary activity. In November 1937 he was appointed assistant to the minister of foreign affairs, and in April of the following year he was sent to Berlin. Andrić's comments on his experiences in Berlin during the early years of the war in Europe have not yet been published, but some insight into his state of mind may be gained from the following entry in his diary for 7 April 1940:

> Whoever has glimpsed, even if only partially and for a moment, the true fate of mankind, can no longer experience untroubled joy; he can no longer look without deep sorrow on a human being stepping into the arena of the sun, onto a winding path with a known end. Composed only of priceless elements from unknown worlds, a man is born in order soon to become a handful of nameless soot and, as such, to vanish. And we do not know for whose glory he is born, nor for whose amusement he is destroyed. He glints for an instant in the clash of contradictions of which he is made, passes alongside other people, but not even with their eyes can they tell one another all the grief of their destinies. So some disappear, and so in cruel ignorance, others are born, and so the incomprehensible history of man runs on.

In March 1941 the Yugoslav government signed the tripartite pact, pledging Yugoslavia's support of Italy and Germany. Extracts from Andrić's letters suggest that he was critical of the government, and on 17 March he asked to be relieved of his duties. Ten days later a coup d'état deposed the regent, Prince Paul, and his seventeen-year-old nephew, Peter, was proclaimed king. Yugoslavia was invaded by the German army. On 17 April the high command of the Royal Yugoslav Army formally capitulated, and the four years of resistance began. Andrić was taken with the rest of the embassy personnel to the Swiss border. Given a choice as to where to go, Andrić went straight to Belgrade, where he lived in isolation, refusing to cooperate in any way with the quisling government for the duration of the war. It is quite likely that without this period of enforced isolation Andrić would not have written the three novels that were published in Belgrade in 1945.

The best known of these, *Na Drini ćuprija* (translated as *The Bridge on the Drina,* 1959), brings together several individual stories set in Višegrad to give a chronicle of certain periods of the town's history, linked by the central symbol of the bridge. The novel offers a vividly illustrated account of a key aspect of Andrić's work: the portrayal of history as a dimension of human life. The succession of stories emphasizes both the insignificance of individual lives and the sense of a community, with a shared history, memories, and experience. Above all, the fine stone bridge, standing steady over the fast-flowing Drina River, represents constancy, the permanence of life itself in which the individual lives all merge.

While *Na Drini ćuprija* takes a broad view of the life of a community through time, *Travnička hronika* (translated as *Bosnian Story,* 1948; *Bosnian Chronicle,* 1963; and *The Days of the Consuls,* 1992) focuses on a seven-year period in the history of the town of Travnik, the seat of the vizier in Bosnia, where French and Austrian consuls served from 1807 to 1814. This novel emphasizes the divisions between sections of the community: Muslims, Christians (Catholic and Orthodox), and Jews. This mixed, divided community forms the background against which the various foreigners, the Western consuls and the viziers themselves, who have also been transplanted into Bosnia from elsewhere, have to negotiate with each other as representatives of their governments, following the fluctuations of their respective foreign policies. Not only are there cultural and religious divisions between individuals, however: when the French consul, Daville, is joined by a young assistant, it is clear that their temperaments, compounded by radically different political views and experience, create equally unbridgeable gulfs. Indeed, Daville's closest contact is apparently with one of the viziers, as they share a boundless admiration for Napoleon. The question of isolation, which dominates Andrić's work, is explored from several points of view: from that of the individual consuls and viziers; from that of the Levantines, Christians from the East, who belong nowhere; and from that of the Jews, representing the isolation of a whole community.

Self-imposed isolation is the subject of Andrić's third 1945 novel, *Gospodjica* (translated as *The Woman from Sarajevo,* 1965), the portrait of a miser dedicated with religious zeal to her obsession with saving and mending.

With the end of World War II and the Communists' successful revolution, the second, socialist Yugoslavia came into being. Andrić participated fully in the intellectual and cultural life of his country, accepting various public positions and devoting himself especially to improving educational opportunities for all. Remembering his own hunger for books as a child, he committed a great deal of time (and his Nobel Prize money) to establishing libraries throughout the country. On 27 September 1958, at the age of sixty-five, he married the recently widowed Milica Babić, to whom he had been devoted for many years. They had only ten years together before she died at age fifty-nine.

Following the awarding of his Nobel Prize in 1961, Andrić was in great demand, traveling extensively until his poor health made it impossible. He continued to work until 1974, when he became seriously ill. He died, after a long struggle, on 13 March 1975. His funeral was attended by some ten thousand citizens of Belgrade.

Andrić's lifetime covers a period of exceptional violence in Europe. While this experience is implicit in his works, it is not often treated directly. The subject matter of short stories he published after World War II covers a range of themes and styles – from tales set in Bosnia under Turkish or Austrian rule to themes from his childhood and timeless reflections set in a contemporary context. Only two stories are concerned exclusively with the theme of the war itself. "Bife Titanik" (The Titanic Bar, 1950) portrays the relationship between the Jewish owner of a little bar in Sarajevo and Ković, a brutal young Fascist, or "Ustasha," who sees Mento Papo as his "own" Jew to persecute and ultimately to murder at whim. In addition to its vivid, often sickening, evocation of the particular circumstances prevailing in Sarajevo in the early stages of the war, this story represents a satisfactory coincidence of universal, generalized themes of fear and persecution. As in the case of the victims in the earlier stories, Papo's vulnerability acts as a magnet to

Andrić receiving the Nobel Prize for Literature in Stockholm, 10 December 1961

Ković's aggression, which in turn functions as a compensation for his own inadequacy.

The violence unleashed by the two world wars is the central theme of "Pismo iz 1920. godine" (Letter from 1920), published in 1946. The story describes the narrator's encounter with an old friend who has decided to leave Bosnia. In a subsequent letter the friend, Max Levenfeld, explains his decision. The letter is a lengthy reflection on the nature of hatred, which he suggests lies just below the surface of relations between the four faiths living side by side in Bosnia.

The experience of living under occupation is the central theme of "Priča o vezirovom slonu" (1947; translated as *The Vizier's Elephant,* 1962), which describes the experience of the people of Travnik under a particularly ruthless vizier. Once he has established his reputation the vizier is hardly seen in the town. But, following a fashion in the Ottoman Empire, he has acquired an exotic pet, an elephant, which is exercised in the town's narrow streets, where it causes havoc and arouses the resentment of the inhabitants. The story builds up the atmosphere of an occupied land, the fear and bitterness, hatred and helplessness of the population caught in an impasse. The townspeople react in different ways to the oppression, depending on their personal power and position. The central point of the story is made in a manner typical of Andrić. One character, Aljo, climbs to a hillside outside the town and from this new perspective is able to see clearly the nature of the impasse in which he and his fellow citizens are trapped. He expresses simply the dilemma that faces them: "Whoever is brave and proud quickly and easily loses his livelihood and his freedom, his property and his life, but whoever bows his head and succumbs to fear loses so much of himself, fear consumes him to such an extent that his life is worth nothing."

The insight offered by altered perspective is a recurrent theme in Andrić's work, and it is one of the main ideas in the story "Osatičani" (The People of Osatica, 1958; translated as "The Climbers," 1966). The town is described as situated both on a hill and in a hollow because of the mountains which rise above it. Everything depends on the point of view of the observer. One of the focal points of the story is the idea that the work of art is superior to ordinary experience: a counterpoint to the relativity and anxiety which mark the villagers' lives is provided by the craftsman who comes to install a cross on the church tower. While the villagers need public confirmation of their exploits, the craftsman works silently in a dark room. His craft is its own justification. He is at one with his task in which confusion and chance are eliminated.

The work of Ivo Andrić confronts the conflict, brutality, and hatred that may be seen as particularly concentrated and close to the surface in his native Bosnia, in order to expose universal patterns of experience. But individual experience is always counterbalanced by further examples, so that the picture emerging from Andrić's work as a whole is subtle and complex. There is nothing negative about the relativity of his statements, however: his unwavering faith in the power of the imagination and the dedication of the craftsman runs through all his works, and there is no doubt of its ultimate triumph. The most concentrated elaboration of this faith comes in the novella *Prokleta avlija* (The Damned Yard, 1954), where the prison yard starkly suggests that the only means of escape from the constraints imposed by society and circumstances of birth is through the imagina-

tion, through the deep human need for stories and storytelling. The imagination provides the capacity to formulate experience, to connect with other peoples and generations in order to begin to understand one's life.

Born of Catholic parents, having lived in Bosnia, Zagreb, and Belgrade, and having spent much of his adult life traveling throughout Europe, Andrić was singularly placed to observe and trace the fundamental currents of life in the troubled lands for which he became so eloquent a spokesman. The importance of his work is acknowledged throughout the territories that made up Yugoslavia between 1918 and 1991. It has a new significance now for all who seek to understand that country's violent collapse.

Bibliography:
Ivo Andrić. Bibliografija dela, prevoda i literature, 1911–1970 (Belgrade: Srpska Akademija Nauka i Umetnosti, 1974).

Biographies:
Miroslav Karaulac, *Rani Andrić* (Belgrade: Prosveta / Sarajevo: Svjetlost, 1980);
Radovan Popović, *Ivo Andrić: Život* (Belgrade: Jugoslovenska Revija, 1989); translated by Karin Radovanović as *Ivo Andrić – A Writer's Life* (Belgrade: Jugoslovenska Revija, 1989);
Vanita Singh Mukerji, *Ivo Andrić. A Critical Biography* (Jefferson, N.C. & London: McFarland, 1990).

References:
Gun Bergman, *Turkisms in Ivo Andrić's 'Na Drini Ćuprija' examined from the Points of View of Literary Style* (Uppsala: Almqvist & Wiksells, 1969);
Mary P. Coote, "Narrative and Narrative Structure in Ivo Andrić's *Devil's Yard,*" *Slavic and East European Journal,* 21 (Spring 1977): 56–63;
Thomas Eekman, "The Later Stories of Ivo Andrić," *Slavonic and East European Review,* 48 (July 1970): 341–356;
Alan Ferguson, "Public and Private Worlds in *Travnik Chronicle,*" *Modern Language Review,* 70 (October 1975): 830–838;
E. D. Goy, "The Work of Ivo Andrić," *Slavonic and East European Review,* 41 (June 1963): 301–326;
Celia Hawkesworth, *Ivo Andrić: Bridge between East and West* (London & Dover: Athlone Press, 1984);
Hawkesworth, "Ivo Andrić's Unobtrusive Narrative Technique with Special Reference to *Kuća*

na osami," Annali dell' Istitutio Orientale di Napoli, 20, no. 1 (1979): 131–153;

Želimir B. Juričić, *The Man and the Artist: Essays on Ivo Andrić* (Lanham, Md.: University Press of America, 1986);

Ante Kadić, "The French in *The Chronicle of Travnik,*" *California Slavic Studies,* 1 (1960): 134–169;

J. Kragalott, "Turkish Loanwords as an Element of Ivo Andrić's Literary Style in *Na Drini ćuprija,*" *Balkanistica,* 2 (1975): 65–82;

Albert Lord, "Ivo Andrić in English Translation," *American Slavic and East European Review,* 23 (September 1964): 563–573;

John Loud, "Between Two Worlds: Andrić the Storyteller," *Review of National Literatures,* 5, no. 1 (1974): 112–126;

Loud, "Zanos in the Early Stories of Ivo Andrić," Ph.D. dissertation, Harvard University, 1971;

Claudio Marabini, "La Narrativa di Ivo Andrić," *Nuova antologia di lettere, arti e scienze,* 499 (1967): 474–490;

Vasa D. Mihailovich, "The Basic World View in the Short Stories of Ivo Andrić," *Slavic and East European Journal,* 10 (Summer 1966): 173–177;

Mihailovich, "The Reception of the Works of Andrić in the English-Speaking World," *Southeastern Europe,* 9 (1982): 41–52;

Regina Minde, *Ivo Andrić. Studien/ber seine Erzählkunst* (Munich: Otto Sagner, 1962);

Njegoš M. Petrovií, *Ivo Andrić, L'homme et l'oeuvre* (Ottawa: Les Editions Lemeac, 1969);

Felicity Rosslyn, "The Short Stories of Ivo Andrić: Autobiography and the Chain of Proof," *Slavonic and East European Review,* 67 (January 1989): 29–41;

Vida Taranovski-Johnson, "Bosnia Demythologized. Character and Motivation in Ivo Andrić's Stories 'Mara Milosnica' and 'O starim i mladim Pamukovićima,' " *Die Welt der Slaven,* 25 (1981): 98–108;

Taranovski-Johnson, "Ivo Andrić's *Kuća na osami:* Memories and Ghosts of the Writer's Past," in *Fiction and Drama in Eastern and Southeastern Europe,* edited by Henrik Birnbaum and Eekman (Columbus, Ohio: Slavica, 1980), pp. 239–250.

Elisaveta Bagryana

(16 April 1893 – 23 March 1991)

Kleo Protokhristova
University of Plovdiv

BOOKS: *Vechnata i svyatata. Stikhotvoreniya* (Sofia: Pechatnitsa "Knipegraf," 1927);

Tŭrkulnata godinka. Stikhotvoreniya za detsa (Sofia: Chipev, 1931);

Zvezda na moryaka. Stikhotvoreniya (Sofia: Chipev, 1932);

Sŭrtse choveshko. Stikhotvoreniya (Sofia: Khemus, 1936);

Zvezdichki. Stikhove za detsa (Sofia: Khemus, 1938);

Gospozhata, by Bagryana and Matvey Vŭlev (Sofia: Khemus, 1938);

Chudnata elkha. Stikhove za detsa (Sofia: Khemus, 1942);

Pet zvezdi. Stikhotvoreniya (Sofia: Bŭlgarski pisatel, 1953);

Samolet za Moskva. Poemka za detsa (Sofia: Bŭlgarski pisatel, 1953);

Chudesen sŭn (sred nasekomite). Piesa za detsa v shest kartini, by Bagryana and Mariya Popova (Sofia: Narodna mladezh, 1953);

Vlak. Stikhove za preduchilishtna vŭzrast (Sofia: Narodna mladezh, 1955);

Obicham te, Rodino! Izbrani stikhotvoreniya za detsa (Sofia: Narodna mladezh, 1956);

Orlyakŭt izlita. Izbrani stikhove za detsa i yunoshi (Sofia: Bŭlgarski pisatel, 1960);

Ot bryag do bryag. Stikhotvoreniya (Sofia: Bŭlgarski pisatel, 1963);

Ptichki lekokrili. Stikhotvoreniya za detsa (Sofia: Bŭlgarski pisatel, 1971);

Maysko utro. Stikhove za detsa (Sofia: Bŭlgarski hudozhnik, 1972);

Kontrapunkti. Stikhotvoreniya (Sofia: Bŭlgarski pisatel, 1972);

Drugarche v putya (Sofia: Narodna mladezh, 1975);

Svetlosenki. Stikhotvoreniya, 1973–1977 (Sofia: Bŭlgarski pisatel, 1977);

Na brega na vremeto. Stikhotvoreniya (Sofia: Profizdat, 1983);

Antologiya manuskripta (Plovdiv: Khr. G. Danov, 1983).

Elisaveta Bagryana

Editions and Collections: *Izbrani stikhotvoreniya* (Sofia: Narodna kultura, 1955);

Izbrani stikhotvoreniya (Sofia: Bŭlgarski pisatel, 1957);

Stikhotvoreniya (Sofia: Bŭlgarski pisatel, Biblioteka za uchenika, 1966);

Izbrana lirika, 2 volumes (Sofia: Bŭlgarski pisatel, 1973);

Izbrani stikhotvoreniya (Varna: G. Bakalov, 1982);

Izbrani proizvedeniya, 2 volumes (Sofia: Bŭlgarski pisatel, 1983);

Izbrani stikhotvoreniya, 3 volumes (Sofia: Bŭlgarski pisatel, 1988).

OTHER: *Izbrani prevodi,* translated by Bagryana (Sofia: Narodna kultura, 1979);

Antologiya na bŭlgarskata poeziya, 3 volumes, edited by Bagryana (Sofia: Bŭlgarski pisatel, 1981).

Elisaveta Bagryana is one of the most outstanding representatives of contemporary Bulgarian poetry. She belongs to the generation that came on the scene during the years after World War I, but she was also a contemporary of several more poetic generations, sustaining a career that lasted for more than sixty years. Her verse is considered one of the greatest achievements in Bulgarian literature.

Elisaveta Bagryana is the pseudonym of Elisaveta Lyubomirova Belcheva, born on 16 April 1893 in Sofia to Maria and Lyubomir Belchev. The first of their seven children, she attended school in Sofia. In 1906 she finished intermediary school, and the following year she enrolled in the Girls' High School in Veliko Tŭrnovo, where her father had been sent on service. There, at age fourteen, she first attempted to write verse. In 1907 she studied for a few months at a high school in Sliven, her father's native city, which she considered the same all her life. The natural beauty of the area surrounding the city played an important role in her artistic development. That setting is represented in one of her most famous poems, "Stikhii" (The Elements). From 1908 to 1910 she studied at the First Girls' High School in Sofia. After graduating in 1910 she worked for a year as a schoolteacher in the village of Avtane (now Nedyalsko) in the county of Yambol. This experience was significant for her because there she first came into contact with country people, who came to figure in her poetry. She was also influenced by the folk songs she heard in the region.

In the autumn of 1911 Bagryana enrolled in the Slavic department of the University of Sofia "St. Kliment Okhridski." At the same time she had walk-ons at the National Theater and sang in the chorus of the National Opera. During her years at the university she read poetry by Bulgarian and foreign authors, and she entered the circle of young writers that included Georgi Raychev, Yordan Yovkov, Dimcho Debelyanov, Konstantin Konstantinov, Khristo Yasenov, and Dimitŭr Podvŭrzachov. Bagryana was writing poetry herself, but, being rather shy and diffident, she needed outside encouragement to face the public. Yovkov recognized her talent and published two of her poems in the journal *Sŭvremenna misŭl* (Contemporary Thought) in 1915: "Vecherna pesen" (An Evening Song) and "Zashto?" (Why?).

In autumn of the same year Bagryana was appointed as teacher in the Girls' High School in Vratsa. She continued to write poetry but did not publish it. In 1918 she was appointed to the Girls' High School in Kyustendil, the location of the Bulgarian Army headquarters. She met Capt. Ivan Shapkarev, son of the well-known folklorist Kuzman Shapkarev. Bagryana married Ivan Shapkarev in 1919, and at the end of the year their son, Lyubomir, was born. The following two years were a time of personal and artistic doubts for the young poet, and she did not publish any poetry. However, it was a period of self-development for Bagryana, and her circumstances put her in touch with the complexity and variety of daily life. In 1921 some of her poems were printed in *Vestnik na zhenata* (The Women's Newspaper). Her literary career began in earnest at this time; she wrote for some of the most outstanding and popular periodicals of the day – *LIK* (Literature-Art-Culture), *Sŭvremennik* (A Contemporary), and *Zlatorog* (The Golden Horn). Her pseudonym first appeared in *Zlatorog,* accompanying three poems in the October 1922 volume. Konstantinov wrote an article on her poetry for *Vestnik na zhenata* (21 October 1922).

Bagryana's marriage turned out to be a disaster. Literally escaping in September 1923, she left for Germany, traveling along the Danube and spending several weeks in Berlin. In November she moved to Munich and stayed there until the end of the year, mingling with a group of Bulgarian writers, actors, and artists: Raychev, Nikolai Liliev, Svetoslav Minkov, Dechko Uzunov, Olga Kircheva, Fani Mutafova, and Chavdar Mutafov. She studied German, visited galleries, and attended concerts. She wrote the poems "Na 'Helios'" (On "Helios"), "Maychina pesen" (Mother's Song), and "Snyag" (Snow) during those months.

When Bagryana returned to Sofia, she was awarded the Ministry of Education's prize for poetry. Soon after her arrival the poem "Kukuvitsa" (Cuckoo) was published in Konstantinov's newspaper, *Ek* (Echo). Strongly influenced by the folk-song style, it declares the woman-wanderer's inability and unwillingness to build a nest and nourish her children. Months later Bagryana was accepted as a member of the Union of Bulgarian Writers, and in November 1924 she took part in a public poetry reading for the first time. During this period she met Boyan Penev, who was to play a significant role in her life. In January 1925 *Zlatorog* published her cycle of poems "Vechnata i svyatata" (The Eternal and Holy), and she received a prize from the Union of Bulgarian Writers.

In April Bagryana finally abandoned her marriage completely, leaving her husband's home and divorcing him. In July she went to France with Penev. They spent the remainder of the summer in Paris and a village in Brittany. The impressions of love and happiness from this period are reflected in Bagryana's "Bretanski tsikŭl" (The Brittany Cycle). In the anthology *Pet godini* (Five Years, 1925) Bagryana's verse is presented along with works by the most prominent Bulgarian authors from the generation following World War I: Mutafov, Nikola Furnadzhiev, Asen Raztsvetnikov, and Khristo Smirnenski.

In 1925 Bagryana was again awarded the Ministry of Education's prize for poetry. She devoted the years 1926 and 1927 to her love for Penev. Sharing his friends and interests, Bagryana entered the world of spiritual striving and intensive poetic quest that she so eagerly needed. However, Penev died unexpectedly in June 1927. Bagryana poured out her pain and despair in "Requiem," one of her best works, in which love is equated with self-sacrifice.

Bagryana's first book was published at the end of this dramatic year. The collection *Vechnata i svyatata* at first seems dedicated to a single theme – love. A closer reading reveals how multifaceted Bagryana's idea of love is. Love is a cry for freedom – "Intérieur" (Interior); a strong and demanding feeling – "Otplata" (Retaliation), "Videnie" (Vision), and "Potomka" (Heiress); eager exaltation – "April," "Amazonka" (Amazon), and "Lyubov" (Love); giving oneself to the unknown – "Bezumie" (Folly) and "Unes" (Reverie); and grief for the beloved – "Requiem."

The second dominant theme of the book is the striving for freedom and unattainable distances. In "Amazonka" the poetic speaker feels akin to the nomadic tribes who wandered ages ago through her fatherland. It is her Amazon blood that brings the thirst for far-off seas, unknown lands, and exciting experiences.

Some of Bagryana's most enlightened poems are about motherhood. In the title poem, "Vechnata" (The Eternal), she praises the holiness and mystery of the continuation of life, crystallized in the image of the eternally reincarnating young and beloved woman. The idea of the indestructibility of life appears in other versions in other poems. In "Requiem" the shock of the loss of her lover is overcome by the wise insight that love is inexhaustible, and, being the chain of life, it will always keep the balance between misery and happiness.

The appearance of a debut book when an author is already well known and accepted by the public is not a frequent event in literary history. For Bagryana it was the result of a long, self-denying labor through the years. The book had a remarkably good reception and placed her high among the best authors of the time. *Vechnata i svyatata* impressed contemporary readers with its unusual vigor. The Bulgarian society of the 1920s was still preserving a patriarchal and rather strict atmosphere. The poems declaring the young woman's desires and a cult for the pleasures of this world were quite a shock, with the rejection of centuries-old moral conventions. The second edition (1927) was equally successful. The third and fourth editions were published in 1941 and 1943, each with a printing of two thousand copies – a large number for a poetry collection, especially in a small country such as Bulgaria.

Bagryana traveled a great deal during the next two years. In 1928 she visited various places in Bulgaria for public readings of her poetry. In the autumn she left for France, staying in Paris for ten months. Her artistic interests broadened; she attended modern ballet performances, plays, concerts, exhibitions, and literary readings. She made the acquaintance of such writers as Marina Tsvetayeva, Vladimir Mayakovsky, Ilya Ehrenburg, and André Breton. On her way back to Bulgaria in June of the following year, she stopped in Venice for several days, taking part in an international writers' meeting.

In 1929 the largest publishing house in Bulgaria, Khemus, offered Bagryana a contract, which she signed, to publish all her books and pay her a monthly salary. During the next two years references to her poetry began appearing abroad. In May 1931 an "Evening of Bulgarian Poetry" in Warsaw featured translations of Bagryana's works, along with those of Khristo Botev, Pencho Slaveykov, and Peyo Yavorov. During the same month Bagryana was a member of the Bulgarian delegation to the International Congress of Writers' Unions, held in Paris. In 1931 she published her first book of poems for children, *Tŭrkulnata godinka* (The Year Rolled Away). In 1932 *Révue mondiale* (World Review) published some of Bagryana's poems, along with a review giving a highly favorable evaluation of her works. During the same year Bagryana first visited Yugoslavia, where she wrote the cycle "Evenings in Vikrce," published as "Slovenski vecheri" in *Sŭrtse choveshko* (The Human Heart, 1936). Then she took part in the P.E.N. Congress in Budapest. Her second collection of poems, *Zvezda na moryaka* (The Mariner's Star), was published that year.

Zvezda na moryaka reveals an important stage of Bagryana's creative development. Although she remains true to some of the characteristic themes of her earlier poetry (love and the thirst for freedom), the dominant themes of the second collection come from another sphere of poetic experience: the sea, the striving for unknown and fascinating worlds, and the journeys to far-off countries. New imagery, based on her experiences in big cities and with technological progress, is also evident in the poems.

A striking feature of the collection is the predominating pessimistic mood, so much different from the primal vitality of her earlier verse. The disillusionment with life reinforces the idea of the uselessness of poetry – its inadequacy to the real demands of human existence. The opening poem, "S.O.S.," which is representative of the entire collection, draws a cosmopolitan picture of modern times reaching far beyond national borders. The symbols of technologically advanced civilization provide the framework for the world that the poet longs to experience and absorb. Paradoxically, Bagryana is at the same time fascinated with and repelled by the scientific inventions. She is attracted by their novelty but horrified by their inhuman nature. Welcoming them, she nevertheless believes them to be in discordance with her instinct for the natural and the human, for the primal elements of life. The striving for the wide world is counterbalanced by the reflection on the complexity of modern Bulgarians' mentality – the conflict between striving toward distant horizons and the irresistible sentimental bonds to one's country, home, and family.

The enchantment with distant horizons that forms the kernel of the cycle "Zovŭt na moreto" (The Call of the Sea) – in which the image of the sea functions as a symbol of the vast, unattainable, yet tempting world of the unknown – is another realization of Bagryana's dominant theme: the striving for freedom, no longer concerned with imprisonment by social hypocrisy. The abstract idea of the sea is combined with the poet's vivid memories of summers spent at the seaside, thus forming the basis for the cycles "Zovŭt na moreto" and "Nessebŭr Dream." The charming seascape, the mornings, the shrieks of the gulls, the summoning sirens of the ships, the dazzling sun, the caressing sands, the enchanting smell of the salty air, the threatening and destructive elements of the waves – all these objects are contemplated in Bagryana's verse.

Along with the new images and emotions that enrich Bagryana's poetry, there is an evident ten-

Portrait of Bagryana by Dechko Uzunov, 1926

dency in *Zvezda na moryaka* toward a different form. Its primary characteristic is a broad composition similar to that of the lyrical poem. The poet vigorously breaks up the verse, abandoning the traditional syllabic rhythms. In this collection Bagryana achieves a verse style that flows like a river. It functions as a metaphorical expression of her emotional capacity, which bursts forth through the words, creating a free and broad rhythm that corresponds to her love for the spaciousness of the ocean, the vigor of the waves, and the intangibility of the dreams and mirages.

The following years offered Bagryana the opportunity of new professional activities. In 1933, 1934, and 1935 she took part in the P.E.N. Congresses in Dubrovnik, Barcelona, and Paris, respectively. In 1935 she journeyed to Istanbul and Ankara. That trip forms the basis for the cycle "Express d'Orient." In 1936 her next collection of verse, *Sŭrtse choveshko,* was published. It seems to repeat the main topics of the previous one. The burning thirst for new lands is combined with nostalgia. Impressions of countries and people's faces are the impulse for poetic creation in such poems as "Ekspres v pustinyata" (Express in the Desert), "Lavri" (Laurels), and the cycle "Slovenski vecheri." Love is the other dominant theme. The love poems are calm and serene, different from her earlier vigorous lines, burning with passion. Love is viewed as a treasure that fills one's being with bliss and courage, helping one to face the hours of trial.

In June 1938 Bagryana was again a delegate to the P.E.N. Congress (in Prague). In 1939 she returned to Paris, taking part in an evening of Bulgarian poetry and music. In 1940 she wrote the cycle "Golemiyat tsirk" (The Big Top), in which she expresses her share of the fear of the horror threatening the world's future. The cycle depicts a vast circus, where a giant clown (an allegorical image of Adolf Hitler) is proclaiming the beginning of World War II with a sinister smile. The picture is apocalyptic. Although terrified by the world of cruelty and futurelessness, the poet felt that there was no way back to the past. The persistent image of old bridges being broken down became a key feature in her poetry. During the period from 1937 to 1943 she wrote the poems for "Most" (The Bridge), which remained unpublished at the time.

In 1944 Bagryana married Aleksandŭr Likov, a publicist, critic, and political figure. During the bombardment of Sofia they were buried under the ruins of their home but miraculously survived. However, most of the poet's papers were destroyed by fire. In 1946 she visited Romania with a group of Bulgarian writers. In 1950 she received the Dimitrov Prize, the highest honor awarded by the state. In the following years she visited the Soviet Union. Her impressions from that trip and her attempt to write civic poetry in a new manner resulted in the collection *Pet zvezdi* (Five Stars, 1953). Although the book was awarded the Order of the People's Republic of Bulgaria, it marks a waning in Bagryana's artistic strength.

For Bagryana the 1950s were a period of slow and somewhat painful transformation, forced by the political changes in the country – a fate Bagryana shared with other generations of poets living and writing during this time. Personal unhappiness added to the trial of the years. In 1954 her husband died. The Boyana cycle, one of Bagryana's finest works, is dedicated to him; it is included in the collection *Ot bryag do bryag* (From Shore to Shore, 1963). From the pain of personal loss Bagryana found a new direction for her poetry, thus remaining true to her creative ability to perceive the world through her intimate experiences. But the violent

pain and desperation evident in "Requiem" gave way to a quiet sadness and resignation.

The next fifteen years were marked by several publications of Bagryana's selected works. She traveled to Belgium (for the Biennale of the Poets at Knock-de-Zoet, 1956), Brazil (as a delegate to the P.E.N. Congress, 1960), Italy (1962), Greece (1965), Sweden (delivering a lecture in Uppsala on Slaveykov in 1966, the centenary of his birth), and Paris (1967). In 1963 she was awarded the title People's Cultural Worker, the greatest public recognition in Bulgaria at the time, and in 1969 she received the gold medal of the International Poetry Association. Her books were published in Paris (1957), Moscow (1959), Warsaw (1961), Prague (1963), Zagreb (1965), Rome (1966), and Bucharest (1967).

Bagryana's most remarkable feat from these years, however, is the collection *Ot bryag do bryag,* which conveys her impressions of Brazil and her experiences while traveling there. In a manner characteristic of her poetic vision, in Brazil she contemplated not so much the exotic landscapes but human lives. Therefore most of the poems are meditative, but poetic imagery and intensive emotions are still present. Among her best are "Nostalgiya" (Nostalgia) and "Shepa snyag" (A Handful of Snow), a heartbreaking account of personal tragedy and loss, of love and humanity. Besides the poems expressing Bagryana's sorrow for her husband in the Boyana cycle, there is a key poem, "Kledenetsŭt" (The Well), in which the central image symbolizes her poetry's deep roots in native tradition. Some brilliant lines depict Mount Vitosha, visualized as a source of strength and wisdom, while others describe Boyana Church, with its magnificent medieval frescoes.

During the 1970s Bagryana, still in remarkably good health, continued her artistic and public activities. She continued to travel – to France (1970), Lebanon (1971), Greece and Czechoslovakia (1972), Poland (1973), and Belgium (1974). In 1972 her collection of verse *Kontrapunkti* (Counterpoints) was published and awarded the prize of the Union of Bulgarian Writers. In these poems her love for humankind and homeland and her inexhaustible curiosity for the mysteries of being find new expression. At the center of the collection is "Nestinarska sŭdba" (The Firedancer's Fate), which considers the role of fate in the poet's life, in her homeland's history, and in her personality. Memories of the past frequently occupy Bagryana's verse in this collection; she recalls both the happy and unhappy days – the "black and white," which became the key image of her later works.

In 1973 Bagryana's eightieth birthday was officially celebrated in Sliven. Still in good health, she had one more active decade to go. She traveled regularly, wrote verse, edited a three-volume anthology of Bulgarian poetry (1981), and published collections and new editions of her earlier works. She also wrote children's books and produced two new collections of poetry: *Svetlosenki* (Light and Shade, 1977) and *Na brega na vremeto* (At the Time's Strand, 1983). Her verse in these volumes is preoccupied with the issues of time, philosophy of life, and values in human existence. The dominating image is the day and the sequence of days — an essential part of her poetry from the earliest years — but one specifically crystallized in her later works. The image bears the rhythm and meaning of existence — a concentrated image of life itself.

Bagryana contemplated the world with never-fading astonishment, living fully to her last day and acquiring a somewhat mythical status in Bulgarian literary history. She is revered for her vitality; for her long and active life, which seemed so much like immortality, even to herself; and for her evolving poetic vision, which nevertheless retained a basic constancy. Bagryana is not only the greatest Bulgarian female poet, she is also one of the best poets in Slavic literature, her name taking its place beside those of Anna Akhmatova and Marina Tsvetayeva.

Interviews:

Vanya Boyadzhieva, "Pri Elisaveta Bagryana. Tvorcheska anketa," *Literaturna misŭl,* 3 (1967): 140–146;

Ivan Sarandev, *Elisaveta Bagryana. Literaturna anketa* (Plovdiv: Khr. G. Danov, 1990).

Bibliographies:

Georgi Tsanev, ed., *Rechnik na Bŭlgarskata literatura,* volume 1 (Sofia: BAN, 1973), pp. 63–66;

Elena Ognyanova, *Kratki danni za Elisaveta Bagryana i tvorchestvoto i,* in Bagryana's *Izbrana lirika,* volume 2 (Sofia: Bŭlgarski pisatel, 1973), pp. 253–258;

Mariya Gareva, "Bibliografska spravka za Elisaveta Bagryana i 'Vechnata i svyatata,' " in Bagryana's *Vechnata i svyatata* (Plovdiv: Khr. G. Danov, 1980), pp. 103–107.

Biographies:

Blaga Dimitrova and Yordan Vasilev, *Mladostta na Bagryana i neynite spŭtnitsi* (Plovdiv: Khr. G. Danov, 1975);

Dimitrova and Vasilev, *Dni cherni i beli. Elisaveta Bagryana – nablyudeniya i razgovori* (Sofia: Nauka i izkustvo, 1975);

Dimitrova and Vasilev, "Krŭstoputishta. Elisaveta Bagryana. Silueti ot neynoto vreme," *More,* 1–2 (1990): 5–86.

References:

Zdravko Cholakov, "Nablyudeniya vŭrkhu poetikata na Bagryana," *Plamŭk,* 8 (1973): 69–73;

Petŭr Dinekov, "Dve knigi – dva vŭrkha" and "Elisaveta Bagryana v bŭlgarskata poeziya," in his *V zhivota i literaturata* (Sofia: Nauka i izkustvo, 1982), pp. 69–77, 78–95;

Dinekov, "Poeticheskiyat pŭt na Bagryana," *Plamŭk,* 8 (1973): 61–68;

Dinekov, ed., *Elisaveta Bagryana. Novi izsledvaniya* (Sofia: BAN, 1989);

Svetlozar Igov, "Vechnata i svyatata," *Plamŭk,* 5 (1983): 5–13;

Dora Koleva, *Za poetikata na Bagryana* (Sofia: Bŭlgarski pisatel, 1983);

Bozhanka Konstantinova, *Elisaveta Bagryana* (Sofia: Otechestvo, 1989);

Rozaliya Likova, "Elisaveta Bagryana," in her *Istoriya na bŭlgarskata literatura – poeti na 20-te godini* (Sofia: Nauka i izkustvo, 1979), pp. 210–267;

Ivan Meshekov, "Grekhovnata i svyata pesen na Bagryana," in his *Eseta, statii, studii, retzenzii* (Sofia: Bŭlgarski pisatel, 1989), pp. 702–723;

Milena Tsaneva, "Elisaveta Bagryana," in her *Petima poeti* (Sofia: Bŭlgarski pisatel, 1974), pp. 35–79;

Tsaneva, "Poetichniyat svyat na Bagryana," in her *Profili i etyudi* (Sofia: Bŭlgarski pisatel, 1968), pp. 57–111;

Pantelei Zarev, "Svetŭt na Bagryana," *Literaturna misŭl,* 4 (1968): 3–41.

Khristo Botev
(25 December 1847 – 20 May 1876)

Lyubomira Parpulova-Gribble
Ohio State University

BOOK: *Pesni i stikhotvoreniya ot Botyova i Stambolova. Knizhka pŭrva,* by Botev and Stefan Stambolov (Bucharest: Pechatnitsa na vestnik *Zname,* 1875; facsimile, Sofia: Nauka i izkustvo, 1979).

Editions and Collections: *Sŭchineniya: Stikhotvoreniya. Politicheski statii. Podlistnitsi,* edited by Zakhari Stoyanov (Sofia: Bŭlgarska narodna pechatnitsa, 1888);

Pŭlno sŭbranie na sŭchineniyata, 3 volumes, edited by Mikhail Dimitrov (Sofia: Nov svyat, 1940; revised and enlarged edition, Sofia: Nauchen institut Khristo Botev, 1949–1950);

Sŭbrani sŭchineniya, 3 volumes, edited by Petŭr Dinekov and others (Sofia: Bŭlgarski pisatel, 1976).

Editions in English: *Selected Works,* edited by Stefana Tarinska, translated by Petko Drenkov (Sofia: Sofia-Press, 1976);

Poems, edited by Theodora Atanassova, translated by Kevin Ireland (Sofia: Sofia-Press, 1974; revised edition, 1982).

Khristo Botev is considered the greatest poet in modern Bulgarian literature. Although he was also a gifted writer of journalistic prose, his literary fame is founded mainly upon some twenty superb poems. The rare combination of a powerful poetic talent, an extraordinary life, and a heroic death made him a national hero and a role model for future generations of Bulgarian poets.

Khristo Botev Petkov was born in the town of Kalofer on 25 December 1847 (6 January 1848 in the modern Gregorian calendar). His parents, Botyo Petkov, a Russian-educated schoolteacher and prominent local citizen, and Ivanka Drenkova, gave their firstborn son the name Khristo (a Bulgarian form for *Christ*) following the Bulgarian tradition of naming a child after the saint on whose feast day the baby was born. In 1863, after graduation from the Kalofer school, fifteen-year-old Khristo departed for Russia to complete his high-school education in Odessa. During the two years he spent there, Botev grew increasingly dissatisfied with the instruction in the gymnasium, neglected his schoolwork, and was finally expelled.

In both Kalofer and Odessa, Botev read extensively, although not systematically. His passion for reading significantly expanded his knowledge of literature and fortified his rebellious inclinations. The young man became interested in the ideas of the radical Russian literary and political figures as well as the French Socialists. He even got involved in a Russian revolutionary circle, several members of which were later arrested. Botev also found kindred spirits among the Polish revolutionary activists whose main goal was the restoration of the independent Polish state. Some of the people who knew him as a student in Odessa recalled that he wrote poetry, which he would recite to his friends. Unfortunately, none of these works has survived.

At the beginning of 1867, after about a year of teaching and producing revolutionary propaganda in various villages, he returned to Kalofer, where he substituted for his sick father as a schoolteacher. However, the speech he delivered on the major Bulgarian school holiday, the feast of Saint Kiril and Saint Metodiy, irritated both the rich Bulgarians and the Turkish authorities with its criticism of social injustice and thinly veiled call for an independent Bulgarian state. In order to avoid persecution he had to leave the country. Initially he intended to return to Russia, but he later decided to stay in Romania.

During his sojourn in Kalofer, Botev published his first poem, "Maytse si" (To My Mother), on 1 April 1867 in Petko R. Slaveykov's newspaper, *Gajda* (Bagpipe). Slaveykov probably chose the text from a notebook with several other poems that Botev had sent to him in order to garner the opinion of the most prominent Bulgarian poet of the time. Regrettably, this notebook, along with Slaveykov's entire archive, later perished in a fire. "Maytse si" is dominated by the theme of death. The love for his mother is the only thing that the lonely, disappointed lyrical persona still cherishes, but it is about to fade away because of his approaching death. The text reads like the work of an accomplished master, not the debut of an aspiring poet.

The rest of Botev's poems were written during his years in Romania (1867–1876). *Restless, difficult,* and *exciting* are probably the words that best describe

his life as an émigré. Between 1868 and 1872 the poet lived mostly in Braila, where he worked as a typesetter in Dimitŭr Panichkov's printing shop, as an actor in Dobri Voynikov's theatrical troupe, and as editor of his own newspaper, *Duma na bŭlgarskite emigranti* (Word of the Bulgarian Émigrés). Like many other journalistic enterprises of the period, *Duma* lasted for only a few issues because of lack of financial support. In mid 1872 Botev moved to Bucharest to work for the newspapers *Svoboda* (Freedom) and *Nezavisimost* (Independence), which were published by Lyuben Karavelov. In April 1873 Botev started another journalistic venture, the satiric newspaper *Budilnik* (Alarm Clock), which ceased publication in May because of lack of money. In 1874 he became a teacher in the Bulgarian school in Bucharest.

During his Bucharest period (1872–1876) Botev became a central figure in the left wing of the Bulgarian political émigrés. At first he worked with Karavelov as a leader of the Bŭlgarski revolyutsionen tsentralen komitet (Bulgarian Revolutionary Central Committee). The committee's goal was to establish a revolutionary organization inside Bulgaria to help achieve national independence. Around 1874 Karavelov shifted toward the camp of the so-called enlighteners, while Botev remained a convinced revolutionary. In August 1874 he joined the new Central Committee and became the editor of its newspaper, *Zname* (Banner). Because of some disagreements with the new leadership, Botev left the committee in September 1875, but he continued to work for the cause.

The year 1875 was full of important events for Botev. He married a widow, Veneta Rasheva; his mother and two of his brothers came to live with him after the death of Botyo Petkov; and he published his only collection of poetry, *Pesni i stikhotvoreniya* (Songs and Poems), which included pieces by Stefan Stambolov, another revolutionary and a far less talented poet. Botev's last journalistic enterprise, the newspaper *Nova Bŭlgaria* (New Bulgaria), was short-lived. After the first issue the poet left for Bulgaria to help his compatriots in their struggle against the Turks during the April Uprising.

Pesni i stikhotvoreniya contains sixteen of Botev's poems. Compared to "Maytse si," "Kŭm brata si" (To My Brother) is much more explicit about the isolation and pessimism of the poet: he knows neither joy nor freedom because no one, not even his brother, answers his call to help the suffering people. Here the poet's love for his countrymen is paralleled not by severe depression, as in "Maytse si," but by wrath aroused by the indifference of the "fools" who surround him. Wrath and hostility as the opposite side of passionate love are also the common emotional dominants of "Elegiya" (Elegy), "Borba" (The Struggle), "Moyata molitva" (My Prayer), "V mekhanata" (In the Tavern), "Strannik" (Stranger), and "Patriot" (Patriot). The first four poems convey their messages rather directly, using a powerful mix of biblical references and offensive, lower style expressions, such as "chosen scum," "sanctimonious drivel," "idol of the fools," and "idiots." The last two works are caustic satires. The themes of personal and national freedom and national and social oppression are another common element of these texts.

Botev rarely wrote about romantic love. The only poem entirely devoted to this traditional subject of poetry is "Ney" (To Her). In "Do moeto pŭrvo libe" (To My First Love) the love theme is fully incorporated into the set of concerns typical in Botev's writings. The conflict between the poet's infatuation with a beautiful woman and his love for his people is firmly resolved by the statement of the lyrical persona that if he were to choose between his beloved and his duty to his country, the love for his homeland would prevail. Botev believed that the moral imperatives advocated in his writings had to govern his life as well. His decision to leave his family and cross the Danube leading a detachment of volunteers to aid in the Bulgarian uprising is one of the most impressive examples of this unity between poetry and personal life. On 17 May 1876, before sailing off on the Austrian steamboat *Radetski,* he wrote a letter to his wife; his stepson, Dimitŭr; and his baby daughter, Ivanka, telling them that after his homeland they were the ones he loved most.

Botev and his family lived in poverty and endured various hardships. This situation was a source of deep pain and sorrow for the poet. And yet, whenever he had some money, he did not hesitate to put it into publishing his newspapers. He regarded them as the means for serving the great cause of his life: winning freedom and social justice for his people. The conviction that no sacrifice — even one's own life — is too high a price for achieving this goal is present in the best of Botev's works, including "Na proshtavane" (On Parting), "Prista-nala" (Eloped), "Khayduti" (Outlaws), and "Khadzhi Dimitŭr." Botev's poems are usually passionate lyrical monologues, but the last four also include a well-developed epic component. The stories they tell — sometimes based on real events, sometimes purely fictitious ones — are strongly influenced by the imagery and style of Bulgarian folk ballads.

For example, "Na proshtavane" is linked to a specific event from Botev's life. In 1868 he decided to enlist in a detachment of volunteers organized by Zhelyo Voyvoda that went to Bulgaria to fight for freedom. The undertaking failed because, on the one hand, the *voyvoda* (captain) could not raise enough money to arm his followers and, on the other, because the Romanian police arrested him at the request of the Turkish government. The poem, although first published in 1871, was most likely written in connection with Botev's decision to join the rebels. It was probably intended as the poet's last testament before embarking on this dangerous road. In a manner typical of the *khaydushki pesni* (folk outlaw songs), the young rebel bids farewell to his mother as he is about to leave with his detachment. He asks her, in case he is killed, to tell his younger brothers about him, hoping that they will follow in his footsteps. The poet-rebel also draws a more optimistic picture, in which he will return to his native village as a victorious hero and embrace both his mother and his beloved girlfriend. The text is fascinating not only for its high poetic qualities but also for its prophetic portrait of the circumstances of Botev's death. The lyrical persona envisions that he will be killed in the mountains, where the earth will soak up his blood and eagles will carry his flesh over the crags. Indeed, on 20 May 1876, in a battle between his volunteers and Turkish military units, Botev was shot dead in the mountains near the town of Vratsa, and the detachment was destroyed. The location of his grave, if he ever had one, remains unknown.

"Khadzhi Dimitŭr," the most exquisite of Botev's poems and regarded by many as the greatest masterpiece of Bulgarian poetry in general, contains similar prophetic insights. Khadzhi Dimitŭr, Botev's friend, was also a born rebel. He spent years as an émigré in Romania, led a detachment of volunteers to Bulgaria in 1868, and was killed during a battle in the same mountains where Botev perished. The site of his grave, if he ever had one, also remains unknown. For several years there were rumors that the announcements of his death were false and that he was waiting for the right time to rejoin the struggle to liberate Bulgaria. The rumors were founded on the old, widely spread folk motif about the great hero who does not die but hides in a secret place, waiting to return at a certain moment to help his people (as in the legends of King Arthur and the South Slavic epic hero Prince Marko). This belief demonstrates that the otherwise insoluble conflict between life and death can be resolved with the help of poetic imagination. It is reflected in the

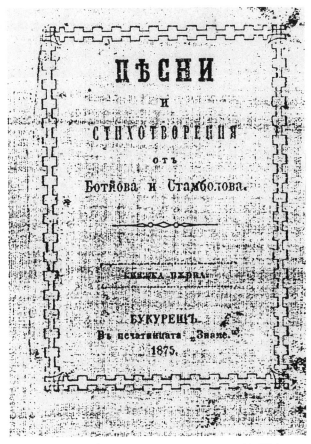

Title page for the only book Botev published in his lifetime

famous fifth stanza of the poem: "He who falls fighting for freedom / never dies; earth and sky, / beast and nature mourn him / and minstrels sing of him." Many feel that in these lines Botev once again foresaw his own fate.

"Khadzhi Dimitŭr" combines all the major themes of Botev's poetry: striving for freedom, national oppression, death, and the poetry of the mountains. The last theme transforms the tragic victim into an inspiring hero. The final hours of Khadzhi Dimitŭr are divided between two different realms. There is the real world with the scorching sun of a midsummer day; the sorrowful song of a harvester in the distant fields of wheat; and a lonely, mortally wounded hero, his broken weapons scattered around him, bleeding and cursing the entire universe from the top of the mountain. There is also the fantastic world of folk poetry where an eagle, a falcon, and a wolf care for their "brother"; the mountains sing "a rebel's song" in the starry night; three beautiful wood fairies come to dress his wound; and the hero's last wish is to learn the fate of the men from his detachment. The fifth stanza keeps the two realms together by transferring the

issue of death from the material world to that of the spirit. As a result the overall mood of the poem is optimistic in spite of the inevitable death of the hero.

Botev's last work, "Obesvaneto na Vasil Levski" (The Hanging of Vasil Levski), is not part of *Pesni i stikhotvoreniya.* The poem, which Roman Jakobson considers the highest point of Botev's quest for new forms of poetic expression, was first published in a wall calendar for 1876. It is devoted to another friend of the poet, Vasil Levski, who was a truly exceptional man and the chief driving force behind the secret revolutionary committees that were working for the liberation of the country. His death was a severe blow not only to the revolutionary network but also to the morale of its activists. Botev was probably devastated by Levski's death because he does not include any optimistic notes in this text. Levski's execution in February 1875 inspired the metaphoric winter landscape in the profoundly tragic conclusion of the ballad: "The winter sings its baleful song, / squalls chase thistles on the plain / and cold and frost and hopeless tears / overwhelm your heart with pain." Unlike "Khadzhi

Dimitŭr," "Obesvaneto na Vasil Levski" did not win immediate critical approval. There were even suggestions that it was not written by Botev. Gradually, however, literary critics recognized what ordinary readers had sensed from the beginning – that it is a piece of truly remarkable poetry.

Both of these poems, like many of the others, became popular shortly after they were published. Complete with melodies, they circulated widely as folk songs, yet the people who sang them often did not know that Botev was the author. According to Petŭr Dinekov, the main reason for the publication of *Pesni i stikhotvoreniya* was Botev's desire to use the book for propaganda purposes during the preparation of the April Uprising. This intent explains why he included Stambolov's poems, which, although of inferior poetic quality, were also popular as revolutionary songs at that time. Various letters from that period testify that the book was in great demand and that copies of it were smuggled to Bulgaria in boxes of bullets. Another testimony to the appeal of the songs based on Botev's poems is found in Levski's pocket notebook, where he included the text of "Na proshtavane" among his favorite songs.

While many of these songs are no longer part of the active repertoire of contemporary Bulgarians, "Obesvaneto na Vasil Levski" and "Khadzhi Dimitŭr" still retain their popular appeal. The circumstances in which one can hear them, however, have changed considerably. Nowadays they are not performed at informal gatherings but are associated with two special occasions. The first song is always broadcast on the national radio on 19 February, the day of Levski's death, which has become a national holiday. In the evening hundreds of people gather at the monument to Levski in Sofia to lay flowers and join professional and amateur choirs in performing the song. The second song is traditionally broadcast on 2 June (the day of Botev's death, according to the Gregorian calendar now used in Bulgaria). Choirs sing it in the evening as part of the solemn ceremonies across the country commemorating Botev and all the others who have died for the independence of Bulgaria. After World War II the Communist government changed the definition of the holiday, making it a memorial day for the fighters "against capitalism and fascism" as well. The fall of the Communists from power in 1989 will certainly entail another redefining of the holiday, but it is highly unlikely that any politically motivated changes will affect the connection of the song to it.

Botev died at age twenty-eight. During his short life he managed to accomplish so much that after the liberation of the country in 1879 he became a revered national hero. Because of his status as a national symbol, many political parties have tried to enlist him as their ideological forefather and use his authority for propaganda purposes. Their arguments are founded mostly on the social and philosophical convictions expressed in his journalistic writings and political actions. The Communist party was especially eager to picture him as its venerable precursor on the basis of his calls for social justice and equality, his criticism of the institution of the church and the clergy, his infatuation with the ideas of utopian socialism, and his connections with Russian radicals and nihilists. The most effective pieces of evidence legitimizing such claims are the telegram Botev sent to express support for the Paris Commune (1871) and his "Credo of the Bulgarian Commune" (1871). However, in a 1991 article on these two texts, Iliya Todorov comes to the conclusion that neither of them should be regarded as Botev's original.

The fate of Botev's poetic legacy is rather complicated. He is widely regarded as a great poetic talent; most Bulgarians are able to quote at least a few lines of his poetry. Many of the best Bulgarian poets have devoted special poems to him, and his works have been translated into twenty-five languages. And yet he has no direct students among contemporary poets, perhaps because later generations have realized that they cannot surpass his literary achievements while closely following in his path.

On the other hand, the image of the poet created by the fusion of Botev's exquisite poetry, prophetic insights, devotion to civic duties outweighing purely personal problems, and untimely tragic death has become an influential role model for Bulgarian poets. Many have tried and some (such as Peyo Yavorov, Pencho Slaveykov, Dimcho Debelyanov, and Nikola Vaptsarov) have mastered successful variations of this model. Botev's image as a poet has also been instrumental in shaping the expectations of the Bulgarian reading public. In spite of all the efforts to convince a wide audience that the personal life of a poet does not have to follow the ideas expressed in his/her works, still – especially for those authors whose writings emphasize social and political concerns – the unity between poetry and biography remains the ultimate test for national recognition.

Biographies:

Zakhari Stoyanov, *Khristo Botyov: Opit za biografiya* (Ruse, 1888);

Ivan Klincharov, *Khristo Botyov: Biografiya* (Sofia: Knizharnitsa I. G. Ignatov, 1910);

Nikola Nachov, *Khristo Botyov: Biografichna skitsa* (Sofia: Kooperativno prosvetno druzhestvo "Razvitie," 1918);

Mikhail Dimitrov, *Khristo Botev: Biografiya* (Sofia: Nauchen institut Khristo Botev, 1948);

Donka Petkanova, *Khristo Botev: Biografichen ocherk* (Sofia: Natsionalen sŭvet na Otechestveniya front, 1961).

References:

Georgi Bakalov, *Khristo Botev: Zhivot, idei i sŭchineniya* (Moscow: Tsentralizdat, 1938);

Stoyko Bozhkov and Zara Genadieva, *Rechnik na ezika na Khristo Botev* (Sofia: Izdatelstvo na Bŭlgarskata akademiya na naukite, 1960);

Konstantin N. Derzhavin, *Khristo Botev: Zhizn i tvorchestvo* (Moscow: Akademiya nauk SSSR, 1962);

Petŭr Dinekov, *V sveta na Khristo Botev* (Sofia: Bŭlgarski pisatel, 1976);

Roman Jakobson, "K srukture poslednikh stikhov Khr. Boteva," in his *Selected Writings,* volume 3: *Poetry of Grammar and Grammar of Poetry* (The Hague, Paris & New York: Mouton, 1981), pp. 519–535;

Docho Lekov, "Khristo Botev," in *A Biobibliographical Handbook of Bulgarian Authors,* edited by Karen L. Black, translated by Predrag Matejic (Columbus, Ohio: Slavica, 1981), pp. 132–137;

Charles A. Moser, "The Bulgarian Renaissance (1762–1878)," in his *History of Bulgarian Literature* (The Hague & Paris: Mouton, 1972), pp. 35–90;

Ivan Paunovski, ed., *Bŭlgarskata kritika za Khristo Botev* (Sofia: Bŭlgarski pisatel, 1983);

Boyan Penev, *Khristo Botev* (Sofia: T. F. Chipev, 1931);

Stefana Tarinska, *Prozata na Khristo Botev* (Sofia: Nauka i izkustvo, 1966);

Iliya Todorov, *Nad Boteviya stikh: Tekstologichni izsledvaniya* (Sofia: Bŭlgarski pisatel, 1988);

Todorov, "Simvol-veruyu na bŭlgarskata komuna," *Letopisi,* 1 (1991): 118–137;

Ivan Undzhiev and Tsveta Undzhieva, *Khristo Botev: Zhivot i delo* (Sofia: Nauka i izkustvo, 1975); revised as *Khristo Botev: Zhivot i tvorchestvo* (Sofia: Otechestven front, 1983);

Lev Vorobev, *Khristo Botev: Zhizn i deyatelnost* (Moscow: Goslitizdat, 1953).

Papers:

Botev's papers are housed in the Bulgarian National Library, "Kiril and Metodiy" (Bŭlgarski istoricheski arkhiv, fond no. 86, Khristo Botev).

Ivan Cankar

(10 May 1876 – 11 December 1918)

Irma M. Ozbalt

BOOKS: *Erotika* (Ljubljana: Kleinmayr & Bamberg, 1899; revised edition, Ljubljana: L. Schwentner, 1902);

Vinjete (Ljubljana: L. Schwentner, 1899);

Popotovanje Nikolaja Nikiča (Ljubljana: Slovenska Matica, 1900);

Jakob Ruda: Drama v treh dejanjih (Ljubljana: L. Schwentner, 1900);

Knjiga za lahkomiselne ljudi (Ljubljana: L. Schwentner, 1901);

Tujci (Ljubljana: Slovenska Matica, 1901);

Za narodov blagor: Komedija v štirih dejanjih (Ljubljana: L. Schwentner, 1901);

Kralj na Betajnovi: Drama v treh dejanjih (Ljubljana: L. Schwentner, 1902); translated by Henry Leeming as *King of Betajnova,* in *Scena,* 7 (1984): 25–44;

Na klancu (Ljubljana: Slovenska Matica, 1902);

Ob zori (Ljubljana: Ig. pl. Kleinmayr & Fed. Bamberg, 1903);

Življenje in smrt Petra Novljana (Ljubljana: Slovenska Matica, 1903);

Hiša Marije Pomočnice (Ljubljana: L. Schwentner, 1904); translated by Henry Leeming as *The Ward of Our Lady of Mercy* (Ljubljana: Državna založba Slovenije, 1976);

Križ na gori: Ljubezenska zgodba (Ljubljana: Slovenska Matica, 1904);

Gospa Judit (Ljubljana: Lavoslav Schwentner, 1904);

Potepuh Marko in Kralj Matjaž [and] *V mesečini: Zgodba iz doline šentflorjanske* (Ljubljana: Slovenska Matica, 1905);

Nina (Ljubljana: L. Schwentner, 1906);

Martin Kačur: Življenjepis idealista (Ljubljana: Slovenska Matica, 1907);

Smrt in pogreb Jakoba Nesreče (Ljubljana: Slovenska Matica, 1907);

Aleš iz Razora (Ljubljana: Narodna založba, 1907);

Krpanova kobila (Ljubljana: L. Schwentner, 1907);

Hlapec Jernej in njegova pravica (Ljubljana: L. Schwentner, 1907); translated by Sidonie Yeras and

Ivan Cankar

H. C. Sewell Grant as *The Bailiff Yerney and His Rights* (London: John Rodiker, 1930);

Novo življenje (Ljubljana: Slovenska Matica, 1908);

Zgodbe iz doline šentflorjanske (Ljubljana: L. Schwentner, 1908);

Pohujšanje v dolini šentflorjanski: Farsa v treh aktih (Ljubljana: L. Schwentner, 1908);

Za križem (Ljubljana: L. Schwentner, 1909);

Sosed Luka: Kmečka novela (Celovec: Družba sv. Mohorja, 1909);

Kurent: Starodavna pripovedka (Ljubljana: L. Schwentner, 1909);

Bela krizantema: Mojim recenzentom (Ljubljana: L. Schwentner, 1910);

Hlapci: Drama v petih aktih (Ljubljana: L. Schwentner, 1910);

Troje povesti (Celovec: Družba sv. Mohorja, 1911);

Volja in moč (Ljubljana: L. Schwentner, 1911);

Milan in Milena: Ljubezenska pravljica (Ljubljana: L. Schwentner, 1913);

Podobe iz sanj (Ljubljana: Nova založba, 1917); translated by Anton Druzina as *Dream Visions and Other Stories* (Willoughby Hills, Ohio: Slovenian Research Center of America, 1982);

Moje življenje, edited by Dr. Janko Šlebinger (Ljubljana: Zvezna tiskarna, 1920); translated by Elza Jereb and Alasdair MacKinnon as *My Life and Other Sketches* (Ljubljana: Državna založba Slovenije, 1971);

Mimo življenja (Ljubljana: Ig. pl. Kleinmayr & Fed. Bamberg, 1920);

Grešnik Lenart: Življenjepis otroka (Ljubljana: L. Schwentner, 1921);

Romantične duše: Dramatična slika v treh dejanjih (Ljubljana: L. Schwentner, 1922).

Collections: *Zbrani spisi,* 20 volumes, edited by Izidor Cankar (Ljubljana: Nova založba, 1926–1935);

Izbrana dela, 10 volumes, edited by Boris Merhar (Ljubljana: Cankarjeva založba, 1951–1959);

Zbrano delo, 30 volumes, edited by Anton Ocvirk and others (Ljubljana: Državna založba Slovenije, 1967–1976).

PLAY PRODUCTIONS: *Jakob Ruda,* Ljubljana, Deželno gledališče, 16 March 1900;

Kralj na Betajnovi, Ljubljana, Deželno gledališče, 9 January 1904;

Za narodov blagor, Prague, Pištekovo lidové divadlo na Král. Vinohradech, 28 February 1905;

Pohujšanje v dolini šentflorjanski, Ljubljana, Deželno gledališče, 21 December 1907;

Lepa Vida, Ljubljana, Deželno gledališče, 27 January 1912;

Hlapci, Trieste, Slovensko gledališče, 31 May 1919;

Romantične duše, Ljubljana, Narodno gledališče, 6 October 1922.

At the turn of the century Slovene literature underwent a metamorphosis: stilted realism and formalistic versification were swept away by a group of young talents, whose work was commonly called *Slovenska Moderna* (Modern Slovene Art). Among them was Ivan Cankar, who is considered the greatest Slovene writer of all times. He introduced into Slovene literature the latest European styles and transformed Slovene language into a cadence of rhythmic prose verging on poetry.

Ivan Cankar was born on 10 May 1876 in Vrhnika, a small town in western Slovenia. His father, Jožef, was a jobless tailor. Twelve children were born into the family, but only eight survived. The burden of providing for them fell upon the shoulders of their mother, Neža. She took any occasional work she could get and was often forced to beg for food.

Cankar was a bright student in Vrhnika elementary school, and some town dignitaries offered to send him to a Ljubljana high school. As a charity project he lived in miserable conditions, rooming in overcrowded dwellings with sanctimonious landladies; most of the time he was starving. He attended *realka,* a high school that emphasized science. In his junior years he was an excellent student, but later he barely passed, excelling only in Slovene. At the age of fourteen he began writing poems that consisted of patriotic exclamations, naive moralizing, and borrowed eroticism. Yet even in this early versification are some themes that were to become Cankar's own: dedication to his mother and social satire. Some of this poetry was preserved in a handwritten book dated January 1891 and titled, "1. zvezek. Pesmi Ivana Cankarja" (Volume 1, Poems by Ivan Cankar).

In high school Cankar was the leader of a literary club and chief contributor to the school's almanac. He was also a severe critic of his peers' contributions. Through the help of his teacher of Slovene, his poems and short prose were soon accepted by literary magazines. While his prose followed the rules of school compositions, his poetry reflected the influence of Anton Aškerc, who attracted him with his dramatic ballads and with his attitude toward social problems. Under Aškerc's spell Cankar soon rejected dogmatic and political Catholicism and directed his poetic vision away from romantic fantasy and toward the life that surrounded him.

In October 1896 Cankar registered with the faculty of engineering at the Vienna University. But the courses bored him so much that he stopped attending lectures almost immediately. Instead he sank into the study of contemporary European literature and the philosophy of Ralph Waldo Emerson, Benedict de Spinoza, and Friedrich Nietzsche. He also began studying French and Italian. In the evenings he frequented smoke-filled cafés, where he participated in literary discussion presided over by Fran Govekar, the chief proponent of the short-lived period of naturalism in Slovene literature. Under Govekar's influence Cankar became an enthusiastic naturalist. In 1896 he published nine short stories in the conservative newspaper *Slovenec,* which clearly showed this influence. Yet they also include some definite traits of Cankar's own personality and style: his evaluation of situations and his presence in the stories were obvious, even though he theoretically subscribed to the determinism and objectivism of the naturalistic approach.

In cosmopolitan Vienna, Cankar soon encountered other literary currents. He became fascinated with Maurice Maeterlinck, Paul Verlaine, Henrik Ibsen, August Strindberg, and Russian novelists, and he was overcome by the decadents, whose style he considered "naturalism turned inside-out." Thus, while still professing allegiance to naturalism, he created decadent poems and short stories. When he sent them to Ljubljana for publication, some editors were perplexed; some were shocked; and Govekar was angry.

Decadence was just a brief episode in Cankar's art. Sensualism was foreign to his temperament. His "sins" — the world of courtesans, passion, and blasphemy — were a literary pose, far removed from the reality of his poverty-stricken life in Vienna, where he lived on the meager income from articles he wrote for Ljubljana newspapers. In March 1897, unable to cope with his precarious existence any longer, he returned home, presumably for the Easter holidays. He remained in Slovenia for more than a year. At Vrhnika he spent his days corresponding with editors and friends and polishing the manuscript for his first book, *Erotika* (Erotica, 1899), in which he collected his best poems, including the decadent "Dunajski večeri" (Vienna Evenings). He sold it to the Ljubljana publisher Bamberg just in time to pay for the funeral of his beloved mother, who had read her son's poems with pious admiration.

After his wife's death Jožef Cankar moved to Pula to live with one of his daughters. Ivan joined him there for a few months. In Pula he worked on a play, *Jakob Ruda*. It was a tragedy dealing with his mother's death, for which he blamed his weakling father. Under the influence of Ibsen, however, the play grew into a psychoanalytic drama of larger proportions, dramatizing the economic and spiritual collapse of the protagonist. It was published and staged in 1900.

In October 1898 Cankar returned to Vienna, determined to finish his studies, but he did not register at the university until March 1899. He was even poorer than in 1896 and bombarded his publishers with pleas for money. In fall 1899, however, his situation improved when he found new accommodations with a working-class family, a young divorcée seamstress and her four children. The Löfflers provided him with a home for the next ten years, and Albina Löffler became his mistress. He pooled his resources with hers, but they were always short of money. In this struggle for survival Cankar wrote frantically. Whenever he sold a manuscript he handed some money to Albina and spent the rest for drinks. Until 1902 he occasionally attended lectures, but then he dropped all pretenses of being a student. It had become clear to him that his only vocation was writing. From time to time he thought about getting a steady job, but he never accepted one. Financial pressures became extremely severe after he changed his affection from his landlady to her fifteen-year-old daughter Steffi, but Albina Löffler was practical: she continued pampering him and considered him Steffi's fiancé.

In 1899 Bamberg finally published *Erotika*. It caused a scandal. The critics declared it a corrupt book, and the bishop of Ljubljana bought up all available copies and had them burned. Cankar was not too upset; by then he had outgrown his decadent stage. In the same year another Ljubljana publisher, L. Schwentner, published *Vinjete* (Vignettes), a collection of Cankar's naturalistic and decadent prose, and short stories written in a style he had by then adopted as his own: symbolism. Cankar embraced the philosophy of symbolism as formulated by Emerson and Maeterlinck, but he manipulated its stylistic devices in accordance with his own artistic nature and method. In the epilogue to *Vinjete* he consciously disassociated himself from any theories, and from then on he exploited styles of different schools, blending them into a distinct manner that was soon labeled *cankarjanstvo* (cankarism). The source for some of Cankar's vignettes was life in the Vienna slums, but most of the collection comprises satirical sketches exposing the narrow provincialism of Slovene literary and political life. The critics, who were confused about the symbolism in *Vinjete,* rejected Cankar's characters as unreal, his style as affectation, and his themes as indecent and hallucinatory.

By then Cankar was already involved in new projects. His next collection of short stories, *Knjiga za lahkomiselne ljudi* (A Book for Frivolous People, 1901), includes some lyrical sketches about abused children, but it is mainly a combination of fantasy and satire, colored by Nietzschean philosophy. The stories overflow with character types that were to become Cankar's trademark: fat, stupid, dishonest politicians and clergy. Stylistically many of these stories are grotesques. When the book came out in 1901, the critics angrily rejected it, calling the stories blasphemous, cynical, and corrupt.

At about the same time Cankar produced a longer narrative, *Popotovanje Nikolaja Nikiča* (Travels of Nikolaj Nikic, 1900), which depicts the tragic fate of the young poet Dragotin Kette, for whose death he blamed an unfeeling society. His next work, *Tuji* (Strangers, 1901), is based on personal experience and deals with the theme of artists who are unrecognized in their homeland and live as misfits. The critics praised Cankar's elegant style but deplored his pessimism and lack of Christian values.

The same indignation that permeated his stories also inspired three plays Cankar wrote at the turn of the century. When *Jakob Ruda* was performed at the Ljubljana theater in March 1900, the critics rejected it for its lack of positive heroes. Aškerc and Govekar criticized it for personal reasons: they were reaping applause in the theater with their romantic, folklore-based plays, and Cankar was a dangerous intruder.

Cankar's second play, a biting political satire, *Za narodov blagor* (For the Good of the People, published in 1901), was written after he had settled down with the Löfflers. It depicts intrigue and corruption in the two leading Slovene political parties, the conservatives and the liberals. The liberals and the Govekar-led management of the Ljubljana theater refused to stage the play until 1906, after its 1905 premiere in Prague. Most reviewers rejected the play: the right accused Cankar of siding with anarchists, while liberals labeled his satire an exaggeration, stemming from the fact that it was written in Vienna by a man who had lost contact with Slovene reality.

Cankar's third play, *Kralj na Betajnovi* (King of Betajnova, published in 1902), is a sociopsychological dissection of a battle between a tyrant-superman and a rebel-intellectual. The critics declared it unsuitable for the stage, calling the idea of superman ugly, an elaboration of the Nietzschean philosophy. The play was performed in 1904, most likely against Govekar's wishes.

As if to escape from the unpleasantness of the sociopolitical scene in Slovenia, Cankar began writing a novel, *Na klancu* (On the Hillside, 1902), whose subject, his mother, he considered unmarred by evil. Yet his poetic, symbolistic portrait grew into a socio-economic analysis not only of Vrhnika and its "hillside of the poor," but of all Slovenia. The scenes and characters are depicted realistically, but with poetic liberties and symbolic overtones. The critics proclaimed the novel Cankar's best work and recognized the author as a brilliant writer, calling his style intoxicating. They suggested that he forget foreign cities and foreign models and con-

Portrait of Cankar, 1909

tinue writing about people and places in his homeland.

In 1904 Cankar collected some of his short stories that had been published in various magazines in a book titled *Ob zori* (At Dawn). The sketches in this third collection differ from those in his first two in that they are written in a simple, realistic style. Instead of anger and cynicism, they display compassion for the children of the Vienna slums. The liberal critics praised the book, but the conservatives rejected it as gloomy and blasé, swarming with prostitutes and crazy vagabonds.

Cankar wrote about abused, physically and mentally crippled children of Vienna again in a short novel, *Hiša Marije Pomočnice* (The House of Our Lady of Mercy, 1904), which depicts the suffering of fourteen girls shut in a hospital ward for the terminally ill. Some of them have been exposed to sexual abuse. The novel, which consists of self-contained episodes, grew out of Cankar's visits to Amalia Löffler, Steffi's sister, who lived in such a hospital. The cyclical symbolization of the girls' life stories shows the development and refinement of

Cankar's symbolistic style, in spite of many naturalistic descriptions. The critics, however, were not interested in the message or stylistic devices of the novel; they pounced exclusively upon the chapters they considered sexually explicit, and labeled the novel "artistically exquisite pornography." Cankar was deeply hurt, maintaining that the message of *Hiša Marije Pomočnice* was "as pure as a mountain spring." In addition to the theme of the child martyr Cankar continued developing his old motif of the artist-stranger.

The immediate stimulus for his short novel *Križ na gori* (Cross on the Mountain, 1904) was the success of the Slovene Impressionists' exhibition in Vienna. The story is, therefore, optimistic: its young hero-artist does not need to search for glory abroad; he finds happiness with his humble girlfriend from the Gully – another Hillside – a symbol for his homeland.

The new perception of the artist-stranger who has come home was further developed in the parable *Potepuh Marko in Kralj Matjaž* (Vagabond Marko and King Matjaž, 1905). Using a folklore motif, Cankar wanted to show Govekar how folk art could be incorporated into modern literature. It is interesting that Govekar assessed the story positively, while the conservatives deplored the character type of the hero-vagabond.

In 1905 Cankar began dealing with a new theme: teachers, a segment of Slovene intelligentsia, whose existence depended on the whims of political change. The story *Martin Kačur: Življenjepis idealista* (Martin Kačur: A Biography of an Idealist, 1907) describes an eager young teacher and his downfall among the backward people in a remote village. Heavily realistic scenes intermingle with dreams and hallucinations in this novel, which has a compact structure and a dramatic plot. After World War II it was made into a film.

In 1906 Cankar turned his attention to the controversial theme of illegitimate children in two stories, "Smrt in pogreb Jakoba Nesreče" (Death and Funeral of Jacob Badluck) and "Aleš iz Razora" (Aleš from Razor). Both stories are bitter condemnations of society's attitude toward such children. "Aleš iz Razora" also incorporates the theme of religious hypocrisy.

In 1907 L. Schwentner published Cankar's *Krpanova kobila* (Krpan's Mare), a collection of polemical articles and stories that represent the culmination of lengthy exchanges between Cankar and Govekar. The title, based on a classical Slovene tale, ridicules Govekar's "national" plays.

In spite of his literary activities over these years, Cankar felt trapped in his life with the Löfflers. He was becoming aware of the futility of his relationship with tender-hearted Steffi, who could not understand her fiancé's writings. The situation became painfully clear to him in 1907, when he went to Slovenia for the May elections as the Social Democrats' candidate to represent the Sava mining region in the Austro-Hungarian monarchy's National Assembly. In Ljubljana he met a young student, Mici Kessler, with whom he fell deeply in love.

Cankar's acceptance of a political role surprised everybody; yet it was a logical step for the writer who was born, grew up, and worked among the poorest working-class people and who incessantly demanded justice and decried the exploitation of the helpless. During his election campaign he set out to write a brochure about the plight of farm laborers. Instead he produced one of his finest works, *Hlapec Jernej in njegova pravica* (Servant Jernej and His Rights, 1907), a novelette that reads like a ballad and a biblical parable. The work depicts the fate of an aging farm laborer who gets fired and then seeks justice in courts and in the church. Finally he sets the farm on fire and is burned to death. The critics assessed the story in superlatives. They especially praised Cankar's biblically solemn language. *Hlapec Jernej* has been repeatedly dramatized and staged and has been translated into many languages.

After his unsuccessful candidacy in the elections, Cankar dutifully returned to Vienna. He decided to marry Steffi immediately and even obtained a loan to pay for the wedding. He kept postponing the event, however, and instead buried himself in work. He soon returned to an old theme: abused children. He prepared *Za križem* (Following the Cross, 1909), a collection of new and previously published short stories. Many of the stories are set in Ottakring, where he lived and where the buildings were crowded with industrial laborers, toiling seamstresses, Czech immigrants, and pale, timid children. Other stories, based on his memories of his Vrhnika childhood portray hungry altar boys, orphans, the mentally handicapped, illegitimate children, emigrants, and vagabonds. The introduction to the collection is a symbolic passage in which Christ, wearing a red robe, leads a procession of the downtrodden toward Golgotha and salvation. The epilogue is a poem dedicating the book to Mici Kessler. Among the reviews of the book, the most interesting one tried to define the by-then-established term *cankarjanstvo*.

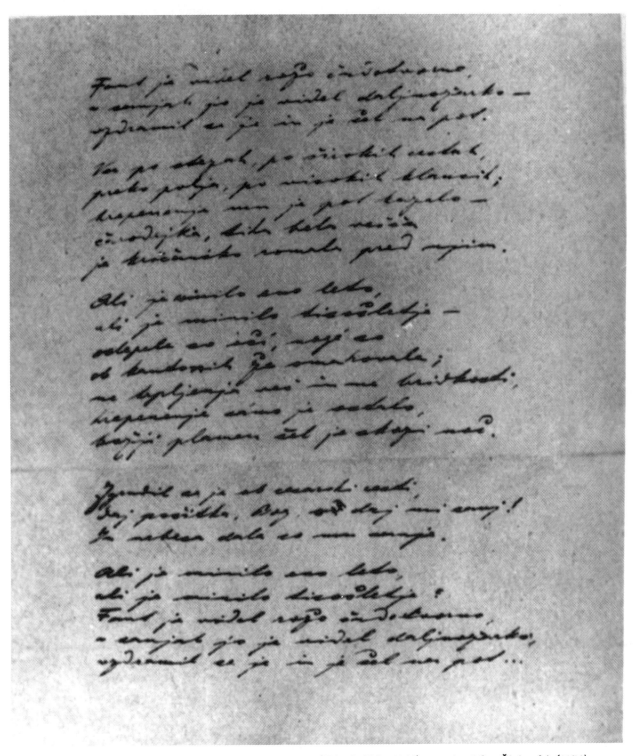

Page from the manuscript for Cankar's play Lepa Vida *(Vida the Fair, 1912); reproduced from* Živi orfej *(1970)*

In 1908 Cankar prepared a collection of satirical stories, *Zgodbe iz doline šentflorjanske* (Tales from the Valley of Saint Florian), and a published play, *Pohujšanje v dolini šentflorjanski* (Corruption in the Valley of Saint Florian). Together they represent a new cycle in his work. They combine two of his old motifs: the artist-stranger; and the bigoted, amoral bourgeois. Stylistically they combine lyrical fantasy and satirical grotesque. They are Cankar's most provocative reckoning with "dolina šentflorjanska," his homeland.

In the stories and the play the hero-artist-wanderer returns incognito to the Valley of Saint Florian, accompanied by his beautiful girlfriend. They settle in a hut above the valley. The community is deeply shocked; but at night the dignitaries prowl around the lovers' nest to feast their eyes on other people's sins. The lovers flee. When the farce was performed at Ljubljana, the critics dismissed it as the product of the ungrateful author's vengeful imagination.

In the same year, because of his perpetual search for new publishers and sources of income, Cankar wrote a story for the Catholic publisher Mohorjeva družba (Saint Mohor Society). Although *Sosed Luka* (Neighbor Luka, 1909), is a didactic version of the sin-and-atonement motif, the conservative critics rejected it. They were annoyed that a Catholic publisher would inflict upon unsuspecting readers stories by the leading Slovene nihilist and cynic. This attack hurt Cankar deeply, especially because he had already prepared another book, a collection of three stories, for the same publisher, who was now reluctant to accept it.

In spite of all the misunderstandings and attacks on his work, Cankar's dedication to his homeland never faltered. In summer 1909 he produced one of his most poetical works, a tale titled *Kurent* (a mythological character). The main theme of this symbolistic work is the emigration of the impoverished Slovene peasants, but it is conveyed through the unreal world of fairy tale and folklore, a sphere Cankar had touched upon in *Potepuh Marko*. The text is full of fantastic elements, which intertwine with highly stylized scenes from real life. At the end of the story Kurent, a fiddler-vagabond, leads the procession of the doomed toward the ship that will take them away. The laments of the impoverished folk and Kurent's hymns to his beloved homeland are written in a solemn, rhythmic prose.

Kurent was the last work of Cankar's Vienna period. In September 1909 he left for a visit with one of his brothers, a priest in Sarajevo. There Cankar added to *Kurent* an epilogue in the form of three sonnets, in which he expressed a newfound joy, an awakening from doom and despair, a belief in God. This catharsis might have stemmed from his feeling of physical and spiritual liberation from the Vienna bondage. The critics rejected *Kurent* as incomprehensible, and one of them decided that Cankar's work had no literary value because his mellifluous language conveyed nothing.

After he had completed *Kurent,* Cankar concentrated on a new play. *Hlapci* (Servants; published, 1910; produced, 1919) deals with the fate of teachers after the conservatives' victory in the 1909 elections. Having presented a teacher-idealist in *Martin Kačur* and the frightened teacher Šviligoj in *Pohujšanje,* Cankar now depicted a whole gallery of intimidated teachers in a Slovene village, who, afraid for their jobs, become obedient servants of the new regime. The only rebel among them is destroyed economically and psychologically.

In November 1909 Cankar left Sarajevo for Ljubljana, settling in a hotel in Tivoli Park to await the première of *Hlapci*. The play, however, was censored and never performed during his lifetime. It was published in book form in January 1910. The critics called Cankar's portrayal of teachers a falsified picture, and the conservatives even urged teachers to answer Cankar's accusations, labeling *Hlapci* an inferior product of a money-hungry, deteriorating author. The teachers took up the challenge and published a declaration against Cankar's defamation of their profession.

While waiting for the censor to release his play, Cankar wrote *Bela krizantema* (A White Chrysanthemum, 1910), a bitter reckoning with his assorted critics, especially Govekar. The book is a combination of a lyrical essay and short stories. Its title is symbolic: the white chrysanthemum in the lapel of a beggar represents the art, including Cankar's, of the economically impoverished Slovene nation. When the book was published, the critics angrily labeled Cankar a mentally unstable megalomaniac, calling his art an artificial chrysanthemum.

By the time Cankar finished writing *Bela krizantema,* he had decided not to return to Vienna. Thus ended the most productive, if the most difficult, period in his life. In the spring of 1910 he found a new home at a pleasant inn atop Rožnik, a hill above Tivoli Park. He lived there almost until his death. For a while the Löfflers continued prodding him to "come home," but Steffi eventually married and lived a long, contented life.

During the last eight years of his life, the aggressiveness of Cankar's Vienna period gave way to a gentler kind of humanism, which concerned itself with ethical rather than sociopolitical questions. He now contemplated the psychological complexities of the human soul, and with merciless honesty confessed his own misdeeds and imperfections. Such musings also determined the form of his writings: instead of realistic dramas and novels, he wrote mostly short, lyrical sketches including memories and reflections. His language underwent its final tuning: the rhythm of his sentences obliterated the borderline between poetry and prose.

Cankar's last play, the highly symbolic *Lepa Vida* (Vida the Fair), is set in a dilapidated Ljubljana sugar refinery, a home for the homeless, in which the author had witnessed the death of two friends, talented young poets. *Lepa Vida* depicts their suffering and unfulfilled dreams. The heroine, Vida, is based on a character in Slovene folklore, but in Cankar's play she is the symbol of art and of longing for love and purity. *Lepa Vida* was staged in January 1912. The critics dismissed it as unsuitable for the stage but praised its language. Oton Župančič, the main poet of the *Moderna* group, called the play "the high mass of the Slovene language."

Cankar's last two full-length narratives were *Volja in moč* (Will and Power, 1911) and *Milan in Milena* (Milan and Milena, 1913). They deal with the theme of spiritual dualism: body, the source of evil, versus soul, the source of purity. In both works the heroes reject the physical aspect of love and conclude that the only salvation from evil lies in the negation of man's biological existence, a philosophy similar to that in Leo Tolstoy's *Kreutzer Sonata* (1890). The critics, who discussed philosophical questions instead of the artistic value of Cankar's stories, declared that the author lacked a scholarly mind for such analyses.

Cankar's short stories of his last period, often tiny lyrical sketches, were first published in magazines and daily papers. He prepared some of them for publication in book form. The first of such collections, *Moja njiva* (My Field), which was not published during Cankar's lifetime, includes his memories of the people who had been close to him and whom he had hurt; among these he most often thinks of Steffi and of his father, who had died, neglected and alone, at Vrhnika. Some stories are thematically connected with the Saint Florian cycle and represent the last specimens of Cankar's satirical prose. A few deal with a new motif: animal life around the Rožnik inn. The accomplished group, "Ob svetem grobu" (By the Sacred Grave), is dedicated to Cankar's mother. In these stories he does not portray his mother as a representative of a social class or as a symbol, as he did in *Na klancu;* he

shows her as a woman with tremendous moral strength and an unlimited capacity for love, at the same time confessing his guilt of youthful arrogance and unpaid debts. The cycle "Ob svetem grobu" became the best known of his lyrical sketches and has been repeatedly republished and translated.

The second collection, *Moje življenje* (My Life), a string of sketches from Cankar's childhood, was his attempt at autobiography. It was published in book form in 1920, after the author's death. In these sketches Cankar reminisces about his childhood home, carefree games, his first experience of injustice in the school he hated, his first encounter with death. *Moje življenje,* too, has often been republished and translated, and it is considered the key to Cankar's personality.

Another collection of autobiographical sketches, *Grešnik Lenart* (Sinner Lenart, 1921), deals with Cankar's high-school years in Ljubljana. Written in the third person, it has as its main event a petty theft that a starving student commits against his benefactor. The psychological crisis is finally resolved by Lenart's mother's understanding and forgiveness.

World War I disrupted Cankar's life in a ruthless manner. From 23 August until 9 October 1914 he was jailed because of his publicly expressed sympathies for the Serbs and for a future union of the South Slavs. A year later, in spite of his frail physical condition, he was drafted into the Austrian army. He was suffering from nervous tension and heart disease, as well as from enuresis, a lifelong source of humiliation. He ate little and drank too much. He was dismissed from the army within six weeks and returned to Rožnik.

The events of the war overshadowed his personal memories. He perceived war as torture and humiliation of all humanity and a dangerous threat to the existence of the Slovene nation. From these feelings grew the contents of his last collection *Podobe iz sanj* (Dream Visions), which was published in 1917. The sketches in *Podobe iz sanj* are hardly stories: events are described rarely, and the "visions" are mostly meditations. In a highly symbolistic style verging on expressionism, they display horrors at the front, villages collapsing into rubble and ashes, a world governed by insanity, evil, destruction, and death. Only toward the end does Cankar express hope, and finally belief in salvation; the collection culminates in a solemn allegory of a "high mass."

Podobe iz sanj was accepted by critics and readers as his finest. The artist had finally come home; he was not a stranger anymore. Like his three collections of memories, *Podobe iz sanj* has been republished and translated many times.

By the time *Podobe iz sanj* came out, Cankar was no longer living at Rožnik. The inn had changed hands, and he did not feel welcome there any longer. In September 1917 he moved to downtown Ljubljana. At the end of October 1918 he fell on the stairs of the building where he lived and injured his neck. A month later he contracted pneumonia, and on 11 December 1918 he died. He is buried in Ljubljana in a common grave with fellow members of the *Moderna* group, the poets Dragotin Kette and Josip Murn.

During his lifetime Cankar was the central personality in Slovene literature. Nearly all writers of his time succumbed to the magic of his style, imitating it consciously or subconsciously. The expressionism of his last book influenced the postwar expressionists to such a degree that they gave some of their magazines the names of his books (*Lepa Vida, Križ na gori*). With his analysis of social injustice Cankar also prepared the way for the social realism of the 1930s. His art, which had been incomprehensible to most critics during his lifetime, became the subject of scholarly research. Between 1926 and 1935 his *Zbrani spisi* (Collected Writings) were published in twenty volumes by his cousin Izidor Cankar. After World War II many professional and amateur theater groups began staging his plays, especially *Kralj na Betajnovi, Pohujšanje v dolini šentflorjanski,* and *Hlapci*. Between 1951 and 1959 his *Izbrana dela* (Selected Works) were published in ten volumes, and between 1967 and 1976 the scrupulously precise *Zbrano delo* (Collected Works) appeared in thirty volumes. Essays on different aspects of Cankar's personality and art inundated literary magazines and scholarly reviews. In addition to Slovene problems Cankar dealt with themes that are common to all humanity; therefore, his work has been translated into many languages, including English.

Letters:

Pisma Ivana Cankarja, 3 volumes, edited by Izidor Cankar (Ljubljana: Državna založba Slovenije, 1948);

Pisma I – V, volumes 26–30 of *Zbrano delo,* edited by Jože Munda (Ljubljana: Državna založba Slovenije, 1970–1976).

Bibliographies:

Fran Petrè, *Rod in mladost Ivana Cankarja* (Ljubljana: Slovenski knjižni zavod, 1947);

Lojz Kraigher, *Ivan Cankar,* 2 volumes (Ljubljana, 1954, 1958);

France Dobrovoljc, *Bibliografija literature o Cankarjevi dramatiki* (Ljubljana: Mestno gledališče, 1960);

Damnjan Moračić, "Bibliografska gradja o Ivanu Cankaru," *Književnost i jezik,* 23 (1976): 255–259;

Albert Širok, *Moja srečanja s Cankarjem* (Trieste: Založništvo tržaskega tiska, 1976).

References:

Francè Bernik, *Cankarjeva zgodnja proza* (Ljubljana: Cankarjeva založba, 1976);

Bernik, "Problem Cankarjeve lirike," *Slavistična revija,* 16 (1968): 169–202;

Wilhelm Heiliger, *Nostalgie bei Ivan Cankar* (London: Slavic Press, 1972);

Janko Kos, "Cankar in problem slovenskega romana," *Sodobnost,* 24 (1976): 413–423;

Janko Lavrin, "The Conscience of a Small Nation (On Ivan Cankar)," in his *Aspects of Modernism* (London: Nott, 1935), pp. 197–207;

Joža Mahnič, *Obdobje Moderne,* in *Zgodovina slovenskega slovstva,* volume 5, edited by Lino Legiša (Ljubljana: Slovenska matica, 1964);

Miha Maleš, *Podoba Ivana Cankarja: Spominski zbornik,* I. del (Ljubljana: Bibliofilska založba, 1945);

Irma M. Ozbalt, "Social Misfits in Morley Callaghan's and Ivan Cankar's Fiction," Ph.D. dissertation, McGill University, 1977;

Dušan Pirjevec, "Ivan Cankar in naturalizem," *Slavistična revija,* 13 (1961–1962): 1–48;

Anton Slodnjak, "Ivan Cankar in Slovene and World Literature," *Slavonic and East European Review,* 59 (April 1981): 186–196;

Slodnjak, *Slovensko slovstvo* (Ljubljana: Mladinska knjiga, 1968), pp. 268–279, 306–336;

Helena Stupan, *Od Prešerna do Cankarja* (Maribor: Založba Obzorja, 1955), pp. 239–258;

Josip Vidmar, *O Ivanu Cankarju* (Ljubljana: Državna založba Slovenije, 1976);

Vidmar, Štefan Barbarič, and Fran Zadravec, eds., *Simpozij o Ivanu Cankarju* (Ljubljana: Slovenska matica, 1977);

Božo Vodušek, *Ivan Cankar* (Ljubljana: Hram, 1937);

Wolfram Walder, *Ivan Cankar als Kunstpersönlichkeit* (Graz & Cologne: Hermann Bolhaus Nacht, 1954);

Franc Zadravec, "Subjektivne in objektivne osnove Cankarjeve satire," *Slavistična revija,* 24 (1976): 57–70.

Miloš Crnjanski

(26 October 1893 – 30 November 1977)

Nicholas Moravcevich
University of Illinois at Chicago

BOOKS: *Maska: Poetička komedija* (Zagreb: Nakl. Društva hrv. književnika, 1918);

Lirika Itake (Belgrade: S. B. Cvijanović, 1920);

Priče o muškom (Belgrade: S. B. Cvijanović, 1920);

Dnevnik o Čarnojeviću (Belgrade: Sveslovenska knjižara, 1921;

Naše plaže na Jadranu (Belgrade: Izdanje Jadranske straže, 1927);

Seobe (Belgrade: Geca Kon, 1929); translated by Michael Henry Heim as *Migrations* (New York: Harcourt Brace, 1994);

Ljubav u Toskani (Belgrade: Geca Kon, 1930);

Sabrana dela, 2 volumes (Belgrade: Narodna Prosveta, 1930);

Knjiga o Nemačkoj (Belgrade: Geca Kon, 1931);

Sveti Sava (Belgrade: Zadruga Profesorskog društva, 1935);

Belgrade (Belgrade: Bureau Central de Presse, 1936);

Seobe; Dnevnik o Čarnojeviću (Subotica: Minerva, 1956);

Konak (Belgrade: Minerva, 1958);

Itaka i komentari (Belgrade: Prosveta, 1959);

Seobe i druga knjiga Seoba, 2 volumes (Belgrade: Srpska književna zadruga, 1962);

Lirika, proza, eseji (Novi Sad: Matica srpska, 1965);

Serbia, Seobe, Lament nad Beogradom (Novi Sad: Matica srpska, 1965);

Tri poeme (Belgrade: Prosveta, 1965);

Kod hiperborejaca (Belgrade: Prosveta, 1966);

Sabrana dela, 10 volumes, edited by Roksanda Njeguš and Stevan Raičković (Belgrade: Prosveta, 1966);

Izabrana dela, 4 volumes (Belgrade: Prosveta, 1967);

Lirika (Belgrade: Prosveta, 1968);

Kap španske krvi (Belgrade: Nolit, 1970);

Roman o Londonu, 2 volumes (Belgrade: Nolit, 1971);

Priče o muškom, Suzni krokodil, Maska (Belgrade: Beogradski izdavačko-grafički zavod, 1973);

Miloš Crnjanski

Sabrane pesme (Belgrade: Srpska književna zadruga, 1978);

Knjiga o Mikelandjelu (Belgrade: Nolit, 1981);

Sumatra i druge pjesme (Sarajevo: Veselin Malseša, 1981);

Embahade (Belgrade: Nolit, 1983);

O Banatu i o Banaćanima (Novi Sad: Književna zajednica Novog Sada, 1989);

Politički spisi (Belgrade: Sfairos, 1989);

Eseji i prikazi (Novi Sad: Književna zajednica Novog Sada, 1991).

Edition in English: Selection of Crnjanski's poems in *Serbian Poetry from the Beginnings to the Present,* various translators, edited by Milne Holton and Vasa D. Mihailovich (New Haven: Yale Center for International and Area Studies, 1988), pp. 234–240.

OTHER: *Antologija kineske lirike i Pesme starog Japana,* edited and translated by Crnjanski (Belgrade: Narodna biblioteka Srbije, 1990).

The work of Miloš Crnjanski, which includes novels, poetry, short stories, essays, and travel books, ranks among the highest accomplishments of modern Serbian literature. While the range and depth of both his prose and his verse place him in the forefront of twentieth-century Serbian writers, the singularity of his style gives him an even more extraordinary place.

Crnjanski was born on 26 October 1893 in Čongrad, Hungary, to an impoverished Serbian family – Thomas, a local notary public, and Mary Crnjanski. Completing his primary education in Pančevo, where he stayed with his maternal grandfather, Crnjanski subsequently entered a high school in Temesvar, where he lodged with a poor schoolteacher named Dušan Berić, who according to Crnjanski's recollections was as influential in his intellectual development as his parents. After the death of Crnjanski's father in 1909 his mother moved to Temesvar (now Timisoara), and Crnjanski lived with her until his graduation in 1912. He then entered the export academy in the Adriatic port city of Rijeka. After a year of study he moved to Vienna. Until the outbreak of World War I he oscillated between his interests in philosophy and art history and the bohemian existence of a poetic, carefree young man.

Drafted into the Austro-Hungarian army and sent to the Serbian front, he soon ended up in a hospital in Vukovar after an epidemic of cholera and later was transferred to Rijeka. In the hospital there he started to write poems for his first collection of verse, *Lirika Itake* (Lyrics of Ithaca, 1920), and to compose his first play, *Maska: Poetična komedija,* (The Mask: A Poetic Comedy, 1918).

In the summer of 1915 he was sent back to his regiment in Bečkerek and shortly thereafter departed with it to the eastern front in Galicia. Though he participated in several battles around Zlota Lipa, he still found time that autumn to begin composing his first novel, *Dnevnik o Čarnojeviću* (The Diary about Čarnojević, 1921). Toward the end of 1915 he was again in a hospital, in Krakow. Through the help of his aunt, a nun, he was transferred to the hospital of her monastery in Vienna. In the following year, again through his aunt's connections, he was spared further frontline duty and was sent instead to Šegedin to serve as a telephone switchboard operator at a railroad station, which allowed him to continue work on his poetry and prose.

Early in 1917 he met Julije Benešić, editor of the Zagreb literary journal *Savremenik* (The Contemporary), who soon published four of his poems. That winter Crnjanski completed a short training course in the reserve officers' school in Ostrogon and was ordered to report to the army headquarters on the Italian front. On the way he stopped in Zagreb to meet Benešić, who seemed willing to publish some of the young writer's prose as well.

Crnjanski saw no combat in Italy in the opening months of 1918; only a few weeks after his arrival he was again recuperating in a military hospital, this time in Opatija, where he concentrated on his literary work. In September he had to return to the Italian front, but in a matter of days he obtained a three-month leave for Vienna – ostensibly to take university examinations, although in 1913 he had left the export academy without completing any graduation requirements.

With the political and military collapse of the Austro-Hungarian Empire a few months later, Crnjanski returned home, now in the Banat village of Ilandža, where he spent the first postwar winter with his mother while working on *Dnevnik o Čarnojeviću*. That year *Savremenik* printed a dozen of his short stories and poems, while the Society of Croat Writers published the poetic comedy *Maska*.

In the spring of 1919 Crnjanski went to Belgrade to begin studying comparative literature at the university. In addition to his prose and verse contributions to various journals, the publisher S. B. Cvijanović brought out *Lirika Itake*. The book was an instant success, establishing Crnjanski as a notable contemporary author within the Belgrade literary community. The poems are characterized by a distinctly expressionistic protest against war and carnage, full of bitter irony and denial of the conventional myths surrounding warfare. They also express an equally fervent yearning for some cosmic ecstasy epitomized through dreams about the purity and peace of the faraway snowy peaks of the Urals and the unknown expanses of exotic islands, seas, and diamond-pure constellations of unreachable stars. His lyricism mixes this quest for the unattainable with the melodiousness and elegiac sadness of the romantic expression of the early Serbian poet Branko Radičević.

During his first year at the University of Belgrade, Crnjanski met Vida Ružić, his future wife. Upon his graduation in the spring of 1920 he departed for Paris for further study at the Sorbonne. Though he was displeased with the publisher of *Dnevnik o Čarnojeviću*, who demanded a drastic shortening and revision, Crnjanski maintained his creative momentum by publishing some of his shorter prose and verse works and his collection *Priče o muškom* (Tales of the Masculine, 1920). However, the book had only a lukewarm reception. In Paris, Crnjanski concentrated on his studies and in his spare time undertook to translate into Serbian Chinese poetry he encountered in French and English translations.

In the fall of 1921 Crnjanski was compelled to return to Yugoslavia for a short tour of reserve military training in the Bosnian town of Mostar. Beforehand, however, he spent three months in Italy, meeting his girlfriend Ruzić and an already prominent writer of his generation, Ivo Andrić, who was then a secretary of the royal Yugoslav embassy in the Vatican. While staying in Florence with Vida, Crnjanski wrote his well-known long poem "Stražilovo.

In October, after his military training in Mostar – where he was often in the company of Aleksa Šantić, a prominent poet of the older generation – Crnjanski departed for Belgrade to marry Ružić. He also started to collaborate with Stanislav Vinaver, Rastko Petrović, and a few other Belgrade modernists gathered around the literary journal *Zenit* (Zenith). Toward the end of 1921 this circle became known as the Belgrade Literary Union Alpha and entered publishing with its Albatros imprint, which as its first offering published *Dnevnik o Čarnojeviću*. Like Crnjanski's first poetry collection, this short novel was imbued with his expressionistic anguish over the horrors of war and destruction. It offered a many-faceted picture of the disturbed psychology of a young man who left the unspeakable carnage of the war totally changed, disturbed, and mistrustful

of old verities yet still given in his imagination to yearnings for something new that would be higher and more beautiful.

In search of a permanent job after his marriage, Crnjanski first accepted the position of a gymnastics teacher in the high school of Pančevo and in the following year succeeded in obtaining a transfer to a Belgrade high school as a history teacher. Later, to supplement his small earnings, he turned to journalism. In 1923 he published fragments from his travels through Italy, joined the staff of the prestigious newspaper *Politika* (Politics), and was drawn deeper into the political life of the country. He also turned to theatrical criticism, worked with Marko Ristić on the journal *Putevi* (Roads), and published his *Antologija kineske lirike* (Anthology of Chinese Lyrics, 1923).

Two years later he joined the staff of the newspaper *Vreme* (Time), began to participate in the periodicals *Naša krila* (Our Wings) and *Almanah Jadranske Straže* (Almanac of the Adriatic Guard), and published a poem, "Serbia." In 1926, while writing a series of journalistic reports on the Royal Yugoslav Air Force, he quarreled with and insulted an officer with whom he afterward fought a duel, which ended without harm to either participant.

In 1927 Crnjanski published a booklet, *Naše plaže na Jadranu* (Our Adriatic Beaches), and gave the manuscript of his major novel, *Seobe* (1929; translated as *Migrations*, 1994), to the prestigious journal *Srpski književni glasnik* (Serbian Literary Herald) for serial publication. A year later he followed with another booklet, *Boka Kotorska* (The Bay of Kotor), and an anthology of Japanese poetry titled *Pesme starog Japana* (Songs of Old Japan). Later that year he became press attaché in the Royal Yugoslav embassy in Berlin and soon after began to write his travel book *Knjiga o Nemačkoj* (A Book on Germany, 1931). Throughout the following year he participated from Berlin in a heated newspaper debate concerning the rejection of his travel books from Italy by the Srpska književna zadruga (Serbian Literary Cooperative).

The year 1929 was important for Crnjanski's literary career, for the appearance of his novel *Seobe* was a major literary event. The novel is a vast panorama of eighteenth-century Serbian life in the swampy borderlands of the Austro-Hungarian Empire after a vast segment of the Serbian nation had been compelled to abandon its Ottoman-oppressed medieval homeland to settle there. The idea of migration in search of a new and better homeland is the central motif of the entire work and the dominant obsession of its protagonist, Maj. Vuk Isa-

Crnjanski in 1932 (photograph by Milan Bogdanović)

ković. Though a warrior of lesser rank, he is drawn in a sufficiently exalted manner to give the novel a truly epic foundation.

The quest starts with Vuk Isaković's vague yearning for some special, unknown, and yet intensely familiar region of peace and tranquillity, a place that would be his and his people's ultimate haven — the long-awaited terminus of all their spatial and spiritual wanderings. At first this hallowed abode exists only in his feverish imagination as an abstract vision of a celestial domain seen as an "endless blue circle with a star in it." Eventually, while he and his Serbs trudge off to yet another pointless Austro-French war in the distant valleys of Alsace, this dream of a privileged region of harmony and calm becomes identified in his mind with the image of distant Russia. Vuk is irresistibly drawn to it by the force of his faith in "sweet orthodoxy" and the ancestral ties of racial and linguistic kinship. With every new misfortune that befalls him and his men in their irrelevant foreign campaign, this dream of a great new journey, this urge for an ultimate, conclusive migration to that distant, holy Russia, gains in

intensity and color. Yet the story of Vuk's striving to transcend the glum reality of his misspent life ends inconclusively. While he continues to hold on to the idea of an impending resettlement to the end of the novel, the conflict between his desire to embark on a great new journey and his reluctance to leave his settled existence in pursuit of such a venture remains unresolved, and the resultant impasse torments him like a disease for the rest of his life.

In 1930 Crnjanski returned to Yugoslavia just as his controversial book of travel pieces from Italy, titled *Ljubav u Toskani* (Love in Tuscany), appeared. In Belgrade he returned to his former position of high-school history teacher and continued his journalistic work. In the same year he saw the appearance of his *Sabrana dela* (Collected Works) in two volumes, with an introduction by Milan Bogdanović, a prominent contemporary literary critic. Crnjanski received two literary awards for *Knjiga o Nemačkoj*. In 1931, as the essays from that book continued to feed the fires of literary debates in Belgrade and Zagreb, Crnjanski was for the first time labeled a reactionary by his left-oriented modernist literary friends. The journalistic controversies even led to court trials, with Crnjanski bringing legal charges against two of his critics.

In 1932 the rift between Crnjanski and the leftists widened even more, since by then their literary arguments had spilled over into ideological and political disagreements aired in court proceedings that were widely publicized in the papers. While the debate was in full swing, *Vreme* serially published his novel about Lola Montez, entitled *Kap španske krvi* (A Drop of Spanish Blood, 1970). Both the literary critics and the reading public found this work distinctly inferior to his achievements in *Seobe*. This reaction, on top of all the disappointments and vexations he had experienced in his antileftist stand, prompted him to turn away from literary work and dedicate himself to journalism.

In 1935 he published only a booklet on Saint Sava and a series of short travel pieces from his visit to Spain. In addition, he started the journal *Ideje* (Ideas), for which he wrote many conservative political editorials. That year he entered the diplomatic service of Yugoslavia and returned to Berlin. During his two-year sojourn in Germany he traveled to Denmark, Spain, England, Sweden, and Norway. Throughout this period he kept up his journalistic ties with *Vreme,* and his journeys resulted in a series of foreign-affairs reports.

In 1939 Crnjanski was transferred from Berlin to Rome, and he continued to send to *Vreme* his foreign-affairs reports about the deteriorating political situation on the eve of World War II. At this time he also began to compose his extensive travel-memoir, *Kod hiperborejaca* (With the Hyperboreans, 1966), and his essays on Italian art, *Knjiga o Mikelandjelu* (A Book about Michelangelo, 1981). When Italian-Yugoslav political and diplomatic relations worsened even more in 1940, he sent his wife back to Yugoslavia and remained in Rome, increasingly isolated.

In April 1941, after Italy had declared war on Yugoslavia, he was under house arrest for some time until the Yugoslav government ordered its Italian embassy staff to move to Lisbon. With his wife, who joined him on the trip west, Crnjanski spent several months in Portugal and then joined the Yugoslav government in exile in London. During the war years he was politically active but published nothing. With the creation of a Communist-dominated Yugoslavia at the end of the war, he chose to remain in London. To reorient himself and start a new career in his fifty-second year, he enrolled in international affairs at the University of London. In 1946 he wrote an unpublished novel in English titled "The Shoemakers," hoping that this would help establish him on the British literary scene. Yet his work remained unnoticed, and his desperate attempts to find employment – as a receptionist in a hotel, a distributor of books, or a shoe-store employee – failed one after another. For a considerable length of time he and his wife were supported only by her receipts from the door-to-door sales of the dolls sewn by her in their tiny apartment in the London suburb of Finchley.

In 1949, through some connections of Crnjanski's wife, the émigré couple was given a modest apartment in the stable area of an estate belonging to a wealthy British gentlewoman, Lady Padget, the wife of a former viceroy of India. Because Vida Crnjanski, in exchange for that charity, was obliged to keep company with her benefactor and serve her in demeaning household chores, Crnjanski found the circumstances insulting and kept out of sight as much as possible. To extricate them from what seemed to him an unacceptable, beggarly existence, he placed all his employment hopes in his completed hotel management degree. When his efforts failed, he tried to overcome his misery and frustration by concentrating on a new literary project, the sequel to *Seobe*. The second book of the two-volume *Seobe* proved not to be a direct sequel to the first except thematically and through its interest in the world of the eighteenth-century Austro-Serbian diaspora. It begins in the spring of 1752, seven years after the conclusion of Vuk Isaković's last military

campaign. Vuk does not appear, except as the subject of an occasional reminiscence or argument, and its hero is his adopted son, cavalry captain Pavel, who is the moving force behind the decision of the entire Isaković clan to leave Austria and who is the main organizer of his people's eventually successful resettlement in Russia.

Pavel's resolve to accomplish this task involves him in a series of picaresque adventures. Through these bildungsroman wanderings he is gradually transformed into the full-fledged inheritor of his stepfather's obsessive quest for personal tranquillity and happiness and a rightful place under the sun for his uprooted, grief-surfeited people. Though the symbolic and lyrical suggestions of the central significance of that striving are not as heavily accentuated in this work as they were in the preceding one, the already-familiar archetypes of the morning star, blue skies, and the feeling of ascent are as prominent in Pavel's imagination as they were in Vuk's. So is his dream of Russia. From the beginning of the Austrian reforms in Vojvodina, designed to lessen the freedoms of the Serbs in the frontier lands, Pavel's disgust with Austria is as deep as that of his stepfather a decade before; his trust in deliverance through a move to Russia is essentially as mythopoeic. However, after he establishes his first contact with the Russians in Vienna, Pavel gradually begins to see the flight to Russia not as the ultimate goal of his people's quest for a home but as a necessary intermediate move on the path to final delivery from both Turkish and Austrian oppression. From that moment the idea that the Austrian Serbs should migrate to Russia so that they could later sweep down into the Balkans with the Russians to liberate their ancient homeland becomes Pavel's central obsession, a cardinal fixation that remains at the foundation of all his subsequent spiritual longings. Yet Pavel's clear understanding of his spiritual yearning for a true home only provides him with a greater sense of loss when, upon his arrival in Russia, he finally faces the truth that he and his people's great migration was not a temporary move but an irrevocable act of irreversible estrangement and ultimate disappearance through assimilation.

Pavel's search for a true haven, though clearer, bolder, and far more tangible than Vuk's, also comes to nothing at the end of the novel. However, the stubborn and quixotic persistence with which he pursues his quest for the impossible allows him to pass, very much like Vuk, through both the bright and dark areas of his misspent life with the dignity and decorum of a genuine tragic hero. Even aside

МИЛОШ ЦРЊАНСКИ КАП ШПАНСКЕ КРВИ

НОЛИТ

Cover for Crnjanski's 1970 book, Kap španske krvi *(A Drop of Spanish Blood), which was first published serially in the newspaper* Vreme *in 1932*

from the heroic dimension of Vuk's and Pavel's personal quests for tranquillity and home, Crnjanski's narrative in both parts of the novel gains much of its epic texture from his presentation of the motif of migration as a collective phenomenon involving not only the destiny of the Isaković clan led first by Vuk and later by Pavel, but that of the entire Austro-Serbian diaspora as well. The sections of the second book of *Seobe* that show details of the Serbian exodus to Russia produce the impression that the entire country is on the move toward the magic goal of the promised land, and the vastness of that long trek eastward impresses the reader with its own momentum and symbolism.

The completion of the second book of *Seobe* brought no improvement in the ill fortune of the Crnjanski family. Though in 1951 Crnjanski's wife received her diploma as a fashion seamstress and he graduated from the University of London with a de-

gree in international affairs, the promised position at Cambridge did not materialize. They remained stranded at Lady Padget's estate, although by then Crnjanski refused to have any personal contact with their benefactor. After a while he even gave up looking for a job and spent all his time writing.

In 1956, during a short vacation at Cooden Beach near London, he composed his major long poem "Lament nad Beogradom" (Lament over Belgrade), which illustrates better than anything the extent of his nostalgia and sadness over a misspent life in exile. However, that year also marked the beginning of his resurrection in Serbian literature, for the publishing house Minerva in the Vojvodinian town of Subotica decided to republish *Seobe* and *Dnevnik o Čarnojeviću*. The positive reaction of both critics and the reading public prompted Crnjanski to establish contact with Yugoslavia's leading literary paper, *Književne novine* (Literary Gazette), and the prominent journals *Književnost* (Literature) and *Savremenik* (Contemporary). This led to a notable increase in his artistic visibility in a country where he was still considered politically undesirable.

In 1957 segments of the second book of *Seobe* were serialized in *Književnost;* in the following year Minerva published the play *Konak* (Hostel), and in 1959 the country's leading publishing house, Prosveta (Enlightenment), followed with the complete text of *Itaka i komentari* (Ithaca and Comentaries). The enormous interest in Crnjanski's work that these publications generated in Yugoslavia led not only to an avalanche of his additional contributions to various literary journals but also to discussions of the possibility of his return. In 1965 these initially tentative probes resulted in an official government invitation to terminate his exile. After some hesitation Crnjanski decided to accept the offer, despite his awareness that such a move would serve the propagandist aims of Yugoslavia's Communist regime bent on furthering its legitimization in the West and on discrediting the anti-Communist stand of the Serbian intelligentsia in exile.

In 1966, a year after Crnjanski returned to Belgrade, Prosveta came out with his *Sabrana dela* (Collected Works) in ten volumes, and in 1967 he sent to press segments of his then-unpublished works, including *Embahade* (Embassies, 1983), a volume of memoirs from his diplomatic service; *Knjiga o Mikelandjelu,* containing his study of the great artist and of the Italian Renaissance in general; and his last major novel, *Roman o Londonu* (A Novel about London, 1971), the most autobiographical of all of his works, which covers the two postwar decades of his agonizing émigré existence in England. In 1971

Nolit published the entire two-volume edition of that work. Though the book was awarded the prestigious NIN award as the best prose publication of that year, in the judgment of several literary critics it was not equal either in scope or profundity to *Seobe*. Yet it is a powerful, poignant tale of the human fall brought on by the futility and emptiness of life in exile. The narrative follows the experiences of a couple of Russian émigrés, a husband and wife, displaced by their country's revolution and desperately struggling – just as Crnjanski and his wife did – to retain their dignity in the phantasmagorically hostile, gray city of London, which robs them of every hope and aspiration. Caught in the webs of the city's numbing, impersonal strangulation, the hero of the work, a proud Russian nobleman and a former imperial army officer named Nikolai Ryepnin, gradually retreats deeper and deeper into isolation and despair, until he finally reaches the point of total alienation and lethargy that leads to his suicide. Since most of the incidents depicted from Ryepnin's life are a direct transposition of those that Crnjanski encountered in England during his long exile, his weaving of distinctly autobiographical material into the threads of his plot adds special poignancy to this work, making it a fitting conclusion to a lifelong literary career in which the idea of the rise and fall in the search for spiritual tranquillity and home is a predominant and ever-present symbol.

From 1972 to 1977, the year he died, Crnjanski did not write anything new, though during this period, in addition to a few more editions of his collected and selected works, there appeared several lengthy critical studies about him and his work, confirming that his place in Serbian literature is secure for years to come.

Bibliography:

Stanka Kostić, Ružica Stojković, and Marija Ševković, "Bibliografija," in *Književno delo Miloša Crnjanskog,* edited by Predrag Palavestra and Svetlana Radulović (Belgrade: Institut za književnost i umetnost/BIGZ, 1972), pp. 347–412.

References:

Petar Džadžić, *Prostori sreće u delu Miloša Crnjanskog* (Belgrade: Nolit, 1976);

Nikola Milošević, *Roman Miloša Crnjanskog* (Belgrade: Srpska književna zadruga, 1970);

David Norris, ed., *Miloš Crnjanski and Modern Serbian Literature* (Nottingham, U.K.: Astra Press, 1988);

Norris, "Time in the Novels of Miloš Crnjanski," Ph.D. dissertation, University of Nottingham, 1989;

Predrag Palavestra and Svetlana Radulović, eds., *Književno delo Miloša Crnjanskog* (Belgrade: Institut za književnost i umetnost, 1972);

Aleksandar Petrov, *Poezija Crnjanskog i srpsko pesništvo* (Belgrade: Argue, 1971);

Svetlana Velmar-Janković, "Miloš Crnjanski," in her *Savremenici* (Belgrade: Prosveta, 1967), pp. 39–83;

Velimir Visković, "*Seobe:* njihovo mjesto u stvaralaštvu Miloša Crnjanskog," *Književna istorija,* 5 (1973): 606–631;

Radovan Vučković, "Ekspresionističke zamisili Miloša Crnjanskog u posleratnoj književnosti," *Život,* 50 (1976): 365–382.

Vučković, "Struktura i osnovne crte simbolike *Seoba* Miloša Crnjanskog," *Letopis Matice srpske,* 5 (1970): 443–484;

Marin Držić

(circa 1508 – 2 May 1567)

Henry R. Cooper, Jr.
Indiana University

BOOK: *Pjesni Marina Držića ujedno stavljene s mnozim druzim lijepim stvarmi* (Venice, 1551 [nonextant]; republished, 1607, 1630).

Collection: *Marin Držić: Djela,* edited by Frano Čale (Zagreb: Sveučilišna naklada Liber, 1979).

Editions in English: *Uncle Maroje,* translated by Sonia Bićanić (Dubrovnik: Dubrovnik Summer Festival, 1967);

Grižula, translated by Ljerka Djanešić and Kathleen Herbert (Dubrovnik: Dubrovnik Summer Festival, 1967).

Three writers define the course of the Croatian-Dalmatian Renaissance. At the beginning stands Marko Marulić of Split (1450–1524), the "father of Croatian literature," a world-renowned writer in Latin, a priest of great piety, and the link between the Croatian Middle Ages and the Italian Renaissance. At the end of the period stands Ivan Gundulić of Dubrovnik (1589–1638), a pious layman who composed the *Osman* (circa 1621–1638), Croatia's national epic, and effected the transition in Croatian letters from the Renaissance to the baroque. Between these two is found Marin Držić of Dubrovnik, a priest with no apparent religious calling, a prolific playwright who published little, a historical enigma whose definitive biography may never be written for lack of reliable facts. Držić marks the height of Renaissance culture not only in Dalmatia and Croatia but throughout the Slavic world.

The first mention of Marin Držić in the Dubrovnik archives is dated 1526, when as a young *klerik* (seminarian) he was awarded by his uncle Andrija an income from two Dubrovnik parishes, Svih svetih (All Saints', commonly known as Domino) in the city and Opatija sv. Petra na Koločepu (Abbey of Saint Peter on Koločep). Nothing, unfortunately, is known of his early education, though most sources assume it took place in Dubrovnik, or of his subsequent seminary career. Indeed, of his life be-

fore the age of about thirty, all that can be reliably deduced is that he was descended from an illegitimate branch of a once-powerful and wealthy family of Dubrovnik mercantilists. His forebears, in addition to their commercial interests, also had their fair share of clerical vocations. Džore Držić (1461–1501), another of Marin's uncles, was the first of Dubrovnik's poets to achieve fame in his own name. In the course of the sixteenth century Držić's father and brothers lost what little inherited wealth they had and were reduced to the more modest, worldly position of employees for major Dubrovnik trading concerns. Of the family's subsequent fortunes it would seem Držić's nieces and nephews – he had no known children – took pride in their uncle's literary achievements, for in 1607 and 1630 they had republished at considerable expense the only book he ever produced. By the great earthquake of 1667, which leveled Dubrovnik and destroyed forever its commercial fortunes, the Držić family had died out. Knowledge of the playwright and his works remained scant until the end of the nineteenth century, and an actual revival of his plays as theatrical pieces had to wait until the twentieth.

The only other data revealing details of Držić's life are the records preserved in the Dubrovnik archives, which catalogue his many debts and legal squabbles; manuscripts for his plays – later, often defective copies of lost originals; a few letters containing his alleged plans for overthrowing the government of Dubrovnik; and random mentions in the archives of the Italian city of Siena regarding his stay there. Making a coherent chronology of the playwright's life has been an ongoing concern of Croatian and Serbian critics. By and large, however, it must be said that the only reliable picture of Držić to emerge since his "rediscovery" one hundred years ago can be drawn from his plays. In them his Renaissance spirit shines. No dusty archival record matches them for their wit, inventiveness, and skill.

Držić probably acquired his profound insight into Renaissance comediography while at the university in Siena from the fall of 1538 to January 1545. Though he may have been studying law there, the only extant data on his stay indicate that he was elected vice rector of the university for a year, beginning in June 1541 (probably for lack of a more acceptable candidate rather than because of any inherent administrative talents of his own); at the same time he oversaw the residence for foreign students (the "Domus sapientiae"), and he was detained briefly by the Sienese police for having acted in a play performed illegally in a private home. It would appear he never completed his course of study in Siena, and of his travels, study at other universities in Italy or beyond, and writing activities in this period one can only speculate.

Record of Držić surfaces again in December 1545, when he signed on as companion and translator for a disgruntled Austrian nobleman, Duke Christoph von Rogendorf, who intended in a fit of pique to defect to the Turks. At the last moment, however, the duke reconciled himself with the Hapsburg court, and he and Držić traveled to Vienna, where Držić, who had sold five years of his parish income to his brother in order to have money to travel, evidently grew quickly weary of his duties. After about three months he made a leisurely return trip to Dubrovnik by way of Klagenfurt and Venice. In August 1546 the duke again appeared in Dubrovnik and this time did proceed to Istanbul, taking Držić with him. When Rogendorf refused to convert to Islam in order to join the Turkish government, however, the sultan had him thrown in jail. Eventually he was released, thanks to the intercession of the French ambassador. Renouncing the duke and all his schemes, as well as the duke's other companions, some of whom were in bad odor in Dubrovnik, Držić again returned to his native town, no doubt fiscally worse off but rich in the kind of experiences young men of Dubrovnik avidly sought. Having seen the world, or at least as much of it as was relevant for him, and fast approaching middle age, he settled into Dubrovnik and remained there for the next twenty years. Sometime in 1548 or 1549, after having been church organist, student, vice-rector, traveling companion, and seminarian, he finally took holy orders and became a deacon; by May 1550 the records refer to him as a priest. Most historians assume he allowed himself to be ordained because of his wretched financial status and not out of any sense

Statue of Marin Držić by Ivan Meštrović in Dubrovnik Art Gallery

of religious vocation. His extant writings would seem to confirm that suspicion, for not one of his texts has a Christian (or for that matter even moral) intent.

Shortly after his return home, Držić began his literary career. His first work was the comedy *Pomet* (literally snowstorm or squall but in the play the name of the principal character); it was probably written in 1548, but the text has been lost. Working with a speed that would characterize his writing for the next ten years, he next produced *Tirena,* a popular pastoral comedy (one of only three plays actually published in the playwright's lifetime). It was performed outdoors before the prince's palace during the pre-Lenten carnival festivities of 1549 and was so well received that some of Držić's enemies thought that he had stolen it from Mavro Vetranović (1482–1571), a talented and highly respected Dubrovnik writer; Vetranović himself, however, publicly proclaimed Držić the author. Set in the woods outside Dubrovnik, the play revolves around the love of the shepherd Ljubmir for the *vila* (wood nymph, sprite) Tirena and the numerous impediments to their happiness. It follows all the conventions of Italian Renaissance rustic comedies, including antique gods and idealized peasants; its dialogue is in double-rhymed dodecasyllabic verse. Most important, it establishes many of the contrasts Držić would use throughout his playwriting career to milk his fairly standard situations for all their intrinsic humor. In a list from the Croatian critic

Frano Čale, the editor of Držić's collected works (1979), these include the symbolic versus the authentic, the mythic versus the rustic, the fantastic versus the realistic, the elevated versus the trivial, the idyllic versus the urban, and the Petrarchan versus the anti-Petrarchan. One might also add local Slavic material versus borrowed Italian elements, including a richly macaronic language derived from a Croatian base with numerous dialectal variations and extensive Italian intrusions.

About a year later, for the *pir* (an elaborate, multiday wedding feast) of Martolica Džamanjić – the well-to-do of Dubrovnik outdid each other in the splendor of their nuptials – Držić composed *Novela od Stanca* (The Joke about Stanac, 1550), a brief comedy (316 double-rhymed dodecasyllables, as opposed to the 1,690 in *Tirena*) set in Dubrovnik during carnival. Briefly, it is the tale of a gullible old peasant who comes to town and is made the butt of jokes by young city slickers, in the spirit of carnival merriment. It is strictly urban and realistic (no antique gods or spirits except as masked revelers), and it conveys a wonderful sense of Dubrovnik's proud but not overbearing image of itself. Not only was *Novela od Stanca* popular in Držić's own lifetime (it too was published in 1551), but it was the first of Držić's works to enter the modern repertory, being produced in Zagreb on 2 January 1895.

Držić's third extant play, *Pripovijes kako se Venere božica užeže u ljubav lijepoga Adona u komediju stavljena* (The Tale of How the Goddess Venus Enflamed the Lovely Adonis with Love, Made into a Comedy, 1551), was written for the *pir* of a distant and wealthy relative of the playwright's, Vlaho Držić. It is another of his rustic comedies in verse, featuring Roman deities and Slavic peasants. Its Italianate humanism contrasts with the folkloric setting and the topical references to Dubrovnik events. The alternation of scenes between one and the other exemplifies, as it were, the Croatian Renaissance itself: structures and themes came in abundance from Italy, but the content and the wit were distinctly local. Thanks to Vlaho Držić's patronage, the playwright's friends were able to raise sufficient funds to have this play, together with the preceding two and some Petrarchan love lyrics of Držić's, published in Venice in 1551 (the publishing house is unknown, and no copy of the book is extant). Titled *Pjesni Marina Držića ujedno stavljene s mnozim druzim lijepim stvarmi* (The Poems of Marin Držić Placed Together with Many Other Lovely Items), it was the only publication of Držić's writing in his lifetime.

The year 1551 marked the apogee of Držić's career, not only thanks to the printing of his work but because during the pre-Lenten carnival of that year his best-known and most successful comedy, *Dundo Maroje* (Old Man [or Uncle] Maroje) was staged in the *Vijećnica* (council chamber) of the Dubrovnik senate. Like all the rest of his plays not included in his book, it has come down only in defective manuscripts (it was not actually published until 1867, when it appeared in a Dubrovnik anthology of prose and verse). Nevertheless, as Držić's longest and most elaborate work, it reveals the playwright's genius like no other of his plays. Since its first modern staging (in an adaptation by Marko Fotez in 1938), it has become a staple of the Serbo-Croatian–speaking theater.

Though it is set in Rome (to which some think Držić traveled for the holy jubilee in 1550), *Dundo Maroje* is imbued with the hopes and traumas of commercial Dubrovnik at the height of its wealth and power. In the prologue to the play the author himself boasts of stealing his theme from Plautus, and clear borrowings are to be found as well from Terence, Niccolò Machiavelli, Baldassare Castiglione, Giovanni Boccaccio, and the commedia dell'arte (to name only the best-known sources). The subject itself is ancient: a son receives money from his father to undertake commercial activities in a distant land; instead of trading, however, the son engages in riotous living abroad. The action of the play involves the father's arrival at the scene of the son's debauchery, with all the attendant confusion, maneuverings, deceptions, revelations, and accusations. Unfortunately, the end of the play is missing from the extant manuscripts, but the action itself is so stereotyped that happy endings for all can be safely predicted.

The characters are standard as well: dissolute youths; a miserly father; servants who are cunning, lazy, or dishonest; prostitutes; a jilted fiancé; a Jewish merchant; and a German with an execrable Italian accent. The morality is hackneyed: Maro, the prodigal son, knows he has done wrong and fears his father's wrath. Yet he does not repent, and in the end he is rewarded (for the wily always win in Držić's world). What is new and attractive about the play is the author's lack of moralizing, his complete commitment to fun and humor at the expense of highmindedness. Moreover, the dialogue is extraordinarily rich. Dialects distinguish one Dalmatian from another; macaronisms separate the educated from the show-offs; the vocabulary of commerce is nuanced and varied, while the language of love and seduction rings so true that it is hard to believe the scenes were written by a (presumably celibate) Catholic priest. Whole scenes are in Italian.

Conclusion of a letter by Držić (reproduced from volume 3 of Povijest hrvatske književnosti, 1990)

Multilingual puns abound, especially as the result of the more stupid characters' misunderstandings. Despite the play's great length (almost two hundred pages in modern typesetting), the action races forward, and interest is not allowed to flag. The only serious characters are Pomet, the honest servant, who in a series of monologues at the beginnings of many scenes gazes objectively on events, and Dugi Nos (Long Nose), the necromancer who appears only in the prologue to announce that the world is an eternal battleground between *ljudi nazbilj* (the good [or "for real"] people) and *ljudi nahvao* (the bad [or boastful] people) and that the former must do everything in their power to triumph over the latter. While modern critics, particularly in the second half of the twentieth century, have tried to wring a revolutionary meaning from these ideas, a less ideological reading would seem to suggest that Držić was describing manners, not class warfare. To be enjoyed, *Dundo Maroje* should be taken as an indulgent and well-intentioned poke at Dubrovnik's foibles and preoccupations. Držić was profoundly aware of how insubstantial all good human inten-

tions are: his goal was to depict with humor how people get into and out of the relationships and situations they devise for themselves and how, despite themselves, they survive and carry on. A committed bon vivant himself, he happily left the moralizing to others.

What modern audiences see in *Dundo Maroje* is less clear. To be accessible, the play must be shortened and adapted (fluency in Italian, for example, could be assumed for a sixteenth-century Dubrovnik audience but not for a twentieth-century Croatian one). The amorality of many of the characters is a bit embarrassing, and of course the stereotypes underlying several of them, especially the servants, are less and less familiar. Nevertheless, the play is performed to acclaim: its witty language, comic encounters, exaggerated characters, delicious and predictable complications, and its intertwined multiple happy endings strike the same chord in Croatian and Serbian viewers that William Shakespeare's comedies strike in English speakers or Molière's do in France. When one remembers that all three playwrights drew from the same antique and Renaissance wells and that Držić was the first among them to do so, then the bard of Dubrovnik's real achievement in *Dundo Maroje* can be given its rightful due.

After the banner year of 1551 it is uncertain what Držić was about: poverty caused by his inveterate overspending dogged his steps. At one point, perhaps in 1553, he was reduced to working in the Salt Bureau of Dubrovnik, which was a sinecure of sorts for impecunious clergy. He is known to have refused further employment there in 1556. It is hard to imagine that his finances had improved by then — in fact, various suits against him suggest the opposite — but another circumstance may have forced his hand. As a result of the Council of Trent, which met intermittently from 1545 to 1563, the lives and particularly livelihoods of the Roman Catholic clergy came under increasing scrutiny. Positions outside the church were discouraged and clerical discipline tightened. Dubrovnik in this regard was no exception, and from about 1556 on the local clergy were under ever greater pressure to conform. In 1562 Držić settled a ten-year lawsuit with his brother, and in December he left for Venice, where he became chaplain to the archbishop. (Despite the title it was not an important position.) He returned to Dubrovnik in late 1563, but perhaps only briefly. One hears nothing of him again until summer 1566, when he wrote four peculiar letters from Florence, denouncing the government of his native city and calling for its violent overthrow. When nothing came of those — the Florentine princes to whom they were addressed surely ignored them as the ravings of a madman — he returned to Venice, where he died on 2 May 1567. He was buried in an unmarked grave in the Church of Saint John and Saint Paul (Zanipolo in the local dialect). Clearly in the last decade or so of his life Držić was bitter and disaffected, perhaps as a result of having been forced to submit to the discipline of a religious calling he never really felt he had. In any event the sources of his comedic voice and vision began to decline in this period, and they probably failed altogether when he abandoned his native soil.

After a pause of a few years, Držić produced another lengthy prose comedy, *Skup* (the name of the principal character, which suggests the word for *miser* in Slavic), for the *pir* of one Sabo Gajčin, perhaps in 1554. An "erudite comedy" (based on Italian Renaissance reworkings of classical models) along the lines of *Dundo Maroje*, *Skup* retells Plautus's tale of the classical miser, using, however, domestic details. The commercial and banking vocabulary is particularly rich, though the constant repetition of words such as *zlato* (gold) and *tezoro*

(wealth) grows boring. The ending of the play is missing, but it surely was a happy one, with everyone's getting the partner of choice and Skup's keeping his gold. Držić may have written another play in 1554, *Džuho Krpeta* (the name of the main character), for the *pir* of Rafo Gučetić. Only fragments of the play, in an eighteenth-century copy, survive.

Držić's last great play was written for the 1556 *pir* of Vlaho Sorkočević. It too lacks the last few lines of text. For the most part the dialogue is in prose, with an occasional poetic interlude. As in all of Držić's plays, there are five acts with many scenes in each. The play is titled both *Grižula* (the name of the principal character) and *Plakir* (Pleasure, the son of Cupid and another character in the play), but its focus is on the lot of the *godišnice*, maids usually from the country who were hired by city households on yearly contracts (hence their name, from Serbo-Croatian *godina*, "year"). Grižula, an old man who has fled from the city to live in the country outside Dubrovnik, meets Omakala, a *godišnica* who has fled back to the country from her cruel city employer. Though rustic in setting, the play is urban in theme, and despite the presence of the classical gods and virtues, not to mention peasants, it speaks eloquently of the vicissitudes of city life. Some critics speak of a certain mannerism in this play, for it is a shade darker and its lines are drawn a bit deeper than in Držić's earlier pieces.

Perhaps then it is not surprising that Držić's last dated writing is not a comedy at all but the translation into his native dialect of Lodovico Dolce's Italian translation of Euripides' tragedy *Hecuba* (spelled *Hekuba* in Croatian). As such it is the first tragedy in Croatian literature, and some critics have cited elements of originality in it (guessing that Držić may have worked from the original Greek, or at least from a Latin translation, rather than exclusively from Dolce). The translation was probably done in 1558, and it was twice banned from the stage by the nervous Dubrovnik authorities before it was performed on 29 January 1559 (the last mention of a performance of one of Držić's plays in his lifetime). It consists of 2,733 octo- and dodecosyllabic verses (making it Držić's longest verse composition). Until 1959 it was assumed that not Držić but the pious Vetranović had done the translation because the play is so out of keeping with the rest of Držić's oeuvre. But archival research and a more profound understanding of the darkening mood of Držić's final years have proved *Hekuba* to be the comediograph's. The play speaks clearly to Držić's skill as well as to the sophistication of the literary culture of his day. Once again those Renaissance works that prompted other European dramatists to create their finest plays came earlier to Dubrovnik to find their first creative home away from home.

Little need be said about Držić's other fragmentary and undated plays: *Tripče de Utolče* (also called *Mande,* named after the principal male and female characters of the play respectively), a love-triangle play based on the work of Giovanni Boccaccio but set in neighboring Kotor and involving Turks, who are surprisingly absent from Držić's other works; *Arkulin* (the name of the principal character), about an old tightwad bachelor who chases a girl for her dowry; *Pjerin* (the name of the main character), which survives in fragments and seems to be based on a theme from Plautus; and *Karanje: Dživko Oblizalo i Savo Vragolov* (Scolding: Dživko Licklips and Savo Foecatcher), a medieval farce that several critics do not attribute to Držić at all.

Though never completely forgotten either in Dubrovnik or the rest of the Serbo-Croatian–speaking world, Držić and his plays were largely ignored from the end of the sixteenth century until the end of the nineteenth. His departure from Dubrovnik, subversive activities in Florence, and untimely death in Venice may have colored his memory at home and made his works less popular there. Without a printing press of its own, Dubrovnik could perpetuate the works of its poets and playwrights only in manuscripts, which are prey to loss and destruction, as was clearly the case with Držić's plays. But perhaps most important the tastes of literary consumers themselves began to change, so that the High Renaissance frivolity so characteristic of Držić came to be shunned in favor of a growing mannerism that would soon end in a full-blown baroque aesthetic. It would not be until romanticism that Držić and the Dalmatian Renaissance as a whole came back into vogue, partly for their literary interest but largely as a political program for the eventual liberation of the South Slavs from foreign domination. Moreover, because of the obscurity into which he had fallen and the sorry state of the manuscripts in which his works were recorded, Držić had to wait even longer, well into the twentieth century, for his full restoration to a place of honor in the Croatian, South Slavic, and European literary pantheons, until scholars had painstakingly recovered his work and details of his life. Only now, comparatively speaking, can audiences appreciate the range and depth of his genius and savor the richness of his dialogue. Only now can one confidently place Marin Držić at the head of a generation of European

Title page for a 1781 edition of Držić's poems

writers – some of the greatest the world has ever known – who looked to Italy and its Renaissance for inspiration and instruction but derived their characters and contexts from the world in which they lived and moved. One clever critic has posited Držić's direct influence on Shakespeare, if only it could be proved that Shakespeare knew Serbo-Croatian. But nothing of the kind is necessary, for Držić, Shakespeare, and others were simply all cut from the same cloth, that is, homespun after an Italian pattern.

Letters:
Marin Držić: Djela, edited by Frano Čale (Zagreb: Sveučilišna naklada Liber, 1979).

Bibliography:
Jakša Ravlić, ed., *Marin Držić: Zbornik radova* (Zagreb: Matica hrvatska, 1969).

Biographies:
Živko Jeličić, *Marin Držić Vidra* (Belgrade: Nolit, 1958; Zagreb: Naprijed, 1961);

Slobodan Prosper Novak, *Planeta Držić: Držić i rukopis vlasti* (Zagreb: Cekade, 1984).

References:

Henrik Birnbaum, "Renaissance Poets and Playwrights in Dubrovnik," *Die Welt der Slaven,* 33 (1988): 102–120;

Dražen Budiša, "Humanism in Croatia," in *Renaissance Humanism: Foundations, Forms, and Legacy,* edited by Albert Rabil, Jr., volume 2: *Humanism beyond Italy* (Philadelphia: University of Pennsylvania Press, 1988), pp. 265–292;

Frano Čale, "Marin Držić between Philosophy and Politics," in *Comparative Studies in Croatian Literature,* edited by Miroslav Beker (Zagreb: Zavod za znanost i književnosti Filozofskog fakulteta u Zagrebu, 1981), pp. 125–157;

Ivo Frangeš, *Povijest hrvatske književnosti* (Zagreb & Ljubljana: Nakladni zavod Matice hrvatske-Cankarjeva založba, 1987);

Vera Jaravek, "Marin Držić: A Ragusan Playwright," *Slavonic and East European Review,* 37 (December 1958): 141–159;

Ante Kadić, "Marulić and Držić: The Opposite Poles of the Croatian Renaissance," in his *The Tradition of Freedom in Croatian Literature: Essays* (Bloomington, Ind.: Croatian Alliance, 1983), pp. 19–33;

Miroslav Pantić, ed., *Marin Držić* (Belgrade: Zavod za izdavanje udžbenika Socijalističke republike Srbije, 1964);

Dragoljub Pavlović, "Novi podaci za biografiju Marina Držića," in his *Starija jugoslovenska književnost* (Belgrade: Naučna knjiga, 1971), pp. 153–163;

Franjo Petračić, ed., *Stari pisci,* volume 7: *Marin Držić* (Zagreb, 1875);

Michael Boro Petrovich, "Croatian Humanism and the Italian Connection," *Journal of Croatian Studies: Annual Review of the Croatian Academy of America, Inc.,* 27 (1986): 78–90;

Milan Rešetar, ed., *Stari pisci hrvatski,* volume 7: *Marin Držić,* second edition (Zagreb, 1930);

Franjo Švelec, *Komički teatar Marina Držića* (Zagreb: Matica hrvatska, 1968);

Josip Torbarina, "A Croat Forerunner of Shakespeare: In Commemoration of the 400th Anniversary of the Death of Marin Držić (1508–1567)," *Studia romanica et anglica zagrabiensia,* 24 (1967): 5–21.

Jovan Dučić

(5 February 1871 – 7 April 1943)

Vladimir Miličić
Western Washington University

BOOKS: *Pjesme* (Mostar: Zora, 1901);
Pesme (Belgrade: Srpska književna zadruga, 1908);
Pesme (Belgrade: S. B. Cvijanović, 1911);
Sabrana dela, 10 volumes (volumes 1–6, Belgrade: Narodna prosveta, 1929–1932; volumes 7–10, Pittsburgh: Srpska narodna odbrana, 1942–1951) – comprises volume 1: *Pesme sunca* (1929); volume 2: *Pesme ljubavi i smrti* (1929); volume 3: *Carski soneti* (1930); volume 4: *Plave legende* (1930); volume 5: *Gradovi i himere* (1930); volume 6: *Blago cara Radovana* (1932); volume 7: *Grof Sava Vladislavić* (1942); volume 8: *Staza pored puta* (1951); volume 9: *Moji saputnici* (1951); volume 10: *Jutra sa Leutara* (1951);
Lirika (Pittsburgh, 1943);
Sabrana djela, 6 volumes (Sarajevo: Svjetlost, 1969);
Sabrana dela, 5 volumes (Belgrade: Slovo ljubve, 1982).
Edition in English: *Plave legende – Blue Legends,* bilingual edition, with English translations and an introduction by Vasa D. Mihailovich (Columbus, Ohio: Kosovo, 1983).

Jovan Dučić is considered by many specialists to be the best Serbian writer of lyric poetry. Almost single-handedly, he changed the tone and sensibility, the themes, the vocabulary, the style, the rhythm, and the form of Serbian poetry, brilliantly bringing it up to European standards. As no one before or after, Dučić succeeded in integrating pictorial and symbolic representations, words and sounds, versification and music, original visionlike intuitive analyses, and descriptions of nature, culture, and the human soul to such an unheard-of degree that it was easy, as well as pleasurable, for many lovers of poetry to learn his poems by heart. Together with Milan Rakić, another great Serbian poet and contemporary, Dučić brought the alexandrine (a twelve-syllable line) and the eleven-syllable line to near perfection. It has often been said that Dučić composed many more high-quality poems

Jovan Dučić

than any other Serbian poet. The originality and depth of his thought; the richness of his ideas; the excellence of his linguistic expressions; the abundance of his appropriate metaphors and symbols; the aristocratic elegance, simplicity, and musicality of his poetry and his prose – all have led to a revival of interest in his works among Serbian literary specialists.

Dučić was born on 5 February 1871 near the city of Trebinje, in the province of Herzegovina. His father, Andrija Dučić, was a merchant; his mother, Joka (née Sušić), already had two children – a son, Risto, and a daughter, Soka – from an earlier marriage. After the death of her first husband, she had married Andrija Dučić, by whom she also had two children: Jovan and a daughter, Mileva. During the Herzegovinian uprising in 1875, Dučić's mother and all four children escaped to nearby Dubrovnik. After the uprising ended, Andrija Dučić also went to Dubrovnik and died there several years later. His childhood stay in beautiful Dubrovnik must have greatly influenced Dučić. Dubrovnik was the city that he loved most, visiting it whenever he could and drawing inspiration for his poems from its elegant beauty. After his father died, the family moved to the city of Mostar, where his mother raised her four children. Her struggles inspired Dučić's first published poem, "Samohrana majka" (Self-Supporting Mother, 1886). By that time Risto, the poet's half brother, having become the breadwinner of the family, put Jovan through school, first in Mostar, then in Metković, in Herzegovina, and in Sombor, in the province of Vojvodina, where the family had moved. In Sombor he prepared himself to be a teacher, and for a while he taught schools in Bosnia and in Herzegovina. He started a literary newspaper, *Zora* (Dawn, 1896–1901), with compatriots Aleksa Šantić and Svetozar Ćorović, both of whom also became well-known Serbian authors. Having received financial help from a Bosnian cultural society and a stipend from the Serbian government, he went on to study in Geneva and in Paris from 1896 to 1906.

During his studies in those two leading cultural centers of Europe, Dučić succeeded in becoming a well-educated person, particularly in literature and in the arts, obtaining a degree in social sciences in Geneva and becoming quite worldly, with a pronounced interest in high society. Many of his contemporaries considered him a snob. An almost-unanimous opinion exists that he was an exceptionally vain and sensitive person when it came to any criticism of his literary works or personal traits. Later, when he became a career diplomat, a whole series of anecdotes about real or presumed shortcomings of his character were recorded. According to one of them he was always sensitive about his age: when a friend of his told him once that he had aged, Dučić retorted: "Well, Giga [Jakšić], even when I do get old, I'll age like a Stradivarius violin

and will appreciate with time. And you? You'll grow old like a worn-out military boot ready to be thrown out in the garbage." His biographer Kosta St. Pavlović (a Yugoslav diplomat who knew Dučić all his life and worked closely with him for three and a half years) describes Dučić as having dark-brown hair, an aquiline nose, and blue eyes and says that he was a tall, attractive man with an athletic build.

Following his return from abroad in 1906, Dučić started preparing himself in Belgrade for diplomatic service. He was already regarded as the best poet of the young generation, and he knew how to use his status to achieve his goal. His diplomatic career started in 1910 and ended with World War II. He never married, but his reputation as a ladies' man is well known.

In the approximately four hundred poems Dučić published, he dealt with many themes, but, unlike any other Serbian poet, he addressed himself systematically, almost programmatically, to seven great perennial themes: love, God, nature, woman, solitude, life, and death.

Pjesme (Poems, 1901), Dučić's first book, reflects the influence of Vojislav Ilić, one of the most popular Serbian poets of the time. Like Ilić, Dučić was interested in the classical past and in decorative form, but unlike Ilić's poetry, Dučić's early verse was romantic and sentimental. Quite a few of the poems already included the seeds of his future interest in beauty and form – as well as several of his characteristic themes, something that never left him. During his decade-long stay as a student in Geneva and Paris, he had found related souls among the French Parnassians and symbolists. He already shared their concern with form, a labored-for beauty, and a detached attitude toward daily social life. Charles Baudelaire was one of his favorite poets because Baudelaire preserved an intimate approach to individual suffering, commenting on despair, agony, and bitterness – an approach also important to Dučić. He especially liked the suggestive quality of the symbolists' poetry, a trait which he himself would master.

His second book of poetry, titled *Pesme* (Poems, 1908), reveals his readings as a student. The feelings expressed in his love poems, dealing with tears and suffering, are not yet authentic, functioning as a decoration of love. The poems successfully exhibit the atmosphere, interests, and the artificiality of life in the French Belle Epoque. He gave Serbian poetry a new rhythm for the alexandrine and a superbly elegant sonnet, as well as a new sensibility that comes from a new poetic vocabulary of

An 1897 letter from Dučić to Ivan Ivanić informing him that Dučić has just become the new manager for a journal to which Ivanić has contributed words in strikingly original combinations, as in these images: "the gardens were dying with painful impatience"; "the dust of the silvery stars"; "in a tranquil violet night where the stars rustle." Another feature that he brought to his poetry was the abundance of light: his "Jadranski Soneti" (Adriatic Sonnets, 1901) delight the reader with the omnipresence of light, sun, space, and sky. His predilection for aristocratic life and feeling led him to write poems about Dubrovnik during the baroque period ("Dubrovačke poeme" [Poems of Dubrovnik], 1908) and medieval Serbia (*Carski Soneti* [Imperial Sonnets], 1930). The poems about Dubrovnik are charmingly sketched pictures and masterly narrated portraits of patricians and the life and people of the city, with an abundance of celebration, dancing, feasting, and music. The *Carski Soneti* are somewhat less successful, perhaps because he felt closer to Latin rather than old Serbian culture. Only a few of the sonnets succeed in conjuring up the life and the atmosphere of Czar Dušan's fourteenth-century Serbia. In his thirty-seven prose poems, *Plave legende* (Blue Legends, 1930), he shows himself to be a highly cultured poet in whom sensibility regularly prevails over emotion. These poems are beautiful poetic sketches, romanticized and spiritualized descriptions of particular moments and events in human life, alone or in relation to anthropomorphized nature and animals. Many of them end with a generalized descriptive or philosophical punch line such as, "For things assume the shape given to them by our soul"; or, "But when they turned into darkness, one could no longer distinguish the man from the dog."

Dučić wrote better poetry after 1910, during the period which coincides with his diplomatic service for the kingdom of Serbia and, later, Yugoslavia. He began as first secretary in Sofia, and before becoming the first Yugoslav ambassador when he was sent to Bucharest in 1939, he served in various diplomatic functions, twice in Rome, twice in Athens, twice in Madrid (the second time, 1940–1941), once in Geneva, twice in Cairo, and once in Budapest. By becoming a diplomat he seems to have achieved his dream of an aristocratic way of life; high living was finally realized. There is a near-consensus among Dučić specialists that he composed his best poems after 1920. They are represented by the cycles of "Jutarnje pesme" (Morning Poems), "Večernje pesme" (Evening Poems), and "Pesme Sunca" (Poems of Sun) – all published in *Pesme sunca* (Poems of Sun, 1929) and *Pesme ljubavi i smrti* (Poems of Love and Death, 1929); and in *Lirika* (Lyric Poems, 1943). In them he succeeded in establishing the sought-after harmony between him-

self as a poet and himself as a human being. His poetry was no longer "a quiet pale little girl that dreams." Instead it was like his soul, "all dressed in a wonderful light." He finally began to feel how "the gentle words of the eternal. . . . pass through his heart and mouth."

A Serbian reader of Dučić's best poetry finds him a magician of form who transforms life into an enchanting art, spiritualizing and beautifying everything that he touches, turning it into a delightful musical language. His versification is, in general, impeccable, his rhymes rarely stale or predictable. The great majority of his poetry is written in eight-, nine-, eleven-, or twelve-syllable lines with a caesura. His meter is predominantly trochaic or iambic. Only during the last decade of his life did he compose some poems in an accentual meter.

Dučić's mastery of form occasionally ascends to the sublime, with the form itself becoming meaningful. For example, "Povratak" (The Return), which is addressed to God, consists of five four-line stanzas and is written in a nine-syllable iambic line with a caesura after the fifth syllable. Only one line deviates from this norm, when an *i* (and) is inserted after the fifth syllable, thus erasing the expected caesura. That *and* is a magical one: it also erases the boundary separating the poetic hero from God, becoming the bridge uniting them: "Tad neće više biti medje / Izmedju tebe i izmedj mene" (Then there will be no boundary / Between you and between me.)

Several of Dučić's disputed artistic and ontological positions could be viewed as normal growth in a practicing poet, or they could be explained as the artist's attempt to achieve a fullness in his art by depicting life in all of its richness and variety. With regard to his attitude toward religion, he was constantly torn between beauty and love. One part of him was on the side of beauty and therefore drew him toward pre-Christian paganism, particularly classical Greek and Roman; but as he grew older the theme of love – including Christian love – began to prevail. He was, therefore, both a pagan and a Christian in his lifetime. Concerning his relationship with nature, he kept one part of it intact, material and spatial (writing remarkably realistic descriptions of nature with little interpretation), while making the other part idealized and spiritualized. His striving for fullness is also apparent in his great themes of loneliness and woman. He intentionally separated himself from the grayness of everyday life and from other people, saying, in a Nietzschean manner, "I weave my nest above your head." But he also felt that he was condemned to loneliness against his will, as a part of an existential fate from which there is no escape:

> I know of lonely, boring hours,
> Of bitter, dejected Autumns;
> All things stand like friends united,
> Only my soul is solitary.

His love poetry dealing with women, or, better stated, dealing with a nonexistent woman, can stand as a sign for a good part of his canon. His woman and his love of women are equally real and artificially created, natural and contrived, deep and superficial, true and feigned, sincerely and falsely emotional, but also intellectual. His emotions toward women and the feelings that they can evoke in him are, on the whole, subordinated to his abstract and generalized reflections. Although woman, or Woman, resides somewhere in the depths of his heart, she is so deep within that she remains a dark secret. His Woman is woven from the night. She appears to be both an idea and an ideal. The last two stanzas of the five-stanza "Pesma ženi" (Poem to Woman, in *Pesme ljubavi i smrti*) state Dučić's essential view:

> You are all woven out of my specter,
> Your cloak of sun is knitted out of my dreams;
> You were my alluring thought;
> The symbol of all vanities, ruinous and frigid.

> And you don't exist nor have you ever existed;
> Born in my silence and boredom,
> You only shone on the sun of my heart:
> For all that we love we created ourselves.

Yet his striving for fullness did not completely leave out real woman and real emotions. Indeed, a woman of flesh occasionally inhabits his poems, as in the opening lines of the five-stanza poem "Čednost" (Chastity, in *Pesme ljubavi i smrti*):

> While you sleep, an invisible hand
> Devotedly sculpts your little breasts all night,
> Wipes off and corrects, pulls, runs together,
> Moves tranquil lines and makes curves.

Finally, his poetic credo, as expressed in poems from different periods of his life, may also serve as an example of his tendency toward fullness. In his earlier period, the sonnet "Moja poezija" (My Poetry, 1904) depicts his poetry as a marblelike, pale little girl who dreams. The poet asks her to be too beautiful, so that not everybody would love her; to be too virtuous, in order not to become a leader of a rushing crowd; and to stand

Cover for a 1969 edition of Dučić's poems

impassively, while around her body hovers a patch of mysterious fog instead of an ornate and luxurious dress. A later counterpart to this poem is "Pesma" (Poem, 1935), which exemplifies a different poetic credo:

> The Lord sowed me all the time,
> And everywhere I am a new word and a symbol –
> The first seed in the white bread,
> The first stone in a fortress.

> And the first kiss of those in love,
> And the knife in the hand of a bandit,
> And the prayer from modest hearts,
> And the dream of a hungry snake in the sand.

> The Lord sowed me by handfuls
> In the fields which the eternal suns flood,
> In order to be his sign among the people,
> His golden trumpet of glory.

> And the shipwreck in daybreak,
> And the desperate person's cry for strength;
> And the brilliant cedar in Lebanon,
> And the frightful army in front of Carthage.

The Lord sowed me with his whole hand,
In the bright hour and the huge one,
To be the morning of every day,
And his voice and the key of everything.

On the empty road an atom of dust,
In the sky the sun's circle and the image,
The focus in the house of a poor person,
The tear in the eye of a martyr.

Dučić remained a poet even in his prose work *Gradovi i himere* (Cities and Chimeras, 1930), a collection of travelogues. The various "letters" in this book were written either during his visits as a student, a diplomat, or a tourist to various Mediterranean and European places, including Greece, Egypt, Jerusalem, Spain, France, and Switzerland. His "letters" appear to be only a pretext for him: to escape to a distant past populated with important historical figures and events that he admired more than the contemporary reality in which he lived; to put to practice his capacity for poetic descriptions in prose reflections on the past glory of historically important places, on the beauty and value of old myths, and on the destiny and meaning of the bygone nations and cultures he admired. They also provide him occasion to comment on the philosophy of history, human mores, love, life, and women, in addition to a plethora of human traits. His observations include "It appears that everything great and holy had to be imposed upon people by force" and "Christianity perhaps would not even have created its art if it consistently followed the gospel, or if – luckily – the art instinct in humans were not more vital and bigger than the religious one." He knew how to adorn even his prose writing in luxurious form, full tropes, and figures, from simple, but effective and erudite, comparisons and similes to original and striking metaphors and metonyms – all expressed in a language full of music. In many cases he transformed the reality he saw into magical visions that readers somehow want to believe are true and really exist. In many instances even the simplest descriptive sentence can resonate in the reader longer than might be expected, creating more synesthetic effects than an entire poem: "The white stripe of this long road extends from here to the sea, disappearing in the distance as a silver voice."

Blago Cara Radovana (Czar Radovan's Treasure, 1932), on which Dučić toiled at least four years, is his longest work, a collection of his own philosophical cogitations and paraphrased thoughts of other thinkers. Meditations on poets, love, woman, happiness, old age and youth, heroes, prophets, and many other subjects are couched in beautiful language. These reflections, often derivative but witty, supply the reader with useful information about Dučić's intellectual interests. In many instances his musings turn into maxims, valuable poetic observations, or interesting but controversial assertions, as in statements such as "People become fanatics faster than becoming educated"; "A smile is the daybreak or the dawning of the [human] body"; "We are truly good only when we are truly happy. Misfortune ruins the heart and destroys character"; "there are, in fact, only two creators in the cosmos: God and poets. The first one starts everything, the second one completes it"; and "A lyric poet will become a great poet only after he succeeds in telling great truths about the three greatest motifs ... which control our destiny: God, Love, and Death."

Grof Sava Vladislavić (Count Sava Vladislavić, 1942) is a biography of a supposedly distant relative of Dučić's who served as Russian ambassador to China in the early eighteenth century. The book is composed of excerpted texts about the count which Dučić found in the libraries and archives of several European cities. For each excerpt he wrote an introduction and a conclusion.

Staza pored puta (Path by the Road, 1951) comprises poetic sketches of Peter I, King of Serbia; Nikola Pašić, a Serbian politician; Aleksandar, King of Yugoslavia; and several other political, military, and diplomatic dignitaries of Dučić's time. Although Dučić said that "One learns art from artists, not from critics," he nevertheless wrote a volume of literary criticism, *Moji saputnici* (My Traveling Companions, 1951). His penetrating analysis and evaluation helped establish the places of seven authors in Serbian literature.

Jutra sa Leutara (Mornings from Leutar, 1951) is a continuation of *Blago Cara Radovana*. These new philosophical reflections are presented in simpler sentences and exhibit more original thoughts than those of the earlier work. This time he deals with tranquility, hatred, dance, jealousy, vanity, fear, disappointment, patriotism, character, and courtesy.

Dučić also translated some 150 published poems from six languages, mainly Russian, French, and German. These translations are yet to be evaluated. His own poems have been translated into many languages, beginning with the German in 1904.

Serious analysis and evaluation of Dučić's literary work is yet to come. As the ideological antipode of pre–World War II Yugoslav dogmatic Marxists and of leading political and artistic ideologues of Tito's Yugoslavia, Dučić was either attacked or neglected. The Communists were proletarians in their ideology; he was an aristocratic parvenu. They were for socialist realism and later the equally dogmatic socialist aestheticism; he was more on the side of art for art's sake. They asked for an active social involvement with the masses, whereas he was an individualist who cared more for the Muses than the masses. They were for the dictatorship of the proletariat; he would probably have favored a modern and enlightened monarchy.

Another group is still attempting to denigrate the value of Dučić's works: advocates of free-style poetry, for whom Dučić's traditional versification represents an anachronism. Yet each type of versification possesses possibilities and advantages that the other does not. It is in the concept of the fullness of poetry that a better understanding of Dučić's contribution to literature resides. He believed that lyric poetry is based on principles of art that are not inferior to the principles of cognition. For him lyric poetry was one of the most complex creations of the human mind, representing a metaphysical theory of aestheticization of the world and, consequently, occupying the highest level of metaphysics. His work as a writer epitomizes a powerful proof for such a belief.

Taking his whole body of work into account, it would not be incorrect to say that it satisfies our need for spirituality, that it affects our emotions, that it involves our senses and sensibilities, that it engages our intellect, and that it fulfills our need for — and feeling for — beauty and aesthetic form to a higher degree than the poetry of any other Serbian poet in the twentieth century.

Dučić died on 7 April 1943 in Gary, Indiana, where he spent the last year and a half of his life, having come from Lisbon in December 1941 after his country was overrun by the Nazis.

Biographies:

Živko Milićević, "Jovan Dučić i njegovi saputnici," *Prilozi za književni jezik i folklor,* 31 (1965): 229–243;

Kosta St. Pavlović, *Jovan Dučić* (Milan, 1967);

Radovan Popović, *Istina o Dučiću* (Belgrade: Književne novine, 1982).

References:

Midhat Begić, "Modernistička gama Dučićeva," in his *Raskršća I* (Sarajevo: Svjetlost, 1957), pp. 171–198;

Božo Bulatović, *Jovan Dučić* (Belgrade: Rad, 1962);

Vuk Filipović, "Priroda u poeziji Jovana Dučića," in his *U svetu književnog dela* (Priština: Jedinstvo, 1966), pp. 116–161;

Zoran Gavrilović, "Jovan Dučić," in his *Poezija od Vojislava do Bojića* (Belgrade: Nolit, 1966), pp. 163–187;

E. D. Goy, "The Poetry of Jovan Dučić," in *Gorski Vijenac: A Garland Offered to Professor Elisabeth May Hill,* edited by R. Auty, L. R. Lewitter, and A. P. Vlasto (Cambridge, Mass.: Modern Humanities Research Association, 1970): pp. 165–178;

Vladimir Jovičić, "Jovan Dučić, 'Himna pobednika'," *Književna istorija,* 4 (1972): 455–462;

Vasilije Kalezić, "Pesnik Jovan Dučić," in Dučić's *Izabrana dela* (Belgrade: Narodna knjiga, 1964), pp. 5–24;

Milan Kašanin, "Sudbine i ljudi: Usamljenik," *Letopis Matice srpske,* 401 (1968): 351–372;

Vladeta R. Košutić, "Uticaji na Dučića," in *Parnasovci i simbolisti u Srba* (Belgrade, 1967), pp. 1–88, 191–200;

Slavko Leovac, "Dučićevo sagledanje Helade," *Savremenik,* 8 (1962): 339–358;

Vasa D. Mihailovich, "Jovan Dučić," in *Critical Survey of Poetry: Foreign Language Series,* 5 volumes (Englewood Cliffs, N. J.: Salem Press, 1984), I: 426–434;

Nikola Mirković, "Jovan Dučić," *Slavische Rundschau,* 4 (1932): 302–323;

Mirković, "Jovan Dučić," *Srpski književni glasnik,* 48 (1936): 335–344, 424–433;

Miodrag Pavlović, "Jovan Dučić, danas," *Delo,* 10 (1964): 1191–1228; also in his *Osam pesnika* (Belgrade: Prosveta, 1964), pp. 7–51;

Kosta St. Pavlovic, "Yovane Doutchitch: Prince des poètes serbes," *Etudes Slaves et Est-Européennes,* 12 (1967): 99–113;

Bogdan Popović, "Jedna kritička analiza," *Srpski književni glasnik,* 32 (1914): 33–40, 126–137, 200–217; also in his *Ogledi* (Belgrade: Prosveta, 1959), pp. 190–227;

Popović, "Teme i misli u Dučićevom pesništvu," in Dučić's *Pesme Sunca,* volume 1 of his *Sabrana dela* (Belgrade: Narodna prosveta, 1929), pp. xi–xxii;

Jovan Skerlić, "Jovan Dučić: *Pjesme,*" *Letopis Matice srpske,* 210 (1901): 77–86;

Pero Slijepčević, "Jovan Dučić," in his *Sabrani ogledi* (Belgrade, 1956), I: 93–148;

Pavle Zorić, "Od estetizma do religioznosti," *Savremenik,* 4 (1958): 322–335.

Elin Pelin
(Dimitŭr Ivanov Stoyanov)
(18 July 1877 – 3 December 1949)

Lyubomira Parpulova-Gribble
Ohio State University

BOOKS: *Razkazi,* 2 volumes (Sofia: St. Atanasov, 1904, 1911);

Pepel ot tsigarite mi (Sofia, 1905);

Ot prozoretsa (Sofia: Ya. Yakimov, 1906);

Kitka za yunaka: Razkazi (Sofia, 1917);

Pizho i Pendo: Khumoristichni stikhove, razkazi i dialozi na shopski dialekt (Sofia: Knigoizdatelstvo na bŭlgarskite pisateli, 1917; revised edition, Sofia: Khemus, 1918);

Gori Tilileyski: Prikazki za detsa, naredeni v stikhoŭ (Sofia: Khemus, 1919);

Sladkodumna baba: Narodni prikazki (Sofia: Al. Paskalev, 1919);

Svatbata na Chervenushko: Vesela istoriya v stikhove za detsa (Sofia: Al. Paskalev, 1924);

Tsar Shishko: Prikazki v stikhove (Sofia: Ministerstvo na narodnata prosveta, 1925);

Pravdata i krivdata: Narodni prikazki (Sofia: Khemus, 1927);

Pesnichki (Sofia: Ministerstvo na narodnoto prosveshtenie, 1927);

Zemya: Povest (Sofia: Ministerstvo na narodnoto prosveshtenie, 1928);

Cherni rozi (Sofia: T. F. Chipev, 1928);

Tri babi (Sofia: Khemus, 1930);

Potocheta bistri: Stikhove za detsa (Sofia: Ministerstvo na narodnoto prosveshtenie, 1931);

Yan Bibiyan: Neveroyatnite priklyucheniya na edno khlape (Sofia: Khemus, 1933);

Yan Bibiyan na lunata (Sofia: Khemus, 1934);

Az, ti, toy: Mili rodni kartinki (Sofia: Khemus, 1936);

Pod manastirskata loza (Sofia: Khemus, 1936);

Dyadovata rŭkavichka (Sofia: Khemus, 1937);

Zlatni lyulki: Stikhove za detsa (Sofia: Grazhdanin, 1938);

Sŭchineniya, 5 volumes, edited by Todor Borov (Sofia: Khemus, 1938–1942);

Kumcho Vŭlcho i Kuma Lisa: Stsenirana prikazka (Sofia: Khemus, 1939);

Elin Pelin (Dimitŭr Ivanov Stoyanov)

Shturche-svirche: Veseli stikhcheta za momicheta i momcheta (Sofia: Khemus, 1940);

Geratsite: Povest (Sofia: Khemus, 1943);

Strashen vŭlk: Prikazki v stikhove (Sofia: Khemus, 1944);

Sŭbrani sŭchneniya, 10 volumes, edited by Todor Borov and others (Sofia: Bŭlgarski pisatel, 1958–1959).

Editions in English: *Short Stories* (Sofia: Foreign
Languages Press, 1965);
Short Stories, edited by Mercia Macdermot, trans-
lated by Maguerite Alexieva (Sofia: Foreign
Languages Press, 1972);
Bag Boys (Sofia: Sofia Press, 1975).

Elin Pelin and Yordan Yovkov are considered
the two outstanding Bulgarian prose writers in the
period between the two world wars. "Bard of rural
misery," "classic of Bulgarian literature," and "*shop*
writer" are the epithets most commonly used to describe Elin Pelin. The first two, based mostly on
short stories he wrote before World War I, indicate
the thematic scope of his works and his prominent
place in the history of Bulgarian literature. The
third one refers to his humorous sketches written in
the dialect of the *shopi* (peasants living in the villages
around Sofia) and to the typical locale of his works.

Dimitŭr Ivanov Stoyanov, who began using
the pen name Elin Pelin in 1897, was born on 18
July 1877 in the village of Baylovo in the Sofia district. He was the youngest son in the large family
(five sons and two daughters) of Ivan Stoyanov and
his wife, Tota. Ivan Stoyanov, the only literate person of his generation in the village, was an ardent
supporter of education. Around 1868 he had invited
a teacher to the village and opened a school in the
basement of his house. In later years, in spite of his
modest financial means, he developed the habit of
buying books with part of the money he earned
from sales at the farmers' market in Sofia. He was
determined to give a good education to his sons.
Dimitŭr, the future Elin Pelin, was the only son
who did not earn a high-school diploma. He studied
in Panagyurishte (1892–1894), Sofia (1894–1895),
and Sliven (1897–1898), but he ran into trouble everywhere, mainly because of his unwillingness to
work on subjects that did not interest him. Elin
Pelin was a passionate reader, however, especially
of literature, and thus he compensated to a large extent for his lack of higher education. A nine-month
stay in France (1906–1907), arranged by Minister of
Education Ivan Shishmanov, allowed Elin Pelin to
learn French and expand his knowledge of the
Western world. A trip to Italy in 1905 and another
one to Russia in 1913 further broadened his awareness of European culture.

Initially Elin Pelin lived and wrote under
rather difficult financial circumstances. He was a
teacher in Baylovo (1896–1897), left for a year,
then returned and stayed for two more years (1898–
1899). In 1899 he moved to Sofia, where he worked
various literary and journalistic jobs to earn a living. In 1903 Shishmanov furnished the young
writer his first permanent employment. He was
hired as a teacher in a gymnasium in Sofia, but in
fact his assignment was to serve in the university library. In 1908 Elin Pelin went to work in the National Library. During World War I he was drafted
into the army and given a position on the editorial
board of the newspaper *Voenni izvestiya* (Military
News) and the journal *Otechestvo* (Fatherland). In
1926 he became director of the Ivan Vazov Museum, remaining there until he retired in 1944. This
position provided him with a secure although relatively modest income, allowing him to devote more
attention to his literary work while supporting his
wife, Stefana, and their two children, Elka and
Boyan.

Elin Pelin's works usually appeared first in
contemporary periodicals; then he would collect
some in a separate book, which would undergo several editions. Elin Pelin's active participation in the
humorous paper *Bŭlgaran* (a distorted form of the
word *Bulgarian,* 1904–1909) and in the literary
newspaper *Razvigor* (the name of a spring wind,
1921–1924) had serious consequences for his career
as a writer because it meant also that he associated
with specific literary groups and their aesthetic pro-
grams. *Bŭlgaran* was published by a group of young
and talented artists, critics, and actors who favored
a jocular attitude toward life and art. To a certain
extent their paper served as a counterbalance to
Misŭl (Thought), the most prestigious literary periodical of the time, which promoted a serious and
somewhat elitist view of literature and culture.
Razvigor, without being a predominantly humorous
newspaper, provided an alternative to *Zlatorog*
(Golden Horn), the leading serious literary journal
of the period between the two world wars. As a result, Elin Pelin's stories were never published either
in *Misŭl* or in *Zlatorog.* Elin Pelin also worked as editor of the literary journal *Slŭnchogled* (Sunflower,
1909) and the children's newspapers and magazines
Veselushka (Little Merrymaker, 1908–1910), *Chavche*
(Little Daw, 1913–1914), *Svetulka* (Firefly, 1920–
1932), *Pŭteka* (Path, 1933–1934), and *Septemvriyche*
(A Child of September, 1945–1949).

His extensive experience with literary periodicals enhanced Elin Pelin's natural sensitivity to the
expectations of his audience. He chose as his literary persona a jovial skeptic who observes life in all
of its variety and contradictions. This image was
highly successful because it suited Elin Pelin's personality and was little exploited by other Bulgarian
men of letters. The general public was not the least
disturbed by the fact that the persona combined sev-

Elin Pelin

eral distinctive personalities, such as a writer with intimate knowledge of both the beauty and the misery of village life, a witty and down-to-earth *shop,* an avid hunter and fisherman, a man of letters with bohemian inclinations, and an adult who advises the youngsters but is also ready to explore, laugh, and play with them. Readers were actually amused by the ability of the writer to wear so many different hats so well. Literary critics, however, accustomed to the predominant model of monolithic authorial figures, have always had trouble with this multifaceted persona. They usually pick out one personality, or even a facet of it, declare it the most essential, and argue with those who have made a different but equally simplifying choice.

It is difficult to understand how the same author who published such finely crafted psychological pieces as "Spasova mogila" (Saint Saviors' Hill) and "Iglika" (a girl's name meaning *primrose*) could publish at the same time the frivolous sketches collected in *Pepel ot tsigarite mi* (Ashes from My Cigarettes, 1905) and *Ot prozoretsa* (From the Window, 1906). Nor is it easy to explain how Elin Pelin managed to retain his reputation as an outstanding author for so many years after he virtually stopped writing the kind of stories that made him well known. Yet he did indeed become famous and remained so until his death. The young writer who once fainted from hunger in the office of the publisher of *Letopisi* (Chronicles) later became chairman of the Union of Writers (1940). The former high-school dropout became a member of the Bulgarian Academy of Sciences (1940). The village boy who used to go hunting with his father became a friend and hunting companion of the Bulgarian king. The twenty-fifth anniversary of Elin Pelin's literary activity was enthusiastically celebrated in 1922, during the capitalist period of Bulgarian history, and in 1948 the Union of Bulgarian writers and other cultural organizations celebrated his seventieth birthday (until Krŭstyo Genov's 1956 book, 1877 was believed to be the year of his birth). In 1949 he was honored further with a nationwide celebration organized by the Communist government of Bulgaria.

Elin Pelin started writing in high school, publishing his first short story at the age of seventeen (1895). As a student in Sofia, he put out two handwritten newspapers, *Toyaga* (Stick) and, later, *Fiu* (a whistling sound to attract attention or express surprise), intended to amuse the tenants in the inn where he was renting a room. During the first years of his literary career, Elin Pelin was attracted by socialist and populist ideas, although he never fully embraced them and never became a member of the Socialist party. These early ideological inclinations are displayed most clearly in his articles, poems, and stories in the short-lived journal *Selska razgovorka* (Rural Conversation), which he edited in 1902–1903. From 1905 on Elin Pelin moved away from radical political ideologies and abandoned the militant tone in his early criticism of social injustice. He never stopped weaving general democratic and humanistic ideas into his works, however; Vivian Pinto justly called him the "humanist of Shopsko."

Elin Pelin's literary production includes short stories and novelettes, humorous sketches, and works for children. The two volumes titled *Razkazi* (Stories, 1904, 1911) laid the foundation for Elin Pelin's literary fame during the interwar period. The first volume includes twenty-eight short stories, some revised and improved versions of previously published works and some new ones. Another thirteen short stories and the novelette *Geratsite* (The Gerak Family) appear in the second volume. Among the republished stories are his first mature works: "Vetrenata melnitsa" (The Windmill), "Napast bozhiya" (Divine Plague), "Gost" (Guest), "Izkushenie" (Temptation), and "Proletna izmama" (Spring Delusion), all written during his second stay in Baylovo. Typically the quality of Elin Pelin's first mature works is as high as that of the later ones. In the prehistory of nearly every one of his stories – early and late – there is a real event that set his imagination in motion. The action takes place in the country, and the main characters are simple people (peasants, village teachers, priests, and monks). An element of humor or satire is usually present.

For example, the real event that inspired the story "Vetrenata melnitsa" was the failed undertaking of Elin Pelin's father to build a windmill during a year of terrible drought; "Napast bozhiya" was inspired by diphtheria epidemics in Baylovo and Elin Pelin's efforts to convince the people not to use a contaminated well. Behind "Proletna izmama" is the disappointment of an amorous herdsman when he discovers that the white spot amid a field of green wheat is not the kerchief of a pretty woman, but a horse skull impaled on a stick (a magic way of protecting crops against the evil eye). Yet the plots of these stories take courses different from those of the real events. In "Vetrenata melnitsa" the windmill is only an object in the background, while the action is centered on the dance of one of the windmill builders, Lazar Dŭbaka, and Khristina, the beautiful granddaughter of the other builder. They bet that she will marry Dŭbaka if he proves to be better than she in this dance. In "Napast bozhiya," a story strongly influenced by Elin Pelin's populist ideas, the epidemics are just the cause that provokes the main event: the conflict between the village teacher, who advocates the scientific point of view, and the local priest, who champions the old ways. In "Proletna izmama" the protagonist is not a herdsman but a monk, and, consequently, the conflict between the vow of celibacy and the temptations of the flesh becomes the main theme. Humor is an important component of the first and third works, while the second one is dominated by satire.

Because Elin Pelin built each of his stories around a single central event, showing it at the most crucial stage of its development – right before the final outcome of the conflict – the time span of the action is usually short. Elin Pelin once said he could not sit down to write unless he knew the end of the story. The simplicity of his sentence structure helps to create the sense of a naturally flowing narrative. In his best stories this seemingly effortless mode of delivering is nonetheless paired with a rich texture of images, emotions, and ideas. Initially attracted by the easy unfolding of the story, the reader is later surprised and captivated by the wide range of possible interpretations.

Elin Pelin's strengths as a short-story writer, however, made it difficult for him to write longer works. He never finished his novel "Nechista sila" (Unclean Power) although he invested much time and effort in it. He completed his second novelette, *Zemya* (Land, 1928), only under unrelenting pressure from the editor of the journal in which it was serialized in 1922. The only longer work he completed without such prodding is the novelette *Geratsite,* and it took him from 1904 to 1909 to write it. This novelette describes the disintegration of the extended patriarchal family of a wealthy peasant. It involves a gallery of characters: the industrious patriarch Yordan Geraka, his three sons – greedy Bozhan, good-hearted but weak Petŭr, and the lazy and irresponsible Pavel – their wives (especially Elka, the pure and suffering wife of Pavel), and some of their children. In *Geratsite* the idyllic side of village life, which is the subject of many of Elin Pelin's stories – including "Vetrenata melnitsa," "Kumovi gosti" (A Visit to the Godparents), and "Kosachi" (The Mowers) – appears only as a contrast to make the characters' moral degradation even more horrifying. *Zemya* is an exploration of the devastating effect that greed, particularly a peasant's greed for land, can have on human soul. The unfinished "Nechista sila" probes into yet another dark corner of the human psyche: the destructive force of male sexual desire when it is exploited by an unscrupulous temptress.

During the interwar period Elin Pelin published two collections of short narratives. *Cherni rozi* (Black Roses, 1928) includes thirty "poems in prose," many of which he wrote before the war or in 1921. In these prose poems Elin Pelin capitalizes on his ability to draw emotionally charged nature scenes. Unlike the short stories, in which the landscape always introduces a lyrical undercurrent that expands the possibilities for interpreting characters and events, the prose poems completely eliminate plot and use the nature scenes as allegories. Each description of nature is accompanied by a brief philosophical statement that spells out the author's intended meaning. For example, in "Lyato" (Summer) a vivid picture of a hot summer day ends with five sentences implying that this setting is an allegory of human maturity as opposed to youth or old age.

Pod manastirskata loza (In the Monastery Arbor, 1936) is a collection of eleven "charming little stories," to use Charles A. Moser's words, written over twenty-five years. In the opening piece, "Otets Sisoy" (Father Sisoy), the author tells his readers that he spent "one blissful summer" in a small monastery, where he heard the stories that will follow from the wise abbot Father Sisoy while dining with him in the monastery arbor. Along with this mostly

A 1947 letter from Elin Pelin to his sister Irina Argirova

formal connection, the texts are united also by an interpretation of Christian norms and values, which makes one recall Fyodor Dostoyevsky's novel *The Brothers Karamazov* (1879–1880). The true essence of Christianity, according to *Pod manastirskata loza,* is not extreme asceticism or religious zeal inspired by hatred, but forgiveness and love for God's creation. Unlike Dostoyevsky's Father Zosima, who expresses his ideas in the form of straightforward religious instruction, however, Father Sisoy uses brief

tales or, as the author calls them, "fables," which involve various paradoxes and a certain dose of good-hearted humor. Some of the stories – such as "Och-ite na Sveti Spiridon" (The Eyes of Saint Spiridon) and "Ogledaloto na Sveti Khristofor" (The Mirror of Saint Christopher) – rework subjects from saints' lives; others – such as "Zanemelite kambani" (The Silenced Bells) and "Edna obikolka na Sveti Georgi" (One Tour of Saint George) – use motifs from Bulgarian folk legends; and still others are

Elin Pelin's own creations. Of the last group "Zhenata sŭs zlatniya kosŭm" (The Woman with the Golden Hair) deals with a topic rarely found in Elin Pelin's writing: life in a small provincial town.

Least important as literary achievements are the stories published during World War I. In 1917 Elin Pelin gathered them in *Kitka za yunaka* (A Wreath for the Hero). Most of the pieces are rather simplistic illustrations of the official patriotic line. Although the book had five more editions (1918, 1925, two in 1942, and 1944), Elin Pelin must not have had a high opinion of it; "Sreshta" (A Meeting) is the only story from this book which he included in the five-volume collection *Sŭchineniya* (Works, 1938–1942).

Elin Pelin's humorous writings include sketches in *Pepel ot tsigarite mi* and *Ot prozoretsa*; the *shop* stories, letters, and dialogues – in prose or verse – most of which were collected in *Pizho i Pendo* (the names of the two main *shop* characters, 1917); and the belletristic feuilletons in *Az, ti, toy* (I, You, He, 1936). Many of the works in *Pizho i Pendo,* the book that sealed Elin Pelin's reputation as a *shop* writer, were initially published in *Bŭlgaran*. One member of the *Bŭlgaran* group recalled that the idea for these pieces came from witty disputes in *shop* dialect frequently improvised by Elin Pelin and the well-known cartoonist Aleksandŭr Bozhinov during their evening gatherings. According to Bozhinov, the name Pizho was borrowed from one of his cartoon characters, while Pendo was the name of a real *shop,* whom he and Elin Pelin met in the village of Gorublyane.

The feuilleton "Chovekŭt, za kogoto vsichki se grizhat" (The Man Everybody Is Concerned About) is considered the best example of the works collected in *Az, ti, toy,* especially by critics interested in Elin Pelin's social message. Its simple plot is embellished by grotesquely exaggerated details. By mistake a poor man enters a conference room where a committee is meeting. Its members, who have never before seen the poor people whose problems they are supposed to solve, decide to detain the unexpected visitor and study his needs, but the committee becomes engaged in debates over bureaucratic procedures, forgetting about the poor man, who dies of hunger. The implied point is that such committees are useless because they neither know nor care about the poor. Critics who are not interested in this sort of social satire find little literary value in *Az, ti, toy,* pointing out that in later years Elin Pelin said he was ashamed of the book. Yet he did include *Az, ti, toy* in *Sŭchineniya*. In general, Elin Pelin's humorous writings are topical, written on

the spur of the moment to satisfy the needs of various periodicals. Most of them are now of interest only to literary historians.

Elin Pelin's children's stories, especially his tales in verse, are a lasting contribution to Bulgarian children's literature. *Gori Tilileyski* (Tililey Mountains, 1919), *Svatbata na Chervenushko* (Chervenushko's Wedding, 1924), *Tri babi* (Three Grandmothers, 1930), *Dyadovata rŭkavichka* (Grandfather's Mitten, 1937), and *Strashen vŭlk* (A Frightening Wolf, 1944) are extremely popular among Bulgarian children. Elin Pelin also wrote prose renditions of folktales, carefully preserving all the important characteristics of genuine folk narratives. His many poems for children are uneven in quality. Some of them now sound fairly dated, while others continue to appeal to young readers. The majority of these poems are collected in *Pesnichki* (Little Songs, 1927), *Potocheta bistri* (Clear Brooks, 1931), and *Shturche-svirche* (Little Cricket–Little Musician, 1940). *Yan Bibiyan: Neveroyatnite priklyucheniya na edno khlape* (Yan Bibiyan: The Unbelievable Adventures of One Kid, 1933) and its sequel, *Yan Bibiyan na lunata* (Yan Bibiyan on the Moon, 1934), are still popular. These novels present an amusing combination of fantasy and science fiction.

Elin Pelin's humorous writings and works for children help a great deal to maintain his reputation. He mentioned the popular appeal of his works with special pride in a speech to the Union of Writers, "Kak pisha" (How I Write, 1949), pointing out that in the first decades of the twentieth century his stories quickly became part of the repertoire of so-called literary matinees and evenings organized primarily by teachers all over Bulgaria. He also reminisced about the success of his own readings at such gatherings in Sofia. Another indication of the popularity of his works is the fact that all of his books have been frequently republished. The most popular seems to be the novelette *Geratsite,* which appeared in eleven separate editions between 1943 and 1987.

Surprising as it may be, Elin Pelin's impact upon the Bulgarian literature is little studied. Since his best stories were written in a realistic mode, there has been a general assumption that all the realist writers after him must have been influenced by his achievements. Yet Elin Pelin's literary lessons have been most successfully used not by a critical or socialist realist but by Yordan Radichkov, widely considered the best short-story writer in Bulgarian literature today, who blends a serious outlook on life with laughter and elements of realism with the grotesque and the absurd.

Interview:

Petŭr Tikholov, *Elin Pelin: Intervyuta i razgovori* (Sofia: Nauka i izkustvo, 1964).

References:

Aleksandŭr Balabanov, *Elin Pelin: Sbornik* (Sofia: Al. Paskalev, 1922);

Manon Dragostinova, *Za realizma v tvorchestvoto na Elin Pelin* (Sofia: Nauka i izkustvo, 1964);

"Elin Pelin," in *A Biobibliographical Handbook of Bulgarian Authors,* edited by Karen L. Black, translated by Predrag Matejić (Columbus, Ohio: Slavica, 1981), pp. 180–184;

Krŭstyo Genov, *Elin Pelin: Zhivot i tvorchestvo* (Sofia: Izdatelstvo na Bŭlgarskata akademiya na naukite, 1956);

V. Mirolyubov [Krŭstyo Krŭstev], "Pevec na selskata nevolya," in his *Mladi i stari* (Sofia, 1907);

Charles A. Moser, "From War to War (1917–1944)," in his *A History of Modern Bulgarian Literature* (The Hague & Paris: Mouton, 1972), pp. 181–250;

Vivian Pinto, "Elin Pelin (1878–1949): Humanist of Shopsko," *Slavonic and East European Review,* 41 (December 1962): 158–181;

Penyo Rusev and others, eds., *Elin Pelin: Sto godini ot rozhdenieto mu* (Sofia: Izdatelstvo na Bŭlgarskata akademiya na naukite, 1978);

Ognyan Saparev, "Elin Pelin i problemite na komichnoto," in his *Literatura i interpretatsiya* (Plovdiv: Khristo G. Danov, 1988), pp. 136–172;

Vladimir Vasilev, "Ot 1920 do dnes: Elin Pelin," *Zlatorog,* 14 (March 1933): 105–119.

Ivan Gundulić

(8 January 1589 – 8 December 1638)

Thomas Eekman
University of California, Los Angeles

BOOKS: *Pjesni pokorne kralja Davida* (Rome, 1621);
Od veličanstva božijeh (Rome, 1621);
Suze sina razmetnoga (Venice, 1622);
Arijadna (Dubrovnik, 1633);
Osman (Dubrovnik, 1826); translated by E. D. Goy
(Zagreb: Yugoslav Academy of Sciences and
Arts, 1991);
Ljubovnik sramežljiv (Dubrovnik, 1829);
Dijana; Armida (Dubrovnik, 1837);
Dubravka (Dubrovnik, 1877); translated by Goy in
British-Croatian Review, 3, no. 9 (1976): 1–24;
Prozerpina ugrabljena od Plutona (Dubrovnik, 1877).
Collection: *Djela,* edited by Djuro Körbler and
Milan Rešetar (Zagreb: JAZU, 1938).

Portrait of Ivan Gundulić

The writings of Ivan (or Djivo Fran) Gundulić mark the culmination point of a cultural development (especially in poetry and the theater) in the free city of Dubrovnik that lasted for almost four centuries, until the city lost its independence in the nineteenth century. He is generally recognized as the greatest Dubrovnik poet.

The son of Frano Gundulić and Djiva Gradić (de Gradi), Ivan Gundulić was born on 8 January 1589 in Dubrovnik, on the Dalmatian coast. He was descended from the old noble family Gundulić/Gondola, which had played a prominent role in Dubrovnik public life since the early thirteenth century. He spent most of his life in this flowering Adriatic commercial town. Among his high-school teachers were the Italian Camillo Camilli, who wrote a sequel to Torquato Tasso's epic *La Gerusalemme liberata* (1581), and Petar Palikuća, a translator of Italian. Gundulić acquired the nickname Mačica (Pussycat), probably during his school years. After graduating from high school, he did not study at one of the Italian universities, as some of his coevals did, but remained in Dubrovnik (then also known as Ragusa) and occupied increasingly more important administrative posts successively. When he was nineteen (in 1608) he became a member of the *Veliko vijeće* (Great Council); twice, in

1615 and 1619, he held the temporary function of *knez* (commissary or governor) of Konavli, an area southeast of the city. From 1621 until his death he held some office in the city government every year; in 1636 he became a senator, in 1637 a judge, in 1638 a member of the *Malo vijeće* (Small Council). Had he lived a little longer, he would probably have been elected *knez* of the Dubrovnik Republic, the highest function that was held for one month only by meritorious, at least fifty-year-old gentlemen. His father, who died in 1624, had been *knez* five times, and Ivan's son Šiško later held the same position.

In 1628 Gundulić married Nika Sorkočević; they had three sons (all of whom later became members of the *Veliko vijeće*) and two daughters. He had a relatively uneventful life and died on 8 December

61

1638 in his native city, after a brief illness. He was buried in the Franciscan Church in Dubrovnik. His wife died in 1644. The oldest son, Frano, became a colonel and later a general in the Austrian army, married Countess Octavia Strozzi, lady in waiting of Empress Eleonora, and died in Vienna in 1700. His second son, Šiško, and Šiško's son Djivo were both poets.

Gundulić grew up in a literature-oriented ambience and in an atmosphere of patriotic ardor. His earliest writings were gay pastoral plays with predominantly mythological themes and amorous plots. He once listed ten plays that he had written: *Galatea, Dijana, Armida, Posvetilište ljuveno* (The Sacrifice of Love), *Prozerpina ugrabljena od Plutona* (Proserpina Abducted by Pluto), *Čerera, Kleopatra, Arijadna, Adon,* and *Koraljka od Šira* (A Coral from Šir). Of these plays, texts for only four have been preserved, possibly not in their original form: *Dijana* and *Armida,* two short plays; *Arijadna,* an adaptation of the Italian Ottavio Rinuccini's *Arianna* (1608); and *Prozerpina.* They are comedies in the Italian manner and also typical of Dubrovnik theater in his time, with music, songs, and dance — the forerunners of the melodrama and opera. Gundulić's plays were apparently staged with much success in Dubrovnik, but soon Gundulić renounced them. In the preface to his first published work, *Pjesni pokorne kralja Davida* (King David's Humble Songs, 1621), a translation of David's seven penitential psalms, he calls his plays "idle and empty songs" that he preferred "to leave in the dark."

After these juvenile creations Gundulić turned to work that expressed a more serious and sober outlook on life; this seriousness became characteristic of his later oeuvre. A factor in this changed attitude seems to have been the influence of the Jesuits, who played an increasingly important role in Dubrovnik intellectual life of the seventeenth century (in the Gundulić family there were several prominent Jesuit clerics). Several poems from Gundulić's early period have been lost, and some poems have been attributed to him without proof of their authenticity. He planned and probably started to translate Tasso's *Gerusalemme liberata.* It is doubtful that he ever finished it, and whatever portion he did complete is not extant. Gundulić's *Ljubovnik sramežljiv* (The Timid Lover), a free translation of *Amante timido* (1619) by his Italian contemporary Girolamo Pretio, was published in 1829.

An allegorical pastoral play in three acts, *Dubravka,* which Gundulić wrote in 1627, was performed in Dubrovnik in 1628, probably on the name day of Saint Vlah, the patron of the city and defender of its freedom and independence. Although the play, in its form and in some of its mythological features, is not free from foreign influences, its contents are quite original: it is dedicated to Dubrovnik, its liberty and prosperity, and takes place in an imagined, idyllic pastoral place called Dubrava (*dub* [oak], *dubrava* [oak forest], from which the name Dubrovnik is also derived), where traditionally on the annual Freedom Day the shepherds get together and choose the handsomest young shepherd and shepherdess, who then will be engaged. This year, the fairest maiden is Dubravka, the comeliest young man Miljenko; corruption has entered this idyllic entourage, however, and the old, ugly Grdan has bribed the voters to vote for him so he will get Dubravka as his bride. His scheme seems to succeed, but after the couple has entered the temple of the god Lero for the marriage ceremony, Lero shows his displeasure with peals of thunder and an earthquake. Grdan has to flee; Miljenko enters the temple and is united with the beautiful Dubravka. At the end all those seduced to do wrong solemnly pledge to mend their ways, and they sing a song to celebrate freedom, the highest blessing God has bestowed on them ("O lijepa, o draga, o slatka slobodo": Oh wonderful, dear, sweet freedom!). The play includes several secondary characters and interludes (monologues and dialogues of satyrs, shepherds, and friends); part of the action is narrated by a messenger. Its language and its action are simple, attractive, and understandable — even to a contemporary public — and from 1888 onward it has been staged in Dubrovnik every year.

In 1635 or 1636 Gundulić wrote a hymn of praise to "Visini privedroj Ferdinanda II, velikoga kneza od Toskane" (His Serene Highness Ferdinand II, Grand Prince of Tuscany) on the occasion of his marriage. He praises him for his supposed valor and militancy against the Turks but also for his love of the Slavic language that he was learning (his teacher was the poet's relative Marin Gundulić). On this occasion Gundulić expatiates on the Slavic language and people that spread "from the Dubrovnik area all the way to the icy Polar Sea" — an indication that the idea of connection and coherence of the various Slavic nations was well known in Dubrovnik. Of course, he also extols Ferdinand's glorious ancestors and relatives, among whom was the Austrian emperor, and he appeals to him to fight the dangerous and treacherous Muslims.

Gundulić also wrote "Žalosno cviljenje u smrt gospodje Marije Kalandrice" (Elegy for Mrs. Maria Calendari's Demise). This Dubrovnik lady died in 1637, and the 314-line poem was probably Gundulić's last creation, or at least the last one that has been preserved. It is replete with images of and reflections on death, which "transforms an exquisite, beautiful flower into trash."

His major work is the long lyrical epic *Osman*, written between 1621 or 1622 and the end of his life. Of its twenty cantos, two are nonextant: the fourteenth and fifteenth (or, according to other scholars, the thirteenth and fourteenth). Since the poem was not published for nearly two centuries after Gundulić wrote it, it may not seem surprising that *Osman* was not preserved in its entirety; yet the epos was copied hundreds of times – handwritten copies have been found all over the Serbo-Croatian linguistic territory. Djuro Körbler, one of the editors of the first complete scholarly edition of Gundulić's *Djela* (Works, 1938), used about forty different manuscripts for this edition and looked at some forty others. None of these manuscripts includes the two missing cantos, suggesting that Nikola Ohmučević, who copied the work as early as 1651–1653, was right in assuming the missing parts were never written. His opinion was shared by Vsevolod Setschkareff in his 1952 study of Gundulić. Some later Croatian poets have attempted to supply the two missing cantos; the best known of these texts, by Ivan Mažuranić (1844), has often been added as an appendix to editions of *Osman*.

The eighteen extant cantos comprise some eleven thousand lines in Gundulić's short, trochaic, octosyllabic meter, with a caesura after the fourth syllable and alternating, feminine rhyme. This prosodic form was by far the most common in Gundulić's versification, though in some works he also used twelve-syllable lines. Following the Italian habit, he took the liberty of counting two successive vowels as one syllable (also when a *j* is between the vowels); consequently, the line "caru Osmanu biješe ostala" has eight, not eleven syllables. His *osmerac* (eight-syllable line) is shorter than the *deseterac,* the popular line of the South Slavic epic folk song, and shorter than any other line used in virtually all other epic poems in world literature. Short lines are, in fact, not well suited to the narrative epic style, but Gundulić succeeded in creating a compact, pithy manner of writing, in which he managed to include not only epic action, but also reflections and digressions. Because of its short lines, the *Osman* possesses a lightness and freshness that give it a place apart in world literature.

In the first canto Sultan Osman, commander-in-chief of the Turks, complains in a monologue of his misfortune and of the weakness of his army, as a result of which he has been badly defeated by Polish forces near Hotim (Khotin on the Dniestr in Moldavia). In reality the outcome of this 1621 battle was ambiguous; both parties suffered heavy losses, and there was no real victor. At the end of canto 1, Osman decides to gather a new army in the East, hoping for military successes. In canto 2 his counselors advise him to marry a high-born girl and to conclude peace with Poland to avoid trouble with this formidable neighbor-state during his absence. Then, in canto 3, the *poklisar* (envoy) Ali-paša sets out on a journey to Warsaw to conclude peace. He passes the battlefield of Khotin in canto 4 and tells his traveling companion about the war of the previous year. Then he meets Krunoslava, the wife of the Polish knight Korevski (the historical Korecki), and informs her that her husband is in Turkish captivity (canto 5). She decides to go to Constantinople disguised as a man and to try to set him free (canto 6). In canto 7 Kazlar-aga, who has been charged with finding a fair and noble bride for the sultan, travels through Greece, carrying a whole company of young ladies with him as prisoners. Near Smederevo in Serbia he meets old Ljubdrag with his daughter, Sunčanica; after Ljubdrag has told the sad story of how his twelve sons were all killed, Kazlar-aga carries away Sunčanica (canto 8). In canto 9, set in Poland during a commemoration of the first anniversary of the battle at Khotin, the Tatar Amazon Sokolica appears with her suite and takes some Polish women prisoner. In the ensuing struggle she is defeated, but Prince Vladislav (the Polish crown prince Wladyslaw) appears and takes her under his protection. (In reality Wladyslaw had been ill and lying in his tent during the entire battle; but Gundulić viewed him as the great victor and hero.)

In canto 10 Ali-paša arrives in Warsaw, where he is received by King Šišman (King Zygmunt). In the royal palace Osman views tapestries depicting the battle of Khotin (canto 11). Canto 12 deals with Krunoslava's adventures in Constantinople, where she ends up in prison with her beloved. In canto 13 the devil orders his infernal powers to stir up a revolt among the Turks. The next extant cantos describe the events in Constantinople: mutiny in the army, which demands extradition of the sultan's adviser, Grand Vizier Dilaver (canto 16); a conspiracy of former Sultan Mustafa's mother and her son-in-law Daut to liquidate Osman (canto 17); Dilaver's defense of Constantinople against the insurgents (canto 18); Dilaver's death (canto 19); and finally the appearance of Osman, who has been arrested,

Title page for Gundulić's 1621 translation of seven psalms attributed to David

before the reinstated Sultan Mustafa; Osman is taken to prison and murdered by order of Daut (canto 20).

Gundulić's *Osman* was published for the first time in 1826; many editions followed. The standard text is still the one in Djuro Körbler and Milan Rešetar's edition of Gundulić's *Djela* (Works, 1938); other important editions include Milan Ratković's (1955), J. Ravlić's (1964), and Miroslav Pantić's (1967). There was an Italian translation as early as the late eighteenth century; a German translation was published in 1918, a Polish one in 1934, and an English one in 1991. Many scholars have studied and commented on the work: on the mystery of the two absent cantos, the question of its unity, of its genesis, its purport, Gundulić's sources, and the artistic as well as ideological qualities of the epic. There is no doubt that the battle of a strong Turkish army under Osman against a Polish army (formally led by Wladyslaw, but in fact by Gen. Karol Chodkiewicz) was the stimulus for Gundulić to write his heroic poem, even though the entire ac-

tion takes place after the war and is viewed in retrospect. Combined with Gundulić's pro-Christian, anti-Muslim, and basically patriotic Slavic, political theme there is the more general moral theme (frequently deliberated in baroque literature) of human pride, craving for power, and heedlessness that must end in collapse. Milan Rešetar advanced the hypothesis that *Osman* may be divided into two parts: the original epic and cantos 2–13, which do not belong to the core epic because they are not essential for the story of Osman's death and its causes as announced by Gundulić in the first canto. Rešetar's arguments, in his introduction to the Polish translation, are not quite convincing although *Osman* does not distinguish itself by a strong structural unity. Gundulić, however, does emphasize the decisive importance of the victory, the ensuing decline of the Turkish empire (wishful thinking in those times), and the senselessness of Osman's ambition. His fall, precipitated by the revolt of the janissaries, is attributed to the defeat at Khotin, which is historically incorrect but important for the point Gundulić wants to make. The introduction of fantastic episodes with fictitious or partly fictitious characters (Korevski, Ali-paša, Ljubdrag, and others) and Amazons (Krunoslava, Sokolica) who have their romantic adventures is a feature Gundulić borrowed from the Italian epic works he used as his models; such digressions are a normal quality of the baroque epos. Gundulić did not in every respect imitate Italian models or follow the rules drafted in the sixteenth century by Tasso, Julius Caesar Scaliger (Giulio Cesare Scaligero), and others. In his epic Gundulić introduced occasional elements of humor and used some proverbs and locutions, a practice not in accordance with the serious character of the heroic epic. Gundulić's dependence on Tasso has been stressed by scholars such as Alfred Jensen, Franjo Marković, Albert Haler, Roman Brandt, and Vsevolod Setschkareff; but others have pointed to elements from South Slavic folk poetry in many episodes, turns of speech, expressions, and epithets in *Osman*.

A certain dichotomy can also be found in the serious part of the work. On the one hand, there is the theme of human pride and its downfall embodied in the young Sultan Osman; on the other, the theme of glory and victory for Christianity and Slavdom, embodied in the valiant Wladyslaw. Gundulić, however, keeps to the old rule requiring a certain objectivity or sportsmanship toward the antagonist of the epic; he paints Osman as presumptious, ambitious, and headstrong but as valiant and not uncongenial, as a victim of the discontent of the janissaries and the perfidity of his rivals. The work is named after him, it deals with his *gesta* and tragic death. But the real hero, of course, is Wladyslaw. Notwithstanding his minimal role in the whole war, he traveled shortly afterward to Rome and visited several European countries, where he was met with praise and enthusiasm: some Italian poets wrote laudatory poems in his honor. This enthusiasm for the Polish prince (justified to some extent by the fact that he had proven himself a valiant and capable military leader on other occasions) was bolstered by the hope and expectation in southern and eastern Europe that the Turkish power would soon be broken.

Yet, in some places the reader gets the impression that Gundulić viewed the struggle between Poles and Turks as a game, in spite of the acute danger of Turkish conquest in seventeenth-century southeastern Europe. In canto 9 one of his fictitious characters, Sokolica, an ally of the Turks, cruelly kills a large number of Poles; yet in the beginning of canto 10 the Poles engage in joyous merrymaking, and Wladyslaw does not blame Sokolica for her misdeeds; he treats her with the utmost courtesy. Likewise, the Turk Ali-paša and the Polish prince Zbaraski treat each other with courtesy and kindness in canto 9.

Some scholars – including Jensen, Rešetar, and O. Makovej – have expressed the opinion that Gundulić knew little about Polish history and about the recent battle at Khotin; others – including Brandt and Stjepan Musulin – point out that his reproduction of the events is, generally speaking, more or less in accordance with the historical facts. Musulin shows that Gundulić must have had ample oral and/or written information about the situation in Poland and on the battlefield on the Dniestr, incorporating in his epic more of these data than others had assumed. Yet the fact remains that the battle itself and all details about it are reproduced in *Osman* rather vaguely and sometimes obviously at variance with historical authenticity. It is uncertain whether Gundulić did not know the real course of events or consciously distorted the facts, interpreting them in his own way in order to make them tally with his own conception of the war or the rules of epic art. After all, he was not in the first place a chronicler of facts (the same episode was chronicled in detail by several of his contemporaries) but a poet.

For example, he does not concede any Polish losses (except the slaughter brought about by the fictitious Krunoslava). He fails to mention General Chodkiewicz's death and his succession by the het-

man Lubomirski, whose part in the war was almost as important as Chodkiewicz's. Gundulić includes Polish commanders who were not even present on the Khotin battlefield and omits others who did play a decisive role. On his journey to Italy shortly after the war, Prince Wladyslaw was in Ancona, where he apparently visited a di Gondola family, a branch of the Gundulić family. It is possible that this event was known to the poet or that he met the prince there. If so, this family connection may have given the poet the impulse to extend his epic about Osman with a "Wladyslawiada," a second theme about the Khotin war and Wladyslaw's heroic part in it. A prominent place in his *Osman* is assigned to the Polish commander Korecki, who in reality did not play a very active role in the battle and was twice taken prisoner by the Turks; after the first time, he managed to escape and passed through Dubrovnik. Gundulić may have heard about Korecki's stay in the town and may even have met him, which may have instigated him to attribute to Korecki such an important function. He clearly did not aim at giving an objective account, accurately weighing what was historically and factually true and worth reporting. Although interpolating totally imagined stories (for example, that Osman's life was saved by Grand Vizier Dilaver, as described in cantos 1 and 4, or that Wladyslaw with his own hand killed Paša Karakas in canto 4), in many instances he keeps fairly close to history, probably drawing on books and other materials on Poland in the Dubrovnik State Archive and on verbal information.

From an artistic, not a historiographical point of view, Gundulić has been criticized by Armin Pavić and by Albert Haler. Haler especially complains of Gundulić's indigestible rhetorical pathos and his constant application of baroque formulas without any poetical spontaneity or real inspiration. Haler considers the *Osman* devoid of all poetical value, a product of a propagandistic religious moralist, and he provides numerous examples to demonstrate that Gundulić's epic is only a weak imitation of Italian models and worthless from an aesthetic viewpoint. This extreme opinion is untenable, and most critics and investigators value Gundulić's work highly. Setschkareff, for example, calls Gundulić "undoubtedly the greatest Slavic baroque poet," while Jensen says he wrote "the greatest heroic epos in Ragusan and perhaps in all Slavic poetry, at least before the nineteenth century."

As Miroslav Pantić pointed out in the introduction to his edition of *Osman* (1967), it was Gundulić's tragedy that his principal creation, the crowning piece of his oeuvre, on which he had worked for many years, remained in unpolished form due to his premature death, with repetitious lines, thoughts not fully developed, inconsistencies, and anachronisms. An additional misfortune was that the text fell into the hands of well-meaning, but incompetent copyists, who in the course of almost two centuries have done much harm to it, sometimes changing the order of the lines or even adding their own lines. Modern textual criticism and literary-historical research have more or less eliminated these deficiencies. This research has also enabled us to estimate the extent of Gundulić's originality. It is obvious that he studied Aristotle, knew the classical Roman poets, and of course was familiar with Ariosto and especially Tasso. He must have been also familiar with Giambattista Marino, his contemporary, whose ideas on writing good poetry (that initiated the baroque era in literature) Gundulić applied in his epic. Gundulić was convinced that poetry was not only supposed to be well constructed, pleasing to the ear and eye, and written according to specific classical rules, but it also had to be moralistic, conveying a serious message to the reader. Those were his basic guiding principles. In *Osman* — and to a certain degree also in *Suze sina razmetnoga* (The Tears of the Prodigal Son, 1622) — the main ethical idea is that of the frailty and uncertainty of happiness, of human vanity, and of insolence that will end in disaster: "naučite, ljudi oholi, / ki živete bez pripasti, / da nije tvrdje krepke toli / kâ ne može časom pasti" (learn, you arrogant people, who live without scruple, that there is no fortress so strong it cannot fall in one moment). He illustrates this lesson not with an example from ancient times or from the Bible but with a recent and topical "true" story. This subject must have heightened the interest of readers. (Though not printed for a long time, his *Osman* and several other works were frequently copied and widely circulated in manuscript.)

The edifying tone of *Osman* is never overdone, and the short rhyming lines lend the work a surprising lightness. *Osman* could be viewed as a transition from renaissance to baroque: based on sixteenth-century principles and prescriptions, it simultaneously manifests typical baroque features, with its strong contrasts and catastrophes, its fantastic elements, its demons and Amazons, the antitheses that characterize its language and style, the hyperboles and oxymora, the frequent metaphors and the terms and figures of speech typical of the seicento. Despite Tasso's undeniable influence, *Osman* has its own character and a special message (the vigilance in view of the Turkish danger in southeastern Europe) that is not present in the Italian epic literature of his or the preceding epoch. Mainly in two works, *Dubravka* and *Osman,* Gundulić has exhibited his poetic talent, his creative power, his rich imagination, and his mastery of the Serbo-Croatian language.

References:

Antun Barac, "Esej o Gunduliću," in his *Knjiga eseja* (Zagreb: Mlada Jugoslavija, 1924);

Roman Brandt, *Istoriko-literaturnyj razbor poèmy Ivana Gunduliča "Osman"* (Kiev, 1879);

Henry R. Cooper, Jr., "Poles on Croats: A Recent Polish Work on Ivan Gundulić's *Osman,*" *Canadian-American Slavic Studies,* 10 (1976): 419–425;

Arturo Cronia, "L'influenza della Gerusalemme liberata del Tasso sull' Osman di Giovanni Gondola," in *L'Europa orientale,* volume 2 (Rome, 1925);

Dunja Fališevac, "Ivan Gundulić," in *Hrvatska književnost u evropskom kontekstu,* edited by Aleksandar Flaker and Krunoslav Pranjić (Zagreb: Liber, 1978), pp. 259–277; republished in *Comparative Studies in Croatian Literature,* edited by Miroslav Beker (Zagreb: Zavod za znanost i književnosti Filozofskog fakulteta u Zagrebu, 1981), pp. 199–221;

E. D. Goy, "*Osman* and The Death of Smail-Aga Ćengijić," *Scottish Slavonic Review,* 7 (1986): 17–30;

Albert Haler, *Gundulićev "Osman" s estetskog gledišta* (Belgrade, 1929);

Nikola Ivanišin, "*Osman* Djiva Gundulića," in his *Dubrovačke književne studije* (Dubrovnik: Matica hrvatska, 1966);

Alfred Jensen, *Gundulić und sein Osman* (Göteborg, 1900);

Ante Kadić, "Ivan Gundulić (1589–1638)," *Journal of Croatian Studies,* 30 (1989): 89–96;

Mihovil Kombol, "Gundulić u hrvatskoj književnosti," *Hrvatska revija* (Zagreb), 11 (1938): 602–604;

Djuro Körbler, "Četiri priloga Gunduliću i njegovu *Osmanu,*" *Rad* JAZU (Zagreb), no. 205 (1914): 135–220;

Vinko Lozovina, "Gundulić, the Poet of the Ragusan Republic," *Slavonic and East European Review,* 17 (1939): 668–676;

O. Makovej, "Beiträge zu den Quellen des Gundulić'schen *Osman,*" *Archiv für slavische Philologie,* 26 (1904): 71–100;

Franjo Marković, "Estetička ocjena Gundulićeva *Osmana,*" *Rad* JAZU (Zagreb), nos. 46 (78–

165), 47 (129–221), 50 (96–175), 52 (1-140) (1879–1880);

Stjepan Musulin, *Poljaci u Gundulićevu "Osmanu"* (Zagreb: JAZU, 1950);

Miroslav Pantić, "Arhivske vesti o dubrovačkom pozorištu u doba Gundulića i Palmotića," *Pitanja književnosti i jezika,* 4 (1957);

Armin Pavić, "Gundulićev 'Vladislav,'" *Rad* JAZU (Zagreb), no. 55 (1881): 1–115;

Pavić, "O kompoziciji Gundulićeva *Osmana*," *Rad* JAZU (Zagreb), no. 32 (1875): 104–150;

Pavić, *Postanje Gundulićeva "Osmana"* (Zagreb, 1913);

Herbert Peukert, *Ivan Gundulićs "Osman" in Deutschland* (Berlin: Akademie Verlag, 1969);

J. Ravlić, "Prilozi proučavanju Gundulićeva *Osmana,*" *Gradja* (Zagreb), no. 28 (1962);

Milan Rešetar, "Gundulićev *Osman,*" *Bratstvo* (Novi Sad), 17 (1923): 117–155;

Rešetar, "Die Metrik Gundulića," *Archiv für slavische Philologie* (Vienna), no. 25 (1903): 250–289;

Rešetar, "Pjesme pripisivane Gunduliću" and "Glavne osobine Gundulićeva jezika," *Rad Hrvatske Akademije* (Zagreb), no. 272 (1941);

Hans Rothe, "Unutrašnja forma u književnom baroku slobodnog grada Dubrovnika. Ivan Gundulić: *Suze sina razmetnoga,*" in *Croatica,* volume 16 (Zagreb: Hrvatsko Filološko Društvo, 1985), pp. 55–81;

Vsevolod Setschkareff, *Die Dichtungen Gundulićs und ihr poetischer Stil* (Bonn: Athenäum Verlag, 1952);

Franjo Švelec, "O Gundulićevoj poeziji," *Republika,* 11–12 (1954);

Švelec, "Ivan Gundulić," in *Povijest hrvatske književnosti,* volume 3 (Zagreb: Liber-Mladost, 1974), pp. 177–211;

V. K. Zajcev, "Istoričeskaja osnova i idejnoe soderžanie poèmy I. Gundulića *Osman,*" in *Literatura slavjanskix narodov,* volume 2 (Moscow, 1957);

I. Zore, "Alegorije u Gundulićevoj *Osmanidi,*" *Rad* JAZU (Zagreb), no. 94 (1889): 199–236;

Zore, "O kompoziciji Gundulićeva *Osmana,*" *Rad* JAZU (Zagreb), no. 39 (1877): 151–192.

Vuk Stefanović Karadžić

(6 November 1787 – 7 February 1864)

George Vid Tomashevich
State University of New York at Buffalo

BOOKS: *Mala prostonarodna slavenoserbska pesnarica* (Vienna, 1814–1815);

Pismenica serbskoga jezika po govoru prostoga naroda (Vienna: Pečatnja G. Ionna Šnirera, 1814);

Srpske narodne pripovjetke i zagonetke (Vienna, 1821; revised and enlarged edition, 1854);

Danica: Almanah (Vienna, 1826–1834);

Miloš Obrenović, Knjaz Serbiji (Budim, Hungary: Štamparija kralj. univers. peštanskoga, 1828);

Žitije Hajduk-Veljka Petrovića (Vienna: Zabavnik, 1828);

Srpske narodne poslovice (Vienna, 1836);

Montenegro und die Montenegriner (Stuttgart & Tübingen: J. G. Cotta, 1837);

Kovčežić (Vienna, 1849);

Praviteljstvujušći Sovjet Serbskij za vremena Kara-Djordjijeva ili Otimanje ondašnjijeh velikaša oko vlasti (Vienna: Štamparija Jermenskoga manastira, 1860);

Život i običaji naroda srpskoga (Belgrade, 1867);

Skupljeni gramatički i polemički spisi, 3 volumes (Belgrade: Štamparija Kraljevine Srbije, Državno izdanje, 1894–1896);

Prvi i drugi srpski ustanak (Belgrade: Prosveta, 1947);

Sabrana dela, 39 volumes (Belgrade: Prosveta, 1964).

OTHER: *Lexicon Serbico-Germanico-Latinum* [*Srpski rječnik*], edited by Karadžić (Vindobona [Vienna]: Typis Congregationis mechitaristicae, 1818, revised and enlarged, 1851–1852; revised and enlarged edition, Belgrade: Tipographia regni Serbiae, 1898; Tipographia regni Yugoslaviae, 1935);

Novi zavjet, translated by Karadžić (Vienna: British and Foreign Bible Society, 1847);

Srpske narodne pjesme, 9 volumes, edited by Karadžić (Belgrade: Štamparija Kraljevine Srbije, 1891–1900; revised edition, Belgrade: Državna Štamparija Kraljevine Jugoslavije, 1920–1930); translated by John Bowring as *Servian Popular Poetry* (London: Privately printed, 1827).

Portrait of Vuk Stefanović Karadžić, circa 1816

In the thirteenth century Prince Rastko Nemanjić, later Saint Sava, turned Serbian culture toward the East; in the eighteenth the philosopher Dositej Obradović turned it toward the West; and in the nineteenth the peasant genius Vuk Stefanović Karadžić turned it toward itself. More than anyone else, he made his people realize that, in addition to their splendid heritage of high-medieval civilization, they also had a rich and humane folk culture of which any nation could be proud and that, after long centuries of declining Ottoman oppression, they were rejoining the West not as empty-handed barbarians but as an old and historically experienced people bringing to the world a gift of beauty and universal value.

Karadžić was born on 6 November 1787 in the village of Tršić, near the town of Loznica in Jadar in northwest Serbia. He was the sixth child of Stefan and Jegda Zrnić Karadžić, who had lost five children before him to various illnesses. The name *Vuk,* which in Serbian means "wolf," was supposed to protect him from witchcraft. Vuk learned the alphabet from a literate relative, the local merchant Jevto Savić-Čotrić, and began to write in a solution of gunpowder on pieces of paper from discarded cartridges. In 1796, after a brief stay in the Loznica grammar school, he spent a short time in the monastery of Tronoša until his father took him home to watch over his goats.

In 1804, the year of the first Serbian insurrection against the Turks, Karadžić was not able to join the fighters because of physical underdevelopment and lameness already apparent in his left knee. Instead he became a secretary to the local insurrectionist Djordje Ćurčija. In the fall of the same year Karadžić went to Sremski Karlovci, where he studied Latin, Church Slavonic, German, arithmetic, and catechism under Archimandrite Lukijan Mušicki, a renowned poet of Serbian classicism. Karadžić was not admitted to the local high school because he could not produce a certificate of elementary education. Therefore he moved to Petrinja, Croatia, where he hoped to perfect his knowledge of German.

On his return to Serbia in 1807, he served as a secretary to the insurrectionist hero Jakov Nenadović and later to the Serbian Governing Council in Belgrade. In the liberated capital he met philosopher and educator Obradović, founder of the Velika Škola (later the University of Belgrade) and Serbia's first minister of public instruction. As the first major Serbian writer to introduce substantial elements of the spoken language of the common people into his transitional mixture of lingering Old Church Slavonic, Slaveno-Serbian, and Russo-Serbian and as Karadžić's teacher, Obradović was an important precursor to Karadžić. In 1812 Karadžić was sent to eastern Serbia and Bulgaria with special credentials from Karageorge's government to negotiate with the Turks, and in 1813 he served as a deputy judge and local administrator.

Fleeing from the reconquest of Serbia by the sultan's armies in 1813, Karadžić crossed into Austria and reached its capital in November. As soon as he was settled he wrote a pamphlet on the catastrophe in his homeland. The piece attracted the attention of Jernej Kopitar, a learned Slovenian Slavicist and the official censor of Austrian publications. Kopitar recognized in Karadžić a master of the Serbian language and introduced him to some of the most outstanding German, Russian, and Czech scholars of his time. Karadžić thus became acquainted with the German Romantic Clemens Brentano; the famous brothers Jacob and Wilhelm Grimm; the illustrious poet-philosopher Johann Wolfgang von Goethe; the Russian historian Nikolay Mikhailovich Karamzin; the Czech father of Slavic philology, Josef Dobrovsky; and the gifted folklorist Therese Albertine Luise von Jakob (Talvj), his much admired "gospodja Talvija" (Mrs. Talvija).

At Kopitar's urging he began to gather his first collection of Serbian oral literature, *Mala prostonarodna slavenoserbska pesnarica* (A Small Slaveno-Serbian Songbook of the Common People). Published in 1814–1815, the work includes both lyric and epic folk poetry. With it Karadžić declared war on the so-called Slaveno-Serbian language of the stuffy literary elite and began to use the spoken, living language of the illiterate masses. For this hitherto despised medium he wrote a grammar, *Pismenica serbskoga jezika po govoru prostoga naroda* (Orthography of the Serbian Language According to the Usage of the Common People). Published in 1814, the treatise was composed in Budapest with the help of Luka Milovanov.

In 1815 the great German folklorist Jacob Grimm sent Karadžić a formal request, in the name of the German Folklore Society, to start collecting Serbian poems, traditions, customs, and other materials. In 1817 Karadžić coedited, with Kopitar, Davidović's Vienna-based newspaper *Novine Srbske* (Serbian Newspaper). The following year, when Karadžić married Anna Kraus, the daughter of a Viennese tailor, his Slovenian friend and teacher served as his best man.

Karadžić's revolutionary work on the reform of his people's language and orthography was based on his logical and scientific principle: "Write as you speak and read as is written!" In place of the forty-six letters of the old Slaveno-Serbian orthography, he reduced the Serbian alphabet to only thirty graphemes corresponding to the thirty segmental phonemes of the Serbian language and the four suprasegmental phonemes governing stress, pitch, and intonation. This meant leaving out all unnecessary signs and introducing new ones previously absent

Karadžić's restored house in Tršić

from Serbian spelling. He discarded some useless letters of the outdated Russo-Slavonic orthography and stylized the characters for certain sounds still without a symbol of their own.

He also effected a major reform in the Serbian language itself. Since his ancestors were originally from Hezegovina, he wrote in the so-called southern or Jekavian dialect, resolutely rejecting the inconsistent mixtures of the Slaveno-Serbian and Church Russian languages. At the outset of the 1800s Serbian authors used a hybrid language — mainly Serbian, but heavily sprinkled with Church Slavonic and Russian words and constructions. Karadžić introduced into Serbian literature the pure, living speech of the village folk and the crystalline language of the great Serbian epics, folktales, and proverbs. He was not bothered by the depth of the Turkish impact on the Serbian language and culture in his people's daily speech.

Anticipating the discovery of the phoneme (unit of sound) as both an acoustic phenomenon and a linguistic concept, Karadžić's system of spelling based on a fixed one-to-one relationship between sound and its symbol is one of the most scientific and phonetic spelling systems in use. Foreshad-

owed by Sava Mrkalj, Serbian monk and teacher, as well as by the German romantic Karl Leberecht Immermann, this system of perfectly phonetic writing is not bound to the Serbian language or the Cyrillic alphabet. As a universal principle it is applicable to all languages and alphabets.

In 1818 Karadžić published his important *Srpski rječnik* (Serbian Dictionary), officially titled *Lexicon Serbico-Germanico-Latinum.* Its first edition, the result of painstaking scholarship, includes twenty-six thousand words; the second, issued in 1851–1852, had forty-seven thousand. A third edition, prepared in Belgrade in 1898, includes thousands of additional entries found among his posthumous manuscripts. This great dictionary still serves as a standard reference work. Most of the items in it were actually heard and gathered by Karadžić and his correspondents from living informants. Each is marked with accents indicating stress, pitch, and intonation and translated in German and Latin. The dictionary also includes a brief grammar and short essays illustrating the sociolinguistic and situational contexts of the terms they accompany and offering a gold mine of information on Serbian folklife, customs, and history. Far ahead of its time, the dictionary represents a monumental achievement not only in lexicography but also in ethnography, folklore, and historiography. In addition, Karadžić was not an armchair scholar: although lame and never physically robust, he was a tireless field-worker long before fieldwork became a methodological imperative in the professional training of modern Western anthropologists.

His rejection of the artificial Slaveno-Serbian literary language was a more problematic matter than his decisive rejection of its obsolete spelling. He first suggested that each author should use the dialect of his or her native region but soon came to realize that this would almost surely result in linguistic chaos. Besides, by rejecting the declension of certain Serbian verbal forms he restricted the flexibility of the Serbian sentence and imposed the necessity of using substitute dependent clauses that serve as roundabout expressive devices. This and other ambivalent results of his reforms were discussed by the modern Serbian writer Meša Selimović in his essay *Za i protiv Vuka* (For and Against Vuk, 1967). Selimović's interesting work is a belated echo of the old dispute between Karadžić's supporters and his opponents, which divided the Serbian literati throughout most of his lifetime and long thereafter.

Both of his reforms were strongly resisted by certain representatives of the Serbian Orthodox church and most of the Vojvodinian intelligentsia, yet Karadžić refused to retreat. He defended his ideas with energy and eloquence in a series of polemics. Particularly well known are his critiques of Milovan Vidaković's novels and, still more, his trenchant *Utuci* (Retorts), including *Utuk na utuk* (A Retort to a Retort), exchanged with his chief adversary Jovan Hadžić (Miloš Svetić). These are collected in *Skupljeni gramatički i polemički spisi* (Collected Grammatical and Polemical Writings, 1894–1896).

Between 1823 and 1833 Karadžić published four volumes of ballads and folk songs. A later edition, published between 1841 and 1846, grew to six volumes, followed by the definitive Serbian government edition of all his available materials in nine volumes, published between 1891 and the early 1900s. According to the American Slavicist George R. Noyes, "These books are still the most important collection of Serbian folk poetry; in fact, Karadžić is regarded as the greatest of all Slavic collectors of such materials. Through countless popular reprints, the best ballads that he published have become familiar to the whole Serbian people." Karadžić's collection *Srpske narodne pripovjetke i zagonetke* (Serbian

Folktales and Riddles, 1821) was considerably enlarged in a later edition.

In his lifetime his work was more favorably received abroad than among his own people. In 1819 he became a member of the Saint Petersburg Society of the Lovers of Russian Literature, in 1823 an honorary doctor of the University of Jena, and in 1825 an honorary doctor of the University of Göttingen. He received a pension from the Russian government starting in 1826 and starting in 1836 a small assistance from the government of Serbia. For a while he served as a member of his country's legislative commission and as presiding judge, but soon he returned to Vienna, where he resumed his scholarly activities. Throughout most of his seventy-six years, despite the recognition that came to him early, Karadžić and his family struggled with material hardships and almost-incessant academic and political turmoil.

Between 1826 and 1829 and in 1834 he published the almanac *Danica* (The Morning Star), which contains valuable articles on language, geography, and ethnography as well as some anecdotal and humorous material. Between 1834 and 1835 he traveled through Primorye, Boka, and Montenegro. His purpose was to become still better acquainted with the living language of his people and its wealth of proverbs. The most valuable result of this field trip was his *Srpske narodne poslovice* (Serbian Folk Proverbs, 1836). He also collected anecdotes, epigrams, and even some folk erotica. His excellent book on Montenegro and its people, *Montenegro und die Montenegriner* (Montenegro and the Montenegrin, 1837), was a German abridgment of a longer Serbian text, now lost, that was never published.

Karadžić was also a serious contributor to Serbian and European historiography, especially as a chronicler of his own age. His most important works in the field include *Miloš Obrenović, Knjaz Serbiji* (Miloš Obrenović, Prince of Serbia, 1828) and *Praviteljstvujušči Sovjet Serbskij* (The Serbian Governing Council, 1860). He also wrote *Žitije Hajduk-Veljka Petrovića* (A Life of Haiduk Veljko Petrović, 1828), one of the most objective works of modern Serbian historiography. The German historian Leopold von Ranke based his major study on the Serbian people's struggle for independence, *Die serbische Revolution* (1829; translated as *A History of Servia, and the Servian Revolution,* 1847), on the oral and written information provided by Karadžić.

In 1847 Karadžić published his translation of the New Testament, in which he leaned on the Russo-Slavonic translation of 1820, to a lesser extent on Martin Luther's sixteenth-century German

Karadžić and his wife, Anna

text, and at particularly difficult junctures on Kopitar. Karadžić's translation is classic, but it departs somewhat from his principle of popular speech and occasionally Serbianizes some Old Church Slavonic and Russian words as well as some residual Turkisms, from which he coined interesting neologisms.

In addition to bitter enemies, Karadžić had several faithful friends. At the outset of his career he greatly benefited from Kopitar's help and, in its later phases, from the support of philologist Djura Daničić and poet Branko Radičević. Daničić's work *Rat za srpski jezik i pravopis* (The War for the Serbian Language and Orthography, 1847) was a welcome boost to Karadžić's efforts at a crucial turning point in his public life. In his vigorous, successful defense of Karadžić's linguistic claims, Daničić used scholarly arguments that have survived the test of time.

The same year saw the publication of *Pesme* (Poems) by Radičević, the leading Serbian Romantic, whose poetry demonstrated that Karadžić's popular idiom was admirably suited even for poetry of high artistic value. Thus the victory of Karadžić's

reforms finally became obvious even to the greatest skeptics among his own people.

In 1853 Karadžić prepared the second edition of his *Srpske narodne pripovjetke i zagonetke,* and his daughter, Mina Vukomanović, translated them into German. They were published in 1854 with a preface by Jacob Grimm. Karadžić's work was also admired by such figures as Aleksandr Pushkin in Russia, Adam Mickiewicz in Poland, and Prosper Mérimée in France; in addition, after marrying an American named Edward Robinson, Talvj wrote about it in America.

Karadžić's principal ethnographic work, *Život i običaji naroda srpskoga* (The Life and Customs of the Serbian People), appeared in 1867. In this book he points out that the most sacred things to every people are its *zakon,* by which he means primarily religion rather than law, and then language and customs. The legal meaning of the work *zakon,* which literally does mean "law," is subsumed under the term *običaji* (customs), which includes legal traditions and precedents. More controversial is his 1849 almanac *Kovčežić* (Treasure Chest). In the article "Srbi svi i svuda" (Serbs All and Everywhere), Karadžić tries to prove that the Croatian name properly belongs only to the speakers of the so-called Čakavian dialect and that the Kajkavians are actually Slovenes. These statements are still a source of acrimony between Croatian and Serbian scholars. Yet they are not a permissible excuse for imputing to Karadžić preposterously exaggerated claims he never made.

It is well known that Karadžić was an ardent patriot, a fighter for constitutional guarantees, and even a nationalist, but he was never a chauvinist. Had he ever been known as such, it is hard to imagine that he would have won and kept the respect of such great figures as Goethe, the Grimms, Talvj, and von Ranke, not to speak of other illustrious literati who saw fit to praise and honor him. Goethe called him "der brave, tüchtige Mann" (the upright, capable man), and he surely would not have wasted his time on a narrow-minded, bigoted type. Had Karadžić really harbored such dangerous delusions, they almost certainly would have been detected and used by his many enemies.

As the great reformer of the Serbian literary language and orthography and a significant early modern linguist, Karadžić brought the pioneering efforts of his predecessor Obradović to their logical conclusion and built upon them a foundation for post-Turkish Serbian culture and literature. By collecting and publishing the most beautiful and hitherto unknown creations of the Serbian folk mind and securing for them the recognition and admiration of the most illustrious personalities of civilized Europe, he more than anyone else reawakened his people's pride and self-confidence and contributed to the development of modern Serbian national consciousness. Largely self-taught, he acquired his enviable erudition through extensive reading and traveling as well as conversation and correspondence with learned friends. His work powerfully influenced other South Slavic peoples and certainly contributed to the awakening and growth of their national consciousnesses as well. It also reminded them of their similarities, ethnolinguistic kinship, strong community of interests, and often-overlapping elements of a shared cultural heritage. These efforts found their formal expression in the *Književni dogovor* (Literary Agreement) concluded in Vienna in 1850 between leading Serbian and Croatian intellectuals for the introduction of the same literary language among both peoples. Although Zagreb, the capital of Croatia, speaks the Kajkavian dialect, and Belgrade, the capital of Serbia, the Štokavian variant of the Ekavian dialect, the linguistic link between the two peoples is provided by the eastern and western Štokavian variants of the southern, Jekavian speech of Herzegovina.

Whatever the future of Yugoslavia, and especially of Serbo-Croatian political relations, Karadžić's work is likely to endure because it rests on sound and imperishable foundations. This father of Serbian alphabet, orthography, lexicography, grammar, literature, folklore, ethnography, and historiography was also a significant contributor to the development of Serbia's constitutional democracy and its post-Ottoman legal system. His famous 1832 letter from Zemun to Miloš Obrenović, full of scathing criticism of the prince's personal tyranny and of all tyrannies, is a milestone in the evolution of Serbian democracy, political freedom, social justice, and human rights.

Like so many other Serbian expatriates from medieval to modern times, he spent most of his physical life abroad, but he maintained loving memory of the land of his birth, to which his remains were solemnly transferred from Vienna in 1897 and buried, beside those of his teacher Obradović, at the portal of the cathedral of Belgrade.

Letters:
Pisma (Belgrade: Prosveta, 1947).

Biographies:
Ljubomir Stojanović, *Život i rad Vuka Stef. Karadžića* (Belgrade & Zemun: "Makarije" A.D., 1924);

Duncan Wilson, *The Life and Times of Vuk Stefanović Karadžić, 1787–1864: Literacy, Literature, and National Independence in Serbia* (Oxford: Clarendon Press, 1970).

References:
Ivo Andrić, *O Vuku kao piscu – O Vuku kao reformatoru* (Belgrade: Prosveta, 1950);

Aleksandar Belić, *Vukova borba za narodni i književni jezik* (Belgrade: Prosveta, 1948);

Milan Bogdanović and Božidar Kovačević, *Vuk Karadžić – Njegov život i kulturno-revolucionarni rad* (Belgrade: Kolarčev narodni univerzitet, 1947);

Zlata Bojović, ed., *Vuk Karadžić i njegovo delo u svome vremenu i danas* (Belgrade: Medjunarodni slavistički centar, 1988);

Henry R. Cooper, Jr., "Vuk Karadžić's Serbian New Testament (1847) and the Paradigm of Modern Slavic Vernacular Bible Translations," *Serbian Studies,* 5, no. 1 (1989): 25–42;

Vladimir Ćorović, "Vuk Karadžić (1787–1864)," *Slavonic and East European Review,* 16 (April 1938): 667–677;

Andra Gavrilović, ed., *Spomenica o prenosu praha Vuka Stefanovića Karadžića iz Beča u Beograd* (Belgrade: Srpska kraljevska akademija, 1898);

Knjiga o Vuku Karadžiću (Belgrade: Jugoslovensko profesorsko društvo, 1938);

Yvonne R. Lockwood, "Vuk Stefanović Karadžić: Pioneer and Continuing Inspiration of Yugoslav Folklorists," *Western Folklore,* 30 (January 1971): 19–32;

Živomir Mladenović, "Unpublished Folk Poems of Vuk Karadžić," *Slavonic and East European Review,* 50 (July 1972): 372–385;

Miljan Mojašević, *Jakob Grim i srpska narodna književnost* (Belgrade: Srpska akademija nauka i umetnosti, 1983);

Viktor Novak, *Vuk i Hrvati* (Belgrade: Naučno delo, 1967);

Novak, ed., *Vukov zbornik* (Belgrade: Srpska akademija nauka i umetnosti, 1966);

George R. Noyes, "Karadzic Vuk Stefanovic," in *Slavonic Encyclopedia,* edited by J. S. Roucek (New York: Philosophical Library, 1949), pp. 567–568;

Predrag Palavestra, "Vuk's Legacy and Medieval Serbia," *Relations,* 1–3 (1989): 173–180;

Monica Partridge, "Vuk Karadžić: His English Connections," *Zeitschrift für Slawistik,* 33 (1988): 681–691;

Michael Boro Petrovich, "Karadžić and Nationalism," *Serbian Studies,* 4, no. 3 (1988): 41–57;

Miodrag Popović, *Vuk Stefanović Karadžić, 1787–1864* (Belgrade: Nolit, 1964);

Nikola R. Pribić, "Vuk Stefanović Karadžić: Founder of Comparative Balkan Folklore," *Synthesis*, 2 (1975): 107–111;

Miljana Radovanović, *Vuk Karadžić – Etnograf i folklorist* (Belgrade: Srpska akademija nauka i umetnosti, 1973);

Meša Selimović, *Za i protiv Vuka* (Novi Sad, Yugoslavia: Matica srpska, 1967);

Biljana Šljivič Šimšić, "Vuk Stefanović Karadžić," in *Landmarks in Serbian Culture and History,* edited by Vasa D. Mihailovich (Pittsburgh: Serb National Federation, 1983), pp. 174–193;

Šljivič Šimšić, "The Woman in Serbian Folk Proverbs: On the Material Collected by Vuk St. Karadžić," *Serbian Studies,* 1 (1980): 41–50;

Izmail Ivanovič Sreznievski, "Vuk Stefanović Karadžić, biografska i bibliografska skica," *Srpski književni glasnik,* 52 (November 1937): 383–399;

Benjamin A. Stolz, "Kopitar and Vuk: An Assessment of Their Roles in the Rise of the New Serbian Literary Language," in *To Honor Jernej Kopitar, 1780–1980,* edited by Rado L. Lencek and Cooper (Ann Arbor: University of Michigan Press, 1982), pp. 151–167;

Talvj, "Slavic Popular Poetry," *North American Review,* 43 (July 1836): 85–116;

Dragiša Živković, "Vukova borba i srpski pesnički jezik," in his *Od Vuka do Andrića* (Belgrade, 1965), pp. 26–53.

Jure Kaštelan
(18 December 1919 – 24 February 1990)

Dasha Čulić Nisula
Western Michigan University

SELECTED BOOKS: *Crveni konj* (Zagreb: Zadružna štampa, 1940 [destroyed]); republished in *Crveni konj i Pijetao na krovu* (Zagreb: Grafički zavod Hrvatske, 1980); republished as *Crveni konj* (Zagreb: NZMH, 1990);

Pijetao na krovu (Zagreb: Zora, 1950);

Biti ili ne (Zagreb: Mladost, 1955);

Malo kamena i puno snova (Zagreb: Lykos, 1957);

Lirika A. G. Matoša (Zagreb: Rad JAZU, 1957);

Pijesak i pjena (Zagreb: Zagrebačko dramsko kazalište, 1958);

Čudo i smrt (Zagreb: Naprijed, 1961);

Izbor pesama (Belgrade: Srpska književna zadruga, 1964);

Zvjezdana noć: Izbor pjesama, selected by Nikola Milićević (Zagreb: Školska knjiga, 1966);

Približavanje; prolegomena za liriku Antuna Branka Šimića (Zagreb: Razlog, 1970);

Prazor, Forum, nos. 7–8 (Zagreb, 1972);

Izabrane pjesme (Belgrade: Rad, 1976);

Otvorena pjesma: Veliki školski čas (Kragujevac: Spomen-park Kragujevački oktobar, 1976);

Divlje oko (Zagreb: Znanje, 1978);

Pjesme o mojoj zemlji (Banja Luka: Glas, 1981);

San u kamenu i druga vidjenja, selected by Šime Vučetić (Zagreb: Mladost, 1981);

Pjesme, edited by Nedeljko Mihanović (Sarajevo: Veselin Masleša, 1982);

Izabrana djela, edited by Ante Stamać (Zagreb: NZMH, 1983);

Jure Kaštelan (Valjevo: Grafičko-izdavačka radna organizacija "Milić Rakić," 1983);

Miroslav Krleža: Criticism and interpretation 1893–1981 (Zagreb: JAZU, 1985);

Krilali Konjanik (Zagreb: NZMH, 1991).

Editions in English: Poems translated by Vasa D. Mihailovich, Ronald Moran, and Maria Malby, *The Bridge,* 19–20 (1970): 24–26;

Poems in *New Writing in Yugoslavia,* edited and translated by Bernard Johnson (Baltimore: Penguin, 1970), pp. 69–72;

Poems in *Contemporary Yugoslav Poetry,* edited by Mihailovich, translated by Charles Simic, Mihailovich, Moran, and Malby (Iowa City: University of Iowa Press, 1977), pp. 20–23;

Poems in *Contemporary East European Poetry,* edited by George Emery, translated by Peter Kastmiller (Ann Arbor: Ardis, 1983), pp. 351–353.

PLAY PRODUCTIONS: *Pijesak i pjena,* Zagreb, Zagrebačko dramsko kazalište, 1958;

Prazor, Split, Dioclecian palace, 4 July 1976;

Otvorena pjesma: Veliki školski čas, Kragujevac, Spomen-park, 21 October 1976.

OTHER: *Makedonske narodne pjesme,* selected and translated by Kaštelan (Zagreb: Novo pokoljenje, 1948);

Oganj i ruža: Pjesme narodne revolucije, edited by Kaštelan (Zagreb: Kultura, 1956);

Antun Branko Šimić 1898–1925, Pjesme i proza, edited by Kaštelan (Zagreb: Matica hrvatska, 1963);

Ljudi: Izbor iz poezije o revoluciji i za revoluciju, edited by Kaštelan (Belgrade: Komunist, 1969);

Živadin M. Stevanović – Likovi i susreti: pripovetke, introduction by Kaštelan (Brestovac kod Kragujevca: Živadin M. Stevanović, 1969);

Dragutin Tadijanović: Pjesme i proza, edited by Kaštelan (Zagreb: Matica hrvatska, 1969);

Voćka poslije kiše: Izabrane pjesme i memoarski zapisi Dobriše Cesarića, selected, with an afterword, by Kaštelan (Zagreb: Mladost, 1978);

Dragutin Tadijanović: Zbornik radova o pjesniku, edited by Kaštelan, Marijan Matković, and Nedeljko Mihanović (Zagreb: Mladost, 1980);

Oton Gliha, *Gromače,* illustrated texts by Kaštelan, Vladimir Marković, and Zdenko Tonković (Zagreb: SNL, 1983);

Sabrana djela Ivana Gorana Kovačića 1913–1943, edited by Kaštelan, Marijan Matković, and Dragutin Tadijanović (Zagreb: JAZU, 1983);

Marin Franičević: Izabrana djela, edited by Rafo Bogišić, Kaštelan, and Ivan Katušić (Zagreb: NZMH, 1986).

Post–World War II Croatian poetry finds its roots in the works of two poets: Jure Kaštelan and Vesna Parun. These two writers broke with the prewar generation and set the stage for what was to come – a freer, more flexible poetic expression. A leading postwar Croatian poet, Jure Kaštelan introduced several modern trends into Croatian poetic expression. Especially noteworthy is the personal tone with which he addressed such themes as suffering, sacrifice, war, love, and death. He is also known for linguistic associations and surrealistic wordplay and a subtle lyricism that has been compared to the poetry of Federico García Lorca. Other examples of Lorcian influence on Kaštelan include traditional folk intonation, short lines, loosely structured stanzas, parallelism and repetition, and his habit of posing questions which remain unanswered. The themes of nature and lost childhood also appear in the work of both poets. In addition to being a leading postwar lyrical poet, Kaštelan, in his role as a professor of literature, wrote many scholarly works on contemporary writers, including his

doctoral dissertation on Antun Gustav Matoš, which was published in 1957, and prolegomena for poetry by A. B. Šimić (1970). He also edited and wrote introductions for important collections of works by Dobriša Cesarić, Ivan Goran Kovačić, Miroslav Krleža, Dragutin Tadijanović, and many other writers.

Jure Kaštelan was born on 18 December 1919 in the village of Zakučac, near Omiš on the Dalmatian coast, in Croatia. His father, Stipe Kaštelan, was a noted historian in the Poljica region near Split. Kaštelan completed high school in Split and then in 1938 enrolled in the philosophy department at the University of Zagreb.

When in April 1941 the Germans attacked Yugoslavia, the war which Kaštelan had dreaded became a reality. In 1942 he joined the partisans as a journalist. For the next three years he witnessed the horrors of war but also the ability of the human spirit to endure in spite of them. Many of his later poems germinated in this atmosphere. After the war he returned to complete his studies in Slavistics at the University of Zagreb. He then worked as a journalist for the newspaper *Vjesnik* (Herald) and as an editor for the journal *Republika* (Republic).

In 1949, having completed his studies, Jure Kaštelan became an assistant professor of Yugoslav literatures at the University of Zagreb, where he also later chaired the section on literary theory. From 1956 to 1958 he taught Croatian at the Sorbonne. His doctoral dissertation on the lyrical poet Matoš was published in 1957. Kaštelan retired in 1980.

The theme of war pervades Kaštelan's poetry. Repeatedly in his collections there appears the figure of a horse, symbolic of the dignity and nobility associated with the endurance of human suffering for the sake of the motherland. In the later collections the horror of war is replaced by an underlying tone of anxiety over man's condition in the twentieth century. Nature is also featured prominently in most of his collections.

Kaštelan's comments as a critic contribute to the understanding of his intrinsic poetic style. In writing about the poet Dobriša Cesarić, Kaštelan noted that "real poetry is like an element, simple and inexplicable. To relate it in rational concepts is always in part an effort in vain." What must be done with a poem, according to Kaštelan, is not to examine its superficialities but rather to explore its mysteries.

Kaštelan's first poems date from 1937, and his first collection of poems, *Crveni konj* (Red Horse, 1940), appeared in print when Kaštelan was twenty-one. Appearing at the dawn of World War II, this collection was particularly relevant to the times. He was keenly aware of the destruction the civil war in Spain had brought about and had a sense of foreboding that war would spread throughout Europe. His collection reflects this presentiment and also his obsession with death. Unfortunately, because of its dealing openly with such subjects, the collection was seized by censors and destroyed.

Kaštelan's poetry speaks of his own loss of innocence in turbulent times, describing himself as a stranger in a big city. His poetry reveals social malaise, the search for solutions, and the struggle for a better life. The poem "Predosjećaj jeseni na velegradskom pločniku" (The Foreboding of Autumn on the Big City Sidewalk) is a good example of Kaštelan's work in this vein.

By the 1950s Kaštelan's poetry acquired a kind of Whitmanesque grand manner and effusive style marked by repetitious descriptions of nature — the gray-green color of sage, the greenery of the countryside, the blue-green sea, and the paleness of the stone color of the barren land. Indeed, critics have suggested that Kaštelan was influenced not only by García Lorca but by Walt Whitman as well. If Kaštelan did not read Whitman in the original, exposure to Whitman's poetry became possible with Augustin (Tin) Ujević's translation of *Leaves of Grass,* which appeared in Zagreb in 1951. Kaštelan's well-known poem "Salut et fraternité" (Safety and Fraternity, a poem about man's freedom) may be an homage to the American poet. The influence of Whitman's reliance on parallelism and anaphora is noticeable in Kaštelan's next two collections.

Pijetao na krovu (The Rooster on the Roof, 1950), though published ten years after Kaštelan's first book was destroyed, still has war as its primary theme. His poetic expression has matured in terms of its metaphorical language and musicality. The humanitarian note in the poems reveals a desire for a better world, one of freedom and peace.

There are nine cycles of poems in this collection, all of which associate the function of revolution with that of poetry. Kaštelan says, "Revolutions are not made so poems can be written about them. Rather, poems and revolutions are born to safeguard the dignity of man, his basic human right to peace, freedom and creativity."

The most frequently quoted cycle is "Tifusari" (Sick with Typhus), a good example of poetry inspired by the revolution. Its structure, intonation, and images are inspired by national epic poetry. "Tifusari" consists of six poems, each rhythmically different, each representing a step closer to death.

Kaštelan in 1958

Throughout the first four poems the tone is dark, mimicking the mental state of a patient whose condition fluctuates between delirium and clarity. In the fifth poem the cycle moves to a stage of lightness and optimism, but in the sixth darkness sets in again, and the cycle ends in an atmosphere of gloom.

The simplicity of Kaštelan's style can be seen in a poem from "Susreti" (Encounters), where Kaštelan's notion that the dead live within the living sounds an optimistic note. This same view has been explored by other postwar Croatian poets, mainly Parun and Irena Vrkljan. In Kaštelan's poem repetition even of single-word statements emphasizes the theme: "Mrtvi žive u nama. Rastu. Rastu. / Mladi i raspjevani moji drugovi. / Mrtvi žive u nama." (The dead live in us. They grow. They grow. / Young and happy my friends. / The dead live in us.)

The last cycle, "Čarobna frula" (The Magic Flute), includes love poems. The lovers are idealistic and innocent, maybe even shy: "Volio bih da me voliš / da budem cvijet u tvojoj kosi. / Ako si noć, ja ću biti zora / i bljesak svjetlosti u rosi" (I would like you to love me / that I be a flower in your hair. / If you are night, I will be dawn / and a flash of light in the dew).

Biti ili ne (To Be or Not to Be, 1955) expands the thematic and technical concerns of Kaštelan's first two books. The very title of the collection expresses a question pondered by Greeks and mulled over by William Shakespeare. Hamlet's question, according to Kaštelan, remains the unanswered question of the twentieth-century person.

In the next collection, *Malo kamena i puno snova* (A Few Stones and Plenty of Dreams, 1957), Kaštelan again focuses on the nature of life and death. He sees life as a road toward death, a road that obviously is not the same for each individual. This collection, some critics point out, is especially reminiscent of García Lorca. There is more free verse, and there are tones of surrealism. The images – rich in sea flora, olive trees, evergreens, and agave – depict the environment of his home, Dalmatia. He, like Parun, sings of the sea and longs for the environment of his childhood.

Besides being a poet and essayist, Kaštelan was also a lyrical dramatist and a short-story writer. The main theme of the lyrical drama *Pijesak i pjena* (Sand and Foam, 1958) is love, its birth, growth, beauty, and unfulfilled dreams. Another dramatic piece is *Prazor* (Predawn, 1972). The fate of the figure JA (I) in the play is presented as that of a single individual; yet he speaks for all mankind (other characters play the role of the chorus). In fact, everything in the play moves from the specific to the general and back; from the dramatic to the poetic and back; from the depths to the heights and back; from light to shadows and from love to tyranny and back. Kaštelan's third play, *Otvorena pjesma* (Open Song, 1976), is a recital in seven parts, which was commissioned for the Big School Hour, which takes place every year in Kragujevac in memory of those schoolchildren who were killed there by Germans during World War II. The Kragujevac tragedy can be rendered only in a heavy tone. Kaštelan was able, however, to juxtapose the depiction of these terrible events with a vision of man's humanness, dignity, and belief in a better future.

Just as in his poetry, Kaštelan attempts to deal with the complexities of life in the modern world in *Čudo i smrt* (Wonder and Death, 1961), a collection of fourteen short stories with strange plots and characters that are mere types (a teacher, a traveler, an elder). Their metaphorical language and its rhythm have led the critics to call the stories poetry in prose.

In Kaštelan's collection of poetry *Divlje oko* (A Wild Eye, 1978), published nearly twenty years after *Malo kamena i puno snova*, he took a different perspective on the same road of life. His language remains direct and clear, but his focus has turned more inward, examining man's (his own) reality from an existential perspective. Man in his "here and now" lives in the world of "darkness," followed by short periods of "light." The whole collection alternates between dark and light, reflecting on the evil and goodness of the human condition. Simplifying his verse, Kaštelan turned to a kind of folk speech in clear dactosyllabic lines, reminiscent of old Croatian national epics.

In these poems there is irony and even satire. He seems to dwell on local peasant expressions, and he has rescued words that belong to the past. Perhaps he placed them in verse in order to safeguard them, to preserve them. The most prevalent tone in this collection is one of acceptance and peace, something Jure Kaštelan seems to have been seeking for most of his life. When asked which of his poems he preferred, Kaštelan replied: "I don't know whether I have written my favorite poem because one is as dear to me as another, as my left hand is dear to me as the right one, as my right eye is dear to me as the left one."

Kaštelan, like perhaps only Miroslav Krleža in the twentieth century, was able to combine in his career writing poetry and writing about poetry. Though Kaštelan's work is yet to be fully examined, he already holds an important place in the development of postwar Croatian poetry and in the overall development of Croatian literature.

References:

Miodrag Bogičević, "Kaštelanova poruka jave i sna," in his *Prisutnosti* (Sarajevo: Svjetlost, 1966), pp. 70–81;

Tode Čolak, "Jure Kaštelan," in his *Ka piscu i delu* (Sarajevo: Svjetlost, 1978), pp. 299–322;

Ante Kadić, "Postwar Croatian Lyric Poetry," *American Slavic and East European Review*, 17 (1958): 509–529;

Božo Milačić, "Mrtvi žive u nama," in his *Suze i zvijezde* (Zagreb: NIP, 1956), pp. 7–27;

Nikola Milićević, "Poezija Jure Kaštelana," in his *Riječ u vremenu* (Zagreb: Mladost, 1981), pp. 125–142;

Predrag Palavestra, "Pesničko iskustvo Jure Kaštelana," *Savremenik*, 28 (1968): 212–217;

Ivo Šmoljan, "Jure Kaštelan," in his *Pjesnik i pjesma* (Zagreb: Zora, 1965), pp. 7–64;

Ante Stamać, Foreword to Jure Kaštelan, *Izabrana djela* (Zagreb: NZMH, 1983), pp. 7–22.

Edvard Kocbek

(27 September 1904 – 3 November 1981)

Michael Biggins
University of Washington

BOOKS: *Zemlja* (Ljubljana: Nova založba, 1934);
Tovarišija: dnevniški zapisi od 17. maja 1942 do 1. maja 1943 (Ljubljana: Državna založba Slovenije, 1949);
Strah in pogum: štiri novele (Ljubljana: Državna založba Slovenije, 1951);
Groza (Ljubljana: Slovenska matica, 1963);
Slovensko poslanstvo: dnevnik s poti v Jajce, 1943 (Celje: Mohorjeva družba, 1964);
Listina: dnevniški zapiski od 3. maja do 2. decembra 1943 (Ljubljana: Slovenska matica, 1967);
Poročilo: pesmi (Maribor: Obzorja, 1969);
Eros in seksus (Ljubljana: Naše tromostovje, 1970);
Svoboda in nujnost: pričevanja (Celje: Mohorjeva družba, 1974; revised and enlarged edition, Celje: Mohorjeva družba, 1989);
Žerjavica (Trieste: Založništvo tržaškega tiska / Koper: Lipa, 1974);
Domotožje: eseji (Ljubljana, 1975);
Krogi navznoter (Ljubljana: Slovenska matica, 1977);
Zbrane pesmi, 2 volumes, edited by Tone Pavček (Ljubljana: Cankarjeva založba, 1977);
Pred viharjem (Ljubljana: Slovenska matica, 1980);
Sodobni misleci (Celje: Mohorjeva družba, 1981);
Dnevnik 1951–1952, edited, with commentary, by Dimitrij Rupel (Zagreb: Globus, 1986);
Dnevnik 1945, 5 volumes, edited by Inkret (Ljubljana: Cankarjeva založba, 1991);
Dnevnik 1946, 2 volumes (Ljubljana: Cankarjeva založba, 1991);
Kamen skala, edited by Andrej Inkret (Ljubljana: Nova revija, 1991);
Osvobodilni spici, 2 volumes, edited by Peter Kovačič-Peršin (Ljubljana: Društvo 2000, 1991, 1993);
Zbrano delo, 5 volumes, edited by Inkret (Ljubljana: Državna založba Slovenije, 1991–1994);
Dnevnik 1947 (Ljubljana: Cankarjeva založba, 1993).
Edition in English: *Na vratih zvečer – At the Door at Evening*, bilingual edition, with English translations by Tom Ložar (Ljubljana: Aleph / Dorion, Quebec: Muses' Company, 1990).

Edvard Kocbek in 1974 (courtesy of Matjaž Kocbek)

Poet and publicist, religious reformer and social revolutionary – ultimately an internal exile speaking with more force than any of his contemporaries – Edvard Kocbek lived an eventful, controversial life that in recent years has become emblematic of the fundamental dilemmas facing Slovenia in the twentieth century. Since the early 1980s, as Slovenes have begun to take stock of their recent past without the government-imposed biases of previous decades, Kocbek's name has begun to appear virtually everywhere – from overviews of Slovene literature to histories of World War II and the Yugoslav Communist regime to general intellectual histories of the century. There is a growing acknowledgment of his importance in crystallizing the issues that have divided his society. It was in Kocbek's outspoken nature to spearhead opposition to abuses of power, whether they emanated from the Catholic church or the Communist party, and yet he was at different times intimately aligned with both as a means of attaining what he saw to be the highest goals of each. He viewed writing, and above all, poetry, as the ideologically neutral ground where he could communicate to others his deeply personal vision of the possibility of perfection. As diffuse and irreconcilable as the varied elements of his vita may seem, Kocbek's life and work were all of a piece. Writing and social commitment were both responses to a moral imperative, experience in one breeding new revelations in the other, and Kocbek was the rare individual who embodied a high measure of talent for both.

He was born on 27 September 1904 in the town of Sv. Jurij na Ščavnici (Saint George on Ščavnica, now Videm na Ščavnici) in the far northeastern corner of Slovenia, then part of the Austrian province of Styria. His father, Valentin – who was born in the region but had traveled to Ljubljana to study church music – was drawn to Sv. Jurij by the opportunity of working in the parish church as organist and sexton, positions which together afforded the Kocbek family an adequate income. Edvard and his siblings later recalled that both father and mother (Matilda, née Plohl) worked to provide their four children with as secure a childhood as possible, and a nostalgic tone pervades the children's later recollections of growing up.

Accompanying his father on duties in the parish church – which was just across from the Kocbek house – pumping the organ bellows, or serving as altar boy at mass, young Kocbek's experience of Catholicism was acute. Like most rural literary prodigies, he exhausted his town's book supply early on. When he finished elementary school in Sv. Jurij at the age of thirteen, his father arranged to board him at a classical gymnasium in Maribor, a small city some forty miles away. In his autobiographical sketch "Kdo sem" (Who I Am), Kocbek characterizes his transition to Maribor as the first real jolt of his life. He eventually mastered the practical challenge of having to adapt overnight to city life after a childhood spent entirely in the country, but the disparity he perceived between the two ways of life wrought a lasting change, as his later inspiration seems to have been suspended between a longing for the rural utopia of his childhood and a recognition that his destiny would inevitably draw him toward the city.

In 1919 the family withdrew Kocbek from school in Maribor and enrolled him in a less expensive trade gymnasium in far more provincial Ptuj, mostly for reasons of economy. Despite the outward austerity of his life during his four years there, this period was the time when he was definitively won over to poetry. His subject in these earliest attempts was, to use his own words, his intoxication with the earth and particularly with the natural and folkloric phenomena of the Slovenian countryside. They provided the basis for his first collection of poems, *Zemlja* (Earth), published in 1934. By 1923, after having amassed an outstanding school record, he devised a plan for returning to Maribor and finishing his studies that at the same time would put less of a financial burden on his parents. He applied and was accepted in a preparatory seminary in Maribor, on condition that after graduation he commit himself to theology and ultimately the priesthood. His last years of secondary school (1923–1925) and two years as a student of theology, also in Maribor (1925–1927), witnessed Kocbek's maturation as a social activist. The crucial step, one which would prefigure a series of similar crossroads decisions throughout his life, came when he unexpectedly withdrew from the seminary and returned to Sv. Jurij. His family was perplexed and hurt at what they perceived to be the self-destruction of so promising a career; and the parish priest, Kocbek's former mentor, withdrew his favor from Edvard and the Kocbek family altogether for years to come. Kocbek's explanation to his family, related by his younger brother Jože, was simply that he had realized he could serve his fellow man better from outside the church than from within. While this was an underlying rationale, the act itself was apparently undertaken to protest an injustice that had befallen a fellow student in Kocbek's residence at the seminary.

During the next few years Kocbek organized, on short notice, a major retreat of socially minded Catholic youth, the published proceedings of which had a profound effect in liberal Catholic circles; he moved to Ljubljana and enrolled in Romance languages at the university. At the same time, he assumed the editorship of the Catholic youth magazine *Križ* (The Cross), and as editor he served as the focal point for a group of young writers who sought to liberate Slovene Catholicism from the heavy overlay of dogma and conformity that had alienated them from it. For decades, if not centuries, the church hierarchy had dominated virtually every aspect of public life in Slovenia, and the young intellectuals grouped around *Križ* exhorted their countrymen to form more-personal, direct relationships with both God and Caesar.

Several terms of foreign study, first in Berlin (1928–1929) and then in Paris (1931–1932), brought Kocbek in contact with writers he had admired since boyhood, as well as with French personalists such as Emmanuel Mounier, who had then just founded the seminal journal *Esprit*. The new personalist philosophy articulated with force precisely what Kocbek and his circle were arguing to the Slovenes – that divinity is immanent in mankind and manifests itself foremost in the relations between individuals. Kocbek maintained long-lasting relationships, primarily through correspondence, with several of the writers that he met during his stay in Paris.

After graduating from the University of Ljubljana in 1930, he was assigned to a teaching post in the Croatian town of Bjelovar, not that far from home geographically, but nonetheless an entire culture away, especially considering that Kocbek spoke no Croatian. His unofficial exile there, subtly engineered by the authorities in Ljubljana to neutralize his radical effect at home, lasted until 1936, including three years teaching school in the provincial capital of Varaždin, a few dozen miles from the Slovene border. In the same year Kocbek finally managed to win himself a transfer to a teaching position in Ljubljana. Once there, he threw himself into the activist scene with renewed vigor, publishing controversial tracts on the Slovene national question, the ideal shape of Christianity, and the relationship between it and Marxism. He established contacts with leading figures in the Slovene national movement, including Edvard Kardelj and Boris Kidrič, both of them prominent Marxists who would play important political roles in Tito's Yugoslavia. In all his dealings with Marxists then and later, however, he proclaimed his disapproval of Marxist theory and methods, while conceding that their envisaged end result – the conquest of personal alienation through the establishment of a more egalitarian social structure – was very near his own. Then, in 1937, in the prestigious Catholic monthly *Dom in svet* (Home and World) he published a tract titled "Premišljevanja o Španiji" (Reflections on Spain), in which he threw an undeniable challenge at organized Catholicism by charging it with an innate tendency to encourage the lowest expectations of the bourgeoisie and, consequently, to support the rise of fascism. His protest further sharpened the establishment's image of Kocbek as a renegade and even brought about a one-year suspension of the journal. Kocbek pursued his cam-

Kocbek, left, with his mother, Matilda, and brothers Slavko and Jože, 1914 (courtesy of Matjaž Kocbek)

paign by founding a new, independent journal, *Dejanje* (Action), which he published from 1938 until the German invasion of Yugoslavia in 1941 – the beginning of a new era for the poet.

While the body of Kocbek's published literary work is not large, virtually each of his books provoked such a strong reaction that it had some sort of lasting effect on the Slovene writing that followed. *Zemlja* (Earth, 1934), his first collection of poems, comprises one extended hymn of praise to the Slovene countryside. The poems are grouped into seven sections by genre or theme: the first section consists of short, rhymed verses, some of them reminiscent of Slovene folk songs, while the seventh and last section introduces a climactic sequence of Whitmanesque (or more appropriately for Kocbek, who knew no English – biblical) psalms addressed to his native land, and constructed on long, anaphoric lines. The five sections in between are all thematic arrangements of verse in unconventional forms with headings such as Poems for Night and Day, Autumn Poems, Love Poems, and Poems About Earth. Many of the individual pieces in these sections are prose poems, divided typically into two parts with short lines. Each of them captures in detail a specific image – dynamic, yet, viewed from a distance, impersonal and static – that the poet has witnessed: a group of peasant women singing in chorus as they walk barefoot through a meadow from work, a village captured in the light of sunset, two oxen pulling a cart down a trail toward the vanishing point. Some are Dionysian outpourings of a sense of unity with nature, a loss of fixed reference points except for the barest essentials – roots, dirt, wind. But even when the central poems give an appearance verging on disorder or derangement, they are still counterbalanced, either at the last minute or in a following poem, by an underlying sense of order, of a divine nature present in all things. The framework of *Zemlja* serves much the same redeeming function – the traditional forms of the first section and the psalms' detailed and loving inventory of Slovene rural life in the last ease the reader into and out of the unconventional poems and moods of the middle sections. Yet this lull surrounding the turbulent eye of the storm is deceptive. The collection ends on an uncertain note. The final images of a new order – whose elements are "nothing but metal, copper, steel, lead, the earth's variegated guts" – intrude, even if only tentatively, on the dominant harmony, the composite picture suggesting the ambiguity and irony that in Kocbek's next collection of poems, thirty years later, would become pervasive.

Autobiography and imaginative prose fuse in Kocbek's next major published work, *Tovarišija* (Comrades), the diary that he kept from 1941 to mid 1943 and which was published in 1949. Its companion piece, *Listina* (Document), consists of his diary entries for the rest of 1943 and was originally intended for publication at the same time, but in fact it did not come out until 1967, in the same year as the long-delayed second printing of *Tovarišija*. After the fall of Yugoslavia to invading German forces in April 1941, Kocbek remained in occupied Ljubljana for about a year. He maintained close contacts with the Slovene resistance, attending clandestine organizational meetings in the city, while the core of the militant opposition had already fled and regrouped in remote mountainous regions nominally under Italian control. The Osvobodilna fronta (the Slovene Liberation Front), or OF, was formed soon after the invasion as a coalition of left-leaning militant organizations, the Communist party foremost among them. Later evidence has shown that enlisting Kocbek in the OF as a member of its executive committee proved an effective way of demonstrating the movement's legitimacy to large numbers of ideologically centrist and leftist Catholics, who then joined or offered their support. In fact, the OF was largely manipulated by its strong Communist center almost from the start, although during the first two war years the appearance of a pluralistic structure was maintained. In mid May 1942 Kocbek left Ljubljana to join the Partisan forces in the field, convinced that German plans for those regions of Slovenia that had been incorporated into the Reich included the physical elimination of his nation. This sense of ultimate peril helps to explain the tenacity with which he supported the OF, despite its increasingly totalitarian leanings. In spring 1943 Kocbek and other representatives of non-Communist constituent bodies were invited to sign what became known as the Dolomite Declaration, in which the non-Communist members of the OF formally recognized the primacy of the Communist party in governing the body. His signature on this document eventually proved to be one of his most controversial acts, exposing him to later charges of weakness and betrayal, although it is more likely that his hopeful idealism was responsible.

Both *Tovarišija* and *Listina* consist of Kocbek's synopses of field reports, summaries of his day's work in the agitprop section of the Partisan command, descriptions of close calls and an occasional rout at the hands of the occupiers, transcripts of his conversations and disputes with other Partisan leaders, and fragments of speculative essays – all interspersed with passages of high lyricism. Throughout the war he kept several notebooks simultaneously, each serving a different purpose or genre, and after 1945 he edited them together into a continuous narrative. Both books provide a firsthand, if necessarily restricted, view of events near the center of power during those years; at the same time they document the vast fluctuation of Kocbek's internal states; his enthusiasm for the movement in its broadest, liberating sense; his reaction to events around him; his naiveté in matters of Realpolitik; and his growing distrust of the center as it increasingly manipulated him. Yet most of these accounts, even the ones at first straining for objectivity, are ultimately and unmistakably a poet's.

In both books glimpses of the Slovene countryside provide the one constant amid all vicissitudes. Despite the wartime setting, they give the impression of a pantheist's idyll. Again and again, Kocbek lovingly describes the varied natural surroundings in which he finds himself. Slovenia's past and present as a land prove indistinguishable to his eye, transcending and dwarfing the temporary rule of invaders, even the struggles of his own liberation front and its ideological squabbles:

> We look out over the expanse of forested valley floor that separates us from the German border. It's less than a kilometer, as the crow flies, to the German guardposts. In fact, though, from here we can't see any German soldiers or the border. Only sunlit hillsides strewn with hamlets and chapels. Only cart trails, coppices, meadows and ravines. There is something celebratory in the air. And in fact, a short while later bells begin to ring. Then they start to ring from three, all four sides. . . . The bells fade. My eyes glaze and I see more clearly. Earth and sun begin to speak. An ancient language. The hidden remains of antediluvian monsters begin moving through the earth. Everything that I see was once beneath the sea. From that time to now this land has seen so many natural and historical disasters. Waters have surged, tempests raged, billions of seeds have germinated and perished. Battles waged between nature and man, between man and man, between heaven and earth. Pestilence and famine, the movement of tribes, Turkish incursions, peasant uprisings, Protestant fervor, religious pilgrims, graveyards, folk songs, moonlight, sin, shamed and glorified humanity (*Tovarišija*, 23 September 1942).

Despite his periodic suspicions of the party's intentions for Slovenia, Kocbek served a full tour of duty with the partisans. He was with Tito's forces near Drvar, Bosnia, when one of the severest German offensives of the war forced them to evacuate to the Adriatic island of Vis. From there, in 1944, he was dispatched on a diplomatic mission to the Vatican; and in 1945 he accompanied Partisan forces as they finally occupied Belgrade after the German withdrawal. Over the next few years he held the posts of minister for Slovenia in the newly formed Communist federal government, as well as vice-president of the regional Slovene Assembly. In 1946 he and other high officials made a monthlong goodwill tour of the Soviet Union. His diary entries for this period are replete with praise for the great social experiment being conducted in the Soviet Union and now in his own country. Contradicting this mood, they also provide periodic glimpses of Kocbek's disillusionment at the full implications of the revolution's failure. These crass contradictions hint at a profound internal struggle that he would soon either have to submit to or reconcile.

The year 1951 saw the publication of his first and only book of prose fiction, *Strah in pogum* (Fear and Courage), a collection of four novellas set in wartime Slovenia among the partisans. All four stories focus on protagonists forced by circumstances into the greatest moral dilemmas of their lives. The final story, "Blažena krivda" (Blessed Guilt), confronts the medic of an encircled Partisan unit with the necessity of liquidating one of his comrades-in-arms, identified in a recently received dispatch as a German spy. The unit's political commissar intentionally singles out the young intellectual to carry out the execution, justifying his choice by saying that it will "do him the most good." Torn between his personal values and what is repeatedly represented to him as the good of the cause – the demands of history – he resists at first, but finally acquiesces and sets out with his unsuspecting victim on a bogus mission, in the course of which he is expected to perform the deed. The rest of the narrative depicts his psychological turmoil as he first tries to steel himself, then repeatedly offers his victim an out, and finally lashes himself (or rather, is lashed by unknown forces) into such a homicidal fury that he cannot help but pull the trigger. Ultimately he realizes that in a personal sense he, not history, has also committed a primal act, and that by implication no one could have fully grasped the circumstances that led his victim to whatever treachery he may have committed.

The biblical overtones of Kocbek's style are pronounced in the original. The narrator's speculations on the nature of the human spirit are the dark underside of the New Testament message, the Sermon on the Mount minus the Beatitudes. The protagonists' only hope resides in grace, which they both find when they are brought together in the same farmhouse by a freak coincidence and nursed from their wounds. Needless to say, this attitude was anathema to politically orthodox bearers of the Yugoslav revolutionary spirit, who required strict two-dimensionality of the court iconographers. Yet even though *Strah in pogum* was proclaimed taboo and not republished until the more liberal 1980s, its meteoric appearance in 1951 marked the virtual end of socialist realism in Slovene literature. Though author and artifact quickly faded from the cultural scene and although some writers still persisted in manufacturing books according to the regime's precepts, perceptive and talented writers took courage from Kocbek's example and were soon managing to publish less ideologically stilted work.

Throughout early 1952 Kocbek and his book were pilloried in the Slovene periodical press in

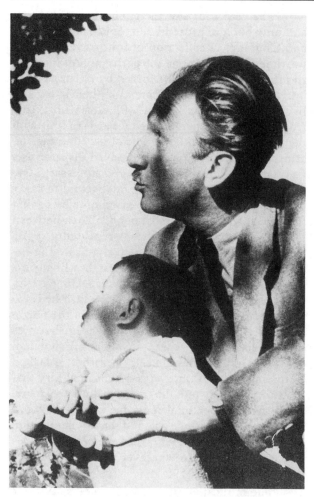

Kocbek with his son Matjaž in 1949 (courtesy of Matjaž Kocbek)

Prešeren Prize, Slovenia's preeminent literary award, for his second collection of poems, *Groza* (Horror, 1963), this award coming at the insistence of the younger generation of writers and over the objections of the party establishment.

Although *Groza* consists of poems written over three decades – the mid 1930s through the early 1960s – there is a unity to the collection that is determined partly by the continuity of its historical framework and partly by its persistently recurring motifs and themes. The poems are presented chronologically in six untitled sections spanning the prewar and postwar periods and wartime. The title is a terse expression of man's state in face of the omnipresent reality of death. But as death implies regeneration, it is precisely through these moments of horror that the poet attains the clarity of vision that allows him to reintegrate man into the universal fate of nature, and so establish the basis for faith. The images that lead to these realizations are either quintessentially Slovene – a roadside crucifix, the view from a mountainside, characters recalled from folk tales – or they occur archetypally, outside time and space. Because the poems in *Groza* originated over such a broad span of time, there is a noticeable progression in the collection's tone. The sections dating to the war years are full of both horror and hope; the postwar sections show a steady drift toward disillusionment, a loss of faith in the subject's ability to have any effect on the world around him. A characteristic poem, about the Black Sea, is at once a threnody on the erosion and uselessness of all human accomplishment, as well as a discreet but devastating lament of Slovenia's futile geographic position, symbolized by the eastward current of its rivers, away from Europe.

During the decade from 1963 through 1972 a relaxation of political strictures occurred all over Yugoslavia as the individual republics gradually arrogated more and more autonomy to themselves. The fact that Kocbek could now publish, travel abroad, make public appearances, and participate in the founding of new journals was just one manifestation of the much-broader societal changes that were taking place. In 1964 he was able to publish excerpts from his second volume of war diaries as *Slovensko poslanstvo* (The Slovene Mission), which details the trek from Slovenia to Bosnia that Kocbek and other members of the OF made to pledge their loyalty to the larger Yugoslav antifascist movement (AVNOJ) under Tito. Publication of the entire second volume (*Listina*) was delayed until 1967, primarily because of the increasingly frequent doubts Kocbek had expressed in it about the course the re-

what more closely resembled an ideological witch trial than a literary dispute, and he was finally expelled from the corridors of power in which he had been steadily growing superfluous. The early 1950s were his absolute low point. He published little – and that pseudonymously, made few appearances, and supported himself largely by translating novels and children's literature from French and German, including works by Honoré de Balzac, Guy de Maupassant, Prosper Mérimée, Antoine de Saint-Exupéry, Max Frisch, and others. For the rest of his life the authorities would periodically snipe at him, either one-on-one or using the media for a public display. His internal exile lasted throughout the 1950s. In retrospect Kocbek viewed it as a developmental cordon sanitaire between two major periods of activity, although in fact he would never fully lose the stigma – or aura – of social marginality. Partial rehabilitation came in the early 1960s and more definitively in 1964, when he was awarded the sistance movement was taking under the growing domination of the Communist party.

His third collection of poems, *Poročilo* (A Report), appeared in 1969. As the title implies, it is meant as a communication between the poet and his audience, as though over a great distance. In a series of mostly ironic poems, Kocbek reports to the Slovenes on the wreck of his ideals, his subsequent exile, and isolation. He is a "heron in the swamp, a stork in fog ... , / an Egyptian hermit who has stepped / from his pillar onto a mirage / a lone lighthouse in the ocean / with decades of silence in my throat." In a more grotesque vein he portrays himself as an aging, portly Hamlet who regrets not having made a more timely exit. He shows a great predilection for paradox, the most blatant form of irony: "There is nothing darker / than clear speaking / and nothing truer than a poem, / which reason cannot assault."

The poems give a composite picture of Kocbek himself as he looks back on his career and confronts the indignities that exile presses on him in the present. One three-page poem consists of sheer invective directed at a microphone that the authorities have planted in his apartment. In another he reflects on the absurdity, in retrospect, of his role in the Slovene revolutionary movement: "And then they sent me into history, / the way they send a child out for bird's milk. ... " But given all the superfluousness of his frustrated ideals, he is still far less grotesque than the figures that populate Ljubljana society, of which occasional poems provide a glimpse.

For much of his later life Kocbek believed privately that Communist power in postwar Slovenia had been founded on a few key deceptions – among them the outright denial of the massacres that Partisan units committed at war's end against Slovene *domobranci* (home guards), military units of the wartime Slovene collaborationist government. In April 1945, fearing capture by the partisans, tens of thousands of Slovene home guards, Croatian *ustaša* troops, some Serbs, and civilian camp followers escaped to Austria, where they were rounded up by the British occupation forces and repatriated by sealed train to Yugoslavia. Partisan forces unloaded them at stations all along the way through Slovenia and Croatia, leading them on forced marches to remote rural sites, where they were systematically killed. On several occasions in the late 1940s Kocbek had confronted colleagues in the government, including Milovan Djilas, with rumors he had heard about the massacres. Each time the allegations were denied. By the early 1950s he had gathered enough independent evidence to substantiate them, but for a long time he was in no position to go public. His own sense of guilt for the massacres, deriving from his complicity with the ideology that led to them, made his stance toward the issue still more complex.

By 1975 the time was right for revelations. In 1974 the regime launched an attack against Kocbek in the press as an attempt to counter the celebrity that the public observance of his seventieth birthday had brought him. No longer willing to tolerate indignities and feeling contrition for his own long silence, Kocbek arranged to give an interview on the subject of the postwar massacres and the circumstances surrounding the Dolomite Declaration to Boris Pahor, a Slovene writer from Trieste, where it was published as part of a monograph on Kocbek. Soon afterward it reappeared in the Ljubljana weekly *Naši razgledi* (Our Perspectives), where for many readers it had the effect of an explosion, provoking their first serious doubts about the regime's legitimacy. Within a short time he was summoned to a series of police interrogations, threatened with prosecution, and once again attacked in the Yugoslav press and other public forums. Attention drawn to his case throughout Western Europe, and in particular the efforts of German novelist Heinrich Böll, helped to minimize the effects of this wave of persecution.

The two-volume *Zbrane pesmi* (Collected Poems), appearing in 1977, was Kocbek's last major publication during his lifetime. The edition includes two previously unpublished collections – *Pentagram,* consisting largely of poems from wartime, and *Nevesta v črnem* (Bride Dressed in Mourning), late poems with a distinct valedictory air – alongside the three earliest books of poetry and *Žerjavica* (Ember), a short collection first published in Trieste in 1974. Although still unmistakably Kocbek, *Žerjavica* and *Nevesta v črnem* show signs of an evolution away from the harsh irony of *Poročilo* toward a milder acceptance of fate. The poems are now more conscious of being merely poems, of falling short of the infinite mark, a failing which turns into a strength as they all become part of the greater game (or play, *igra*) of words, the game of poetry that perpetually attempts to reconcile conceptual opposites, to dissolve dualities, knowing full well that this goal can never be achieved in any lasting way. In the same spirit he continues to play with antinomies, sometimes stringing together so many at once that they have the effect of the incantation that would break their own spell. Still characteristic of Kocbek are the long, coordinated periods, numerous simple sentences linked into one breathless chain, pressing forward and conveying impressions following each other in such rapid sequence that the lyrical "I" can only register, but not rationalize them. The style is incantational, its aim poetic bliss. The poems themselves begin to form such a succession of impressions, freely borrowing from each other, repeating themselves, always leaving something in the blind spot, always somehow falling short, and consciously so, until "Suddenly the famous painter drew / a straight line and knew that he was dying, / for all his life he'd struggled / to draw a straight line, but / never could. . . ."

Kocbek once commented to a friend that he was confident his time would come, even though he doubted he would still be present when it did. Since his death on 3 November 1981 that prediction has been steadily fulfilled. Yugoslavia's unraveling through the 1980s not only made widespread appreciation of his work possible, but – much more noticeably – it also culminated in the realization of the Slovenes' millennial dream of national sovereignty. If the new state has a spiritual father, personally exacting but also forgiving of human shortcomings, it is indisputably Kocbek.

Letters:
Peščena ura: Pisma Borisu Pahorju 1940–1980 (Ljubljana: Slovenska matica, 1984);
"Enaindvajset pisem Edvarda Kocbeka dr. Antonu Trstenjaku," *Sodobnost,* 34, no. 10 (1986): 925–953.

Interviews:
Boris Pahor, "Pogovor z Borisom Pahorjem," in *Edvard Kocbek: Pričevalec našega časa* (Trieste: Zaliv, 1975); republished in *Naši razgledi,* 9 May 1975; republished again in Kocbek's *Svoboda in nujnost,* second edition (Celje: Mohorjeva družba, 1989);
"Odgovori Loysu Lampretu," in *Nova revija,* 19–20 (1983): 2034–2037.

Biographies:
Andrej Inkret, "Škica za življenjepis Edvarda Kocbeka," *Nova revija,* 1, nos. 7–8 (1982–1983): 676–681;
Janez Gradišnik, ed., *Človek je utihnil: Spominu Edvarda Kocbeka* (Celje: Mohorjeva družba, 1983);

Anton Trstenjak, "Edvard Kocbek – ekstatična osebnost, ne politik," *Sodobnost,* 34, nos. 8–9 (1986): 711–719;
Jože Kocbek, "Moj brat Edvard Kocbek: Otroška ptujska in mariborska dijaška leta," *Sodobnost,* 35, nos. 8–9 (1987): 828–842;
Boris Pahor, *Ta ocean, strašno odprt: Dnevniški zapisi od julija 1974 do februarja 1976 – sledi zapis iz leta 1980* (Ljubljana: Slovenska matica, 1989).

References:
France Bernik, "Etika in ideologija v Kocbekovi vojni prozi," *Slavistična revija,* 34, no. 3 (1986): 233–246;
Andrej Capuder, "Edvard Kocbek – pesnik jaza," *Celovški zvon,* 2, no. 5 (1984): 70–77;
Helga Glušič, "The Prose and Poetry of Edvard Kocbek, 1904–1981," *Slovene Studies,* 8, no. 2 (1986): 65–72;
Igor Grdina, "Vojni dnevniki Edvarda Kocbeka," *Slavistična revija,* 36, no. 4 (1988): 427–436;
Spomenka Hribar, *Edvard Kocbek in Križarsko gibanje* (Maribor: Založba Obzorja, 1990);
Hribar, *Krivda in greh* (Maribor: Založba za alternativno teorijo, 1990);
Andrej Inkret, "Pričevanje o brezumni slasti in o zadnji grozi: Kocbekove štiri partizanske novele," *Problemi,* 22, no. 8 (1984): 69–88;
Taras Kermauner, "Več Kocbeka!" *Sodobnost,* 29, no. 12 (1981): 1114–1119;
Lev Kreft, ed., *Edvard Kocbek: Poezija, kultura, politika* (Ljubljana: Komunist, 1988);
Boris Pahor, *Edvard Kocbek, pričevalec našega časa* (Trieste: Zaliv, 1975);
Boris Paternu, "Slovene modernism: Župančič, Kosovel, Kocbek," *Cross Currents Yearbook,* 7 (1988): 321–326;
Dimitrij Rupel, "The Heresy of Edvard Kocbek," *Slovene Studies,* 10, no. 1 (1988): 51–60;
Rupel, ed., *Kocbekov zbornik* (Maribor: Obzorja, 1987);
Michael Scammell, "Slovenia and its Poet," *New York Review of Books,* 24 October 1991, pp. 60–61;
Drago Šega, "Idejni profil Kocbekove poezije," in his *Eseji in kritike* (Ljubljana: Cankarjeva založba, 1966), pp. 73–91;
Franc Zadravec, "Kocbekova prednovelistična proza," *Sodobnost,* 34, nos. 6–7 (1986): 643–657.

Aleko Konstantinov

(1 January 1863 – 11 May 1897)

Charles A. Moser
George Washington University

BOOKS: *Do Chikago i nazad: Pŭtni belezhki* (Sofia: B. Shimochek, 1894);

Bay Ganyo: Neveroyatni razkazi za edin sŭvremenen bŭlgarin (Sofia: Pencho Spasov, 1895); translated by Francis Salter and Stuart Durrant as "Bai Ganiu: The Incredible Tales of a Contemporary Bulgarian," *Canadian-American Slavic Studies,* 7–9 (1973–1975);

Sŭchineniya, 2 volumes (Sofia: Komitet za uvekovechavane pametta na Al. Konstantinov, 1901–1903);

Sŭchineniya, 3 volumes (Sofia: A. Paskalev, 1921–1922);

Sŭchineniya, 2 volumes, ed. by Petŭr Pondev (Sofia: Bulgarski pisatel, 1957);

Sŭbrani sŭchineniya, 4 volumes, ed., by Iliya Todorov, Petŭr Pondev, and Tikhomir Tikhov (Sofia: Bulgarski pisatel, 1980–1982).

Aleko Konstantinov – often referred to familiarly by his first name or by one of his favorite pen names, *Shtastlivets* (the lucky one) – occupies a special place in the history of late nineteenth-century Bulgarian literature. Although the dominant figure of his time was Ivan Vazov, now considered the national writer of Bulgaria, Konstantinov carved out an important literary niche for himself as a humorist and social commentator during a period of political turmoil in newly liberated Bulgaria. His chief literary creation, Bay Ganyo, ranks among the best-known literary figures in Bulgaria as the distillation of all that is most unattractive in the Bulgarian character. In addition, Konstantinov's death at the hand of a political assassin fixed his personality in the Bulgarian historical memory.

Aleko Konstantinov was born on 1 January 1863 in the small city of Svishtov, located in north central Bulgaria on the Danube, which forms the boundary between Romania and Bulgaria. His family home in Svishtov is now preserved as a museum containing artifacts and memorabilia.

Aleko Konstantinov (photograph © Di "Seltemvri")

Konstantinov's family life was never particularly happy. His three sisters were sickly and all died young, as did his mother; by 1890, when he was only twenty-seven, all the other members of his family were dead. His father was an overbearing man with whom Konstantinov never got along especially well. In adulthood Konstantinov never married and apparently never even had any serious affairs of the heart. In his travel notes on his 1893 visit to America he remarks that he had never been in love, and there is little mention of love relationships in his works.

However, Konstantinov did obtain some benefits from his family. He received a good education, first in his hometown, then in the well-known Gabrovo school, and finally in Nikolaev, Russia, where he was sent in 1878 to continue his studies. He read Russian authors and translated works of such poets as Aleksandr Pushkin and Mikhail Lermontov into Bulgarian. His first publication was a poem, "Ogledalo" (The Mirror), which appeared in February 1880. However, Konstantinov's favorite writer was Ivan Turgenev, and like him Konstantinov is remembered as a prose writer.

After completing his secondary education in 1881 Konstantinov went to the university at Odessa to study law. Upon completing his studies in 1885 he went to Sofia and obtained a legal position, only to be deprived of it during a period of political turbulence under the administration of Prime Minister Stefan Stambolov in 1888. He then tried to support himself through private legal practice. Proving unsuccessful, he turned increasingly toward literature. When literary resources were scarce, he tried lawyering from time to time, but he never had much luck because of his inability to organize even his personal life.

Another positive legacy Konstantinov derived from his father was a love for travel and an interest in foreign lands. In a brief questionnaire in 1894, "Moyata izpoved" (My Confession), he defined his "favorite fragrance" as that of "steamships and railroads." In 1889 he visited the World's Fair in Paris and two years later made a trip to Prague. He also went to Chicago for the World's Fair in 1893, which provided him the opportunity to see something of the New World and retell his impressions in *Do Chikago i nazad* (To Chicago and Back, 1894), perhaps the best-known Bulgarian travel book.

Konstantinov set out on 20 June 1893 with two traveling companions, a doctor and a civil servant, neither of whom knew any more English than he did. Upon his arrival in New York, immigration officials first decided he was from Hungary and then from Turkey when he showed them his homeland on the map. After marveling at "wondrous" New York with its gigantic fifteen-story buildings, he made his way by train to Chicago, where the Bulgarian pavilion (its sign read "Bulgarian Curiosities") was a much more modest, one-story affair. From Chicago the friends traveled to Washington, D.C., then continued through Philadelphia to Boston, where they took ship for the Old World, visiting Paris and London before returning to Bulgaria. Afterwards, again in "Moyata izpoved," Konstantinov recalled the American trip as one of the two fin-

est moments of his life, and France as his favorite foreign country.

Konstantinov's attitude toward what he saw in the United States was simultaneously admiring and critical. His reading, Konstantinov says, had stimulated great admiration within him for "American liberty, equality, and its governmental system," so he was predisposed toward the country. Indeed, he found much to admire: the Brooklyn Bridge, for one thing, made a powerful impression on him. Then there was Broadway in New York. Until he saw Broadway, he wrote, he had considered the Ringstrasse in Vienna the most beautiful avenue he had seen. "The Ringstrasse," he decided, "is an elegant beauty wrought in marble. Broadway is a wonderful, eternally dancing ballerina decked in all the colors of the rainbow." He considered Washington one of the most beautiful cities he had ever visited. Niagara Falls he found almost indescribable: it was as though, he recalled, "one encountered God himself rather than one of his creations." He thought the railroads remarkably well run and was pleased that external class distinctions hardly seemed to exist in the United States: the rich and the poor consorted cheek by jowl, and in some places, he claimed, one could not find any poorly dressed people.

On the other hand, Konstantinov formed some negative impressions of American life. Soon after arriving in New York the Bulgarian travelers met a Serbian immigrant who authoritatively assured them that corruption was rampant and that the almighty dollar was king in the United States, which shook Konstantinov. He could observe something of the power of the dollar at least indirectly: the ship coming over was filled with immigrants drawn to America primarily by the promise of easy wealth, for example. Also, the impression made on him by the fine railroad system was blunted by manifestations of greed such as competing lines publishing maps emphasizing only cities they served, which Konstantinov found exaggeratedly sinister. A trip to the Chicago stockyards and slaughterhouses – which for some odd reason formed part of the itinerary of many visits to Chicago at the time – nauseated him, making him exclaim, "To what monstrous things does the thirst for money drive human beings!" He discovered reinforcement for an anticapitalist viewpoint in the works of Edward Bellamy, which he quotes at some length in his book.

Still, when Konstantinov frees himself from the negative opinions of others and draws upon his own observations, he provides a balanced view of things. For example, though he likes the equality of American society, he finds American life too rushed and busy to suit his taste. On the whole he offers his readers a travel book that is both entertaining and instructive and that includes a fairly accurate picture of what the New World was like some one hundred years ago. This was important for his Bulgarian audience, few of whom would ever have the opportunity to discover America for themselves.

Konstantinov was fortunate enough to have the opportunity to travel abroad on several occasions, but he did not neglect his small homeland, whose natural beauties he extolled in several shorter travel sketches. However, his admiration for scenic beauty was inextricably intertwined with an enthusiasm for technological and industrial progress. Thus one of his last sketches, "Sofia-Mezdra-Vratsa: Putni belezhki" (Sofia-Mezdra-Vratsa: Travel Notes), begins with a fine description of the rugged valley of the Iskur river and ends with an appreciation of the countryside around Vratsa, but it also reveals that he was sent to Vratsa to write a report on the newly opened Sofia-Roman railroad line, which he hails as a great engineering achievement. Its formal opening was a genuine celebration, he writes, and he hopes there will be many more such achievements, for they ensure the "people's progress and happiness," not celebrations with "firecrackers" attended by "ecclesiastical gendarmes." Also, in Vratsa he is pleased to meet a Bulgarian who has raised himself by his own bootstraps to organize such enterprises as a shop for manufacturing elegant cabriolets and carriages. Such men as these, Konstantinov believes, will build a prosperous Bulgaria in the future.

Do Chikago i nazad and the other travel sketches are of course not works of fiction. Konstantinov acquired a reputation as a fiction writer primarily through his Bay Ganyo sketches. By the early 1890s he had many connections in literary circles, including links to such publications as the journals *Misŭl* (Thought), *Bŭlgarski pregled* (Bulgarian Review), and *Zname* (Banner). He was also the center of an informal group called *Vesela Bŭlgaria* (Merry Bulgaria), at whose gatherings the figure of Bay Ganyo was first introduced. The Bay Ganyo sketches began appearing in *Misŭl* in 1894 and came out in a separate edition in 1895.

As originally conceived, Bay Ganyo was a provincial Bulgarian clod, a walking compendium of the ignorance, narrow-mindedness, and insensitivity to be found in greater or lesser degree in any society, including Bulgarian society. These negative traits stand out in greatest relief when Bay Ganyo is

Cartoon by Iliya Beshkov, in which Bay Ganyo kills his author (photograph © Di "Seltemvri")

abroad, and many of the original sketches were set in foreign countries, including Germany, Switzerland, and Russia. For example, in one of these sketches, "Bay Ganyo in Dresden," the narrator describes a climbing accident in which Bay Ganyo's sister has perished with her American companion, a young man. Summoned to the scene, Bay Ganyo enters with his headgear on, clumping along like a horse and loudly inquiring as to the whereabouts of his sister. When he discovers that the two young people have been laid side by side in death, he declares himself absolutely scandalized over such moral laxity.

Another sketch describing Bay Ganyo abroad, with wider political implications, is "Bay Ganyu na izlozhenieto v Praga" (Bay Ganyo at the Prague Exhibition), which is based upon the trip Konstantinov and the Vesela Bŭlgaria group took to Prague in 1891. In the sketch the group of Bulgarians in the train wax patriotic as they head for the Serbian border. But when they cross it at evening and it turns out that illuminating candles have not been provided for the passengers, Bay Ganyo is at the fore-

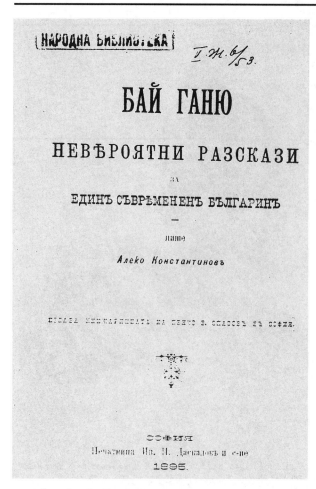

Title page for Konstantinov's collection of sketches about
Bay Ganyo

cations, decide on the spur of the moment to publish a newspaper. After the decision has been made they debate over what name to choose for it: *Justice* is one suggestion, then *People's Wisdom, Bulgarian Pride,* or *Popular Grandeur.* All these proposed titles are satirical digs at the actual names of periodicals of the time, publications with as little behind them as Bay Ganyo's enterprise. The next step is knowing how to produce an editorial properly. One begins by flattering the prince, says Ganyo:

> Put in something about *Your humble children, Our father and parent, in the dust of Your most august feet,* set up a whole series of these things, you know how to do it. Then don't forget the couple of words you should have about the people. . . . And then give the opposition a real dressing down: start off with, Those traitors, those . . .
>
> "Traitors" is a little old-fashioned now, so let's call them "swine" . . . , [replies a colleague].

The emergence of the satirical element in the Bay Ganyo sketches stems from Konstantinov's own political evolution. For most of his life, though a lawyer, he remained relatively apolitical, but in 1894 he joined the Democratic party and stood from his hometown of Svishtov in the parliamentary elections of that year, only to be defeated. His experience with the machinations of his political enemies disillusioned him and brought him to see Bay Ganyo as more than a buffoon – in fact, as a political threat. Consequently, he turned in the last, short period of his life to the political article as his principal instrument. He began in 1894 with "Po 'izborite' v Svishtov" (On the 'Elections' in Svishtov).

Thereafter Konstantinov appeared frequently in periodicals with political articles on various topics. His literary ally, the critic and editor of *Misŭl,* Krŭstyo Krŭstev, later wrote that "each of Aleko's articles was a social and literary event that stirred every thinking person in Bulgaria and aroused in him sometimes merry laughter, sometimes anger and indignation." He also found in Konstantinov a "painfully sensitive conscience" that was the "mother of ridicule, irony, anger, indignation, and national shame" – a sense of shame that informed both his Bay Ganyo sketches and his directly political sketches.

One bitter sketch of this type, "Izbiratelen zakon" (Election Law), dates from early 1895. It parodies a legal document that makes explicit what he had concluded was implicit in Bulgarian electoral practice. Thus, for example, article six of section two defines voters as "those Bulgarian citizens who are unafraid of the Ottoman criminal code and dis-

front of those claiming that such an oversight must have been the fault of some foreigner. As the train moves through Serbia, Bay Ganyo, having consumed his own provisions, scrounges food and drink off the other passengers in a masterly fashion, using such outrageous flattery that the victim is scarcely able to resist him. When the train reaches the border, where the local population has organized a warm welcome for their "brother Bulgarians," Bay Ganyo leaves the train, brushes past a little girl offering him a welcoming bouquet, enters the toilet, and then emerges still adjusting his clothing. The narrator is overcome with shame when he recalls how all the other Bulgarians reacted to this welcome: they simply jammed their heads out the windows of the train and stared.

Konstantinov later shifted the target of his satire from the cultural, as in "Bay Ganyo in Dresden," to the political. "Bay Ganyu zhurnalist" (Bay Ganyo the Journalist) is an example. Bay Ganyo and his friends, who possess not the slightest qualifi-

pose of powerful muscles and various weapons."
The following are not permitted to vote:

1. Those jailed without trial;
2. Persons who fill out their ballots without official permission;
3. Those who think for themselves;
4. The physically weak; and
5. The poor.

Finally, if such definitions as these are insufficient to guarantee a government victory, the election law states:

> As soon as the voting is concluded, the chairman of the electoral commission, without inspecting the ballots, shall declare those previously designated to have been elected, and shall compel the armed voters to sign a telegram thanking [the government] for these free elections.

The satire in this sketch was extremely heavy-handed, but it quickly saw print so that the government could not be accused of suppressing free speech in the political arena.

However, one does not write political and social satire of this sort, especially in Bulgaria, without earning political enemies. Konstantinov also received warnings that his life was in danger. That danger became real on 11 May 1897, the feast of Saints Cyril and Methodius, long a major national and religious holiday in Bulgaria. Konstantinov left Plovdiv for the town of Peshtera, where he spent a pleasant day. Toward evening he set out for Tatar-Pazardzhik with a traveling companion. After dark the men were overtaken by hired assassins, and the badly wounded Konstantinov died before he could reach Pazardzhik. He was buried in Sofia. Though his inimitable literary voice was silenced, he had already made his mark on Bulgarian literature.

Bibliography:
Petya Dyugmedzhieva and others, *Aleko Konstantinov 1863–1897: Bio-bibliografski ukazatel* (Sofia: Narodna biblioteka "Kiril i Metodiy," 1983).

Biographies:
Georgi Konstantinov, *Aleko Konstantinov: Biografiya* (Sofia: Khemus, 1946);
Stoyan Mikhaylovski, Aleko Konstantinov, G. P. Stamatov v spomenite na süvremennitsite si (Sofia: Bŭlgarski pisatel, 1963), pp. 127–352.

References:
Stefan Elevterov, *Poetikata na Aleko Konstantinov i nasheto literaturno razvitie* (Sofia: Nauka i izkustvo, 1978);
Krŭstyo Krŭstev, *Aleko Konstantinov: Literaturen siluet* (Tutrakan: Mavrodinov, 1907);
Aleksandur Nichev, *Aleko Konstantinov, 1863–1897* (Sofia: Bŭlgarska akademiya na naukite, 1964);
Tikhomir Tikhov, ed., *Bŭlgarskata kritika za Aleko Konstantinov* (Sofia: Bŭlgarski pisatel, 1970).

Srečko Kosovel

(18 March 1904 – 27 May 1926)

Peter Scherber
University of Göttingen

BOOKS: *Pesmi,* edited by Alfonz Gspan (Ljubljana, 1927);

Izbrane pesmi, edited by Anton Ocvirk (Ljubljana: Tiskovna zadruga, 1931);

Zbrano delo, 3 volumes in 4, edited by Ocvirk (Ljubljana: Državna založba, 1946–1977; volume 1, revised, 1964);

Moja pesem, edited by Lino Legiša (Maribor: Obzorja, 1964);

Integrali '26, edited by Ocvirk (Ljubljana: Cankarjeva založba, 1967; revised, 1984); translated by Wilhelm Heiliger as *Integrals* (Santa Barbara, Cal.: Mudborn Press, 1983);

Moja pesem, edited by Ocvirk (Koper: Lipa 1976);

Pesmi in konstrukcije, edited by Gspan (Ljubljana: Mladinska knjiga 1978).

Despite his short lifetime of twenty-two years and the brief creative period that it implies, Srečko Kosovel stands – with Ivan Cankar and Oton Župančič – among the most important Slovene poets of the twentieth century. Kosovel, more so than nearly all of his contemporaries, absorbed the cultural, political, and social impulses in the Europe of his time and integrated them intensely in his poetry and essays. For this reason he belongs to European and world literature. His complete works were not published until fifty years after his death. Many of his individual poems have been translated into several major and minor languages, but complete translations of his works exist only in French and German.

Srečko Kosovel was born on 18 March 1904 in Sežana, about ten miles to the east of Trieste, in the Slovene region Karst, which gives its name to the mountain plateau north of Trieste and east of the Isonzo River.

Several years later his father, Anton Kosovel, and mother, Katarina (née Stres), took their family to live in the nearby town of Tomaj, where Anton Kosovel soon earned a reputation as a teacher, choir leader, and musician. Srečko was the youngest of five children and remained for the rest of his life emotionally bound to his birthplace and the Karst. His brother Stano, who was nine years older, became known as an author and journalist, and their sister Karmela achieved recognition as a pianist.

The stormy political history of the Karst in the twentieth century exerted a dominant influence on Kosovel's life. The area surrounding Trieste, predominantly inhabited by Slovenes, was part of Austria until the end of World War I, when it was joined to Italy. Particularly under the Fascist dictatorship of Benito Mussolini, Slovene culture was suppressed, and the Slovenes were denied their cultural and political rights. In the mid 1920s the political situation for the Slovenes was desperate: a return to Austria was impossible, but a new state of Serbs, Croats, and Slovenes (SHS) seemed undesirable as well; to Kosovel it threatened to become no less totalitarian than its German, Russian, and Italian equivalents. After 1945 the Karst, with most of the Slovene coastal region, was united with the other parts of Slovenia as a constituent republic of Yugoslavia.

During World War I Kosovel's father had decided to send his son to school in Ljubljana, instead of in nearby Trieste, hoping Srečko would become a forestry engineer who would make the melioration and reforestation of the Karst his life's task. During his school years Kosovel was interested in literature and, prompted by his school friend Branko Jeglič, he was involved in the Kres circle, whose never-published anthology Kosovel enriched with his first poems. While he was still in school, he contributed to other minor publications such as *Jadran* (Adriatic), *Preporod* (Rebirth), and *Mlado Jutro* (Young Morning). In 1922 he began to study Romance and Slavic languages and literatures at the University of Ljubljana and simultaneously to participate actively in the literary life of the city as a writer, reciting and publishing his works and doing editorial work, chiefly for political or cultural circles.

Srečko Kosovel

In 1922 he edited the journal *Lepa Vida* (Beautiful Vida), of which only a few issues were published. For Slovenes this name has two associations: it reminds them of the Slovene ballad about beautiful Vida, which expressed to some extent the national and cultural aspirations of the Slovene people; and it alludes to Slovene writer Cankar, whose poetic drama *Lepa Vida* (1912) served as a literary model for Kosovel's postwar generation. Also in 1922 Kosovel contributed to the short-lived journal *Trije labodje* (Three Swans), published by the first generation of the Slovene avant-garde: Marij Kogoj, Anton Podbevšek, and Josip Vidmar. Kosovel's brief employment as an editor of the academic magazine *Vidovdan* (Saint Vitus Day) ended in 1923 as it became obvious that its attitude was hostile to the interests of Slovene students.

A journal, "Slovenska revija" (Slovene Review), belonged to Kosovel's many unrealized plans. He wanted to publish it in Geneva, the seat of the League of Nations, so that he could acquaint the world with the desolate situation of the Slovenes, caught between the developing Yugoslav and Italian dictatorships. The League of Nations was, according to Kosovel, the representative of the "European lie," in which the larger nations set the tone, although they were long since discredited morally. The slogans "Evropa umira" (Europe is dying) and "društvo narodov laž" (The League of Nations is a lie) run through his entire work, his diaries, and his letters. He planned to write a tragedy titled "Evropa umira," but he never finished it, nor did he complete "Na pragu človečanstva" (On the Treshold of Humankind), a satire on the League of Nations.

In 1924 he planned with some friends to establish a club of young authors, *Klub mladih* (Club of the Young), but the project broke down in the early stages. The year 1925 brought the establishment of the literary-dramatic circle "Ivan Cankar," which Kosovel helped to organize. This group was able to function successfully and decisively for a time in the literary life of Ljubljana.

Kosovel made his cultural-political and literary-critical credo known in several articles published during his lifetime. Among these are the essays "Umetnost in proletarec" (Art and the Proletarian),

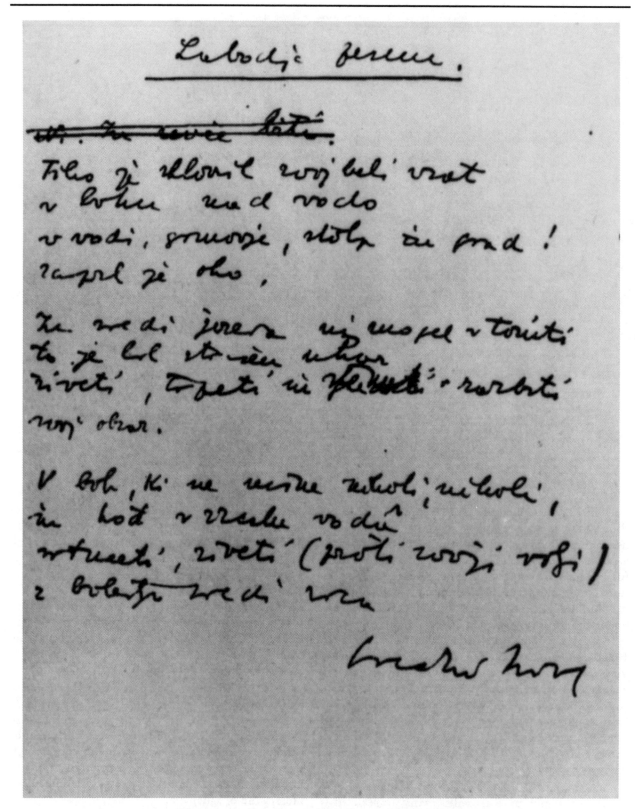

Manuscript for Kosovel's poem "Labodja pesem" (Swan's Song)

"Razpad družbe in propad umetnosti" (The Decay of Society and the Decline of Art), "Manifest svobodnim duhom" (A Manifesto for Free Spirits), and "Kaj je kulturno gibanje?" (What is a Cultural Movement?). Their publication was possible because in autumn 1925 Kosovel, along with his closest colleagues and friends, was able to take over the editing of the Slovene Farmer's party magazine for young people, *Mladina* (Youth), and could shape it according to his own aesthetic and political notions. He was less fortunate with *Zlati čoln* (Golden boat), a booklet of his poems he prepared in 1925. The poems remained unpublished until years after his death.

In the winter of 1925–1926 the Cankar circle organized some spectacular literary evenings in Ljubljana and in the coalfield of Trbovlje, which attracted the attention of a broader public. In the beginning of 1926 Kosovel, who had always been frail, caught a chill and became seriously ill. A return to his home in Tomaj could not restore his health. He was suffering from meningitis and complications arose. When Kosovel died in his home at Tomaj on 27 May 1926, he had published only a few of his poems, a handful of essays and reviews, and practically none of his prose.

Not until the 1970s could one gauge Kosovel's significance in Slovene and European literature. Despite the presence of the Italian police at his funeral, his friends Bratko Kreft and Ivo Grahor expressed their nationalist feelings. In Ljubljana Slovene officials suspected Kosovel of having had radical leftist leanings. Therefore, until World War II only politically bowdlerized, abridged editions of his works could be published. *Pesmi* (Poems, 1927), financed by his friends and edited by Alfonz Gspan, offered — with only sixty-six poems — a well-meant but seriously unrepresentative picture of his creative work.

Stano Kosovel submitted his brother's literary estate to Anton Ocvirk, later a professor of comparative literature, who published a somewhat larger selection of Kosovel's poems, *Izbrane pesmi* (Collected Works), in 1931. The first volume of Kosovel's *Zbrano delo* could not be published until 1946, when — due to the upheaval of political and social structures in postwar Yugoslavia — Kosovel's poetry had come to be regarded as progressive and exemplary. In editing volume one of *Zbrano delo* Ocvirk used his own, limited criteria of poetic quality as the basis for his deciding which poems should be published and included only part of Kosovel's published works and only the previously unpublished material that conformed to Ocvirk's notions of quality. Therefore, until the middle of the 1960s, for the

most part only Kosovel's so-called Karst poetry and some of his expressionistic oeuvre were known. After delays in releasing the rest of his collected works were criticized repeatedly in the press, a second edition of the first volume appeared in 1964 with hardly any new text.

Presumably as a reaction to the contemporary debate about the avant-garde movements, Ocvirk published Kosovel's constructivist poems in 1967 as *Integrali '26* (Integrals '26), a title that might suggest incorrectly that the contents of the book were written by Kosovel shortly before his death in 1926. This book attracted enormous interest from the Slovene public, particularly among critics and authors of the then-active post-avant-garde. In 1977 Ocvirk brought the publication of his edition of Kosovel's collected works to a conclusion, but it cannot be ruled out that additional, as yet unknown texts will come to light. An important part of his collected works is Kosovel's letters to his friends and relatives, which made possible new insights into his literary plans and thoughts.

The availability of Kosovel's entire opus created a basis for a serious scholarly discussion of avant-garde phenomena and Kosovel's important role in their history. The Slovene avant-garde may be divided into three phases: an early anarchistic one, which is embodied in the works and happenings of Anton Podbevšek; a middle, constructivist phase, of which Kosovel's works form the center; and a final phase focused on the theater group Novi oder and the journal *Tank,* both organized by Ferdo Delak and Avgust Černigoj.

"Moje življenje je moje, slovensko, sodobno, evropsko in večno" (My life is mine, Slovene, contemporary, European, and eternal), Kosovel wrote in a 1924 letter to a friend and in his diary as well. Thus he gave both the spatial and the temporal dimensions to his thoughts. In his works Kosovel returned again and again to the conflict between a regional model of the world and those of Yugoslavia and Europe. The region is Kosovel's central spatial concept; he relates other spatial concepts (Ljubljana, Yugoslavia, or Europe) to this one. In significant portions of his poetry and prose he thematized the Karst as a region that represents a certain perfection, a sort of microcosm in which life is intact and in which a humane future can be imagined. These possibilities were not present in his other spatial concepts. In Europe, Yugoslavia, and Slovenia a future worth living was possible only by bringing about a humanization of these areas, which he could imagine only through a transformation in a "humanistic" revolution. The fact that Kosovel saw in the Communist-Socialist path a possibility for realizing such ideas is not surprising: at that time this was a common hope among Europe's left-wing intellectuals.

Kosovel's concept of region has a utopian component. As a place of self-discovery it offered an alternative to life in the European metropolis, a refuge or an oasis: "Potem je upati, da vstane ta Kras, ta čudno nerodoviti Kras, oaza sredi lažnjive civilizacije Evrope, tako rekoč zatočišče romantikov" (Then one can hope that this Karst, this strange unfertile Karst will rise, an oasis in the middle of the lying civilization of Europe, so to speak a refuge of romantics), he said in a dialogue he wrote in his diaries.

The evolution of Kosovel's style could be discussed only after the appearance of *Integrali '26*. Until then there had been a certain consensus about the beginnings of his poetry, seen in the context of modernism or more exactly of impressionism, and about his later, socially committed work, viewed as an aspect of European expressionism. *Integrali '26* forced scholars to reconsider how Kosovel's avant-garde style was formed, to see his development as three chronologically overlapping stylistic layers.

These three phases in Kosovel may be viewed as corresponding to three literary models suitable for structuring a crude analysis of his total work. The impressionistic model of his poetry, present in his so-called Karst poems and some other poems, contrasts thematically the "sunny" Karst and the "foggy" Ljubljana. The second, expressionistic model includes the poems in which Kosovel oriented himself toward European expressionism – as characterized in the texts of the anthology edited by Kurt Pinthus, *Menschheitsdämmerung* (Dawn of Humankind, 1920). In his expressionistic poems Kosovel targeted the political and social problems of his time and simultaneously corresponded formally to his European contemporaries (Ernst Toller, Walter Hasenclever, Ivan Goll) in breaking with the traditional poetic form. In his "Ekspresionistična pesem" (Expressionistic poem) Kosovel explicitly referred to this model, and he expressed his mood as a poet in the refrain: "jaz sem drevo brez vej" (I am a tree without branches). In "Ekstaza smrti" (Ecstasy of Death), which provoked much excitement when Kosovel recited it during a public appearance in November 1925, Kosovel placed his mood between the extremes of Oswald Spengler's cultural pessimism and Socialist criticism of capitalist society. The peaks of his expressionist phase comes in the cycles "Rdeči atom" (Red Atom) and "Tragedija na oceanu" (Tragedy on the Ocean), expressing his hope for revolutionary change and his deeply seated pessimism regarding the fulfillment of this hope.

The poems he called *Konstrukcije* (Constructions), which became known in their full extent only with the publication of the *Integrali '26* in 1967, form the third, constructivist model, especially his *Kons* texts: short, graphically and typographically unconventional poems and his *Lepljenke* (stick-on poems), texts which he put together out of newspaper headlines. With the manifesto "Mehanikom" (To the Mechanics), which he wrote in July 1925, he placed himself in the tradition of declarative self-assessment as it was practiced in postrevolutionary Russian literary groups. In it he opposed the old, "mechanical" worldview with a new "electrical" one, to go with the New Man. The manifesto concludes with the slogan: "Vsi mehanizmi morajo umreti! NOVI ČLOVEK PRIHAJA!" (All mechanisms must die! The New Man is coming!)

Kosovel's stand with respect to the Slovene and Yugoslavian avant-garde of his time was subject to constant change. As time went on he developed from a partisan and comrade-in-arms in the group surrounding Podbevšek to a critical fellow traveler, insofar as he stood aloof from events whose only purpose was to shock the petit-bourgeois of Ljubljana. Referring to those members of the avant-garde group *Zenit* (Zenith) in Slovenia (Zenit was active in Belgrade and Zagreb as well), Kosovel remarked that he loved the Zenitists but not Zenitism. Kosovel's contributions to the avant-garde were characterized by an integration of political and artistic content in spoken and written word and in cultural activities, as were, for example, Russian constructivist works by Ilyá Selvínsky and K. Zelinsky.

If we look at Kosovel's acknowledged literary and spiritual models, we see, next to the dominant impact of Cankar and the Slovene so-called Moderna, Kosovel's Croatian contemporary Miroslav Krleža and the German expressionists. As far as the spiritual basis of his thought is concerned, the influence of Friedrich Nietzsche and especially of Rabindranath Tagore should not be overlooked. The direct influence of Russian literary constructivism on Kosovel's work cannot be proved, but he must have been familiar with constructivism, in the visual arts at least, through his friends Grahor and Černigoj.

The critics Franc Zadravec and Janez Vrečko have shown convincingly that Kosovel created, autonomously and without extensive international contacts, one of the few examples of European literary constructivism. Research on Kosovel's texts, especially on his constructivist works, is still in its early stages. His *Kons* poems, his graphic poetry put together from newspaper headlines, as well as his — for the most part still-undeciphered — diaries promise many interesting discoveries.

Letters:

Zbrano Delo, 3 volumes in 4, edited by Anton Ocvirk (Ljubljana: Državna založba, 1946–1977), III: 261–588.

References:

Drago Bajt, "Russian Constructivism, the Slovenes and Srečko Kosovel," in *Slovenische historische Avantgarde/Slovene Historical Avant-garde,* edited by Aleš Erjavec (Ljubljana: Aesthetic Society/ Gesellschaft für Ästhetik, 1986), pp. 7–17;

Gino Brazzoduro, "Kosovel, Our Contemporary: A Constructivist Reading of *Integrals,*" *Le livre slovène,* 22, nos. 2–3 (1984): 61–69;

Aleksandar Flaker, "Kosovelova konstruktivna poezija i jugoslavenski kontekst," in *Obdobje ekspresionizma v slovenskem jeziku, knjiťevnosti in kulturi,* volume 2 (Ljubljana: Univerza Edvarda Kardelja, 1984), pp. 173–182;

Alfonz Gspan, *Neznani Srečko Kosovel* (Ljubljana: Državna založba, 1974);

Anton Ocvirk, *Literarna umetnina med zgodovino in teorijo: Razprave,* 2 volumes (Ljubljana: Državna založba, 1978–1979), volume 2, pp. 255–525;

Boris Paternu, "Slovene Modernism: Župančič, Kosovel, Kocbek," *Cross Currents,* 7 (1988): 321–336;

Marija Pirjevec, *Srečko Kosovel: aspetti del suo pensiero e della sua lirica* (Trieste: Stampa triestina, 1974);

Dimitrij Rupel, *Srečko Kosovel* (Ljubljana: Delavska enotnost, 1976);

Srečko Kosovel v Trstu (Trieste: Zaliv, 1970);

Janez Vrečko, "Kosovel med *Integrali* in *Konsi,*" *Sodobnost,* 33 (1985): 64–72;

Vrečko, *Srečko Kosovel, slovenska zgodovinska avantgarda in zenitizem* (Maribor: Obzorja, 1986);

Franc Zadravec, "Konstruktivizem in Srečko Kosovel," *Sodobnost,* 14 (1966): 1248–1256;

Zadravec, *Srečko Kosovel: 1904–1926* (Koper/Trieste: Lipa & Tržaški tisk, 1986).

Papers:

Kosovel's papers are in the National and University Library (NUK) in Ljubljana.

Ante Kovačić

(6 June 1854 – 10 December 1889)

Maria B. Malby
East Carolina University

BOOKS: *Baruničina ljubav* (Zagreb: Vijenac, 1877);
Fiškal (Senj: H. Luster, 1882);
Izabrane pjesme (Zagreb: Sokolova biblioteka, 1908);
Sabrane pripovijesti (Zagreb: Društvo hrvatskih
    književnika, 1910);
U registraturi (Zagreb: Matica hrvatska, 1911);
Ukupna djela Ante Kovačića, 3 volumes (Zagreb:
    Hrvatski izdavački bibliografski zavod, 1944);
Stihovi (Zagreb: Jugoslavenska akademija znanosti i
    umjetnosti, 1949);
Djela, 2 volumes (Zagreb: Zora, 1950);
Medju žabarima (Zagreb: Novo pokoljenje, 1951);
Feljtoni i članci (Zagreb: Jugoslavenska akademija
    znanosti i umjetnosti, 1952);
Prve pripovijesti (Zagreb: Jugoslavenska akademija
    znanosti i umjetnosti, 1953);
Fiškal; Medju žabarima (Zagreb: Mladost, 1978).

Ante Kovačić

The author of one of the most significant Croatian novels of the nineteenth century, Ante Kovačić did not live to see the publication of his masterpiece in book form. After years of financial hardship and of harassment by the church and the representatives of a foreign government in his country, he died prematurely in a state hospital.

During his lifetime Kovačić either published his works in literary magazines or paid for the publication of monographs, always suffering a loss. After his death his wife, Milka, left with four children and pregnant, sold his manuscripts and copyrights to St. Kugli of Zagreb. She neither saw her husband's works published promptly, as had been stipulated, nor did she receive the entire sum of the pittance on which they had agreed. Kovačić's masterpiece, *U registraturi* (At the Registry, 1911), and several collections of his other works appeared in print about two decades later, after positive critical statements on his writings.

Kovačić lived during particularly trying times in Croatia. Still part of the Austro-Hungarian Empire, the country came under an ever-increasing control by the Hungarians during his lifetime. The two major political parties of this period were at odds, pitting the few members of the intelligentsia against each other. Furthermore, the country, in transition from feudalism to capitalism, was undergoing an economic crisis. Impoverished peasants flocked to the cities or went abroad in search of work and education, often finding themselves permanently displaced. Persecuted by reactionary forces in the country, members of the Pravaši (Rights) party criticized negative phenomena in Croatian social, political, and economic life. Their list was endless, as was their anger. Although lacking a real program, they were vociferous and articulate. One of the boldest and angriest among them was Kovačić.

Born on 6 June 1854 in Oplaznik, a hamlet near the Slovenian border, Ante Kovačić grew up as a typical Croatian peasant boy of the second half of the nineteenth century. His father, Ivan, was a vineyard overseer at a baron's estate. Although he and his Slovenian-born wife, Anica, née Vugrinc, provided adequate support for their two children, they could not afford further education for their son after he had completed grammar school in Marija Gorica, a nearby village. However, since young Ante was a bright pupil, his parish priest Tomo Gajdek, later a canon, made it possible for him to attend high school in Zagreb. Kovačić had to do chores for the clergy to earn his room and board. Eventually he tutored some of his classmates as well.

Two years before graduating from high school Kovačić was persuaded to enter the seminary, but he left it promptly after receiving his diploma. From then on he had to support himself. He took a job as a clerk in a legal practice and started studying law. At the same time he worked for several literary journals, in which he published some of his own articles and literary works.

Kovačić began writing poetry while still in high school. His early work, consisting of love poems and patriotic and historic songs, was of slight literary value. One such poem, "Car Bajazet" (Emperor Bajazet), was published in 1871 in *Nada* (Hope), a minor literary magazine, marking his debut into the world of literature. Kovačić's poetry later became more serious and purposeful. Motivated by his own hard life and his disillusionment with the city, Kovačić started to criticize. Emulating the style of Ante Starčević, one of the most influential figures of the Rights party and notorious for his sarcastic speeches, Kovačić introduced satire and sarcasm into his poetry. Attacking social injustices, human vices and shortcomings, political cowardice, and naiveté, Kovačić wrote approximately seventy poems, most of which were published posthumously. Those that appeared in magazines while Kovačić was still alive greatly annoyed their targets. Several decades later critics, on the contrary, delighted in them, as they did in Kovačić's feuilletons, his three completed novels, his unfinished novel, and his short stories. The critics after World War II proclaimed certain passages from these works to be perfect examples of critical realism.

Although he often attacked upper- and middle-class immoral and unethical behavior, Kovačić was primarily concerned about the fate of Croatian rural people. He empathized with their hardships, delighted in their occasional attempts to outwit those who exploited them, and depicted their painful adaptation to city life. At the same time he was angry with those who, after receiving an education, returned to the country to exploit people there or to introduce ideas that he considered dangerous. Both types, the opportunists and the pseudointellectuals, were assigned some of the most unpleasant roles in Kovačić's fiction. By portraying such characters Kovačić recorded the development of the Croatian middle class as he focused his attention on the sad predicament of his beloved peasants.

In 1878 Kovačić published a poem titled "Metamorfoza" (Metamorphosis), to which August Šenoa, the father of modern Croatian literature, reacted negatively. Šenoa contended that by failing to restrain his wild imagination "according to the laws of aesthetics" Kovačić had created a kaleidoscope. Šenoa thus urged the young writer to purify his fantasy, which Kovačić could never do. His instinct for realistic observation and realistic portraiture notwithstanding, Kovačić had an uncontrollably vivid imagination. As the suffering in his life intensified, this wild, irrational side of Kovačić's psyche prevailed over the rational part, leading to tragic consequences. Among Kovačić's papers one can read a prophetic remark, "Est aliquid in cerebro," and his subjective, partially incorrect translation: "There is something painful in the brain."

Nowhere is Kovačić's wild imagination more evident than in his portrayal of male/female relationships. A passionate man, he saw women either as angels or demons. While such a classification was typical of many Romantic writers, some of whom were still active in Kovačić's time, his demonic women take on new dimensions. Always responsible for the hero's and their own undoing, they become the personification of fate. Since fate in Kovačić's writing has the proportions of Greek tragedy, his works usually end up cluttered with dead bodies.

In Kovačić's first novel, *Baruničina ljubav* (The Baroness's Love, 1877), one can already perceive his obsession with fate. Here a mother unwittingly falls in love with her own son. On the day of their engagement the truth, too shocking to endure, is revealed to them. Pavao kills himself while his mother, Baroness Sofija Grefstein, enters a nunnery. In spite of all the vestiges of Romanticism in the novel, such as the seduction of a maiden, descriptions of bacchanalia and foreboding dreams, and references to a duel and to poisoning, the elements of realism are also present. Once seduced and abandoned by Julijo, the unworthy man she had loved, the baroness is doomed as are those yet to come into contact with her. From the point of view of modern psychology this is quite sound: because of a severe trauma, a person can easily become affected for life. However, critics thus far have failed to give proper attention to the cause of pathological behavior in some of Kovačić's heroines.

Frequently Kovačić shows in his work cases of an innocent person's contamination by evil, which then becomes endemic. In the endless chain of events that follows it is not easy to discern who the real perpetrator is, especially since Kovačić assigns his violated women the role of chief aggressor. Intrigued by if not obsessed with women, Kovačić makes his traumatized heroines express aggression through their sexuality. Once seduced, they are apt to go on a sexual rampage, destroying every male in their path. If and when such a demonic woman tries to break the vicious circle of her actions, it is too late. Either her latent yearning for goodness is soon overshadowed by the evil she now embodies, or it is simply a matter of poetic justice. Baroness Grefstein, after living for many years as a damned woman and her seducer's "friend in Satan," suddenly becomes attracted to young Pavao. Just when she seems ready to change her ways, however, she must face the monstrous truth and her son's suicide.

Kovačić's main purpose in this novel is to expose upper-class immorality. Though aware of her troubled past, he feels no empathy for his protagonist because she is a noblewoman of German descent. Kovačić despised foreign elements in his country, German in particular, and accordingly he expressed this antipathy in most of his works. The baroness's entourage consists of equally corrupt numbers of domestic landed gentry. An exception is Ivan Martinić, who teaches the baroness Croatian and falls in love with her. With him Kovačić initiates in his work the theme of the struggle of a young man from the country to obtain an education. Although Ivan is by no means a peasant, he has financial problems in common with other country youths who seek an education in the city.

Several works that followed this novel show Kovačić's negative feelings toward the push for education advocated by Šenoa and his followers. In "Ljubljanska katastrofa" (Ljubljana's Catastrophe, 1887), a romantic autobiographical story about two men's trip from Zagreb to Ljubljana, Kovačić expresses his views in the form of a dialogue. Disguised as Andrija, one of the traveling companions, he argues his point with Sornig, who believes neither in God nor in people but wants enlightenment for the masses. Pointing out the contradictions in this man's statements, Kovačić has a chance to speak out against supposed German civilization and materialism. Though he always expressed anticlerical views, he asserts here that what people need most is faith.

Aside from a romantic plot in which two girls fall in love with Andrija and he with them, making it imperative that he simply leave, the story has a serious component, showing Kovačić's preoccupation with the relevance of education and his fear of the spreading of Socialist ideas. Since these ideas were coming primarily from Germany, he rejected them in spite of his concern for the poor.

In "Zagorski čudak" (The Crank from Zagorje, 1888), Kovačić describes a true casualty of education. A boy from sturdy peasant stock, Juraj Sporčina, is sent to a seminary. He starts attending dances and begins to date while still in school. Juraj learns that the two women he has become involved with are of the "demonic" kind, and he has sense enough to abandon them both during a confrontation in Vienna. Although one of them is pregnant, he simply walks out, hat in hand and with a bow. After he returns to his village following a long stay abroad, the reader is left wondering what might have been had this earthy man not been uprooted from his soil.

The year 1880 was eventful for Kovačić. He received a law degree; married Milka Hajdinova, a teacher from Petrinja, with whom he had six children (one of whom died in infancy); and published several new works. These show an increasing involvement with social and political concerns. In the short story "Ladanjska sekta" (Landed Gentry, 1880), he focuses on the decadence of Croatian upper- and middle-class society and the spreading of Darwinist and Socialist ideas in the country. Tomaš Branac, a teacher who comes to disseminate these ideas into the quiet backwaters of Zagorje – Kovačić's native region – is a man with a shady past. Sofija, a daughter he had out of wedlock, arrives to announce her engagement to another teacher. Even though Branac had befriended Pepo, a member of the board of education and the landed gentry, Pepo now plots his ruin in order to force Sofija into marrying him instead. Ugly and common in spite of his social position, Pepo was unable to complete his university studies because of limited intelligence. A fine example of the pseudointellectual type Kovačić despised, he fits well into the company of other such types, Sofija's fiancé and his friends included. Some of these characters shock the villagers with their loose moral behavior. Perhaps to dramatize the infiltration of all sorts of negative influences from the city into the country, Kovačić concludes this story with three deaths.

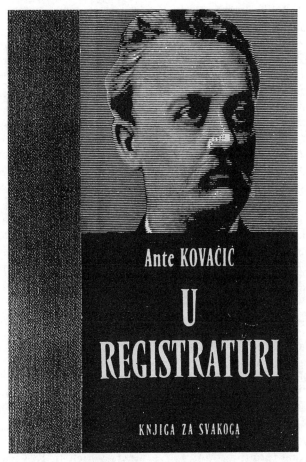

Cover for a 1965 edition of Kovačić's best-known work, first published
in the journal Vijenac in 1888

Another interesting work published in 1880 was a parody of a well-known Croatian epic, Ivan Mažuranić's, *Smrt Smail-Aga Čengića* (The Death of Smail-Aga Čengić, 1846). Kovačić entitled his poem "Smrt babe Čengićkinje" (The Death of Old Woman Čengić). This highly satiric work cannot be appreciated without a familiarity with the original work and the political situation in Croatia to which Kovačić was referring. To reduce Mažuranić, the well-known poet and governor, to "Old Woman Čengić" and to compare the persecution of the Rights party by the government to the sufferings of Montenegrins during Turkish rule showed great boldness on Kovačić's part.

In 1882 Kovačić published his second novel, *Fiškal* (The Lawyer). Kovačić uses here a pejorative term, which sets the tone for the entire work. The lawyer is Jakob Podgorski, a boot maker's son living in a small provincial town. There he practices law, takes bribes, and engages in usury, making the most of his education in the worst sense. With Podgorski and his assistant Dugan, Kovačić zeroed

in even closer on pseudointellectuals and middle-class society in general. A calculating man and an emotional vacuum, Podgorski spends a lot of time trying to manipulate a noblewoman into marrying him and thus secure her estate for his illegitimate daughter. In the background of his maneuvers are descriptions of various illicit relationships, pointing to a lack of moral fiber in Croatian society. Such a demoralizing atmosphere is accentuated by three deaths and several forthcoming ones. This novel sets the stage for *U registraturi,* which depicts total chaos in both city and country.

Kovačić's third novel, *Medju žabarima* (Among Petty People, 1951), is a satire of a provincial town and its people. Kovačić worked in the town, Karlovac, as a legal assistant upon receiving his law degree. The novel appeared serially in the journal *Balkan* (Balkans) in 1886 but it was never finished because the people of Karlovac demanded that the publication of the novel be stopped.

Kovačić's next novel was his masterpiece, *U registraturi.* After appearing in *Vijenac* (Wreath) in

1888, it was first published in book form in 1911, securing his place in Croatian literature. All of his previous writings lead up to this work, since *U registraturi* is a synthesis of all of Kovačić's themes. Everything he had to say, everything he ever felt, is contained in this novel. Both positive and negative traits of his writing are intensified, the linguistic and stylistic imperfections noticeable in other works are heightened, and nowhere is his penchant for the fantastic more disturbing. At the same time the highly autobiographical descriptions of the protagonist's boyhood and of the disintegration of village life constitute some of the finest pages of Croatian realism and naturalism.

Kovačić previously had used several methods of narration in his fiction, but the one used in this novel is his most ingenious: *U registraturi* opens as various papers and documents at the registry converse with the protagonist's diary. The body of the novel is made up of the diary's confession, and at the end the author tells how the protagonist in an act of madness torched his diary, all the papers, and himself. Symbolically the registry represents Croatia, where worthless documents gather dust with no apparent hope for action. This sense of hopelessness sets the tone for the entire novel. The book traces Ivica Kičmanović's life from his rather happy childhood in the country through his nightmarish existence in the city, his retreat into the country, and his eventual return to the city. The main message, Kovačić's last, is an open question: education at what cost?

A bright peasant boy, Ivica is taken to a city mansion to help a distant relative, Žorž (Jurić), perform his duties of a butler and to study. While there he meets the master's mistress, sixteen-year-old Laura, and becomes infatuated with her. Having lost his innocence, Ivica loses in due time everything else. The encounter with Laura is the beginning of the end for him. A product of rape, Laura has an incestuous relationship with the master of the house, referred to as Mecena (Maecenas). After Laura kills this man and finds out that he was her natural father, her already-affected psyche suffers a terrible blow. Once a dear little girl whose childhood was a cross between a nightmare and a fairy tale, Laura intends now to live the rest of her life spending Mecena's money with Ivica. But when Ivica wants to legalize their union, Laura is compelled to refuse. Only Ferkonja, an utterly evil man, seems to understand her reasons. When Ivica decides to marry Anica, a girl from his own village, Laura pleads for another chance. Rejected, she forms a band of robbers, goes on a sexual rampage,

and massacres several people in Ivica's wedding party. While the readers and critics were baffled by some of these episodes, members of the church reacted strongly, accusing Kovačić of immorality – a judgment he tried to refute.

Like other women traumatized when young, Laura loses early her chance for a normal life. Through her errant ways she becomes both the embodiment and the symbol of all the negative forces on earth. When Kovačić was writing *U registraturi,* he felt that he and all of humanity were faced with a cruel fate; beyond that he could see nothing else. With the completion of this novel he escaped into madness, only months after he had finally been allowed by the reactionary government of Khuen Hedervary to open his own legal practice in Glina.

His pessimism notwithstanding, Kovačić is remembered today for his love of rural Croatia and its people. His descriptions of village life have been enjoyed by generations of readers. His darker creations, such as Mecena, his servant Žorž, and the poet Bombardirović-Šajkovski in *U registraturi,* have no parallel in all of Croatian literature. Moreover, Kovačić's sharp, realistic criticism of Croatian society was continued by the next generation of writers. Among them was Miroslav Krleža, who coined the word *laurinizam* to express that which Kovačić's Laura personified, achieving a synthesis of various elements which in Kovačić create a cacophony. By doing so, Krleža picked up from where Kovačić left off and placed Croatian literature in the international spotlight.

Letters:

Krešimir Kovačić, "Iz korespondencije i zapisaka Ante Kovačića," *Hrvatsko kolo,* 3, no. 1 (1950): 103–108.

Bibliographies:

Milan Ratković, "Bibliografija radova Ante Kovačića," in Kovačić's *Djela,* volume 1 (Zagreb: Zora, 1950);

M. Selaković and M. Živančević, in *Leksikon pisaca Jugoslavije,* volume 3 (Novi Sad, Yugoslavia: Matica srpska, 1987), pp. 349–351.

References:

Vladimir Anić, *Jezik Ante Kovačića* (Zagreb: Školska knjiga, 1971);

Antun Barac, "Kovačićeva 'Ladanjska sekta' prema Lazarevićevoj 'Školskoj ikoni'," *Prilozi za književnost, jezik, istoriju i filozofiju,* 14, nos. 1–2 (1934): 153–173;

Barac, "Čitajući Kovačića," *Hrvatsko kolo,* 21 (1940): 142–163;

Višnja Barac, "Tragovima lektire Ante Kovačića," *Filologija,* 2 (1959): 111–119;

Aleksandar Flaker, "Ante Kovačić i ruska književnost," *Filologija,* 1 (1957): 101–121;

Flaker, "Kovačić's Novel *In the Registry* and the Stylistic Formation of Realism," in *Comparative Studies in Croatian Literature,* edited by Miroslav Beker (Zagreb: Zavod za znanost i književnosti Filozofskog fakulteta u Zagrebu, 1981), pp. 297–316;

Flaker, "Osebujnost hrvatskog književnopovijesnog procesa XIX stoljeća," *Radovi za slavensku filologiju,* 10 (1968): 69–85;

Ivo Frangeš, "Budjenje Ivice Kičmanovića," *Umjetnost riječi,* 1 (1957): 29–46;

N. Ivanišin, "Optička nijansa hrvatskog lirskog ekspresionizma," *Croatica,* 3 (1972): 133–154;

Krešimir Kovačić, "Književna ostavština Ante Kovačića," *Republika,* 5 (1949): 929–935;

Kovačić, "Odnos grada i sela u književnim djelima Ante Kovačića," *Republika,* 6 (1950): 143–144;

Zvonimir Kulundžić, "Tri priloga o Anti Kovačiću," *Republika,* 29 (1973): 1058–1069;

Milan Marjanović, "Dr. Ante Kovačić," *Savremenik,* 2, no. 2 (1907): 74–84;

Marjanović, "Književni profili: Dr. Ante Kovačić," *Savremenik,* 2 (1907): 74–84;

Marjanović, "Prvaci hrvatskoga realizma," *Brankovo kolo,* 6, nos. 31–32 (1900): 1004–1011;

Antun Gustav Matoš, "Štiocu, predgovor Sabranim pripovijetkama A. Kovačića," in Kovačić's *Djela,* volume 7 (Zagreb: Matica hrvatska, 1938);

Milan Ratković, "Nepoznati rukopisi Ante Kovačića," *Gradja za povijest i književnost Hrvatske,* 14 (1939): 187–240;

Duško Roksandić, "Iz dječačkih uspomena Ivice Kičmanovića," *Umjetnost riječi,* 4, no. 1 (1960): 56–64;

M. Selaković, "Ante Kovačić," *Izvor,* 3, nos. 1–2 (1950): 33–39;

Selaković, "Stihovi Ante Kovačića," *Izvor,* 3, no. 9 (1950): 632–635;

Miroslav Šicel, *Gjalski* (Zagreb: Globus, 1984);

Vice Zaninović, "Ante Kovačić," *Hrvatsko kolo,* 1 (1950): 20–34.

Silvije Strahimir Kranjčević

(17 February 1865 – 29 October 1908)

Ellen Elias-Bursać

BOOKS: *Bugarkinja* (Senj: Marijan Župan, 1885);
Izabrane pjesme (Zagreb: Naklada Matice hrvatske, 1898);
Trzaji (Tuzla: N. Pissenberger and J. Schnürmacher, 1902);
Pjesme (Zagreb: Društvo hrvatskih književnika, 1908);
Odabrane pjesme omladini (Sarajevo: Danijel A. Kajon, 1909);
Pjesnička proza (Zagreb: Društvo hrvatskih književnika, 1912);
Izabrane pjesme (Geneva: Biblioteka jugoslovenske književnosti, 1918);
Pjesme (Zagreb: Matica hrvatska, 1926);
Djela, 4 volumes (Zagreb: Minerva, 1933–1934);
Pjesme (Zagreb: Matica hrvatska, 1943);
Pjesme (Zagreb: Nakladni zavod Hrvatske, 1948);
Sabrana djela, 3 volumes (Zagreb: Jugoslavenska akademija znanosti i umjetnosti, 1958–1965);
Silvije Strahimir Kranjčević: Pjesme, pjesnička proza, kritike, o sebi (Zagreb: Matica hrvatska/Zora, 1964);
Iza spuštenijeh trepavica: Izbor pjesama; Silvije Strahimir Kranjčević (Zagreb: Matica hrvatska, 1989).
Editions in English: Selected poems in *An Anthology of Modern Yugoslav Poetry in English,* translated and edited by Janko Lavrin (London: Calder, 1962), pp. 87–90; and *Introduction to Yugoslav Literature,* edited by Branko Mikasinovich, Dragan Milivojević, and Vasa D. Mihailovich (New York: Twayne, 1973), pp. 335–338;
"Pogled," translated by Carolyn Owlett Hunter as "The Glance," *Journal of Croatian Studies,* 28–29 (1987–1988): 176–179.

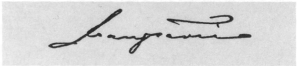

The poetry of Silvije Strahimir Kranjčević spans the turn of the twentieth century: his first volume of poems, *Bugarkinja* (Keening), appeared in 1885, and his last, *Pjesme* (Poems), shortly after his death in 1908. Never fully emancipated from the Romantic and realist postulates of his predecessors, he built on the lyrics of patriotism and love by Petar Preradović, August Šenoa, and August Harambašić before him, yet the new depths he brought to his verse laid the way for the Croatian *Moderna* (modernism), which soon found its voice in the years before World War I.

Pain is the single strongest emotion in Kranjčević's poetry. Though he wrote occasional lyric love poems, his finest poems breathe with his pain. The sincerity of his suffering and the profundity of his anguish for the fate of his community, for his native Croatia, and for humanity are the greatest gifts his verse brought to Croatian and South Slavic literatures.

His life was defined by the Catholic faith his mother cherished and the freethinkers to whom he was drawn. He perceived his struggle as a poet in rejecting a dogmatic definition of life, instead embracing a vision of humanity in nature sustained by toil and suffering in hopes of a better future. This vision is due in part to the fact that Kranjčević was a frail man left to his own resources at a time when all the writers and artists he knew led brief, tragic lives. Thus with the political climate of repression under Austrian governors Benjamin Kallay in Bosnia and Kheun Hedervary in Croatia, which fed the pervasive atmosphere of fin de siècle pessimism, it becomes easier to grasp the despair permeating young Kranjčević's poetry.

Silvije Kranjčević was born in the coastal town of Senj on 17 February 1865. He added his middle name, Strahimir, later in life as the Croatian version of his given name. The third of six children, Kranjčević grew up in a relatively affluent family. His father, Spiridion (Špiro), was a clerk in the Senj magistrate's office; his mother, Marija, was a vital, temperamental woman – well-read, fanatically devout, and given to visions and hallucinations. Kranjčević was also known for his visions as a child and was fond of playing a game called "little altar," popular during his childhood, in which boys built their own altars. His wife in her memoirs says he clung to his mother as a child, preferring to sit with her in the kitchen instead of playing with friends. She died in 1880 when he was fifteen, followed five years later by her husband, leaving Kranjčević to fend for himself.

Kranjčević was drawn during his high-school years to political activity, which took the form of membership in the anticlerical Stranka prava (Party of State Right) movement led by Ante Starčević. A former seminarian, Starčević inevitably drew either intense hatred or intense admiration from his audience. He championed a Croat national radicalism that countered Illyrianism, the literary and political movement dating from the mid eighteenth century that promoted a South Slavic identity and language, insisting on the right to Croatian statehood while boldly denying the very existence of Slovenes and Serbs, claiming instead that they were originally Croats. This inflammatory, emotional rhetoric so fired Kranjčević in the turbulent late 1870s that he offended the Franciscans who ran his high school; his participation in political demonstrations during his final year of schooling provoked them to refuse him permission to matriculate. His father exerted

what authority he could muster in Senj to send Kranjčević to Rome for ecclesiastical study at the Collegium Germanico-Hungaricum, where he was expected to spend the next seven years in study and then join the priesthood.

Kranjčević arrived in Rome in November 1883, but after only six months of lectures in philosophy at the Roman papal university he decided to return home. His letters from Rome convey his despair: "I will be staying seven years here . . . seven long, long years – farewell my homeland, farewell my father's house, and farewell all memory."

These months in Rome decided the young man's mind on several counts. He flatly rejected the dogma of the church or any future professional affiliation with Catholicism. He was resolved to become a teacher and poet; while still in Rome he began to write poems in earnest. This emerging set of convictions, however, cut him off from any support from home in his further studies, catapulting him into the world of pauper-intellectuals at large.

Fearful of his father's wrath, he went to Zagreb rather than Senj upon his return from Rome in 1884. He attended the Zagreb teachers' college, where he earned his teaching certificate in March 1886, aided by support from his benefactor Bishop Josip Juraj Strossmayer. Little is known of his two years spent in Zagreb except for the fact that his father died and that he published his first volume of poetry, *Bugarkinja,* in Senj, both in 1885.

A childhood friend, Milan Gruber, wrote of the circumstances leading up to the publication of Kranjčević's first book of poetry. A local printer, Marijan Župan, had asked Gruber to propose the names of several writers for a series of literary works he could publish to inaugurate his new printing company. Gruber urged his friend to consider publication, and the two pored over the sheaves of poems Kranjčević brought him, polishing the verses that, Gruber recalls, Kranjčević was quick to compose. Their considerations were both artistic and political. Kranjčević, as an impassioned Starčević supporter, wrote not only of the cultural plight of Croatia but of its colonial political position; in particular, the defiant poem "In Tyrannos" was rejected for its volatile political message. The poem was finally published in 1948, forty years after the poet's death.

At first Kranjčević thought to dedicate his first book to a young woman. He changed his mind, however, and decided instead on a dedication to Starčević, but Gruber felt such a controversial political dedication would be far too provocative. Gruber suggested Kranjčević's benefactor Strossmayer, but Kranjčević would not agree because Strossmayer was Starčević's political rival. Finally, they settled on Šenoa, a historical novelist and poet of the Illyrian tradition and one of Kranjčević's key models. The title, *Bugarkinja,* a Slavic custom of keening or wailing in lamentation, was chosen once the collection of poems was more or less complete.

Kranjčević strove to make himself a purely Croatian poet by choosing syllabic schemes closely akin to those used in oral epic poetry, with their eight-, ten-, twelve-, and even sixteen-syllable lines. His poems are generally lengthy and often narrative. He adheres to conventional rhyming schemes. In this first volume there are several lyric poems toward the end, including a fifteen-part collection of sonnets, but he is best remembered for his poems of social and political consciousness. He is consistent throughout in his use of štokavian ijekavian, the Croatian dialect selected by his predecessors the Illyrian writers, as the literary language but also the dialect of his native Senj region.

In 1886, upon earning his certificate as a teacher, he petitioned to the local authorities for a teaching position in Bosnia, for there were no teaching jobs available at that time in Croatia. Kranjčević was assigned to a teaching position in Mostar in late August 1886. Bosnia had come under temporary Austrian custody only a few years before, and the authorities frowned on explicit references to Croatian or Serbian language, culture, or identity. Teachers were expected to teach Bosnian language and literature without mentioning Croatian or Serbian origins. With Kranjčević's long-standing commitment to Starčević's party and his clearly articulated identity as a Croatian poet, such censorship of national identity must have collided directly with his most deeply held convictions and can further explain the emphasis on suffering articulated in his poetry. Once settled in Bosnia and Herzegovina, Kranjčević gradually moved away from a strictly pro-Starčević approach to cultural questions. Despite his youthful enthusiasm for Starčević's platform, he demonstrated a moderation and tolerance in his contacts with, and admiration for, Serbian writers – particularly Jovan Dučić, Jovan Jovanović Zmaj, Ljubomir Nedić, and others – that went far beyond the binding constraints of Starčević's ultra-Croatian views.

During the next seven years Kranjčević was transferred four times. He stayed in Mostar for no more than six months and was then reassigned, supposedly after a minor political incident, to a post in Livno, where he spent the remainder of the school year and all of the next. He then went to Bijeljina for a longer stay of four years. After this he re-turned for a year to Livno, and finally in October 1893 he was dispatched to Sarajevo, where he lived until his death in 1908. He never relinquished the hope of finding employment in the Zagreb area and petitioned the authorities on several occasions to find a position in Croatia, but to no avail. The years Kranjčević spent moving from one Bosnian town to another, when he wrote his finest verse, were also his most productive as a poet. His poems first appeared in literary magazines in Croatia and Bosnia, particularly in *Vijenac* (Wreath) in Zagreb.

Upon moving to Sarajevo he was first assigned a teaching post but was soon transferred by the local authorities to an editorial position in the newly founded *Nada* (Hope), a literary magazine started in 1894. His work as an editor further established him in the literary world in Zagreb and Sarajevo by allowing him to cultivate contacts with writers. The journal was designed to provide the population with writing, prose, and poetry to meet their cultural needs and inform other South Slavic communities of the literary and cultural events in Bosnia and Herzegovina. The national identity of all contributing authors was to be deemphasized in the journal, as it had been in Kranjčević's teaching positions, in keeping with the repressive Austrian cultural policy of the day, which perceived a threat to the stability of the region in nurturing an awareness of membership in the Croatian and Serbian communities.

During his eight years with *Nada,* Kranjčević wrote numerous essays, reviews, and short prose pieces, but these are not accorded the same significance as his poetry. One such prose piece, "Pogled" (translated by Carolyn Owlett Hunter as "The Glance"), can be found in the *Journal of Croatian Studies.* Though literary translation was not a major preoccupation for Kranjčević, he also tried his hand at rendering some of Heinrich Heine's verse and fragments of Lord Byron's *Mazeppa* (1819) and William Shakespeare's *Julius Caesar* (1599).

In 1898, after having worked at *Nada* for four years and become an established literary figure through his first book and periodical publications, Kranjčević married Ela Kašaj, daughter of a military frontier officer. They continued to live in Sarajevo, where she worked as a teacher. They had one child, a daughter named Višnja. Eight days after their wedding Kranjčević proposed the publication of a collection of poetry to the renowned firm Matica Hrvatska in Zagreb, and it was accepted.

Izabrane pjesme (Selected Poems), with sixty-three poems and the oratorio *Prvi grijeh* (First Sin), came out in 1898 in Zagreb. Four of the poems were taken from *Bugarkinja* and presented in revised form.

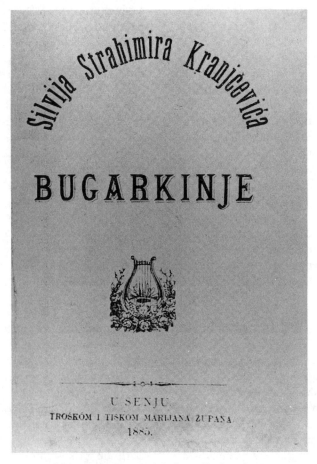

Title page for Kranjčević's first collection of poems

The others had appeared in periodicals, with the exception of ten poems published for the first time. This collection represents Kranjčević at his finest, including "Iza spuštenijeh trepavica" (Behind Lowered Lashes), "Lucida intervalla," "Eli! Eli! lamâ azâvtani?," "Zadnji Adam" (The Last Adam), "Mojsije" (Moses), and "Moj dom" (My Home). Mostly lengthy poems, some of them are sweeping laments such as "Mojsije" (206 lines in seven irregular stanzas):

> Lead my people out, O Lord.
> Lead them out of doleful bondage.
> And cast off from drowsy lids
> Scales encrusted, scales still direful
> That now shackle up their eyes!
> Call to mind how cheerless slavery
> Like that ponderous tombstone there
> Weighed upon my brother's shoulders;
> How our torturers condemned
> In our women's wombs our children:
> Great Jehovah! Be thou kind!
> Cast a curse on torturing tyrants

> And my people save, O Lord!
> – English translation by I. Titunik

Others are more regular in form, such as "Moj dom" (twelve four-line stanzas):

> Indeed I have a homeland; my heart is where it dwells,
> Replete with hill and plain;
> I seek a place where my paradise I may spread,
> And . . . swallow my pain.

The oratorio *Prvi grijeh,* first published in 1893 in *Vijenac* in Zagreb, was written as a libretto for composer Ivan Zajc. Apparently Kranjčević was commissioned in 1892 by the Kolo choral society in Zagreb to write the libretto. It was first staged as a concert with three performances at the Croatian National Theater in Zagreb in April 1907. In 1912 it was held four times to celebrate Zajc's eightieth birthday, and in 1948 segments of it were given at the Croatian National Theater in Zagreb to commemorate the fortieth anniversary of Kranjčević's death.

In 1902, three years after *Izabrane pjesme* appeared, Kranjčević's third volume of verse, *Trzaji* (Strumming), was published in Tuzla, Bosnia, with forty-three poems, including ten predating *Izabrane pjesme;* the others were new. While Janko Polić Kamov speaks of this collection with admiration – "and (herein) the tragedy of our Silvije approaches a catastrophe, one that is quiet, profound, modern" – Augustin ("Tin") Ujević dislikes the book, preferring Kranjčević's earlier work.

A major controversy broke out between Catholic literary critics, on the one hand, and freethinking anticlerical critics, on the other, upon the publication of Kranjčević's second and third volumes of poetry in 1898 and 1902. The dogmatic Catholic critic Antun Mahnič was the first to attack the antidogmatic implications in Kranjčević's philosophy of people finding solace and strength in work and nature rather than in the church. He published angry reviews of *Izabrane pjesme* and *Trzaji* in the journal *Hrvatska straza* in 1903 under the pseudonym "Criticus," accusing Kranjčević of Socialist inclinations – Kranjčević expressly names work as a source of human salvation – and of being a Darwinist. Regarding form and artistic skill Mahnič admits that Kranjčević stands above his contemporaries, but though Kranjčević uses the name of God in his verse Mahnič sees this as no more than a mask to conceal the "starkness of his godless sciences" of materialism, pantheism, and Buddhism. He accuses Kranjčević of replacing faith in God with faith in his own strength and labor, claiming that these beliefs spring directly from modern socialism.

Other Catholic literary critics responded to Mahnič's scathing attacks with a more compassionate reading of Kranjčević's poetry. Jakša Čedomil speaks of the poet with sympathy, finding in even the least religious of his poems elements of Christian virtue, compassion for suffering, absolution, and forgiveness. Ferdo Rožić criticizes Kranjčević for overglorifying the role of reason yet concludes with the prediction that Kranjčević will one day become a "resonant Christian genius."

Milan Marjanović, a freethinking Zagreb literary critic, responded by praising Kranjčević for all the very traits of his writing that the church found offensive and applauding his libertarian rejection of dogma. It is apparent, however, that both Marjanović and his Catholic literary rivals read Kranjčević only for his political message, dwelling only briefly if at all on his qualities as a poet.

Later poets, writers, and scholars, however, gave Kranjčević's work more serious and studied consideration. Antun Gustav Matoš says of Kranjčević that with the "force of his altruism and the impact of his powerful voice he was the first modern name of Croatian literature, the purest voice, indeed, of Croatian consciousness." Miroslav Krleža defines Kranjčević's most fundamental trait as "his breakthrough from timeworn clichéd phrases into the realm of the unsaid." Kamov says that Kranjčević "suffered but was no ascetic; he wrote of love, not infatuation; his was passion without joy, pleasure without happiness, and laughter without humor." Antun Barac claims that Kranjčević's poem "Mojsije" can be compared to Alfred De Vigny's poem "Moïse," but that Kranjčević's is stronger than De Vigny's. In intensity and adequacy of expression Kranjčević stands as an equal, while only from an organic standpoint is he weaker.

In 1903 *Nada* was terminated. A lively debate ensued between the local authorities and dignitaries of the Sarajevo Catholic church regarding Kranjčević's next post. He was proposed either for the position of principal of the Sarajevo women's teachers' college or superintendent of girls' and women's education there. The latter was immediately opposed by Josip Štadler, archbishop of Sarajevo. Štadler accused Kranjčević of having written "travesties bereft of all Christian spirit, aggrievously injuring religious Christian sentiment." He refused to allow such a godless man to act as superintendent for the Catholic girls' school in Sarajevo.

In response the Sarajevo administration agreed to have Kranjčević's books read and these accusations considered, but they defended the poet against the church authorities. Kranjčević was granted the job of superintendent, but he was cautioned that he would not be able to exercise his authority in the Sarajevo Catholic schools. The swing in favor of Kranjčević in this case reflects a wave of liberalization in the Bosnian administration, which coincided with the death of the Austrian governor Kallay, whose earlier repressive policies had constrained Kranjčević in his years as a teacher.

Kranjčević had little time to enjoy the relative prosperity of his new and rather prestigious position. Complaints related to kidney and bladder problems began to afflict him with increasing seriousness. There may have been a first operation in Sarajevo in 1902; in fact, letters and other sources suggest that the complaint may have dated back to the 1890s. In September 1906 Kranjčević finally decided the Sarajevo doctors were not offering him adequate treatment and decided to go to Vienna. The operation in Vienna took place in late November, but Kranjčević's convalescence was so protracted, the wound so slow to heal, that he could not leave

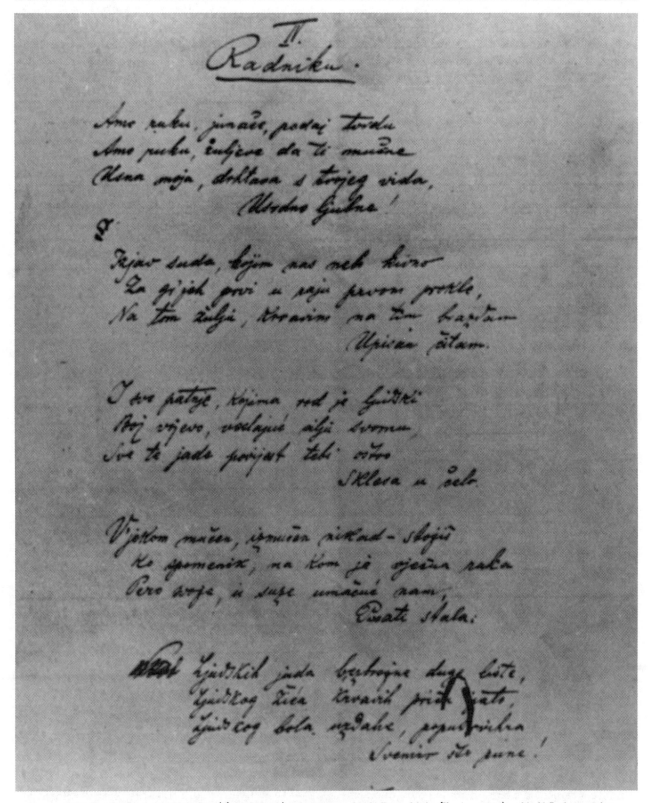

Manuscript for Kranjčević's poem "Radniku" (To the Laborer), which appeared in his Bugarkinja *(Keening, 1885) and in his* Izabrana pjesme *(Selected Poems, 1898); manuscript located in Sarajevo*

the hospital until August 1907. During his stay in Austria he wrote almost daily to his wife in Sarajevo, leaving those interested in him and his work a poignant record of the acute suffering he underwent in those months. His letters to Ela indicate that he was visited by several prominent cultural figures while at the hospital, including Ivan Meštrović and his wife Ruža, Josip Kosor, Milan Ogrizović, and Adela and Andrija Milčinović.

Ela Kranjčević went to Vienna to help her husband return to Sarajevo in June 1907, but she had to wait two months for him to recover from a bout of fever. When he finally did leave the hospital he was so frail that he could hardly walk. The incision from the November operation never healed properly. They first went to visit her sister and brother-in-law in Zagreb on their way back to Sarajevo. Another bout of fever subsided by mid-August, permitting them to continue on to Sarajevo.

The costly treatment and hospitalization drained the Kranjčevićs' financial resources. The Croatian Writers' Association gave them small sums of aid twice and decided in 1908 to publish a volume of his collected poetry; the proceeds from the publication would be sent to help defray his medical costs. However, they came too late. The collection was published by the association shortly after his death as *Pjesme* (Poems). It includes twenty-one poems, four of which had come out before 1902.

He went in for one last operation in Sarajevo in July 1908 but never recovered, and he died on 29 October 1908 at the age of forty-four. His wife died three years later of tuberculosis at the age of thirty-five. Just as his life had been a source of ongoing controversy, so was his death. A Sarajevo bishop hurried to his bedside to administer the last rites while Kranjčević was unconscious, against the poet's express wishes to the contrary. Matoš attended the funeral and commented on it bitterly. The church was so apprehensive that the funeral might be used as an occasion for antidogmatic attacks that they would allow no one to speak at the graveside. The cultural figures who attended, most of them from Sarajevo and outlying areas, gathered outside the entranceway to the cemetery, where they held their speeches. Matoš was outraged that no one from the Croatian Writers' Association had come. When a later initiative called for exhuming Kranjčević's body from the Sarajevo cemetery and taking it to Zagreb to be buried at the Mirogoj cemetery, the Croats in Bosnia were offended at the belated expression of interest and refused to allow it.

Like many of his contemporaries, Silvije Strahimir Kranjčević never received a full education. Thwarted by his refusal to accept a church education yet constrained in financial support for other educational opportunities, he was forced to limit himself to a rudimentary teacher's training, which did not allow him to develop fully as a writer. Later writers find his poetry repetitive, particularly in the anthologies after 1900, and choose only a few of his poems to admire, yet all agree that, fueled by his rebellious nature and his deep commitment to Croatian culture, Kranjčević wrote verse that brought a new depth to the understanding of the Croatian plight and a more serious role for literature. More than merely patriotic, his poems are genuinely tragic. As his illness claimed what hope he held as a young man, his pessimism grew until bitterness and despair were the prevalent sentiments his poems expressed. Although he was quickly seen as an important poet after the publication of *Bugarkinja* and *Izabrane pjesme,* he could not boast of support from the writing community in Croatia; this was an age when writers throughout the South Slavic community fared poorly. His poetry, for all its depth and tragic sense of suffering, did not break away enough from the Romantic examples of his predecessors to earn him the status of an innovator; rather, he is considered a link between the Romantic realists of the nineteenth century and the modernists of the prewar turn of the century.

No book-length translations of his work exist in English, but three poems – "Mojsije" (translated by I. Titunik in an excerpt), "Hristova slika" (The Painting of Christ, translated by G. Komai), and "U želji ljubavi" (Love's Desire, translated by Komai) – appear both in Janko Lavrin's *Anthology of Modern Yugoslav Poetry*, and in the anthology *Introduction to Yugoslav Literature.*

Letters:

Illija Kecmanović, ed., *Prepiska Silvija S. Kranjčevića* (Sarajevo: Svjetlost, 1966).

Biography:

Illija Kecmanović, *Silvije Strahimir Kranjčević: Život i delo* (Sarajevo: Narodna prosvjeta, 1958).

References:

Antun Barac, "De Vigny, Carducci, Kranjčević," *Hrvatsko kolo*, 10 (1929): 194–220;

Vladimir Ćorović, "Lektira Silvija Strahimira Kranjčevića," *Gradja za povijest književnosti hrvatske*, 10 (1927): 1–100;

Ivo Frangeš, "Rani Kranjčević," *Letopis Matice srpske,* 144 (December 1958): 443–465;

Marin Franičević, "Današnji Kranjčević," in his *Pisci i problemi* (Zagreb: Kultura, 1948), pp. 105–134;

Milan Gruber, "Iz djetinjstva imladosti S. S. Kranjčevića," *Obzor,* 257–262 (1933): n.p.;

Albert Haler, "O poeziji Silvija Strahimira Kranjčevića," *Srpski književni glasnik,* 27 (1929): 265–274, 356–361, 434–443;

Ante Kadić, "Kranjčević's Jesus on the Barricades," in his *The Tradition of Freedom in Croatian Literature* (Bloomington, Ind.: The Croatian Alliance, 1983), pp. 181–215;

Janko Polić Kamov, "Silvije Strahimir Kranjčević, *Bosanka vila* (1910): 12–13;

Miroslav Krieža, "O Kranjčevićevoj lirici," *Hrvatska revija,* 4 (March 1931): 137–158;

Branimir Livadić, "Život i poezija Silvija Strahimira Kranjčevića," foreword to Kranjčeviľs *Pjesme* (Zagreb: Matica hrvatska, 1926), pp. iii–liii;

A. G. Matoš, "U sjeni velikog imena," *Savremenik,* 3, no. 12 (1908): 705–714;

Dragutin Tadijanović, "Napomene uz *Sabrana djela Silvija Strahimira Kranjčevića,*" in *Sabrana djela Silvija Strahimira Kranjčevića,* (Zagreb: Jugoslavenska akademija znanosti i umjetnosti, 1958), I: 535–562, II: 493–528;

Tin Ujević, "Trnokop u Silvijevoj bašti," *Pregled,* 7 (November 1933): 631–639;

Šime Vučetić, "Kranjčević," in his *Izmedju dogme i apsurda* (Zagreb: Matica Hrvatska, 1960), pp. 78–162.

Papers:

Kranjčević's papers are kept in several places. The Muzej grada Sarajeva (City Museum of Sarajevo) holds poetry, personal manuscripts, and documents, as does the Nacionalna sveučilišna biblioteka (National University Library) in Zagreb. Other repositories of his personal effects and related documents are the Zemaljski muzej (Regional Museum) in Sarajevo and the Institut za teatrologiju i književnost, HAZU (Croatian Academy Institute for Theater Studies and Literature).

Miroslav Krleža

(7 July 1893 – 29 December 1981)

Ante Kadić
Indiana University

BOOKS: *Pan* (Zagreb, 1917);
Tri simfonije (Zagreb: Društvo hrvatskih književnika, 1917);
Hrvatska rapsodija (Zagreb: Djordje Ćelap, 1918);
Pjesme, 3 volumes (Zagreb, 1918–1919);
Lirika (Zagreb: Jug, 1919);
Hrvatski bog Mars (Zagreb: Narodna knjižnica, 1922);
Novele (Koprivnica: Vinko Vošicki, 1923);
Vučjak (Koprivnica: Vinko Vošicki, 1923);
Sabrana djela, 3 volumes (Koprivnica: Vinko Vošicki, 1923–1926);
Vražji otok (Zagreb: Neva, 1924);
Izlet u Rusiju (Zagreb: Narodna knjižnica, 1926);
Gospoda Glembajevi (Zagreb: Društvo hrvatskih književnika, 1928);
Knjiga pjesama (Belgrade: Geca Kon, 1931);
U agoniji (Belgrade: Srpska književna zadruga, 1931);
Knjiga lirike (Zagreb: Minerva, 1932);
Povratak Filipa Latinovicza (Zagreb: Minerva, 1932);
Eseji (Zagreb: Minerva, 1932);
Moj obračun s njima (Zagreb, 1932);
Glembajevi (Zagreb: Minerva, 1932);
Sabrana djela, 9 volumes (Zagreb: Minerva, 1932–1934);
Simfonije (Zagreb: Minerva, 1933);
Hiljadu i jedna smrt (Zagreb: Minerva, 1933);
Podravski motivi (Zagreb: Minerva, 1933);
Legende (Zagreb: Minerva, 1933);
U logoru. Vučjak (Zagreb: Minerva, 1934);
Evropa danas (Zagreb: Biblioteka aktuelnih pitanja, 1935);
Balade Petrice Kerempuha (Ljubljana: Akademska založba, 1936);
Pjesme u tmini (Zagreb: Biblioteka nezavisnih pisaca, 1937);
Novele (Zagreb: Biblioteka nezavisnih pisaca, 1937);
Deset krvavihgodina (Zagreb: Bibliotekanezavisnih pisaca, 1937);
Golgota (Zagreb: Biblioteka nezavisnih pisaca, 1937);
Djela Miroslava Krleže, 11 volumes (Zagreb: Biblioteka nezavisnih pisaca, 1937–1939);

Miroslav Krleža

Banket u Blitvi I (Zagreb: Biblioteka nezavisnih pisaca, 1938);
Knjiga proze (Zagreb: Biblioteka nezavisnih pisaca, 1938);
Na rubu pameti (Zagreb: Biblioteka nezavisnih pisaca, 1938);
Eppur si muove: studije i osvrti (Zagreb: Biblioteka nezavisnih pisaca, 1938);
Banket u Blitvi II (Zagreb: Biblioteka nezavisnih pisaca, 1939);

Dijalektički antibarbarus (Zagreb: Biblioteka nezavisnih pisaca, 1939);

Knjiga studija i putopisa (Zagreb: Biblioteka nezavisnih pisaca, 1939);

Račić (Zagreb: Nakladni zavod Hrvatske, 1947);

Goya (Zagreb: Nakladni zavod Hrvatske, 1948);

O Marinu Držiću (Belgrade: Prosveta, 1949);

Djetinjstvo u Agramu 1902–1903 (Zagreb: Zora, 1952);

Govor na Kongresu književnika u Ljubljani (Zagreb: Zora, 1952);

Pijana noć četrnaestog novembra 1918 (Zagreb: Zora, 1952);

Sabrana djela, 27 volumes (Zagreb: Zora, 1952–1972);

O Erazmu Rotterdamskom (Zagreb: Zora, 1953);

Kalendar jedne bitke godine 1942 (Zagreb: Zora, 1953);

O parlamentarizmu i demokraciji kod nas (Zagreb: Zora, 1953);

Kako stoje stvari (Zagreb: Zora, 1953);

Davni dani (Zagreb: Zora, 1956);

Eseji (Belgrade: Prosveta, 1958);

Aretej (Zagreb: Zora, 1959);

Eseji I–IV, 4 volumes (Zagreb: Zora, 1961–1967);

Banket u Blitvi I–III, 3 volumes in 2 (Zagreb: Zora, 1964);

Zastave I–IV (Zagreb: Zora, 1967);

Put u raj (Zagreb: JAZU, 1970);

Panorama pogleda, pojava i pojmova I–V (Sarajevo: Oslobodjenje, 1975);

Zastave I–V (Sarajevo: Oslobodjenje, 1976);

Dnevnik I–V (Sarajevo: Oslobodjenje, 1977);

Iz naše književne krčme (Sarajevo: Oslobodjenje, 1983);

Ratne teme (Sarajevo: Oslobodjenje, 1983);

Sa uredničkog stola (Sarajevo: Oslobodjenje, 1983).

Editions in English: "The Hut Five B," translated by Dorian Cooke, *New World Writing,* no. 11 (1957): 176–188;

The Return of Philip Latinovicz, translated by Zora Depolo (London: Lincolns-Prager, 1959; New York: Vanguard Press, 1969);

"Hodorlahomor the Great," translated by Drenka Willen, and "The Love of Marcel Faber-Fabriczy for Miss Laura Warronigg," translated by Branko Lenski, in *Death of a Simple Giant, and Other Modern Yugoslav Stories,* edited by Lenski (New York: Vanguard Press, 1965), pp. 55–83, 85–99;

"The First Mass of Alojz Tiček," translated by Svetozar Koljević, in *Yugoslav Short Stories,* edited by Koljević (London: Oxford University Press, 1966), pp. 236–289;

The Cricket Beneath the Waterfall, and Other Stories, edited by Lenski (New York: Vanguard Press, 1972);

On the Edge of Reason, translated by Depolo (New York: Vanguard Press, 1976);

"Kristofor Kolumbo," *Scena,* 1 (1978): 135–147;

"Croatian Rhapsody," translated by B. S. Brusar, *Most,* 1–2 (1982): 93–108;

"The Battle at Bistrica Lesna," translated by Brusar, *Most,* 3 (1984): 62–77;

"Kraljevo," translated by Alan McConnell-Duff, *Scena,* 7 (1984): 50–64;

"The Noble Glembays," translated by Tim Bowen, *Scena,* 9 (1986): 253–291;

"At the Mind's Edge," translated by McConnell-Duff, *Scena,* 12 (1989): 182–200.

OTHER: *Enciklopedija Jugoslavije,* 8 volumes, edited by Krleža (Zagreb: Leksikografski zavod, 1955–1971).

Miroslav Krleža, generally considered the greatest Croatian writer of the twentieth century, was born in Zagreb on 7 July 1893. After completing high school, he was sent to Hungary, first to the officers' school in Pecs and then to the military academy in Budapest. At that time many Croatian intellectuals hoped that Serbia's role in the struggle for national liberation and unification would be similar to the central part of the Piedmont in the unification of Italy. Although an Austro-Hungarian officer, Krleža, who espoused this ideal, crossed the border and volunteered to serve in the Serbian war against the Turks (1913). Serbian authorities became suspicious of Krleža, however, and expelled him. He was subsequently arrested by the Austrians, deprived of his rank, and, after Austria-Hungary declared war on Serbia in July 1914, was sent to the front as a private.

During World War I, in Galicia and on other Austrian fronts, Krleža came into close contact with Croatian peasants and workers, who were being killed en masse for the "despised German kaiser." These simple and honest people had a deep yearning for decent family life and social justice and desired the expulsion of all exploiters from their fields and villages.

Disillusioned over his "nationalistic" dreams and suffering with the underprivileged, Krleža greeted the October 1917 revolution in Russia as a starting point for a new and better world. Alone or with other leftist writers, Krleža edited literary journals, including *Plamen* (Flame, 1919), *Književna republika* (Literary Republic, 1923–1927), *Danas* (Today, 1934), and *Pečat* (Stamp, 1939–1940). Although most of them were short-lived, being banned by police authorities, they played an important role in orienting many Yugoslav intellectuals toward "progressive" goals.

Miroslav Krleža

During World War II Krleža was in constant danger; rumors were spread abroad that he was dead. He wrote a great deal, but this work was not published until later. Since he did not join the Partisans during the war, he was in disgrace for a while after 1945, but soon he was rehabilitated by Tito. From 1952 on, Krleža was a driving force in liberalizing Yugoslav culture. In 1967 he sided with Croatians defending the use of their own language, but after the drastic ukase of Tito against Croatian political leaders and prominent intellectuals (1 December 1971), Krleža kept silent.

From 1950 until 1977, when he became ill, Krleža was director of the Lexicographic Institute in Zagreb. He was also the editor in chief of *Enciklopedija Jugoslavije* (Encyclopedia of Yugoslavia, 1955–1971). Unfortunately, it overpraises the Partisan fighters and slanders or omits discussion of the enemies of communism.

Krleža's first published work was the antireligious play *Legenda* (Legend, 1914) in *Književne novosti* (Literary News). In it he portrays Jesus and his relations with Mary, sister of Lazarus. She is in love with Jesus; he knows it but prefers to reject her advances. His shadow, or alter ego, tries to convince him that he should not fly too high because only ter-restrial things have real substance and can procure worthy pleasure; the rest is smoke and purely cerebral invention. The play, full of historical allusions and premonitions, is difficult to perform; its unity lies in the writer's conviction that Jesus was untrue to himself and his better feelings.

In the same spirit and pattern – a mixture of history, materialist preaching, and rejection of religious belief – Krleža wrote other "legends," such as *Cristoval Colon* (Christopher Columbus, 1917), and *Mikelandjelo Buonaroti* (Michelangelo Buonarroti, 1918).

Although *Legenda* is filled with lyrical elements (moonlight, stars, birds, and two lovers who speak in the language of the Song of Solomon), *Mikelandjelo Buonaroti* is more poetic. In this play Krleža does not indulge in lyrical phraseology; his Michelangelo is a sensitive soul who loves roses, caresses a spider within its web, feeds mice, sings to the rays of the sun, and is enchanted by the magic power of colors. Krleža's Michelangelo reminds one of Francis of Assisi, and at certain moments one is aware that the author is recalling Francis's *Cantico di Frati Sole* (Canticle of Brother Sun, early thirteenth century).

Michelangelo was willing to renounce legitimate pleasures, such as wine and women, for the solitary path of artistic creation. To paraphrase Anton Chekhov's statement, an artist may have a legitimate wife (his daily job) but his mistress (art) is dearer to him than his wife. Michelangelo and Krleža were each happy in the exclusive company of their mistresses.

Christopher Columbus is the most consistent among Krleža's visionaries. Christ dies so that others will cherish his memory, while he is aware that his cause is forever lost. Michelangelo degrades himself to create beauty for which mankind would gladly forgive him his weakness. Columbus discovers the New World, but he immediately senses that his great discovery will serve purposes totally alien to his goals – in the new continent, as in the old, there will be interest and profit, banking enterprises, greed, slaves, rulers and ruled, rich and poor. Columbus lets "the pygmies" enjoy the fruits of his labors. He is one of those predestined to dream because no reality can satisfy their yearning. Even stars become muddy, they say, in contact with the earth and its inhabitants.

Krleža continued to depict important historical figures as legendary heroes, visionaries, individuals tormented by anxiety over the validity of their own goals or the capacity of the masses to follow them. Lenin too, in Krleža's subsequent writing, has much in common with all those who have suffered for their ideals. Lenin is not a real man, such as we know him from history; he is a myth, an idol whom Krleža had adorned with superlative qualities. He is the saint whose shrine is in the middle of Moscow, and Krleža is happy to worship there.

In 1917 Krleža published the "expressionistic" poem *Pan,* in which he chants the beauty of nature and joys of life as opposed to Christian self-abnegation. He is sure that the final triumph will be with man's natural inclinations. Krleža's "symphony" is "Ulica u jesenje jutro" (A Street in an Autumn Morning, 1919): his countrymen boast about military success, forgetting that their dear ones are hungry and their roofs are falling in.

The same or similar themes — war and its horror, the rejection of the past and belief in a brighter future, peace of mind found in the midst of the native landscape — are interwoven in Krleža's subsequent collections of poetry. The most important are: *Lirika* (Lyrics, 1919); *Knjiga lirike* (A Book of Lyrics, 1932); and *Pjesme u tmini* (Poems in the Darkness, 1937).

Krleža was revolted by his war experiences, and he returned to the theme of this trauma in all of his writings. Thus, in the poem "Rat" (War) he sees darkness reigning everywhere and hears sleeping humans crying in their blood-filled dreams. To protect themselves they

> At the scorching fury of the war
> strike nails into their doors
> as into coffin lids.
>
> But in the night Someone Unknown
> will shake and break those locks
> and hang black banners from the roofs.

Death is a daily phenomenon; in vain the people try to escape it, but it reaches them where they least expect. Even when he walks through the snow, the poet feels a pain:

> I know all this will pass,
> and traces of myself will vanish
> even quicker than the snow beneath my feet.
> And none will know that I was here and then gone.

In his "Plameni vjetar" (Burning Wind, 1918) Krleža foresees the final destruction of all "lies," and in his well-known "Noć u provinciji" (Night in the Province, 1930) he compares reactionaries to dogs barking at the moon:

> Dogs bark. They bark furiously, senselessly, frantically,
> dogs bark stupidly, vainly, fanatically

at everything that moves: at lights, noises and shadows,
at the moon, suspicions, people unknown. . . .

> Oh canine congress, you bark, the caravans move on,
> hooves are heard, creaking wheels, the sound of harness.
> Vainly your barking pours your hate on passers,
> all move on, disappear, you on chains like blind shadows
> wait for fate, to die a dog's death with you here beside the
> fence.

Having rejected his pristine Christian faith, Krleža saw Jesus as a man of questionable teaching and dubious moral values. Krleža wrote that Jesus' mother was easy prey because nobody knows who made her pregnant. When he visited churches, he was interested only in examining their architecture; afterward he became bored and began dozing:

> Sitting and dreaming, bleak and dumb in the grey
> of the church. Blissfully drowsing the time away.
> Dead saints and mildewed books, God dead and gone.
> Outside the bleating of sheep goes on and on.

Krleža's masterpiece of form and style is *Balade Petrice Kerempuha* (The Ballads of Petrica Kerempuh, 1936), written in the kajkavian (northern Croatia) dialect. Kerempuh is an equivalent of the German Till Eulenspiegel, a peasant clown who enjoys playing tricks on persons of higher rank. In *Balade Petrice Kerempuha* Krleža describes the sufferings of the Croatian peasants from the time of Matija Gubec and his comrades (1573) to the present. The Illyrian movement (the Croatian political and cultural revival) and abolition of serfdom (1848) did not change their intolerable situation. As Krleža wrote in "Galženjačka" (The Song of the Gallows Bird):

> Through all times and eternity
> the gallows are the only remedy.
>
> Streams of blood will flow away,
> flow for ever and a day.
>
> From out this hell there is no way:
> the rich grow fat — poor Tom must pay.

In Petrica's songs, heavily influenced by folk poetry, Krleža speaks bitterly, but effectively, against noblemen, clergymen, and bureaucrats. His protest is conveyed in a masterful way.

The hardships of the Croatian peasants — particularly during World War I — and the decadence of the aristocrats and the middle class are the main themes of Krleža's short stories and plays; in these two forms he reached his greatest achievement.

Krleža with Ivo Andrić in Zagreb, 1960

In his deeply moving collection of short stories *Hrvatski bog Mars* (The Croatian God Mars, 1922), dealing with the Croatian *domobrani* (home guards), there are two stories that merit particular attention. "Bitka kod Bistrice Lesne" (A Battle at Bistrica Lesna) describes the tragic end of seven Croatian peasants in Galicia, while at home their children are starving; their wives drink out of desperation; and their fields remain uncultivated. "Baraka pet be" (The Hut Five B) deals also with the bloody fighting in Galicia and points to its consequences: a hospital full of patients who are divided into three categories — those with broken and protruding bones, those with amputated legs and arms, and those whose last moment is rapidly approaching. Similarly, the play *Hrvatska rapsodija* (The Croatian Rhapsody, 1918) is a vision of Croatia and its centuries-long suffering under the cruel Magyar dominations. A train is carrying the entire nation toward the battlefield; sick, hungry, mad, desperate, and bigoted people are sketched in the same tableau. Krleža is convinced that such a train must fall into an abyss to make room for a more logical existence.

Among Krleža's stories dealing with bourgeois society, "Prva misa Alojza Tičeka" (The First Mass of Alojz Tiček, 1921) is usually cited as representative of his work. In it he describes the Old World, when the closely knit powers of home, police, and church tried to suppress all manifestations of individual freedom. Alojz, the eldest son of the police sergeant Tiček, is sent to the seminary so that his brother Ivica can go to the high school. Ivica is a Jacobin and Darwinist and would give his life to see "a real revolution with the guillotine cutting people's heads off, the 'Marseillaise' sung at the top of everyone's voice, and the city burning." The third and youngest brother, a soldier, justifies his choice of career with the following argument: "If there were no barracks, there would be no church. And if there were no church, there would be no God." Many talented children of poor families entered the ecclesiastical or military ranks to escape the sad destiny of their kin. In this otherwise plausible tableau, however, Krleža includes some dramatic (or grotesque) and unnecessary episodes. The same day that he celebrates his first mass, Alojz secretly meets his girlfriend. He loves her, but he sacrifices their future happiness together for fear of displeasing his bigoted and selfish parents. During a banquet a fat monsignor, who has had a scandalous love affair with a baroness, sits at the head of a table and utters nonsensical platitudes. Krleža, a gifted writer, at times succumbed to the temptation to ridicule — to the point of caricature — those whom he disliked.

In another story, "Cvrčak pod vodopadom" (The Cricket Beneath the Waterfall, 1937), the narrator is disturbed by the doctors who give him various medications, some of which create symptoms that others are then supposed to cure. In a tavern the narrator meets a friend, Doctor Siroček, an incurable optimist who suggests to him that he take off his dark glasses. He invites him into the latrine where once he heard the voice of a cricket beneath the flushing water. Dr. Siroček carries bread crumbs in his pocket to feed the cricket. This astonishing tale, which begins with the confession of someone who has suffered a nervous breakdown and holds long conversations with the dead throughout the night, ends by saying that there is beauty everywhere, if only one can see it.

As many other writers have done, Krleža has depicted a particular family in several works. Attempting to portray the ascent and decline of capitalist society in eleven stories and three plays about the Glembay family, Krleža shows how this Croatian clan, whose peasant ancestor acquired riches by killing a Styrian goldsmith, gradually moves into higher circles. Its descendants are bankers, businessmen, government officials, and generals. Their moral dissoluteness grows in proportion to their wealth. They can prosper only in the antinational and antisocialist Austro-Hungarian monarchy, of which they are obedient servants. When the dual monarchy disintegrates in 1918, all the Glembays become nervous wrecks, ready to commit crimes or suicide. In the moment of their downfall Krleža shows them as degenerates and criminals, castigating the capitalist system that they represent.

Whereas in legends Krleža was romantic and symbolistic (in the manner of Oscar Wilde) and in his "expressionistic" *Hrvatska rapsodija* he concentrated on external action, in his dramas about the Glembays, under the influence by Henrik Ibsen, he tried a new method: a psychological dialogue, with few characters and extremely limited action.

Gospoda Glembajevi (The Glembays, 1928) centers on the conflict between Ignjat Glembay and his son Leone; whereas the old Glembay is an embodiment of the negative aspects of his class, Leone is an educated and refined gentleman. In the first act the audience senses an oncoming storm in the innuendos of the intense dialogue between father and son. In the second and third acts, when hidden passions and hatred surge to the surface, all semblances betray their real natures.

U agoniji (In Agony, 1931), Krleža's best play, was written in the same year as *Gospoda Glembajevi*. In the first act Baron Lenbach commits suicide after a humiliating quarrel with his wife, Laura. For three years Laura has loved the lawyer Ivan Križovec and hoped to be his wife, but now she discovers that his interest in her was only transient.

Laura's faint suspicion suddenly becomes certitude; she is now able to draw conclusions from certain expressions and movements. She has noticed these same details before but has been unable to comprehend them because she was blindly in love. Now, when it is too late, she grasps everything:

I remember in the semidarkness of the auditorium I felt your body, you, and I was unable to control myself; I put out my hand toward you and I looked at you. At that moment, in the auditorium, everything happened between you and me that could possibly have happened. The light was shining on you. To your right, two rows in front of us, sat an unknown woman. You were flirting with her. All that was like a flash, and then it went out. I forgot it, but now I see that what happened in that flash was everything. Your glance in the eyes of that strange woman, my movement toward you, that

was everything! I wanted a child by you that night. Yes, I so wanted to feel your hand, but you . . . .

Lenbach was a degenerate and a drunkard; Križovec is an egoist and careerist, while Laura vibrates with intelligence, passion, and sincerity. There are few, if any, pages in South Slavic literature where psychological perception and intensity are so superb.

In the eighth edition (1962) of *U agoniji* Krleža added a third act; Laura attempts suicide at the end of the third act instead of at the conclusion of the second. In this new version of the play the audience learns more about Križovec, an extremely evasive character, and his capacity for presenting the most selfish motives as the benevolent gestures of a gentleman; but the question nevertheless remains whether this third act adds to one's understanding of the protagonists.

As with Chekhov's *The Cherry Orchard* (1904), critics are still discussing whether Krleža's third Glembay play, *Leda* (1930), is a comedy or a tragedy. Krleža calls *Leda* "a comedy of a carnival night," and certain stage directors put the accent on comedy when presenting the play. *Leda* follows as a logical conclusion to the two previous plays in the Glembay cycle. Besides Oliver Urban, a Glembay aristocrat, there is Klanfar, a parvenu Yugoslav industrialist whose social consciousness is no better than that of the Glembays. The old and new exploiters are symbolically rejected by a cleaning woman, who feels only disgust while sweeping up the remnants of their debauchery.

Thirty years later, in 1959, Krleža published *Aretej* (Aretheus), his "fantasy" about a Roman physician from the third century who, to preserve his position at the imperial court, kills an innocent person, and about Mr. Morgens, "the glory of European medicine," who in 1938 is in an identical position but does not surrender, being helped in his decision by the resuscitated Aretheus. Krleža transports us from one epoch to the other so we can witness how human blood has been shed in the same way over the centuries and under totally identical conditions. It is hard to grasp Krleža's views on mankind and its progress; while one character remarks that "the human hand is a consummate masterpiece," the other stresses that man was still an ape during Roman times and has remained one.

To discover who they are, what happened to them at definite moments in their lives, what shaped them so fundamentally that they are as unable to escape their psyches as their bodies, Krleža's heroes — including some members of the Glembay family —

often examine their own roots; so does Kamilo, a stand-in for the author and the main character of *Zastave I–IV* (Banners, 1967), his last roman-fleuve.

This digging into the past, this recollection of things in some ways gone forever but nevertheless always present in memory, is most characteristic of Krleža's first and most popular novel, *Povratak Filipa Latinovicza* (1932; translated as *The Return of Philip Latinovicz*, 1959). Toward the end of the novel the reader is told that Philip was "ceaselessly digging in his own darkness with a lamp in his hand, like a miner buried under the layers of a collapsed mine, when on all sides everybody is feverishly tunneling to get out."

Philip has been away, probably in Paris, for a long period, during which he has become famous as a painter. When he returns home, he is assailed by memories of his unhappy childhood. He does not know his father's identity, and he has no respect for his loose-living mother. He involves himself with a nymphomaniac named Bobočka, who is later killed by her neurotic husband. Confronted with the same sort of society found in the Glembay stories and plays, Philip stands above others because he searches for the meaning of life in general and of his own life in particular. Mladen Engelsfeld convincingly demonstrates that Philip is doing his utmost to discover his identity, that he is not devoid of national feelings, and that, for this reason, he tries to understand and help his backward and underprivileged countrymen. Moreover, although he has rejected Catholic dogmas, he has remained an admirer of Jesus Christ, and his Catholic education has left a deep mark on his mental outlook.

Philip is not a simple man; he is tormented by contradictory tendencies within himself. At times he is similar to the character Dr. Kyriales, a former revolutionary who, being without roots and rejecting all moral values (for example, he throws a boy into a burning furnace for no reason), commits suicide in despair. Philip speaks about women in the most derogatory terms, but he is enchanted with Bobočka, in whom he finds qualities that are a product of his own imagination or naiveté. He is unhappy at his inability to produce broad canvases of his native Pannonia; yet he is basically saved because he had never lost contact with the Croatian soil and with the people who live there. Having matured, he is aware that he must accept them as they are and endeavor with them to lay foundations so that human relations will be more bearable. Critics (such as Ivo Frangeš and Engelsfeld) seem correct when they say that, though the novel concludes with Philip looking at Bobočka lying dead in a pool

of her blood, he will come out of her room feeling a greater solidarity with other human beings.

Povratak Filipa Latinovicza interestingly depicts the psyche of a painter who "thinks" with his senses, unmasking the moral nakedness of selfish individuals. Full of sophisticated discussions – epitomized by Philip's existential questioning: Who am I, and how am I supposed to fulfill my life? – the book was unlike most Croatian literature of the 1930s.

Two of Krleža's novels appeared in 1938: *Na rubu pameti* (On the Edge of Reason) and the first volume of *Banket u Blitvi* (Banquet in Blitvia); the second volume was published in 1939, and the third not until 1964.

Na rubu pameti depicts an unnamed lawyer who revolts against the privileged social class to which he belongs through education, position, and wealth. When his boss boasts that he has killed four peasants who tried to steal some wine from his cellar, the lawyer-hero calls him a criminal. The hero is then condemned by the court and thrown into jail, where he discusses with a Communist various philosophical-political viewpoints, insisting that nobody has the right to imprison or kill people for their opinions. The Communist confesses that he would liquidate all those who do not agree with him. The lawyer also befriends a simple peasant whom he finds more human and less hypocritical than his previous associates. After he is released from prison, the lawyer is rejected by these acquaintances and then travels to Italy, where he visits the Sistine Chapel. Being insulted by a petty merchant, he punches him in the nose; he is expelled from Italy and confined to a mental asylum. When we realize that Krleža wrote this daring attack against all totalitarian systems, including Stalinism, in the late 1930s, we understand why he is nicknamed "the first revisionist" by his fervent followers.

Although the events in *Banket u Blitvi* take place in Lithuania and Latvia, it is apparent that Krleža again has in mind all the dictators of the period between World War I and II, including the king of Yugoslavia. Many European countries were then drifting toward undemocratic systems. The main character is Barutanski, a cretin who considers himself an emanation of divine will and rules Blitvia in a most arbitrary way. Barutanski is killed at a banquet, where victory over Blatvia is being celebrated. In the third book his main opponent, Niels Nielsen, refuses to side with an opposition party and returns home from exile, invited by a new revolutionary regime. It is not clear whether he will collaborate with the regime. As an émigré Nielsen has "realized that each isolated individual effort in the struggle against crime and lies ends as a romantic adventure." The author concludes that "the only thing upon which one can count is the printed word; this is the best weapon which man has invented in defense of human dignity."

In *Zastave* the novelist gives a broad panorama of the events between 1912 and 1922, mixed with autobiographical reminiscences. The central theme is the intimate, often troublesome relations between a high government official ready to serve all regimes and his only son, Kamilo, carried away at first by nationalism and later by revolutionary goals. Krleža did not write often about the entangled relations between a particular man and woman. Probably he was aware of his weakness in this area. In the roman-fleuve *Zastave* the least successful chapters are those in which he describes Kamilo's encounters with Ana Borongaj, his flame from adolescence. Although as a whole not well integrated, *Zastave* gives a detailed picture of Croatia in the 1920s and includes fascinating fragments that could be considered separately as first-class short stories or novellas.

Perhaps Krleža's most interesting book is *Izlet u Rusiju* (A Trip to Russia, 1926). Although he was favorably disposed toward the new Socialist regime when he traveled to the Soviet Union, he does not write as a propagandist; he points out both the positive and negative sides of Soviet life. Krleža was glad to observe the enthusiasm of a workingman in rebuilding the country, but he also saw the bureaucrats enjoying many privileges and presenting a great obstacle to the normal development of socialism. This travelogue is a lyrical and human document. Krleža even understood the tragedy of those who were dethroned by the new order, proving himself an artist who looks with open eyes at those he loves. He was convinced that final victory would lie with the proletariat, and, therefore, he was not afraid to point to weaknesses in the Soviet system.

Krleža wrote many essays on both foreign and South Slav writers. His superb analyses of writers and poets such as Erasmus, Charles Baudelaire, Marcel Proust, and Endre Ady are still valuable today. These authors – together with Ernest Renan, Arthur Schopenhauer, Ludwig Feuerbach, and Friedrich Nietzsche – exercised a decisive influence on his artistic and philosophical-political development.

Being deeply involved and temperamental, Krleža was less objective and consistent when dealing with the Croatian cultural past; what he wrote depended on his mood. At first he bombastically declared that the five-centuries-long literary tradition of Croatia was "a lie," but in 1966 he joined his countrymen when they celebrated the 130th anniversary of the Illyrian movement. At various times he wrote positively or negatively about the same people. Thus, in *Balade Petrice Kerempuha* he praised Ante Starčević as a farsighted politician, but in the 1950s he minimized his significance. In 1926 he attacked Stjepan Radić, the founder of the Peasant party, but two years later, when Radić was shot in the Belgrade parliament, he eulogized him, feeling that the entire nation was in mourning. He ridiculed the sculptor Ivan Meštrović for "believing in God," but three decades later he masterfully evaluated his art. At first he held the novelist Ksaver Šandor Djalski in low esteem, but in the postwar period he extolled him as a gifted writer.

Krleža's treatment of Juraj Križanić (1618–1683) – one of the pathetic and heroic figures of Krleža's "legends," about whom he also intended to write a novel and a drama – typifies Krleža's oscillations and exemplifies his subjective approach. Krleža did not care who Križanić was in reality. In Krleža's portrayal of Križanić in the epilogue to *Aretej* the prisoner of Tobolsk is not Križanić but Krleža. A devout Catholic priest, supposedly he no longer believes in God and his providence, and he has rejected the Catholic faith and thinks that all his efforts were in vain. Krleža wrote the epilogue to *Aretej* when he did not know – living in Zagreb under surveillance by the *ustasha* (the Croatian government during World War II) – whether he would survive.

In reading Krleža's essays one should expect neither absolute accuracy nor objective judgment but appreciate his persuasive and expressive power. When he writes, he quarrels with himself and with other real or imaginary protagonists. Krleža's knowledge was indeed encyclopedic: he wrote about the writers, sculptors, painters, musicians, philosophers, and politicians, domestic and foreign. He loved Goya and classical music (including Johann Sebastian Bach, Wolfgang Amadeus Mozart, and Frédéric Chopin). He did not care for contemporary art. His favorite instrument was the violin; he thought that only the sound of a violin was able to elevate the human beast to the level of God.

While the majority of critics – including Milan Bogdanović, Marko Ristić, Marijan Matković, Šime Vučetić, Miroslav Vaupotić, Ivo Frangeš, Mladen Engelsfeld, Stanko Lasić, and Predrag Matvejević – consider Krleža the most outstanding Croatian and Yugoslav writer, others – such as Ivo Lendić, Stanislav Šimić, Vasilije Kalezić, Mića Danojlić, and

Bogdan Raditsa – have tried hard to discredit him and minimize his significance.

Krleža did not keep silent. A man of strong convictions and temperament, he defended himself and his beliefs. In his *Moj obračun s njima* (My Squaring of Accounts with Them, 1932), there are autobiographical items concerning his "nationalistic" (pro-Serbian) enchantment and later disappointment. In December 1939 Krleža published in *Pečat* a vitriolic diatribe against the "orthodox" socialist realists (such as Ognjen Prica, Radovan Zogović, Jovan Popović, and Milovan Djilas). Panic, disarray, and turmoil grew in leftist circles. Krleža was attacked as a renegade and revisionist. The party hierarchy considered him a stubborn and incorrigible individualist and heretic.

In postwar Yugoslavia, Krleža continued to defend creative freedom. Thus, in his speech at the 1952 Writers' Congress in Ljubljana he brilliantly condemned any kind of Zhdanovism (government-controlled literature) or bureaucratic intervention in the cultural domain.

From his arrival on the literary scene in 1914 until 1941 and again after 1948, Krleža was often in the forefront of culture in Yugoslavia. His materialistic convictions – conveyed with strong emotional impetus, his Marxist and liberal philosophy, his socialism mingled with a sincere defense of personal freedom, and his readiness to defend his point of view with his own life – made Krleža highly controversial and unacceptable to both nationalists and rigid Communists. In Krleža's view a writer should have individual and progressive ideas and present them as he thinks best. Until 1941 Krleža's skirmishes with "Socialist" theoreticians were just as bitter and dangerous as were those with the bourgeois camp.

Krleža was and has remained controversial not only as an artist but also as a human being: he was sociable, friendly, and tender but also quick to react with sarcasm and ridicule. He employed clerics and nationalists in his institute but did not hesitate to interrupt promptly all conversations, even with his old friends, when they disagreed with him. He himself doubted the value of some of his many works, but woe to that critic who expressed publicly a similar opinion. He was a Croatian patriot, deeply rooted in Croatian tradition and their national grievances, but he wrote derogatory pages about his countrymen and their culture. He was in his inner being a dissident and rebel, but in his old age, probably afraid of losing the unbelievable privileges bestowed upon him, he showed signs of opportunism, and he bowed to powerful men. He no longer be-lieved in socialism when it became a police apparatus (see his interviews with Predrag Matvejević) but allowed "the new class" to defend itself with his writings.

Krleža was and shall remain a pivotal figure, and no one interested in twentieth-century Croatian and South Slavic literature can ignore him. With the passage of time Krleža's personal foibles and certain of his works will be forgotten, but he fully deserves to be ranked among the luminaries of contemporary world literature. The future generations of his countrymen will rightly be proud of his contributions to their cultural heritage.

Interviews:

Predrag Matvejević, *Stari i novi razgovori s Krležom* (Zagreb: Spektar, 1982);

Enes Čengić, *S Krležom iz dana u dan,* 4 volumes (Zagreb: Globus, 1985).

Bibliographies:

Davor Kapetanić, "Bibliografija djela Miroslava Krleže," in *Zbornik o Miroslavu Krleži,* edited by Marijan Matković (Zagreb: JAZU, 1963), pp. 601–773;

Kapetanić, "Literatura o Miroslavu Krleža," in *Miroslav Krleža,* edited by Vojislav J. Durić (Belgrade: Prosveta, 1967), pp. 335–451;

Kapetanić, "Bibliografija Miroslava Krleže," *Revija,* 5 (1968): 80–133;

Gojko M. Tešić, "Bibliografija o Miroslavu Krleži 1968–1973," *Književna istorija,* 6 (1973): 351–434.

Biographies:

Jan Wierzbicki, *Miroslav Krleža* (Warsaw: Wiedza powszechna, 1975; Zagreb: Liber, 1980);

Marijan Matković, *La vie et l'oeuvre de Miroslav Krleža* (Paris: UNESCO, 1977);

Ivan Očak, *Krleža-Partija* (Zagreb: Spektar, 1982);

Stanko Lasić, *Krleža. Kronologija života i rada* (Zagreb: Grafički zavod Hrvatske, 1982);

Zvane Črnja, *Sukobi oko Krleže* (Zagreb: Mladost, 1983).

References:

Ralph Bogert, *The Writer as Naysayer: Miroslav Krleža and the Aesthetic of Interwar Central Europe* (Columbus, Ohio: Slavica, 1991);

Enes Čengić, *Krleža* (Zagreb: Mladost, 1982);

Branimir Donat, *O pjesničkom teatru Miroslava Krleže* (Zagreb: Mladost, 1970);

Mladen Engelsfeld, *Interpretacija Krležina romana Povratak Filipa Latinovicza* (Zagreb: Liber, 1975);

Ivo Frangeš, "Stvarnost i umjetnost u Krležinoj prozi," in *Hrvatska književna kritika,* volume 10 (Zagreb: Matica hrvatska, 1969), pp. 249–274;

Darko Gašparović, *Dramatica krleziana* (Zagreb: Centar za kulturnu djelatnost, 1977);

Vasilije Kalezić, *U Krležinom sazvježdju* (Zagreb: August Cesarec, 1982);

Mladen Kuzmanović, *Kerempuhovo ishodište. Geneza "Balada Petrice Kerempuha"* (Rijeka: Izdavački centar Rijeka, 1985);

Stanko Lasić, *Struktura Krležinih Zastava* (Zagreb: Liber, 1975);

Reinhard Lauer, *Miroslav Krleža und der deutsche Expressionismus* (Göttingen: Vandenhoeck & Ruprecht, 1984);

Josip Lešić, *Slika i zvuk u dramama Miroslava Krleže* (Sarajevo: Veselin Masleša, 1981);

Mate Lončar, "Krležini književni časopisi," *Književna istorija,* 24 (1973): 673–700; 25 (1974): 109–126; 26 (1974): 255–284;

Darko Suvin, "Voyage to the Stars and Panonian Mire: Miroslav Krleža's Expressionist Vision and the Croatian Plebian Consciousness in the Epoch of World War One," *Mosaic,* 6, no. 4 (1973): 169–183;

Miroslav Vaupotić, *Siva boja smrti* (Zagreb: Znanje, 1974);

Ivo Vidan, *Ciklus o Glembajevima u svom evropskom kontekstu* (Zagreb: JAZU, 1968);

Šime Vučetić, *Krležino književno djelo* (Sarajevo: Svjetlost, 1958; Zagreb: Spektar, 1982);

Viktor Žmegač, *Krležini evropski obziri. Djelo u komparativnom kontekstu* (Zagreb: Znanje, 1986).

Laza K. Lazarević

(13 May 1851 – 28 December 1890)

Vasa D. Mihailovich
University of North Carolina at Chapel Hill

BOOKS: *Šest pripovedaka* (Belgrade: Kraljevska srpska državna štamparija, 1886);

Pripovetke, 2 volumes (Belgrade: Srpska književna zadruga, 1898–1899);

Dela (Zemun: Napredak, 1912);

Izabrane pripovijetke (Zagreb: Matica hrvatska, 1917);

Celokupna dela (Belgrade: Narodna prosveta, 1929);

Pripovetke (Belgrade: Geca Kon, 1932);

Izabrane pripovetke (Belgrade: Prosveta, 1946);

Izabrane pripovetke (Zagreb: Prosvjeta, 1950);

Pripovetke (Belgrade: Rad, 1956);

Sabrana dela (Belgrade: Prosveta, 1956);

Pripovetke (Novi Sad: Matica srpska / Belgrade: Srpska književna zadruga, 1958);

Dela (Novi Sad: Matica srpska / Belgrade: Prosveta, 1970);

Celokupna dela (Belgrade: Prosveta, 1981).

Translations in English: "The Robbers," translated by Edna Worthley Underwood in *Short Stories from the Balkans,* edited by Underwood (Boston: Marshall Jones, 1919), pp. 145–164;

"The First Matins with My Father," translated by Pavle Popović in *Jugo-Slav Stories,* edited by Popović (New York: Duffield, 1921), pp. 19–50; translated by James W. Wiles as *First Morning Service with Father* (Belgrade: B. Cvijanović, 1929); translated by Svetozar Koljević in *Yugoslav Short Stories,* edited by Koljević (London: Oxford University Press, 1966), pp. 1–18;

"By the Well," translated by Popović in *Jugo-Slav Stories,* edited by Popović (New York: Duffield, 1921), pp. 123–150; translated by I. Altaraz in *Great Short Stories of the World,* edited by B. H. Clark and M. Lieber (Boston: Heath, 1925), pp. 833–845;

"The German Girl," translated by Branko Mikasinovich in *Introduction to Yugoslav Literature: An Anthology of Fiction and Poetry,* edited by Mikasinovich, Dragan Milivojević, and Vasa D. Mihailovich (New York: Twayne, 1973), pp. 73–83.

Laza K. Lazarević

Laza K. Lazarević was a leading realist in Serbian literature in the second half of the nineteenth century. Although he came from a small town and wrote mostly about the townsfolk, he also wrote about village people, thus contributing to a prominent genre of that time, the "village short story," practiced by other leading Serbian writers such as Milovan Glišić and Janko Veselinović. What sets Lazarević apart is his tendency to probe deeper into the psyche of his characters, thus making him a founder of psychological prose in Serbian literature. He wrote only a few short stories, but the small quantity is offset by high artistic quality unequaled in all of Serbian literature up to his appearance.

Lazarević was born on 13 May 1851 in Šabac, a middle-sized town near the Sava and Drina rivers in western Serbia. His father, Kuzman, an immigrant from the neighboring village and a merchant, died when Lazarević was ten. His mother, Jelka, née Milovanović, became the head of the family and managed to provide a setting of strong family values typical of Serbian patriarchal society of that time. Lazarević finished elementary and junior high school in his native town and then moved to Belgrade, where he completed high school and graduated in law from the University of Belgrade. He lived with the family of his brother-in-law; the setting provided an atmosphere similar to the patriarchal life in his hometown. At this time he made his first attempts at writing. He was also exposed to liberal social and political movements, but instead of embracing liberal causes he developed rather conservative views, remaining loyal to the traditional values acquired in the patriarchal life at home. With a state scholarship he went to Berlin in 1872 to study medicine. In addition to being exposed to a highly civilized German and western European society, Lazarević had a romantic affair with a German girl; this experience inspired him to write his first short story, "Švabica" (translated as "The German Girl," 1973). Upon graduation he returned to Serbia in 1879. By then he had already written a few short stories, which he began to publish that year.

The rest of his life Lazarević spent in performing his duties as a physician, writing short stories, and participating in the burgeoning life of a small capital awakening from centuries of stagnation in the backwaters of Europe. He became the personal physician of King Milan Obrenović, was elected to the Serbian Academy of Sciences, and took part in the Serbo-Bulgarian War of 1885 as a member of the medical corps. Such an active life limited his time for what he liked most – writing. It may have also contributed to his tuberculosis, a disease from which many people in Serbia of that time perished, including many intellectuals and writers. Lazarević's marriage in 1881 brought peace and joy in his private life, although this was not reflected in his literary works. He continued to write and publish at a reduced pace. In 1886 he saw the publication of his first short-story collection, Šest pripovedaka (Six Short Stories). The success of this book prompted him to further literary endeavors, but his death from tuberculosis in 1890 cut him down in the prime of his life; by then he had been able to finish only nine stories, leaving eight stories unfinished and many plans unfulfilled.

Lazarević's first published story, "Prvi put s ocem na jutrenje" (first translated as "The First Matins with My Father," 1921), is in many ways his best story, exemplifying to the fullest his entire outlook on life and his approach to literature. It belongs to a cycle of stories about life in a provincial town. It also reveals Lazarević's favorite topic: the family as a nucleus of social life threatened by vices or onrushing changes. Mitar, the head of a small family, a loving husband and father, and a good provider, succumbs to his only vice – gambling. When he gambles away all his possessions, he decides to commit suicide but is saved at the last moment by his faithful wife. She restores in him a faith in the future, reminding him in a dramatic final scene of past difficulties that they had overcome together, convincing him that they will do those things again together. Even though the change in Mitar is somewhat abrupt, it serves the purpose of showing that a strong family is indestructible when its interests are placed first and foremost. The positive ending is typical of many of Lazarević's stories, expressing his optimism even when the situation calls for a more pessimistic outcome. The potential didacticism is overshadowed by his skillful plot, lively and credible dialogue, and masterfully depicted psychological states of the characters.

Another story from the same cycle, "Vetar" (The Wind), has a similar setting – the life of a merchant family in a provincial town. The merchant in the story, Janko, places his love for his mother above everything else, but he has a warm spot also for other people – the friends of his father – who are not as fortunate. The mother is again depicted as good-natured, serious, loving, and compassionate – in short, a pillar of the family, even if the husband is nominally the head. In "On zna sve" (He Knows Everything) Lazarević returns to a small-town merchant family, except this time the two brothers, Vidak and Vučko, possess different characteristics. The conflict and eventual resolution arise when the younger brother shows individualistic tendencies. However, when the older brother suffers a debilitating accident, the younger takes over and saves the family property. In all these stories Lazarević is highly optimistic of the final outcome, the good in his characters and around them triumphing in the end. This somewhat idealized stance is in line with his basic, even if not omnipresent, optimism.

This is not the case with the final story of the provincial-town cycle, "Sve će to narod pozlatiti"

Anna Gutiar, the inspiration for Lazarević's autobiographical story "Svabica" (The German Girl)

(People Will Make Up for Everything). Here the father expects his wounded son back from the war, but when he returns without his legs, the father tries to console himself by saying that the people, for whom his son had sacrificed himself, will take care of him. The ominous scene of passersby dropping alms in the cripple's lap hints at the more realistic outcome – begging. This is the most pessimistic of Lazarević's stories. Coming as it does toward the end of his career, it may have foreshadowed the lessening of his inveterate optimism, although some social criticism, even accusation, presented in his earlier stories should not be overlooked. It may also reflect Lazarević's sharp eye for realistic detail, focusing here on the devastating effects of the lost war.

Lazarević's stories about village life show an affinity with the town stories in their conflict between community and individuals, the transformations of the main characters and the same idealistic belief in the basic goodness of humanity. What is new is the clash between the old and the new, which in the rural setting is more vivid simply because rural life is more conservative and therefore a natural target. The best example is found in "Školska ikona" (A School's Icon). The undisputed authority is represented by the village Orthodox priest, a barely educated but honest and good person who wields his authority by example rather than by preaching. But when a new teacher, a young firebrand with progressive ideas, takes up his position in the village, the stage is set for a clash of major proportions. To make matters more dramatic, the priest's daughter, who has just returned from her schooling in the city, falls in love with the teacher and elopes with him, having found it impossible to conform to the old-fashioned rules of her father any longer. The village school catches fire, and the priest is mortally injured trying to save the school icon. The remorseful daughter returns in her father's dying moments and answers his plea to stay in the village as a teacher, accepting in a symbolic gesture the rescued icon of Saint Sava, the earliest and foremost Serbian educator. Its somewhat naive plot and idealistic connotations aside, the story sharply delineates the encroaching clash between the old and the new: the old personified by an old-fashioned priest aware of the need for change but not to the degree that the teacher advocates, and the new personified by a revolutionary teacher. The teacher is shown in negative colors: ill-natured, very knowledgeable but ignorant of the true nature of the peasants he is supposed to educate, and impatient with the "backward" state of the villagers. The most important aspect of the story is the insidious encroachment of new and foreign ideas into the patriarchal way of life that has existed for centuries, enabling Serbian society to survive centuries of Turkish occupation and enforced retardation.

A similar conflict is built into the story "Na bunaru" (translated as "By the Well," 1921, 1925). The conflict is provided by a young girl, Anoka, who is unwilling to subject herself to the rigorous order of the *zadruga,* a cooperative system that has ruled the Serbian village for untold generations. Instead of obeying the elders – the foundation of *zadruga* life – she demonstrates her strong will and rebelliousness, desiring to subject others to her will. Her obstinacy is slyly overcome by the *zadruga* head's order to others to satisfy all her wishes, which eventually bores her and leads to her transformation. Again, the change in Anoka is somewhat abrupt and unrealistic, but it underscores Lazarević's point that individuals have to sacrifice their wills for the good of the commune, without which the nucleus of Serbian rural order is severely undermined. The liberal winds blowing in Serbian society in the second half of the nineteenth century are shown here to have pernicious effects, which Lazarević, a traditionalist and conservative, tries to stem. Again, didacticism is neutralized by genuine characters and their psychological credibility.

The final story in this group, "U dobri čas hajduci" (Just in Time, Hajduks; translated as "The Robbers," 1919), is devoid of deep significance, but it is lively and skillfully told. Interestingly, Lazarević did not understand village life as well as Glišić or Veselinović, to name a few village prose writers; he used the village motifs to further his basic views and to exercise his dexterity in building good plots and credible characters.

The last group, consisting of two stories, stands outside the above tendencies. These stories are almost entirely autobiographical – to be sure, most of his stories harbor some autobiographical elements. "Švabica" depicts his romantic encounter with a German girl during his studies in Germany. However, the story goes beyond autobiographical reminiscences or a romantic affair. It presents the fine psychological dilemma of a young Serbian student facing a marriage to a foreign girl, with all the potential problems involving her life in an entirely different world in Serbia. Knowing Lazarević's traditional and conservative views, it is clear why the student cannot make such a decision, for his own sake and the girl's, at a time when Germany and Serbia are like two different planets. Told in an epistolary form, the story is highly dramatic and full of the sincerity of a youth finding himself in the strange world for the first time. Because of its autobiographical nature, "Švabica" was not published during the author's lifetime and was left somewhat unpolished. The other story, "Verter," is his weakest. Modeled after Johann Wolfgang van Goethe's *Die Leiden des jungen Werthers* (1774; translated as *The Sorrows of Werther*, 1779), Lazarević's story is a pale copy, void of originality and verve and even of the stylistic excellence and psychological nuances usually found in his writings.

The eight incomplete stories are unfortunately left in fragments and cannot be adequately judged as artistic achievements. This is indeed a tragic loss for Serbian literature because some of these sketches could have become very good stories.

The contribution of Laza K. Lazarević to Serbian literature is significant from both historical and artistic angles. He appeared at the height of the Serbian realistic period, joining a group of talented writers who had liberated Serbian fiction from the Romantic notions of emotionalism, folklore, and nationalism. Lazarević took Serbian fiction a step fur-

ther by way of an eclectic choice of universal themes – within a local framework, of course – and through the refined psychological elucidation of characters, a step taken only by one other writer, Svetolik Ranković. Both Lazarević and Ranković developed under a heavy influence of the nineteenth-century Russian writers; Lazarević is sometimes compared to Ivan Turgenev. Just as important is Lazarević's artistic acumen. In addition to his selection of exquisite themes, he had a good sense for plot structure, natural dialogue, easy-flowing narrative, and, above all, characterization. His language is authentic. Most of his stories possess a highly dramatic power; "Prvi put s ocem na jutrenje" was made into a movie in the United States by Vukadin Kecan. With all these qualities, Lazarević occupies a prominent place in all of Serbian literature.

Bibliographies:

Golub Dobrašinović, "Bibliografija radova Laze Lazarevića," in Lazarević's *Sabrana dela* (Belgrade: Prosveta, 1956), pp. 584–593;

Damnjan Moračić, "Bibliografska gradja o Lazi Lazareviću," *Književnost i jezik,* 23 (1976): 391–395.

Biographies:

Arturo Cronia, *Lazar K. Lazarević* (Rome: Istituto per l'Europa orientale, 1932);

M. Djorić, *Lazar K. Lazarević: Lekar i pisac* (Niš, Yugoslavia: Gradina, 1958);

Vladimir Jovičić, *Laza Lazarević* (Belgrade: Nolit, 1966).

References:

Milan Bogdanović, "O Lazi K. Lazareviću," *Književnost,* 12 (1951): 437–467;

Živojin Boškov, "Laza K. Lazarević i ruska književnost," *Mostovi,* 7 (1976): 3–14, 154–158;

Marko Car, "Laza K. Lazarević," in his *Moje simpatije,* volume 2 (Mostar, 1897), pp. 115–143;

Vlada Cvetanović, "Jedan vid odnosa prema ženskin likovima u pripovetkama Laze K. Lazarevića," *Stremljenja,* 23 (1982): 1–86;

Velibor Gligorić, "Laza K. Lazarević," in his *Srpski realisti* (Belgrade: Prosveta, 1954), pp. 141–179;

Edward D. Goy, "Laza K. Lazarević: A Study in Theme and Background," *Slavonic and East European Review,* 35 (December 1956): 129–156;

Saša Hadži Tančić, "Paralelni svetovi: Tradicijski pripovedački model i njegova savremena invokacija," *Delo,* 30, no. 4 (1984): 27–42;

Dušan Ivanić, "'Verter' Laze Lazarevića," *Književna istorija,* 2 (1970): 755–774;

Zlatko Klatik, "O stilsko-jezičkim osobinama Lazarevićeve pripovetke 'Prvi put s ocem na jutrenje,'" *Književna istorija,* 2 (1970): 739–753;

Božidar Kovačević, "Laza K. Lazarević," in Lazarević's *Sabrana dela* (Belgrade: Prosveta, 1956), pp. vii–xxxi;

Antun Gustav Matoš, "Lazar K. Lazarević," *Mlada Hrvatska,* 1, no. 3 (1902): 71–79; republished in his *Eseji i feljtoni o srpskim piscima* (Belgrade: Prosveta, 1952), pp. 13–23;

Ljubomir Nedić, "Laza K. Lazarević," *Srpski književni glasnik,* 13 (1904): 36–44;

Milija Nikolić, *Forme pripovedanja u umetničkoj prozi Laze Lazarevića* (Belgrade: Naučna knjiga, 1973);

Miloš Savković, "Laza Lazarević," in his *Ogledi* (Belgrade: Prosveta, 1952), pp. 227–272;

Jovan Skerlić, "Laza K. Lazarević," *Srpski književni glasnik,* 17 (1906): 672–679, 743–752, 834–846;

Živojin Stanojčić, *Sintaksa jezika Laze K. Lazarevića. I: Sintagmatski odnosi* (Belgrade: Institut za srpskohrvatski jezik, 1975);

Dimitrije Vučenov, "Psihološko slikanje u pripoveci 'Sve će to narod pozlatiti,'" *Književnost i jezik,* 22 (1975): 403–414.

Desanka Maksimović

(16 May 1898 – 11 February 1993)

Biljana Sljivic-Simsic
University of Illinois at Chicago

SELECTED BOOKS: *Pesme* (Belgrade: S. B. Cvijanovií, 1924);

Zeleni vitez (Belgrade: Misao, 1930);

Ludilo srca (Belgrade: Srpska književna zadruga, 1931);

Gozba na livadi (Belgrade: Misao, 1932);

Srce lutke spavaljke i druge priče za decu (Belgrade: Geca Kon, 1933);

Kako oni žive (Belgrade: Geca Kon, 1935);

Nove pesme (Belgrade: Srpska književna zadruga, 1936);

Raspevane priče (Belgrade: Geca Kon, 1938);

Dečja soba i ostale priče (Belgrade: IPROZ, 1942);

Zagonetke lake za prvake djake, by Maksimović and Jovanka Hrvaćanin (Belgrade: Jugoistok, 1942);

Patuljkova ljuljaška (Belgrade: IPROZ, 1943);

Šarena torbica (Belgrade: IPROZ, 1943);

Oslobodjenje Cvete Andrić (Belgrade: Centralni odbor AFŽ Jugoslavije, 1945);

Pesnik i zavičaj (Belgrade: Prosveta, 1946);

Reka pomoćnica (Belgrade: Novo pokolenje, 1948);

Izbrane pesme (Zagreb: Zora, 1950);

Otadžbino, tu sam (Belgrade: Prosveta, 1951);

Vetrova uspavanka (Belgrade: Dečja knjiga, 1953);

Otvoren prozor (Subotica: Minerva, 1954);

Prolećni sastanak (Belgrade: Dečja knjiga, 1954);

Strašna igra (Belgrade: Prosveta, 1954);

Miris zemlje (Belgrade: Prosveta, 1955);

Bajka o Kratkovečnoj (Belgrade & Sarajevo: Svjetlost, 1957);

Ako je verovati mojoj baki (Belgrade: Mlado pokolenje, 1959);

Buntovan razred (Subotica & Belgrade: Minerva, 1960);

Zarobljenik snova (Cetinje: Narodna knjiga, 1960);

Čudo u polju (Belgrade: Mlado pokolenje, 1961);

Govori tiho (Belgrade: Mlado pokolenje, 1961);

Medvedova ženidba (Sarajevo: Svjetlost, 1961);

Pisma iz šume (Belgrade: Prosveta, 1961);

Sunčevi podanici (Belgrade: Mlado pokolenje, 1962);

Patuljkova tajna (Sarajevo: Svjetlost, 1963);

Desanka Maksimović in 1960

Pesme (Belgrade: Prosveta, 1963);

Ptice na česmi (Zagreb: Mladost, 1963);

Tražim pomilovanje (Novi Sad: Matica srpska, 1964); translated by Celia Hawkesworth as "I Seek Clemency" in *Relations* (Belgrade), 2 (Summer 1988): 5–38;

Hoću da se radujem (Sarajevo: Veselin Masleša, 1965);

Djačko srce (Belgrade: Mlado pokolenje, 1966);

Pesme (Belgrade: Srpska književna zadruga, 1966; revised and enlarged edition, Belgrade: Prosveta, 1976);

Ne zaboraviti (Subotica & Belgrade: Minerva, 1969);

Pesme (Novi Sad: Matica srpska / Belgrade: Srpska književna zadruga, 1969);

Sabrana dela, 7 volumes (Belgrade: Nolit, 1969);

Praznici. Putovanja (Belgrade: Slovo ljubve, 1972);

Nemam više vremena (Belgrade: Prosveta, 1973);

Letopis Perunovih potomaka (Belgrade: Nolit, 1976);

Pesme iz Norveške (Belgrade: Prosveta, 1976); translated by Robert De Bray as *Poems from Norway* (Belgrade: Idea, 1984);

Snimci iz Švajcarske (Belgrade: Slovo ljubve, 1978);

Sabrane pesme, 5 volumes (Belgrade: Nolit, 1982);

Slovo o ljubavi (Belgrade: Srpska književna zadruga, 1983);

Priča starog kamena (Zagreb: Mladost, 1984);

Trenutak u zavičaju (Kruševac: Bagdala, 1984);

Pradevojčica (Belgrade: BIGZ / Priština: Jedinstvo, 1985);

Miholjsko leto (Belgrade: Prosveta, 1987);

Sabrane pesme, 6 volumes (Belgrade: Prosveta, 1987);

Pamtiću sve (Belgrade: Nolit, 1988);

Ozon zavičaja (Belgrade: Književne novine, 1990);

Sabrane pesme, 6 volumes (Belgrade: Prosveta, 1990).

Editions in English: *Poems by Desanka Maksimović: Greetings from the Old Country / Pesme: Pozdravi iz Starog Kraja,* edited by Milan Surdučki, various translators (Toronto: Yugoslavica, 1976);

Selections in *Contemporary Yugoslav Poetry,* edited by Vasa D. Mihailovich, various translators (Iowa City: University of Iowa Press, 1977), pp. 5–8;

Shaggy Little Dog (London: Abelard / North-South, 1983);

Selections in *Serbian Poetry from the Beginnings to the Present,* edited by Milne Holton and Mihailovich, various translators (New Haven: Yale Center for International Area Studies, 1988), pp. 253–257;

Visions: Selected Poems, various translators (Belgrade: Nolit, 1988);

Selections translated by Marie Schulte in *Scottish Slavonic Review,* 12–13 (1989): 142–153.

OTHER: *Ruske narodne bajke,* edited and translated by Maksimović and S. N. Slastikov (Belgrade: IPROZ, 1945);

Bugarske deče pesme, edited and translated by Maksimović and Slastikov (Belgrade: Prosveta, 1946);

J. Kastelic, ed., *Antologija slovenačke poezije,* 2 volumes, translated by Maksimović (Belgrade: Nolit, 1961);

Oton Župančić, *Izbrana dela,* translated by Maksimović (Belgrade: Srpska književna zadruga, 1961);

Petnaest sovjetskih pesnikinja, edited and translated by Maksimović (Belgrade: Nolit, 1963);

Francè Prešeren, *Sonetni venac,* translated by Maksimović (Belgrade: Srpska književna zadruga, 1968);

Prešeren, *Sonetni venac i druge pesme,* translated by Maksimović (Belgrade: Rad, 1969);

Približavanje: Bugarske pesnikinje u prevodu Desanke Maksimović, edited and translated by Maksimović (Niš: Gradina, 1971);

Anton Aškerc, *Pesme,* translated by Maksimović (Belgrade: Obelisk, 1972).

Desanka Maksimović appeared on the Serbian literary scene in 1920 and graced it with her presence for more than seventy years. From her first published verses, with which she established herself as an important lyric poet, her poetry, though rooted in Serbian tradition, has remained new and fresh, always changing yet always unmistakably her own. A minute and seemingly frail woman, she persistently and successfully pursued her own literary path, never formally belonging to any group, school, or trend. Any influences were filtered through the prism of her own talent and fully and harmoniously integrated into an entirely original poetic opus. From her early confessional love poetry of the 1920s and 1930s, which is permeated with sun rays and scents of her native area's forests and meadows, morning mists, and mysterious moonlit landscapes, to her universally acclaimed collections *Tražim pomilovanje* (1964; translated as "I Seek Clemency," 1988) and *Nemam više vremena* (My Time Is Running Short, 1973), Maksimović matured both as a person and as a poet, growing in stature among her peers and her people until she became the undisputed first lady of Serbian poetry — and, above all, a true Serbian national poet, firmly embedded in her cultural heritage. The recipient of innumerable national and international literary awards and honors for her poetry, prose, travel books, children's books, and translations, she was a member of the Serbian Academy of Sciences and Arts since 1959. She is so popular with her readers that almost everyone refers to her by her first name.

Desanka Maksimović, whose ancestors came to Serbia from Herzegovina sometime in the late eighteenth century, was born in the village of Rabrovica, near Valjevo, to Mihailo Maksimović, a schoolteacher, and his wife Draginja, née Petrović. When Desanka was only two months old her father was transferred to Brankovina, a small town in the heart of Serbia rich with history and traditions, where her maternal grandfather, Svetozar Petrović, served as a Serbian Orthodox priest. Both her father and grandfather loved books and possessed large libraries for that time. Her father wrote poems for children and patriotic plays. She learned early about traditional Serbian values and acquired a love for studying and reading even before she started elementary school. The oldest of eight children and surrounded by a large and loving family in the luxuriant, unspoiled natural setting of the Brankovina area, she lived a happy, memorable childhood. Even though her family moved to Valjevo when she was ten years old, settling permanently in Belgrade in 1918, she never forgot Brankovina and always considered it her native town. She returned there often, in her poetry and in person, as if those contacts with her native soil — its people, sky, trees, and flowers — were essential for renewing her poetic inspiration, refreshing her poetic language, and providing comfort in difficult moments of her life.

In Valjevo, Maksimović finished elementary school and in 1909 enrolled in high school. World War I interrupted her education and brought her first personal tragedy: soon after the war began, her father, to whom she was very close, died of typhoid fever as a soldier in the Serbian army. Many years later, in her collection *Nove pesme* (New Poems, 1936), she reminisced about her father: "Only now I dare think of him / After so many mournful years and days. . . ." During the war, to find solace in her sorrow and fill the time away from school, she learned French on her own by repeatedly reading the works of Hippolyte Taine and a few French novels she had at her disposal. When the war was over she stayed in Valjevo until 1919 to finish high school. Then she went to Belgrade to join her family and begin her studies of comparative literature and art history at the University of Belgrade. By the time she left Valjevo she had filled a couple of school notebooks with her verses. She took them to Belgrade and soon contacted the poet Sima Pandurović, who was her German teacher in Valjevo before World War I. She asked him to read and evaluate her poetry, hoping that he could recommend at least a few of her poems for publication in the journal *Misao* (Thought), of which he was an editor. Indifferent and aloof, Pandurović passed the notebooks to the editor in chief of the journal, Velimir Živojinović Massuka, who agreed to read them only as a favor to Pandurović, although he did not ex-

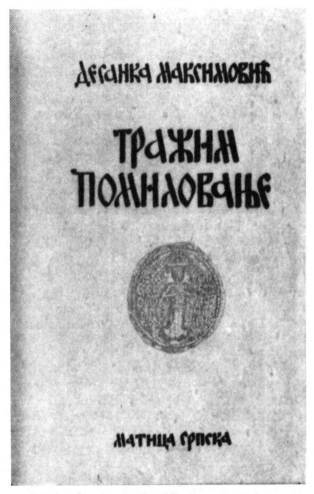

Cover for Maksimović's Tražim pomilovanje *(1964), her best-selling collection of poems*

pect much from poems written by a young, provincial girl who had just graduated from high school. After World War II, Massuka recollected this event in an interview for Radio-Belgrade:

At first, I was pleasantly surprised. . . . As I was reading, my initial surprise and astonishment were gradually transformed into excitement. This was something fresh, warm, sincere, and original, clad in a beautiful form. . . . Simple and all woven of the same thread, these poems, however, were different from one another. Experiences were told sincerely, almost naively, yet without any banality; very intimate feelings were expressed openly, in a manner almost embarrassing for those times, yet, somehow, still discreetly and innocently. That was a kind of confessional poetry that was cultivated by all the best poets of all times, from Sappho and Pindar, . . . via Petrarch, Shakespeare, Goethe, Lermontov, Byron, Heine . . . to Anna Akhmatova and Elisaveta Bagryana. . . . Yet, except for the basic structure, there was nothing in the notebooks that belonged to the old models, either foreign or ours . . . Maksimović's experience had a new content and was different from anything I knew; her verse had a completely different, never before used cadence; there was music in it, it had an internal metric harmony but without a strict metric rhythm.... There was something elusive, soft, feminine, and sparkling in that verse created with confidence and only seemingly shy and anxious....

The entire collection of poems that Maksimović took to Belgrade was published in *Misao* in 1920 and 1921. In *Antologija najnovije srpske poezije* (Anthology of the Newest Serbian Poetry), compiled by Pandurović and published by *Misao* in 1921, Maksimović was the most represented poet. Her "Strepnja" (Anxiety) was voted by the readers as the best poem, her first literary award. In 1922 the most prominent Belgrade literary journal, *Srpski književni glasnik* (Serbian Literary Herald), also began to accept her poems for publication, and that same year three of her most popular poems — "Strepnja," "Čežnja" (Yearning), and "Pokošena livada" (A Mowed Meadow) — were included in *Antologija jugoslovenske lirske poezije* (An Anthology of Yugoslav Lyric Poetry), compiled by Mirko Deanović and Ante Petrović.

In 1924 Maksimović graduated from the University of Belgrade and received a French government fellowship to study for a year at the Sorbonne in Paris. That same year she also published her first collection, titled *Pesme* (Poems). By that time she was already a well-known young poet in Belgrade literary circles. Her first collection of poems received positive reviews in general. In *Jugoslovenska njiva* (Yugoslav Field), a prominent Croatian critic, Antun Barac, wrote that "Maksimović's poems are the best ever written in our language by a woman and are, undoubtedly, among the best created in our country in the last several years.... Those are poems of youth, with its abundant ecstasies and its vague longings.... In this book there are several poems of a perfect beauty, with a rhythm that captures every vibration of human soul, with feelings that are in themselves a synthesis of refinement, discreetness, devotion, and longing." In 1925 Maksimović received a Saint Sava medal from the Serbian government for her achievements in poetry and was appointed professor in the elite First High School for Girls in Belgrade. With a brief interruption (1941–1944), she taught there until her retirement in 1953.

In Serbian literature the 1920s were years of turmoil created by a new wave of rebellious poets whose well-organized groups and journals advocated destruction of the traditional, established poetic norms and authorities and called for a new literature that would be able to uncover the subconscious, explain modern humanity, take it to cosmic heights, and express its feelings and thoughts in a form free of all constraints. At the time this new wave, well organized and determined to triumph at any cost, was referred to as the New Modernism, even though there were several distinct isms, imported and domestic, grouped together under that name, including expressionism, surrealism, zenithism, and hypnoism. The New Modernists did not like Maksimović, and she became one of their targets in the late 1920s and early 1930s, when the surrealists emerged as advocates of Communist ideas and propagators of revolution. They criticized her not only because of her adherence to the traditional poetic norms that they tried to destroy but also for her lack of interest in the politically engaged literature they supported. She withstood these attacks with dignity while continuing to pursue her own poetic path. "I would not have had as many friends as I have now if I had not been able to forget the biting jokes or critical remarks about my poetry and myself," she once noted.

In fact, the circle of Maksimović's friends and admirers among Belgrade intellectuals steadily grew in the meantime. Besides keeping her friendships from her student days, even with those whose literary ideology was different from hers, such as Miloš Crnjanski, she associated with many prominent poets, authors, artists, and actors of the *Misao* circle. They gathered in the home of Smilja Djaković, the owner of the journal, and spent hours together discussing poetry, new books, exhibits, and cultural life in Belgrade. In the P.E.N. club in the 1930s she also became friendly with poets Jovan Dučić and Milan Rakić, two of the idols of her youth, and was honored when in 1935 Dučić wrote that she was a first-class lyric poet. That same year she received the prestigious Seven Arts Award for her poetry.

In 1933 Maksimović married Sergej Nikiforovič Slastikov, a Russian émigré born in Moscow. They had a happy marriage and a productive literary union. Even though they never had children of their own, a good part of their creative life was devoted to children and young people. Besides translating, individually or together, many classical Russian authors and poets, they also translated Russian folktales and literature for children. Slastikov also published two collections of his own works for young readers. Her husband's death in 1970, following the death of her mother in 1969, inspired Maksimović to write the beautiful poems of her collection *Nemam više vremena,* to thank her late husband "for embracing, even in death, our soil...."

Retired against her will by the quisling government in occupied Serbia in 1941, Maksimović spent World War II between Brankovina, Valjevo, and Bel-

*Biographer Miodrag Blečić with Maksimović and her husband, Sergej
Nikiforovič Slastikov*

grade. To survive, she taught and made dolls to
sell. She also sewed children's clothes and exchanged them for food in Brankovina and surrounding villages. She walked from Belgrade to the
nearby Mount Avala to collect wood to heat their
apartment. Except for a few books for children, she
did not publish anything during the war even
though some of her patriotic poems, inspired by the
horrors of the war, were written at that time. The
collection *Pesnik i zavičaj* (Poet and His Native Land,
1946) includes Maksimović's best patriotic poems, in
which she expresses her pride in her nation's freedom-
loving tradition, as in "Ustanici" (The Rebels), and
brave resistance to the German occupiers during
World War II, as in "Srbija je velika tajna" (Serbia Is
a Deep Secret). The best-known of these poems is
"Krvava bajka" (A Legend of Blood), a poetic requiem for the schoolboys of Kragujevac massacred by
the Germans in 1941. In it Maksimović effectively
chose a form of a legend in verse to reflect on a monstrous crime committed by the Germans against

> a far-off land of peasants
> among the Balkan hills, where
> martyrdom befell
> a class of schoolboys gay —
> all in one day.

Maksimović's patriotic poems are lyrical and gentle
in tone, very much in tune with her entire poetic

opus; they give strength to resist rather than ignite
a desire to attack.

Maksimović's sixtieth birthday in 1958 was
widely celebrated by her nation. She received many
awards and was nominated a corresponding member of the Serbian Academy of Sciences and Arts;
she was elected early the following year. It was generally thought that her work was complete and that
it was time to acknowledge her contribution to Serbian and Yugoslav literatures in an appropriate
manner.

In 1964 Maksimović celebrated the fortieth anniversary of her first collection by publishing a
volume of reflective and mature poetry, *Tražim
pomilovanje*. It impressed both the critics and the
reading public by its original structure and powerful
poetic message. Subtitled "Lirske diskusije s
Dušanovim zakonikom" (Lyrical Discussions with
Czar Dushan's Code of Laws), the collection begins
with an introductory poem titled "Proglas" (The
Proclamation [of the Code]). Some of the poems
that follow have as their subject the well-known
fourteenth-century Serbian czar Dushan the Powerful. In a solemn voice the czar authoritatively presents principles of his justice through various poeti-
cized "articles" of his Code of Laws, including "O
carskom selu" (On the Czar's Village), "O poklisaru"
(On the Envoy), and "O odbeglu robu" (On the Run-
away Slave). He carefully delineates the social differ-
ence between the feudal lords and the serfs on which

that justice was based. In response, the lyric persona of other poems, representing the voice of the poet, seeks mercy for all men and women exposed to sufferings and injustice and ostracized by czars, God, or others, regardless of their social class and whether they are guilty or innocent. The collection glorifies forgiveness and compassion for all human beings, "the same as we are or different from us."

The procession of people for whom the poet seeks mercy begins with the lowly male and female serfs: "Za sebra" (For the Serf), and "Za sebarske žene" (For Female Serfs). It continues with the monk and the heretic, the soldiers killed in wars ("Za vojnička groblja" [For Military Graveyards]), those stripped of power and the powerful ones, the misunderstood, the naive, the shy and clumsy ones ("Za one koji se spotiču preko praga"[For Those Who Stumble over the Threshold]), the prisoners who were granted amnesty but have never been forgiven, Mary Magdalene, the Cinderellas of this world, barren women, people who mock everyone, those who like magicians destroy or build at will the reputations of others, and many more. The czar's presence is felt constantly, because the poet occasionally addresses him directly. Both poetic subjects know, however, that the czar belongs to a distant, feudal era, and his crude principles of justice, no matter how humane they might have seemed to his subjects, are unacceptable to the poet and must not be perpetuated in modern times. In the closing poem, "O praštanju" (About Forgiveness), the czar defends himself – "I am not God. / Only He is strong enough / to forgive . . ." – because, if God forgives, no man would dare accuse him of being either weak, "or a dreamer and a *poet.*"

Tražim pomilovanje, published when Marshal Tito's regime had already begun to show its weaknesses and corruption, created a sense of euphoria in Serbia and catapulted the poet to heights of fame and popularity she had not experienced before. The book became a best-seller and in less than a year was reprinted three times. Shows in which her lyrical discussions with Czar Dushan were read by leading actors, actresses, and choirs to sold-out theater halls sprang up all over the country. As a result, between 1964 and the celebration of her seventieth birthday in 1968, Maksimović was highly honored many more times. In 1965 she was elected a full member of the Serbian Academy of Sciences and Arts, and in 1967 the Supreme Soviet of the Soviet Union awarded her a Medal of Honor.

In 1973 she again surprised everyone with a new collection, *Nemam više vremena,* inspired by three recent deaths in her family, especially that of her husband in 1970. The central theme tying all the poems of this collection together is the calm resignation with which the aging poet meets and accepts death as a component of life. She prepares herself for the last journey without fear, in expectation that her loved ones will be there to meet her. For her, death means returning to nature and merging with eternity:

> We are earth.
> Every particle and thread of us
> the earth will soak up slowly,
> we are going to quench the thirst of the roots of oaks,
> and of some refuge of insects, underground.
> We are earth
> and death will drain us
> with innumerable straws and siphons.

Another best-seller, *Nemam više vremena* brought Maksimović more awards, including the Special Vuk Award for Life Achievement in 1975, which previously had been awarded only to Ivo Andrić, Serbia's first and sole recipient of the Nobel Prize for Literature.

In 1976 Maksimović published *Letopis Perunovih potomaka* (A Chronicle of Perun's Descendants). The individual poems of this collection are structured into two cycles, centered around a war and a religious controversy, both during the tenth century. The war theme introduces the Serbs and Croatians as allies, united by the will of their gods against Bulgarian aggression. The religious theme poetically evokes the times when the Croatians adopted the Latin service in their churches and broke their ancestral ties with the Serbs. She harmoniously combines elements of South Slavic ancient history and mythology in order to present universal human problems of discord among neighborly nations, senseless wars, and the suffering of innocent people brought about by leaders' greed and vanity. Perhaps nowhere else in her poetry does Maksimović create such a rich, metaphoric language in which archaisms, folklore elements, and neologisms blend so harmoniously as in this collection. However, the reviewers were not unanimous in their praise. Some of them wrote that this collection compares unfavorably to those of 1964 and 1973, mainly because it was devoted to the "banal" and "stale" theme of the relations between the Serbs, Croatians, and Bulgarians. In the light of the events of the early 1990s that ripped Yugoslavia apart, Maksimović's poetic chronicle acquires a prophetic dimension. She saw the deterioration of Serbian and Croatian relations much more clearly and much earlier than many of her contemporaries and tried to warn her people.

During the 1970s and 1980s Maksimović traveled extensively. Besides many European countries, including Great Britain and the Soviet Union, she also visited Australia, Canada, the United States, and China. In both Philadelphia and Chicago in 1980 she was the guest of the North American Society for Serbian Studies and received a plaque to commemorate her visit. After her trip to Norway she published a collection of poems, *Pesme iz Norveške* (1976; translated as *Poems from Norway*, 1984), and two years later she wrote a travel book, *Snimci iz Švajcarske* (Snapshots from Switzerland).

In 1988, while her readers and friends honored her in numerous ways on her ninetieth birthday, Maksimović published a new collection, *Pamtiću sve* (I Shall Remember Everything). The last poem of the collection, "I gavran reče" (Quoth the Raven), paraphrases Edgar Allan Poe's raven and could indicate her intention to conclude her poetic output with *Pamtiću sve*:

> Quoth the raven: never more,
> In vain the spring denies it
> and the nests of nightingales and black birds
> and also the chirping of the crickets deny it,
> they are outshouted by the blind owl
> and by my heart, which whispers softly, very softly: never
> more.

The dominant themes of the collection are farewell to life and the poet's effort to prepare for death properly.

With its accent on love in all of its varieties, on the beauty of nature, and on universal ethical principles, Desanka Maksimović's superb poetry represents her most valuable contribution to Serbian literature. She has also presented to Serbian readers classical and modern Slavic and French writers, such as Fyodor Dostoyevski, Aleksandr Pushkin, Anton Chekhov, Anna Akhmatova, Francè Prešeren, Oton Župančič, Elisaveta Bagryana, Elin Pelin, Honoré de Balzac, and many more in excellent translations. Her many works for children and young adults include poetry, short stories, and several novels, all of which are aimed not only at entertaining young readers but at developing in them traditional ethical values cherished by the poet and love and respect for their fellow human beings.

Interview:

Biljana Sljivic-Simsic, "Flowers Have Been My Friends: An Interview with Desanka Maksimović," *Serbian Studies,* 1 (Spring 1981): 85–92.

Bibliography:

Ljubica Djordjević, *Pesničko delo Desanke Maksimović* (Belgrade: Filološki fakultet Beogradskog univerziteta, 1973), pp. 337–441, 468–497.

Biographies:

Miodrag Blečić, *Desanka Maksimović: Život praćen pesmom* (Belgrade: Slovo ljubve, 1971);

M. Blečić, "Život," in *Desanka Maksimović: Život, Pesme, Kritike,* edited by Mirjana Vasiljević (Belgrade: Slovo ljubve, 1978), pp. 13–86;

Velizar Bošković, *Pesnikinja izbliza: Tihi nemiri Desanke Maksimović* (Belgrade: Stručna knjiga, 1992).

References:

Joanne Delavan, "Desanka Maksimović," *Review* (Belgrade), 1–2 (1985): 33–34;

Ljubica Djordjević, *Pesničko delo Desanke Maksimović* (Belgrade: Filološki fakultet Beogradskog univerziteta, 1973);

Miroslav Egerić, "Verses of Love and Nature," *Relations* (Belgrade), 1 (1985): 45–48;

Dragan Nedeljković, *Desanka Maksimović: Pesnik naše sudbine* (Sombor, Yugoslavia: Gradska biblioteka "Karlo Bjelicki," 1974);

Elizabeth Pribić, "Desanka Maksimović's Translations of Bulgarian Literature," *Festschrift für Nikola R. Pribić,* edited by Josip Matešić and Erwin Wedel (Neuried: Hieronymus, 1983), pp. 271–284;

Marie B. Schulte, "Images of Women in the Works of Desanka Maksimović," M.A. thesis, Oxford University, Corpus Christi College, 1991 — includes an appendix with more than twenty poems translated by Schulte;

Biljana Sljivic-Simsic, "The Collective Hero-Victim in Desanka Maksimović's *Letopis Perunovih potomaka* (1976)," *Southeastern Europe,* 9, nos. 1–2 (1982): 70–83.

Ranko Marinković

(22 February 1913 –)

Cynthia Simmons
Boston College

BOOKS: *Proze* (Zagreb: Matica hrvatska, 1948);
Geste i grimase (Zagreb: Zora, 1951; revised edition, Zagreb: Znanje, 1979);
Ruke (Zagreb: Kultura, 1953; revised edition, Belgrade: Kultura, 1962);
Pod balkonima (Belgrade: Prosveta, 1953);
Glorija (Zagreb: IBI, 1956; corrected edition, Belgrade: Nolit, 1966; revised edition, Belgrade: Nolit, 1972); translated by David Miladinov and Roberta Reeder as "Gloria" in *Five Modern Yugoslav Plays,* edited by Branko Mikasinovich (New York: Cyrco Press, 1977), pp. 147–266;
Poniženje Sokrata (Zagreb: Naprijed, 1959);
Koštane zvijezde (Sarajevo: Svjetlost, 1961);
Karneval i druge pripovijesti (Zagreb: Naprijed, 1964);
Kiklop (Belgrade: Prosveta, 1965);
Novele (Zagreb: Školska knjiga, 1966);
Zagrljaj i druge novele (Belgrade: Prosveta, 1968);
Tri drame: Albatros, Glorija, Politeia ili Inspektorove spletke (Zagreb: Znanje, 1977); *Politeia ili Inspektorove spletke* translated by Ellen Elias Bursać as "Politeia or The Inspector's Intrigues," *The Bridge,* 55 (1978): 17–32;
Zajednička kupka (Zagreb: Biblioteka Hit, Znanje, 1980);
Sabrana djela Ranka Marinkovića, 6 volumes (Zagreb: Grafički zavod Hrvatske, 1982);
Nevesele oči klauna (Zagreb: Globus, 1986).

PLAY PRODUCTIONS: *Albatros,* Zagreb, Croatian National Theater, 29 March 1939;
Glorija, Zagreb, Croatian National Theater, 29 December 1955;
Politeia ili Inspektorove spletke, Zagreb, Croatian National Theater, 16 October 1977.

Dalmatia has bequeathed great storytellers to Croatian literature, including Vladan Desnica, Vjekoslav Kaleb, Petar Šegedin, and Vladimir Nazor. Yet Ranko Marinković stands out among them. The corpus of his creative works may be modest in comparison to some, but his work is finely honed

Ranko Marinković

and of universal appeal. Even when the settings of his tales are provincial, Marinković's meditations on the modern human condition are applicable to all. For that reason, certain works by Marinković have been widely translated, and he has done much to promote his nation's literature on the contemporary European literary scene.

Ranko Marinković was born on 22 February 1913 on the island of Vis. He led an isolated early childhood, which coincided with World War I. His formal education began in 1919, just after the war. He attended elementary school on Vis and high school in Split and Zagreb. Infected with the spirit of "world crisis" during his secondary school years, he began to write.

In the years leading to his degree from the Philosophy faculty of the University of Zagreb,

Marinković published poems, stories, essays, and criticism in magazines and newspapers, including *Novo vrijeme* (New Times), *Mladost* (Youth), *Politika* (Politics), *Učiteljska riječ* (The Teacher's Word), and *Dani i ljudi* (Days and People). The mood or theme of some poems found a more mature dramatic or narrative expression in later works – for example, "Monolog na konopcu" (Monologue on a Rope) in his play *Glorija* (1956; translated as "Gloria," 1977), "Podnevno kupalište ili ja, što se davim u oceanu duhovne borbe da doživim renesansu" (The Midday Swim or Whether I Who Am Drowning in the Ocean of Spiritual Struggle Will Live to See the Renaissance), and in the parodic prose of Marinković's most recent novel, *Zajednička kupka* (Shared Bath, 1980). The same can be said for the early prose – leitmotivs from the stories "Debut doktora Budikovca" (The Debut of Doctor Budikovac), "Dva mrtvaca" (Two Corpses), "Maestrali s mora" (Mistrals from the Sea), and "Vigilije" (Vigils) are further developed in *Karneval i druge pripovijesti* (Carnival and Other Stories, 1964), *Proze* (Prose Pieces, 1948), and elsewhere. Marinković's essayistic and critical writings of these years reveal not only his appreciation of literary freshness and independence, particularly in the works of Tin Ujević and Miroslav Krleža, but also his receptiveness to modern irony and satire – attitudes that better characterize his later works, especially his novels.

Marinković's connection with Krleža in the first phase of his career and up to World War II was, in fact, quite direct. The already well known Krleža invited the young writer to collaborate with him on the literary journal *Pečat* (Stamp). Marinković had plans of his own, however. In 1937 he founded his journal *Dani i ljudi* (Days and People). Although it ceased publication after only a few issues, it documents the advent on the Croatian literary scene of a significant group of progressive young intellectuals. Two years later Marinković accepted Krleža's offer of collaboration and presented several of his own works in *Pečat*, a journal considered to be the primary forum at that time for modernist experimentation and dialogue. Ivan Goran Kovačić, a promising young writer of the interwar period, recognized in Marinković's stories, such as "Sunčana je Dalmacija" (Sunny Is Dalmatia) and "Hiljadu i jedna noć" (One Thousand and One Nights), an "exceptional gift." During this period Marinković also saw his first play, *Albatros* (Albatross, 1939), staged at the Croatian National Theater under the direction of Freda Delak. This play, its anticlericalism and antifascism reminiscent of Krleža, suggests a grim denouement of the story of

civilization on its contemporary course. Significantly, it appeared on the eve of World War II.

In 1941 Marinković was captured by the Italians in occupied Split and spent two years in a camp in Ferramonte. After the capitulation of Italy in the fall of 1943, he spent a year at the refugee camp at El Shatt, Egypt, where he was able to resume writing. In 1945 he organized an exhibit in freed Split of refugees from El Shatt and took up official posts in the Croatian Ministry of Education and the government publishing house, Nakladni zavod, of the republic.

From 1946 to 1950 Marinković was the director of the Croatian National Theater. In 1951 he became a professor of drama at the Zagreb Academy of Dramatic Art. Thus, in addition to the considerable influence Marinković has had on modern prose writers and playwrights, he has served as teacher and mentor to generations of students of dramatic performance as well.

After the war Marinković published fewer essays and criticism and more prose works. His first book, *Proze*, received a literary award from the Federal Yugoslav Committee on Culture. Like many other writers from Dalmatia, Marinković favored in these and earlier stories, such as those published in *Pečat*, the customs and speech patterns of his native region. Yet the universal appeal of his clerics, landowners, and provincial officials suggests interpretations of his works that carry meaning beyond the strictly regional. In "Cvrčci i bubnjevi – Samotni život tvoj" (Crickets and Drums – Your Lonely Life), for example, the inadequacies and, perhaps, insincerity of the local Catholic priests are revealed against the backdrop of Dalmatia's stunning and regenerative natural beauty. The local color provides an engaging context for the dialectic of the spiritual versus the material. Nonetheless, underlying this first collection was a suggestion of what was to come. As Marinković notes in *Proze*, "the fragments are written as building material for some novel."

The masterpieces of Marinković's short prose and drama appeared in the 1950s. The best-known collection of his short stories, *Ruke* (The Hands), was first published in 1953 and was honored that year by a literary award from the city of Zagreb. This first edition varies considerably from the second edition of 1962. The overriding theme that connects the stories of the original collection – "Mrtve duše" (Dead Souls), "Karneval" (Carnival), "Suknja" (The Skirt), "Andjeo" (The Angel), "U znaku vage" (Under the Sign of Libra), "Koštane zvijezde" (Bony Stars), "Prah" (Dust), "Benito Floda von Reltih" (a parodic amalgam of Benito

Mussolini's first name and *Adolf Hitler* spelled backwards), "Ruke," and "Zagrljaj" (The Embrace) – is the fear of war. Marinković's dread of war had characterized earlier works as well, which before World War II were often noted for their atmosphere of foreboding. Preoccupation with fear and death, in retrospect, struck some critics as an obsession.

The title story of the collection is Marinković's most translated work. The common war themes of morality versus loyalty and violence or barbarism versus humanity here receive a virtuosic treatment. The story commences with a narrator's obfuscated observation of "them" thrown across the back, the left one being caressed in the embrace of the right one. Despite the suggestion of the title, the reader does not immediately comprehend the situation. Only after the introductory paragraphs, with a switch to dramatic dialogue, is it clear that the surreal situation is a conversation between two hands. The right hand is the more capable, powerful, intelligent, and serious one. It is also more "civilized" than the left hand. The more atavistic and instinctual left hand criticizes the right hand for its complicity in "his" transgressions. The right hand signed the death sentence of a man who "sinned" in word but not deed; that evening, it caressed a woman, having forgotten – or worse, having been emboldened by – its role in the "criminal's" cruel fate. The argument continues until the left hand endures an affront to its honor – a notion the left hand had ridiculed just before, with regard to the military code of honor. A young boy spits on the left hand after it has playfully tweaked the boy's nose. The right hand rises to the left hand's defense, and when the boy's father confronts the hands, the right hand again comes to the left hand's defense. Despite the differences between them, the hands join in kinship to defend themselves against the "enemy." With the reference to the swastika that the right hand wears on its sleeve, the reader can assume that the argument rages over the Croatian right hand's collaboration with the Nazi occupiers. However, the fact that the controversy is depicted by means of the metonymic images of hands encourages a wide range of interpretations.

The barbarism and betrayal that characterize the wartime mentality of "Ruke" are complemented by the sense of suspicion, oppression, and persecution of that period conveyed in another well-known story from the collection, "Zagrljaj." As in "Ruke," some mystery surrounds the opening scene. The narrator peers through a keyhole at a man at a desk attempting to write. The writer, the narrator ex-

plains, is afraid of someone, and that fear is realized on the little bit of text that the writer has managed to produce by an ink blot that falls on the paper and begins to spreading, obscuring the words. Another assault on the writer's prose comes from an ant that mistakes a letter for fly droppings and attempts to carry it off. In exasperation, the writer gets up to go out. The narrator follows and describes the writer's encounters with what the reader comes to realize are the real-life counterparts of the fictional characters with whom he was wrestling in his room. All are intimidated by an armed police officer who dares them even to look at him askance. The story takes a surprising twist when the writer, in defiance of the narrator's warnings, follows the police officer to a secluded spot, sneaks up on him, and grabs him from behind. This is the "embrace" referred to in the title. The writer has decided to sacrifice himself – to hold "a piece of disgusting, filthy life" until they both perish. The writer has been vanquished by authoritarian oppression, the ink blot on his prose – but he is capable of one heroic deed so that others may live freely – and write.

Marinković's admission that he considered his earlier *Proze* to be fragments of a future novel may have predisposed some critics to observe a similar incompleteness or fragmentation in some of the stories of *Ruke*, especially in "U znaku vage." Both Vlatko Pavletić and Borislav Mihajlović recognized in *Ruke* the promise of a novel. For whatever reason, Marinković was unsatisfied with the composition of this second collection, and when it was republished in 1962 he replaced "Mrtve duše," "U znaku vage," and "Karneval" with the revised prose poem "Cvrčci i bubnjevi – Samotni život tvoj" from *Proze*, titled here simply "Samotni život tvoj."

Marinković's recognition as a world-class playwright came with the premiere of *Glorija* at the Croatian National Theater in 1955. The play was hailed as a masterpiece of contemporary drama and was produced the following year in several other Yugoslav cities and European capitals. *Glorija* was received not only as a supercharged tragedy but also as a poetic lament on the modern human condition. Characters in the play are powerless before the forces controlling either the spiritual realm (the church) or secular, material existence, symbolized by the circus.

The pressures from the priests – spiritual and secular "fathers" – and the public, which destroy the title character Glorija, would be minimized if not negligible if the protagonist were not a woman. Glorija, in her "incarnation" as Sister Magdalene, is brought to a Dalmatian village church to help the local bishop and his secretary, Father Jere, provide their parishioners with a "miracle." Glorija is the stage name of Jagoda, a former acrobat who, when she lost her nerve, left the circus and her father to join a convent. She is brought in as an accomplice to the priests' scheme because of her assumed dramatic talent. Sister Magdalene's task is to stand motionless in the niche of the statue of the Virgin Mary and only occasionally give some "miraculous" sign. Complications arise from two sources, specifically from two men.

By coincidence Sister Magdalene's father, Kozlović, arrives at the parish at the same time she does. He has been wandering about, trying to interest a parish in his own "miracle" – a mechanical Jesus who moans and bleeds red ink. Because he recognizes his daughter as she is led into the church, he refuses to leave the town when his device is rejected. In the meantime Father Jere finds fault with Sister Magdalene's "performance" – she is too womanly, her eyes are too lively, she lacks the pure and otherworldly stare of the Madonna, and she seems to be too interested in displaying her own beauty. The fact is that Father Jere falls in love with Sister Magdalene and finds her guilty for his attraction to her. She quickly reaches a stage of mental and emotional turmoil, torn between her father, who visits the church and calls to his daughter to recognize him, and Father Jere, whom she loves but also resents for his impossible expectations of her. The situation becomes critical when an old woman who has prayed to the "Madonna" to heal her son, and from whom she has received a sign, returns to the church crying hysterically and yelling that the Virgin is a fraud, for her son has died. Horrified by her deception of the faithful and enraged at Father Jere's exploitation of her, Glorija decides to leave with her father.

In the last scene Glorija prepares for her first performance since returning to the circus. She plans to attempt an unheard-of double somersault without a net. Her old fears remain, and, in addition, she tells her friend (one of the clowns) that she now hears voices – they come from the church – and she hears the Bach fugue that Father Jere used to play to her as the Madonna. Just as she is about to go on, Father Jere appears unexpectedly. She soon realizes that he has not changed and that his life is troubled more as a result of his failed ambitions than by his moral hypocrisy. Nonetheless, he has come to warn Jagoda, as he begins to call her, not to perform. He feels that some of his sin – the ruse of the Madonna – has entered her, and she will perish. Jagoda reacts toward Father Jere with pity until he begins to

blame her father for sacrificing her to *his* own ambitions. She asks the priest to leave. Now on the scene, Kozlović encourages Jagoda to perform, and the loudspeaker announces her act. With a sense of resignation, she goes on. When the clown comes running to Jagoda's father to warn him that she is not concentrating, his response is that it is too late – the show has begun. Jagoda has asked the orchestra to play Bach's fugue, and to that accompaniment she falls to her death. Thus Jagoda is lost to the personas created for her – by her father as the trapeze artist Glorija Flesh, and by Father Jere as the whore, Magdalene, playing the Madonna. She never was allowed, as she protests at the end of the play, even to ask why.

The play goes beyond postwar anticlericism in the Communist world in its argument – in the Slavic tradition of Fyodor Dostoyevsky, Yevgeni Zamiatin, and Mikhail Bulgakov – against the enslavement of free will through mystery and miracle. *Glorija* must also be considered in the context of Marinković's grand motif of the circus. The circus world is the exclusively human sphere, where human foibles can prevail but also where one might witness a genuine earthly miracle.

In 1959 Marinković published an authoritative revised edition of his selected short prose, *Poniženje Sokrata* (The Humiliation of Socrates). Included are the title story, "Sanjiva kronika" (Sleepy Chronicle), "Balkon" (The Balcony), "Ni braća ni rodjaci" (Neither Brothers Nor Kin), "Karneval," "Mislilac nad osam grobova" (A Ponderer over Eight Graves), and "Oko božje" (God's Eye). Some of the stories had appeared in an earlier collection, *Pod balkonima* (Under the Balconies, 1953). Typical of Marinković's early works, the action takes place in the locales of his childhood – small island towns of Dalmatia. As with his other Dalmatian stories, the author's observations on the sometimes-eccentric behavior of the islanders carries universal significance. Other collections of selected works followed shortly thereafter, including *Karneval i druge pripovijesti*.

With the publication of his first novel, *Kiklop* (The Cyclops, 1965), Marinković achieved the same immediate recognition in that genre as he had with his play *Glorija*. In that year he received the NIN prize for the best novel of the year, an award from the city of Zagreb, the Goran prize, and the annual award from the Vladimir Nazor Fund. For many critics, *Kiklop* secured a place for Croatian literature in the history of the twentieth-century novel.

Despite its epic sweep, *Kiklop* is characterized by its fragmentation, which is motivated by the encounters, discussions, ruminations, and dreams of the protagonist, the journalist Melkior. The implied place and time is Zagreb in the early days of World War II. The wartime atmosphere mentioned in his short stories – of chaos, intrigue, fear, and aggression – is even more intensified. Melkior, before, during, and after his time in the army, ponders the cyclic nature of history, especially the inevitable return of the forces of evil. The message is not cynical, however. Significantly, those in the fictional Zoopolis infected with the fever of war hail from the intelligentsia. As stated in the novel, "Life has chosen the intelligentsia for its games; it doesn't make history with idiots." Perhaps from such meditations the reader can discover the sources of disintegration and a new humanity. Marinković's ultimate intent is to escape the eye of the cyclops.

The next addition to Marinković's dramatic works was the vaudeville *Politeia ili Inspektorove spletke* (1977; translated as "Politeia or The Inspector's Intrigues," 1978). It is a timeless political farce on the police state and those who enforce oppression. Many critics consider it uncharacteristic of the playwright and not on a par with similar dramas in this vein. Nonetheless, the dialogue offers many successful tragicomic moments.

When Marinković's collected works were first published in six volumes in 1982, they included a new and still-unperformed play, *Pustinja* (The Desert). Another tragicomedy, it dramatizes the overwhelming scope of human deceit and yet is not utterly cynical or postmodern. The main character, Fabije, pronounces, "My home is a desert, there I see my mirage." If one can identify the mirage, can one then improve upon reality?

Marinković's second novel suffers in comparison to *Kiklop. Zajednička kupka,* published in 1980, fifteen years after the first novel, has been described as a contemporary feuilleton. The twenty short pieces, though related through the cast of characters, lack any organic unity. Through a series of life situations the reader wonders at human resilience or explores the frontier of the real and the imaginary. For example, the Candidesque Jakobson is convinced that despite his travails, even if he must bathe in excrement, he can find contentment. In defense of this latest work of fiction, it can be viewed simply as an extension of Marinković's experimentation with the genre, in which he has abandoned all conventions of composition and style.

Interview:

Radovan Popović, "Yugoslav Dramatists Speaking," *Scena,* 2 (1979): 123–130.

References:

Ljubomir Cvijetić, *Književno djelo Ranka Marinkovića* (Sarajevo: Svjetlost, 1980);

Branimir Donat, "From Individual to Mythic Experience," *The Bridge,* 3–4 (1966): 89–92;

Darko Gašparović, "Ranko Marinković: 'Politeia or The Inspector's Intrigues,' " *The Bridge,* 55 (1978): 33–35;

Petar Marjanović, "Ranko Marinković: 'Gloria,' " *Scena,* 7 (1984): 154–159;

Milivoje Marković, *Prostori realizma* (Subotica: Minerva, 1981);

G. R. Tamarin, *Teorija groteske* (Sarajevo: Svjetlost, 1962);

Šime Vučetić, *Izmedju dogme i apsurda* (Zagreb: Matica hrvatska, 1960).

Antun Gustav Matoš

(13 June 1873 – 17 March 1914)

Dubravka Juraga
University of Arkansas

BOOKS: *Iverje: Skice i sličice* (Mostar: Izdavačka
   knjižara Pacher i Kisića, 1899);
Novo iverje: Skice i sličice (Zagreb: Knjižara Franje
   Suppana, 1900);
Ogledi: Studije i impresije (Zadar: Hrvatska knjižar-
   nica, 1905);
Vidici i putovi: Eseji i impresije (Zagreb: Knjižara Lav-
   oslava Kleina, 1907);
Umorne priče (Zagreb: Knjižara Mirka Breyera, 1909);
Tri humoreske (Zagreb: Humoristična knjižnica,
   1909);
Naši ljudi i krajevi: Portreti i pejzaži (Zagreb: Knjižara
   Josipa Sokola, 1910);
Moralista i druge satire (Zagreb: Naklada Humoristične
   knjižnice, 1911);
Život za milijune (Zagreb: Naklada Humoristične
   knjižnice, 1912);
Pečalba: Kaprisi i feljtoni (Zagreb: Društvo hrvatskih
   književnika, 1913);
Djela A. G. Matoša, 17 volumes (Zagreb: Binoza,
   1935–1940);
Dragi naši savremenici, Djela, volume 10 (Zagreb:
   Binoza, 1940);
Pripovijetke (Zagreb: Zora, 1951);
Sabrana djela, 20 volumes, edited by Dragutin
   Tadijanović and others (Zagreb: Jugoslavenska
   akademija znanosti i umjetnosti, 1976).
Editions in English: "The Neighbor," translated by
   Ivan Mladineo in *Great Short Stories of the
   World,* edited by Bennett Harper Clark and
   Maxim Lieber (New York: McBride, 1925),
   pp. 824–830;
"A Time to Remember," translated by Eugene E.
   Pantzer in his *Antun Gustav Matoš* (Boston:
   Twayne, 1981), pp. 91–126.

Antun Gustav Matoš

Antun Gustav Matoš was an important and
controversial Croatian modernist writer whose
work participated in the sense of turmoil and
change that swept across turn-of-the-century Europe. Partially due to the unsettled and contradictory times in which he lived and partially because of
his own disposition, Matoš's work is distinguished
by a remarkable range of attitudes and opinions on
a variety of issues. He maintained a belief in the
power of laughter and a consistently ironic attitude
toward his own life and work, but he never lost
sight of the importance of his task. Matoš was an intellectual and a writer who sought to introduce European standards into Croatian culture and literature, and his work had considerable influence on
later Croatian and Serbian writers of the twentieth
century.

   He wrote in a variety of genres, including
poems, short stories, and essays; literary and the-

ater criticism; travel books; commentaries on contemporary life and culture; and book reviews. Of these, he is now best known for his poetry; though he wrote only about eighty poems, perhaps twenty are now considered masterpieces. His stories and essays show a variety of influences – Edgar Allan Poe and Charles Baudelaire are especially important – while still resonating with the new voices of modernism and its credo of "making it new." Matoš also left an important volume of criticism, in which he lucidly and masterfully appraised various Serbian, Croatian, and European writers such as Stendahl, Isidora Sekulić, Lord Byron, Oscar Wilde, Sima Pandurović, Jovan Veselinović, Jovan Dučić, Vladimir Nazor, Dinko Šimunović, Émile Zola, Laza K. Lazarević, August Šenoa, and many others.

Matoš was born on 13 June 1873 in Tovarnik, near the town Šid in Srem. He was the second of five children of August Matoš and Maria Schams Matoš. His father, originally from Herzegovina, was an ethnic Croat who taught music. His mother was of Dutch descent. In 1875 the family moved to Zagreb, where Matoš spent his childhood and early youth. He continued to regard Zagreb as his home throughout his bohemian career, much of which was spent in exile. He attended the Zagreb high school, where he studied French and cello. Matoš was not a successful student; he was independent-minded and studied only what interested him. After getting three failing grades, one of which was in Croatian, he dropped out of school at age seventeen. From 1891 to 1892 he attended veterinary school in Vienna but dropped out due to illness.

In 1892 Matoš published his first story, "Moć savjesti" (The Power of Conscience), in the prestigious journal *Vijenac* (Garland). The next year he was drafted into the Austro-Hungarian Imperial Cavalry and sent to Slavonia. Freedom loving and independent, Matoš found this new military environment oppressive. After eight months of cleaning stables and tending to horses, he was reassigned to a farrier's school in Zagreb but could not adjust to military life. In August 1894 he and another soldier deserted to flee to Serbia. On the way he was captured and imprisoned in the Petrovaradin fortress in Novi Sad, but he soon escaped and finally reached Serbia by October 1894.

The next three years Matoš spent in Belgrade. He worked at various jobs – as a tutor, a cellist, a journalist, and a writer – living the life of a true bohemian. Often he would have only enough money to eat once a day; he was constantly in debt for his room, and he had to spend sharp Continental winters wearing his summer clothes. When he did earn money he would immediately spend it paying debts. If anything was left, he would spend it with his friends in the café Dardaneli, the heart of Belgrade's literary and bohemian life at the time.

Matoš plunged into Belgrade's literary circles, making friends and receiving their support for his work. His friendship with Janko Veselinović, a prominent Serbian writer, was among the most important, as Veselinović helped him to establish ties within the literary communities in Belgrade and Sarajevo. Veselinović introduced Matoš to Kosta Hörman, the editor of the Sarajevo journal *Nada* (Hope). Hörman recognized Matoš's talent and published his numerous essays and pieces. Matoš's literary contributions to *Nada* were the most important and steady source of income that he had at the time. He was determined to live off his writing throughout most of his life. This determination led him to a life of poverty and ill health, but he was probably the first genuinely professional writer in South Slavic literature.

Matoš enjoyed the literary and intellectual life he found in Belgrade. He befriended many figures from artistic, theatrical, and literary circles there. In his numerous literary essays Matoš described the social life of Belgrade and many important people who dominated that life; in his reviews of concerts, theater performances, or soirees he commented upon the literary, political, and cultural scene of the time. Belgrade and its life became Matoš's favorite theme, and he is one of the best chroniclers of this period in the Serbian capital.

Despite constant poverty and a struggle to survive, Matoš managed to study, write, and publish prolifically. Regardless of the friendships he made, he gave priority to his work as a literary critic, and his fierce criticisms of various writers for their bad work sometimes led to strained relationships. His peaceful life in Belgrade came to an end when he wrote a negative review of Veselinović's recently published novel *Hajduk Stanko* (Rebel Stanko, 1896). This was the last straw for the Belgrade society, as Matoš had already alienated many people with his biting observations and criticisms. After the review was published, he was regarded as an ingrate; many attacks on him were published in various journals. He lost his job as a cellist and was even labeled an Austrian spy. He became a persona non grata in all of Belgrade's circles.

Unable to support himself and dissatisfied with the atmosphere that encircled him, Matoš regretfully left Belgrade in January 1898, intending to go to Paris. A false passport enabled him to travel through Austria so that he could visit his friends and his sister Danica in Vienna. There he was recognized by a soldier from his former regiment, and he hastily left for Munich. He spent a carefree month there, during which he wrote little. From Munich he went to Geneva, where he read a great deal and studied in order to educate himself further. There he wrote letters to *Nada* about various subjects, one of which was Jean-Jacques Rousseau's birthplace. He also wrote an important essay about Voltaire. His first collection of stories, *Iverje: Skice i sličice* (Chips: Sketches and Pictures), appeared while he was in Geneva in 1899. The collection consisted of stories that Matoš had published since 1892: "Moć savjesti," "Nezahvalnost" (Ingratitude), "Čestitka" (Greetings), "Pereci, friški pereci" (Pretzels, Fresh Pretzels), "Kip domovine leta 188-" (A Monument to the Homeland, Year 188-), and "Miš" (A Mouse).

Most of these stories are realistic and written in a mildly satirical tone. They often deal with political issues, as when Matoš focuses on the occupation and oppression of Croatia by Austro-Hungary in "Kip domovine leta 188-." Here he depicts the death of an old woman, a symbol of the Croatian people, crushed under the hooves of the Austrian cavalry. In this story he manages in only a few words to bring alive centuries of serfdom and humiliation.

But Matoš can also be romantic and optimistic; in "Pereci, friški pereci" Matoš depicts a young and tender love relationship between a hussar and his poor girlfriend. "Moć savjesti," Matoš's first story, is a combination of the realistic and fantastic tendencies that color his storytelling. In this story the realistic portrayal of a corrupt provincial bureaucrat is transformed into the fantastic account of a Gogolian nightmare. "Miš" is Matoš's psychological study of the unconscious mind of a man, Mihajlo Milinović, tormented by guilt over the suicide of his pregnant girlfriend. In this suspenseful story, informed by an atmosphere reminiscent of Poe, Mihajlo's conscience takes its toll and induces him inadvertently to become the victim of his own "suicide."

In Geneva, Matoš had so little money and the royalties for his published work came so rarely that he was forced to ask various people for help. In August 1899 he secretly left his unpaid quarters in Geneva and headed for Paris. He was excited when he finally arrived in the heart of European art and culture. In Paris he lived in cheap hotels or rented rooms that he could not afford to heat; he often went hungry. But Paris and its effervescent life had a strong appeal for Matoš. He had an open and

Matoš with his fiancée, Olga Herak, in 1910

eager mind thirsty for artistic and cultural life in the metropolis, and that intensive life strongly influenced him in his literary development. One of the places Matoš never tired of visiting in Paris was the library, where he spent countless hours studying and writing.

For the next five years his life in Paris followed a pattern similar to that in other places he had lived: with little or no money, he was often hungry and in need of good clothing and a warm room. But his enthusiasm for literature and writing and his determination to earn his keep as a man of letters never diminished. His financial situation improved slightly in 1900 when he held a position as a press attaché in the Bosnian Pavilion at the Paris Exposition. He tirelessly wrote letters, published mainly in *Hrvatsko pravo* (Croatian Right) in Zagreb, in which he discussed Parisian, Croatian, and cosmopolitan themes. He also discussed various people from the artistic, literary, and cultural worlds.

This period also had a tremendous impact on Matoš as an essay writer. His essays on Stendahl,

Voltaire, Rousseau, Baudelaire, Paul France, Maurice Barrès, Oscar Wilde, and Friedrich Nietzsche are among his finest.

Matoš made numerous friends in Paris, but his friendships with André Rouveyre and Edouard Champion were the most important. Rouveyre generously offered to share with Matoš the security of his warm rented room and his meager financial means. Champion's father owned a well-known bookstore, where Matoš had an opportunity to meet some of the most important writers and intellectuals of the time.

His Paris period was the most important of Matoš's creativity. There he wrote about fifteen stories, which are considered to be among his best and most mature work. While in Paris he published his second book of collected stories, *Novo iverje* (New Chips, 1900). The stories in this collection include "Nekad bilo – sad se spominjalo" (Once Upon a Time – Now Only Remembered; translated as "A Time to Remember," 1981), "U čudnim gostima" (A Strange Visit), "Camao," "Božićna prič" (A Christmas Story), "Iglasto čeljade" (A Needlelike Being), and "Samotna noć" (A Lonely Night). As in the first collection, these stories follow two patterns. Several are realistic depictions of life in his native Croatia, with tones ranging from critical and satirical to openly sentimental. Others are bizarre and fantastic, filled with strange elements and symbols by which Matoš attempts psychological analyses of his characters, usually eccentric intellectuals through whom Matoš depicts modern humanity and the crises with which it has to struggle. In these stories he does not attempt to achieve realistic representation but searches for an aesthetic truth. Love is a common theme in his stories. Love is often juxtaposed with death, and in contrasting them Matoš suggests the antithesis of the banal and the ideal and their dramatic conflict. Stories such as "Camao," "Iglasto čeljade," or "U čudnim gostima," "Miš" or "Samotna noć" have a nightmarish quality and are reminiscent of Baudelaire or Poe.

Matoš follows similar patterns in his third story collection, *Umorne priče* (Tired Stories, 1909). Among the most interesting stories from this collection are "Lijepa Jelena" (Beautiful Jelena) and "Balkon" (Balcony). Both stories show destructive forces at work. In "Lijepa Jelena" Matoš portrays a painter who is destroyed by his constant search for ideal beauty. In the wonderfully lyrical "Balkon" the narrator is unable to accept and appreciate his real life because of his similar yearning for an impossible ideal. Such stories are representative of Matoš's complex poetics. On the one hand, his

work is informed by an aesthetic quest for beauty and harmony – he was something of an idealist. On the other hand, Matoš frequently deals with the cruel disjunction between the real and the ideal.

Though he lived the life of an emigré and a cosmopolitan intellectual, Matoš's main interest always lay in his homeland of Croatia. He sought in his writing to help Croatia rise from the backwardness caused by hundreds of years of Austrian domination. He bitterly fought against the narrow-minded provincialism of those who tried to close off Croatia from the rest of the world. Instead, he argued that Croatian culture could best grow and flourish through exposure to the best that European culture had to offer.

By 1902 he again became bored and restless and wanted to leave Paris. He considered going to the United States but opted for Belgrade instead in order to be closer to Olga Herak, a girl in Zagreb with whom he had established a warm correspondence. This second stay in Belgrade lasted almost four years, from 1904 to 1908. It was among the most trying periods of Matoš's difficult life. Some of his disappointment lay in the fact that he was coming from Paris, a metropolis with which Belgrade could hardly compare. But other things contributed as well: many of his former bohemian friends had left the city or died. His income was again very meager; he often had to live in unheated, damp, and expensive rooms. Partially due to such conditions, his right hand became crippled by Dupuyterin's disease, and he had to start writing with his left hand while in constant fear that this hand might eventually succumb as well.

As soon as he arrived in Belgrade he became involved in various debates, especially with the renowned critic Jovan Skerlić and the poet Jovan Dučić. These polemics and numerous other essays and theater reviews were published in journals such as Belgrade's *Slobodna reč* (Free Speech), *Srpska zastava* (Serbian Banner), Zagreb's *Hrvatsko pravo, Prosvjeta* (Education), and others. Matoš made new friends among the new generation of Belgrade's bohemian writers, artists, and actors. "Traveling is poetry," he wrote, "and poets and poetic people are the best travelers." While in Belgrade, some of his travel pieces were published in the collection of essays *Vidici i putovi* (Horizons and Roads, 1907). For Matoš adventures, the search for freedom, and the hunger for the new and the unknown give the life of modern humanity its energy and substance.

In his essays Matoš delineated his artistic credo. He insisted on beauty as the highest value that brings sense to life and makes it bearable.

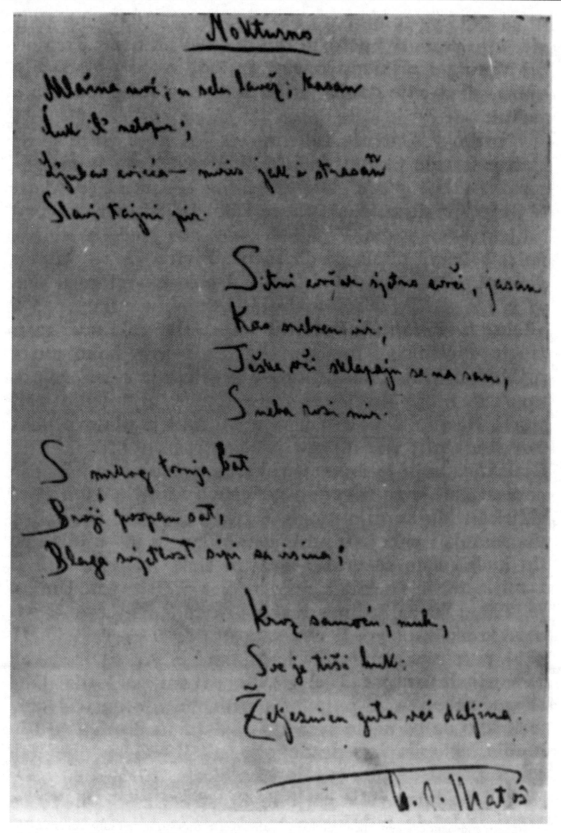

Manuscript for Matoš's sonnet "Notturno" (Nocturne), his last poem (reproduced from Mirko Žeželj's Tragajući za Matošem, *1970)*

Human stupidity, on the other hand, he identified as his most important foe. Though much of his own writing was political, he railed against any imposition of other functions and purposes, such as social concerns, on art. In his essay "Realizam i artizam" (Realism and Artism) Matoš explains:

> We are for the quite natural idea that an artist must be an artist in the first place and that a literary work must first of all be a work of art. Artism is nothing else but the emancipation of art from all other elements that are not artistic and that do not contribute to the freeing of the artist from other considerations. The infamous *l'art pour l'art* [art for art's sake] means only that the aim of art can be only art, only beauty, that art is just as free and independent as is science. The only measure of artistic value is the power of the aesthetic impression. A work of art is not a pure work of art if in it the aesthetic moment, the pure artistic moment, is not the strongest, if it is not stronger than the ethical and intellectual moment.

After spending more than a decade in exile, Matoš was ready to return home. He was eager to be with his future fiancée, Olga Herak, to visit his family and friends, and to settle down. However, due to his desertion from the army in 1893 he could not safely return to Croatia, though he secretly visited Olga in Zagreb four times from 1905 to 1907. Throughout his stay in Belgrade he continuously appealed to the Austrian government to let him return to Zagreb. Confident that amnesty would soon be granted – it was granted that fall – Matoš returned to his beloved Zagreb on 22 January 1908.

He was disappointed by changes that had occurred in Zagreb in his absence. The new, bourgeois part of the city and its philistine mentality were alien to him, while the old, aristocratic part, which for Matoš had formerly set the city's cultural tone, had almost disappeared. Nevertheless, during this period he formed a circle of young poets and intellectuals who admired him and tried to follow in his footsteps. Most prominent among his protégés was Augustin ("Tin") Ujević, though Ujević and Matoš later split and became bitter enemies.

Matoš actively participated in the political and cultural life in Zagreb. He engaged in numerous heated controversies and literary debates, often insulting and offending his opponents, sometimes unfairly. In these later years his attacks became bitter and sarcastic, and he became sensitive and easily offended. His relationship with his fiancée was also difficult. Matoš was a passionate and jealous man, and Olga was an independent and open-minded woman. Meanwhile, his habitual financial difficulties continued. In order to provide himself finally with some source of stable income, he passed exams that would enable him to become a high-school teacher. Then, after a particularly tumultuous quarrel, Olga broke their engagement.

His collection of essays *Naši ljudi i krajevi* (Our People and Regions) appeared in 1910, including important essays such as "O modernosti" (On Modernism), "Književnost i književnici" (Literature and Writers), "Jovan Skerlić," "Iz Samobora" (From Samobor), and "Oko Lobora" (Around Lobor). In 1912 Matoš wrote his only play, the unsuccessful comedy *Malo pa ništa* (A Little Next to Nothing). That same year he compiled many of his polemical essays, epigrams, and satires in a book, *Dragi naši savremenici* (Our Dear Contemporaries), which included not only his work but the work of his opponents. The book was not published until 1940. In 1913 he published *Pečalba* (Migrant Work), a collection of pieces that had appeared from 1902 to 1912. Some of the essays included here are on Isadora Duncan, Leo Tolstoy, P. T. Barnum, and others.

Matoš wrote his first poem when he was sixteen. However, his best poetry was written in the Zagreb years after 1909. This poetry was not well received during his lifetime, but he is now regarded as an important early-modernist Croatian poet. His poems are strongly influenced by Baudelaire. In the sonnet "Mladoj Hrvatskoj" (To Young Croatia) Matoš puts forward his poetic credo. A poem searches to express only rare impressions; it communicates only with the chosen few who are sensitive and refined enough to understand beauty. The aim of poetry is to achieve pure beauty. Matoš insisted on the formal perfection of a poem and argued that the sonnet is the best poetic structure because its restrictions help the poet to achieve perfection. However, his best poems seem informed more by emotion than by theory, as in "Notturno" (Nocturne), "Canticum Canticorum" (Song of Songs), or "Mora" (Nightmare). Matoš's poems are all personal and subjective, but his themes are diverse. He wrote about the unsuccessful search for love, beauty, and happiness. He also wrote patriotic poems with strong social commentary, as in the poems "Gospa Marija" (Lady Marija), "Mora," and "1909."

Matoš succeeded in obtaining a teaching position (he never actually taught – the position was a sinecure) and he was finally without financial worries. But his health continued to deteriorate. During the last decade of his life Matoš suffered from the effects of alcohol abuse and from laryngitis and a sore throat. Doctors suspected tuberculosis of the throat and treated him, unsuccessfully, for that disease; his real ailment turned out to be throat cancer. Hoping to find a cure in the warm Italian climate, Matoš traveled to Florence in 1911 and Rome in 1913. On these trips he wrote several travel pieces, including "Pod florentinskim šeširom" (Under the Florentine Hat) and "Od Firence do Zagreba" (From Florence to Zagreb). He died of throat cancer in 1914 at the age of forty.

Matoš was a complex and controversial writer who contributed immensely to both Croatian and Serbian literature. His essays and letters provide a vivid chronicle of intellectual and artistic life in Zagreb and Belgrade during important and complex times. His poems and stories provided important models for a new generation of modernist writers in Serbia and Croatia. He tirelessly wrote literary criticism in an attempt to raise the artistic and aesthetic level of those literatures and to move them closer to the artistic level of Europe of his time. Temperamental and impulsive, he was often contradictory, but he never forgot that his aim was the search for beauty through art. Despite his travels, he remained devoted to his Croatian homeland, but his principal allegiance was to his art.

Bibliographies:

JAZU, *Sabrana djela Antuna Gustava Matoša, Sv. 20* (Zagreb: Liber, 1973);

Dubravko Jelčić, *Literatura o A. G. Matošu 1896–1974* (Zagreb: Liber, 1976).

Biographies:

Mirko Žeželj, *Tragajući za Matošem* (Zagreb: Matica Hrvatska, 1970);

Dubravko Jelčić, *Matoš* (Zagreb: Globus, 1984).

References:

Antun Barac, "A. G. Matoš," in his *Hrvatska književna kritika* (Zagreb: JAZU, 1938);

Barac, "Uz Matoševu prozu," in his *Članci i eseji* (Zagreb: Matica Hrvatska, 1968), pp. 259–291;

Tode Čolak, *Portreti iz novije hrvatske književnosti: Knjiga prva* (Belgrade: Sloboda, 1967);

Ivo Frangeš, "Antun Gustav Matoš: *Jesenje veče*," in his *Matoš, Vidrić, Krleža* (Zagreb: Liber, 1974);

Frangeš, "Stil Matoševe novelistike," in his *Matoš, Vidrić, Krleža* (Zagreb: Liber, 1974);

Velibor Gligorić, *U vihoru* (Belgrade: Nolit, 1975);

Olga Grahor, *France in the Work and Ideas of Antun Gustav Matoš* (Munich: Otto Sagner, 1973);

Jure Kaštelan, "Lirika A. G. Matoša," *Rad JAZU,* 310 (1957): 5–145;

Dubravka Oraić, *Pejzaž u djelu A. G. Matoša* (Zagreb: Matica Hrvatska, 1980);

Eugene Pantzer, *Antun Gustav Matoš* (Boston: Twayne, 1981);

Jovan Pejčić, "Književnost, kritika, modernost: Teorijski pogledi Antuna Gustava Matoša," *Izraz,* 32 (January–February 1988): 78–88;

Bruno Popović, *Matoš i nakon njega* (Zagreb: Studentski centar sveučilišta Zagreba, 1972);

Tin Ujević, "Em smo Horvati" *Savremenik,* 9 (1914): 238–244.

Papers:

Major holdings of Matoš's manuscripts are at the Institut za Književnost Jugoslavenske akademije znanosti i umjetnosti in Zagreb.

Ivan Mažuranić

(11 August 1814 – 4 August 1890)

Ljerka Debush
Harvard University

BOOKS: *Smèrt Čengić-age* (Zagreb: Iskra, 1846); revised as *Smrt Smail-age Čengića* (Zagreb: Albrecht, 1857); translated by James Wiles as *The Death of Smail-Aga* (London: Allen & Unwin, 1925) and by Charles A. Ward as "Smail-Aga Čengić's Death" in *The Bridge,* 17 (1969): 5–34;
Hèrvati Madjarom (Karlovac: Prettner, 1848);
Pjesme Ivana Mažuranića (Zagreb: Narodne Novine, 1895; revised edition, Sušak: Primorski štamparski zavod, 1924);
Djela, edited by Slavko Ježić (Zagreb: Zora, 1958).

OTHER: *Deutsch – Illyrisches Wörterbuch,* compiled by Mažuranić and Jako Užarević (Zagreb: Gaj, 1842);
Ivana Gundulića OSMAN u dvadeset pievanjah, with books 14 and 15 and a dictionary by Mažuranić (Zagreb: Gaj, 1844);
"Nekoliko manje poznatih rečih, štono se nalaze u statutu krčkom," *Arkiv za povestnicu jugoslavensku,* 2 (1852): 297–307.

In the period between 1835 and 1848 the literary output in Croatia echoed the precepts of European romanticism. A multitalented and enterprising generation of writers set out to modernize Croatian culture, to codify a literary language, to unify an orthography, to document folk literary genres, and to reaffirm and strengthen the importance of a national literature for both the upper class and the emerging middle class. This generation is known as the Illyrian movement. All of its members were polyglots, educated abroad, well-read in major European literatures, and aware of the current romantic theories. Ivan Mažuranić was one of its central figures.

Croatian romanticism was not a reaction to the neoclassical aesthetic canon. On the contrary, it sought to integrate the neoclassical literature of Dubrovnik with the current European romantic theories of art. The leaders of the Illyrian movement had to overcome Croatian regionalism and contend with a threatening Hungarian nationalism. Their goal was to

Portrait of Ivan Mažuranić

raise the Croatian national consciousness of an old, uninterrupted, and unifying literary culture functioning as a part of a larger whole – South Slavdom. Croatian poets became vocal proponents of these ideas.

Mažuranić's reputation as the greatest Croatian romantic poet rests almost entirely on his narrative poem *Smèrt Čengić-age* (The Death of Smail Aga Čengić, 1846; revised as *Smrt Smail-age Čengića,* 1857). This poem of a mere 1,134 lines is as yet unsurpassed in Croatian literature for its style and beauty: it is a fusion of classical and modern, of archaic and innovative, of symmetry and asymmetry, of the contemporary and the timeless. But Mažuranić was not only, or even primarily, a poet. He was also a politician, lawmaker, translator, philologist, author of dictionaries, writer of political speeches and manifestos, mathematician, and astronomer. During his tenure as *ban* (governor) of Croatia, a university was founded in Zagreb, major school reform took place, and the juridical system was overhauled.

Ivan Mažuranić was born on 11 August 1814 in Novi, a small town on the Adriatic coast, as the fourth of five sons in a well-to-do peasant family. He attended a German-language elementary school in his hometown and then went on to a Latin high school in Rijeka. There he also studied Italian and Hungarian. In 1833 he went to Zagreb to study philosophy. The following year he continued his studies in Szombathely. A lively correspondence with his older brother Antun kept him abreast of events in Zagreb. He read the Illyrian manifesto by Ljudevit Gaj as well as the new periodicals *Danica* (Morning Star) and *Novine horvatske* (The Croatian Newspaper). Mažuranić became an early contributor to these publications. During 1835 about a dozen of his poems were published in *Danica*. In the same year Mažuranić returned to Zagreb to begin his studies at the law school there. He graduated in 1838 and soon moved to Karlovac to start a law practice. In 1841 he married Alexandra Demeter, the sister of the well-known poet Dimitrije Demeter. Mažuranić's most significant literary activity took place between 1842 and 1848.

Mažuranić's early poems were written mostly in Croatian, but some are in Hungarian. An influential figure for his literary development was the Hungarian poet Ferenz Császár, one of his teachers in Rijeka. In addition, his brother Antun provided incessant encouragement. After receiving Gaj's Illyrian manifesto, Ivan wrote to his brother in October 1834: "Čitajučega oglasu, koju svrhu domorodnih novinah meni poslao jesi, takov svrbež poetičeski od radosti jest primio, da srdcu nikako odoliti ne mogoh, več da illiričkoj danici odu jednu sočinim, koju (kakva jest da jest) eto ovde k' listu priklopio jesam. Čitaj i razsudi ju." (As I was reading the announcement which you sent me together with the domestic newspaper, I was overcome by such a joyous poetic frenzy that I couldn't resist and I composed an ode to the Illyrian morning star which I now enclose [just as it is] with this letter. Read it and evaluate it.)

Over the next ten years Mažuranić published quite a few lyrical poems, but a large part of his involvement with literature was the study of poetry and translation. He read classical Roman poetry and con-

temporary Italian, French, Polish, and English verse. He also read and analyzed earlier Croatian literature, primarily the works of the Dubrovnik poet Ivan Gundulić. He translated Horace, Ovid, and Adam Mickiewicz, among other poets. In his own poetry Mažuranić initially experimented with classical meters, but later he also tried his hand at the ten-syllable line of oral folk poetry. A good example of a symbiosis of models and influences is his 1838 poem *Vjekovi Ilirije* (The Age of Illyria), where the bucolic imagery is inspired by Virgil and the flow of history from a golden age to the age of man is reminiscent of Ovid, while the description of the Illyrian homeland evokes Anton Mihanović and Gundulić. The verse is the ten-syllable line of oral poetry organized in eight-line stanzas.

The greatest work of Croatian literature before Mažuranić's time was the epic poem *Osman,* by Gundulić, a seventeenth-century Dubrovnik poet. Books 14 and 15 of the poem, however, were irretrievably lost. Mažuranić took upon himself the formidable task of completing Gundulić's masterpiece. He went about it in his quiet, methodical, scholarly fashion. He first compiled a dictionary of all the words Gundulić used in *Osman,* and used only these words and forms of words in his addition. In composing the missing books, Mažuranić developed and finished several subplots, providing a masterful link between the first thirteen and the last five books of the epic. Yet his addition turned out to be more than just a part of a larger whole. It exists as a whole and complete poetic work unto itself. In a string of lyrical miniatures and images Mažuranić tinged Gundulić's fatalism with his own romantic spirit. The first edition of *Osman* with Mažuranić's additions was published in 1844.

Two years later, in 1846, Mažuranić created and published his masterpiece, the narrative poem *Smèrt Čengić-age* (better known under the revised title *Smrt Smail-age Čengić*). The 1,134-line poem consists of five loosely connected parts: *Agovanje* (Aga's Rule), *Noćnik* (Night Traveler), *Četa* (Troop), *Harač* (Tribute), and *Kob* (Fate). By 1992 this poem had been published in more than 150 editions at home and abroad and had been translated into most European languages. The enormous amount of literary criticism on it continues to grow.

The plot revolves around a Turkish *aga* (lord) named Smail Čengić, a vain, cruel, and courageous man, renowned for his horsemanship and skill with saber and javelin. He exacts tribute in the cruelest of fashions from the Christian peasants under his rule. In book 1 (*Agovanje*) he orders the execution of several imprisoned Montenegrins (Christian Slavs). He also puts to death an old man named Durak, a con-

Ivan Mažuranić

done, the sun has set, the moon has risen in the sky. Having witnessed his father's execution and having pleaded for mercy in vain, Novica decides to go over to the Christian side and leaves the camp at night. He travels through the wilderness with only the darkness as his ally. Both the Turks that he has abandoned and the Montenegrins he has not yet joined are now his enemies. Frightened of every unknown sound or movement in the night and alone in the rugged mountains, he forges ahead, led by the thought of doing what is morally right. This trek through the night is Novica's road to Damascus: he goes through a moral, spiritual, and, later, a religious conversion. As an outward sign of this change, he has removed the Turkish turban from his head. In his heart he prays to God for safe passage. Finally, as dawn breaks, he arrives in the town of Cetinje. Having stated his purpose and surrendered his arms to the guards, he is let into the commander's residence. The night is over; the sun is about to rise. As Novica walks through the gate, the last flickering star is fading in the sky: the star of *aga* Čengić.

In book 3 a troop of young Montenegrins gathers in the dark. Like Novica in the previous section, they travel in the night, led by righteousness and protected by God. They walk through the mountains in a menacing, solemn silence, enveloped by the darkness of a starless and moonless night in which only the steel blades of their weapons occasionally flicker. They move with a steady pace of inexorable fate. As the sun comes out, the troop is met by an old priest who strengthens their resolve and gives them God's blessing. His sermon sums up Mažuranić's ethical credo, the belief in the ultimate triumph of good over evil, of right over wrong. As they pray, Novica comes to the priest, asking to be baptized. Afterward they all take communion. The sun sets, and the troop goes on.

At 623 lines, *Harač*, book 4, is longer than the other four books combined. It also forms a compositional whole and could stand as a poem in its own right. The action is set in motion by *aga*'s wrath. He has arrived in the area of Gacko to exact tribute and has ordered his servants to bring the Christians to his camp for torture. While practicing the javelin throw, the *aga* aims at a shackled peasant, but his horse stumbles, and the javelin hits a Turk, Safer, in the eye. The *aga*, already frustrated by the mediocre sums of tribute collected, believes his pride to be further wounded by the fact that he, the great hero, has missed the target. When the Christian peasants laugh at him, the *aga* orders the most horrible tortures for them. The peasants cannot pay tribute be-

vert to Islam, who advised him to set the prisoners free or else be a target for revenge. This advice infuriated the *aga* because for him the release of prisoners is not an act of mercy but rather a sign of personal weakness. As he observes the executions, the *aga* stands tall, strong, and brave, a proud, implacable, awe-inspiring warrior. The Christians do not plead for mercy. They die defiantly, in silence. While the *aga* experiences neither pity nor remorse, he is suddenly shaken by a cold shiver of fear: the Christians, the lowly infidel slaves he despises, are dying in a manner worthy of a noble hero like himself; their kin will want to avenge their deaths. The *aga* shows no outward signs of this brief spell of fear and dismisses the thought quickly. Durak is the only one who begs for his life, and his son Novica also pleads for his father to be spared, but the *aga* executes the old man anyway as a lesson to the other Turks: no Muslim should fear a Christian.

Book 2 begins with a verse echoing Genesis, in the style of folk poetry: the deeds of the first day are cause they have nothing to give, and the *aga* cannot forget his humiliation. As night falls and the Turks sit down to dinner, thunder roars ominously in the distance, and Montenegrin troops advance toward the camp. His fury still unassuaged, the *aga* asks for a song. The singer, Bauk, improvises a mocking song that parodies the *aga*'s mishap, blowing it out of proportion. He sings of an *aga* who humiliates the Christians by leaping over them on his horse. Suddenly, the horse stumbles, and the *aga* falls to the ground. The account of this disgraceful fall spreads quickly, carried by folk singers throughout the land. Listening to Bauk, *aga* Čengić is consumed by anger. He suddenly understands that, no matter what he does, the memory of the event will always be there, immortalized in a song. Posterity will remember him only for this one inexplicable twist of fate. His impotent fury is now aimed at Turks and Christians alike for they have all witnessed his loss of honor. As he is about to renew his torturing of Christians, the camp is attacked by the Montenegrins. The first shot hits Safer in the other eye. Just as Safer's first loss of an eye prefigured *aga*'s fall from grace, so the loss of the other eye prefigures the *aga*'s death. As he moves to mount his horse, he is felled by a bullet. In the ensuing brief battle most of the Turks are slain, as well as some of the Christians, including Novica.

Book 5 is quite short. Somewhere high up in the mountain of Lovćen is a hermit's hut, and in it a puppet. The puppet is fully attired in clothes and arms of a noble Turkish lord. Whenever anyone steps in front of it, it bows and clasps its hands. The poem ends with alternating lines of questions and answers, questions that a visitor would ask of the hermit. The puppet represents *aga* Čengić; the saber and the other weapon are Čengić's, as are the puppet's gold-embroidered jacket, which has now lost its luster, and his turban, which hangs to one side. These faded possessions are all that remain of the great *aga*.

Critics have analyzed the poem in great detail, searching through every verse to untangle the multilayered web of links and sources: Virgil, Ovid, Homer, the Bible, Gundulić, oral folk poetry, current Romantic literature in Europe, including contemporary writings in Croatia. Among the Croatian influences the most significant are the poem *Grobničko polje* (Grobnik Field, 1842), by Dimitrije Demeter, and a travelogue, *Pogled u Bosnu* (A View of Bosnia, 1842), by Mažuranić's younger brother, Matija.

Despite strong links with classical poetics and Gundulić's neoclassicism, Mažuranić created a work that was clearly influenced by Romantic theo-

ries of his time. *Smrt Smail-age Čengića* defies several precepts of the neoclassical aesthetic canon, including the rules that genres should be clearly separated and all parts of a literary work should form a cohesive composition. *Smrt Smail-age Čengića* is a narrative poem, a genre which eludes a single, standard definition. Its parts form separate autonomous wholes with their own titles, beginnings, and endings. At the same time they follow the development of a narrative in a linear sequence. The unity of the poem as a whole is achieved not only through the single theme, but also through a close link between the overall title and the fifth part. The dominant rhythm is that of heroic epic poetry, a fact which is further underscored by a dramatic setting of scenes and monologues. This order is upset in three important ways. Mažuranić introduced passages with lyrical overtones, descriptions of nature and of surroundings complete with creatures such as ghosts and demons, and voices of the dead — all favored by the Romantics. Furthermore, he played with line length using eight- and ten-syllable lines. Both can be found in oral poetry, but the eight-syllable line is primarily associated with Gundulić's *Osman*. Finally, he turned the classical order of an epic song on its head: what one would expect to be an introduction comes at the end. The *arma* and *vir* are introduced in book 5. The death of the *aga*, announced in the title, acquires its deeper meaning at the end of the poem.

Other parts of the poem have inner connections as well. Thus book 1 is echoed and its themes are repeated in book 4, while the theme of book 2 is elaborated in book 3. Viewed from this angle the entire poem reveals its well-thought-through structure of beautiful asymmetry.

Mažuranić the Romantic is also revealed through sharp oppositions between good and evil, light and darkness, courage and cowardice, the mighty and the oppressed, and, certainly, through a strong patriotic message. At the same time Mažuranić the neoclassicist saturated his lines with allusions to antiquity. The wrath and wounded pride of the *aga* is reminiscent of the wrath of Achilles, the old priest reminds the reader of Tiresias, while the peasants dragged by Turkish horses are directly compared to Hector and are addressed by the poet as Trojans abandoned by gods. The *aga* himself unites opposites too. He is not a typical Romantic antihero, a rebel against society and established rules. On the contrary, he is very much a product of the Turkish societal hierarchy and its values. He functions within rules and expectations for a man of his stature. Being a cruel, coldhearted tyrant, he deserves punishment and death. At this point, however, one can detect a certain Romantic ambivalence in Mažuranić. In book 5 the *aga* is ostensibly humiliated as much as possible, reduced to a puppet that limply and mechanically bows to visitors. At the same time the little hut and the puppet function as a shrine. The *aga*'s fate is a warning that all tyranny is doomed to fail. The *aga* himself is an awe-inspiring hero.

Most of Mažuranić's writing after 1846 was directly connected with political events of his day and with his increasingly important role in public life. In the revolutionary year 1848 he published a pamphlet, *Hèrvati Madjarom* (Croats to Hungarians), as a response to strong Hungarian nationalism. He represented the voice of the emerging middle class. As a believer in justice, Mažuranić called for equal rights of all nations in Hungary.

In the period between 1850 and 1860 Mažuranić rapidly advanced through several high government positions, putting aside all literary work in the belief that he could serve his country better as a politician than as a poet. He had a reputation as an erudite man of even temper and sound judgment. In 1861 he became the first chancellor for Croatia within the Austro-Hungarian Empire. In 1866 he withdrew briefly from the political arena, but he returned in 1873 to serve as *ban* of Croatia – the highest political office. He was the first commoner to hold this office. During his seven-year tenure he actively promoted reforms in education and other aspects of cultural life. After stepping down in 1880, Mažuranić withdrew completely from politics and spent the last decade of his life studying mathematics, astronomy, and philosophy. He died in Zagreb on 4 August 1890.

Ivan Mažuranić is a distinctive figure in Croatian literary history. With a handful of verse he created works of timeless beauty, holding a masterly balance between classical and contemporary, oral and artistic, the Orient and the West, barbarians and civilization, Islam and Christianity. Writing in an era in which the modernization and unification of a literary language were of primary importance, he created a polished and compact style that left its mark on many generations of Croatian poets.

Letters:
Sabrana djela Ivana Mažuranića, edited by Ivo Frangeš and Milorad Živančević (Zagreb: Liber, 1979).

Biographies:
Tadija Smičiklas, *Ivan Mažuranić, predsjednik "Matice Ilirske" od god. 1858 do god. 1872* (Zagreb: Matica hrvatska, 1892);

Milutin Cihlar Nehajev, "O Ivanu Mažuraniću kancelaru i banu," *Hrvatska revija,* 3 (1930): 525–536, 637–651;

Antun Barac, *Mažuranić* (Zagreb: Matica hrvatska, 1945);

Milorad Živančević, *Ivan Mažuranić* (Novi Sad: Matica srpska, 1964).

References:

Ivo Frangeš, "Mažuranićeva umjetnost," *Forum,* 3, nos. 7–8 (1964): 75–95;

Frangeš, "Mažuranićev pjesnički jezik," *Kolo,* 3, nos. 9–10 (1965): 404–423;

Frangeš, "Za konačni tekst *Smrti Smail-age Čengića,*" *Croatica,* 4, no. 5 (1973): 131–149;

Branko Gavella, "Pjesnička gradja Mažuranićeva *Smail-age,*" *Književnik,* 3 (1961): 644–652;

E. D. Goy, "The Tragic Element in *Smrt Smail-age Čengića,*" *Slavonic and East European Review,* 44 (1966): 327–336;

Goy, "*Osman* and *The Death of Smail-Aga Čengijić,*" *Scottish Slavonic Review,* no. 7 (1986): 17–30;

Rudolf Horvat, "Ban Ivan Mažuranić," *Hrvatsko kolo,* 11 (1930): 41–84;

Ljudevit Jonke, "Mažuranićev ep i narodne pjesme koje pjevaju o smrti Smail-aginoj," *Rad Jugoslavenske akademije znanosti i umjetnosti,* 264 (1938): 97–122;

Svetozar Koljević, "Mažuranić, Njegoš and the Folk Tradition," in *South Slav Perspectives: Liber Amicorum in Honour of E. D. Goy* (Kruševac & London: Bagdala & School of Slavonic and East European Studies, 1989), pp. 11–19;

Risto Kovijanić, "Starac dobri Mažuranićeva speva," *Zbornik za književnost i jezik,* 14 (1966): 87–133;

Franjo Marković, "Ivan Mažuranić," in *Smrt Smail-age Čengića* (Zagreb, 1876), pp. ii–xlvi;

Muhsin Rizvić, "Smrt i život Čengić-age: Nekolike metodološke pretpostavke," *Izraz,* 38 (1975): 472–518;

Ivan Slamnig, "Ivan Mažuranić i dubrovačko jezično i književno nasljedje," *Dubrovnik,* 13 (1970): 5–11;

Milorad Živančević, "Nedogled kritike o Mažuraniću," *Letopis Matice srpske,* 404 (1969): 75–84;

Živančević, "Ilirizam," in *Povijest hrvatske književnosti,* 5 volumes (Zagreb: Liber-Mladost, 1976), IV: 1–217.

Momčilo Nastasijević

(23 September 1894 – 13 February 1938)

E. D. Goy
Cambridge University

BOOKS: *Zapis o darovima moje rodjake Marije* (Belgrade: Pokret, 1925);
Iz tamnog vilajeta (Belgrade: Cvijanović, 1927);
Pet lirskih krugova (Belgrade: Privately published, 1932);
Celokupna dela, 3 volumes (Belgrade: Izdanje prijatelja, 1938);
Sedam lirskih krugova (Belgrade: Prosveta, 1962);
Momčilo Nastasijević (Belgrade: Nolit, 1963);
Izabrana dela, 2 volumes (Belgrade: Prosveta / Zagreb: Naprijed / Sarajevo: Svjetlost, 1966);
Sabrana dela, 4 volumes (Belgrade: Srpska književna zadruga, 1991).

Editions in English: Selected poems translated by E. D. Goy in *Serbian Studies,* 1, no. 3 (1981): 31–49; *Serbian Studies,* 4, nos. 1–2 (1986–1987): 30–49; and *Southeastern Europe,* 9, nos. 1–2 (1982): 53–69;

"Silentia" and "Words in Stone," translated by Goy, *Scottish Slavonic Review,* 8 (1987): 40–55;

Poems, translated by Goy, in *Relations, Serbian Quarterly Review,* 1 (1988): 7–26;

Poems, translated by Charles Simic, in *Serbian Poetry from the Beginning to the Present,* edited by Milne Holton and Vasa D. Mihailovich (New Haven: Yale Center for International and Area Studies, 1988), pp. 259–264.

Momčilo Nastasijević

During his lifetime Momčilo Nastasijević was less well known than some of his contemporaries, such as Miloš Crnjanski and Rastko Petrović. His literary output was not large, and it gained immediate appreciation only in a narrow circle of intimate friends. Although he published poems regularly in leading literary periodicals such as *Misao* (Thought) and *Srpski književni glasnik* (Serbian Literary Herald), he remained relatively unnoticed. He privately published his one volume of poetry, *Pet lirskih krugova* (Five Lyrical Cycles, 1932). One reason for this lack of recognition was that – with his individual views of poetry and literature and the problems of the development of the Serbian literary language –

he was outside the trends of expressionism and surrealist Marxism dominant in Belgrade at the time. Another reason was that his compression of style and his individual imagery make him an extraordinarily difficult poet, especially for those who seek a paraphrasable meaning in poetry. For this reason he has been accused of being hermetic by some critics. In truth he is hermetic in the same sense as is Stéphane Mallarmé. In terms of English poetry, one might hazard a comparison with Gerard Manley Hopkins and Dylan Thomas; yet Nastasijević is more dialectal than Hopkins and more compressed than Thomas. Only since the 1950s has Nastasijević come to be recognized as one of the great poets of the Serbian language, and his influence on Serbian poetry has been of paramount importance.

Born in Gornji Milanovac, one of seven children of Nikola Nastasijević, a builder who specialized in church building and masonry, Momčilo Nastasijević was one of a gifted family. His elder brother Živorad was a painter. His younger brother Svetomir became a well-known composer, and a third brother, Slavomir, wrote popular historical novels.

Educated at the high schools in Čačak and Kragujevac, Nastasijević showed a considerable talent for music. He played the flute and, later, the violin, cello, and piano. He spoke fluent French and German and had reading knowledge of Russian and English. In 1912 he went to Belgrade, where he enrolled in the high school for boys. Among his close friends there was Gavrilo Princip, the assassin of the Austrian archduke in Sarajevo. In 1913 Nastasijević enrolled as a student in Belgrade University to read French language and literature. It would appear that he also had a talent for mathematics, but of his many interests poetry and language appear to have dominated.

The outbreak of war in 1914 interrupted Nastasijević's studies. He returned to Gornji Milanovac, where he was declared physically unfit for army service. Yet he joined the army as a volunteer and in 1915 was taken prisoner by the Austrians. He managed to escape and, after many adventures, returned to Gornji Milanovac, where he remained in virtual hiding until the end of the conflict.

In 1919 he returned to Belgrade University and in 1921 took his degree. He was then appointed as teacher of French at the Belgrade high school for boys, where he served until his death from pneumonia in 1938.

From an early age Nastasijević had written poetry. His early poems show the influence of Jovan Dučić and the Parnassian style approved by the Belgrade school led by the critic Bogdan Popović. As early as 1915 Nastasijević was writing short stories in an unremarkable straightforward realistic style. On the other hand, his early poetry shows a considerable talent. Had he written nothing else, his two poems "Allegro" and "Adagio" (1916) are worthy of inclusion in any anthology of poetry of that period. As a student he published translations in the literary supplements of various newspapers of the day. These included works by Jean de la Bruyère, Edgar Allan Poe, and José Maria de Heredia.

A turning point in Nastasijević's work was his 1922 essay "Nekoliko refleksija o umetnosti" (A Few Reflections about Poetry), in which he shows himself as much a theoretician as a writer. The adoption by Dučić and others of French Parnassianism and the alexandrine seemed to Nastasijević to be a desertion of the essential tone and individuality of the Serbian language. Every language possesses its own syntax and the natural color of expression that is its tone. Tone comes before semantics — not the phonetic tones, but rather the syntactically suggested tone of voice. He considered critical principles of style to be mere abstraction. Style, he wrote, is like bricks. One may build a wall and then dismantle it, but try doing the same thing with a flower. True style is not a constructed house, but a grown tree. Form and content are indivisible. The artist's task is to tear the veil from the truth of being, to be a bridge between reality and surreality.

This essay was to be the first in a series of articles on art and music. In 1923 Nastasijević gained a scholarship and spent his summer vacation in Paris, where he was apparently deeply interested in the writings of Marcel Proust and of Jean Cocteau. In "Nekoliko refleksija o umetnosti" one might suspect the influence of Joris-Karl Huysmans's supernatural naturalism. That Nastasijević had read *A rebours* (Against the Grain, 1884) and *Là-bas* (Down There, 1891) cannot be excluded. Yet, if there is any French resemblance, it would seem to be in the strange parallel between Nastasijević and that other high-school language teacher (of English) Mallarmé. Both lived superficially uneventful lives in a small circle of friends. Both were theoreticians of poetry as well as poets. One cannot avoid thinking of Mallarmé's "Relativement au vers" as one peruses Nastasijević's essays. Geoffrey Brereton wrote of Mallarmé: "Since the fluent command of language which the majority of great poets have enjoyed was not for him, he made the most — sometimes, perhaps, more than the most — of the words of which he did dispose." These words might easily be applied to Nastasijević and his poetry.

For Nastasijević poetry was a search for the intimate expression and attainment of the thing expressed. The individual language was a unique instrument. In "Za maternju melodiju" (For Mother Melody, 1929) he wrote, "The voice is far more essential than the word." The musicality of verbal expression is its essential meaning. For the poet his native language, its color and tone, are the sole true material. Thus translation from one language to another is like transcribing or arranging a piece written for the violin so that it may be played by another instrument, or, worse still, like the transplantation of an exotic plant into a foreign soil. Thus in his works Nastasijević was to turn back to the language of the Serbian medieval writers and folk songs. Yet, like the symbolists, he saw the need for tackling the barrier between expression and the thing expressed. Surreality may not be comprehended, only experienced, and such intimation may be gained only through the existentially profound individuality of one's native language. Always, in all expression, there is an "escaped mystery."

This search and struggle was to direct the development of Nastasijević's style in drama, prose, and, especially, poetry, leading to his straining of syntax and compression into what often seems almost telegraphic statement. His poetry needs to be read without too much worry about its literal meaning. If one relaxes and lets the tone and imagery work its will, allowing due value to pauses and rhythm, much of the "hermetic" nature of the poetry will cease to matter. As Nastasijević wrote, "The beauty of anything is its mystery."

In 1925 Nastasijević published *Zapis o darovima moje rodjake Marije* (My Relative Mary's Wedding Gifts), a story with an eerie, supernatural atmosphere reminiscent of Poe. In Serbian this sort of fiction was completely new and received instant recognition. In 1927 Nastasijević published it again with a series of other, similar stories under the title *Iz tamnog vilajeta* (From the Twilight Zone) and was awarded a literary prize. Most of the tales are striking for their atmosphere and also for their dialectal and syntactically individual language.

In 1927 Nastasijević entered the sphere of drama. He had already written two fairly conventional plays, *Nedozvani* (The Uninvited) and *Gospodar Mladenova kćer* (Master Mladen's Daughter). *Nedozvani* was performed by a minor company in 1931, and in 1933 a group of amateurs performed *Gospodar Mladenova kćer*. These early plays were, perhaps, of lesser significance than three plays that involved music. The first was *Medjuluško blago* (The Treasure of Medjulug, 1927), a musical drama with music composed by Svetomir Nastasijević. Two more dramas in which music was intended to play an essential part in supporting the tone and atmosphere were *Djuradj Branković* (1933), on a theme from Serbian medieval history, and *Večita slavina* (The Eternal Tap, 1936). None of these dramas was published until 1938, and they have yet to be given the attention due to them. *Medjuluško blago* is a symbolic, poetic play, a first step that, perhaps, goes little further than the lyrical plays of William Butler Yeats. *Djuradj Branković* and *Večita slavina* show an advance toward an existential awareness of being and history. The latter is dominated by a tone of resignation. History, one senses, is the life of one man, overlapped by others. It repeats and repeats.

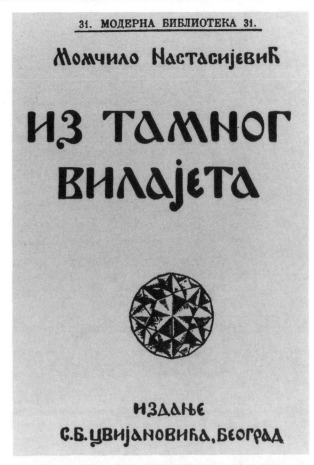

31. МОДЕРНА БИБЛИОТЕКА 31.

Момчило Настасијевић

ИЗ ТАМНОГ ВИЛАЈЕТА

ИЗДАЊЕ С.Б. ЦВИЈАНОВИЋА, БЕОГРАД

Title page for Nastasijević's Iz tamnog vilajeta *(From the Twilight Zone, 1927), a collection of stories*

In 1929 Nastasijević wrote a group of stories about the history of his native Gornji Milanovac, "Hronika moje varoši" (A Chronicle of My Town). Compared with *Iz tamnog vilajeta,* the style is obscure and difficult. It is "poetic" prose. As an attempt to apply his views of "musical" poetry to prose, it is perhaps not a success.

The essential value of Nastasijević's work is in his poetry. In 1932 he published *Pet lirskih krugova* (Five Lyrical Cycles). The five cycles are *Jutarnje* (Morning Poems or Matins), *Večernje* (Evening Poems or Vespers), *Bdenja* (Vigils), *Gluhote* (Silentia), and *Reč u kamenu* (Words in Stone), fifty-five poems in all. Two other cycles, *Magnovenja* (Moments) and *Odjeci* (Echoes), remained unpublished until 1938. Many of the poems in all seven cycles had already been published in various literary periodicals, in slightly differing versions. This is typical of Nastasijević. He seems to have had a limited scale of imagery, which he developed always in the direction of an absolute expression. In the five cycles of 1932 individual poems are brought together so that

Nastasijević in the 1920s

does my joyous breath / Mournfully echo in the valley?" Is it the flute of Mallarmé's faun or the real flute Nastasijević played? Most likely both. The theme appears to be that of communication. The poem seems to say "I am driven to express a thing, because to express is to possess. Yet my expression, by its very nature, destroys the reality of what I express, alters it, conditions it. It is not the thing, but I and my words. Thus I am excluded by the fateful nature of my being and, so, utterly alone." The final poem of the cycle, "Dafina" (The Oleaster), ends with a tone of menace:

> When the unloved dies,
> The air is pungent
> Of passion.
>
> At the moment of fading
> The bud flares up to over-blowing.
> Death awakens the unloved.
>
> Set no oleaster upon the grave,
> its breath is pungent,
> Ghostly beckoning into the darkness.
>
> But roll on it a heavy stone,
> Heavier than the buried thirsting,
> When the unloved dies.

The situation is tragic. One cannot resign the struggle, no matter how impossible. Frustration is a vampire.

The sense of a frustration inherent in expression haunts Nastasijević's poetry. "Reć svoju nemu" (Dumb, my word) is almost the key to the poems. Through the next four cycles the style gradually distills into a telegraphic utterance in which tone suggests itself and plays the main role. Thus of expression, in the fourth cycle, *Gluhote,* the compressed statement is validated by its urgency:

> And by a drop only,
> By a drop
> This ineffability into a word,
>
> With doom would it drown the living,
> With doom all things.

In *Jutarnje* and *Bdenja* the problem is related to the encounter with the other, to love, and to death. The same rigid separation haunts all being. Loneliness is insuperable. Even birth and parents are questioned: "I am not my father." Love itself, considered in the borrowed imagery of the sixteenth-century love poetry (the poets of Dubrovnik as likely as Pierre de Ronsard and Joachim du Bellay), is no cure for the sickness. Yet, though all this be

the total is united in a single statement. The effect is a total experience close in its nature to that of music. One may recall what T. S. Eliot called the "auditive intuition." The poems are a struggle on the levels of both style and theme. Form and content are indeed identical; yet the reader may find it natural to consider them separately. The first cycle, *Jutarnje,* suggests both. First it is an excursion into parody. The folk songs, especially the lyrical songs with their compressed and dialectal syntax, provide the basis of the poem "Izvoru" (To the Spring). "Jasike" (The Aspens) is a parody on Dučić. "Rumena kap" (The Red Drop) and "San u podne" (A Midday's Dream) recall Mallarmé's *L'après-midi d'un faune* (Afternoon of a Faun, 1876) in their sense of dreamy, turgid sensuality. The first poem, "Frula" (The Flute), sets the real theme of the cycles. Ignoring Nastasijević's warnings about translation, it might be transposed into English as: "Flute, why true and vain, Nastasijević writes in *Gluhote* that the urge of being is to accept the wounds as beauty and life. "Yet I wish, for so is it, / If wound there be, / It be deeply alive." The fifth cycle, *Reči u kamenu,* brings style and theme together in a new and original compression. The answer to living is that one must live. This is beauty. The "escaped mystery" must, perhaps, be accepted, or so one might conclude from the following lines:

Solidly
Between lives a wall.

Stonily
For each loaf
Calloused upon the palm
A corn.

And a lock,
And beyond the lock,
The key of keys in the door of doors.

To treason this
The more silently insinuates.

One is not let off. The writhing struggle between opposites that dominates the cycles ends only with a musical resolution: "And so and so / And ever so." Yet to suggest a theme in this way is to invalidate what is the real quality of the poetry. It is better to consider the poems as a musical variation on a theme. Reading the poems leads one to realize how much Nastasijević achieved his aim of making tone more than the word. *Pet lirskih krugova* comes close to a symphony in words.

The final cycles, *Magnovenja* and *Odjeci,* give the impression that they are less finished and less harmonized than the first five. An outstanding characteristic of Nastasijević's poetry is the combining of opposites. One needs only mention the title of the poem "Radosno opelo" (A Joyous Requiem) from *Magnovenja.* In the sixth poem in *Gluhote* the poet uses the term *nem* (mute) for his expression: "Beauty blinds me / Though mute." For the English reader these lines may recall Dylan Thomas: "And I am dumb to tell the crooked rose." Again, in "Tuga u kamenu" (Sorrow in Stone) from *Magnovenja:* "Not word, nor verse, nor sound / Speaks my sorrow." Rather like Petar Petrović Njegoš, living is experi-

enced as a harmony between opposites, between joy and suffering, pain and happiness.

Nastasijević's early death meant that much was left undone. As it is, the poetry he left presents a lyrical experience that is generally rare in poetry and seems to arise out of his profound feeling for his native language. For this reason he has been greatly respected by some of the leading modern Serbian poets, such as Vasko Popa and Miodrag Pavlović. Small as his output was, Nastasijević's poetic achievement is certainly one of the greatest, if not the greatest, in the Serbian language of the twentieth century.

References:

E. D. Goy, "The Cycle *Bdenja* from the *Pet lirskih krugova* by Momčilo Nastasijević," *Serbian Studies,* 4, nos. 1–2 (1986/1987): 30–49;

Goy, "The Cycle *Jutarnje* from the *Pet lirskih krugova* by Momčilo Nastasijević," *Southeastern Europe,* 9, nos. 1–2 (1982): 53–69;

Goy, "The Cycle *Večernje* from the *Pet lirskih krugova* by Momčilo Nastasijević," *Serbian Studies,* 1, no. 3 (1981): 31–49;

Goy, "The Poems *Gluhote* and *Reči u kamenu* by Momčilo Nastasijević," *Annali dell' Istituto Universitario Orientale, Napoli, Sezione Slava,* 9 (1966): 161–196;

Radomir Konstantinović, "Momčilo Nastasijević," in his *Biće i Jezik,* 8 volumes (Belgrade: Prosveta, 1983), VI: 7–70;

Miloš M. Marković, *Nastasijevići* (Gornji Milanovac, 1984);

Petar Milosavljević, *Poetika Momčila Nastasijevića* (Novi Sad: Matica srpska, 1966);

Miodrag Pavlović, "Momčilo Nastasijević," in *Izabrana dela* (Zagreb & Belgrade: Naprijed, 1966);

Svetlana Velmar-Janković, "The Reception of Momčilo Nastasijević in Serbia and Yugoslavia since 1938," *Serbian Studies,* 5, no. 4 (1990): 41–53;

Slobodanka M. Vladiv, "The 'Lyrical Drama' of Momčilo Nastasijević: Problems of Poetics and Translation," *New Zealand Slavonic Journal,* 1 (1988): 51–66.

Vladimir Nazor

(30 May 1876 – 19 June 1949)

Cynthia Simmons
Boston College

BOOKS: *Slavenske legende* (Zagreb, 1900);
Živana: Mitski epos u devet pjesama (Zadar, Croatia: Nagradjana štamparija Vitaliani, 1902; revised edition, Zagreb, 1936);
Pjesma o narodu hrvatskomu (Zadar, Croatia, 1902);
Knjiga o kraljevima hrvatskim (Zadar, Croatia: Hrvatske knjižarnice, 1904);
Krvava košulja: Uspomene iz doline Rase (Pula: J. Krmpotić, 1905);
Krvavi dani (Zagreb, 1908);
Veli Jože: Istarska priča (Ljubljana: Naklada "Matice slovenske," 1908);
Lirika (Zagreb: Dionička tiskara, 1910);
Hrvatski kraljevi (Zagreb: Matica hrvatska i Matica dalmatinska, 1912);
Istarske priče (Zagreb: Izdanje Matice hrvatske, 1913);
Nove pjesme (Zagreb: Z. and V. Vasića, 1913);
Mrtvo ostrvo (Zagreb, 1914);
Intima (1913–1914) (Zagreb: Z. and V. Vasića, 1915);
Medvjed Brundo: Životinjski ep (Zagreb: Naklada izdavača, 1915);
Pjesni ljuvene (Zagreb: Z. and V. Vasića, 1915);
Stoimena: Priče (Zagreb: Izdala Matica hrvatska, 1916);
Utva Zlatokrila: Romantički ep u pet pjevanja (Zagreb: Tiskom Boranića i Rozmanića, 1916; revised edition, Zagreb: Tisak Jugoslovenske Štampe, 1928);
Pabirci (1892–1917) (Zagreb: Naklada Branka Vodnika, 1917);
Djela, 5 volumes (Zagreb: Naklada Branka Vodnika, 1918);
Arkun: Priča iz slavenske prošlosti (Zagreb: Breyer, 1920);
Tri priče za djecu (Zagreb, 1920);
Carmen vitae: Antologija, edited by M. Marjanović (Zagreb: Izd. Narodne knjižnice, 1922);
Legenda o sv. Hristoforu (Zagreb, 1922);
Niza od koralja (Zagreb, 1922; revised edition, Zagreb: Knjižara Z. and V. Vasića, 1930);

Vladimir Nazor

Priče iz djetinjstva (Zagreb: Hrvatski štamparski zavod d. d. nakl. odjeljenje, 1924);
Crvenkapica (Zagreb, 1925);
Lirske pjesme (1900–1925) (Belgrade: Grafički zavod "Narodna misao," 1925);
Bjelouška (Zagreb, 1926);
Genovefina košuta (Zagreb, 1926);
Gubavac (Zagreb, 1926);
Otac (Zagreb, 1926);
Sarac i divičan grad (Zagreb, 1926);
Snježana (Zagreb, 1926);
Pjesme o četiri arhandjela (Sušak, 1927);
Priče s ostrva, iz grada i sa planine (Zagreb: Matica hrvatska, 1927);
Boškarina: Istarska priča (Gorica, 1928);

156

Šarko (Zagreb: Z. and V. Vasića, 1928);

Oče nas: Pjesma (Belgrade, 1929);

Sabrana djela, 29 volumes (Zagreb: Z. and V. Vasića, 1929–1933);

Andjeo u zvoniku (Zagreb, 1933);

Topuške elegije (Zagreb, 1933);

Pastir Loda: Zgode i nezgode bračkog fauna, 2 volumes (Zagreb, 1938–1939);

Dedek Kajbumščak: Nova pričanja o drevnom krapinskom čovjeku (Zagreb: Dvorska knjižara Vasić, 1939);

Večernje bilješke (N.p., 1942);

Djela, 8 volumes (Zagreb: Hrvatski izdavalački bibliografski zavod, 1942);

Pjesme partizanke 1942–1945 (London: Ujedinjeni odbor Južnih Slavena, 1944);

O mlitavcima na zemlji i u paklu (Kordun, Yugoslavia: Naprijed, 1944);

Ahasver (Zagreb: Izdanje knjižare R. N. Horvata, 1945);

Istranke (Zagreb: Nakladni zavod Hrvatske, 1945);

S partizanima 1943–1944 (Zagreb: Nakladni zavod Hrvatske, 1945);

Djela Vladimira Nazora, 15 volumes (Zagreb: Nakladni zavod Hrvatske, 1946–1950);

Kurir Loda (Zagreb: Izd. Matice hrvatske, 1946);

Legende o drugu Titu (Zagreb: Matica hrvatska, 1946);

Partizanka Mara (Zagreb: Nakladni zavod Hrvatske, 1946);

Podzemna Bosna (Zagreb: Nakladni zavod Hrvatske, 1946);

Puškibuški (Zagreb: Nakladni zavod Hrvatske, 1946);

Stare istarske balade (Rijeka: Nakladni zavod Hrvatske, 1946);

Pepeljuga (Zagreb: Nakladni zavod Hrvatske, 1947);

Pionir Grujo (Zagreb: Nakladni zavod Hrvatske, 1947);

Istarski gradovi (Zagreb: Novo Pokoljenje, 1949);

Izabrane pjesme, edited by Marin Franičević and Vladimir Popović (Belgrade, 1949);

U zavičaju (Zagreb: Izdavački zavod Jugoslavenske akademije, 1949).

OTHER: *Spomen-knjiga proslave 60-godišnjice zastupnika naroda prof. Vjekoslava Spinčića u Kastvu 22. i. 23. oktobra 1908,* edited by Kazimir Jelušić and Nazor (Kastav, 1909);

Spomenica istarskih Jugoslavena za mirovni kongres u Parizu, edited by Nazor (Zagreb, 1919);

Čitanka iz hrvatskoga ili srpskoga jezika za I, II, III i IV razred srednjih škola, compiled by Nazor

(Zagreb: Izdanje Jugoslovenske Štampe, 1927–1929);

Heinrich Heine, *Pjesme,* translated by Nazor (Zagreb: Z. and V. Vasića, 1932).

A versatile and prolific writer whose productive years spanned a formative half century in Croatian history, Vladimir Nazor is not only a monumental literary figure in his homeland but also a cultural hero of the twentieth century. At the beginning of his career his nontraditional metrics, adulation of pagan Slavic heritage, and lyrical tribute to the natural beauty of the Istrian countryside and Dalmatian coast contributed to the ongoing process of antirealist opposition and modernist innovation. Yet he was also capable of mimetic exactitude and social engagement. Nazor responded personally to the vicissitudes of the Croatian literary and cultural scene from colonialism through partisan revolt to Socialist independence in his poems, epics, long and short prose fiction, essays, criticism, memoirs, and even textbooks.

Vladimir Nazor was born on 30 May 1876 in Prostira, on the island of Brač off the Dalmatian coast of Croatia. He was one of six children born to Petar and Marija (Vulić) Nazor. Petar Nazor was a customs official of Croatian, French, and perhaps Turkish descent; Marija was the daughter of a customs official and of Croatian and Italian heritage. Although possibly of aristocratic ancestry, the Nazors at the time of Vladimir's birth owed their prosperity to Adriatic commerce. As was common in the region, the family spoke both Italian and Croatian fluently.

The young Nazor attended elementary and secondary schools in Dalmatia. Due to his poor performance at the classical high school in Split, he transferred to the more science-oriented *realka.* There, at age twelve, he met the future modernist poet Milan Begović, who was instrumental in encouraging Nazor in his earliest attempts at poetry; his first recorded poem, written in Italian, dates from this period. Begović is also credited with convincing Nazor to write in Croatian. During this period Nazor was engaged in translation as well – from French (Alfred de Musset, Victor Hugo) into Croatian and from Croatian and Serbian (Begović, August Šenoa, August Harambašić, Zmaj, Josip Badalić, Petar Preradović, Djura Jakšić) into Italian. The poet and translator then went on to earn an advanced degree in the natural sciences at the University of Graz in Austria.

For most of his professional life Nazor worked also as an educator – first as a teacher in Split, in

Vladimir Nazor as a young man

Writers' Union. He also received an honorary doctorate of philosophy from the University of Zagreb.

Although women played a pivotal role in Nazor's life – he doted on his elderly mother, his sister Irma cared for him in his later years, and he immortalized his infatuations in verse – he never married and left no direct descendants. His life and work lend themselves to the reductionist stereotyping of woman as either "madonna" or temptress.

Nazor's first collection, *Slavenske legende* (Slavic Legends), appeared in 1900. Poems such as "Perun," "Momir i Grozdana," "Kosovo," and "Kraljević Marko" sing of pagan Slavic gods and legendary Slavic heroes and celebrate past eras of Slavic pride and independence. Often identified as an influence on these verses is Natko Nadilo's study *Religija Srba i Hrvata* (Religion of the Serbs and Croats, 1888); also influential was Nazor's acquaintance at an early age with Italian poets, particularly Giosuè Carducci and Gabriele D'Annunzio, and the classical literature of his father's library. His first book received little attention among the literary establishment, but young writers and critics, including Petar Skok, Milan Marjanović, and Milutin Cihlar Nehajev, hailed the work as a new direction in poetry – synthetic, dynamic, and magical, in opposition to the pessimism that seemed to reign among the younger generation.

Nazor's second book, the epic poem *Živana* (1902), continued the theme of the battle of light and dark in Slavic mythology, and it received a similarly cool response. Nazor often returned to this poem and reworked it; he published a second edition in 1936. Despite its critical failure, the epic poem remained thematically central to his work and served as a workshop for his experimentation in metrics. Nazor's 1904 collection, *Knjiga o kraljevima hrvatskim* (A Book on Croatian Kings), also belongs to this mythological-legendary period of his poetry.

Many critics consider the poetry and prose of Nazor's Istrian period (1903–1918) to be the most important in the development of his art. The early works of these years are not the strongest: the cycle of sonnets *Istarski gradovi* (Istrian Towns, later published in 1949); the ballads *Krvava košulja* (The Bloody Shirt, 1905); and the historical novel *Krvavi dani* (Bloody Days, 1908). Yet they demonstrate his turn from the metaphysical and mythological to the relatively realistic, even if he remained focused on the past. The works were culturally significant as well. Like the title ballad "Krvava košulja," which symbolically depicts the freeing of the serfs in 1848, they contributed to a renewed sense of national identity among the Istrians.

Zadar, and in several towns in Istria, including Pazin, Kopar, and Kastav; then, between the wars, as director of an orphanage in Crikvenica, and, finally, as director of a high school in Zagreb. His responsibilities did not seem to interfere with his creative writing. In fact, his years in Istria were his most productive. Although he was revered as a poet even before World War II, Nazor's status as a hero can be attributed to his decision, during the Nazi occupation of Croatia, to leave Zagreb with his young friend, the poet Ivan Goran Kovačić, to join Marshal Tito and the Partisans – a path not taken by another well-known writer, Miroslav Krleža. Accounts of Nazor's hardships as well as of his privileges among Tito's forces became legendary, and his faithfulness and sacrifices were acknowledged with several appointments and awards. His nonproletarian art and demeanor notwithstanding, Nazor was president of numerous bodies and organizations, including the anti-Fascist organization known as ZAVNOH, Narodni Sabor (the National Parliament of Croatia), the Presidium, the publishing house Matica hrvatska, and the Croatian

The same effect was achieved by some of Nazor's best work of the period, the stories published in *Istarske priče* (Istrian Tales, 1913). In *Veli Jože* (Great Joe, 1908) he returned to the lyrical and epic mode of his first collections in creating a legendary Istrian hero. Veli Jože leads the serfs in a revolt against the masters and provides Nazor's contemporary Istria with a symbol of the nation's hidden strength. "Boškarina" deals more directly and realistically with social issues. The "heroine" of the story is a cow, Boškarina, who, although small, lean, and missing one horn and her tail, proves more productive in the meager pastures of Istria than a hefty cow from another region. Despite its realistic detail, this story, like "Veli Jože," carried symbolic significance for the Istrian people.

In the modernist spirit, Nazor was most compelled during the Istrian years to seek new modes of expression. *Lirika* (Lyrics, 1910) includes both the dithyrambic exultation at nature and, in the concluding cycle – later titled "Robovi" (Slaves) – a patriotic yet self-critical stance. His challenge to his compatriots in an "unheroic time" was likened to the massive avenging figures sculpted by Ivan Mestrović. Nazor's patriotic poems signaled the start of a nationalistic period in his writing, as in *Nove pjesme* (New Poems, 1913), *Medvjed Brundo* (Bear Brundo, 1915), *Stoimena: Priče* (1916), and *Pabirci* (Gleanings, 1917), that lasted ten years. *Lirika* was well received, and Nazor's influence on the rebellious, individualistic, and nationalistic youth was strengthened.

With the start of World War I, Nazor's verse became more lyrical and introspective. Waiting to be called to war and under the assumption that he would not survive, he wrote *Pjesni ljuvene* (Love Songs, 1915). An edited version of this collection, with *Intima (1913–1914)* (1915) and the earlier *Lirika* and *Nove pjesme,* were published as *Lirika* in his *Djela* (Works, 1918) and include many of Nazor's love poems. Poems on this theme during his time in Kastav may have been inspired by a particular love interest, teacher Marija Parčić. However, the object of the poet's affection in these and other love poems is usually best understood as the "eternal feminine," a synthesis of woman, poetry, and the divine, which Nazor sought to the end of his life.

During the 1920s Nazor lived in relative isolation as the superintendent of an orphanage in Crikvenica. He attributed much of what he learned about storytelling to his experience with his young wards, and during that period he wrote, in addition to pedagogical materials, the delightful autobiographical

collections *Priče iz djetinjstva* (Stories from Childhood, 1924) and *Priče s ostrva, iz grada i sa planine* (Stories from the Island, the City, and the Mountain, 1927), as well as a novel about his dog, *Šarko* (1928).

The best known and most translated of the stories in *Priče iz djetinjstva* is "Andjeo u zvoniku" (Angel in the Belltower). It tells of five-year-old Vlado's conviction that the church bells are rung by an angel. Caught one day in the bell tower looking for angels, he is returned to his anxious mother by the village priest, who reassures her that no matter what happens to him, the little boy will always be one of those who believes in God and his angels.

Nazor produced a collection of religious poems as well, *Pjesme o četiri arhandjela* (Songs about Four Archangels, 1927). The collection received critical praise, and he was acknowledged as a Catholic poet. Nazor's work was again compared to Meštrović's sculptures. One critic observed that the two artists had traveled parallel paths from *Slavenske legende* and the fragments of St. Vitus's Day Temple (Vidovdanski hram) across visions of war to the angels of later religious motifs.

In order to understand these works fully, however, they must be interpreted within the context of Rudolph Steiner's anthroposophy and its effect on the poet during his tenure in Crikvenica. The majority of the poems in *Pjesme o četiri arhandjela* appeared after Nazor had read Steiner's four lectures on the archangels given in 1923. They are incomprehensible without recourse to Steiner's discussions of the phases of the universe and the angels, who, as higher spiritual beings, direct human fate and work to make the individual "master of his destiny." The final poem, "Oče nas, koji jesi na nebesi" (Our father, who art in heaven), is a direct paraphrase and gloss of Steiner's lecture "Our Father." Similarly, the autobiographical *Priče iz djetinjstva* and *Priče s ostrva, iz grada i sa planina* represent more than charming reminiscences. Nazor had been considering writing his memoirs of childhood since the end of World War I. It was only after reading Steiner, however, that he came to recognize the symbolic significance of his memories and then felt compelled to document their "higher" power.

The work of Nazor's Zagreb period – of the 1930s up to December 1942, when he left to join the Partisans – is usually viewed as less productive, and his literary efforts were generally of a different sort. He wrote a travel book and engaged in literary criticism. He wrote articles on metrics – a continuous interest throughout his career – and he kept a journal, *Večernje bilješke* (Evening Notes, 1942). Toward the end of the 1930s he published a two-volume

Frontispiece for Nazor's Nove pjesme *(New Poems, 1913), which is more nationalistic than his earlier work*

Vladimir Nazor is best known in his later years as the author of "Partisan poems" and recollections of these guerrilla warriors and their leader Tito: *Pjesme partizanke 1942–1945* (Poems of the Woman Partisan 1942–1945, 1944), *S partizanima 1943–1944* (With the Partisans 1943–1944, 1945), and *Legende o drugu Titu* (Legends about Comrade Tito, 1946). He is credited with recording some of the most accurate impressions of the early war years among the Partisans and the people, although he is also faulted for his blind constancy to Tito and his allies, particularly after the war.

Nazor is a legendary figure in the history of Croatian literature. His long literary career spent alternately within society and withdrawn from it, which culminated with his adventures among the Partisans, invites investigation and speculation. His versatility in genre and metrics was impressive. No doubt that versatility was not only the expression of his remarkable talent but also a symptom of an emotional or psychological ambivalence that left the writer torn between classical balance and economy and lyrical romantic excess.

Bibliographies:

Moša Pijade, *Vladimir Nazor,* in his *Partizanske varnice,* volume 1 (1944);

Nedeljko Mihanović, "Literatura o Vladimiru Nazoru (1898–1969)," *Croatica,* 3 (1972): 289–376.

Biographies:

Vladimir Dedijer, *Dnevnik,* 3 volumes (Belgrade: Drzavni izdavački zavod Jugoslavije, 1945–1950);

Mirko Žeželj, *Tragom pjesnika Vladimira Nazora* (Zagreb: Stvarnost, 1973).

References:

Antun Barac, *Vladimir Nazor* (Zagreb: Jug, 1918);

Rafo Bogišić, "Vladimir Nazor i hrvatska renesansna poezija," *Forum,* 32 (1976): 149–175;

Josip Čelar, *Umetnost Vladimira Nazora* (Šibenik, 1928);

Vida Flaker, "Vladimir Nazor and European Modernism," in *Comparative Studies in Croatian Literature,* edited by Miroslav Beker (Zagreb: Zavod za znanost i književnosti Filozofskog fakulteta u Zagrebu, 1981), pp. 399–407;

Mladen Iveković, *Nepokorena zemlja* (Zagreb: Nakladni zavod Hrvatske, 1945);

Ante Kadić, "Vladimir Nazor," *Journal of Croatian Studies,* 17 (1976): 64–72;

novel of epic proportions, *Pastir Loda* (The Shepherd Loda, 1938–1939). Running some six hundred pages and spanning two thousand years in the history of Nazor's native Brač, the mythical novel laments human fallibility but symbolizes the human capacity for endurance and regeneration in the Dalmatian shepherd. This figure represents for Nazor the indefatigable human spirit, the hero who has persisted since the Greeks and who will outlive the vineyards and the olive trees. This apparent turn to the past, both in theme and style, was judged more generously before than after World War II. In 1940 literary critic Antun Barac described the novel as a synthesis of all that Nazor had done or experienced, and Ljubomir Maraković cited *Pastir Loda* as proof that the productivity of older people does not diminish. However, by 1958 the work was characterized as more storytelling than a novel in the strict sense and as lacking great insight or analysis. In any case, it represented for Nazor a second wind of inspiration.

Milan Marjanović, *Vladimir Nazor kao nacionalni pjesnik* (Zagreb: Hrvatski štamparski zavod, 1923);

Nedjeljko Mihanović, *Pjesničko djelo Vladimira Nazora* (Zagreb: Školska knjiga, 1976);

Milutin Cihlar Nehajev, *Djela* (Zagreb, 1945), volume 8, pp. 63–82; volume 11, pp. 5–21; volume 13, pp. 104–105, 228–241;

Ante Petravić, *Klasična metrika u hrvatskoj i srpskoj književnosti* (Belgrade: Luča, Biblioteka Zadruge professorskog društra, 1939);

Petravić, *Najveći hrvatski pjesnik Vladimir Nazor medju nama* (Zagreb: Vjesnik, 1943);

Vladimir Popović, "Djelo Vladimira Nazora," in Nazor's *Proza* (Zagreb: Naprijed, 1959), pp. 261–305;

Sheoraj Singh Tain, "Indian Reminiscences in Nazor's Etherics," *Most,* 4 (1987): 14–24;

Mirko Žeželj, *Pesnikovim putem* (Belgrade: Naša knjiga, 1960);

Žeželj, *Poezija Vladimira Nazora* (Belgrade: Naša knjiga, 1960);

Žeželj, *Vladimir Nazor: Portret* (Belgrade: Nolit, 1960);

Stanislav Župić, *Čudesni jugoslavenski pjesnik i njegov pjesnički roman kroz dva svijeta* (Zagreb: Vlastita naklada Župić Stanislav, 1968);

Župić, *Nazorova priča* (Belgrade, 1930);

Župić, *Pjesnikove velike čežnje ili dublji smisao Nazorove poezije* (Zagreb: Dubrava, 1945).

Papers:

The major sources for Nazor's correspondence and manuscript material are his diaries (3 volumes) and the archives of the Institut za književnost JAZU (Institute for Literature of the Yugoslav Academy of Sciences). Additional materials are located at the National and University Library in Zagreb and in the town and school archives and museums of Supetar, Ložišća, Split, Zadar, Pazin, Kopar, Kastav, Sušak, Rijeka, Crikvenica, and Zagreb.

Petar II Petrović Njegoš

(1 November 1813 – 19 October 1851)

E. D. Goy
Cambridge University

WORKS: *Pustinjak cetinjski* (Cetinje, 1834);
Liek jarosti turske (Cetinje, 1834);
Luča mikrokozma (Belgrade, 1845); translated by
Clarence A. Manning as *The Rays of Microcosm*
(Munich: Svečanik, 1953); translated by Anica
Savić-Rebac as "The Ray of the Microcosm,"
Harvard Slavic Studies, 3 (1957): 151–200;
translated and edited by Žika Rad. Pivulovich
as *The Ray of the Microcosm* (Salt Lake City:
Charles Schlacks, Jr., 1992);
Ogledalo srpsko (Belgrade, 1846);
Gorski vijenac (Vienna, 1847); translated by James
W. Wiles as *The Mountain Wreath* (London:
Allen & Unwin, 1930); translated by Dan
Mrkich as *Mountain Laurel* (Ottawa:
Commoners' Publishing, 1985); translated
and edited by Vasa D. Mihailovich as *The
Mountain Wreath* (Irvine, Cal.: Charles
Schlacks, Jr., 1986);
Lazni car Šćepan Mali (Zagreb, 1851);
Svobodijada (Zemun, 1854).
Collections: *Celokupna dela,* 2 volumes, edited by M.
Rešetar (Belgrade, 1926);
Celokupna dela, edited by Danilo Vušović (Belgrade,
1936);
Celokupna dela, 9 volumes, edited by Nikola
Banašević, Vido Latković, and R. Bošković
(Belgrade, 1952).
Editions in English: "A Montenegrin to Almighty
God," translated by Dennis Smith, *Yugoslav
Observer* (June 1956): 22;
Selections, in *Serbian Poetry from the Beginnings to the
Present,* edited by Milne Holton and
Mihailovich, translated by Mihailovich and
Anica Savić-Rebac (New Haven: Yale Center
for International and Area Studies, 1988), pp.
147–156.

Petar II Petrović Njegoš stands in Serbian literature rather as William Shakespeare does in English. If Shakespeare developed the English blank
verse (iambic pentameter with no end rhyme) to its

Petar II Petrović Njegoš

capacity, so did Njegoš for the Serbian unrhymed
trochaic pentameter. Njegoš grew up with the trochaic line of the folk epic that Vuk Karadžić had
popularized in his collections as the natural line of
the Serbian language, and he developed it into an
artistic expression that could not be carried further,
only imitated and parodied. In this sense Njegoš
came close to what T. S. Eliot defined as a "classic."
After Njegoš, Serbian poetry gradually moved away
from the folk decasyllabic line (the *deseterac*), for he
had taken it to its maximum of expression.

Born Rade Tomov in the Montenegrin Njeguš
tribe, who lived near and below the mountain plain

of Cetinje, Njegoš belonged to a small nation that was part of the old state of Zeta. Thanks to its mountainous character it succeeded in retaining its independence from the Turkish invaders, first under the dynasty of the Crnojevići and after 1516 as a loose confederation of tribes recognizing the central authority of its Orthodox bishop, or *Vladika*. The many attempts to subdue Montenegro during the seventeenth century failed in the face of skilled mountain fighters and the harsh terrain. The Turkish occupation of Cetinje, its capital, in 1623 lasted only a short time. The area could not support an army of any size, and the Turks were forced to retreat when a shortage of food and water developed. Divided into tribes, each with its own chieftain, the Montenegrins were anything but centralized. At first their *Vladika* was elected. In 1696 Danilo Petrović became the first of the Njeguš tribe to be elected *Vladika*. In 1710 Peter the Great of Russia, engaged in a war with the Turks, attempted to gain support from the Balkan Slavs and sent a delegate to the Montenegrins. In a war in which Peter quickly left his allies to fight on their own with disastrous results, the Montenegrins gained a long-lasting support in the shape of a yearly Russian subsidy. Danilo went to Russia in 1715, beginning a tradition followed by every succeeding *Vladika*. His reputation became such that the position of *Vladika* became hereditary until, after Njegoš, it became a secular principality in 1851 and a crown in 1878. Fanatical hatred of the Turks, a love of freedom, and devotion to the traditions of Orthodoxy were the basis for Montenegro, a nation of warriors brought up to fight and to believe in the glory of death in battle.

Njegoš's uncle was Petar I, one of the best educated and most enlightened of the Vladikas. He took young Rade to serve and learn in the monastery at Cetinje. When later another nephew, Djordje, preferred a military career in Russia, Petar made Rade his successor. Rade learned to read and later studied for a while in a private school in Kotor, then under the Austrians. It appears he read the chronicles he found in the monastery at Cetinje and also learned some Russian from a Russian monk. Perhaps the most important event of his youth was the arrival at Cetinje of the Serbian poet Sima Milutinović Sarajlija, whom Petar I appointed his secretary and tutor to young Rade. An eccentric and romantic figure, a fighter as well as poet and playwright, Milutinović was not an organized teacher. Marching barefoot in the snow to attain Spartan virtues, as well as pistol shooting, played as big a part as any formal education. Yet, in their long

talks, Rade absorbed many of the current Romantic ideas of poetry, as well as an ever deeper respect for the folk songs that he heard every day and sang throughout his life.

On the death of his uncle Petar I, young Rade was confirmed as *Vladika* at the age of seventeen. The following year he was made a monk, taking his uncle's name, Petar, to which he added the patronymic Petrović. He probably added the name Njegoš, an ancient version of his tribal name, on his 1833 visit to Russia, where he rejected the simple name of Petr Petrovich. The position thrust on him was not an easy one for a virile young male. Monkish celibacy must have been a burden. Njegoš never took the church too seriously, rarely wearing clerical dress and taking services only when ceremony absolutely required. In 1840, when the Russian scholar I. I. Sreznyevsky visited him, it was a time for fasting, and Njegoš, excusing himself for not eating what was offered to his guest, said, "That I have to observe such stupidities is no reason for you to do so." Njegoš was tall in stature. Memoirs of him claim he was between six and seven feet in height. "Handsome as Bishop Rade" was a common comparison among Montenegrins. He was reputed to be a crack shot with rifle and pistol and a lover of Havana cigars, which he imported, and of galloping horses. He had two fine steeds taken from Smail Aga Čengić as well as a beautiful Arabian horse, a gift from his blood brother, Ali Pasha Rizvanbegović of Mostar. Matija Ban referred to Njegoš's breakneck riding in 1849, only two years before his death. He had a black beard, high forehead, and eyes which many saw as cunning as well as humorous. According to Sreznyevsky, he was also a good drinker.

In 1833, having been promoted to the rank of Archimandrit, Njegoš went to Russia to be consecrated bishop. His route lay through Vienna, where he met Vuk Karadžić, the great Serbian lexicographer and collector of folk songs. Here also Njegoš experienced the intrigues of diplomatic life. Already he had enemies, and his experiences made him determined to learn French so as to be on an equal footing with the diplomatic world. In Russia he was received with all the ceremony of royalty. Emperor Nicholas I was present at his consecration, and he met many of the leading Russian literary figures of the day. For Njegoš this visit was clearly a cultural turning point in his life. He returned to Montenegro with a printing press and the works of Russian writers, such as Mikhail Lomonosov, Gavrila Derzhavin, Aleksandr Pushkin, and Vasily Zhukovsky, as well as Russian translations of John Milton; Sophocles; George Gordon, Lord Byron; and others.

On his return to Montenegro, Njegoš set about transforming it into a modern state. At Cetinje, where there was little but the old monastery, he built himself a modest "palace," which took the name Bilijarda from the billiard table Njegoš installed there. He also had a hotel built. Under his rule the first schools were opened, and some of the first roads were constructed. Even more important, he imposed taxation on the tribes, forming his own *Garda,* or police force, to enforce his authority. He also set up a ruling senate, consisting of elected tribal chieftains. Clearly none of this was popular with everybody. Njegoš was a ruthless, if just, ruler. He used the death penalty and even resorted to assassination. He had one rival, the *gubernadura,* who held a civil office that stemmed from the days of Venetian influence and had become hereditary in the family of the Radonići. The holder of the title in Njegoš's time, Vanko Radonić, was exposed as an Austrian agent in 1830 and banished from the country; the position was afterward abolished.

In order to develop the country, Njegoš desired peace. His two main dangers came from Austria, with whom he finally settled the question of disputed frontiers, and from the Turks. In 1842 Njegoš made eternal peace with the vizier of Mostar, Ali Pasha Rizvanbegović, becoming his blood brother, but with Osman Pasha Skopljak, the vizier of Scutari, he was to have trouble till the end of his days. In 1843 Osman seized Vrsenjina and Lesendro, two fortified islands in Lake Scutari, which had been Montenegrin. Njegoš never succeeded in getting these islands back. Although he never engaged in war personally, Njegoš was a true Montenegrin. On Cetinje there was a watchtower on which Turkish heads were placed to dry, much to the horror of Njegoš's Russian, German, and British visitors. In 1840 the head of the Herzegovinian Turk Smail Aga Čengić, Lord of Gacko, was sent there. Njegoš is said to have tossed it in the air with a laugh. Čengić's horses and weapons were kept at Cetinje long after.

After his return from Russia in 1833 Njegoš had his first volume of poetry, *Pustinjak cetinjski* (The Hermit of Cetinje, 1834), printed on his new press. It was not impressive, consisting mainly of rather stilted odes to Emperor Nicholas II, Crown Prince Alexander, Prince Golytsyn, and others, but the first poem was different: "Crnogorac k Svemogućemu Bogu" (translated and published separately as "A Montenegrin to Almighty God," 1956), written in octosyllables, offers a key to Njegoš's mature works. It might almost be termed a confrontation with the Deity. The poet sees God in nature –

"The tiniest flower doth praise Thee" – but the poet's mind lacks the categories necessary to perceive God. The human mind is "an oarless boatman." Yet the relation between God and the speaker already has a hint of tragic interaction. Though mortal and fated to be swallowed up in the ocean of eternity, the speaker is also a ruler, like God. Thus, in all the sheer impotence of mortal being, the poet says, "I hope that something of Thine shines in my soul: Unknown and insignificant, still I am proud to share some quality of Thine." Life as a great question remained the leitmotiv of Njegoš's main works.

In the same year Njegoš published *Liek jarosti turske* (A Cure for Turkish Savagery), a decasyllabic poem celebrating the exploits of two Montenegrins, Vido and Mirce. It is little more than a folk epic song. In 1835 he completed *Svobodijada* (The Song of Liberty, 1854), a long epic in ten cantos relating the history of Montenegro's struggles with the Turks. Njegoš again chose the octosyllabic line (even possibly influenced by Ivan Gundulić's *Osman*), perhaps seeking a departure from the popular folk meter, to which he would return and which he would perfect in his later works.

From 1834 to 1842 there was a pause in Njegoš's writing, probably due to the many problems of government which oppressed him. He wrote only a handful of occasional poems in this period. His reforms naturally aroused some opposition, and his opponents presented him to Russia in such a bad light that there was a danger that the czar might withdraw the subsidy on which the country so heavily depended. This problem was the reason for Njegoš's second trip to Russia, in 1837. In Vienna he was delayed and frustrated. He desired to visit Paris before going to Russia, but to his great indignation Prince Metternich refused him a visa. In Russia he succeeded in justifying himself to the czar, but on his return other troubles awaited him. He made peace with Herzegovina in 1842, but then Osman seized the two islands in Lake Scutari in 1843, and the problem of settling frontiers with Austria still remained.

In the meantime Njegoš was learning French from a French tutor. He copied poems by Alphonse-Marie-Louis de Lamartine and Victor Hugo in his daybook, and visitors to him in the 1840s suggest that his French was reasonably fluent. Lamartine's influence may be seen in some of Njegoš's smaller poems, such as "Oda suncu spievata noću bez mjeseca" (An Ode to the Sun, Written on a Moonless Night, 1837). In 1844 his ten-year-old nephew died in Russia, and Njegoš wrote an ode, in twelve-

Njegoš's grave on Mount Lovćen

syllable lines, the alexandrine. In the same year and the same meter he composed his majestic poem "Misao" (Thought). Here again he takes up the theme of the nobility of thought and its tragic insufficiency: "Either you are eternal torment to the body, or the body is for you a temporary prison. By what mysterious law are you bound together?" Man's existence is a great contradiction. In 1846 Njegoš published his collection of folk poetry, *Ogledalo srpsko* (The Serbian Mirror), which he dedicated to Aleksandr Pushkin. Njegoš's creative urges were becoming active again.

For Njegoš writing was probably an escape from the frustrations and isolation of his life as the sole educated man in his tiny country. He saw Montenegro as a center from which to spread freedom to all his Slav brethren. He was an enthusiastic supporter of the Croatian national movement. In 1848 he was prepared to offer military aid to Ban Josip Jelačić, the leader of the newly created kingdom of Croatia, Slavonia, and Dalmatia. He also had great hopes of joining Serbia in liberating Bosnia and Herzegovina. None of these dreams came to fru-

ition. At the zenith of his hopes, Njegoš wrote his two great works, *Luča mikrokozma* (1845; first translated as *The Rays of Microcosm*, 1953) and *Gorski vijenac* (1847; first translated as *The Mountain Wreath*, 1930). For both he chose to return to the folk trochaic pentameter, the natural meter of the folk songs that he sang with his associates on most evenings, often playing the *gusle,* or one-stringed fiddle. Yet he made a different line of it. It is for these two works that he is remembered and for which he deserves a place among the great poets of the Romantic period.

Luča mikrokozma is an epic poem in six cantos, with an introductory dedication to Njegoš's old teacher, Milutinović. The theme is the Fall of Man, which in Njegoš's poem takes place before the creation of the earth. Adam and his legions join Satan in his revolt, but during the ensuing battle Adam repents and betrays Satan. Because of his change of heart, Adam receives a lesser punishment than Satan, who is cast into Hell. Adam is sentenced to live out a mortal life on earth, forgetting his former state of immortality. At the end of life, the term of his punishment, man will either return to his former state of angelic immortality or be sent to join Satan in Hell.

The poem is in the decasyllabic line. Critics have traced its somewhat original theme to various sources, including Milton, Dante, and even Origen and Neoplatonism. In the literary sense, aside from Milton's *Paradise Lost* (1667), the forceful character of the rebellious Satan may also stem from Byron's *Cain* (1821). (A portrait of Byron hung in Njegoš's Bilijarda.) The cosmic view of nature must have been equally influenced by Lamartine's *Méditations poétiques* (1820) and by Victor Hugo's "L'Âme" (The Soul), passages from which Njegoš copied out in his daybook.

The most striking element of *Luča mikrokozma* is in the dedication, certainly poetically the most successful part of the whole poem. In the general ethos of romanticism man's situation is seen as tragic: "Man is to man the greatest mystery." Bound to the physical life of matter, man's mind raises him into the spheres of immortality, only to be pulled back by the material chains of his own being. The scientist and the philosopher can give no answer to the great question of man's purpose and meaning. The mind, by its very mortal structure, is incapable of grasping immortal categories. Only poetic inspiration may, sometimes, afford one a glimpse of the true nature of the mystery. Poetry is, therefore, the one path to Truth. Thus, in the final canto, God offers man one slight, vestigial sense of his true nature, which Njegoš terms "the Spark," the poetic intimation of immortality that comes only through inspiration. God himself is portrayed as the Poet, "occupied in the poetry of creation." This shows how deeply, though indirectly, the Romantic ethos had penetrated Njegoš's view of life.

Poetry is akin to the divine creation. Thus the poet's spirit is led by a guardian angel through the upper cosmic spheres to the center of Heaven, where he sees God and the reenactment of Satan's revolt and man's condemnation. Man is tragically confronted by an abyss on the one hand and the beauty of nature on the other. Yet Njegoš's faith in romanticism and poetic inspiration was not to remain unshaken. *Luča mikrokozma* was his great excursion into romanticism, which in his greatest work, *Gorski vijenac,* he was to bring down to earth in a manner that distinguishes him from the Romantic poets of Europe. Twelve days before his death he wrote to the poet Ludwig August Frankl von Hochwart concerning poetry: "I have never been able to decide whether it is a spark of the immortal fire, or a stormy delusion – the child of our narrow

ambience.... When man rises above himself, then he sees the poverty of humanity."

Luča mikrokozma, perhaps by its very subject, was condemned to poetic failure. The descriptions of the heavenly battle are too reminiscent of a folk epic. Its success is the dramatic portrayal of Satan. Indeed, Njegoš portrays a subtle dialectic in the opposing views of "creation" by God and by Satan. God affirms his aim to be the destruction of Darkness and the universal creation of Light. All was Chaos until God raised his crown, and "This, the first and brightest blow / Shattered their empire to pieces." Satan, on the other hand, states that this view is a lie. Once the universe consisted of equal bright spheres in each of which sat a creator, engaged in his own creation. Then, suddenly, by blind chance, came a vast cataclysm that destroyed everything, except one creator, God, who survived by chance and exploited this fact to become the tyrant. Yet the two contrary descriptions strangely harmonize. Satan's idea of equality and justice is static. It is the harmony of death, of chaos. Its creativity cannot be creative, since there is no struggle. Equality is death. Struggle and inequality are the basis of creation. Thus Satan's own case condemns him, showing him to be a true child of Chaos.

In the final canto Njegoš sees God's decree that man be born into mortality as a punishment. Earth is on the edge of Hell, and man is exposed to the temptations of his old ally, Satan. Satan's spirit of revolt is tempting, certainly to readers, since he appears to stand for individuality. Yet this perception is not so, for individuality can never stem from equality. Njegoš felt his own position, on the edge of Western culture, surrounded and threatened by Muslim "darkness," to symbolize man's position. In the dedication he writes, "I have arisen at the very gates of Tartary." God deprived man of the memory of his true being but allowed him a spark of intimation that would drive him toward a creative sense of his life on earth as a force for his redemption. Njegoš praises the sun worshipers as the first step toward Truth. Then follows a brief account of Christianity. Whether it is but another step upon the road, another emergence of the Spark, or the ultimate religion is not clear. Njegoš may well have considered God above and beyond Christianity. His own position as bishop doubtless forced him to pay lip service; for Njegoš his bishopric was a national duty. Montenegro was his task, his duty, and his creative fate. Christianity was a part of its tradition and an essence of its individual existence. It would be difficult to accept that he was a Christian in the formal sense, as becomes clear in *Gorski vijenac.*

Gorski vijenac is Njegoš's masterpiece. Its link with the philosophy expressed in *Luča mikrokozma* is clear, if only in the fact that he originally thought of calling it "Izvita iskra" or "Izvijanje iskre" (The Emergence of the Spark). The work is in dramatic form and takes as its theme an event from Montenegrin history, one that has only one folk epic to confirm it. Unable directly to subdue the Montenegrins, the Turks began a slow infiltration by converting them to Islam. To accept Islam gave immediate advantages, including freedom from tax. It appears certain that at the turn of the seventeenth century there was a significant number of brotherhoods within the tribes around Cetinje who had converted to Islam. According to legend, Danilo, the first Petrović to be *Vladika,* decided that Islam within the frontiers of Montenegro threatened its very existence, and, with the help of the Martinović tribe, he began to plan the elimination of Muslims around Cetinje. He began his preparations around Whitsuntide and on the following Christmas Eve slaughtered a large number of those who had accepted Islam. Njegoš places the event in 1702, but there is no confirmation even that it really took place. Njegoš saw the event as symbolic of the first conscious affirmation of Montenegro as an independent state and people. In this sense he was linking his own efforts to form a state from a group of tribes with the actions of his ancestor.

Gorski vijenac is a drama, yet not a drama. Its lack of any real structure of acts and scenes, its requiring the presence of hundreds of people on stage, makes it difficult, though not impossible, to perform. Njegoš himself recognized its lack of drama in the classical sense and even thought of improving it in some later edition.

The structure is really made up of scenes, or tableaux, which – while logically following the preparations for the strike against Islam – at the same time represent many facets of the Montenegrin people and their psychology. The framework of the play is European history and the struggle against Islam from Charles Martel onward. Especially it is the history of the Serbian people, the defeat at Kosovo (1389), and the task of avenging it placed by fate upon the Montenegrins. Yet the real, inner theme is that of Danilo, who hesitates to perform an act against people, his own countrymen, and who curses his fate in having to choose such a course. The dramatic form is really dominated by a lyrical poetic element that makes *Gorski vijenac* a dramatic poem rather than a drama to be performed. Njegoš's knowledge of drama was limited to his reading of the Greek tragedies in translation, and,

indeed, he employs the ring dance, or *Kolo,* as a chorus, paralleling events with their historic background and philosophical meaning. All action, as in a Greek play, is offstage. The only other plays Njegoš probably knew were Byron's (which Byron himself said were never intended to be staged) and Pushkin's *Boris Godunov* (1825), which also dispenses with acts and the unities of time and place. More interesting is the possible evolution of dramatic form from the folk epic. In *Luča mikrokozma* Njegoš uses the dialogue of the folk epic, in which extended direct speech is common, as in Homer; Satan's speech, like God's, is direct and thus dramatic.

Gorski vijenac brings the folk decasyllabic line to its greatest expressiveness. Njegoš makes use not only of the metaphor in the sense of contemporary poetry, but also of folk sayings and proverbs in order to express an inner philosophical view of the tragedy of life and history. Many of these sayings have become as readily quoted as are Shakespeare's in the English-speaking world: " 'Tis the blow that finds the spark within the stone"; " 'Tis easy to be good when all goes well, / It is in torture that we learn the hero"; and "The cup of honey no man yet had drunk / Which first the cup of gall has not embittered, / The cup of gall, it seeks the cup of honey." Throughout the incidents of which the work is constructed – the symbolic crossing of lightning below Mount Lovćen, the suicide of Batrić's sister, the marriage scene, the illiterate priest, Draško's satiric description of Venice, Vuk Mandušić's dream, and many other tableaux – there is the unifying movement toward a conclusion over which Danilo hesitates.

The character Danilo raises the question of the tragic clash between historical duty and personality. Danilo, the educated man among a society of primitives, is faced with his own isolation. To his own people the issue is clear, and they rebuke Danilo for hesitation. Danilo begins by cursing the day that gave him birth, with an exact translation of Lamartine's line from "Meditation 30": "Ah, périsse à jamais le jour qui m'a vu nâitre" (Ah, perish forever the day that saw me born), which Njegoš had noted in his daybook. Man cannot choose the circumstances in which he is born, nor the tasks and duties imposed on him by history. Yet he must fight for his own being and that of the people to whom he belongs. Against Danilo is the character of Vuk Mićunović, who lives the very existence that Danilo sees from the standpoint of a more self-aware personality. History imposes a fate and a way of life. Such people as Mićunović exist within this restriction unconsciously and unquestioningly. For him there is no moral question in the slaying of people whom he sees as the enemies of his people and their faith.

In his predicament Danilo, forced by duty to enact a deed that is repugnant to him, reflects Njegoš's own sense of isolation and occasional despair. On 1 November 1847 he wrote to Vuk Karadžić: "God and I alone know my position. A hellish hatred is spreading. The devils of old feared the cross and those of today fear freedom. Were a man as constant as he should be, I would be its most zealous hostage, but at times the bloody and hard struggle overwhelms me and I curse the hour when this spark rose up from the ashes of Dušan's greatness and into these mountains of ours. Why did it too not die where the Serbian hearth was smothered, but it spread up the mountain and glows and brings upon itself the thunderbolts of malice and envy. . . . An ill wind is my constant companion, and there is no refuge for me, save the grave. . . . "

Danilo's predicament is poetically placed in the context of living. The followers of Islam also find beauty in their faith, as expressed by the speech of Mustafa Kadija. History is a tragic conflict of faiths arising from the fact of individual and national being. In the character of Abbot Stefan the problem is universalized. Unlike Danilo, Stefan is not a man of great formal education. He is well traveled as a monk, and at the age of eighty and blind he speaks from natural experience. For him all nature is based on struggle. The winds strive against the sea, creature against creature, plant against plant. All being is a struggle for survival. Amid this struggle man must be heroic. Yet the position becomes more acceptable when it is realized that all human emotions are based upon opposites. There is no light without darkness, no sweet without sour. Happiness is merely a fleeting state that would not exist but for the fact of suffering. "What is man?" Stefan asks. "He must be a man." The challenge of being must be accepted and faced. Yet man has an inherent duty to oppose the tyrant. This view is dominant throughout the work. It relates to what Njegoš terms Čovještvo, which might be translated as "humanity." In the early stages of Gorski vijenac there is a tableau of some little partridges that are caught but released because they had come for shelter from some other danger and, therefore, should not be molested. The term humanity seems to stand for the innate sense of justice, fair play, even something close to sportsmanship. It is the lack of this quality in the Turks that Njegoš attacks. When Danilo went to them on an oath of safe conduct, he

was seized and had to be ransomed. Irrespective of faith or nation, this sense of justice is the individual ethic that is as much part of a man as the rest of his being.

The work ends with what may be seen as a poetic synthesis, evocative of the contradictory nature of Truth. The massacre on Christmas Eve is followed by the New Year. At the news of the successful killing of the Muslims, Danilo, his duty done, weeps, while Stefan laughs. For Danilo it has been a tragedy; for Stefan it is joy at natural and existential duty carried out. Montenegro has found itself, preserved its individuality by being true to itself. As the chieftain Batrić shouts: "A merry Christmas, Montenegro!" The play ends with a humorous interlude of Vuk Mandušić, the rather comic hero who has been off on exploit of his own and has had his favorite rifle broken. He asks Danilo to send it to Venice to be repaired. Danilo laughs, hands him another rifle and says, "In the hands of Vuk Mandušić / any rifle will be good."

Gorski vijenac is Njegoš's one great work, one in which he transcends the romanticism of Luča mikrokozma. In 1849 it became clear that Njegoš was suffering from tuberculosis. In summer 1850 he went to Italy in search of a cure; he returned the following December, traveling through Italy and ending up in Vienna. The news that Omer Pasha Latas, vizir of Bosnia, was planning to attack Montenegro brought Njegoš hurriedly back to Cetinje, where he died on 19 October 1851.

In the year of his death Njegoš published his last work, a historical play, Lazni car Šćepan Mali (The False Czar Stefan the Small). It relates the historic arrival in Montenegro of a mountebank from Dalmatia who claimed to be the dead Peter III of Russia. In the presence of a weak Vladika, Sava Petrović, Stefan ruled Montenegro in all but name from 1767 until his murder in 1774. Though a coward he instituted some law and order and angered the Turks by lending a new rallying point to the Montenegrins. Catherine the Great of Russia was embarrassed and sent Prince Dolgoruky to Cetinje. The Montenegrins, though not believing Stefan to be Peter, nonetheless refused to give him up for punishment.

Njegoš stated that he wrote the play in 1847, just after Gorski vijenac. Perhaps he was still determined to master the dramatic form. The play is divided into five acts and scenes; yet it fails as a drama. Although there are flashes of Njegoš's humor and poetry, Lazni car Šćepan Mali is generally and rightly considered inferior to either Luča mikrokozma or Gorski vijenac.

By both his position and the situation in which he lived, Njegoš is an exception among European poets of the Romantic period. In some essential ways he was almost a living model for many Romantic heroes. True, he learned much from the Romantics, from Pushkin, Lamartine, and Hugo, but he also learned from Milton, Dante, the Greek dramatists, and, above all, the language and music of the folk poetry. Yet in a profound sense Njegoš was a new voice in European poetry, unfortunately hidden from view by the fact that his language was generally unknown. Isolated from the general cultural life of Europe, Njegoš was thrown back on the reality of life and existence. His early excursion into Romantic philosophizing soon led to his overstepping romanticism, and in *Gorski vijenac* he produced a work that is more at home with the twentieth-century existentialist writers Jean-Paul Sartre, Albert Camus, and even Eugène Ionesco and Samuel Beckett. These affinities alone make Njegoš worthy of attention from all students of European literature. Unfortunately, as with all great poets, his work loses a great deal in translation. Ultimately, the only way to know it is to read it in the original. Yet such an obstacle does not alter the fact that Njegoš is a European poet of considerable significance whose best work has much to say both to the historian of literature and to the modern world.

Letters:
Pisma Petra Petrovića Njegoša, edited by Dušan D. Vuksan (Belgrade, 1940).

Bibliography:
Ljubomir Durković-Jakšić, *Bibliografija o Njegošu* (Belgrade: Prosveta, 1951).

Biographies:
Vuk Vrčević, *Život Petra II Petrovića Njegoša* (Novi Sad: Matica srpska, 1914);
Vido Latković and Nikola Banašević, *Savremenici o Njegošu* (Belgrade, 1951);

Latković, Miodrag Popović, and Jovan Deretić, *P. P. Njegoš* (Belgrade: Nolit, 1963);
Milovan Djilas, *Njegoš, Poet, Prince, Bishop* (New York: Harcourt, Brace & World, 1966).

References:
Jovan Deretić, *Kompozicija Gorskog vijenca* (Belgrade: Kultura, 1969);
Miron Flašar, *Antičko nasledje u pesmama Njegoševim* (Belgrade: Univerzitetska biblioteka, 1959);
Edward R. Haymes, "Formulaic Density and Bishop Njegoš," *Comparative Literature,* 32, no. 4 (1980): 390–401;
Vera Javarek, "Petar Petrović Njegoš (1813–1851)," *Slavonic and East European Review,* 30 (June 1952): 514–530;
Dimitrije Najdanović, "Njegoš," in his *Tri srpska velikana* (Munich: Svečanik, 1975), pp. 17–70;
Dušan Nedeljković, *Njegoš filozof oslobodilačkog humanizma* (Belgrade: SANU, 1973);
Miodrag Popović, *Njegoš* (Belgrade, 1962);
Pavle Popović, *O Gorskom vijencu* (Belgrade: Geca Kon, 1923);
Žika Rad. Prvulović, *Religious Philosophy of Prince-Bishop Njegoš of Montenegro (1813–1851)* (Birmingham, U.K.: Z. R. Prvulovich, 1984);
Alojz Schmaus, *Njegoševa Luča mikrokozma* (Belgrade, 1927);
Isidora Sekulić, *Njegošu, knjiga duboke odanosti* (Belgrade: Srpska književna zadruga, 1951);
Pero Slijepčević, "Njegoš kao umetnik," *Južni pregled,* 9 (1934): 107–117, 153, 158, 189–197, 202–209;
Krunoslav Spasić, *Petar Petrović Njegoš i Francuzi* (Paris: Sorbonne, 1972);
Slobodan Tomović, *Njegoševa filozofija prirode* (Cetinje: Obod, 1975);
Tomović, *Njegoševa Luča: Studija* (Titograd: Grafički zavod, 1971);
Nikolaj Velimirović, *Religija Njegoševa: Studija* (Belgrade: S. B. Cvijanović, 1911).

Vjenceslav Novak

(11 September 1859 – 20 September 1905)

Maria B. Malby
East Carolina University

BOOKS: *Maca* (Senj, Croatia: H. Luster, 1881);
Pavao Šegota (Zagreb: Matica hrvatska, 1888);
Podgorske pripovijetke (Zagreb: Matica hrvatska, 1889);
Pod Nehajem (Zagreb: Matica hrvatska, 1892);
Informator (Zagreb: L. Hartman, 1894);
Podgorka (Zagreb: Matica hrvatska, 1894);
Majstor Adam (Zagreb: Društvo sv. Jeronima, 1895);
Nikola Baretić (Zagreb: Matica hrvatska, 1896);
Dvije pripovijesti (Zagreb: Matica hrvatska, 1897);
Posljednji Stipančići (Zagreb: Matica hrvatska, 1899);
Dva svijeta (Zagreb: Matica hrvatska, 1901);
Zapreke (Zagreb: Matica hrvatska, 1905);
Disonance (Zadar, Croatia: Hrvatska knjižarnica, 1906);
Tito Dorčić (Zagreb: Matica hrvatska, 1906);
Iz života za život (Zagreb: Naklada hrvatskog pedagoškog zbora, 1907);
Teški životi (Zagreb: Društvo hrvatskih književnika, 1911);
Izabrane pripovijesti, 4 volumes (Zagreb: Matica hrvatska, 1925–1928);
Djela, 12 volumes (Zagreb: Minerva, 1931–1933);
U glib. Iz velegradskog života (Zagreb: Mala knjižnica Biblioteke lijepe knjige, 1941);
Sabrana djela, 15 volumes (Zagreb: Galebovi, 1944–1945);
Iz velegradskog podzemlja (Zagreb: Nakladni zavod Hrvatske, 1948);
Odabrane pripovetke (Belgrade: Novo pokolenje, 1948);
Pred svjetlom (Zagreb: Glas rada, 1949);
Pod Nehajem i druge pripovetke (Belgrade: Novo pokolenje, 1951);
Djela, 3 volumes (Zagreb: Zora, 1951–1952).

Vjenceslav Novak

One of Croatia's most prolific realists, Vjenceslav Novak excelled in the portrayal of the middle class and the working class, or proletariat. Although he entered literature with a romantic story about life in Bosnia during Turkish domination, he soon chose realism as his predominant form of expression. In almost twenty-five years he wrote seven novels, nearly one hundred novellas and short stories, and several textbooks, handbooks, articles, feuilletons, and poems, as well as prose and poetry for children. It is still not known exactly how much he authored, for he wrote some things anonymously or under a pseudonym. What has been gathered, however, is so extensive that even the largest collection of Novak's works (*Djela,* 1931–1933) remains incomplete.

A definitive pronouncement on Novak as a writer has not yet been made. Many of his contemporaries thought of him mainly as a useful source of material to fill the pages of literary journals but unworthy of praise for his endeavors. While it is true that he wrote in haste, at times producing works of uneven quality, he ought to have received more serious attention. Contemporary critics found his writing monotonous, his views contradictory, and his descriptions of everyday life trite. Such statements have come under recent scrutiny. Consequently, at present Novak is perceived in a more favorable light. By now it is acknowledged that he showed great talent in depicting a vast panorama of life in general and the lives of poor people in particular. Although he included in his works all social classes, from aristocrats to the proletariat, it was the introduction into fiction and objective portrayal of the working class that has secured his place in Croatian literature.

Vjenceslav Novak was born on 11 September 1859 in Senj, a town on the Adriatic coast with a complex history. His father, Josip, a Czech, and his mother, Ivka, a descendant of a Bavarian family, died early. Novak went to grammar school in Senj and completed four years of high school in Senj and Gospić. After that he enrolled in the Teachers' College in Zagreb and graduated in 1879. He was offered a teaching position in Senj, where he remained five years. In 1884 he received a fellowship to study music at the conservatory in Prague. Three years later, after completing his studies, he returned to Zagreb as music professor at the Teachers' College, a post he held until his death in 1905.

Novak married early and had seven children. His salary was inadequate for the support of such a large family. Thus he was obliged to supplement his income by writing. Although he wrote poetry and tales for children, Novak is known primarily as a novelist and short-story writer. His first published prose was *Maca* (1881), a story about a Bosnian girl victimized by the Turks. From then until his premature death from tuberculosis, he continued to publish several works each year. The only exception was 1882, when nothing by him appeared in print except for one short poem.

Always pressed for time, Novak could neither polish the style of his fiction nor solidify all of his ideas. The conditions under which he wrote are reflected in an autobiographical sketch published in *Vijenac* (Wreath), "Crtica o Božiću" (Sketch about Christmas, 1899). In it Makso, a man with six children, struggles to make ends meet in a big city. Two days before Christmas he begs a publisher for an advance so he can buy food and a few presents for his children. Even though people are reading his stories, no one wants to lend him money. Disguised as Makso, the author compares himself to a fruit tree. Many enjoy its fruits, but no one thinks of nurturing the tree.

Novak's work addresses four major concerns. To the first belong those works that deal with Senj and its problems. The second deals with Podgorje, a region southeast of Senj. The third treats the Croatian middle class, with the various strata within it; and the fourth introduces into literature the proletariat. At times these categories overlap.

Podgorje, a meager strip of land wedged between the mountain and the sea, where, says one of Novak's characters in his first novel, "one suffers in the winter from hunger and misfortune more than in any other Croatian region," is reflected in many of his works written between 1884 and 1894. In this first novel, *Pavao Šegota* (1888), Mara, a widow from Podgorje, peels four potatoes surrounded by three of her surviving children. The others have died from either hunger or disease. This is just one scene, but it conveys everything that needs to be said about Podgorje. It explains why so many of its inhabitants had to beg in order to survive and why children were chastised if they refused to do so. Mara's surviving three children are spared such a fate because she unexpectedly inherits a fortune. The rest of the novel deals with her son Pavao's education and life as a student in Prague.

When Pavao Šegota arrives in Prague, he is a decent, religious young man. Although he does not wish to become a priest, he is preoccupied with spiritual matters. Hoping to find answers to his queries about God, he buys a book about the origins of humanity. Before long, however, he is pulled into a circle of men who turn him into a debauchee. Three years later he returns to his village near Senj, where he commits suicide after witnessing the devastation he has caused in other people's lives by wasting the family inheritance.

An entire collection of short stories about Podgorje, some of which were published earlier, appeared as *Podgorske pripovijetke* (Stories about Podgorje, 1889). Their main theme is poverty; their secondary theme is love. In fact, love, in the context of humanity's search for happiness, is present in most of Novak's work. His characters yearn for it but seldom attain it. In one of these stories, "Vasiljeva ljubav" (Vasilj's Love), the protagonist is first too timid to confess his feelings to Luce, but when she becomes engaged to Marko he resolves to kill the man. Goodness prevails, however, and Vasilj eventually adopts Luce's son after the boy's parents die from tuberculosis. An even kinder man is Salamon in the story named after him. Though ugly and unintelligent, he has a big heart. When he proposes to Mare, the horrified girl ridicules him and soon marries someone else. Salamon then transfers his love to her child. To alleviate their poverty, he offers to share his home with this young family, an act that costs him his life.

Novak's women in particular have a great capacity for love and self-abnegation. Barica in "Lutrijašica" (The Lottery Player) loses both the man she loves and their child, then works as a servant for an unappreciative family. Upon hearing that Ernest, her late mistress's son, was sent to prison, she sells some of her meager possessions and goes to Zagreb to bail him out. When she does not succeed, she goes home to play the lottery, still hoping to rescue the unworthy man. In the end, after having depleted all her resources, she freezes to death.

Some of the protagonists from Podgorje, such as Petar in "Po smrti" (After Death; published in *Vijenac,* 1890), who grew up as a beggar without a family, are cruel, however. Petar never knew love, so when he marries a good woman he abuses her until she dies. Only then does he experience genuine feelings toward her. Similarly, a dishonest lawyer in "Fiškalova ispovijed" (A Lawyer's Confession; published in *Vijenac,* 1886) causes Marko much pain by having him kidnapped and raised by beggars after the boy's natural father makes him his sole heir. Matteo, the lawyer who wrote the will, appropriates the money but eventually confesses his wrongdoing to a priest. As Matteo now leaves his own property to Marko, he and his beloved Jelica become one of those rare couples who finds happiness in life.

Novak's last contribution to the Podgorje stories is a novella titled *Podgorka* (Woman from Podgorje, 1894). Its female protagonist is Luce, a beautiful young girl who lives in a patriarchal family headed by her blind grandfather. Novak knew that such an old-fashioned system was becoming a thing of the past, so he wanted to capture it on paper before it vanished forever. When Luce falls in love with Mile, who cannot marry her for ten years because the Austrian government forbids guards to marry lest it be forced to provide for potential widows and their children, Mile asks that she, like so many other women, become his common-law wife. Novak was obviously angered by this degrading rule imposed in his country by a foreign government.

In spite of her devotion to her grandfather, who found Mile's proposal unacceptable, Luce would give in to the man she loves if the spirit of her dead mother did not stop her from eloping. Critics have so far ignored this mystical experience, which had great impact on Luce's life. By finding strength to desist from an ill-conceived plan, she forces Mile to resign from a job that violates basic human rights. To find happiness, he has to return to his village and engage in farming, as his ancestors did – a prospect he once found unappealing.

Those protagonists of Novak's works who do not return home in time pay a dear price. This is reflected in many of his works dealing with city life. Young men uprooted from their small villages and pulled away from ancestral ways of making a living, Novak observed, could rarely make a successful transition into the middle class. Critics have found this view disturbing and contradictory to the author's apparent insistence on education. Novak, however, never stated that education was a necessity. He only described the hardships people subjected themselves in order to obtain it. Even when he saw them attain their goals, he had his misgivings. Notebook in hand, recording phenomena that aroused either his curiosity or sympathy, Novak often came across maladjusted young men who were subservient to their superiors and overbearing toward inferiors and women. Their college degrees notwithstanding, such men suffered a lack of confidence, without which they could not find happiness. Some of the students never finished college. They squandered fortunes trying to emulate the lifestyles of city gentlemen and lost themselves. Pavao Šegota, Nikola Baretić, and Tito Dorčić are such maladjusted men. They are the male protagonists of novels with their names that deal with city life and the formation of the Croatian middle class.

Growing up in Senj, a once-prosperous seaport with well-established traditions, Novak witnessed its economic decline and recorded it for posterity. As the world of Senj's patricians – rich sea captains and merchants – collapsed, scores of largely foreign bureaucrats, clerks, and guards came to the fore. Novak describes German-speaking officials and their satellites in his second novel, *Pod Nehajem* (Under the Nehaj, 1892), and he shows the downfall of a patrician family in *Posljednji Stipančići* (The Last of the Stipančićs, 1899). While dealing with sociopolitical problems, both novels also convey personal tragedies in the lives of their protagonists.

In the 1860s, as *Pod Nehajem* opens, the Turks, against whom Fort Nehaj was built, are long gone, yet the people of Senj are still not free. They are at the mercy of Austrians – frequently referred to as Germans – represented by General Gröll and Mr.

The house in Zagreb where Novak spent his last years

Hadaček, a Czech brought up by German clergymen and brainwashed by them. Their opponent is Adolf Huger, a young teacher and a great patriot despite his German name. Novak uses this man as his mouthpiece in arguments with Hadaček, who believes in the superiority of the Germans, and as an ideological contrast to Gröll, for whom Croatian nationalist sentiments are based on pure fiction. While this clash is resolved in a positive way, with Senj becoming part of Croatia in 1871, most protagonists do not see the realization of their dreams. Since Huger dies of tuberculosis, as many of Novak's heroes do, the two women who love him, Ida and Jele, lose their chance at happiness. Jele in particular is destined to go through life experiencing only pain. First robbed of her inheritance, then widowed early, she suffers in silence, forgiving her wrongdoers and even finding compassion for Ida, her rival in love. Rather than seeming a figment of Novak's imagination, Jele is quite real, evoking empathy but not sympathy. She is one of those incredibly good people one often finds in Novak's works, akin to other pure hearts portrayed in world literature. Equally well drawn in this novel are many secondary characters, such as merchants, seamen, and clergymen. In spite of the fact that he wrote quickly, Novak managed to

convey the contrast between the positive and the negative characters well. Because of its many assets, this novel is considered second in his canon only to *Posljednji Stipančići,* Novak's literary masterpiece.

Nikola Baretić, the protagonist of Novak's third novel of the same name, which was published in 1896, is also a former country boy who is out of place in a big city. Describing Nikola's suffering during his student years in Vienna, Novak adds a personal touch, stating that sickness and premature death usually follow such deprivation. Nikola's situation improves after he is hired by a Croatian nobleman in Vienna to teach him his native language, but the hero's ego suffers a blow when the nobleman's daughter, Tereza, vanishes after it becomes apparent that he has fallen in love with her. Nikola eventually meets Marija, a young woman from Zagreb who is in every respect Tereza's double. This second eternal feminine figure in his life puts Nikola once more in touch with God within his own self. Their marriage and life together is a short-lived idyll, however, as the primitive man in Nikola awakens, turning him into an abusive husband and bringing about a separation. Although there is a certain credibility gap here, the reader sees the couple eventually reunited in Nikola's village by the sea.

Purified by years of tribulations, they are given a chance to start life anew.

Posljednji Stipančići deals with an era somewhat earlier than the preceding works. It is set during the start of the Illyrian movement (circa 1830–1850), a rebirth of national consciousness in Croatia and the beginning of a long struggle for emancipation from foreign domination. Ante Stipančić, the protagonist, is a patrician who wavers between the pro-Illyrians and the Germanophiles of Senj. As is his habit, he eventually opts for the wrong side and dies soon thereafter full of regrets. In his dealings with family members he shows equally poor judgment by idolizing his son, Juraj, at the expense of his wife, Valpurga, and his daughter Lucija, called Luce. Treating these two women like objects and confining them to the house, Ante wastes neither time nor money to educate his son. A bright and rebellious child, Luce protests this denial of education, contact with peers, and social life, only to hear her indignant father predict that she will come to no good end. After Ante's death this prophecy comes to pass as Luce is seduced and abandoned by her brother's friend. Both women die in utter poverty, Luce from tuberculosis and her mother from starvation. Juraj vanishes, carrying off the last of the family's money to finish paying for his so-called education in Vienna. He changes his name to György Istvanffy, a sign of disloyalty toward his family and his own people. The tragedy at the end of this novel is intensified by the fact that Martin Tintor, a mason's son and a seminarian, is in love with Luce, but social barriers, more than his future calling, make their union impossible.

The characterization of the protagonists in this novel is exceptional. Ante Stipančić is a dark yet deeply tragic figure, always looking for distinction but dying as a loser. Martin Tintor, the wretched seminarian, dreams of "Slavia" and of Luce, to whom he sends handwritten copies of Petrarch's sonnets. Lastly, the two Stipančić women are among the finest examples of female characters in Croatian literature.

In his next two novels, which deal with the Croatian middle class, Novak gives examples of people who, after receiving an education, find no reward because Croatia simply does not have a place for them. In *Dva svijeta* (Two Worlds, 1901), Amadej Zlatanić, a musician appreciated in Prague, cannot find adequate employment in his country. Elvira Krekić, a young teacher in *Zapreke* (Obstacles, 1905), leaves for America because of a lack of schools and overproduction of teachers in Croatia.

Focusing even more sharply on the poverty of students and working-class people in the city, Novak arrived at the last phase of his creative cycle. This group of works includes portraits – some of the best Novak ever produced – of the Croatian proletariat at the turn of the century. To record their plight for the first time in Croatian literary history, he crawled into their substandard basement dwellings and climbed into the garrets. In doing so, he met starving students deserving of scholarships given to rich students instead, as in *U glib* (Into the Mud, 1901; first published in *Vijenec,* 1941). He encountered countless women laboring as underpaid seamstresses or maids, as in "Janica" (1901) and "Pred svjetlom" (Before Light, 1903), only to be taken advantage of by various men. Both were published in *Vijenec; Prod svjetlom* was published as a book in 1949. He saw workers drowning their despair in alcohol. Probably the most poignant of these stories is "Iz velegradskog podzemlja" (From the City's Underground; published in *Hrvatsko Kolo,* 1905), in which a father, driven to drink because of his insufficient income, accidentally kills his beloved little daughter. To protect him, his distraught wife lies to the police, stating that the child fell.

Tito Dorčić, the third of Novak's major misfits, appears in Novak's last novel, by the same name, published posthumously in 1906. A fisherman's son with an inborn aptitude for this profession, Tito is forced by his father to attend school. Even when he is told by the teachers that his son memorizes lessons without comprehending them, Andrija Dorčić will not be dissuaded. A successful man who is respected by other fishermen, he cannot reconcile himself to his low social status. He is therefore determined to make a gentleman out of his son. Influenced by Charles Darwin's and Chevalier de Lamarck's theories and using Tito as a subject for his study about the correlation between children's aptitudes and their parents' occupations, Mr. Wolff, one of Tito's teachers, urges the boy to drop out. His research leads him to the conclusion that a youngster will do well in life only if he continues in the profession of his forefathers. The school's principal, Reverend Sabljak, concurs. From his own observations, only rarely does a child from a working-class or peasant family appreciate the fruits of culture offered to him; consequently, education for such children is wasted. Furthermore, he argues, Croatia, being an agrarian country, needs people to work the land. These two pronouncements constitute the main message of the novel. It created great controversy, especially since the hero goes mad after having been an incompetent lawyer, an unworthy husband, and a judge who sentenced the wrong man to death. All of these details prove that Novak fully subscribed to the theories expounded by two of his characters.

Compassion for people is the hallmark of Novak's vast literary output, while poverty and love are its leitmotivs. As poverty is practically ubiquitous, love, if found, has little chance to blossom. Therefore, most of Novak's characters display signs of resigned hopelessness. Some critics have frowned upon that, but other writers conveying the same mood attained world fame. In spite of the sense of gloom and doom, Novak does allow for a ray of hope. In *Pred svjetlom* he prophesied, "From below a strong torrent arises. It will grow stronger for one hundred years . . . and when it erupts, it will sweep away maces, miters, and top hats." Because he wrote at a time when the governor of Croatia was Khuen Hedervary, notorious for his persecution of dissidents, Novak did not dare to raise his voice against social injustices any louder. Yet he did bear witness and would have continued to do so had he not, like many of his protagonists, succumbed to poverty-induced disease.

By making the pursuit of happiness one of the main issues in his literary works, Novak emphasized the individual. In doing so, he created a bridge between Croatian realism and modernism, a literary movement of the twentieth century that put the individual in the foreground. This achievement, in addition to his introduction of the proletariat into literature, puts Novak into the foreground of Croatian men of letters.

Letters:
Branimir Livadić, "Iz pisama pokojnoga Vjenceslava Novaka," *Napredak,* 20–21 (1906): 315–317, 332–334;
Andrija Milčinović, "Iz prepiske Kranjčevićeve Novaku," *Savremenik,* 10 (1919).

Bibliographies:
Milan Ivšić, "Bibliografi Vjenceslava Novaka," *Hrvatska revija,* 6 (1933): 692–702;

Slavko Ježić, "Bibliografija radova Vjenceslaw Novak," in Novak's *Djela,* volume 1 (Zagreb: Zora, 1951), pp. 25–40;
Višnja Barac, in her *Vjenceslav Novak,* volume 1 (Zagreb: Matica hrvatska, 1964).

References:
Josip Badalić, "Vjenceslav Novak i njegov nazor o svijetu," *Život,* 7 (1935): 306–316;
Antun Barac, "Vjenceslav Novak," *Savremenik,* 7–10 (1928): 297–304, 355–363, 420–426;
Barac, "Vjenceslav Novak 1859–1905," *Republika,* 11–12 (1951): 785–797;
Milutin Cihlar-Nehajev, "Vjenceslav Novak," *Obzor,* 217 (1905): 217;
Ljudevit Dvorniković, "Vjenceslav Novak: Literarno-psihološka studija," *Nada,* 8 (1902): 147–148ff.;
Mato Džaja, "Pripovijetke Vjenceslava Novaka," *Književnost i jezik,* 5–6 (1957);
Džaja, "Romani Vjenceslava Novaka," *Književnost i jezik,* 3 (1958);
Ivo Frangeš, "Vjenceslav Novak danas," *Riječka revija,* 3–4 (1962);
Marijan Jurković, "Vraćajući se starom Novaku," in Novak's *Izabrana dela* (Belgrade: Narodna knjiga, 1966);
Branimir Livadić, "Vjenceslav Novak," *Savremenik,* 1 (1906): 25–30;
Milivoj Magdić, "Pitanje proleterske književnosti u Hrvatskoj," *Socijalna misao,* 11–12 (1932): 130–133;
Milan Marijanović, "Posljednji Stipančići," *Život,* 6 (1900): 200–202;
Andrija Milčinović, "Vjenceslava Novaka *Teški životi,*" *Savremenik,* 12 (1911): 711–713;
Milčinović, "Vjenceslava Novaka *Tito Dorčić,*" *Savremenik,* 4 (1907): 226–233;
Milan Ogrizović, "Vjenceslav Novak," *Minerva,* 3 (1931): 4–7;
Radoslav Ratković, "Vjenceslav Novak: *U glib,*" *Letopis Matice srpske,* 4 (1951);
Djuro Šurmin, "Podgorka," *Vienac,* 8 (1895): 120–122.

Branislav Nušić

(8 October 1864 – 19 January 1938)

George Vid Tomashevich
State University of New York at Buffalo

BOOKS: *Pripovetke jednog kaplara iz srpsko-bugarskog
rata 1885* (Belgrade, 1886);
Listići iz požarevačkog zatvora (Belgrade, 1889);
Kraj obala Ohridskog Jezera (Belgrade, 1894);
S Kosova na Sinje More (Belgrade, 1894);
Ramazanske večeri (Sarajevo, 1898);
Običan covek (Belgrade, 1900);
Tako je moralo biti (Belgrade, 1900);
Knez Ivo od Semberije (Mostar, 1902); translated by
Luka Djurichich and Bertha W. Clark as "The
Prince of Semberia," *Poet Lore,* 33 (Spring
1922): 85–97;
Opštinsko dete (Belgrade, 1902);
Pučina (Belgrade, 1902);
Šopenhauer (Mostar, 1902);
Kosovo, 2 volumes (Novi Sad: Matica srpska, 1902–
1903);
Rastko Nemanjić (Belgrade, 1906);
Svet (Belgrade: Stamparija "Davidović," 1906);
Ben-Akiba, 3 volumes (Belgrade, 1907, 1932, 1935);
Hadži Loja (Mostar, 1908);
Danak u krvi (Mostar, 1910);
Iza Božjih ledja (Belgrade, 1910);
Jesenja kiša (Mostar, 1910);
Put oko sveta (Belgrade, 1910);
Devetsto-petnaesta (Belgrade, 1921);
Nahod (Belgrade, 1923);
Svetski rat (Belgrade, 1923);
Autobiografija (Belgrade, 1924);
Narodni poslanik (Belgrade: Polet, 1924);
Protekcija (Belgrade, 1924);
Sumnjivo lice (Belgrade, 1924);
Analfabeta (Belgrade, 1931);
Gospodja ministarka (Belgrade, 1931); translated by
Nada Ćurčija Prodanović as "The Cabinet
Minister's Wife," *Scena,* 7 (1984): 70–108;
Mister Dolar (Belgrade: Geca Kon, 1932);
Velika nedelja (Belgrade, 1932);

Branislav Nušić

Sabrana dela, 25 volumes (Belgrade: Geca Kon, 1932–1936);

Beograd nekad i sad (Belgrade, 1933);

Hajduci (Belgrade, 1934);

Ožalošćena porodica (Belgrade, 1934); translated by Prodanović as "The Bereaved Family," *Scena,* 6 (1983): 185–220;

Retorika (Belgrade: Geca Kon, 1934);

Sabrana dela, 20 volumes (Belgrade, 1935);

UJEŽ (Belgrade, 1935);

Dr (Belgrade, 1936);

Pokojnik (Belgrade, 1937);

Dela, 10 volumes (Belgrade: Jež, 1957–1958, 1960–1964);

Sabrana dela, 25 volumes (Belgrade: Jež, 1966).

PLAY PRODUCTIONS: *Narodni poslanik,* 1896;

Prva parnica, 1897;

Knez Ivo od Semberije, 1900;

Običan covek, 1900;

Tako je moralo biti, 1900;

Pučina, 1901;

Šopenhauer, 1901;

Rastko Nemanjić, 1906;

Svet, 1906;

Danak u krvi, 1907;

Hadži Loja, 1908;

Iza Božjih ledja, 1909;

Jesenja kiša, 1909;

Put oko sveta, 1910;

Protekcija, 1912;

Nahod, 1923;

Sumnjivo lice, 1923;

Svetski rat, 1923;

Gospodja ministarka, 1929;

Velika nedelja, 1929;

Beograd nekad i sad, 1932;

Mister Dolar, 1932;

Ožalošćena porodica, 1934;

Analfabeta, 1935;

UJEŽ, 1935;

Dr, 1936;

Pokojnik, 1937.

Despite significant differences in political philosophy and other respects, Branislav Nušić was in some ways his country's Bernard Shaw. According to Serbian critic Vuk Filipović, he was the "magician of laughter in Serbian literature." He was certainly the most beloved and popular Serbian humorist between the two world wars. His profound and unforgettable impact on his people has produced a plethora of stories about him, both authentic and apocryphal. With his precursor Jovan Sterija Popović, he is one of the best-known and most talented Serbian comic writers of all times, whose most successful works, despite their distinctive local color and specifically Balkan atmosphere, continue to be performed on many prestigious stages not only in South Slavic countries but elsewhere in Europe as well.

More than fifty years after his death there is no doubt that Nušić, with all his human imperfections and limitations, was an honorable, kind-hearted, and engaging man of high creative intelligence, keen and penetrating perception, and a contagious and incisive sense of humor. Virtually all critics now agree that this remarkable figure, once described as superficial, farcical, and even pornographic, was one of the most original, versatile, and prolific writers in the history of Serbian and South Slavic literature. Nušić's amazingly diverse opus includes lyrical poems, short stories, novels, dramas, vaudeville skits, newspaper articles, interviews, travel accounts, ethnographic reports, historical memoirs, and almost every other form of literature: his complete bibliography includes more than a thousand items.

Nušić was born on 8 October 1864 in Belgrade, a city whose characteristic spirit, wit, and sense of humor he universalized and immortalized. Brought up in the family of a merchant, he finished his elementary education in Smederevo and his secondary and higher schooling in the capital. He graduated from the Velika škola (later University of Belgrade) with a degree in law and spent a year at the University of Graz.

Although trained to be a lawyer, he was almost everything else but a lawyer. Like Molière, he was not only a major playwright but also an actor. Later, he was a consular official in Bitolj, Thessaloníki, Skopje, Serez, and Priština, a journalist and editor of several political newspapers, a playwright, founder and director of several theaters, deputy director of the Serbian National Theater, chief of the art division of the Ministry of Education, librarian of the National Assembly, and other positions. As a civil servant who found it difficult to hold his tongue, he was forcibly retired at the age of thirty-seven but was later reinstated. In the early 1930s, toward the end of his dynamic, checkered, and restless career, he was even a professor of rhetoric at the Royal Military Academy for a while. For that purpose he put together his highly useful and still unsurpassed *Retorika* (Rhetoric, 1934), which includes not only a learned technical discussion of the subject in general but also valuable sections on its history and excellent examples of world oratory translated into Serbian and classified by types and periods.

Unlike many other young Serbian intellectuals of his epoch, Nušić did not build his political and world outlook on the then-fashionable Socialist philosophy of Svetozar Marković. Yet he was by no means insensitive to the political and social injustices of the regime of the last Obrenovićes, whose dynasty, begun in 1815, ended in 1903. The regime's rampant violations of democracy and the crass corruption of its often poorly educated, semi-primitive, and overbearing provincial bureaucrats and police officials are masterfully exposed and boldly criticized in Nušić's comedies *Narodni poslanik* (A People's Representative, written 1883; produced 1896; published 1924), and *Sumnjivo lice* (A Suspect Person, written 1887; produced 1923; published 1924).

His satiric political poem *Dva roba* (Two Slaves, 1887), a daring swipe at the court of King Milan Obrenović, was inspired by his outrage at the excessive pageantry in honor of the deceased mother of an unpopular but officially favored general, which stood in glaring contrast to the insultingly modest burial of a truly deserving and heroic officer who died at the same time. For that poem, which was interpreted by the authorities as dangerously bordering on lèse-majesté, Nušić was sentenced in 1887 to two years in the penitentiary of Požarevac. During his imprisonment he wrote his famous *Listići iz požarevačkog zatvora* (Feuilletons from the Požarevac Penitentiary, 1889), a humorous work in which he continued to criticize and lampoon the flaws of the regime. In 1889, after serving only one year of his term, he somewhat abruptly and surprisingly entered his country's foreign service, apparently able to distinguish between the internal shortcomings of the government he had just attacked and the external needs and interests of his incompletely liberated nation.

In this and other respects Nušić is reminiscent of his Russian predecessor and role model, Aleksander Sergeyevich Griboyedov, whose powerful satire *Gore ot uma* (The Folly of Being Wise, 1825) was a formative influence on him, as was Nikolay Gogol. Like Griboyedov, while often sharply at odds with his government's autocracy, Nušić was loyal in the service of his country's diplomacy. Yet, unlike his Russian counterpart, who was brutally murdered by a raging street mob in Teheran that sacked the Russian embassy in 1829, Nušić survived his decade of consular service in the Ottoman Empire to tell about the condition of the still foreign-dominated part of his people at that time.

At a time when Serbian literature diverged into two distinct schools, the predominantly subjective and sometimes decadent poetry of late Romanticism and the predominantly objective narrative prose of early realism, Nušić opted for realism. Although he knew the life of his country no less thoroughly in its interior than in its capital city and wrote about it better and more truthfully than all its incipient sociologists put together, most of Nušić's literary output reflects the psychological dislocations and personal conflicts among the burghers of Belgrade caught in a period of rapid social change. These stresses and troubles accompanied the city's hectic transformation from a medium-sized, lethargic Balkan town, orientalized by centuries of slothful Ottoman domination and accustomed to a strictly patriarchal and tradition-bound petit bourgeois mentality, into a rapidly growing and ever more problem-ridden European metropolis.

In his youth, in keeping with local habits, Nušić frequented the popular small *kafanas* (coffeehouses) on the city's former periphery. In these old Balkan gathering places, Nušić met, conversed, joked, and bantered with other known, or merely promising, writers and artistic and intellectual bohemians. The effect of these gatherings on the cultivation of his talent and taste was both negative and positive.

From his *Pripovetke jednog kaplara iz srpsko-bugarskog rata 1885* (The Stories of a Corporal in the Serbo-Bulgarian War of 1885, 1886) until the end of his life in 1938, Nušić was one of the most widely read Serbian authors and a favorite of his country's theatrical audiences. Inexhaustibly creative, inventive, witty, and always in touch with the pulse of his people, he actively contributed to their sociopolitical and moral emancipation. Nušić was affectionately dubbed *Perpetuum mobile* (Perpetual Motion).

One of his best prose works is his collection of short stories *Ramazanske večeri* (The Evenings of Ramadan, 1898), a sympathetic and respectful description of Serbian Muslims. His novel *Opštinsko dete* (A Child of the Community, 1902), conceived as a sad story about the misadventures of a child born out of wedlock, turned in the end into a distinctly funny tale typical of the occasional unevenness and unpredictability of his work.

Though Nušić possessed an almost uncontrollable sense of humor, he had his deeply serious moments and sense of the tragic. On the eve of the Balkan Wars, which liberated the peoples of the area from declining Ottoman oppression, Nušić's dramatic creativity reflected his nation's self-assertive mood. This period motivated most of his patriotically inspired plays, including *Knez Ivo od Semberije* (produced 1900; published 1902; translated as "The Prince of Semberia," 1922), *Rastko Nemanjić* (1906), *Danak u krvi* (Tribute in Blood, produced 1907; published 1910), *Hadži Loja* (1908), and *Nahod* (The Foundling, 1923). Based on familiar historical themes, they were highly popular. His other serious dramas based on contemporary social themes, including *Tako je moralo biti* (It Had to Be So, 1900), *Pučina* (The Main, produced 1901; published 1902), *Jesenja kiša* (Autumn Rain, produced 1909; published 1910), and others, are not regarded by most critics as his highest achievements.

Although these works are in no way inferior literary creations, they are overshadowed by the more lasting popularity of his numerous comedies. Such a fate is not too surprising since Nušić was a comic genius. In addition to *Narodni poslanik* and *Sumnjivo lice,* his most memorable comedies include *Protekcija* (Pull, written 1889; produced 1912; published 1924), *Običan covek* (An Ordinary Man, 1900), *Šopenhauer* (Schopenhauer, produced 1901; published 1902), *Svet* (The World, 1906), *Put oko sveta* (A Voyage Around the World, 1910), *Gospodja ministarka* (produced 1929; published 1931; translated as "The Cabinet Minister's Wife," 1984), *Mister Dolar* (Mr. Dollar, 1932), *Beograd nekad i sad* (Belgrade Then and Now, produced 1932; published 1933), *Ožalošćena porodica* (1934; translated as "The Bereaved Family," 1983), *UJEŽ* (The Association of Emancipated Yugoslav Women, 1935), *Analfabeta* (The Illiterate, published 1931; produced 1935), *Dr* (Doctor, 1936), *Pokojnik* (The Deceased, 1937), and others. These are, for the most part, comedies of manners or intrigue, with occasional elements of farce.

In the opinion of Pauline Albala, Nušić's world "is the varied one of Southeastern Europe, which still shows the traces of a patriarchal tradition, but which already reveals the influences of contemporary materialistic culture. His characters will remain a document on the Balkan man in an epoch of transition." Jovan Skerlić claims that Nušić's lighter plays are "more for viewing than for reading" and that "they contain more theatrical ingenuity than real literature." In Skerlić's opinion Nušić's historical pieces "contain more stage patriotism than literary value." As for his serious plays, the critic insists that even there "he remains general and almost abstract," that "his actions could be taking place almost anywhere and any time," that "his personalities are vague and unindividualized," and that "his style is insufficiently literary." Even Nušić's comedies do not quite measure up to

Nušić's wife, Darinka, in 1893

Skerlić's yardstick. Skerlić is somewhat more generous in assessing Nušić's overall qualities. He admits that, more than anyone before him, Nušić understood stagecraft in its entirety and knew the theatrical business well. Skerlić also admits that "as a writer for the theater, he displayed special inventiveness in finding subjects and types, presenting and developing the situation in a dramatic manner and producing good stage effects."

Nušić's benevolently critical insight into his contemporaries was thorough and psychologically correct. Without explicit ideological preconceptions and political biases, he criticized social injustice as a function of excessive selfishness, unbridled ambition, obsessive material acquisitiveness, and deep-seated, pervasive vanity. He convincingly described the evils of bureaucracy and corruption, the exasperatingly slow pace of procrastinating and inefficient administrations, the flaws and weaknesses of executives and politicians, personality clashes within divided households, and tensions between the family and society.

Nušić was more honest and far wiser and braver than most of his critics. He knew that selfish

Nušić when he was director of a public theater in Novi Sad

and insensitive disrespect for the needs and rights of others, rudeness, brutality, avarice, gluttony, vanity, and sheer stupidity are not peculiar only to slave owners, feudal lords, and capitalists, but occur even among proletarians and their self-styled tribunes as ubiquitous elements of universal human imperfection.

As for Dragutin A. Stefanović's observation that Nušić was "without firm ideological orientation," a charge anticipated by Skerlić, that "in his literary creativity he displayed considerable ideological indefiniteness and inconsistency" and that "his condemnation of the ugly side of capitalist reality was not from the platform of progressive ideology," Nušić was too intelligent and too well educated to confine his social criticism to the straitjacket of a closed and dogmatically interpreted ideology. He realized that the world, including social reality, is too complex, multidimensional, and ineffable to be explained adequately and definitively by any single philosophy.

Beginning in the first decade of the twentieth century, under the scrupulously democratic and liberal constitutional monarchy of King Peter I, Nušić appeared under the pseudonym of Ben Akiba in a series of feuilletonlike contributions to Belgrade's venerable daily *Politika* (Politics). He also fought in

World War I, in which he lost his only son. The war's horrors, sufferings, and destructions, and the cruel personal loss he endured, left a painful and indelible trace that appeared in his work *Devetstopetnaesta* (Nineteen-Fifteen, 1921). This lengthy and moving story is a blend of a travel account with dramatic recollections of Serbia's national catastrophe, which culminated in the Cavalry of the Great Retreat through Albania. He also published *Kraj obala Ohridskog Jezera* (By the Shores of Lake Ochrid, 1894), *S Kosova na Sinje More* (From Kosovo to the Blue Sea, 1894), his two-volume work *Kosovo* (1902–1903), and his *Autobiografija* (Autobiography, 1924). In the 1930s he published his *Hajduci* (The Hajduks, 1934), about traditional freedom fighters viewed as outlaws by foreign occupiers, and several volumes of excellent and entertaining short stories.

Nušić considered women as fellow suffering human beings, especially in their roles of mother, sister, daughter, and spouse. He was too patriarchal and old-fashioned, however, to support their demands for equal participation in all spheres of public life, because he feared that this would interfere with his conservative conception of women's genuine fulfillment and happiness within the confines of the traditional family. His mordant comedy *UJEŽ* mocks a woman who neglects her family obligations in exchange for ambitions in social life. Like other great men, Nušić suffered from certain limitations of his time.

Albala calls him "a constant critic and mild reformer of customs." In fact, he was more a critic of human moral problems than of any particular systems or institutions. His comic situations, created with consummate skill and without sermonizing, point to conclusions that the playwright expected the spectator to reach. As a gadfly of his society and nation, he did not bite too hard or painfully. His treatment of a wide range of assorted human vices and frailties was never bitter or unforgiving. He wrote as a sympathetic fellow sinner made wise and straightened by experience and as though always aware of Johann Wolfgang von Goethe's confession that there is probably no human transgression with which a creative artist is not thoroughly acquainted – at least through observation and imagination – and that, given a set of circumstances, he or she does not feel capable of committing.

In Nušić's earlier works some of his characters were only suggestive hints and sketches. Only in his later years, as his psychological analysis became more comprehensive and profound and his differentiation between the idiosyncratic and local, on the one hand, and the universally human, on the other, became more sophisticated and deliberate, did he mature into a satirist of European stature, a serious judge of his society's moral condition, and a great writer worthy of his election to the Serbian Academy in 1933.

If alive today, he would most certainly be in the forefront of those Serbian intellectuals who, fully aware of their nation's share of universal human shortcomings, resolutely defend its honor, reputation, and rights, unafraid of intimidating allegations of nationalism. When he died on 19 January 1938 in his beloved Belgrade, he was mourned as one of the most popular Serbian writers of all time.

Biographies:

Milivoj Predić, *Nušić u pričama,* 2 volumes (Belgrade: Radomir D. Ćuković, 1937);

Milan Djoković, *Branislav Nušić* (Belgrade: Nolit, 1964);

A. Khvatov, *Nushich 1864–1938* (Leningrad: Iskusstvo, 1964);

Bora Glišić, *Nušić njim samim* (Belgrade: Vuk Karadžić, 1966);

Siniša Paunović, *Bora Stanković i Branislav Nušić iza zavese* (Belgrade: Narodna knjiga, 1985).

References:

Pauline Albala, "Nušić, Branislav," in *Columbia Dictionary of Modern European Literature,* edited by Horatio Smith (New York: Columbia University Press, 1947), pp. 586–587;

Zoran Božović, "Alkibijad Nuša i Antoša Čexonte," *Filološki pregled,* 3–4 (1975): 83–90;

Branislav Nušić (Belgrade: Narodno pozorište, 1964);

Branislav Nušić (Belgrade: Zavod za izdavanje udžbenika, 1965);

Branislav Nušić 1864–1938: Zbornik (Belgrade: Muzej pozorišne umetnosti, 1965);

Jovan Ćirilov, "Branislav Nušić and the Contemporary Belgrade Dramatists," *World Theatre,* 15 (1966): 359–365;

Vuk Filipović, "Branislav Nušić – Stilistika humora i komedije izmedju dva rata," in his *Pisci i vreme,*

volume 2 (Priština: Jedinstvo, 1982), pp. 43–104;

Velibor Gligorić, *Branislav Nušić* (Belgrade: Prosveta, 1964);

Milan Grol, "Branislav Nušić," *Srpski književni glasnik,* 53 (1938): 241–248;

Raško V. Jovanović, "Nušić Fifty Years Later," *Scena,* 13 (1990): 79–94;

Božidar Kovačević, "Branislav Nušić," *Glasnik Jugoslovenskog profesorskog društva,* 13, no. 1 (1932–1933): 5–29;

Josip Kulundžić, "Savremeno scensko tumačenje Nušića," *Letopis Matice srpske,* 394 (1964): 1–28;

Predrag Lazarević, "Nušić's Magical Realism," *Scena,* 13 (1990): 104–112;

Josip Lešić, *Branislav Nušić: Život i delo* (Novi Sad: Sterijino pozorje/Matica srpska, 1989);

Lešić, *Nušićev smeh* (Belgrade: Nolit, 1981);

Vladimir Petrić, "Osobenosti smešnog u Nušićevim komedijama," *Letopis Matice srpske,* 372 (1953): 282–296;

Jovan Skerlić, "Branislav Nušić," in *Istorija nove srpske književnosti* (Belgrade: Rad, 1953), pp. 406–408;

Skerlić, "Humor i satira g. Branislava Nušića," *Srpski književni glasnik,* 19 (1907): 276–285;

Dragutin A. Stefanović, "Branislav Nušić," in *Pregled jugoslovenske književnosti,* 4 volumes (Belgrade: Zavod za udžbenike i nastavna sredstva Srbije, 1972), III: 105–117;

Vasilije Točanac, "Humor ili satira u Nušićevim komedijama," *Književnost i jezik,* 3 (1956): 387–401;

Dragoljub Vlatković, "Prva komedija Branislava Nušića," *Književnost,* 38 (1964): 127–141;

Lav Zaharov, "Gogolj i Nušić," *Književnost,* 12 (1951): 170–178.

Papers:

Selected papers are in the National Library of Serbia in Belgrade.

Dositej Obradović

(1740? – 28 March 1811)

Radmila J. Gorup
Columbia University

BOOKS: *Pismo Haralampiju* [and] *Život' i priključenija Dimitrija Obradovića, narečenoga u kaludjerstvu Dosifea, n'im' istim' spisan' i izdat' (prva čast')* (Leipzig: Breitkopf, 1783); translated by George Rapall Noyes as *The Life and Adventures of Dimitrije Obradović Who as a Monk Was Given the Name Dositej* (Berkeley: University of California Press, 1953);

Sovjeti zdravago razuma Dosifejem Obradovićem složeni (Leipzig: Breitkopf, 1784);

Slovo poučitelno gospodina Georgia Joakima Colikofera . . . s nemeckog jezika prevedeno Dosifejem Obradovićem (Leipzig, 1784);

Ezopove i pročih' raznih' basnotvorcev' s' različni jezika na slavenoserbski jezik' prevedene, sad' prvi red' s' naravoučitelnimi poleznimi izjašnenijami i nastavlenijami izdate i serbskoj junosti posvećene, Basne (Leipzig: Breitkopf, 1788);

Pjesna o izbavleniju Serbije (Vienna, 1789);

Sobranije raznyh' nravoučitelnyh' veščej v' polzu i uveselenije, Dosifejem' Obradovićem' (Vienna: Stefan Novaković, 1793);

Etika ili filozofija naravoučitelna po sistemi g. profesora Soavi Dosifejem' Obradovićem' izdata (Venice, 1803);

Mezimac' G. Dosifea Obradovića – čast' vtora Sobranija raznyh' nravoučitelnyh' veščej v' polzu i uveselenije, edited by Pavle Solarić (Budapest, 1818);

Hristoitija si rječ' blagi običaj . . . (Budapest, 1826);

Vjenac' ot' alfavita . . . , edited by Konstantin Pejčić (Budapest, 1826);

"Prvenac," "Ižica" ili Dositejeva "bukvica," edited by Sevastijan Ilić (Karlovac, 1830);

Dela, 3 volumes (Belgrade: Peto državno izdanje, 1911);

Sabrana dela, 3 volumes (Belgrade: Prosveta, 1961).

Dositej Obradović was the chief representative of the Serbian and South Slavic Age of Enlightenment. His work was of crucial importance for the emergence of modern Serbian literature and culture as well as for the formation of the Serbian national consciousness. In his two-part autobiography, Dosi-

Dositej Obradović

tej left valuable information on his life and his work.

Dimitrije Obradović was born around 1740 in the village of Čakovo, near the present-day Romanian city of Timisoara. His father Djuradj Obradović, a furrier and a merchant, died when Dimitrije was young. Left as a widow with four small children, his mother, Kruna Paunkić, returned with her children to her family in the nearby village of Semarton. She died when Dimitrije was nine or ten years old, leaving him and his two brothers and one sister as orphans. Dimitrije and his brothers went back to Čakovo to live with an uncle. Later Dimitrije joined the household of another uncle, Nikola Parčanin, who wanted to adopt him.

As a young boy Dimitrije showed an avid interest in books and learning. He read both his native Serbian and Romanian, and he even studied Greek for a brief period of time. His uncle hoped to bring him up to become a village priest. Little Dimitrije, however, had different ideas. Exposed to religious literature, in particular hagiographies, he started to dream of becoming a saint. After Dimitrije's attempt to run away with an abbot from Dečani, his uncle decided to distance the boy from books and learning, and he sent him to Timisoara to learn the trade of quilt maker.

In 1757, however, Dimitrije fled the house of his master and found refuge in the monastery of Hopovo at Fruška Gora. The abbot of Hopovo, Teodor Milutinović, took Dimitrije as his helper and disciple. He was impressed with the boy's ability to read well, better than the majority of brothers in the monastery.

Dimitrije spent the following three years at Hopovo, reading *Srbulje,* books written in Serbian Church Slavonic, as well as books in Russian Church Slavonic and Russian. He read lives of saints and sermons of Saint Chrysostom, as well as ascetic works by Ephraem the Syrian and by Dorotheos, a Palestinian abbot of the seventeenth century. On the back cover of one such book Dimitrije wrote: "I, sinful Dositej of Hopovo, an unworthy deacon, finished reading this soul-benefiting book on November 8, 1759."

In Hopovo Dimitrije probably read his first secular books, thirty-six fables by Aesop, some simple Church Slavonic poetry and, among historical books, probably a biography of Peter the Great. He acquired a good reading knowledge of Old Church Slavonic. Accompanying his kind abbot, he traveled to monasteries in Srem, Bačka, and Slavonia.

By 1758 Dimitrije was tonsured and given the name Dositej. Later he was ordained a deacon in the presence of Metropolitan Nenadović. Abbot Milutinović, who sympathized with Dositej's desire to learn, permitted him to leave the monastery and go to a nearby town to study Greek. As time went by Dositej found monastic life more and more stifling. He learned that his fellow monks were intellectually uninspiring and mostly concerned about food and drink. By this time he had read everything he could at Hopovo. Abbot Milutinović had lost his position and was sent to another monastery, where he died, leaving no reason for Dositej to stay at Hopovo. In 1760 he fled, intending to travel to Kiev to further his education.

Dositej spent the winter of 1760–1761 in Zagreb, where he studied Latin. Bishop Danilo Tankosić of Petrinje advised Dositej to take a position as a schoolteacher among Serbs in Dalmatia to earn money for his trip to Russia. Dositej followed this advice and settled in a small town outside of Knin, where he remained for three years. He must have changed his mind about traveling to Russia. In 1763 he set off for Mount Athos in Greece. He became ill in Boka Kotorska on the southern Dalmatian coast and went instead to Maine, Montenegro, where he found a position as a schoolteacher. At Easter 1764 the bishop of Montenegro installed Dositej as a priest. He also read books, mostly Russian, from the bishop's library. Due to his poor health, Dositej returned to Dalmatia. Then he went to Kosovo, where he taught village children. During his stay Dositej sensed the great need of his people for education and for books. He responded by translating into Serbian the best pages of Saint Chrysostom at the request of the daughter of his host, the priest Simić. Arranged in alphabetical order, texts of "Bukvica" (Alphabet) were copied and distributed all over Dalmatia. From Kosovo Dositej went to the Dragović monastery, and in the spring of 1765 he embarked at Split for the island of Corfu, where he resumed his studies of Greek. From there he went on to Greece, to Morea and Mount Athos. He passed the winter of 1765 at the Serbian monastery Hilendar at Mount Athos, but, not finding the particular teacher he was looking for there, he proceeded to Smyrna, where he registered at the school of the well-known master teacher Hierotheos Dendrinos, the "new Greek Socrates." Dositej remained in Smyrna for two years studying theology, philosophy, Greek literature, rhetoric, and church singing. He received an excellent classical education at the highest level possible in the Orthodox world. Critics believe that Dositej's stays in Greece and in Dalmatia were crucial for his development. Had Dositej gone to Kiev as he originally intended, he would have become just another Russian-educated man of the church.

When the relationship between Turkey and Russia began to deteriorate in 1768, Dositej sailed from Smyrna and went – via Naupalia, Corinth, Patras, and Santi Quaranta – to Hormovo, Albania, where he studied Albanian. He returned to Corfu to study rhetoric and Greek literature with Andreas Petritsopolos, and then he went via Venice and Zadar to Plavno, Dalmatia, in 1769. Resuming his profession as a teacher, he spent that winter reading the Italian, Greek, and Slavic books he had bought on his trips. On holidays he preached in the Ortho-

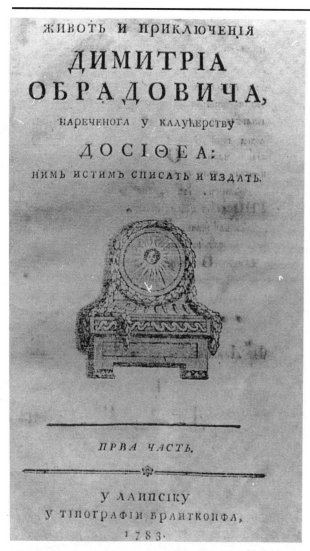

ЖИВОТЬ И ПРИКЛЮЧЕНІЯ

ДИМИТРІА
ОБРАДОВИЧА,
НАРЕЧЕНОГА У КАЛУЋЕРСТВУ
ДОСІѲЕА:
НИМЬ ИСТИМЬ СПИСАТЬ И ИЗДАТЬ.

ПРВА ЧАСТЬ.

У ЛАИПСІКУ
У ТІПОГРАФІИ БРАИТКОПФА,
1783.

Title page for Dositej's first book, which includes his Pismo Haralampiju
(Letter to Haralampije) and the first part of his autobiography

dox monasteries of Krpa, Krka, and Dragović. In Plavno Dositej wrote his second alphabet, *Ižica* (the last letter of the Old Church Slavonic alphabet), a collection of alphabetically arranged pieces of moral advice, which was published posthumously in 1830. He also finished translating into Serbian a Greek book on good manners by Antonios of Byzantium. It was published after Dositej's death as *Hristoitija si rječ' blagi običaj . . .* (1826). In 1770 Dositej composed *Vjenac ot' alfavita* (1826), a collection of moral teachings. After the Catholic church forbade his preaching, Dositej left Dalmatia for Vienna, arriving there in summer 1771.

In Vienna he came in direct contact with western European trends and the ideas of the Enlightenment. Although Dositej had been exposed to European influences earlier, they had been filtered through an essentially Byzantine tradition and its interpretation of Western ideas. Starting with 1771, Dositej was interested primarily in Western literature and ideas, humanistic and secular in character.

He supported himself by tutoring Greek. At the same time he took French, Latin, and German lessons. Later he studied logic and metaphysics. With time he mastered French and became a tutor of French and Italian as well. From his well-educated French teacher he learned much about French and English literature.

In 1777 Dositej entered the service of Vidak, the archbishop of Karlovac, and moved to Modra, near Bratislava, to tutor the archbishop's two nephews. For one year he attended the gymnasium, where he took a course in the philosophy of rationalism with Friedrich Christian Baumeister, who was a disciple of Christian von Wolff. Around this time Dositej started to entertain the idea of writing an autobiography, a popular genre at that time. In 1778 Dositej went to Karlovci, where he used the library of Zaharije Orfelin, a well-known writer. Both Dositej and Orfelin had favorable opinions of the reforms initiated by Empress Marie-Therese. When Dositej realized that Archbishop Vidak would not fulfill his promise to send him to Germany, he left his service and went to Trieste, where he was warmly welcomed by the wealthy Vojnović family and other Serbs.

In Trieste Dositej met Haralampije Mamula, the priest of the local Orthodox church, to whom Dositej's *Pismo Haralampiju* (Letter to Haralampije, 1783) would be addressed. In the company of the Russian Archimandrite Varlam, Dositej traveled through Italy, and then he sailed alone from Livorno to the island of Chios. He intended to go on to Constantinople, but when he learned that a plague was raging there, he remained on Chios for a year, teaching Italian in a local school. He eventually reached Constantinople in 1781, but had to leave soon after his arrival on account of a new outbreak of the plague. From Constantinople he went to Jassy, Moldavia, where he spent a year as a tutor with the wealthy Balsa family.

In fall 1782, with a savings of three hundred ducats, Dositej arrived in Halle, Germany, where he took off his priest's habit for good and enrolled at the university. He attended lectures in physics and the philosophy and aesthetics of German philosopher Johann Eberhard, a disciple of the English moralist philosophy of the seventeenth and eighteenth centuries. In the university records he is registered as "Demetrius Obradovius aus Serbien."

In Halle he became keenly aware of the backwardness of his own people and determined to educate his countrymen, bringing them closer to the European humanistic tradition by writing and printing books in their own, everyday language. He also became acquainted with the ideas of the Enlightenment, which had prompted Emperor Joseph II to modernize the Holy Roman Empire. First as coruler with his mother, Marie-Therese (1765–1780), then ruling alone (1780–1790), the emperor started ambitious church and secular reforms, abolishing serfdom, decreasing the number of monasteries, clergy, and religious holidays, and demanding that education be conducted in the language of the people.

At the time the Serbs were territorially divided. Those living south of the Sava and the Danube were languishing under Ottoman rule. Since the Great Migration of 1690, when the Serbian elite immigrated to Austria, the Austrian Serbs had been subjected to vigorous Catholic propaganda. That forced them to seek help from Russians, and Russian books and teachers were brought in to educate the Serbian youth. The introduction of Russian — and, in particular, Russian Church Slavonic as a language of prestige — interrupted the internal development of a Serbian literary language. Serbian Church Slavonic was abandoned, and Russian Church Slavonic was adopted in its place, creating a linguistic conflict. A new literary idiom was developed spontaneously, based on the local Serbian vernacular with numerous features from Russian Church Slavonic, Old Church Slavonic and Russian. This hybrid, called *slavenoserbski* (Slaveno-Serbian), lacked stability and coherence and was not an effective medium for the spreading of culture. Two separate registers came in existence: the educated men wrote in *slavenoserbski*, and the ordinary people spoke the vernacular.

Affluent middle-class Serbs embraced Joseph II's reforms enthusiastically while the clergy opposed them. Because the Serbs did not have a secular authority to promote reforms, they needed an authority figure who would support the emperor's measures without concern for exposing himself to attacks from the church. Dositej Obradović was singularly equipped to fulfill the mission. He was well educated, had traveled extensively, spoke foreign languages, and was familiar with classical and modern literature and philosophy. He also had serious doubts about religious education and the ability of the Orthodox church to raise the cultural level of its people.

In 1783 Dositej moved to Leipzig to be near the Breitkopf printing shop, which used Cyrillic letters. He wanted to print a collection of moral advice to introduce his readers to his instructive philosophy. Before this work, however, he published two others, in August 1783: his *Pismo Haralampiju* and his autobiography, *Život' i priključenija Dimitrija Obradović a, narečenoga u kaludjerstvu Dosifea, n'im' istim' spisan' i izdat' (prva čast')* (translated as *The Life and Adventures of Dimitrije Obradović who as a Monk Was Given the Name Dositej*, 1953). Even though *Pismo Haralampiju* was dated 13 April, there is no evidence that it was printed separately from the autobiography.

Pismo Haralampiju is the manifesto for Dositej's educational program. In it he informs his friend Haralampije in Trieste of his intention to publish his moral-advice book, which shall be called *Sovjeti zdravago razuma* (Counsels of Common Sense, 1784), written "for the benefit of my nation" and "in our common Serbian language so that all the Serbian sons and daughters may understand it, from Montenegro to Smederevo and the Banat."

In *Život' i priključenija Dimitrija Obradovića narečenoga u kaludjerstvu Dosifea, n'im' istim' spisan' i izdat'*, the first part of his autobiography, Dositej gives an extensive account of his life until the time he left the monastery of Hopovo in 1760. *Život* represents a metaphorical history of Serbian culture. While in *Pismo Haralampiju* Dositej proposed the model of culture to which the Serbs were to aspire, in *Život* he showed by his own example what was wrong with Serbian culture. He attacked the abuses of the clergy and suggested that monasteries be transformed into institutions of learning. He deplored superstition and religious intolerance.

Dositej wrote his autobiography to show the uselessness of monasteries for society and to demonstrate the great need of his people for sound learning. He believed that he would best make these points by recording his own experiences; that is, by illustrating the failure of the monastic system and the advantages of a semisecular education (such as the one he received in Smyrna) or a wholly secular education (such as the one he received in Germany). Above all, he demanded that books be printed for the people, in the language of the people.

Dositej considered the introduction of vernacular elements into the literary idiom necessary because he believed that only one in ten thousand people understood *slavenoserbski* well, whereas the language of the people was understood by all, peasants and educated people alike. With minor dialectal differences, the spoken language was the same in all the areas populated by the Serbs. If books were

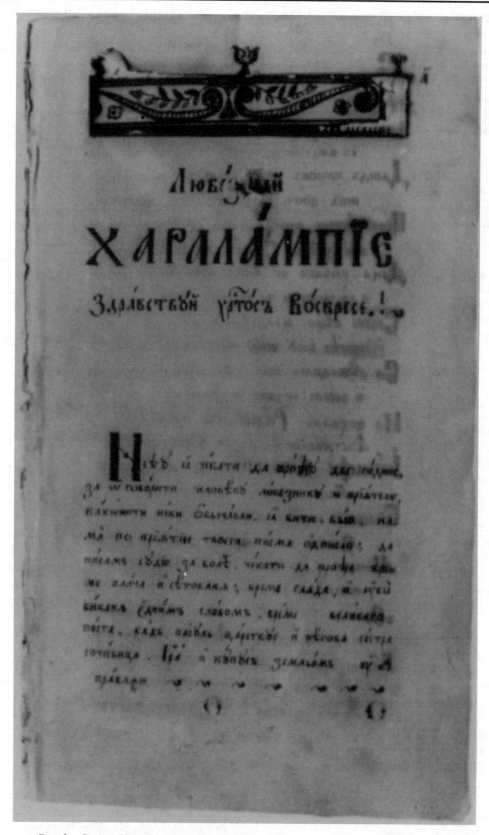

Page from Dositej's Pismo Haralampiju, *in which he announces his intention to publish his writings in Serbian*

printed in the language of the people, they would reach broad segments of population.

Dositej was expressing two essential ideas: the idea of rationalism and the idea of national integration. If people could understand books, they would be motivated to learn. One national language would bridge the differences between Serbs living in different regions of the Austrian Empire and those living south of the Sava and the Danube.

In May 1784 Dositej published his *Sovjeti zdravago razuma,* dedicated to Gen. Simeon Zorić, a wealthy man and a favorite of Catherine the Great. (Zorić had expressed his enthusiasm for *Život* and invited Dositej to come and visit him in Šklov.) In this book Dositej gave the basic outline of his instructive philosophy. The book included advice from famous and wise men, organized in six topical chapters, including Love, Virtue, and Malice. The book also advocated the instruction of girls alongside boys.

At the end of the same year appeared *Slovo poučitelno gospodina Georgia Joakima Colikofera* (An Instructive Discourse by Herr Georg Joachim Zollikofer), Dositej's translation of a discourse by a well-known German preacher. In his commentaries Dositej discussed the need for natural and clear expression.

In 1784 Dositej left Leipzig for London, traveling via Frankfurt am Main, Mannheim, Strasbourg, Nancy, Metz, and Paris. For lack of funds he stayed in Paris only three weeks. He arrived in London in December and remained there for six months, studying English and translating Aesop's fables from Greek into English. He became very enthusiastic about English literature, including books by Joseph Addison, Jonathan Swift, Alexander Pope, and Samuel Richardson.

With a large number of English books Dositej left for Leipzig in May 1785. There a second letter from General Zorić was awaiting him, with a new invitation to Šklov. To earn money for the trip Dositej had to resume his tutoring. At the end of 1787, he finally went to Russia to spend six months in Šklov. There he read books from the general's large library, and he wrote the second part of his autobiography. The general had promised to set up a printing shop for Dositej, and when none was provided for him Dositej sold all his books except the English ones and returned to Leipzig. The general paid Dositej generously for his time, enabling him to print his fables in Leipzig. *Ezopove i pročih' raznih' basnotvorcev' s' različni jezika na slavenoserbski jezik' prevedene sad' prvi red' s' naravoučitelnimi poleznimi izjašnenijami i nastavlenijami izdate i serbskoj junosti*

posvećene, Basne (Fables of Aesop and Various Others Fabulists Translated from Different Languages into Slaveno-Serbian . . .) was printed in late 1788 and early 1789.

Dedicated to the youth of Serbia, the fables were published with moral explanations and instructions. Considering the fable superior to other literary genres because it is appropriate for educated men as well as for simple folks, Dositej translated the fables freely, leaving out all that his audience could not understand or benefit from, while introducing folk proverbs, popular expressions, short poems, and elements of folklore in general with which his readers would be familiar. In the morals section – which surpasses the fables section in length and which Dositej wrote himself – he made reference to both classical and contemporary authors.

To *Basne* Dositej attached the second part of his autobiography, written in the form of letters. In it he gave an account of his life from the time he left Hopovo until 1788. He also included 180 English apothegms and two stories translated from Samuel Johnson's *Rambler* (1750–1752).

In 1789 Dositej left Leipzig for Vienna, where he stayed for twelve years writing and printing books. When the army of Joseph II captured Belgrade from the Turks in October 1789, Dositej wrote *Pjesna o izbableniju Serbije* (Ode to the Liberation of Serbia), in which he glorified both the Austrians and the Russians. Dositej had hopes that this victory meant the deliverance of the Serbian people, but only two years later Belgrade was again in Turkish hands.

One reason for Dositej's long stay in Vienna was the printing shop of Stefan Novaković, a Serb, who bought a printing outfit in 1792 and started to print books in the Cyrillic alphabet. In 1793 Novaković printed one thousand copies of Dositej's *Sobranije raznyh' nravoučitelnyh' veščej v' polzu i uveselenije* (A Collection of Various Moral Articles for Profit and Amusements), an anthology of translated and adapted articles, short stories, Eastern tales, and anecdotes from English, French, Italian, and Latin literature. It also includes a comedy by Gotthold Ephraim Lessing, a poem, and a biography. These articles discussed practical matters of interest to Dositej's reader, and the book is less polemic than Dositej's earlier works. He wanted primarily to entertain his reader, to awaken his interest in belles lettres, and also to encourage young Serbian writers to produce literary works in similar genres.

Dositej's books, including *Basne,* did not sell well. With *Sobranije* he had some initial success but nevertheless made no profit. In financial difficulty, Dositej welcomed an invitation from rich Serbian merchants in Trieste to come there and print books in Serbian at a subsidy of two thousand florins a year. Novaković had sold his printing shop in Vienna, but in Venice, near Trieste, Demetrios Theodosios had started to print Serbian books. Dositej, who arrived in Trieste in 1802, found excellent working conditions there, and his enthusiasm returned. In 1803 he published *Etika* (Ethics, or Moral Philosophy), a translation and adaptation of the popular Italian book *Istruzioni di etica* by G. F. Soave (1743–1806).

At the beginning of the nineteenth century events of far-reaching consequences for the Serbs started to take place south of the Sava and the Danube. After Joseph II died in 1790 his successors proved to be much less enlightened, and Dositej's enthusiasm for the Viennese government cooled considerably. No longer oriented toward western Europe and Austria as a source of national aspirations for the Serbs, Dositej paid more attention to internal factors, looking for forces among Serbians that would aid him in educating his people and raising its national consciousness.

In 1804, under the leadership of Karadjordje, Serbs rose up against the Turks. For the first time since the loss of their medieval empire, the Serbs saw the possibility of establishing an independent state. When he heard of the uprising Dositej collected money for the insurgents from the wealthy Serbs in Trieste, and he added four hundred florins of his own money, one half of his entire savings. He also composed "Pjesna na insurekciju Serbijanov" (Ode on the Insurrection of the Serbs), dedicating it to the brave Serbian warriors and their leader Karadjordje. In 1805 Dositej wrote to his nephew that he would be willing to go to the land of his ancestors. Metropolitan Stratimirović let Dositej know that such a move would be welcomed.

In June 1806 Dositej left his friends in Trieste to offer his services to Karadjordje, seeing the perfect opportunity to apply his rationalistic ideas to a real-life situation. He was the best-educated Serb of the time, and he wanted to help his countrymen build their state by founding schools and printing books to educate Serbian youth. Dositej became a statesman, a nationalist, and a man of the nineteenth century. He was more than sixty years old.

From Zemun on the Danube Dositej secretly crossed to Serbia and met Karadjordje and other leaders. He did not stay long, returning to Zemun,

from which he made several diplomatic missions to help the Serbian cause. He served as an intermediary between Stratimirović and the rebels and between rebels and the Russians. He met in Bucharest with the commander of the Russian army, personally informing him of the Serbian situation and asking for assistance.

Dositej obtained permission from the Austrians to move and settle legally in Belgrade in 1807. Liberated Belgrade enthusiastically welcomed Dositej, who lived there until the end of his life. Even though he and Karadjordje had opposing views on foreign policy, Karadjordje being well inclined toward Austria, while Dositej had become a staunch anti-Austrian, Dositej soon became a confidant of Karadjordje and tutor to his son Aleksa. He served in many capacities, participating in the drafting of the constitution of the new state, directing all the schools in liberated Serbia, and serving on the governing council of the country. He had strong influence both on internal and external affairs.

In September 1808 Dositej opened the Great School, the future University of Belgrade – before members of the governing council, the metropolitan, and the citizens of Belgrade – with an opening address titled "O dužnom počitaniju naukam" (Respect Due to Learning). Vuk Stefanović Karadžić, the future reformer of standard Serbo-Croatian, was one of the first students enrolled. By this time Dositej was well known outside Serbia, and translations of his books were appearing in Romania, Austria, and Russia.

Dositej's health started to fail in 1809. After the fall of the town of Deligrad he refused to leave Belgrade with Serbian refugees but instead remained with Karadjordje. After the Turks' defeat of the insurgents in 1810 and 1811, he traveled to the Russian army command in Wallachia and Bucharest to beg for assistance. In January 1811 he returned from this trip gravely ill. A decree making him secretary of education was waiting for him in Belgrade. He died on 28 March and was buried in the cathedral of Belgrade.

During his stay in Belgrade, Dositej had become a highly respected and venerable public figure. Yet despite his public successes there he had been unhappy that there was no printing shop in Belgrade. Since he could not travel outside Serbia for reasons of security, he could not have his books printed, and he had longed to publish the second volume of *Sobranije.* It was eventually published in 1818 by his disciple Pavle Solarić.

Throughout Dositej's life the program he outlined in *Pismo Haralampiju* remained essentially the same. He worked to bridge cultural differences within the Serbian nation. He opened the door to European influences. He organized the Serbian educational system and established numerous cultural institutions. Even though his writing was mostly didactic, he laid the foundation for modern Serbian literature. He insisted on the increased vernacularization of the literary idiom and, in doing so, paved the way for Vuk Karadžić, who succeeded him as an intellectual leader among the Serbs.

Letters:

Pisma Dositeja Obradovića, edited by Georgije Magarašević (Budapest, 1929);

Pisma Dositeja Obradovića, edited by Borivoje Marinković (Novi Sad: Matica srpska, 1961).

Bibliography:

Dositej Obradović, bibliography in *Sabrana dela,* volume 3 (Belgrade: Prosveta, 1961).

Biographies:

Tihomir Ostojić, *Dositej Obradović u Hopovu. Studija iz kulturne i književne baštine* (Novi Sad: Matica srpska, 1907);

George Rapall Noyes, *Introduction to the Life and Adventures of Dimitrije Obradović* (Berkeley: University of California Publication in Modern Philology, 1951), pp. 3–127;

Mita Kostić, *Dositej Obradović u istorijskoj perspektivi XVIII i XIX veka,* 2 volumes (Belgrade: Posebna izdanja Srpske akademije nauka, 1952), II: 3–304;

Djuro Gavela, *Dositej Obradović* (Belgrade: Narodna knjiga, 1955);

Jovan Deretić, *Dositej i njegovo doba* (Belgrade: Filološki fakultet Beogradskog univerziteta, 1969);

Milka Stanković, *Prometej sa Balkana* (Belgrade: Kekec, 1989);

Andrija Stojković, *Životni put Dositeja Obradovića* (Belgrade, 1989).

References:

Nikola Ćurčić, *The Ethics of Reason in the Philosophical System of Dositej Obradović. His Contribution in This Field to the Age of Reason* (London: University of London, 1976);

Jovan Deretić, *Poetika Dositeja Obradovića* (Belgrade: Vuk Karadžić, 1974);

Radmila J. Gorup, "Dositej Obradović and Serbian Cultural Rebirth," *Serbian Studies,* 6, no. 1 (1991): 35–56;

Vera Javarek, "English Influence on the Works of Dositej Obradović," Ph.D. dissertation, University of London, 1954;

Herta Kuna, *Jezične karakteristike književnih djela Dositeja Obradovića* (Sarajevo: Akademija nauka BiH, 1970);

Pavle Popović, "A Serbian Anglophil Dositheus Obradović," *Quarterly Review,* 232 (1919): 333–351;

Alojs Schmaus, "Lessings Fabeln bei Dositej Obradović," *Zeitschrift für Slavische Philologie,* 8 (1931): 1–47;

Jovan Skerlić, "Dositej Obradović," in his *Pisci i knjige* (Belgrade: Prosveta, 1955);

Miodrag Stojanović, "Dositej's Adaptation of Aesopian Fables," *Balcanica,* 2 (1971): 311–336;

Stojanović, *Dositej i Antika* (Belgrade: Srpska književna zadruga, 1971);

Stojanović, "Historical and Nationalistic Thought in the Works of Dositej Obradović," *Balkan Studies,* 24 (1983): 631–641.

Rastko Petrović

(16 May 1898 – 15 August 1949)

Radmila J. Gorup
Columbia University

BOOKS: *Burleska gospodina Peruna boga groma* (Belgrade: Sveslovenska knjižnica M. J. Stefanovića, 1921); republished as *Burleska gospodina Peruna boga groma i druge staroslovenske priče* (Belgrade: Nolit, 1974);

Otkrovenje: Stihovi i proza (Belgrade: S. B. Cvijanović, 1922);

Afrika (Belgrade: Geca Kon, 1930);

Ljudi govore (Belgrade: Geca Kon, 1931);

Izbor I 1919–1924, edited by Marko Ristić and Vera Stojić (Belgrade & Novi Sad: Matica srpska & Srpska književna zadruga, 1958);

Dan šesti, edited by Milan Dedinac and Ristić, volume 4 of *Dela Rastka Petrovića* (Belgrade: Nolit, 1961);

Izbor II 1924–1935, edited by Ristić and Stojić (Belgrade & Novi Sad: Matica srpska & Srpska književna zadruga, 1962);

Sa silama nemerljivim, edited by Dedinac and Ristić, volume 3 of *Dela Rastka Petrovića* (Belgrade: Nolit, 1963);

Rastko Petrović, edited by Zoran Mišić (Belgrade: Nolit, 1963);

Izabrana dela, 2 volumes (Zagreb: Naprijed / Belgrade: Prosveta / Sarajevo: Svjetlost, 1964);

Putopisi, edited by Dedinac and Ristić, volume 5 of *Dela Rastka Petrovića* (Belgrade: Nolit, 1966);

Izbor i studija Milana Komnenića (Belgrade: Izdavački zavod Jugoslavije, 1967);

Otkrovenje, Poezija, Proza, Ljudi govore (Belgrade: Prosveta, 1968);

Ponoćni delija (Belgrade: Prosveta, 1970);

Otkrovenje, Poezija, Proza, Eseji (Belgrade: Novi Sad: Matica srpska & Srpska književna zadruga, 1972);

Eseji i članci, edited by Dedinac and Ristić, volume 6 of *Dela Rastka Petrovića* (Belgrade: Nolit, 1974);

Poezija, edited by Dedinac and Ristić, volume 2 of *Dela Rastka Petrovića* (Belgrade: Nolit, 1974);

Sabrane pesme (Belgrade: Srpska književna zadruga, 1989).

Rastko Petrović

Edition in English: Poems, translated by Vasa D. Mihailovich and Milne Holton, in their *Serbian Poetry from the Beginnings to the Present* (New Haven: Yale Center for International and Area Studies, 1988), pp. 240–246.

Rastko Petrović is one of the most controversial and influential intellectual writers of modern Serbian literature. He reacted early to the new literary trends of post–World War I Europe, distinguishing himself as an original poet searching for new expressive potentials of poetic language. A poet, essayist, art critic, and travel writer, he is interesting as a representative of his time and as the author of works that are valuable contributions to literature in their own right.

He was born on 16 May 1898 to a middle-class family in Belgrade. His father, Mita Petrović, director of the bureau of taxation, was a passionate amateur historian. One of the best-educated men of his time, he had a considerable talent for drawing, which his children inherited from him. Rastko's mother, Mileva Zorić, a schoolteacher, was a descendant of a well-known family in Titel, Voyvodina. In a loving family that included nine children, Rastko was the youngest. His mother died in 1911, while he was still a young child, leaving an indelible impression on the future poet. Throughout his writing, the motif of mother and motherhood holds a central place. After his mother's death his sister Zora undertook his upbringing.

Petrović's house in Belgrade was a gathering place for leading Serbian and Yugoslav writers, artists, and historians, and young Rastko had an opportunity to meet many of them, including playwright-poet Ivo Vojnović, poet Silvije Strahimir Kranjčević, fiction writer Ivo Ćipiko, and sculptor Ivan Meštrović. The Petrović family and their friends were enthusiastic patriots. A deep love for his country and a strong interest in the cultural tradition of his people are apparent throughout Rastko's writings.

At an early age Rastko showed signs of a rich imagination and a gift for drawing. His siblings also demonstrated talent in art and literature. His oldest sister, Nadežda Petrović, was an accomplished painter; his sister Milica was a poet. Rastko started to write early, while he was still in high school.

The Balkan Wars of 1912 and 1913, and especially World War I (1914–1918), shook the foundations of Rastko's young world. His education was interrupted, and in 1915 he and his sisters followed the Serbian army in its epic retreat from Austrian troops over the snowy and treacherous mountains of Albania. The death and suffering he witnessed on that journey left a deep mark on the seventeen-year-old's psyche. Yet, at the same time, this journey gave him an opportunity to discover the beauty of nature amid destruction and chaos. On the Mediterranean island of Corfu, Rastko published his first poems, in the journal *Zabavnik* (Review).

In 1916, with a group of Serbian students and those members of his family who survived the war, Rastko arrived in France. He finished high school in Nice and then went to Paris to study law. Artists of many nationalities gathered in Paris during the 1920s, giving the modernist movement a truly inter-national character. Petrović became a part of that movement. Erudite and gifted, with fresh experiences from the war, he was well prepared for the artistic revolution that was taking place in Paris. He kept abreast of the newest literary trends and the writers and artists associated with the avant-garde journals *Sic, Action,* and *Nord-Sud.* He attended concerts, visited expositions, and mingled with the literati, making friends with leading figures of Parisian cultural life, including André Breton, André Salmon, Paul Eluard, Philippe Soupault, and Max Jacob. Later he met Pablo Picasso and André Gide. At the same time, he spent long hours in the Bibliothèque Nationale, researching the history of the early Slavs and the oldest records of Serbian culture. His interest in Serbian history and folklore was not based on a desire to discover the past of his people that was revealed in folk poetry. Instead he wanted to establish a connection between that tradition and new literary trends. He turned his attention to lyric poetry, looking for forgotten poetic processes which would enable him to discover new, universal aesthetics. He also studied painting, ethnography, and psychology.

Petrović graduated in 1920 and returned to Belgrade. Over the next few years his talent blossomed. This period was the most productive of his literary career. In Belgrade he became friends with young Serbian modernists, including poets Stanislav Vinaver and Marko Ristić, prose writer Dušan Matić, and painter Aleksandar Deroko. After traveling to Macedonia to visit the monasteries around Lake Ohrid, Petrović went with Deroko to old Ras, the cradle of medieval Serbia, admiring old architecture and frescoes of the medieval monasteries, especially at Studenica and Žiča. With a government stipend he returned briefly to Paris in 1921 to pursue Byzantine studies. His poem "Le Mot de la Soif" appeared in the May 1921 issue of *Action*.

Petrović's first book, *Burleska gospodina Peruna boga groma* (The Burlesque of Mr. Perun, the God of Thunder, 1921), is a Romanesque legend that reveals his interest in the old Slavs as well as his youthful exuberance. The main character, Nabor, lives at the end of the eighth century in the village of Devol. He and the girl he loves die and go together to the Slavic heaven. They enjoy life there, but they must seek refuge in the world of the living after Nabor kills the son of the god Radgost who has been pursuing Urania, Nabor's wife. Nabor reappears six centuries later as a monk, Father Simeon, who gets killed in a raid on his monastery. The lives of Nabor and his later reincarnations – up to the character of Bogoljub Marković, the author's contemporary – serve as only a loose frame for the novel, which has neither a plot nor real characters. It does not follow chronological order and has no beginning or end. Everything happens in the moment, and the reader is never sure whether that moment is present, past, or future. Gods live with people and people with gods, in harmony with nature and passionately devoted to life. The dead visit the living and vice versa. The Slavic gods Perun and Radgost share company with Saint Peter and Saint Ilya. All are happy, healthy, and exuberant. Saint Peter rolls his own cigarettes centuries before Columbus brings tobacco to Europe. Even the painter Vincent van Gogh is in the novel. Laughter, however, dies out in the Christian myths at the end of the book, where joy gets pushed out of life.

Burleska gospodina Peruna boga groma is a literary arabesque, full of optimism and laughter. The poet takes on the task of reviving joy in suffering humanity. While the novel includes no innovative ideas, it is important as a poetic experiment, as an attempt to create a fragmented form of narration that represents as closely as possible the modern artistic sensibility. The subject matter permitted Petrović to revive certain characteristics of folk art, especially exaggeration. The barbarism of the old Slavs finds expression in the language structure and in the breaking down of the established linguistic usages.

When compared to other works of its time, *Burleska gospodina Peruna boga groma* seemed irregular and chaotic. In the middle class of Belgrade the book created a literary scandal, and most readers criticized it harshly. Among the few who defended the book and its author was Ivo Andrić, who felt the book was special even though he found its structure chaotic. Miloš Crnjanski and Isidora Sekulić wrote that *Burleska gospodina Peruna boga groma* announced a new poet "who is deserving of our attention."

In January 1922 the first issue of *Putevi* (Roads), a new journal for art and philosophy, published Rastko's "Spomenik" (Monument). The public reacted violently to this poem, which refers to Christ's sexuality, offending both the general public and the church, which attacked him and threatened him with excommunication.

The conflict between the poet and his middle-class audience had been brewing ever since the publication of *Burleska gospodina Peruna boga groma*. The demands of Petrović's new art challenged middle-class taste. Petrović the poet was offering brave new literary ideas, while Petrović the man could not bear the scorn of his readers. The poet gave in to public pressure and defended himself in the second issue of *Putevi*.

Title page for Petrović's Otkrovenje *(1922), a collection of poems that breaks away from Serbian poetic tradition (drawing by Milo Milunović)*

In spring 1922 he traveled to Paris, where he stayed briefly to replenish his spiritual resources. Then he went again to Old Serbia, Macedonia, Montenegro and Dalmatia. His essay "Dvadeset godina povratka poezije u život" (Twenty Years of Poetry's Return to Life), which appeared in the journal *Misao* (Thought), acquainted his Serbian audience with the main trends and the principal personalities of the cultural scene in Paris. Even though the issue was dedicated to his friend André Salmon, Petrović's essay paid greater attention to Guillaume Apollinaire, who contributed to the creation of a new cultural climate.

On 15 December 1922 appeared Rastko's best book, the collection of poems titled *Otkrovenje* (Revelation). This collection was truly revolutionary in Serbian literature. Breaking old poetic conventions in order to create new ones, Petrović, like the French avant-garde poets, operated on the premise that poetry had to find new linguistic potentials in order to create new realities. It had to rid the word of its normative use, to attack and break it so that it could reveal its original sense, its hidden vitality. Old poetic conventions were completely broken in *Otkrovenje,* and novel language combinations, both harmonious and awkward, were introduced.

Otkrovenje is also significant for what it reveals about Petrović's attitude toward life: its poems exalt natural instincts. The poet feels intense passion, but at the same time he is tormented by the mystery of the corporal. For him inanimate matter acquires poetic and actual life in the ecstasy that takes place in the human body, which he calls "the vessel of life."

Tied to the motif of the human body, which the old Slavs worshiped, is the mythical idea of man's original fall, which is transformed in the poems of *Otkrovenje* into the psychoanalytical notion of the trauma of birth, which is followed by a constant longing to return to the prenatal state, where only biological laws apply.

The forceful verses of *Otkrovenje* seemed heretical to most of Petrović's contemporaries. With only a few exceptions public reaction to the book was unfavorable. Again Isidora Sekulić and Miloš Crnjanski praised the poetic quality of Petrović's writing.

The criticism had a devastating effect on the young poet and perhaps affected his career plans. He traveled to remote areas of Dalmatia, Montenegro, and Macedonia to seek solace in nature. In December 1923 he passed the qualifying exam for a position in the Ministry of Foreign Affairs and soon started to work in Belgrade, where he was entrusted with the reception of foreign dignitaries and with artistic and literary promotion. Many saw this career change as the poet's concession to the pressures of his critics.

He remained active in literary pursuits, however, publishing essays, travelogues, art criticism, short stories, and poems in art and literary journals. The journal *Pokret* (Movement) published his "Mladićstvo narodnog genija" (The Youth of Folk Genius), an essay of great importance for the understanding of the new poetics of the Serbian avant-garde. He dedicated his poem "Putnik" to his fellow poet Stanislav Vinaver. In 1926 he published his long poem "Veliki drug," dedicated to the memory of his thirty thousand peers who perished in the trek across Albania.

That same year Rastko was appointed secretary of the consulate at the Vatican, and a year later he was transferred to the embassy of the Kingdom of Yugoslavia in Rome. The ambassador, poet Milan Rakić, and his wife showed great understand-

ing for Petrović and soon became his friends, helping him in his work.

Srpski književni glasnik (Serbian Literary Herald) started to serialize Petrović's second novel, *Sa silama nemerljivim* (With Immeasurable Powers) in 1927, but it was not published in its entirety until 1963. This novel is a bourgeois melodrama that takes place in postwar Belgrade. The main protagonists are Stevan Papa-Katić, one of the richest citizens of the city, his son Irac, and Marica, the girl whom Irac loves. Antagonized by his father's meddling in his affairs, Irac breaks off relations with his father and with Marica. Soon, however, Stevan forgives his son, and, in what seems to be a happy ending, Irac marries Marica. The following year Irac commits suicide.

Although the young man's conflict with his father was only temporary, he is permanently fighting against the immeasurable forces, "sa silama nemerljivim," that govern his life. Young Irac's obsession with life, which he cannot control, becomes a need to destroy life itself, and he finally sees suicide as the last initiative of his free will.

Sa silama nemerljivim was Petrović's attempt to create an existentialist novel, and some critics have seen a similarity between this novel and *Les Faux-Monnayeurs* (The Counterfeiters, 1926), by André Gide. Petrović's novel, however, remains unconvincing. It is surprising to see him returning to a conventional plot after he was so successful in creating an innovative narrative structure in *Burleska gospodina Peruna boga groma.* The best parts of *Sa silama nemerljivim* are its poetic descriptions of Belgrade and the idyllic life of ordinary people on its river banks.

Thanks to Ambassador Rakić, who approved an extended leave in 1928, Petrović was able to fulfill his lifelong desire to travel to Africa. With a palette and a notebook in hand, he left Marseilles to crisscross the continent by boat, train, and car, and on foot. Petrović was an affectionate traveler and a superb travel writer. He was overwhelmed by the sights and sounds of Africa, but even more by the nude bodies of African women and their free movement in the frenetic rhythm of their dances.

Petrović's lyrical realism found its deepest expression in his travelogues. In his travel writing he was able to give life to real objects by imposing an artistic dimension upon them. This mixing of the objective and the artistic gave multidimensionality to his descriptions. What comes from man and what comes from nature become one. Petrović brings to the reader not only shapes and colors of the objects, but also their taste and smell, allowing readers to experience them and feel the same ecstasy as the author.

This characteristic of Petrović's writing is apparent in his descriptions of trips to the south of Serbia, Dalmatia, Montenegro, Macedonia, Turkey, Spain, Italy, and Libya, which were published in various journals. His enthusiasm for Africa in 1928 resulted in his best travelogue, the long poetic *Afrika,* published in 1930.

In *Afrika* Petrović paints a picture of large expanses parched by the sun, people untouched by European civilization, and their art and music. The ecstasy he feels while watching a nude woman dancing becomes for him the language of gods and the rhythm of creation itself. He tries to transfer visual pictures into words but often feels powerless before his task, and Africa remains a secret for the poet.

In 1930 Petrović was transferred to Belgrade, where he stayed until 1935. During this time he was active in social circles, wrote literary and art criticism for leading journals, and worked on his long novel *Dan šesti* (The Sixth Day, 1961).

In 1931 *Ljudi govore* (People Speak) came out. This rather short poetic prose work is a great achievement in Serbian literature and, in the view of many critics, Petrović's most accomplished work.

Ljudi govore is a bit of many things: novel and novella, poem and travelogue. Although it is based on the poet's trip to Spain, his travels there represent only a frame that gives the poet an opportunity to interact with ordinary people. The book does not have any local color. Its protagonists are fishermen and farmers, living on the shores of a lake and on its two islands, which the poet simply calls Big and Small Island.

Lyric description, so characteristic of *Afrika,* is reduced to a minimum in *Ljudi govore.* The text consists mostly of dialogues. The poet addresses these simple people, and they answer, talking about their conventional lives in simple sentences. Nothing happens to excite intellectual curiosity. Yet from these conversations, which at first appear unconnected, emerge hidden relationships, insights into the lives of the people and their destinies.

The stories of Pipo and Ivona are parallel. Pipo has traveled all around the world as a sailor, but he has had to return home to live the life of a fisherman and thus continue the family tradition. His marriage was arranged, and he does not love his wife. Ivona has loved a local man ever since she was a small girl, but the young man was unaware of her feelings for him. After his family married him to someone else, Ivona lost any interest in marriage and became deeply unhappy. There is no mention

Drawing of Petrović by Aleksandar Deroko

that these two stories are connected. Yet Pipo has named both his fishing boat and his favorite daughter Ivona. As in *Otkrovenje* and later on in *Dan šesti,* the high point of the book represents the ecstasy that the poet and all of nature feel before the act of giving birth.

Ljudi govore represents the high point of Petrović's opus and includes all the motifs on which his poetics is based. The poet's efforts to achieve pure poetry succeed in this book, where all objects and creatures in the universe live and talk just like humans: oars and fishermen's nets speak clearly to the poet. A direct relationship exists between the people and nature. Simple sentences, when spoken by these fishermen and farmers, acquire a new quality, an original freshness.

In 1934 Petrović finished his long novel *Dan šesti,* but his publisher refused to publish it. It appeared posthumously in 1961, edited by two of his friends, poets Milan Dedinac and Marko Ristić. Their edition also includes the second part of the novel, which Petrović wrote much later.

This long novel is a sequel to *Sa silama nemerljivim*. Its protagonist, Stevan Papa-Katić, is the son of Irac and the grandson of Stevan Papa-Katić. Even though the novel presents a fresco of the Serbian retreat to Albania, *Dan šesti* is not a war novel. Petrović describes this tragedy without glorifying the Serbs' suffering. His purpose is to portray a return of human beings to a state of nature, as a sea of humanity – soldiers, students, men and women, and entire families – laboriously crosses mountains and snowcovered slopes, passing through hungry villages and climbing over corpses, trying to reach the sea to ensure their own survival. There are no descriptions of battlefields, and relationships among people – if introduced at all – are presented in flashbacks, usually to peacetime.

The author focuses on the relationship between man and nature. To nature all are equal, rich and poor, soldier and civilian, man and beast. In adverse conditions men's humanity becomes reduced. They lose contact with each other and remain mostly alone. When together, they do not communicate because words no longer have meaning.

Above all, the novel depicts the destruction of man's habitat far from the battleground, the dissolution of civilized life, and a return to the laws of nature. Thrown out of his habitat, deprived of the security it assures and finding himself in a fight with "immeasurable forces," man discovers hidden strength and sources of energy have been suppressed by the same laws and institutions that protected him. These new discoveries are a source of optimism. The old order will descend into chaos; primal matter, symbolized by the sea, will erase all that existed before. Creation will begin again.

As Stevan journeys with his people toward the sea, he frees himself of the trappings of his former life. Things that he held dear now seem completely irrelevant to him. A dog follows him for days, hoping to eat his remains when he dies. He remains alive, discovering new truths and new relationships. He feels the tragedy of life but also its beauty.

The title *Dan šesti* is symbolic. It not only stands as a metaphor for the biblical creation of the world in six days, but also as a suggestion that the novel has six parts. *Dan šesti* is a modern myth about the return to nature, about life and death, and about the perpetual cycle of renewal. At the crucial juncture of the novel, a young mother gives birth to a baby girl and then dies during a storm. Yet for Petrović the vitality of woman is indestructible. She is the biological and intuitive being that will rescue humanity from its crisis. Her body, like the universe, has the ability to regenerate. The new life,

however, will be achieved in the second part of the novel.

Dan šesti has a modern, fragmented structure in which plot is of only incidental importance. There are several narrative lines, as the author follows not only Stevan's life, but also those of many secondary characters, some of whom have only occasional contact with the main character. Situations that arise in the first part are completed to a considerable extent in the second part of *Dan šesti*.

In 1935 Rastko was sent to the consulate of the Kingdom of Yugoslavia in Chicago. He was unhappy to leave Belgrade, fearing that he would never return.

Initially, he was enthusiastic about the United States. He loved its vast landscapes, which he found "just like Romagna or Šumadija, just a million times bigger," as well as its easy way of life. The following year he was appointed chargé d'affaires to the embassy in Washington, D.C.

In Washington his enthusiasm for the United States soon faded, and he complained to his friends in Belgrade and Paris that "life, although it moves at a fast pace, is nevertheless monotonous, empty and limited." He missed his friends and the intellectual climate of Belgrade and Paris. Yet he enjoyed trips to Canada, Mexico, Cuba, and Central America. He was particularly impressed with the art and the culture of the American Indians and became a collector of Indian artifacts, visiting Indian reservations many times. During this time he worked on the second part of *Dan šesti*, which takes place in the United States. Stevan, who has survived the war, severs all his ties with his former life, giving up his large inheritance to establish a new life in the New World. There Stevan meets some of the people with whom he trekked across Albania, including Milica, the baby born in the snowstorm, and he falls in love with her. He often flees civilization, visiting American Indian reservations. In the end Stevan, who has become a famous paleontologist and a Nobel Prize winner, dies the same death as his distant Slavic ancestors, in a deer-hunting accident. The second part of *Dan šesti* does not reach the same high level of artistry as the first part.

In 1941 news that World War II had reached his homeland and that his beloved Belgrade had been bombarded and devastated on 6 April saddened Rastko greatly. His family house was hit, and his personal library, containing some of his manuscripts, was destroyed.

Petrović spent the war years at the Yugoslav embassy in Washington. At the end of World War II and after establishment of the new regime in Belgrade, he pleaded with his friends to arrange for his return, but his repeated requests remained unheeded. Even though he had done nothing to compromise his position with the new regime, he and his writing were in disfavor. No longer an employee of the Yugoslav embassy, he led the life of an ordinary émigré, and his personal and creative life were affected. Far from his homeland, he could not take part in the development of Serbian literature. All he had in America was the memory that he once was an avant-garde poet. Cut off from the sources of his inspiration, he wrote little, and what he did write was not of the same quality as his earlier work.

After 1945 he tried to support himself by writing for journals and newspapers. He wrote poetry and a play in English called *Sibinian Women,* and he worked on a historical novel about the Italian renaissance.

The title he gave his last collection of poems, "Kad padne burma zlatna" (When the Gold Band Falls) suggests the end of his creativity. Published posthumously under its second title, *Ponoćni delija* (Midnight Hero, 1970), this collection reveals a poet who had lost his inspiration. The poems are either laments expressing the poet's nostalgia for the past or poems of the formal exhibitionism that Petrović once detested. Included in this book are fragments of a long poem, "Vuk," on which he had been working since 1923. Segments of it had been published earlier.

Petrović died of a sunstroke on 15 August 1949 and was buried in Washington. He was fifty-one years old. There was no mention of his passing in his native country, while in Paris *Le Monde* published a respectful obituary.

Soon after the demise of socialist realism, Rastko's rehabilitation began in his homeland. Young poets started to read and praise his poetry. His friend Marko Ristić restored Petrović's reputation in "Tri mrtva pesnika" (Three Dead Poets), published in 1954. His poems appeared in anthologies. New editions of previously published works were published, and those left in manuscript – such as *Dan šesti* and *Ponoćni delija* – began to appear. In

1986 Petrović's remains were returned to his homeland and buried in Belgrade.

Petrović holds an important place in the history of Serbian and Yugoslav literatures. He brought to Belgrade the cultural atmosphere of postwar Paris, and he was truly an original poet whose work was accepted by the young modernists as a radical turning point in Serbian literature. He was one of the rare Serbian modernists who did not lose a feeling for national tradition and who attempted a synthesis of Slavic and Serbian traditions and modern literary trends. With his art criticism he directed the future development of the arts in his country. Together with Miloš Crnjanski he set the foundation for the development of the modern Serbian novel. Contemporary writers of fantasy fiction have Petrović as a forerunner. Rastko Petrović was a true Renaissance man, multifaceted and original.

Biographies:

Jasmina Musabegović, *Rastko Petrović i njegovo doba* (Belgrade: Slovo ljubve, 1976);

Radovan Popović, *Izabrani čovek ili život Rastka Petrovića* (Belgrade: Prosveta, 1986);

Gojko Tešić, "Bibliografija radova Rastka Petrovića," in Petrović's *Sabrane pesme* (Belgrade: Srpska književna zadruga, 1989), pp. 341–368.

References:

Zoran Čanović, *Umetnost Rastka Petrovića* (Priština: Jedinstvo, 1985);

Milan Dedinac, "Prevedeno sa uspomenama," *Šesti dan, Delo,* 6, no. 4 (1960): 396–414;

Velibor Gligorić, "Rastko Petrović," in his *Ogledi i studije* (Belgrade, 1959), pp. 167–193;

Milosav Marković, "Great Comrade: Rastko Petrović," *Relations,* 4 (1989): 45–56;

Relations (Belgrade), 5–6 (1982): 59–136;

Marko Ristić, "Tri mrtva pesnika," *Rad JAZU* (Zagreb), 301 (1954): 245–316;

Stanislav Vinaver, "Rastko Petrović – Lelujavi lik sa freske," *Književnost* (1954): 468–488;

Djordjije Vuković, *Književno delo Rastka Petrovića: Zbornik radova* (Belgrade: Institut za književnost umetnost, 1989).

Francè Prešeren

(3 December 1800 – 8 February 1849)

Henry R. Cooper, Jr.
Indiana University

BOOKS: *Krst pri Savici: Povest v verzih* (Ljubljana: Jožef Blaznik, 1836); translated by Henry R. Cooper, Jr., as "The Baptism on the Savica," *Slovene Studies,* 7, nos. 1–2 (1985): 63–80;
Poezíje Dóktorja Francéta Prešérna (Ljubljana: Jožef Blaznik, 1847);
Pesmi Franceta Preširna, edited by Jož. Jurčič and Jož. Stritar (Ljubljana: Oto Wagner, 1866);
Prešeren I: Pesnitve, Pisma, edited by France Kidrič (Ljubljana: Tiskovna zadruga, 1936);
Zbrano delo, edited by Janko Kos, 2 volumes (Ljubljana: Državna založba Slovenije, 1965–1966).
Editions in English: *Selection of Poems by Francè Prešeren,* edited by W. K. Matthews and Anton Slodnjak, various translators (Oxford: Blackwell, 1954); enlarged as *Poems by Francè Prešeren* (London: Calder, 1963);
Selections in *The Parnassus of a Small Nation,* edited and translated by Janko Lavrin and Slodnjak (London: Calder, 1957); enlarged edition (Ljubljana: Državna založba Slovenije, 1965).

An 1850 portrait of Francè Prešeren by Fr. Kurz zum Thurn von Goldenstein in the Prešeren Museum in Kranj

Without doubt Francè Prešeren is the most important and most beloved poet of Slovenia. Each year the anniversary of his death is marked by literary readings, award ceremonies, and other festivities throughout the entire country. Every schoolchild learns his poetry, and as one of its first acts of statehood the newly independent Slovene republic proclaimed his poem "Zdravljica" (The Toast) the national anthem. Prešeren's life was neither long nor easy, but he and his hauntingly beautiful, but pain-fraught, poetry have in many ways come to symbolize and epitomize the Slovene national condition.

On 3 December 1800 Prešeren was born the third of eight children of well-to-do peasants, Šimen and Mina, in the small village of Vrba, north of Ljubljana. He had a serene childhood and was somewhat spoiled by his parents, who perceived early on that he was the most talented of their children. He was sent from home to attend a boarding school in 1810, and in 1812 he moved to Ljubljana,

where he studied until 1821. There, in addition to the academic subjects at which he excelled, he learned the joys of conviviality. He supplemented the money his beloved uncle Jožef sent him by offering to tutor the slower students and happily spent all the extra on carousing with a few close friends. The first decades of the future poet's life were probably his most carefree, without the financial, health, and personal concerns that troubled him later. If there were any problems at this period at all, they might have arisen only because Prešeren was not particularly successful with women; this later would become a leitmotiv of his adult life.

During the 1820s Prešeren studied law at the University of Vienna, returning infrequently to

Ljubljana. Life again was relatively trouble-free in the Austrian capital: though his parents were disappointed and displeased that he did not want to pursue a career in the church, his uncle Jožef, who was a Roman Catholic priest, accepted his decision and continued to support his education. In Vienna Prešeren met Jernej Kopitar, perhaps the most educated and influential Slovene of the day. Kopitar occupied an elevated position in the imperial library and was a scholar with a European reputation. But he never hesitated to help his compatriots and other visitors from Balkan and South Slavic lands who were struggling to make their way in Vienna. Prešeren showed his first poems, written in Vienna during this time, to Kopitar, who suggested that he burn most of them. Prešeren placed one of the surviving texts anonymously in the German-language newspaper in Ljubljana, the *Illyrisches Blatt* (Illyrian Letters) on 12 January 1827 – "Dekletam" (To the Girls). From the outset Prešeren signaled his intention to transcend the moral smugness of the day while demonstrating his innate poetic talent. About a year and a half later Prešeren left Vienna forever to return to Ljubljana, where he lived for most of the rest of his life. The initial warm feelings of trust and friendship toward Kopitar soon disappeared: the poet and the scholar very shortly became bitter opponents in the cultural debates of the 1830s.

Prešeren's professional career did not develop as he had hoped, and until well into his forties he was forced to practice law in firms owned by others. Each of his several attempts to win the right to open his own office was rejected by government authorities, who strictly regulated the number of independent attorneys in Inner Austria, as the Slovene lands were designated at that time. His personal life also remained somewhat subdued: he failed to marry, though he came close once, and he apparently was unable to sustain any long-term attachments. His finances were straitened after the dissolution of his parents' home and especially after his uncle's death in 1835. Only in poetry and literary politics did Prešeren seem to find much joy during the 1830s: the decade was Prešeren's most productive.

The poet had two good friends at this time: Andrej Smolè, a Dionysian character whose company Prešeren sought and enjoyed, and Matija Čop, whom Prešeren had probably known from his school days in Ljubljana but to whom he grew particularly close in the 1830s. Čop was perhaps the best-read man in Ljubljana. A polyglot with an enormous library for the time – how he acquired it on his miserable salary as a public school librarian

is still a mystery – Čop quickly became Prešeren's literary advisor and critic. Furthermore, he began to publish a series of literary anthologies titled *Kranjska čbelica* (The Carniolan Bee), where Preševen was able to place his poems on a regular basis. *Kranjska čbelica* was something of a success, especially when it launched the "Ljubljana ABC War," a strident polemic between Čop, who defended the traditional system of Slovene spelling developed in the sixteenth century, and the powerful Kopitar, who promoted a new alphabet for Slovene that included Cyrillic characters. Underlying this debate was not merely linguistics but cultural orientation in general: while Kopitar hoped to preserve Slovene as a peculiar Slavic dialect uncontaminated by modern and alien elements, Čop sought to develop his mother tongue into a contemporary vehicle for the expression of the Romantic sentiments that were sweeping civilized Europe at the time. Kopitar wanted to enshrine peasant speech as the standard for the nation; Čop wanted to polish the Slovene spoken in the few cities of the country until it could convey the loftiest and most nuanced thoughts of the age. Prešeren was Čop's chosen instrument for raising the level of Slovene discourse above the village trough and peddler's cart. Prešeren did not disappoint him.

With the first volume of *Kranjska čbelica* in 1830 Prešeren composed some of his most important and beautiful poetry, including a translation of Gottfried August Bürger's "Lenore" (1773) that clearly showed the poetic potential of Slovene. Prešeren's original poem "Slovo od mladosti" (Farewell to Youth), also published in the first volume, is regarded by many critics as one of his most accomplished pieces. The poet also joined in the "war" by penning witty and wicked verses against Kopitar and his collaborators, earning in the process the enmity of the establishment, which returned to haunt the struggling lawyer later. In the end Čop and Prešeren prevailed in this battle; in the meantime the poet published his two major works, "Sonetni venec" (The Wreath of Sonnets; published in a supplement of *Illyrisches Blatt*, 1834) and *Krst pri Savici: Povest v verzih* (1836; translated as "The Baptism on the Savica," 1985).

"Sonetni venec" is a marvelously successful elaboration of an old Italian poetic form. (Čop provided Prešeren with information about a great variety of poetic structures from his firsthand knowledge of many European literatures.) It is composed of fourteen sonnets; the last line of each is the first line of the next, and the last line of the last repeats the first line of the first. Furthermore, each first line

Page from the manuscript for Prešeren's copy of the folk song "Lepa Vida" (Beautiful Vida), which provided the basis for his poem of the same title (reproduced from Živi orfej, 1970) becomes a line in the "master sonnet," which is the fifteenth and final sonnet of the wreath. Prešeren added one more device: the first letter of each line in the master sonnet spells out a dedication, "To Julija Primic," a young woman whom he had seen on Easter Eve 1833 and for whom he had conceived a great but unreciprocated passion.

Prešeren's themes in "Sonetni venec" are poetic, erotic, and patriotic; the first two are the most obvious. In working with this complex Renaissance poetic form the poet proved beyond doubt and beyond anything that had been accomplished in Slovene up to that time the expressive potential inherent in the language. His vocabulary, syntax, rhythms, and rhymes are supple, creative, and modern. Unlike his Slovene poetic predecessors, he avoided folksiness in favor of a high style of expressiveness new to the language. Also new was the suggestive eroticism of the verse: "Sonetni venec" provoked an enormous scandal in otherwise placid Ljubljana, prompting denunciations by the clergy and the exclusion of Prešeren from all polite society. But if the verse was fervent, it was not coarse: it shared with its Renaissance forebears much chaste yearning with no suggestion of release. Though this Slovene Petrarch publicly names his Laura, he never lays more than his eyes on her. Still, the passion seems genuine and altogether unendurable and inescapable.

More difficult to discern is the patriotic strand of this poem. The opening line of the cycle, its closing line, and the first line of the master sonnet is "Your poet is plaiting the Slovenes a new wreath." Throughout the work there are regular allusions to the nation, its language, the peril it faces from the fondness Slovenes – especially young Slovene girls – have for German, and the need to bring Slovenes into the modern world of western and central Europe. The poem's patriotism is closely bound to its eroticism, for these two passions together suffice to fire the poet to his greatest creativity. Therefore, it would be a mistake to consider "Sonetni venec" merely a love poem. If it is, it is a love poem written to the whole nation and not to one scandalized young woman whose favor the poet has lost forever. For modern tastes the poetic and patriotic strands of this poem continue to resonate.

One other major work dates from this period: Prešeren's longest piece, *Krst pri Savici,* which many readers consider to be the Slovene national epic. Though he downplayed its significance, calling the poem "a metrical exercise" with which he hoped to "gain the good graces of the clergy," for many critics it is Prešeren's magnum opus, the culmination of the most productive portion of his life and a profoundly insightful and original statement about the nation.

The subject of the poem is the love affair between Črtomir, a Slovene pagan prince, and Bogomila, a Slovene pagan priestess who serves the goddess of love, Živa. Črtomir struggles to defend the Slovene homeland from the relentless and increasingly successful attacks of Frankish Christians, who are trying to convert the Slovenes "by fire and the sword" and coincidentally to subject the Slovene lands to Frankish domination. As Bogomila keeps the pagan home fires burning, Črtomir begins the final engagement, a life-or-death struggle that ends in a total Slovene defeat. Only Črtomir escapes alive, and eventually he wends his way back to Bogomila, planning to flee with her and enjoy at least the remnant of his life in connubial bliss. His surprise and shock are unbounded when he discovers that Bogomila has in the interim converted to Christianity and that she expects him to follow suit.

Prešeren makes a clear distinction, however, between the rapacious Frankish brand of religious militancy and the gentle, more authentic faith preached by missionaries from Italy. It is under the influence of the latter that Bogomila has seen the light, and indeed her conversion has been confirmed by a miracle: she is convinced that Črtomir alone escaped the Slovene rout as a result of her prayers and the intercession of the Blessed Virgin, to whom the former priestess has vowed to commit herself body and soul. Now Črtomir must atone for the slaughter he caused in espousing the Slovene pagan cause – which, however noble and ethnically defensive, was nevertheless in profound error – by becoming a Catholic priest and bringing the remaining Slovene pagans to the church. Coincidentally, he must forgo all thoughts of marriage to Bogomila: their reward will come in heaven, where they will be able to spend eternity together if they are willing to sacrifice the brief pleasures married life would bring them here on earth. Reluctantly Črtomir agrees, whereupon he is baptized in the Savica Falls – a place revered to this day by Slovenes, who ascend to the spot to contemplate its wild beauty and to recite Prešeren's verse. He and Bogomila part, never again to see each other in this life.

Structurally *Krst pri Savici* is quite complex. It is composed of 525 iambic pentameter lines arranged in three unequal parts: an introductory sonnet dedicating the poem to Čop, who died in a swimming accident in the Sava in 1835; twenty-six tercets, which quickly sketch the background situation and describe Črtomir's epic battle with the

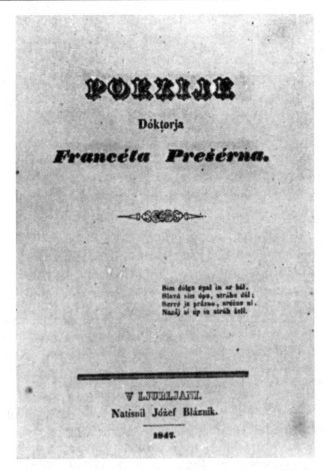

*Title page for the only collection of Prešeren's poems published
during his lifetime*

Franks; and fifty-four eight-verse stanzas, in standard ottava rima, that in serious and leisurely fashion depict the final confrontation between Črtomir and Bogomila. This last section is for the most part dialogue, which may indicate, as some critics have suggested, that Prešeren wavered between the epic and dramatic modes; his surviving correspondence suggests this as well. *Krst pri Savici* includes a few footnotes to indicate the historical and literary sources from which Prešeren drew some of his material, though he hardly offers an exhaustive list. In general, however, the work is pure fiction, so that one must look to its literary qualities and not its historical details for clues to its meaning.

It is easy to read *Krst pri Savici* as an allegory of Prešeren's life, and many critics have done so. Both Črtomir and Prešeren were professional failures, both were rejected lovers, and both seemed doomed to spend the remainder of their days alone. The warrior's resignation and renunciation of happiness in this life echo many of Prešeren's other poems. They also surely duplicate Prešeren's mood after

the death of his close friend Čop. Finally, Črtomir's halfhearted conversion to Christianity is probably equivalent to Prešeren's grim determination that life goes on in any event and that one has no real choice but to live it as well and as dutifully, if not as enthusiastically, as one can.

As in the "Sonetni venec," in *Krst pri Savici* there is a patriotic strand that weaves its own meaning into the text. Whatever one might think of the bloody ways of the Frankish crusaders — and they are explicitly denounced by a "true Christian," the priest who converts Bogomila, lest anyone miss the point — it remains a fact that Črtomir wrongheadedly resists an important cultural and political advancement for his nation by fighting Christianization. Had he been successful in his guerrilla war against the Franks, he would have marginalized the Slovenes by keeping them out of the Christian commonwealth, which was the wave of the future for all of Europe. Thus isolated, they would not have survived: like the Polabian Slavs of north central Europe, they would at best have left behind place-names and a few customs, but ethnically they would have been eradicated. Bogomila and the priest represent the better way, the way of acceptance and adaptation of the new belief. They are willing to renounce the old ways, which provided some of the glue that kept the scattered Slovene tribes together, so that they can work together to ensure that the new way, the Christian way, becomes a new bond for uniting the nation. It is for this reason that Črtomir himself must go off and preach to the people: he will be the link for them between the old and the new. In the process, by putting the people under the protection of the church, he guarantees that the Franks will not be allowed to extirpate the Slovenes as they did the Polabians. For all nations, but particularly for small nations, this process of accommodation with the realities of a more powerful outside world is the key to survival. It is perhaps also the most enduring message in this Slovene national epic, the validity of whose insights seems to have increased rather than diminished over time despite the somewhat dated genre and melodramatic language.

There is a poetic message in *Krst pri Savici* as well. The poem is Prešeren's last attempt to do something new in Slovene literature. This is not to say he stopped writing, nor that he did not create original works after 1835. But he did cease to experiment with new forms, and this cessation can most likely be linked to Čop's death. Čop was Prešeren's intermediary to other European literatures and other literary epochs. He was also Prešeren's first and most sensitive critic. The poem seems to reveal Čop's absence: its unevenness; its now-theatric, now-epic tone; and its overwhelming sadness at the loss of someone close and dear. In a way *Krst pri Savici* is a monument to the close collaboration that had marked Prešeren's most productive period, in which Čop would suggest, Prešeren would execute, and together they would polish. At the same time it is a call to others to do poetically what Prešeren had Črtomir and Bogomila do spiritually: bring Slovenia and Slovene letters into Europe. It is a warning against poetic isolation as well as political apartness. Not only did Prešeren give his nation what most civilized European nations had by then, a national epic, but he warned that if Slovenia did not join the Romantic movement of the time, if it insisted on folk themes sung in the folk way, it would perish culturally, for its own best sons and daughters would look for their entertainment and enlightenment elsewhere, most likely in Austro-German culture. His thoroughly nineteenth-century call to arms was a plea not for religion or nationalism but

for modern poetry on par with the best the rest of Europe had to offer.

It would be an exaggeration to say Prešeren saved modern Slovene culture single-handedly, but he did prepare an enormous and fertile field in which his successors were able to nurture all the arts and sciences. From Prešeren on, therefore, Slovenes were able to make to the European cultural commonwealth their own separate, unique, and particular contributions, not as "Inner Austrians" or "Protestants," "Illyrians" or "Pan-Slavs" — all the designations used until then to characterize politically and culturally the Slavic inhabitants of the eastern Alps. Henceforth they contributed in their own name and right, as Slovenes.

With the loss of family and friends and with never-ending financial difficulties caused by unsuccessful attempts at establishing his own law practice, Prešeren began to decline after the middle of the 1830s. For the remaining decade and a half of his life the most important event of his poetic career was the appearance of a slender volume titled *Poezíje Dóktorja Francéta Prešérna* (The Poems of Dr. Francè Prešeren), which was issued on 15 December 1846 but carried 1847 as its publication date. It included roughly two-thirds of all the Slovene poems he had written; he had planned to issue a companion volume of his German poems as well, but that plan never materialized. Many of the poems in the anthology were revised versions of earlier publications; a few appeared for the first time in the anthology. The works were grouped by genre as follows: lyric poems, ballads and romances, miscellaneous poems and amusing verses, *ghazals,* sonnets (including "Sonetni venec") and the two sonnet cycles "Zabavljivi sonetje" (Amusing Sonnets) and "Sonetje nesreče" (Sonnets of Unhappiness), and finally *Krst pri Savici*. Originally "Zdravljica" was also scheduled to be included among the lyrics, but because the censor objected to a line of it, Prešeren removed the entire poem from the collection, publishing it only after the abolition of censorship in 1848.

Prešeren's lyrics sing of love and loss of love, of patriotism (a gentle love of country, not the ugly nationalism of the twentieth century), and of poetry. Some, such as "Od železne ceste" (About the Railway), are humorous and light, but most, such as the popular "Nezakonska mati" (Unwed Mother), speak with profound sympathy of the emotional agony of the abandoned mother or the jilted lover. More than a few are structurally playful; "Zdravljica," for example, is a picture poem: the verses are arranged so that the stanzas look like wine glasses. The last poem in the section, "Pevcu" (To the Poet) —

whose positioning counterbalances the first poem of the section, "Strunam" (To My Lyre) – is composed of five stanzas, each with an assonant rhyme based on *a, e, i, o,* and *u* in that order. It speaks of the poet as the sacrificial victim of society, the one who articulates and thereby relieves society of its pains by taking them on himself. In "Strunam" he equates poetry with the essential activity of his life, so that for him silence would mean death. Overall, the tone of the lyrics is somber, preparing the reader for the even darker tones of the rest of the volume.

The ballads and romances of the next section are no lighter in substance, but they are faster moving in terms of the language and, as their names imply, musically allusive. "Neiztrohnjeno srce" (The Uncorrupted Heart), for example, can hardly be considered amusing: it tells the tale of a dead poet whose body has decayed away but whose heart remains intact and beating because there are still so many poems left unsung therein. The eroticism of "Ribič" (The Fisherman) – *Ribič* was coincidentally another family name used by the Prešeren clan – is about as heady as anything Prešeren wrote, but the message is very much in keeping with his longstanding point of view that if one must love then one should love without hope of happiness or fulfillment. One who would do otherwise is like the fisherman who pursues the seductive mermaid into the sea: he will only drown.

The section containing various poems is really a combination of a few long and serious pieces and many short and frivolous ones. Among the longer pieces is "Slovo od mladosti" (Farewell to Youth), a splendid work in the European Romantic tradition of lamenting youth's lost illusions. Some consider it Prešeren's best work, especially given that it arose practically ex nihilo in a language that had until then been used, as Prešeren put it, to "teach folks to catch mice," but that now could record some of the loftiest thoughts and profoundest feelings poets of any language might express. Like most of Prešeren's verse, it is a somewhat lugubrious piece, in which all hope is abandoned and love causes unendurable pain. It stands in sharp contrast to the witty epigrams that conclude the section, most of which, however, are quite obscure to the modern reader because the occasions that prompted them have long been forgotten. "Slovo od mladosti," on the other hand, has an eternal quality that will cause it to be read as long as the Slovene language is understood.

Ghazals are a poetic form imported primarily into German literature – Johann Wolfgang von Goethe favored them – from Arabic and Persian sources. Their subjects were more often than not love and drinking wine, and their structural peculiarity involved using the same rhyme – up to half a line long – in every even-numbered verse, while the odd-numbered verses did not rhyme at all. Prešeren introduced this form into Slovene at least in part because the very intricacy of its structure appealed to his poetic genius. The result is a cycle of seven poems – Prešeren's only nonsonnet cycle – that sing of the immortality poetry confers upon lover and loved one and the uncertainty the poet must always face whenever he would love. Implicit in this erotic theme is also a patriotic point: that good and true poetry can crystallize a nation out of a disparate band of tribes.

Unlike the ghazal, Prešeren cannot take the credit for introducing the sonnet to Slovene, but he did perfect it. Of his forty-six Slovene-language sonnets that have survived, he included forty-two in his anthology, furnishing eloquent testimony to the high regard he had for this verse form. Again, this compact form appealed to Prešeren's relish for poetic conciseness. In addition, the very spareness of the form – only 140 to 154 syllables are possible within any given sonnet, and these must be arranged in strictly prescribed ways – favors Slovene, which like English and Italian but unlike Russian or German has many short words that can be flexibly arranged. Prešeren and Čop hoped that the successful adaptation of the sonnet to Slovene would prove beyond all doubt the suitability of the language for high literary purposes, and Prešeren's poetic genius provided the texts.

For the reader who knows both Slovene and Italian, Prešeren's sonnets immediately call to mind Petrarch's, occasionally almost to the point of paraphrasing the Italian master and here and there even mentioning him by name, as in "Je od vesel'ga časa teklo leto" (The Twice Nine Hundred and Thirty-Third Year Has Passed). Love – unrequited, burning, painful, but also sometimes less than sublime and perhaps even a little absurd – is the constant theme. Other topics appear from time to time as well, as in "Sonetni venec," which was reprinted with alterations in the anthology: poetry and patriotism are given their due weight. The range of tones is nowhere wider than in the sonnet section, from the grimmest contemplations of death and destruction to bright, soaring evocations of consummated bliss. One cycle, "Zabavljivi sonetje," is ironic to the point of sarcasm. Here the poet takes wicked delight in skewering his opponents, especially "the old hoof" – Kopitar, that is; *kopita* means "hoof" in Slovene – and his opponents' plans for "reforming" and "preserving" Slovene, which to Prešeren's mind were attempts to strangle the language in its infancy.

The sonnet section closes, however, with a return to painful things. The last cycle is titled "Sonetje nesreče," and it includes some of the most poignant verse Prešeren wrote, especially "O Vrba! Srečna, draga vas domača" (Oh Vrba! Happy, Dear Home Village), an explicitly autobiographical piece that laments Prešeren's lost home and the passing of his only truly happy days. These poems end at death: "Življenje ječa, čas v nji rabelj hudi" (Life Is a Prison, Time the Evil Hangman in It) celebrates the end of life as a release from life's pains; "Memento mori" calls to mind the classic admonition of the pessimist; and finally "Matiju Čopu" (To Matija Čop) concentrates in the sparest verse Prešeren's unbearable pain at the loss of his friend and at the same time introduces the final section of the anthology, *Krst pri Savici*. By the end the poet's despair is relieved only by the consumate intricacy, originality, grandeur, and yet simplicity of his language.

Prešeren's unanthologized verse, most of which was published in his lifetime in various journals, includes Slovene lyrics, ballads, romances, and epigrams as well as his original German poetry and some German versions of his Slovene work. Prešeren was comfortable in German, having heard it from his earliest childhood and then having been schooled in it starting in 1810. His German verse betrays this ease: it is often as fluid and rich as his Slovene work. Some critics have suggested that Prešeren wrote in German in order to promote Slovene: since many educated Slovenes read only in German, composing in German was one way Prešeren could inform his compatriots of what he was doing in Slovene without compelling them to read that language. Whatever the reason, Prešeren's German verse is an important if not always appreciated component of his work. It is also fairly diverse.

Among Prešeren's more amusing verses are the "Literärische Scherze in August Wilhelm Schlegels Manier" (Literary Jokes in August Wilhelm Schlegel's Manner), which repeat in witty German some of the arguments Prešeren had made during the alphabet battles with Kopitar. More typical, however, of Prešeren's artistry are his German sonnets, which in small cycles such as the "Sängers Klage" (Poet's Plaint) lament the sad necessity that he, the Slovene poet, must from time to time compose in German. These are sonnets of defeat, but only if one reads them without Prešeren's Slovene poems in mind. For the reader who knows both parts of Prešeren's work, the German sonnets also contain a bitter irony: that the poet really could write extremely well in Slovene, so he should not have taken so much time with German, whose expressive qualities needed no demonstration. Prešeren's other sonnets speak to the sad bifurcation of his poetic soul as well, and from time to time he gently takes to task those Slavic poets who betray their "natural mother" – their native Slavic language, be it Slovene or Czech or Polish – for their "stepmother" (German usually). Perhaps the most impressive feature of these poems, which are written in a classical, almost old-fashioned German, is their lack of jingoism: for the most part the poet is sadly resigned to the linguistic situation in which he and other Slavs find themselves and seeks to make the best of it.

Perhaps the very best of Prešeren's German verse is a poem he wrote less than three weeks after his friend Čop had drowned, "Dem Andenken des Matthias Čop" (To the Memory of Matthias Čop). In its classical diction and structure it is a controlled but moving lament on the loss of his closest companion and the absurdity of life and death. Yet once again death comes as a release from life's unbearable burdens, so that at least for Čop it might be a blessing in disguise. It is an excruciating resolution, however, for those he leaves behind: death's "sting" is for the living and not the departed. The German elegy to Čop should be read together with the sonnet to him that prefaces *Krst pri Savici*. Written by the same poet responding to the same profound grief, they reveal perhaps more clearly than anywhere else in Prešeren's oeuvre his enormous talent and versatility as well as the depths of his poetic soul. Here he appears truly as a world-class poet at the height of his powers.

Were Slovene more widely spoken, Francè Prešeren would be recognized internationally for his genius. He was the first to raise Slovene letters above the provincial and peripheral, the first to demonstrate the language's expressive range, and the first to articulate a national pride that neither disparaged others nor belittled itself. He was a master of poetic architecture, using the most complex and demanding forms to contain his words and give them an appealing shape. He was extraordinarily creative, combining words and phrases that can still strike today, no matter how well they are known or how often repeated. Though his own life ended in what appeared to be dismal failure and abject poverty, he was enormously successful in stimulating the literary talents of his nation. He was eventually rich in successors, so that his own poetic genius became the model and mold of all Slovene poetry to come. Like every great poet, he transcends both his age and his locale and belongs to the literary heritage of all educated people.

Letters:
Francè Prešeren, *Zbrano delo,* 2 volumes, edited by Janko Kos (Ljubljana: Državna založba Slovenije, 1965–1966) – includes his correspondence.

Bibliography:
Štefka Bulovec, *Prešernova bibliografija* (Maribor, Yugoslavia: Založba Obzorja, 1975).

Biographies:
Francè Kidrič, *Prešeren 1800–1838: Življenje pesnika in pesmi* (Ljubljana: Tiskovna zadruga, 1938);
Anton Slodnjak, *Prešernovo življenje* (Ljubljana: Mladinska knjiga, 1984).

References:
Robert Auty, "Prešeren's German Poems," *Oxford Slavonic Papers,* 6 (1973): 1–11;
Henry Ronald Cooper, Jr., *Francè Prešeren* (Boston: Twayne, 1981);
Janko Kos, *Prešeren in evropska romantika* (Ljubljana: Državna Založba Slovenije, 1970);
Kos, *Prešeren in njegova doba* (Koper, Yugoslavia: Lipa, 1991);

Niko Košir, *Francè Prešeren* (Ljubljana: Partizanska knjiga, 1977);
Janko Lavrin, "Francè Prešeren, 1800–1849," *Slavonic and Eastern European Review,* 33 (1954–1955): 304–326;
Juraj Martinović, *Apsurd i harmonija: Jedno vidjenje Prešernovog pjesničkog djela* (Sarajevo: Svjetlost, 1973);
Boris Paternu, *France Prešeren in njegovo pesniško delo,* 2 volumes (Ljubljana: Mladinska knjiga, 1976–1977);
Paternu, *France Prešeren: Ein slowenischer Dichter 1800–1849* (Munich: Slavica Verlag dr. Anton Kovač, 1994);
Dimitrij Rupel, "Slovenski kulturni sindrom, Razmišljanje o 'Krstu pri Savici,' " *Sodobnost,* 23 (1975): 97–109;
Peter Scherber, *Slovar Prešernovega pesniškega jezika* (Maribor, Yugoslavia: Založba Obzorja, 1977);
Anton Slodnjak, *Geschichte der slowenischen Literatur* (Berlin: De Gruyter, 1958);
Josip Vidmar, "France Prešeren," in his *Slovenske razprave* (Ljubljana: Cankarjeva založba, 1970), pp. 7–77.

Papers:
Prešeren's papers are held in the Narodna in Univerzitetna Knjižnica, Ljubljana.

Kočo Racin

(22 December 1908 – 13 June 1943)

Graham W. Reid
University of Skopje

BOOKS: *Beli mugri* (Samobor, Yugoslavia: Štamparija Dragutina Spulera, 1938); translated by Graham W. Reid as *White Dawns* (Skopje: Macedonian Review, 1974);
Dragovitskite bogomili (Skopje: Zemski odbor na narodniot front na Makedonija, 1948);
Pesme (Belgrade: Nolit, 1952);
Stihovi i tvorbi (Skopje: Kultura, 1966);
Izbor, edited by T. Todorovski (Skopje: Misla, 1987);
Izbrani dela, 6 volumes, edited by P. Korobar and others (Skopje: Naša kniga, 1987);
Pesni (Bitola, Yugoslavia: Misirkov, 1989);
Izbrani stranici, edited by A. and L. Spasov (Skopje: Misla, 1991).

OTHER: *Makedonski narodnoosloboditelni pesni,* 2 volumes, edited by Racin (Mt. Lopušnik, Lazaropole & Debar: illegal party press, 1943);
Stihovi od mladinite (1928–29), in *Kočo Racin: Istorisko-literaturni istražuvanja* by B. Ristovski (Skopje: Kočo Racin, 1983).

SELECTED PERIODICAL PUBLICATIONS – UNCOLLECTED: "Rezultat," *Kritika* (Zagreb), 4, nos. 4–5 (1928): 98;
"Hegel," *Literatura* (Zagreb), 1, no. 6 (1931): 149–156;
"U kamenolomu," *Literatura,* 2, no. 1 (1932): 36–39;
"Veleško lončarstvo," *Vardar,* 1, no. 34 (1932): 12;
"Berači duvana," *Naša stvarnost,* 5–6 (1937): 40–44;
"Podne," *Kultura* (Zagreb), 1, nos. 1–2 (1937): 24–26;
"Ideološki sukobi demokratije i fašizma," as N.P., *Naša stvarnost,* 15–16 (1938): 208–209;
"Blazirane gluposti o osmehu Mona Lize," *Umetnost i kritika,* 1–2 (1939): 88–90;
"Razvitak i značaj jedne nove naše književnosti," *Radnički tjednik,* 1, no. 23 (1940): 5–6;
"Značenjeto na Ilinden," in T. Najdovski, "Novi rakopisi na Kočo Racin," *Kulturen život,* 7, no. 4 (1963): 24–26;

Posthumous sketch of Kočo Racin (Kosta Solev) by Pero Korubar

"Novak," in S. Nikolov, "Novi stranici od ostavninata na Kočo Racin," *Sovremenost,* 31, no. 9 (1982): 66–76;
"Julius," in S. Nikolov, "Novi argumenti za tvorečkite tekovi na Kočo Racin," *Razvitok,* 21, nos. 1–3 (1983): 101–116.

Single-minded in his ideas about the role he considered that poetry, literature in general, and art could and should play in the collective life of a people, Kočo Racin, while best remembered today as a poet, had a renaissance universality – of a socially committed sort – in the variety of creative activities to which he turned his hand. His work from the late 1920s to the early 1940s can be likened to a first functional footbridge where later a more substantial structure would be built, linking the past, largely oral, literature of Macedonia with that of the present and the future.

Kosta Solev, who later took the pen name by which he is better known today from the affectionate form of the name of his youthful sweetheart Raca, (or Rahilka), Firfova (then Firfović), was born on 22 December 1908 into a family of potters in the town of Veles, on the Vardar River, in central Macedonia. The town, a crossroads of ancient communication routes that had largely fallen into abeyance after long centuries of various occupations, showed signs of neglect. Its traditional crafts were decaying, while its industrial potential was as yet undeveloped. Veles nevertheless had already produced two writers of importance in the formation of Macedonian literature, Jordan Konstantin-Džinot and Rajko Žinzifov. In his hometown Racin was compelled by force of economic circumstances to abandon his secondary schooling after only a year and to follow in his father's footsteps as a pottery worker.

In 1926 he began writing journalistic pieces for the trade union paper *Organizovan radnik* (Organized Worker) and followed these a year later with his first attempts at poetry. Between October 1928 and March 1929 he wrote poems later given the title "Pesnite za Raca" (Poems for Raca). Romantically, these lines from his youth were inscribed in calligraphic copperplate on thirty-one postcards sent to his sweetheart. The dates on the cards are now barely legible, but internal evidence points to a partial overlap in composition with the poems collected in the cycle titled "Antologija boli" (Anthology of Sorrow). The six hundred lines, in prose as well as in verse, of the postcards to Raca and the latter cycle devoted to undying love were written in Serbian, the only legally acceptable written language in the region at the time since Macedonian, the language of the rich oral folk tradition Racin had inherited, was then relegated to the inferior position of a substandard tongue. Thanks to the circumstances of living and working in both Serbian- and Croatian-speaking areas and also to his own wide reading, Racin later achieved a greater degree of refinement in his use of those languages; at this stage, however, he showed an awkwardness in using languages – whether Serbian, Croatian, or, occasionally, Bulgarian – other than his native tongue.

From these earliest poems, which like most of his verse remained unpublished during his relatively short lifetime, he went on in the following two years to write poems, again in Serbian, on social subjects. A significant stage in the development of Racin's poetry, they were published separately between 1928 and 1938 in journals in Skopje, Sarajevo, Zagreb, and Belgrade. The title poem of what was later published as a cycle called "Vatromet" (Fireworks) first appeared in 1932.

The milestone in both Racin's work and in the birth and development of a new literature in Macedonia was his composition, from 1936 to 1938, of the cycle of poems in Macedonian called *Beli mugri* (1938; translated as *White Dawns,* 1974). These were published in the printing shop of Dragutin Spuler in Samobor, near Zagreb. The distribution of the edition of four thousand copies was proscribed by the state prosecutor, but by the time the order was issued they had already been taken from the printer in secret and distributed throughout Yugoslavia, mostly in Macedonia, and in Bulgaria. Thus a seminal volume in the history of the development of Macedonian literature – like its important predecessor, the 1861 miscellany of folk songs collected by brothers Dimitar and Konstantin Miladinov – was first printed in Zagreb – only in this case clandestinely.

Into the poems of *Beli mugri,* arranged under twelve headings, Racin poured much of the "great deal of sorrow, the moving tranqility, the grief and the trouble but also the hope" that he wrote he had found in Macedonian folk poetry, giving it a social setting that, while retaining a certain timelessness, was of contemporary relevance. These poems had, and have had ever since, an immediate, strong reaction among Macedonian readers in Yugoslavia and abroad. Anton Popov, a member of the Macedonian Literary Circle led by Nikola Vapcarov in Sofia, while noting what he styled the lack of a strong national theme – for reasons he acknowledges to have been out of Racin's control – greeted them with acclaim and a positive critical analysis. In *Beli mugri* Racin wrote verses in line with his prescription for the future of Macedonian literature as he saw it that were both realistic and based on the heritage of folk literature, "lest they lose their link with the people themselves."

Between 1928 and 1943 Racin wrote other poems, seventeen in Macedonian and three in Serbian, some before and others after *Beli mugri,* some more and others less folkloric in style. These were

К. РАЦИН

БЕЛИ МУГРИ

ПЕСНИ

ЗАГРЕБ

1939

Title page for the 1939 Zagreb edition of Racin's 1938 cycle of poems, Beli mugri *(translated as* White Dawns, *1974), an important work in Macedonian literature*

not included in his collections or cycles and, like most of his poetry, were posthumously published. In the last year of his life, as a member of the Partisan resistance and agitprop worker in the illegal print shop on Mount Lopušnik near Lazaropole and Debar in western Macedonia, Racin published the first of two small collections of songs of Macedonian national liberation, *Makedonski narodnoosloboditelni pesni* (Macedonian Liberation Songs), in an edition of one thousand copies. The second slim volume, also compiled by Racin, of traditional revolutionary songs adapted to the current situation and others written by his fellow Partisans, appeared immediately after Racin's death.

While Racin is best remembered for his poetry, he also wrote and in many cases published short stories, novellas, journalistic pieces, prose sketches, and an attempt at a novel, the manuscript of which was seized by the authorities; only fragments of it have survived. Racin's prose, which can be regarded as a superstructure built on the firm foundation of his poetry, shares themes and motifs with it. A socially committed writer, Racin in his prose illustrates even more explicitly his concern for ordinary people, their everyday needs and worries, and the reality of their existence, whether as impoverished tradesmen or as prisoners caught up in the class struggle. In doing so he presents, usually implicitly but in the case of his journalistic writings sometimes explicitly, the problems confronting his people, the Macedonians, investing them with a universal dimension.

From the outset, with the short story "Rezultat" (Result, 1928) and his award-winning "U kamenolomu" (In a Quarry, 1931), Racin's creative prose can be characterized as a break with more specifically social writing from the earlier and wider concept, espoused in Yugoslav literature by Miroslav Krieža and others, of the social role of art. The characteristic subject matter of this new style of prose is of a contemporary and frequently a utilitarian nature. Racin's subjects and his style provided a starting point for the new Macedonian prose, as his verse did for poetry. His stories deal with subjects, such as the generation gap, presented from a revolutionary viewpoint. His heroes, or Racin as narrator, often tellingly capitalized such conceptual words as *Present, Future, Poverty,* and *Significance.* Racin wrote most of his prose, with a view to publication, in Serbian, although occasionally Macedonian is used in dialogue.

Parallel with his creative writing, Racin was also engaged in journalism, writing for newspapers, journals, and illegal Communist party bulletins on history, philosophy, sociology, literature, and art. He published articles on the medieval Bogomils in Macedonia, Georg Wilhelm Friedrich Hegel, Yugoslav literature, art and the working class, and feminism. During the most fruitful and the last decade of Racin's life he moved several times. This period showed his deepening social and political commitment in a turbulent period of history. In 1932 he moved from Veles to Skopje, where he was employed as a proofreader on the *Vardar* newspaper and was active in the trade-union movement, contributing articles both that year and the next to *Radničke novine* (Worker's Gazette). The close of 1932 saw a reconsolidation of the party's illegal organization in Macedonia, and in mid 1933 Racin was elected to its district committee, with responsibility for agitprop activities, and as editor of and contributor to its paper *Iskra* (Spark).

In 1934 Racin was sentenced to four years' imprisonment for conspiracy, but the amnesty of 5 December 1935 brought his release. In 1936 he moved to Belgrade and worked as a proofreader with *Pravda* (Justice). The following year he worked on

Naš vesnik (Our Herald) brought out by MaNaPo, the Macedonian National Movement, in Zagreb. The same year he published in the *Politika* (Politics) newspaper a full-page feature on the pottery industry and the need for government participation in its modernization. He was also active in trade-union organization in Veles. The same year he contributed an article to the Zagreb periodical *Kultura* (Culture) warning against idealization of the past. In 1938 he wrote on the ideological conflict between democracy and fascism for the Belgrade periodical *Naša stvarnost* (Our Reality) and was a member of the editorial board of another Belgrade journal, *Umetnost i kritika* (Arts and Criticism), to which he contributed two signed texts, one presenting his view of the future as stemming from the working class and the other voicing his opposition to a vulgar materialistic treatment of cultural heritage.

The end of 1939 and the beginning of 1940 were perhaps the most significant period in Racin's journalistic activity. He devoted himself to a systematic treatment of Macedonian history, writing under a pseudonym his view of medieval Bogomilism (a religious sect centered in Bosnia) as a peasant movement, that was opposed to the feudal system on a religious basis. His last work in this sphere in prewar Yugoslavia appeared in *Radnički tjednik* (Worker's Weekly) in Zagreb; in it Racin elaborated his concept of the path that the development of Macedonian should take, a development to which his own creative writing gave impetus.

After 1941 Racin's activity was channeled into illegal party and Partisan resistance work, first as editor of *Naroden bilten* (People's Bulletin), which was clandestinely produced in his house in Veles. The issues Racin edited, in contrast to later ones, show among other things his concern for purity in the Macedonian language. In March 1942 Racin left for Skopje, where he worked as editor of the party central committee's bulletin. In the spring of 1943 he joined the Partisan resistance in western Macedonia as an agitprop worker. His last editorial task was preparing a proclamation in honor of the fortieth anniversary of the Ilinden Uprising against the Turkish rule of 1903. Racin met a tragic end on 13 June 1943 on Mount Lopušnik. Hard of hearing, he was apparently challenged by a fellow Partisan on guard duty and, failing to respond with the password, was shot and killed.

References:
T. Dimitrovski, *Od Pejčinović do Racin* (Skopje: Kultura, 1982);

Dimitrovski, *Rečnik na Beli Mugri na Kočo Racin* (Skopje: Kultura, 1990);

Miodrag Drugovac, *Makedonskata literatura od Misirkov do Racin* (Skopje: Prosvetno delo, 1975);

G. Filipovski, ed., *Svečen sobir posveten na Kočo Racin, 13.VI.1968* (Skopje: MANU, 1970);

Radomir Ivanović, "The Poetics of Kosta Racin," *Macedonian Review,* 7 (1977): 306–316;

Ivanović, *Poetikata na Kočo Racin* (Skopje: Macedonian Review, 1979);

N. Kirkov, *Ilegalniot pečat vo Veles 1941–1942* (Tetovo, Yugoslavia: Polog, 1981);

P. Korobar, *Kočo Racin: Beli Mugri — likovno viduvanje* (Skopje: Makedonska kniga, 1989);

Korobar, ed., *Racin vo spomenite na sovremenicite,* second edition (Skopje: Kultura, 1983);

D. Levkov and Dimitar Solev, eds., *IV Racinovi sredbi* (Titov Veles, Yugoslavia: Sovetot na Racinovite sredbi, 1962);

Dimitar Mitrev and others, *Kniga za Racin* (Skopje: Kočo Racin, 1963);

Duško Nanevski, *Poetot Racin* (Skopje: Studentski zbor, 1983);

S. Nikolov, "Novi argumenti za tvorečkite tekovi na Kočo Racin," *Razvitok,* 21, nos. 1–3 (1983): 101–116;

Nikolov, "Novi stranici od ostavinata na Kočo Racin," *Sovremenost,* 31, no. 9 (1982);

I. Nikolovska, "Tipološki karakteristiki na prozata na Racin," *Stremež,* 30, no. 3 (1986): 167–181;

B. Popov, ed. *Svečen sobir na 40 godišninata od izleguvanjeto na Beli Mugri, 23.XI.1979* (Skopje: MANU, 1980);

Blaže Ristovski, *Kočo Racin* (Skopje: Makedonska kniga, 1983);

Z. Simonovska, *Jazikot na Kočo Racin* (Skopje: Filološki fakultet, 1975);

Aleksandar Spasov, *Baladični elementi folklornog porekla u pesmama Koče Racina i Blaža Koneskog* (Belgrade, Tršić, & Novi Sad: Naučni sastanak slavista u Vukove dane, 1974);

T. Todorovski, *Izučuvanjeto na Racinovata poezija vo srednite uučilišta na SRM* (Skopje: Prosvetno delo, 1976);

Todorovski, ed., *Makedonskata literarturna nauka za Racin* (Skopje: Naša Kniga, 1987);

Tvorečkoto i revolucionerno živeenje na Kočo Racin, X Racinov kongres, 1973 (Titov Veles, Yugoslavia, 1974);

Boris Višinski, *Racin: A Play in Five Scenes,* translated by A. McConnel Duff (Skopje: Macedonian Review, 1979).

Milan Rakić

(2 October 1876 – 30 June 1938)

Michele Bulatovic
University of Louisville

BOOKS: *Pesme* (Belgrade: Štamparija Ace M. Stanojevića, 1903);

Nove pesme (Belgrade: S. B. Cvijanović, 1912);

Pesme Milana Rakića (Zagreb: Nova Evropa, 1924);

Pesme (Belgrade: Srpska književna zadruga, 1936);

Pesme (Belgrade: Prosveta, 1956);

Izabrana dela (Sarajevo: Svjetlost / Zagreb: Naprijed / Belgrade: Prosveta, 1967).

Editions in English: "The Abandoned Church," translated by Oliver Elton in *Slavonic and Eastern European Review,* 21 (1943): 103;

Selected poems translated by Elton in *Slavonic and Eastern European Review,* 24 (1946): 8–10;

Selection of Rakić's poems translated by Mihailo Djordjević in his *Anthology of Serbian Poetry: Golden Age* (New York: Philosophical Library, 1984), pp. 21–63;

Selection of Rakić's poems in *Serbian Poetry from the Beginnings to the Present,* various translators, edited by Milne Holton and Vasa D. Mihailovich (New Haven: Yale Center for International and Area Studies, 1988), pp. 203–208.

Sketch of Milan Rakić by Zuko Džumhur

Milan Rakić is generally recognized as one of the greatest Serbian poets of the twentieth century. He is particularly noted for introducing to the region a new versification imported from western Europe as well as for a series of patriotic poems he wrote about Kosovo, an emotionally symbolic region in Serbian culture and history.

Though Rakić's poetic career began well before World War I and arguably peaked in the first decade of the twentieth century, he is considered part of the vanguard of poets who imposed a modern literary movement on Yugoslavia between the two world wars. During this period many Serbian writers, including Rakić, were members of Yugoslavia's foreign service, perhaps a reflection of the leisured diplomatic life of that time. Also characteristic of many of these poets was that they sought inspiration and spent their formative years abroad.

Rakić traveled beyond his native Serbia to Paris, where the Parnassian movement and the French symbolists shaped his poetic technique and style. He believed, as did the Parnassians, that strict, proportioned lines would prevent heaviness and that this equilibrium was most conducive to illuminating profound emotions and philosophical ideas clearly. Unlike the Parnassians, who were thematically self-consumed, he focused on topics that grew from his heritage. As was common with the Yugoslav poets living abroad, Rakić never lost his devotion to his homeland. This mélange of technique and native themes contributed to the golden age of Serbian poetry (1880–1914).

Born on 2 October 1876 into a prominent family in Belgrade, Milan Rakić became a diplomat like his father, Mita Rakić. Literature and culture were abiding passions in the family. His father translated into Serbo-Croatian, among many other works, Victor Hugo's *Les Misérables* (1862); and his maternal grandfather, Milan Dj. Milićević, was a famous historian, politician, and encyclopedist.

For Rakić the influence of French literature came early, first from his family and then through his formal (though not classical) education in Belgrade. By age fifteen Rakić had developed a discriminating taste for French writers; he admired the Romantics and could recite many of Hugo's poems by heart. Among others, he admired Théophile Gautier's early poems and those of Alfred de Musset.

After completing high school in Belgrade in 1894, Rakić continued to study philosophy and then law at the University of Belgrade. After receiving a scholarship, at the age of twenty-two he traveled to Paris to complete his law degree. Unlike the Croats and the Slovenes, who sought Vienna for literary spirit and inspiration, the Serbs looked to Paris, a wellspring of modern literary movements. Rakić's critical sojourn in this city from 1898 to 1902 had a lasting impact on his poetry. There he came under the influence of French literary movements, namely the Parnassians, and met the man who later was responsible for launching his literary career.

While in Paris, Rakić lived with housemates who were also literary enthusiasts. Occasionally they organized poetry contests, in which the young Rakić read his first sonnets. Unknown to him, the referee of these competitions, Koča Kumanudi, kept the poems. A few years later in Belgrade, Kumanudi received a telephone call from his friend Bogdan Popović, then editor of the Serbian literary journal *Srpski književni glasnik* (Serbian Literary Herald), who desperately needed poems of publishable quality to fill its pages. Kumanudi goaded Rakić into giving his permission to have two of the sonnets published, but only on the condition that he remain anonymous. Thus the March 1902 issue of *Srpski književni glasnik* includes Rakić's philosophical sonnets under the pseudonym "Z." Rakić's dark, pensive voice was already resounding; his first sonnets speak of death, one might speculate, because his father died when Milan was only fourteen. Not until after 1903 and after publishing several poems as

"Z" did Rakić consent to attaching his name to his work published in *Srpski književni glasnik*. Enjoying anonymity was not unusual for him. He was not a socialite, and for him composing verse was a deeply personal endeavor. Keenly sensitive and fastidious, he reluctantly shared his poems. It was only under the intense enthusiasm and camaraderie of his Paris home that Rakić even revealed his poetic flair. He once said that if Serbian literature has anyone to thank for his poems, it is Kumanudi.

Selective as he was about his poems, all of which were written in Serbo-Croatian, Rakić has comparatively few to his name – a total of fifty-two. Of these, twenty-seven were published in *Srpski književni glasnik,* nine in other journals or newspapers, and the remainder in his collections. His first two compilations, *Pesme* (Poems, 1903) and *Nove pesme* (New Poems, 1912), include his best-known works. All of these poems were published as one-volume collections in 1924 and 1936.

Rakić's poems, many of which have been translated into other languages, including English, French, and German, reflect on three major themes – life, love, and patriotism – and all are drawn from his sensitive, philosophical nature. From his first poems to his last, Rakić remained a master craftsman in versification. Critics such as Zoran Gavrilović insist that he raised Serbian poetry to the level of virtuosity. Others add that Rakić's precise form and short, balanced lines, with the added element of a graceful, phonetic Serbo-Croatian devoid of heavy consonant clusters, make his poems musical. Even his earliest sonnets, I and II, have this musical quality, and they, along with those of his fellow poet Jovan Dučić, notably introduced the eleven- and twelve-syllable verse into Serbian poetry, replacing the sixteen-syllable verse of the Serbian poet Vojislav Ilić.

Jovan Skerlić, literary critic and former editor of *Srpski književni glasnik,* claimed that Rakić upheld the Marquis de Vauvenargues's notion that clarity beautifies deep thought. This tendency grew out of his attraction to the Parnassians, such as José Maria de Heredia, and the French symbolists, such as Charles Baudelaire. Deeply pessimistic, Rakić was interested in the tragic predicament of the individual and in deep inner searching. In his decadent, yet not morbid, work Rakić describes misery, decay, and solitude, but he does not drown in his sorrow like Baudelaire, and at times he expresses hope. His wife once said that though he was pessimistic by nature, his life experience made him an optimist.

Pervasive in his poetry from the beginning is the notion that all things are transient, that time

Cover for a 1952 edition of Rakić's Pesme *(Poems)*

is destructive, and that death is a relief from life's hardships. In "Dolap" (translated as "Waterwheel"), based on a memory from his childhood, Rakić describes a black horse whose fate is to turn the wheel and become "weary from the hard work of hard years." "Like me," he says, "you have dreamed of happiness in July's heat." But he adds

> False dreams! Go on, black horse, don't ever stop.
> Don't smell the grass; don't feel the soft, soft spring.
> Heaven will give you praise for your life's work;
> The good, dark grave is all the peace you're earning!
> – translation by Dragana Perović and Milne Holton (in *Serbian Poetry from the Beginnings to the Present,* edited by Mike Holton and Vasa D. Mihailovich, 1988)

The subjects of Rakić's poems correspond to events in his own life, as do the Kosovo poems and "Oproštajna pesma" (A Farewell Poem), written after the death of his sister. "Na kapitolu" (On the Capitol) and "U dansingu" (At a Dance), both writ-

ten during his diplomatic service in Rome, contain subtle reflections of the city under fascism.

In his lyric love poems, most of which he wrote before his marriage in 1905, Rakić sometimes alludes to chivalric heroes and romantic scenes, as in "Ljubavna pesma" (Love Poem). He often speaks directly to a beloved woman whose love he lost as a young man. More common in his love poems is the feeling that love is short-lived, as in "Obična pesma" (A Plain Poem). In "Iskrena pesma" (translated as "A Sincere Poem"), he speaks to a lover who is able to help him forget his mortality so he can feel happiness:

> For that instant of life and delight,
> When I sense the trembling of my entire being,
> For that, let my whole heart bless you!
> But I don't love you, I don't love you, dear!
>
> That is why I shall always say: keep silent!
> Leave the soul alone, let it dream in peace –
> While around us leaves are turning on the trees,
> And darkness descends over sleeping fields.
> – translation by Mihailo Djordjević (in his *Anthology of Serbian Poetry: Golden Age,* 1984)

In 1901 Rakić graduated from the Law School of the University of Paris and soon after returned to Belgrade. He began his career as an official of the Serbian export bank, where he supervised the exporting of dried fruit and preserves, and was later appointed first statistician and then customs official to the Ministry of Finance until 1904. During this period in the world of banking and finance he continued to publish his poems. However, had Rakić not made a career change to diplomacy at age twenty-nine, he might never have been moved to write the patriotic poems that comprise his best-known works.

Thus 1905 not only marks the start of a distinguished twenty-six-year career in the Foreign Ministry of Serbia and then of Yugoslavia but also an important phase in his literary development. His first diplomatic position was as vice-consul in Priština, in the Kosovo district of the Ottoman Empire. That same year, a few months before leaving for Priština, he married twenty-one-year-old Milica Kovačević, daughter of the historian and academician Ljuba Kovačević. Rakić's service from 1905 to 1909 in the Ottoman-ruled cities of Priština, Skopje, and Thessaloníki was a source of immense inspiration for him; what influenced him the most were the years in Priština and his work as a consul from 1909 to 1911.

In 1905 he began writing the seven patriotic poems that are known collectively as the Kosovo cycle. These poems in particular touch the souls of the Serbian people, who take immense pride in their fight at the Battle of Kosovo in 1389. Under the leadership of the strongest of the Serbian rulers, Prince Lazar Hrebeljanović, the Serbs faced the Turks and won a moral victory despite a military defeat. Successive defeats at the hands of the Turks and the threat of the eradication of Serbian life and culture followed.

Turkish tradition and culture, as well as Islamic law, came to permeate everyday life in the Balkans. During his service in the Kosovo region Rakić found only traces of old Serbian culture, with few remnants of Christianity. At the height of the Balkan War of 1912 he wrote "Napuštena crkva" (translated as "The Abandoned Church," 1943), which was inspired by a visit to an abandoned church, where a local peasant begged him to take one of the few remaining icons for safekeeping.

> Sole in that empty church, and ringed by phantom bands,
> The dreadful Christ, despairing, reaches out His hands,
> And waits forever for his flock – but where are they?
> – translation by Oliver Elton (in the *Slavonic and Eastern European Review,* 21 [1943]: 103)

Rakić also began to fathom the widespread destruction of Serbian culture in Kosovo. In the poem "Simonida" Rakić mourns the desecration of the well-known church of Gračanica. Simonida, the wife of King Milutin, a medieval king of Serbia, is depicted there in a fresco, where it is believed that Turks gouged out her eyes – perhaps an act prompted by their religion, which forbids the representation of the human face in sculpture or painting. Looking at her image, he laments

> They have dug out your eyes, you lovely image,
> Alone in this marble place where evening lies.
> They knew no one would witness their pillage;
> A Shiptar with a knife dug out those eyes.

Yet his underlying sense of optimism emerges, and he is still able to feel Simonida's light and inspiration:

> On me today, from your still regal height,
> And from this ancient wall all mired in grime,
> You, sad Simonida, send me that light
> From eyes thus blinded in an earlier time.
> – translation by Kosara Gavrilović and Holton (in *Serbian Poetry from the Beginnings to the Present,* 1988)

Rakić deftly uses religious imagery and the contrast of light and darkness, black and white, and

night and day to express both anguish and hope in these poems. Like "Simonida," other poems in the Kosovo cycle, such as "Jefimija" and "Minaret," reflect his admiration and respect for Serbian monuments, monasteries, and churches. "Kondir" (The Ewer) resurrects the heroes of the past and "Nasledje" (translated as "Heritage") the potent awareness of his ancestors:

> Today, through all my blood, I feel the flow
> Of theirs – my fathers, heroes rude and wild;
> And, on this dull dark evening, well I know
> Why playing at soldiers pleased me as a child.
> – translation by Elton (in the *Slavonic and Eastern European Review,* 24 [1946]: 10)

Though Rakić once said that he never aged so quickly or felt so torn as he did at Kosovo, he had the power to use his personal anguish to express pride and patriotism through his poems. In reading his Kosovo poems, one does not feel immobilized by depression but is, rather, inspired to act. In fact, during Rakić's tenure in Priština from 1909 to 1911, the ideas were planted that later moved him to action. In this period the Young Turk movement, which initially promised liberty to its Christian subjects, eventually set out aggressively to stifle nationalist anti-Turk opposition. This merely aroused, among other things, Serbian patriotism and a stronger desire to drive out the Turks. "Na Gazi Mestanu" (translated as "On Gazi Mestan") best describes these fiery, patriotic passions not only of a soldier but of a people willing to fight to the death for their native land:

> Your looks were dark, you showed no blemish, knew no fears,
> When here, enwrapt in clouds of dust, your onset broke;
> Cold as your own cuirasses, mighty cuirassiers!
> Your gallop, flecked with blood, came like a thunderstroke.
> . . . .
> And now, today, when this last battle is at hand,
> – Though unillumined by the ancient halo, I,
> I too, will give my life for thee, my native land,
> Well knowing what the gift I give, well knowing why.
> – translation by Elton (in the *Slavonic and Eastern European Review,* 24 [1946]: 8)

Perhaps "Na Gazi Mestanu" was an early prediction of Rakić's real passion to defend Serbian land not only with pen but also with sword. After eight years in Kosovo and identifying himself with the plight of the Serbs there, he was compelled to assume a more active role in liberating the Balkans from the Habsburg and Ottoman empires. He left the foreign ministry office and, against the will of his wife and relatives, joined the Serbian irregulars at the outbreak of the Balkan War in 1912. He proudly proclaimed to Milan Ćurčin, a poet known for his free verse, that he was the first to enter the newly liberated Priština and ring the bell of the Orthodox church, which he had been forbidden to do during his diplomatic service in the city.

Rakić resumed diplomatic service during World War I, when in 1914 he was assigned to serve in Niš and then as adviser to the ambassador in Bucharest. In 1916 he became chargé d'affaires in Stockholm and was later transferred to London. He also served as minister in Copenhagen and then in Sofia. His last assignment, from 1927 to 1934, was in Rome. He entered complete retirement from the diplomatic service in 1933 at age fifty-seven because of his failing health.

In 1934 Rakić was honored by his election to the Serbian royal academy and was elected president of the Serbian branch of P.E.N., the international organization of Poets, Playwrights, Editors, Essayists, and Novelists. However, in the last years of his life he was plagued by ill health and endured two unsuccessful operations. He died in Srebrnjak near Zagreb on 30 June 1938, just two days after the 549th anniversary of the Battle of Kosovo.

At age forty-eight Rakić told an interviewer that he dreamed of living alone in Koviona, a small village on the island of Korčula. There he would wear suede suits and ride a bicycle, enjoying the simple pleasures away from the bustle of European cities. Though he never lived to fulfill this dream of serenity, he continually aspired to it through his poetry.

Rakić's contribution to Serbian poetry, though quantitatively modest, remains qualitatively significant and has passed the test of time. Despite the horrors of World War I, when art-for-art's-sake aestheticism completely dissolved and his own "cult of form" seemed anachronistic, his work endured. In Marshal Tito's Yugoslavia, in a political climate that stressed multinational unity and deemphasized ethnic distinctiveness, Rakić's poetry lost official favor. Nevertheless, during the 1980s, on a wave of Serbian nationalism, he enjoyed a resurgence of popularity.

His Kosovo poems, the centerpiece of his verse, have assured him an honored place as one of the greatest Serbian poets. Masterly poetic and profoundly expressive, he is also placed among the creative pioneers of South Slavic poetry. Milan Rakić's critics agree that his originality, clarity, and refinement in his verse render his poems everlasting.

Letters:

Konzulska pisma 1905–1911, edited by Andrej Mitrović (Belgrade: Prosveta, 1985).

Interview:

Branimir Ćosić, "Jedno veče sa G. Milanom Rakićem," in Rakić's *Izabranadela* (Sarajevo: Svjetlost / Zagreb: Naprijed / Belgrade: Prosveta, 1967), pp. 107–120.

Biographies:

Jean Mousset, *Milan Rakitch* (Paris: Boivin et Cie, 1939);

Vojislav J. Djurić, *Milan Rakić* (Belgrade: Prosveta, 1957).

References:

Milan Ćurčin, "Milan Rakić and the Idea of Kosovo," *Slavonic and East European Review,* 18 (July 1939): 170–174;

Mihailo Djordjević, "Milan Rakić," *Serbian Studies,* 5 (Spring 1989): 43–53;

Vojislav Djurić, "Milan Rakić," in Rakić's *Pesme* (Belgrade: Prosveta, 1956), pp. 7–120;

Laura Gordon Fisher, "The Patriotic Poetry of Milan Rakić," *Serbian Studies,* 4, no. 3 (1987): 71–77;

Zoran Gavrilović, *Od Vojislava do Disa* (Belgrade: Nolit, 1958);

Milan Grol, "Iz sećanja na Milana Rakića," *Srpski književni glasnik,* 55 (1938): 262–280, 342–356;

Per Jacobson, *A Concordance to Milan Rakić's Poems* (Copenhagen: Kobenhavns universitets Slaviske institut, 1984);

Želimir B. Juričić, "Milan Rakić: The Diplomat and the Artist," *The Bell of Freedom: Essays Presented to Monica Partridge on the Occasion of Her 75th Birthday,* edited by Peter Herrity (Nottingham, U.K.: Astra Press, 1989), pp. 85–98;

Branko Lazarević, "Versifikacija Milana Rakića," in his *Impresije iz književnosti,* volume 2 (Belgrade: Geca Kon, 1924), pp. 19–24;

Vasa Pavković, *Rečnik poezije Milana Rakića* (Novi Sad, Yugoslavia: Matica srpska, 1984);

Isidora Sekulić, "Milan Rakić," in her *Iz domaćih književnosti,* volume 1 (Novi Sad, Yugoslavia: Matica srpska, 1964), pp. 45–110;

Jovan Skerlić, "Milan Rakić: *Nove Pesme,*" in his *Pisci i knjige* (Belgrade: Prosveta, 1968), pp. 100–105;

Srpski književni glasnik, special issue on Milan Rakić, 54 (July/August 1938).

August Šenoa

(14 November 1838 – 13 December 1881)

Maria B. Malby
East Carolina University

BOOKS: *Zagrebulje,* 2 volumes (Zagreb, 1866, 1880);

Zlatarovo zlato (Zagreb: Dragutin Albrecht, 1872);

Zimzelen (Zagreb, 1873);

Sabrani spisi Augusta Šenoe, 4 volumes (Zagreb: Dionička tiskara, 1876–1878);

Diogenes (Zagreb: Matica hrvatska, 1878);

Prosjak Luka (Zagreb: Matica hrvatska, 1879);

Kletva (Zagreb, 1882);

Izabrane pjesme (Zagreb: Matica hrvatska, 1882);

Sabrane pripovijesti, 8 volumes (Zagreb: Matica hrvatska, 1884–1890);

Sabrane pripovijesti, 7 volumes (Zagreb: L. Hartman, 1910–1920);

Sabrana djela, 16 volumes (Zagreb: St. Kugli, 1919–1932);

Izabrana djela, 20 volumes (Zagreb: Binoza, 1931–1934);

Djela Augusta Šenoe, 12 volumes (Zagreb: Minerva, 1932–1935);

Pjesme (Zagreb: Minerva, 1934);

Sabrana djela Augusta Šenoe, 20 volumes (Zagreb: Preporod, 1943);

Djela, 4 volumes (Zagreb: Zora, 1951);

August Šenoe, 4 volumes (Zagreb: Matica hrvatska, 1962);

Sabrana djela, 20 volumes (Zagreb: Znanje, 1964);

Djela Augusta Šenoe (Zagreb: Globus, 1978).

Edition in English: *The Peasant Rebellion,* translated in abridged form by Branko Brusar (Zagreb: Matica iseljenika Hrvatske, 1973).

PLAY PRODUCTION: *Ljubica,* Zagreb, Zagreb Theater, 26 March 1868.

OTHER: *Vijenac izabranih pjesama hrvatskih i srpskih,* edited by Šenoa (Zagreb, 1873);

Antologija pjesništva hrvatskoga i srpskoga narodnoga i umjetnoga, edited by Šenoa (Zagreb: Matica hrvatska, 1876).

August Šenoa

Dubbed "August I." by Antun Gustav Matoš, a prominent turn-of-the-century Croatian writer and critic, August Šenoa is the father of modern Croatian literature. He appeared on the literary scene at a time when there were no significant writers in Croatia and when those who were writing lacked direction. For two decades (1860–1881) Šenoa led the way in Croatian literature, creating works that surpassed much of what had been written before his time. He wrote lyric and epic poems, narratives in verse, a play, short stories, novellas, novels, critical essays, feuilletons, reviews, and translations and gathered anthologies. All of these had an immense impact both on the reading public and the writers of his time. Generations of children have since been raised reciting his poems written to awaken national consciousness and instill pride in the Croatian national heritage. Today many of his works still receive a warm reception from readers and appear in new editions.

The word *Croat* was sacred to Šenoa. It is said that he died with it on his lips, pleading for more time to complete all his literary projects. Yet his father, Alojz, could not speak Croatian and signed his last name Schönau. The germanized family had moved to Zagreb from Pécs, Hungary, but claimed to be of Czech origin, since the signature Scheynoha appeared in a family prayerbook.

August Šenoa was born on 14 November 1838 in Zagreb. From his mother, Terezija pl. Rabač, he acquired an appreciation for culture in general and literature in particular. Šenoa's son Milan wrote that his grandfather, the bishop's pastry maker, was interested in the theater, painting, and music. Thus young Šenoa was introduced to all these disciplines at home. He attended grammar school in Zagreb. Shortly after his mother's death in 1848 he was sent to live with relatives in Pécs, where he enrolled in high school. A year later he returned to Zagreb, continued his secondary education, and graduated in 1857. Among his teachers were prominent figures in Croatian cultural life who, Austrian rule notwithstanding, imbedded in their students feelings of national pride and love of the Croatian people.

After graduating from high school Šenoa traveled with a schoolmate through Slovenia. There he visited the grave of Francè Prešeren, the foremost Slovenian poet. Later he described his emotions in connection with this pilgrimage in a novella, "Karanfil s pjesnikova groba" (A Carnation from the Poet's Tomb, 1878), and a poem titled "Bohinj," after a lake in Slovenia.

Since he was interested in foreign service, Šenoa took a qualifying exam in Vienna in 1857. Although he passed all the exams with distinction, he was not taken into diplomatic service, apparently due to his Pan-Slavic political orientation. After two years of university studies in Zagreb and Vienna, he was awarded a scholarship by Bishop Josip Juraj Strossmayer to study law in Prague. Here the future

man of letters discovered Czech, Polish, and Russian authors, whose works he read avidly. This stay in Prague was of vital importance for Šenoa's future as a journalist, writer, and civil servant.

In 1865, after receiving a law degree, Šenoa moved to Vienna to become editor of *Glasonoša* (Newsbearer) and *Slavische Blätter* (Slavic Leaflets), political and literary journals. A year later he returned to Zagreb, where he edited *Pozor* (Attention) until this political newspaper was abolished in 1867. His own articles published here included liberal ideas, leading to police surveillance. As a journalist Šenoa developed a keen sense of observation and a predilection for detail. He urged the Croats to follow in the footsteps of Czech politicians in their fight against Austrian imperialism. As a Pan-Slavist he believed in strong ties between the Serbs and the Croats and between all Slavs in general.

Šenoa felt great empathy for the Croatian peasant. Consequently he showed distaste for foreign capitalists in Croatia as well as rich noblemen, largely of foreign descent. The leaders of Croatian political life at this time belonged to the still weak but progressive middle class whom Šenoa wanted to enlighten. For this purpose he wrote not only articles but also verses. In a poem such as "Budi svoj" (Be Your Own Man, 1874) he urges men to do what they must do: not to lose heart, not to waver, just to march forward, no matter what. In "Pjev hrvatskih djaka" (The Song of Croatian Schoolboys, 1873) he glorifies political freedom and extols industriousness, duty, and education.

Šenoa had started writing poetry in high school. He wrote relatively few lyric poems, for he found it difficult to transfer personal emotions onto paper. Only in time, in the collection *Zimzelen* (Evergreen, 1873), was he able to express his innermost feelings adequately.

Šenoa's *povjestice,* narratives in verse with either a folk or historic theme, take a special place in his poetry. These works are didactic, teaching moral and ethical truths, and are usually relevant to contemporary sociopolitical issues. Structurally these poems display varied syllable and rhyme patterns as well as stanza lengths.

Whether he chose a topic from history or wrote an ode to Zagreb or to his former benefactor Bishop Strossmayer, Šenoa always picked words not only for their melodiousness but for vigor as well. Thus, charged with great declamatory power, his poems and verse narratives had a tremendous impact on future generations.

While writing poetry and newspaper articles, Šenoa also wrote feuilletons. These were published in *Pozor* and *Vijenac* (Wreath), which he also edited. Eventually he published some of his feuilletons in two volumes as *Zagrebulje* (Things about Zagreb, 1866, 1880). In them he pointed his finger at social, cultural, and political problems in his hometown.

The year 1868 was a landmark in Šenoa's life. He was chosen for the post of city clerk, was appointed artistic director of the Zagreb theater, married Slavica pl. Ištvanić, and saw the production of his play *Ljubica,* written in 1864 and published in 1866 in *Pozor.* The play folded after the opening night: people either could not or would not admit that such hypocrisy, greed, and pseudocivility as Šenoa exposed in his comedy existed in Zagreb's upper-class society.

As Šenoa saw it, the high life of Zagreb left much to be desired. He viewed both men and women as predatory animals in search of wealth, youth, or both. They plotted and schemed to attain their goals, until the cleverest in the pursuit of personal gratification won the game. In the dialogue Šenoa criticizes the education of upper-class women sent to institutes to be taught the game of entrapment only to end up as unfaithful wives. He also attacks the theater repertoire, which offered third-rate German plays.

In his numerous theater essays, which represent a twenty-year chronicle of the Zagreb theater, Šenoa insists that the theater produce the works of William Shakespeare and plays by great German and French playwrights. In his article "O hrvatskom kazalištu" (About the Croatian Theater, 1865), published in *Glasonoša,* Šenoa uses the term *realism* for the first time in the history of Croatian literature. He also advocates realism in prose in "Naša književnost" (Our Literature), another article published in *Glasonoša* the same year. Literature, according to Šenoa, had the task of depicting Croatian reality, raising the consciousness of the masses, and serving their needs in general.

Accused of dogmatism yet faithful to his dicta, Šenoa tried to lead the way. Although one may say that he turned Croatian literature toward realism, his prose displays many Romantic traits. One could argue, however, that these were often ploys to generate a large reading public rather than flaws indicating an inability to fulfill his own aim.

Šenoa's prose shows an interesting blend of realistic details and romantic scenes. The latter describe great passions and sufferings, loves at first sight, abandoned and illegitimate children, unknown benefactors, rescues at the last moment, and so on. Such episodes are filled with strange characters who entangle and then disentangle the plot. All

this made Šenoa dear to his readers, who were left inconsolable at his premature death.

Shifting from journalism and poetry to prose, Šenoa entered his most mature creative period, which lasted barely ten years (1871–1881). During these years he was extremely prolific, for he wanted to leave as much as possible to posterity. Appointed city councillor in 1873, by day he performed his civic duties as diligently as he wrote by night. It is touching to read about his musings on the luxury of writing full time, with the sun shining on one's pen. Instead he spent sleepless nights at his writing desk. In 1880, after a major earthquake in Zagreb, Šenoa braved the autumn weather for three long months, visiting the survivors, an ordeal he did not survive. As he lay dying, he dictated the end of his novella "Branka" (1881) and parts of his last historical novel, *Kletva* (A Curse, 1882), which was completed by another writer.

Šenoa composed his works with care, mindful of detail and style. Hence he needed time to turn out a finished product. When he wrote about people whom he had met, these people had to pass through his creative process before he was able to turn them into literary protagonists. Similarly, he always visited places that he intended to use as settings for his short stories and historical novels. In this respect he was true to the advice he gave younger writers to visualize every face and every place about which they were going to write. If they could not do that, he told them not to write at all.

As in his poetry, everything in Šenoa's prose, from descriptions to dialogue, flows smoothly. Each protagonist and each scene is depicted vividly with carefully selected words, all in the standard literary language. This was at a time when most people in Zagreb spoke either German or Croatian with overtones of the local "kajkavian" (a dialect spoken around Zagreb). Taking his profession seriously, Šenoa not only did his homework before he started writing but described his research in the foreword. This is particularly true of his historical novels.

Šenoa's first historical novel, *Zlatarovo zlato* (The Goldsmith's Gold), appeared in 1872. From then on until his death Šenoa was the central figure in Croatian literary life. In his remaining years he wrote several short stories and novellas with themes taken from contemporary life: "Prijan Lovro" (Friend Lovro, 1873), "Barun Ivica" (Baron Ivica, 1874), "Mladi gospodin" (The Young Gentleman, 1875), "Iljina oporuka" (Iljayah's Will, 1876), "Karanfil s pjesnikova groba," "Vladimir" (1879), "Kanarinčeva ljubovca" (The Canary's Mistress, 1880), and "Branka," to mention just the highlights.

Title page for Šenoa's first historical novel, about a sixteenth-century class conflict

He also wrote three more historical novels – "Čuvaj se senjske ruke" (Beware of the Hand of Senj; published in *Vijenac,* 1875), "Seljačka buna" (published in *Vijenac,* 1877; partially translated as *The Peasant Rebellion,* 1973), and *Diogenes* (1878) – as well as a novel dealing with life in his own time, *Prosjak Luka* (Beggar Luka, 1879), and the unfinished historical novel *Kletva.* In addition, he worked on translations of foreign literary masterpieces into Croatian and compiled anthologies of Croatian and Serbian poetry. His was such a huge output that even the most complete edition of Šenoa's works, the twenty-volume Binoza edition of 1931–1934, does not include all he wrote.

With *Zlatarovo zlato* Šenoa was recognized as the father of the Croatian historical novel and the best representative of this literary genre. Raised on historical novels by Sir Walter Scott and Victor Hugo, Šenoa became intrigued by Zagreb's past. Fortunately, he lived in an era when several historians tried to shed light on the most prominent epi-

sodes in Croatian history. Their work, as well as the archives of Zagreb, to which he had easy access, provided the material Šenoa needed for this and other historical novels to follow.

The central theme of *Zlatarovo zlato* is class conflict. The citizens of the free city of Zagreb clash with the nobles of neighboring fiefdoms Samobor and Medvedgrad. According to Šenoa, the sixteenth-century conflict, stemming from a land dispute, was aggravated by the infiltration of foreigners into the noble families.

A love story is always the nucleus around which Šenoa builds his plots. Here a young nobleman, Pavao Gregorijanec of Medvedrad, falls in love with Dora Krupić, the daughter of Zagreb's goldsmith. Dora's existence remains undocumented, but Šenoa needed her to dramatize Pavao's refusal to marry the mistress of Samobor, Klara Grubarova. Rejected, Klara swears vengeance. Oscillating between the biblical Susannah and Delilah, figures woven into her tapestries, she might have resisted her impulses, but Grgo Čokolin, the villain, spurs her on. As Klara's new husband, the foreign baron Kristof Ungnad, attacks Dora's hometown to appease his wife, Čokolin poisons the girl for having once rejected him. With Ungnad, Šenoa portrayed not only Klara's unsuspecting accomplice in a diabolic plan but a pawn of the Austrians who, appointed governor of Croatia, wages war against its people.

Klara's obsession with Pavao leads to madness. Evil is thus punished in the end, and life eventually triumphs over death. Because most protagonists, events, and places described in the novel are real, the authenticity of the background gives authenticity to a whole segment of Croatia's past, regardless of romantic exaggerations.

In his second historical novel, "Čuvaj se senjske ruke," Šenoa introduces two love stories, as he writes a tribute to the Uskoks, valiant men used by Austria to repel the Turks. One of the Uskoks' last strongholds after the men's services had become obsolete was the coastal town of Senj. At the beginning of the seventeenth century they led precarious lives there. Since the Austrians refused to pay their wages in time of peace, they engaged in piracy against Venetian ships. Employing a variety of dubious characters, including Senj's Bishop de Dominis and an Italian general, Giuseppe Rabatta, the Austrians and Venetians decide to eliminate the problem. Attacking at night and taking most families hostage, they finally succeed in killing or resettling the Uskoks. With broad strokes of his brush,

Šenoa depicts several tragic deaths, creating an eternal monument to the Uskoks.

At the end of the novel Šenoa lightens the tone by describing the reunion of two couples, Djure and Klara and Juriša and Dume. After many tribulations they start life anew in an almost deserted town. Once again the author puts the wheel of rebirth into motion and attests to the power of divine justice by describing Rabatta's and de Dominis's pathetic ends.

In "Seljačka buna" death seems to have an upper hand, but even here all is not lost. With this novel Šenoa offers an apology for the Croatian peasantry, abused for centuries by domestic and foreign feudal lords. In 1573 a peasant leader named Matija Gubec started a revolt in Stubica, north of Zagreb. Šenoa states that this major historical event was not triggered merely by the fact that the peasants were overworked, hungry, and beaten. Essentially, the uprising started because the ill-famed landowner – Franjo Tahi, a man of Hungarian origin – together with some others randomly dishonored peasant women.

In this novel Tahi rapes Jana, a girl engaged to marry Gubec's nephew Djuro, a free man whom Tahi's soldiers abduct and send off to war with Turkey. Because of treason and reinforcements sent from Slovenia to aid Tahi, Gubec loses his fight. To save others, he gives himself up and is tortured and crowned "king" with a red-hot iron crown in front of Saint Mark's Church in Zagreb.

Although little is known about Gubec, Šenoa could not help but portray him as a decent man who acted out of purely humanitarian motives. Whether he really gave himself up or was captured still remains a question, but this well-researched novel shows that his rebellion was a fight for a just cause. This contradicts the annals, which state that an unruly mob went on a rampage and was justly punished for it. By setting the record straight in this most dramatic of his novels, Šenoa did a great service to the Croatian people.

In a Tolstoyan way Šenoa introduced in this novel many characters: aristocrats, governors, senators, landed gentry, peasants, and women of various classes. Each is seen interacting with others, and each one is accounted for. The central figures are the unscrupulous Tahi and Uršula Henning, a female version of a tyrant. She fights to regain possession of lands Tahi stole from her and stops at nothing to marry off her numerous daughters to rich and powerful men. Here as in Šenoa's other works the protagonists are divided into good and evil. Currently such stereotypes are perceived as a

deterrent to Šenoa's work, albeit less so than some contemporary critics thought. Ironically, he was often attacked by the younger generation of writers whom he had taught to write.

The other two historical novels, *Kletva* and *Diogenes,* deal with Zagreb in the fourteenth and eighteenth centuries, respectively. With them Šenoa completed his saga about the people of Zagreb. *Kletva* shows the clash between townspeople and clergy, which was the beginning of a conflict between the secular and religious halves of Zagreb lasting for many centuries. Šenoa juxtaposes the bishop of Zagreb, Pavao Harvat, who curses the people's section of Zagreb (called Grič), to Živan Benković, the leader of the people and an epitome of human decency. In *Diogenes* that role is played by Antun Janković, a Croatian nobleman fighting utter decadence. This novel describes orgies in the governor's mansion, where power-hungry foreigners congregate. At the end of the novel Governor Baćani (also known as Batthyany), his Hungarian-born wife Tereza, and their entire retinue are outwitted by Janković, the Croatian Diogenes, and his party of righteous men.

With *Prosjak Luka,* focusing on life in nineteenth-century Croatia, Šenoa established himself as the father of the Croatian novel and ushered in Croatian realism. Considered to be his greatest literary achievement, this novel presents the psychology of a foundling whom society has turned into an outcast. Luka becomes a usurer engaging in power games with politicians and playing havoc with peasants to compensate for indignities suffered during his childhood. Like many such demons, he hopes to be redeemed by the love of a beautiful maiden. But when Mara rejects him, he is forever lost and commits suicide. In spite of such a melodramatic conclusion, this is a powerful work based on a real-life story.

Several of Šenoa's short stories were also based on real people he had met on different occasions. In "Barun Ivica" he portrays an illiterate peasant who lost his land to his mother's lover and became a city street sweeper. Similarly, Amalija Lenić Remetinska, the last descendant of an old aristocratic family in "Kanarinčeva ljubovca," becomes destitute because of a dishonest stepmother. Šenoa met this elderly and unattractive "canary's mistress" after she had applied for public aid. As could be expected, she died soon after the demise of her beloved bird. This enabled the writer to reveal the story she had told him as a token of her gratitude for his assistance. Šenoa deals here once more with the damaging effects of child neglect. Amalija's life, he clearly indicates, would have been quite different had anyone ever loved her the way she had loved her canary. Stories such as this one were not well received by the public. Their realism was too painful, but they earned Šenoa the honor of being called father of the Croatian short story. Scores of writers followed in his footsteps and further developed his themes.

In addition to dissipation and loss of property, a theme treated in "Barun Ivica," "Kanarinčeva ljubovca," "Ilijina oporuka," and "Vladimir," Šenoa also showed how thrift and industriousness result in prosperity. This is a parallel theme in "Ilijina oporuka." Šenoa's other subjects in his short stories and novellas include the plight of a country youth sent off to a foreign university in "Prijan Lovro"; the loss of national identity in "Karanfil s pjesnikova groba" and "Branka"; the degradation suffered by nontitled men in the company of nobles in "Mladi gospodin" and "Prijan Lovro"; the disappearance of old aristocratic families in "Vladimir" and "Kanarinčeva ljubovca"; and the struggle of a young female teacher to bring education to the country in "Branka." The protagonists of these stories come from all walks of life, but Šenoa is at his best when he depicts the "little man." The fates of the "humiliated and offended" in particular touched his heart so deeply that these characters often find unexpected rescuers. Hence a priest plays the lottery to win money for the needy in "Mladi gospodin," and a count marries Branka to endow her not only with love but with all his worldly goods so she can help her pupils. In the absence of such benefactors, however, a protagonist may have to take his own life, as in "Prijan Lovro," in which the hero sees no way out of debts incurred as a student.

Šenoa did not write to gain either wealth or fame. As he brought forth people from bygone epochs and his own times, he drew analogies between the past and the present. His main aim was to educate the people and raise their national consciousness. At the same time, he recorded Croatia's struggle against Italian, Austrian, and Hungarian domination, always giving his readers hope for a better future. All his works have one thing in common: the ease with which action flows through words. In passage after passage Šenoa showed that he was both creator and narrator. His literary artistry earned him a reputation as one of Croatia's most prominent writers. Present-day critics agree that time has only enhanced this image.

Letters:

Djela, volume 1 (Zagreb: Zora, 1951);

Sabrana djela, volume 20 (Zagreb: Znanje, 1964).

Bibliographies:

Olga Šojat, in Šenoa's *Djela,* volume 1 (Zagreb: Zora, 1951);

August Šenoa, *Sabrana djela,* volume 20 (Zagreb: Znanje, 1964);

Š. V., "Glavna izdanja djela Augusta Šenoe," in *August Šenoa,* volume 1 (Zagreb: Matica hrvatska, 1964), pp. 35–39.

Biographies:

Milan Šenoa, *Moj otac* (Zagreb: Matica hrvatska, 1933);

Antun Barac, "August Šenoa," in *August Šenoe,* volume 1 (Zagreb: Matica hrvatska, 1962), pp. 5–34;

Slavko Ježić, "August Šenoa," in Šenoa's *Sabrana djela* (Zagreb: Znanje, 1964), vol. 20, pp. 5–281;

Dubravko Jelčić, *August Šenoa njim samim* (Belgrade: Vuk Karadžić, 1966).

References:

Antun Barac, *August Šenoa, Studija* (Zagreb: Narodna knjižnica, 1926);

Barac, "Šenoa kao kritičar," in *Hrvatska književna kritika* (Zagreb, 1938);

Barac, "Šenoina *Seljačka buna,*" in *Savremeni problemi* (Zagreb: Matica hrvatska, 1950), pp. 284–298;

Tode Čolak, "August Šenoa," in *Portreti iz novije hrvatske književnosti* (Belgrade: Sloboda, 1967), I: 7–40;

Gisa Dippe, *August Šenoas historische Romane* (Munich: Otto Sagner, 1972);

Milan Durman, "Pedeset godina nakon Šenoine smrti," *Književnik,* 2 (1932): 31–33;

Aleksandar Flaker, "Šenoa i Turgenev," *Zbornik Radova Slavenskog instituta* (1956): 31–79;

Ivo Frangeš, "Gjalski prema Šenoi," *Forum,* 24 (1972): 345–376;

Frangeš, "Šenoina baština u hrvatskom realizmu," *Croatica,* 1 (1970): 137–166;

Frangeš, "Stogodišnjica *Zlatarova zlata,*" *Forum,* 22 (1972): 517–536;

Ante Franić, "August Šenoa – putopisac," *Zadarska revija,* 30 (March–June 1981): 115–130;

Krešimir Georgijević, "Šenoini pogledi na književnost," *Filologija,* 3 (1962): 65–89;

Janko Ibler, "Šenoine pripovijesti" and "Prvi hrvatski roman: *Zlatarovo Zlato* od Augusta Šenoe," in *Hrvatska književna kritika* (Zagreb: Matica hrvatska, 1961), vol. 2, pp. 43–77;

Dubravko Jelčić, *August Šenoa* (Belgrade: Savremena škola, 1964);

Jelčić, *Šenoa u očima kritike* (Zagreb: Globus, 1978);

Slavko Ježić, *Život i djelo Augusta Šenoe* (Zagreb: Znanje, 1964);

Otokar Keršovani, "O Šenoi," *Republika,* 3 (1945): 197–202;

Franjo Marković, *August Šenoa* (Zagreb: Matica hrvatska, 1892);

Antun Gustav Matoš, "August Šenoa," *Hrvatska smotra,* 11 (1907): 35–36;

Zdravko Mužinić, "Jedna od značajnih etapa hrvatske književnosti," *Mogućnosti,* 28 (November–December 1981): 1130–1134;

Milutin Cihlar Nehajev, "Čim da proslavimo Augusta Šenou?," *Hrvatska revija,* 10 (1929): 586–588, 590–592;

Milan Ogrizović, *Slava A. Šenoi 1881–1921* (Zagreb, 1922);

Duško Roksandić, "Hrvatsko narodno kazalište," *Republika,* 16, nos. 11–12 (1960): 1–10;

Miroslav Šicel, "August Šenoa kao kritičar hrvatske književnosti," *Radovi Zavoda za slavensku filologiju,* 17 (1983);

Zdenko Škreb, "August Šenoa," in his *Comparative Studies in Croatian Literature* (Zagreb: University of Zagreb, 1981), pp. 277–295;

Josip Eugen Tomić, "August Šenoa," *Vijenac,* 13 (1881): 818–820;

Milorad Živančević, "Šenoina vizija Slovenstva," *Savremenik,* 7 (1964).

Pencho Slaveykov

(27 April 1866 – 28 May 1912)

Charles A. Moser
George Washington University

BOOKS: *Momini sŭlzi* (Sofia: K. T. Kushlev, 1888);
Epicheski pesni, volume 1 (Plovdiv, Bulgaria: D. V. Manchov, 1896);
Epicheski pesni, volume 2 (Plovdiv, Bulgaria: Khristo G. Danov, 1898);
Sŭn za shtastie (Tutrakan, Bulgaria: Mavrodinov, 1906);
Epicheski pesni (1882–1907) (Sofia: Misŭl, 1907);
Na Ostrova na blazhennite: Antologiya (Sofia: A. Paskalev, 1910);
Kŭrvava pesen, chast I (Sofia: A. Paskalev, 1911);
Kŭrvava pesen, chast II (Sofia: A. Paskalev, 1911);
Sŭbrani sŭchineniya, 7 volumes, edited by Boyan Penev (Sofia: A. Paskalev, 1921–1926);
Sŭbrani sŭchineniya, 8 volumes, edited by Boris Delchev and others (Sofia: Bŭlgarski pisatel, 1958–1959);
Sŭchineniya, 2 volumes, edited by Angel Todorov and Delchev (Sofia: Bŭlgarski pisatel, 1966).

OTHER: *The Shade of the Balkans,* edited and translated by Slaveykov and Henry Bernard (London: D. Nutt, 1904);
Nemski poeti, edited and translated by Slaveykov (Sofia: A. Paskalev, 1911).

Pencho Slaveykov, scion of a historically prominent literary family, surely hoped to continue along both those lines but had little success in the literary sense and none in the historical. It is easy to confirm the latter, since he was never formally married and died without children. It is more difficult to be certain about the former. He did – along with the other members of the so-called *Misŭl* group – attempt to play a dominant role in the literary culture of his day, but the catastrophe of World War I in large measure severed the normal channels of literary influence, and his achievement had a lesser resonance in the ensuing generation than he expected it would. Still, in his day he was a guiding literary presence, a man who helped shape Bulgarian literary and artistic culture from about 1890 to 1912,

Pencho Slaveykov

down to the eve of the Balkan Wars and World War I.

The son of Petko Slaveykov, an outstanding figure of the Bulgarian Renaissance before the Liberation of 1878, Pencho Slaveykov was born in Tryavna, the youngest of four sons; he also had two sisters. After a period of home instruction he entered the local school in 1875, but his education was soon interrupted by the stormy events of 1876–1878: the April Uprising of 1876, which the Turks suppressed with great brutality, followed by the Russo-Turkish War of 1877–1878, which led to

Bulgaria's liberation after nearly five centuries of Turkish rule on 3 March 1878. The Slaveykov family was then in Stara Zagora, a city that directly witnessed the horrors of Turkish vengeance during this period. Afterward the family wandered about from town to town before settling in Sofia in the fall of 1879.

Even there the political situation was so unstable that in 1881 the Slaveykovs were obliged to remove to Plovdiv, then the capital of Eastern Rumelia, an area still under a form of Turkish rule. This exile was relatively brief, however, and before long the family returned to a house on a central square of Sofia. The square now bears their name.

During these years Slaveykov, whose life was inevitably affected by this series of disruptions, took a serious interest in literature, especially poetry. Ironically, his poor health helped – while young, he was ill for some three years and thereafter could not walk without a cane – for it gave him time for reflection and the cultivation of the then-fashionable pessimistic melancholy characteristic of such verse collections as Stoyan Mikhaylovski's *Suspiria de profundis* (1884).

Unlike most poets of his time, Slaveykov began not by publishing individual pieces in periodicals but with a small collection of verse, *Momini sŭlzi* (A Maiden's Tears, 1888), which included poems he had written in the preceding two years. The quality of his work in this collection was not such as to attract general attention, though.

After a brief period of collaboration on a literary review founded by Ivan Vazov, Slaveykov joined the ranks of contributors to Krŭstyo Krŭstev's journal *Misŭl* (Thought) when it was founded in 1892. Although any direct link with the journal was broken for a considerable time while he studied in Leipzig between 1892 and 1898 – he wrote a dissertation on Heinrich Heine's influence on Russian literature, a topic that combined two of his major interests – he and Krŭstev formed the core of what was generally called the *Misŭl* group. Later they were joined by Peyo Yavorov and Petko Todorov.

While he was still in Germany, Slaveykov's thoughts turned toward his native land, and he began work on the epic poem that claimed his attention off and on for the rest of his career: *Kŭrvava pesen* (Song of Blood), a heroic poetic narrative of the tragic April Uprising of 1876. In so doing, he took his cue from Vazov. In the early 1880s Vazov, feeling that the heroic exploits of the Bulgarians during the liberation were already being forgotten, had written a cycle of poems titled *Epopeya na*

zabravenite (Epic of the Forgotten), in which he exalted the heroes of the recent wars. He followed it with his first and finest novel, *Pod igoto* (Under the Yoke, 1889–1890), which also dealt with the events of the April uprising. No doubt stimulated by his literary rivalry with Vazov, Slaveykov evidently set out to write the "great Bulgarian epic poem." However, it did not appear until 1911, shortly before his death. He did not succeed in his ambition of eclipsing *Pod igoto*, which is now considered the classic Bulgarian novel, since *Kŭrvava pesen* is usually read only in excerpts.

The poem consists of nine cantos with a prologue. In the prologue the poet traces the origins of the poem to the stories and legends he had heard from his mother:

> A small child still, at my mother's knee,
> I would listen to tales and songs of the dreadful
> struggles, sufferings and dark destiny
> of my native land, from its first days, it seems,
> condemned to tears and bloody slavery
> by who knows whose high will.
> Then waking or sleeping, one after another
> pictures, images, and daydreams numberless
> would crowd, rebellious, into my consciousness
> and oppress my soul like some quite evil plague . . . [.]

The memory of the poet's happy childhood contrasts sharply with the history of bloody battles his people had endured, which form the subject of the epic poem. It is set in the fictitious town of Kamengrad and at Shipka, the pass at which Bulgarian volunteers in battle expunged much of the shame of Bulgarian acquiescence to Turkish rule. The Balkan Range, described in impressive verse, that sheltered the anti-Turkish rebels, broods over the human tragedy in the process of unfolding. There is a poetic apostrophe to Oborishte, the remote mountain spot where the revolutionaries met to decide the date of the uprising. The tone and atmosphere of the poem are heroic but distinctly tinged with tragedy: over the entire poem hangs the reader's knowledge that this effort will fail, but also that this failure is necessary for the ultimate liberation of Bulgaria.

Slaveykov's tendency to think in epic terms emerged in works of the 1890s that he called *Epicheski pesni* (Epic Songs), which were published in two volumes in 1896 and 1898 and later gathered in a single volume in 1907. In some of these works Slaveykov indirectly carried on the polemics that the *Misŭl* group had already begun to mount against Vazov and his allies.

There were several points at issue between the two camps. One involved the attitude to be taken toward contemporary modernist currents. Vazov resisted them in favor of the well-tested tenets of realism – Victor Hugo was one of his models – whereas the *Misŭl* group welcomed them, although it refused to accept the more extreme forms of symbolism that it spawned later. Another was the view of the native culture and its place in the international cultural sphere. The Vazov group sought to encourage national feeling and to play down the importance of international influences: among foreign cultures they favored the Russian, though they did not negate those of western Europe. The *Misŭl* group, though it also wished to promote Bulgarian national consciousness, sought to do so within an international cultural context and with an emphasis upon German culture (both Slaveykov and Krŭstev had been schooled in German aesthetic doctrine). They sought to be more intellectual and more self-consciously literary in their approach to writing, which helps to explain why *Kŭrvava pesen* was not especially successful. Over the course of several years around the turn of the century, the two sides exchanged many bitter attacks, each seeking to promote its own supporters at the expense of those in the other camp.

Works such as those contained in *Epicheski pesni* clearly display several of Slaveykov's cultural commitments. His aesthetic views, for example, come to the fore in "Frina," set in ancient Athens. The central character is the extraordinarily beautiful hetaera Frina, who offers a toast to the "goddess above all goddesses – Beauty!" When the mob becomes incensed against her for bringing down upon them the wrath of the gods and when the eloquence of her defender proves inadequate to calm the murderous crowd, Frina removes her robe and displays herself before them. The dazzled mob decides that such a "wondrous body" can only be a "divine revelation" and bears her off to the temple of Aphrodite. Thus does Slaveykov illustrate the power of beauty for good.

Other of Slaveykov's epic poems were more contemporary. The persona of "Cis Moll" (C Minor) is a dark-souled Ludwig van Beethoven embittered by the deafness with which he has been afflicted. Then, recalling that Homer was said to be blind, he accepts the inspiration of his divine sense of art and begins to play, creating unheard-of harmonies: "In the unstructured structure of this proud hymn / there trembled the breath of exalted peace – / the peace of a risen spirit." At the poem's conclusion Beethoven feels the assurance that he has brought the "Promethean fire" to light the "hearts of men" and that he will be "immortal among mortals."

The theme of the heart is prominent in "Sŭrtse na sŭrtsata" (Heart of Hearts), about Percy Bysshe Shelley. It opens with a fine description of the magnificent lake on which he will meet his death. Shelley declares that the heart must be an altar and that the poet must have an "exalted dream of light, / pure aspirations toward higher things, / and a proud, compelling thirst for the ideal" and even defends utopia as a haven for the ideal. Then he sets out across the water in the face of a furious storm and perishes in the deep. The poem ends with a description of the cremation of the poet's body on the shore, the recovery of his heart intact from the flames, and finally the poet's grave in Rome.

Nietzschean themes combine with Promethean ones in "Simfoniya na beznadezhnostta" (Symphony of Hopelessness), in which Prometheus bound plays a central role. Despite his eternal tortures, Prometheus affirms that he will never regret having "illuminated humanity's dark spirit / and its dark destiny in life. . . ." Similarly, modernist themes emerge in "Khimni za smŭrtta na svŭrkhchoveka" (Hymns on the Death of the Superman), which, as the poem's brief introduction says, is set in "the church of St. George in Sofia – originally a pagan shrine, then a Christian church, next a mosque, now deconsecrated but used for Christian services." The poem consists of a complex dialogue among several individual voices and a chorus that chants mystical songs of a religious nature.

By the time Slaveykov returned from his studies in Germany in 1898 he was a well-known writer though still in his early thirties. However, he could not support himself as a literary man and therefore obtained more-mundane employment – first as a teacher and then at the National Library, where he remained for several years. This position enabled him to develop good connections with foreign specialists in Bulgarian literature, including the Englishman Henry Bernard. In 1904 Slaveykov and Bernard published a collection of English translations of Bulgarian proverbs and folk songs titled *The Shade of the Balkans,* one of the earliest works on Bulgarian literature to appear in English.

Slaveykov also enjoyed the warmth of a family circle made up initially of his mother, an elder sister, and a niece. They were joined by another woman in 1903 when he began a liaison with a widow, Mara Belcheva, a poet of considerable talent.

In the middle of the decade Slaveykov worked on a collection of poems titled *Sŭn za shtastie* (Dream of Happiness), which appeared in 1906. This same year he published a long critical essay, "Bŭlgarskata poeziya predi i sega" (Bulgarian Poetry Past and Present), which included among other things an assessment of his own achievements and aspirations. His discussion of past poetry concentrated upon his father, Lyuben Karavelov, and Khristo Botev. Slaveykov paid generous tribute to Botev in particular, admiring the way his life coalesced with his extraordinary poetry, though he claimed that only schoolboys could take Botev's radical political ideas seriously now. Slaveykov might have included Vazov's poetry here, but instead he dismissed it in the section on contemporary poetry as "smooth and without substance ... tender so that it can be munched by toothless gums." He wrote a fair amount about himself, as well as several other contemporary poets, before concluding with a summation that says more about him than about anyone else:

> And if . . . the lives and deeds of our fathers were dedicated to the direct service of life, why our deeds and purposes are different, and more difficult; we are fighting for the soul of modern man, struggling to free his spirit and to implant within his consciousness a sense of *humanity* . . . [.]

Oddly for a writer who scarcely attempted drama as a genre, Slaveykov was interested in the theater and in 1908 received an appointment as director of the National Theater in Sofia. Although he remained in this position for less than a year before returning to the National Library, he was successful in accomplishing certain things on the basis of a clear and exalted vision of the theater's mission, which he set out in November 1909 in an article titled "Natsionalen teatŭr" (The National Theater).

Declaring near the outset that the theater is "one of our most powerful cultural instruments," Slaveykov began with a summary of the early Bulgarian theater from the mid nineteenth century and the history of contemporary playwriting, which was then largely in Vazov's hands. Slaveykov did not miss the opportunity to declare that Vazov's numerous plays were deficient in "language, thought, poetry, conception, composition, action," and even in "simple common sense." If the country lacked a native tradition at this point, the Bulgarians should, he held, turn to good translations of contemporary Western drama in the interim. In addition, since the theater should promote the development of the literary language, the artistic director of the theater

Drawing of Pencho Slaveykov

should be a Bulgarian and not a foreigner, as recent ones had been; and if the National Theater was to be subsidized, it should not be controlled by the state. Finally, Slaveykov argued, the name *Naroden teatŭr* (People's Theater) that it bore was misleading, since it implied light entertainment for the common people. It should instead be rechristened the *Natsionalen teatŭr* and made into a "higher cultural institution, a temple with a liturgy in the Bulgarian language through which we can manifest, in artistic forms and images, our creative powers and outlook on life." Although the theater that he directed still bears the name *Naroden teatŭr,* to a large degree the institution in later years did accomplish the cultural if not semireligious objectives that Slaveykov set for it.

One of Slaveykov's most original contributions to Bulgarian poetry was *Na Ostrova na blazhennite* (On the Isle of the Blessed, 1910), which purported to be an anthology of translations of verse by foreign authors; they were in fact invented. The idea for this collection went back nearly twenty years to the early *Misŭl* years. What emerged at the end was a collection of verses supposedly by writers with such exotic names as Stamen Rosita and Ralin Stubel, with each "author's" contribution prefaced by an appreciation. Through these essays Slaveykov expressed in indirect fashion certain criticisms of contemporary Bulgarian culture. But he was also capable of translating actual poets, as he demonstrated in 1911 with his anthology *Nemski poeti* (German Poets), and for many years he worked on a translation of Adam Mickiewicz's *Pan Tadeusz* (1834). He was also interested in Serbian and Ukrainian authors in addition to German, Russian, and Polish ones.

In 1911, having returned to the National Library some three years before, Slaveykov was dismissed when he came into conflict with an old political enemy who became the minister with jurisdiction over the library. Slaveykov was sent abroad on official travel for a time but then returned and, embittered, collected his resources to enter voluntary exile with his companion Belcheva. She was with him when he died on 28 May 1912 in Brunate, above Lake Como, and she recalled his last days in a moving memoir. His final, unclear word, as she records it, was "Light!" After he breathed his last, she wrote, "I open the curtains.... Outside the sun has set."

In 1921 Slaveykov's remains were returned to Sofia, and he was buried on a small hill where he had loved to sit. Every year on the anniversary of his death Krŭstev organized visits to his grave.

Perhaps Slaveykov was not entirely certain that ensuing generations would give him his due, and therefore he took the liberty of defining his cultural contribution in the poem "Pametnik" (Monument). In this short lyric the speaker sees a marble monument raised to him by future generations, an image of him with a hand upon the heart with which he had "sown the seed of love and beauty / for the future harvest." The last word is given to that new generation that will appreciate him fully:

> And I hear: Our mentor, you have raised
> The finest monument in all the world . . .
> You have raised your monument in all our hearts
> And attained the heights!

Letters:
Pencho Slaveykov, *Pisma do Mara Belcheva* (Sofia: Khemus, 1929).

Bibliography:
Elena Furnadzhieva, *Pencho Slaveykov: Bibliografiya* (Sofia: Narodna biblioteka, 1966).

Biography:
Pencho Slaveykov, P. K. Yavorov, P. Yu. Todorov v spomenite na sŭvremennitsite si (Sofia: Bŭlgarski pisatel, 1963).

References:
Georgi Konstantinov, *Pencho Slaveykov* (Sofia: Bŭlgarski pisatel, 1961);
Malcho Nikolov, *Pencho Slaveykov: Zhivot, lichnost i delo* (Sofia: Khemus, 1940);
Elena Panteleeva, *V poetichniya svyat na Pencho Slaveykov* (Sofia: Nauka i izkustvo, 1984);
Ivan Sarandev, *Pencho Slaveykov: Esteticheski i literaturno-kriticheski vŭzgledi* (Sofia: Bŭlgarski pisatel, 1977).

Borisav ("Bora") Stanković

(31 March 1876 – 22 October 1927)

Biljana Sljivic-Simsic
University of Illinois at Chicago

BOOKS: *Iz starog jevandjelja* (Belgrade: Radikalna štamparija, 1899);

Božji ljudi (Novi Sad: Braća Popović, 1902);

Koštana: Komad iz vranjskog života u četiri čina s pevanjem (Belgrade: Štamparija Petra Jockovića, 1902); translated by Aleksandar Nejgebauer as "Koštana," *Scena*, 7 (1984): 4–19;

Stari dani (Belgrade: Srpska književna zadruga, 1902);

Pokojnikova žena (Belgrade: Knjižarnica Bože O. Dačića, 1907); translated as "The Dead Man's Wife," in *Yugoslav Short Stories*, edited and translated by Svetozar Koljević (London & New York: Oxford University Press, 1966), pp. 96–129;

Nečista krv (Belgrade: Nova štamparija "Davidović," 1910); translated by Alec Brown as *Sophka* (London: Cape, 1932);

Dela Borisava Stankovića, 8 volumes (Belgrade: Odbor za izdavanje dela B.S., 1928–1930);

Pripovetke (Belgrade: Zadruga Profesorskog društva, 1939);

Sabrana dela, 2 volumes (Belgrade: Prosveta, 1956);

Izabrana dela (Belgrade: Narodna knjiga, 1958);

Izbor, edited by Predrag Palavestra (Sarajevo: Svjetlost, 1959);

Nečista krv, Koštana, Pripovetke, 2 volumes (Belgrade: Srpska književna zadruga / Novi Sad: Matica srpska, 1959);

U noći: Pripovetke, Koštana: Komad iz vranjskog života (Belgrade: Prosveta, 1968);

Sabrana dela Borisava Stankovića, 6 volumes (Belgrade: Prosveta, 1970);

Sabrana dela, 6 volumes (Belgrade: Prosveta, 1974);

Dela, 8 volumes (Belgrade: Svetozar Marković, 1983);

Sabrana dela, 7 volumes (Belgrade: Prosveta/BIGZ, 1987).

Editions in English: "Stanoja," translated by V. Dimitrijević in *Slavonic and East European Review*, 6 (1927–1928): 660–666; reprinted in *The Best European Short Stories of 1928*, edited by Richard Eaton (New York: Dodd, Mead, 1929), pp. 270–279; and in *Heart of Europe: An Anthology of Creative Writing in Europe, 1920–1940*, edited by Klaus Mann and Hermann Kesten (New York: Fischer, 1943), pp. 372–377;

"Nushka," translated by M. Stojović and A. T. Atherton, *South Slav Herald* (Belgrade), 23 February 1932, p. 4;

"Christmas Comes, After All," translated by Ernst Pawel in *The World's Greatest Christmas Stories*, edited by Eric Posselt (New York: Prentice-Hall, 1950), pp. 415–426;

"In the Night," translated by Dragan Milivojevic in *Introduction to Yugoslav Literature: An Anthology of Fiction and Poetry*, edited by Branko Mikasinovic, Milivojevic, and Vasa D. Mihailovich (New York: Twayne, 1973), pp. 146–156;

"Our Christmas," translated by Pawel in *American Srbobran*, 7 January 1977, pp. 2–3.

PLAY PRODUCTIONS: *Koštana*, Belgrade, National Theater, June 1900; revised version, Belgrade, National Theater, fall 1901;

Tašana, Belgrade, National Theater, 1 July 1927.

The literary opus of Borisav ("Bora") Stanković is not very large. It includes one finished novel, *Nečista krv* (Tainted Blood, 1910; translated as *Sophka*, 1932), and two unfinished ones, *Gazda Mladen* (Master Mladen, 1928) and *Pevci* (Singers, 1928), collected in *Dela Borisava Stankovića* (The Works of Borisav Stanković, 1928–1930); about forty short stories; and two plays, *Koštana* (produced 1900, 1901; published 1902; translated 1984) and *Tašana* (produced 1927, published 1928 in *Dela Borisava Stankovića*). The short stories range from very short ones, such as the character sketches in the collection *Božji ljudi* (God's Children, 1902), to several long ones, such as "Uvela ruža" (A Wilted Rose), "Jovča," and *Pokojnikova žena* (1907; translated as "The Dead Man's Wife," 1966) that could

Borisav Stanković

be classified as novellas. Stanković wrote his best works between 1898 and 1910. All of them are set in Vranje, his native town, located in southern Serbia. They deal with the life in Vranje in the decades that followed the 1878 liberation of southern Serbia from centuries-long Turkish occupation. This was also the period of Stanković's childhood and teenage years, during which the old-fashioned, Turkish way of life in Vranje underwent significant social and economic changes. Even though seemingly regional in character and tied to a specific and now-distant time, Stanković's best works have occupied one of the central places in Serbian literature for almost one hundred years. Their vitality is due to their universal appeal and modern narrative techniques, which transcend the local time and place and make the author's work a genuine and exciting discovery for every new generation of readers and literary scholars.

Stanković was born on 31 March 1876 into an artisan's family. His father, Stojan, was the only child of Ilija, a shoemaker who had come to Vranje from the nearby village of Kocur, and Zlata, who was the sister of a wealthy Vranje merchant named Jovča. The last two are described by Stanković in his stories "Tetka Zlata" (Auntie Zlata) and "Jovča." Ilija died soon after Stojan was born, and Zlata raised the boy alone. They fell upon hard times, especially when Zlata's second husband also died, but she still managed to provide Stojan with decent training so that, like his father, he became a good shoemaker. Stojan married Vaska, a daughter of prominent Vranje merchant Rista Grk. They soon had their first son, Borisav. The family was not lucky. Borisav's younger brother, Timothy, died as an infant, and by the time Borisav was seven he had lost both his father and his mother. His fraternal grandmother, Zlata, took it upon herself to raise her grandson just as she had once raised his father. With hard work — which she did secretly at home and often during the night so that people would not realize how poor they were — and with the help of friends and Borisav's maternal uncles and aunts, Zlata created a good home for her grandson. He grew up in it pampered and happy. In one of the rooms Zlata collected the valuable pieces of furniture and objets d'art from earlier, better times. They reminded both Borisav and her that their family had been once much better off and their life much more comfortable.

Treated by his grandmother as an only child and as the "man" of the family from an early age, Stanković grew up feeling that he was a special young man, and he expected such treatment from everyone. Life, however, was not generous to him. Extremely sensitive, a dreamer with a poetic soul, and proud, he suffered because of poverty and was easily hurt and offended by his friends, teachers, and people in general. In his high school years he began writing poetry and read it at the high school literary club meetings, where it was admired by his schoolmates. However, when most of his poems were rejected by editors of various literary magazines, he was devastated. He destroyed his entire collection and never wrote another verse again.

As a young man in Vranje he fell in love with a girl from the neighborhood with whom he grew up and whom he expected to marry. His dream about a happy life with her was never realized. His great love left him and married a richer man. Her rejection was a tragedy for the young and extremely vulnerable Stanković, and he never recovered from it. He would never forget his first love, and even though later, in Belgrade, he married another woman, Angelina Milutinović, and had three daughters with her, he never forgot his youth in Vranje and his broken dream, as seen in "Uvela ruža." His best characters all live through similar experiences as he transfers onto them his own regrets for his wasted youth and senseless life without his beloved.

Stanković always felt that he would have done better and been more successful were it not for the poverty in which he was raised. With such an attitude he had difficulties adjusting to adult life, especially when he left his native Vranje and went to Belgrade, where he was an unknown law-school student. Partly because he was heartbroken, devastated by his unhappy love affair, and in general nostalgic for Vranje, and partly because he had to work at demeaning jobs to pay for his room and board, he felt miserable and dejected in Belgrade. He did not want or try to cultivate friendships with people who could help him later in life. He thus remained a loner and never became a part of Belgrade society. After graduating from the Law School he entered civil service but was given mediocre, low-paying clerical jobs that bored him. Before World War I he worked as a customs official, a tax collector, an inspector of the state customs office in the Bajloni brewery, and an official in the Department of Religion and Church Affairs in the Ministry of Education.

Poverty and dissatisfaction followed Stanković throughout his life in Belgrade. Writing became his refuge from the bleak everyday life of a state employee. In his writings he could return to Vranje, to the old house where he was once happy, and to all those who were dear to him and whom he missed, as in "Jovča," *Pokojnikova žena,* "Tetka Zlata," and other stories. He could relive traditional, old-fashioned holiday celebrations in the company of his many relatives and friends, as in "Naš Božić" (translated as "Our Christmas," 1977) and "Stari dani" (Old Times). He could cry over his lonely life and deplore his broken dreams while writing his best fiction.

In 1915 he and his family left Belgrade before the advancing Austrian army. The family remained in the town of Kraljevo, but Stanković continued to retreat with the Serbian army via Niš to Montenegro. There he was imprisoned by the Austrians and interned in Derventa, Bosnia. He was eventually released with the intervention of Kosta Herman, the former editor of the journal *Nada* (Hope) in Sarajevo, who recognized him. Stanković returned to Belgrade, where he was reunited with his family. In 1920 he was appointed an official in the Department of Arts of the Ministry of Education, and he remained in this position until his death on 22 October 1927.

In Stanković's works there are many autobiographical elements, perhaps more than in the work of any other Serbian author. Even though he was only seventeen when he left Vranje, the Vranje of his childhood and adolescent years left upon him indelible impressions. It was his inspiration and refuge. However, Stanković is not a regional author: the old Vranje, masterfully described in his opus, is only the frame, the microcosm, in which are reflected tragic human destinies of universal interest. His most interesting characters are unfulfilled and unsatisfied men and women in some ways similar to him. Their lives are ruined and wasted because of unreasonable yet strict rules and norms of behavior imposed upon the individual by society. Regardless of their gender, all these characters are basically proud, handsome, strong-willed persons whose futures seem brighter than others'. But they are also endowed with strong sensuality. They usually fall passionately in love with the wrong people, and as a result they come into conflict with the established

Stanković's house, now a museum, in Vranje

social order and are forced to give in. Their pride and strong wills are broken, and from once-vibrant, happy, and hopeful people they become the living dead. Their lives and the lives of those around them are destroyed. Sometimes they beat and rape their wives, turn against their relatives, or abstain from sex for the rest of their lives. Sometimes, crushed under the burden of sorrow, they become demented. Whatever the outcome, their existences eventually become equally meaningless and equally empty. Stana and Koja in "Uvela ruža," Jovča and Stanoja from their eponymous stories, Mitke and Koštana from *Koštana,* Sofka from *Nečista krv,* and many others are among such highly sensual characters whose expectations and high hopes for a happy life remain unfulfilled and turn tragic.

The erotic is in general Stanković's strong point. He was the first Serbian author to introduce eroticism to Serbian literature and was a master of depicting with unmatched intensity highly erotic but never pornographic scenes from the lives of his characters. Stanković was also the first to describe in detail a woman's naked body, which was until then considered a taboo subject in Serbian literature. His women are luscious with soft white skin,

sensual eyes, and long black hair that "emanates sweet, sweet scent." They burn with sexual passion, and they are not ashamed. According to social norms they cannot be seen alone with men in public, but they like to tease them by the way they dress and move. They even look at and enjoy each other's bodies or, alone, abandon themselves to erotic fantasies.

In *Nečista krv* the scenes in which the protagonist, Sofka, a young, unmarried woman, marvels at her beautiful, voluptuous body are powerful. She dreams about a handsome, manly husband who will come, sweep her off her feet, and appreciate her feminine charms. Sofka's erotic fantasies overwhelm her. When she sees a retarded, mute young man in their garden, she lures him close to her and forces him to feel her breasts. When the retarded man, aroused by her closeness and encouragement, continues to grab at her breasts and other parts of her body, trying to conquer her, she keeps her cool and, in spite of her own highly erotic mood, does not succumb to the temptation. She will not betray the handsome bridegroom from her dreams. Ironically Sofka, once the most beautiful and richest girl in town, ends her life as a battered woman, abused by her husband both physically and emotionally. At the end of the novel she roams around her big house alone, withered and mostly drunk, surrounded only by her sickly children whom she despises because of their physical and mental disabilities. Her husband is rarely at home; when he is, he treats Sofka cruelly and with disgust. Her servants, all of whom she hired because they are deaf and mute, keep Sofka's desperate sexual exploits with them a deep secret.

In *Koštana* the protagonist is a young and beautiful Gypsy dancer whose beauty, singing, and erotic dancing in a local pub electrifies and polarizes the town. The men spend days and nights in the pub, mesmerized by the beautiful Koštana, including the young Stojan, the son of the most respectable citizen, Haji-Toma, who is one of the wealthiest men in Vranje. On the other hand, the mothers and wives desperately try to keep their men at home and to break the Gypsy's spell over them. Eventually even the old Haji-Toma succumbs to Koštana's charms, and the mayor of Vranje must intervene. Under a police guard Koštana, who is in love with Stojan, is ordered to marry one of her own kind from the neighboring Gypsy village. Her mother cries, "She is still too young to marry, . . . a child . . . , she just began to live . . . ," but the mayor is unmoved, and the cruel wedding robs Koštana of her right to be free to love whomever she chooses. It also brings despair to Stojan and allows the aging Mitke, one of the most memorable of Stanković's characters and the author's mouthpiece, to give Koštana bitter advice on life: "The Fates have come; they are going to take you to be married. . . . And everyone will be happy for you. The bridegroom will come and kiss you but you, you will be crying! The first night you'll cry, and the second one, and you'll cry all your life. . . . Your hands will become rough from housework, your face will lose its color, your eyes will dry out. . . . I know what's coming! Autumn is coming, Koštana, home, housework, my dear, then — only fog and graveyard. . . . That's what's coming. . . . Don't cry, for tears do not help. . . ."

The patriarchal family organization and its devastating effects on women's lives are also masterfully depicted in Stanković's works. Once married, usually by a contract between her father and the father of the groom, and not to the man she loves, the woman is left to the mercy of the husband. He expects her to serve him and be at his disposal. He yells at her, beats her, pulls her by her hair, and in their sexual encounters behaves more as an enemy than a lover, making her feel each time

as if she is being raped. She has no one to whom she can complain because she must pretend in front of others that her husband is a good and honorable man and that she is happy. That is what a decent woman is expected to do. Eventually she cries herself out in the secrecy of her room, her beauty disappears, her self-esteem is lost, and she becomes like a mouse, a shadow of herself, expecting death as liberation. Occasionally emotions, suppressed for a long time, explode, and the woman gives herself to beggars or retarded men since neither her husband nor anyone else seems to be interested in her. However, those desperate acts do not alleviate the woman's pain, because the moral punishment she suffers outweighs the misery that pushes her over the edge.

While recognizing his great literary talent, the critics in Stanković's time, influenced by the dominant school of criticism, unanimously attacked him for his allegedly careless style and disregard for syntax. They pointed out his many broken and unfinished sentences as major proof of his negligence in writing. They also criticized his ability to compose a novel or a play because he did not develop his plot in proper chronological order and because his plays were written without any regard for classical forms. These attacks somewhat lessened Stanković's literary stature among his contemporaries, contributed to his ill feelings toward the Belgrade literary elite, and created a myth about him as a lazy man neglectful of his literary expression. This myth persisted in Serbian literary scholarship until well after World War II. Only in the last two or three decades have literary scholars in Serbia succeeded in dispelling it and in establishing Stanković as one of the great, courageous innovators in modern Serbian literature, both in form and in content. Critics now understand that his broken and unfinished sentences with their unexpected word order, sometimes overly emphatic and sometimes desperately twisted, represent the first internal monologues in Serbian literature. They perfectly correspond to the intensity of emotions the author describes and to his characters' subdued but painful inner conflicts and the often violent outbursts of their long-compressed frustrations.

Stanković was brave enough to break the established literary norms of his times and to introduce to Serbian literature not only a new milieu and new characters but also modern patterns of literary expression. Seemingly a weak man who lived as a loner in relative poverty on the fringes of Belgrade society in the early twentieth century, Stanković has finally emerged as a truly great writer and as a brave and defiant artist. He believed in his talent and preferred to remain true to himself and to his concept of literary art rather than to conform to the literary authorities and prescribed literary norms. Time has proven him right.

Bibliographies:

Ž. P. Jovanović, "Bibliografska gradja o Borisavu Stankoviću," *Književnost,* 6 (1951): 671–681;

D. Vlatković and G. Dobrašinović, "Prilog bibliografiji radova o Borisavu Stankoviću," *Letopis Matice srpske,* 379, nos. 1–6 (1957): 79–83, 187–190, 288–291, 409–412, 540–543, 660–665;

Rista Simonović, *Borisav Stanković i njegovo književno delo: Bibliografija objavljenih radova, članaka i knjiga,* 4 volumes (Vranje, Yugoslavia: Državni arhiv, 1966);

Ružica Milikić-Stojković, "Bibliografski pregled dela Borisava Stankovića," in Stanković's *Sabrana dela Borisava Stankovića,* volume 6 (Belgrade: Prosveta, 1970), pp. 315–362.

References:

Milan Bogdanović, "Realizam Borisava Stankovića," in his *Stari i novi,* volume 1 (Belgrade: Prosveta, 1961), pp. 276–306;

Milan Dedinac, "*Koštana* na beogradskoj sceni," in his *Pozorišne hronike* (Belgrade, 1950), pp. 105–114;

Delo Bore Stankovića u svome i današnjem vremenu (Belgrade: Medjunarodni slavistički centar, 1978);

Jovan Dučić, "Borisav Stanković," in his *Sabrana djela,* volume 4 (Sarajevo: Svjetlost, 1969), pp. 71–98;

Vuk Filipović, *Svet detinjstva u delu Bore Stankovića* (Priština, Yugoslavia: Zajednica naučnih ustanova Kosova i Metohije, 1968);

Velibor Gligorić, "Bora Stanković," in his *Srpski realisti* (Belgrade: Prosveta, 1954), pp. 380–405;

Edward D. Goy, "The Play *Tašana* by Borisav Stanković," *Serbian Studies,* 4 (Fall 1988): 22–33;

Vladimir Jovičić, *Umetnost Bore Stankovića* (Belgrade: Srpska književna zadruga, 1972);

Predrag Kostić, *Bora Stanković* (Belgrade: Nolit, 1956);

Petar Marjanović, "Borisav Stanković: 'Koštana' (1900)," *Scena,* 7 (1984): 19–24;

Boško Novaković, *Sintetička priroda proze Borisava Stankovića* (Kruševac, Yugoslavia: Bagdala, 1970);

Predrag Palavestra, Preface to Stanković's *Nečista krv* (Belgrade: Branko Djonović, 1962), pp. 5–12;

Jaša Prodanović, "Bora Stanković," in his *Naši i strani* (Belgrade: Srpska književna zadruga, 1924), pp. 1–35;

Jovan Skerlić, "Bora Stanković," in his *Pisci i knjige,* volume 3 (Belgrade: Prosveta, 1955), pp. 167–181;

Miodrag Stajić, "Književno delo Borisava Stankovića," *Srpski književni glasnik,* 53 (1938): 340–347, 409–433, 510–522, 588–598;

Dragoljub Vlatković, "Hronologija važnijih dogadjaja iz života i stvaralaštva Borisava Stankovića," in Stanković's *Sabrana dela Borisava Stankovića,* pp. 293–313.

Ivan Tavčar
(28 August 1851 – 19 February 1923)

Timothy Pogacar
Bowling Green State University

BOOKS: *Zimski večeri: Zbirka novelic* (Ljubljana: Narodna tiskarna, 1880);

Povesti, 5 volumes (Ljubljana: Ig. pl. Kleinmayr and Fed. Bamberg, 1896–1902);

Drja Ivana Tavčarja zbrani spisi, 6 volumes, edited by Ivan Prijatelj (Ljubljana: Tiskovna zadruga, 1921–1932);

Visoška kronika (Gorica, Slovenia: Goriška Mohorjeva družba, 1931);

Cvetje v jeseni (Ljubljana: Knjigarna Tiskovne zadruge, 1944);

Med gorami: Slike iz Loškega pogorja, edited by Marja Boršnik (Ljubljana: Državna založba, 1947);

Zbrano delo, 8 volumes, edited by Boršnik (Ljubljana: Državna založba, 1951–1959);

V Zali (Ljubljana: Prešernova družba, 1963);

Izbrano delo, 3 volumes, edited by Franček Bohanec (Ljubljana: Mladinska knjiga, 1963);

Izza kongresa (Ljubljana: Mladinska knjiga, 1979).

Ivan Tavčar

Ivan Tavčar was born on 28 August 1851 in the village of Poljane, located in a scenic farming valley near the medieval town of Škofja Loka in the province of Carniola. This region of steep hills dominated by Mount Blegoš is the setting for most of Tavčar's works and the vivifying source of his worldview. For although Tavčar the lawyer and politician became thoroughly urbanized, he sustained the juxtaposition of city and village, civilized and natural worlds, throughout his career as a writer. The surname Tavčar is possibly linked to the neighboring, more rustic Davča region, which was settled by Bavarians in the seventeenth century and is thus a fitting attribute for a person at the center of Slovene-Germanic relations for most of his adult life.

His first eight years in the poor peasant home of Janez and Neža Perko Tavčar were arduous. Although the household was peaceful, he and his seven younger siblings were poorly clad and subsisted on humble fare while working on their father's three hectares and enjoying outdoor play. Tavčar remained an avid fisherman all his life.

Tavčar's life changed at age nine when, thanks to the help of his twin paternal uncles, both Roman Catholic priests, he left the village school and enrolled in the Saint Aloysius primary school in Ljubljana. In the fourth grade, in 1867, he transferred for two years to the Franciscan school in Novo Mesto in southern Carniola because of a curfew violation he committed when he visited the suburban mansion belonging to an industrialist whose daughter he adulated. This slightly older girl,

Emilija Garz Terpinc, elicited the anguished feelings of adolescent love that became the subject of Tavčar's youthful, unnoteworthy poetry and his early works of fiction. He probably met her through one of his uncles, who visited the Terpinc mansion just outside the city. Emilija's marriage the same year to a wealthy German weighed heavily on Tavčar; her memory occupied him until well after her untimely death in 1884.

Anti-German sentiment was running high in Novo Mesto, so it is not surprising that Tavčar's Slovene nationalist opinions took shape at this time. In 1867 there were also liberal political, judicial, and educational reforms, which were opposed by the Catholic hierarchy. Tavčar's vehement opposition to ecclesiastical involvement in politics also formed at this point. However, political concerns did not yet appear in his writing. One of his first publications, part of an early story titled "Primola" that appeared in *Slavjanski jug*, a short-lived attempt at a common South Slavic literary newspaper, in 1868, initiates the recurrent theme of an educated son's return to his native village.

Tavčar completed his final years of high school in Ljubljana (1868–1871), where his interest in politics and German-Slovene relations intensified. A combination of one-year voluntary military service, writing, and scholarships provided support for law studies in Vienna between 1871 and 1874. Tavčar was a member of the Slovenija club while in the capital but felt progressively more isolated in the large city. His austere living conditions did nothing to improve his mood, and, not being of a truly scholarly bent, Vienna's greater intellectual opportunities offered him little recompense for removal from his homeland and its developing political life. However, during this period Tavčar's acquaintance with European literature grew – primarily German-language (Johann Wolfgang von Goethe, Robert Hamerling, Heinrich Heine, Friedrich von Schiller, Theodor Storm, and others), Russian (Aleksandr Pushkin, Nikolay Gogol, Mikhail Lermontov), ancient (Aeschylus, Plato, Sophocles, Thucydides), Victor Hugo, and William Shakespeare – and his thinking on society and culture deepened. Historians Henry T. Buckle and Wiljem Draper were the greatest influences on Tavčar's historical thinking. Law school was made more difficult because his parents did not support his course of study, preferring instead to see him enter religious life. Tavčar vacationed at home at his uncle's rectory near Novo Mesto during his Vienna years.

With the completion of law school in 1875 Tavčar's formative creative period came to a close.

By then he had published several beginning works reflecting his personal preoccupations – primarily romantic and social – and the type of reading he had been doing, including poetry and a novel, *Zorin* (1870) by the Slovene professor and critic Josip Stritar. The early works can be used, as have Tavčar scholars Branko Berčič and Marja Boršnik, to describe his personal concerns in the late 1860s and early 1870s. For example, his complete published story, "Gospa Amalija" (Madam Amalija, 1875), published in the journal *Zora,* is set in the native village of a narrator who idolizes a young noblewoman who befriends him and teaches him to ride. The woman construes the death of the narrator's younger sister as a premonition of her own impending end, which she soon meets while out riding. Her castle later becomes the focal point of the narrator's sentimental ponderings. In this story and its earlier variants dating to the Novo Mesto years Tavčar relates his infatuation with cultivated women; a yearning for his mother, who is closely associated with his home village; and a fatalistic view of love and life. Boršnik sees in the story a direct reaction to his removal to Novo Mesto, but the motifs are replicated in stories Tavčar later wrote in Vienna. France Bernik summarizes Tavčar's stories during this period as direct expressions of the way he linked women in general with life's tragedies. This view is certainly borne out by the longest story of the period, "Ivan Slavelj" (1876), which, in addition to descriptions of the home village, aristocratic and peasant life, and violent acts instigated by amorous relationships, includes a parody of some Pan-Slavists discussing the Slovene peasantry instead of involving themselves in politics. The last scene is Tavčar's reaction to his older colleagues in Vienna.

Love, weakness, and death are sentimentally linked in other stories. Infirmity brought on by distant admiration is the subject of an old man's reminiscences in the story "Nasproti stari palači" (Opposite an Old Palace, 1874), published in *Zora;* a frail noblewoman is once again the peasant student's object of desire. "Bolna ljubezen" (Sick Love), published in *Zora* the same year, consists of letters to home from a Slovene student in Vienna whose erotic interests in the daughter of a rich German vie with his effusive statements of love for his homeland and deceased mother. When the Viennese woman offers to give herself to him and go to his home, he refuses. The *Slovenski narod* sketch "Margareta" (1875), in contrast, points to later developments in Tavčar's prose. The narrator in this case has, through years of city life, lost touch with nature and love, both of which he rediscovers through a childhood girlfriend. Margareta preserves the essence of childhood for him until she dies in his arms on one of his visits home. "Margareta" is an early example of Tavčar's masterful portrayal of the inhabitants of the hill country around Škofja Loka, although the narrator's subjective world is the true focus here.

In these early works the narrator's ethnic awareness and social origins are pronounced, as might be expected in the case of a young writer who felt himself cut off, even exiled, from home in an alien culture. He found refuge in idealizing his native land, friendship, and love. Counterposed subjective ideals, especially the absolute ideal of love, imbued the spirit of the writer's works from even these earliest, artistically weak examples. As Tavčar matured, his idealization of love was increasingly at odds with his more realistic depiction of the world around him. How Tavčar conceived of love's force in human life at this age can be seen in his association of love with a series of natural motifs, some of them bordering on the violent, that occur throughout his works: flowing water, wind, falling trees, and fleet animals. Thus symbolized, human love becomes an uncontrollable force and thus a part of human fate. On the other hand, the quiet, contemplative scene in nature, which relates to love of the land, is another constant in Tavčar's works. Linking the two sets of imagery is the observer's passivity before the dual vital forces in life, human love and love of the land.

The passive stance his protagonists strike contrasts with Tavčar's well-known public demeanor, particularly in political life. Following the completion of his exams in Vienna, Tavčar was apprenticed to a lawyer in Ljubljana for two years. He was active in a nationalist society, Narodno društvo, a literary club that counted the early realist writers Janko Kersnik and Josip Jurčič among its members, and was secretary of the Drama Society. But, as in Vienna, his ardor for involvement in civic groups did not last long. The developing split between so-called *mladoslovenci* (Young Slovenes) and their older Slovene-minded compatriots in the liberal camp reinforced Tavčar's radical nationalist attitudes, which had already distinguished him from senior students in Vienna. From 1877 to 1880 he worked in the law office of the writer Janez Mencinger in Kranj, not far north of Ljubljana. He served in law offices in Ljubljana for three more years before being licensed to practice in 1883. The following year he opened his own office in Ljubljana, embarking upon a legal career that lasted until his death.

Tavčar gained a reputation as an engaging public speaker in his late twenties and began writing for the newspaper *Slovenski narod* (The Slovene People). His editorials and feuilletons revealed a combative, humorous, and proud nature. For example, the sketch "Birokrat" (The Bureaucrat, 1879) caricatures the upbringing and career of a typical civil servant who is taught to have no truck with Slovenes' "crazy peasant noggins." "V Postojno" (To Postojna, 1881) is a short travel sketch lampooning the author's visit to the thoroughly Germanized town well known for its caverns. Criticism of German cultural predominance in Carniola at the time amounted to opposing government policy as well as the foibles of ethnic Slovenes who aspired to social superiority in urban life.

In the 1880s Tavčar became active in literary journalism and in politics as a leader of the Liberal party. From 1881 to 1884 he was an editor and copublisher of the liberal journal *Ljubljanski zvon* (Ljubljana's Bell). In the spring of 1881 he saw to it that Stritar, the writer and critic he so admired in his younger days, was not offered part ownership: Stritar's pessimistic writing was now a thing of Tavčar's past, and Tavčar saw no reason to share the journal's prestige and income with the older writer. Soon Tavčar also distanced himself from the other two editors, Kersnik and Fran Levec, who were members of the more moderate wing of the Liberal party. However, Tavčar's own reputation as a pro-Slovene radical was compromised by a circular to the Roman Catholic clergy during his unsuccessful candidacy for the provincial parliament, in which he declared that radicalism was dead. The 1883 letter understandably angered other liberals. Another odd action in 1883 was Tavčar's courtship of Baron Andrej Winkler's daughter. Winkler was the first ethnic Slovene to head the Carniolan government, but he was also one of the moderate liberals whom Tavčar so vehemently opposed.

Although 1883 and 1884 were unsettled years in Tavčar's political, professional, and personal life, the early 1880s were among Tavčar's most productive as a writer. A full-length novella titled "Otok in Struga," the names of two castles on the Krka River in southern Carniola, appeared in *Ljubljanski zvon* in 1881. Seven of the twelve stories in the *Med gorami* cycle (In the Mountains, 1876–1888) were published by 1882, including the controversial "Tržačan" (The Boy from Trieste, 1882). Also, Tavčar began seriously working in historical fiction. In this period he abandoned ethereal female characters, who would nevertheless long remain a liability in fencing with his literary and political ad-

Tavčar as a student (photograph in Loški Museum in Škofja Loka)

versaries. As a new writer on the scene when a middle-class Slovene reading public was taking shape, however, Tavčar took advantage of the inherent appeal such characters possessed.

"Otok in Struga," which he began in the mid 1870s, still displays the social and romantic characteristics of his early works in its tale of two lovers from feuding noble families. "Mrtva srca" (Dead Hearts, 1884), published in *Ljubljanski zvon,* treats the enmity of two families, whose shared illicit offspring is one of the protagonists, more philosophically. Each of the main characters makes his or her way in commerce or marriage; the bishop is also corrupted. Only the unstable dreamer and son of both families professes earnest love (of his people and half sister), condemning the entire materialistic age as one of "dead hearts." His principle of renunciation surfaces only much later in Tavčar's works, in his final novel, *Visoška kronika* (The Visoko Chronicle, 1931; first published in *Ljubljanski zvon,* 1919).

Tavčar's stories with historical settings substitute a colorful past for the upper-class milieu of his earlier works and, consonant with the direction established by "Mrtva srca," probe the meaning of contemporary life. "Vita vitae meae" (My Dearest, 1883), published in *Ljubljanski zvon,* coincides with a trip by the fictitious late-sixteenth-century bishop of Ljubljana, Joannes Tavčar, up the Poljanska valley. Two men in the story, Carolus and Jurij Kosem (the nickname of Tavčar's father) — one a Catholic seminarian, the other a persecuted Protestant preacher — speak to the subject of the title. Carolus espouses romantic and mystical love, united in the figure of Mary, as the essence of life. His brother, who is among the group of Protestants that wound Carolus when he returns to his village at night, finds peace in God's word — the translated Bible — and the rejection of all religious and political ideology. The bishop's men once attempted to drown Jurij, Bible in hand, but he retrieved the sacred book and saved himself. In the story's climax Carolus drowns himself when falsely informed that his mother was a Protestant. The narrator concludes, "Blessed is he who is given to die with conscience consoled, for death is indeed the life of our life." With this story

Tavčar found a way to excite reader interest by means of historical color and action while considering universal human issues, not least among them the sacrifice of human life to ideological conflict.

His second major work of historical fiction, "Janez Sonce" (1885–1886), appeared in the journal *Slovan,* which Tavčar founded along with his political ally and the mayor of Ljubljana, Ivan Hribar, after leaving *Ljubljanski zvon.* The 175-page novella demonstrates how well Tavčar was able to combine the expression of intimate concerns and commentary on current politics in an entertaining story line, loosely based on events in the life of Janez Sonce in the first four decades of the seventeenth century. Tavčar knew of Sonce from the first Slovene historian, Janez Vajkard Valvasor, and other sources, but he transferred the events to 1660, the year of the emperor's visit to Ljubljana, in order to form a parallel with Franz Josef's visit in 1883. He likewise took political advantage of Sonce's conflict with the governor and weak estates, who strip him of his knighthood for having dueled the emperor's designate. But as Boršnik points out, such cloaked jibes by Tavčar were more personal than political in nature. On a personal level, Sonce's marriage to a much younger burgher resembled Tavčar's courtship of nineteen-year-old Franica Košenini, whom he married in May 1887. Sonce's defense of his honor reflected Tavčar's own along with his great fear that he might fail in his courtship.

Tavčar's marriage at age thirty-five took place twenty years after that of Emilija, his first love, and became the next most significant event in his life after his departure from Poljane as a peasant boy. Now he quickly ascended the social ladder, changing from the radical popular speaker who had impressed Ivan Cankar in 1882 into one of Ljubljana's first citizens. A month after the wedding Tavčar purchased a large two-story house on the Ljubljanica River. In 1884 he was elected to the city council. In 1887 he became chairman of the Drama Society, and in 1888 he was elected chairman of the national publishing house. Its purchase of *Ljubljanski zvon* led to Tavčar's again editing the journal (1891–1894) and publishing in it his own sharp satire of clerical extremists, "4000" (1891).

Tavčar's public jousting with clergymen, who especially disapproved of his erotic subjects, possessed both literary and political importance in the 1880s. Tavčar sought to defend the autonomy of literature from ideological oversight – which is not to say that it could not be used to express liberal political points of view, about individual rights and the condition of the peasantry, for example. However,

as shown by his treatment of the Protestant characters in "Vita vitae meae," he deeply mistrusted dogmatism. The issue for Tavčar was not the portrayal of amorous relationships but the danger that social strictures pose to human freedom and the fundamental expression of freedom, human love. The political aspect of the clerical attacks on Tavčar's works, led by the Gorizian educator Anton Mahnič, proved more threatening in the long run because the clergy's growing role in party politics eventually undermined the liberals' support in rural areas. Tavčar was a believer, and he sympathized with what he saw as the old-style clergy who shared their parishioners' hardships, even if they were frequently in conflict, and presented a common front with them to higher authority. The modern clergy, according to Tavčar, concerned itself with matters outside of its province, such as politics. The satire "4000," described in the subtitle as a story from future ages fitting to the time, depicts the clerical hegemony that results in the burning of books – Francè Prešeren's poetry – and of people for suggesting an end to the rule of celibacy and for having erotic thoughts. Scholarship and technology are disdained in the Latin-speaking Catholic province; the inhabitants live according to the decrees of the papal administrator, in which Mahnič is satirized. The entire work is cast as a travelogue, with Tavčar disguising his resurrected self as a Siberian pilgrim. The travelogue traditionally served as a form of protest in nineteenth-century Slovene literature, which underlined the literary aspect of Tavčar's satire.

However, Tavčar's most significant literary achievement to this point was his completion of the *Med gorami* cycle. The remainder of the cycle depicting life in the Poljane valley appeared from 1887 to 1888 in *Zova, Ljubljanski zvon,* and *Sloven.* The twelve sketches vary in length from approximately five to thirteen pages. They are notable for their narrative balance, masterful use of peasant speech, and realistic description of characters and nature. The reserve that the narrators maintain belies the characters' extreme motivations. The story that elicited the most public attention was "Tržačan," which recounts how a disfigured man finally finds a wife and adopts a boy from Trieste. However, after the couple has their own child, the father begins beating the boy and depriving him of food, eventually causing his death on the same day that the father is trounced by a neighbor. The adult narrator's expert handling of his childhood recollection comes out in biblical parallels and a mixture of speech styles. The public could not accept the realistic possibility of such behavior, the less so because of the austere, powerful

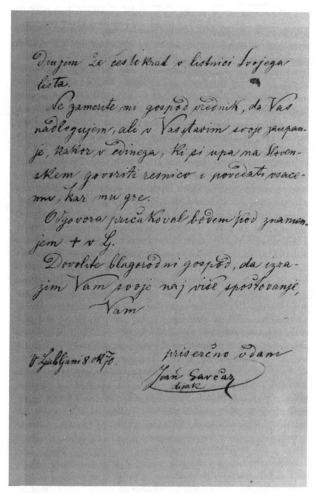

Letter from Tavčar to Zvon (Bell) editor Josip Stritar, 8 October 1870 (manuscript department, People's and University Library, Ljubljana)

manner in which Tavčar described it. In fact, the only implausible point is that the father does little to conceal the family's mistreatment of the boy.

Meta in "Šarevčeva sliva" (Šarevč's Plum Tree, 1887) is motivated by greed and fear to bury the dowry her father left her and to save money from the abundant yield of her plum tree. When she cannot locate the buried gold after a storm, she decides that she has been robbed and then cuts down her plum tree to prevent its theft. The next day the neighbors find her beneath the fallen tree, and the narrator concludes that she did indeed save herself from penury, though her life was poor.

Tavčar's sketches of village life are artistically unique but part of a larger corpus of village stories that reached a peak in production during the 1870s and 1880s. They differ from his early prose about the village in that they tell of ordinary characters with extreme motivations rather than about odd types, as in earlier stories. In scope and themes, Tavčar's sketches differ from longer examples of

Slovene prose about village life written roughly between 1900 and 1940.

Tavčar returned to his native valley in 1893 when, with the help of his wife's aunt, he purchased the manor of Visoko, not too distant from Poljane. Boršnik believes that the decision to buy Visoko was prompted by a challenge to his professional integrity in the same year he married and that this serious event embittered him against his professional colleagues and city life in general. In any event, Visoko became a place of rest for the writer and his family for the remainder of his life. Many of Tavčar's papers were lost from Visoko during World War II. A statue of the writer now stands on the grounds, but the house itself awaits restoration.

The Liberal party entered a steady decline in the late 1890s due to the growing might of the Catholic People's party. The latter's increase was a reflection of the church's more active role in European politics under Pope Leo XIII, but the Slovene bishops were less enlightened than their colleagues abroad. The Liberals' choice of the German party and German capital as allies against the Catholic party and young social democrats proved to be a fatal mistake, although the Liberal-German coalition held sway in the parliament from 1896 to 1908. The towns and the upper class remained the Liberals' base while their support in the countryside eroded. Election reform in 1908 led to an absolute majority for the Catholic party. While Tavčar's national influence waned, he continued to serve in the provincial parliament (1908–1912), was a Carniolan representative in Vienna (1901–1906), and was elected mayor of Ljubljana (1911–1921). He performed his mayoral duties well, especially during the difficult years of World War I. His faithfulness to the Hapsburgs – he could not conceive of an alternative for the Slovene provinces – was practically justified during the war. When younger politicians engineered the formation of Yugoslavia, Tavčar still had a role in Slovene government, as director of food supplies. He served only briefly as an elected representative to the constitutional negotiations in Belgrade in 1920, returning home because of his deteriorating health. Tavčar's impressions of the assembly in the 1921 essay "Beogradu" (In Belgrade), published in *Slovenski narod,* reveal his enthusiasm for the new country and admiration for the Serbian nation and their political leaders. At the end of the twentieth century, however, the legacy of Tavčar's Liberal party at its height in the 1880s proved stronger than the intervening experiments of Yugoslavism and social democracy, to which Tavčar was bitterly opposed.

In the last two decades of his life Tavčar published his three longest works: *Izza kongresa* (Concealed at the Congress, 1979; first published in *Ljubljanski zvon,* 1905–1908), *Cvetje v jeseni* (Flowers in Autumn, 1944; first published in *Ljubljanski zvon,* 1917), and *Visoška kronika. Izza kongresa* describes social and personal events surrounding the 1821 meeting of the Holy Alliance in Ljubljana. The colorful novel was intended to appeal to popular reading tastes, but it also provides topical commentary on Ljubljana society and politics. Metternich is the central character; his love for a young Slovene noblewoman receives more attention than the monarchs' flirtation with local women. The work stands alone in the least productive years of Tavčar's literary life and is of a kind with his feuilletons and perhaps the satire "4000." Its publication corresponded to the decline in Tavčar's political fortunes and his open conflict with modernist writers such as Ivan Cankar, who was also active in the social democratic opposition.

Tavčar's antipathy toward Cankar was due to unfortunate misunderstandings as well as political differences and envy of Cankar's literary acclaim. (Tavčar had personally supported many young writers, including Cankar, opening his Ljubljana house to them.) Following *Izza kongresa* Tavčar was thought to be finished as a writer.

The appearance of the idyllic yet sober *Cvetje v jeseni,* a frame novel set once again in the Poljane highlands, was thus a notable event in Slovene literature. The author-lawyer as narrator relates the tale of his "pure love" for a peasant who dies after he buys a farm by her village and before their marriage can take place. He doubts that his listeners in the frame, a group of city women, can comprehend such great love. The novel also includes a peasant love story and the tale of a feud between two families that is similar to the stories in the *Med gorami* cycle, except here Tavčar glorifies the Slovene peasant, in particular the woman, whose spirit triumphs in spite of trying circumstances and base human motivations.

Visoška kronika remains one of the most well-wrought Slovene novels, despite being only the first part of a projected trilogy about the rich Kalan peasant family beginning in the early seventeenth century. The main character, Izidor Kalan, suffers from his blind faith in authority, both paternal and ecclesiastical, and the related personal flaws of passivity and belief in fate. In the compact space of two hundred pages he chronicles his own coming to terms with his failings, which nearly result in the execution by drowning of his beloved Agata, who is accused of witchcraft after Izidor brings her to Visoko in order to right one of his father's wrongs in the Thirty Years' War. After Agata's trial by water in Škofja Loka, Izidor renounces Visoko, and his brother Jurij marries her. Izidor joins the army and returns years later, cleansed by the renunciation of material wealth and the sufferings of war, to live out his life. Agata and Jurij, however, press him into marriage to his first love, Margareta, who now lives with them. (Izidor's courtship of Margareta was broken off by his father in connection with the need to entitle Agata to her share of Visoko.) Their son adds an epilogue to the novel that relates his father's and uncle's deaths and his own calling to the priesthood. *Visoška kronika* is Tavčar's most psychologically profound work. It displays the writer's masterful compositional skills in the careful arrangement of events, his vivid characterization through dialogue and setting, and his occasionally lusty, occasionally acid humor. The novel has traditionally been considered a historical work for young readers but deserves more careful critical attention, as Marjan Kramberger's book devoted to it demonstrates.

Perhaps because of his politics Tavčar has not been accorded the critical attention that he deserves. In addition, the excitement of the modernist movement in Slovene literature served to render his last two novels almost anachronistic. While he had aided young modernist writers, he resented their success; this resentment may have waned only in his last two years.

Interview:
Izidor Cankar, *Obiski* (Ljubljana: Nova založba, 1920).

Biographies:
Branko Berčič, *Mladost Ivana Tavčarja* (Ljubljana: Slovenska matica, 1971);
Franček Bohanec, *Ivan Tavčar* (Ljubljana: Partizanska knjiga, 1985).

References:
France Bernik, "Erotika v nekaterih Tavčarjevih proznih delih," *Slavistična revija,* 22, no. 1 (1974): 41–53;
Marja Boršnik, *Ivan Tavčar, leposlovni ustvarjalec* (Maribor: Obzorja, 1973);
Boršnik, "Prijatelj in Tavčar," in *Prijateljev zbornik,* edited by Stefan Barbarič (Ljubljana: Slovenska matica, 1975);
Miran Hladnik, "Slovenski ženski roman v 19. stoletju," *Slavistična revija,* 29 (1981): 259–296;

Matjaž Kmecl, "Okvirna pripoved pri Tavčarju," in Tavčar's *V Zali: Cvetje v jeseni* (Ljubljana: Mladinska knjiga, 1975), pp. 182–197;
Gregor Kocijan, *Kratka pripovedna proza od Trdine do Kersnika* (Ljubljana: Državna založba, 1983), pp. 158–253;
Marjan Kramberger, *Pazlivejša branja* (Ljubljana: Mladinska Marjan knjiga, 1975), pp. 153–201;
Kramberger, *Visoška kronika: Literarnozgodovinska interpritacija* (Ljubljana: Mladinska knjiga, 1964);
Jože Mahnič, "Zgradba in slog *Visoške kronike*," *Prostor in čas,* 6, nos. 1–2 (1974): 76–86;
Marija Mitrović, "Destrukcija avtoritarnosti in Marija deklarativnosti," in Tavčar's *Visoška kronika* (Ljubljana: Mladinska knjiga, 1987), pp. 251–281;
Mitrović, "Elementi modernog v romanu *Visočka hronika* Ivana Tavčara," *Književna istorija,* 59 (1983): 359–368;
Boris Paternu, *Slovenska proza do moderne* (Koper, 1957), pp. 105–141;
Timothy Pogacar, "Childhood in the Works of Ivan Tavčar: A Comparison of the Early Works and the Novel *Visoška kronika*," *Slovene Studies,* 10, no. 2 (1988): 149–160;
Breda Pogorelec, "Stilno predhodništvo v Tavčarjevih delih," *Jezik in slovstvo,* 24, nos. 7–8 (1982–1983): 285–292;
Franc Zadravec, "Tavčarjev literarni in politični nazor v letih 1919–1921 ter Ivan Cankar," *Slavistična revija,* 22 (1974): 1–30.

Augustin ("Tin") Ujević

(5 July 1891 – 12 November 1955)

Dubravka Juraga
University of Arkansas

BOOKS: *Hrvatska u borbi za slobodu* (Belgrade: Pijemont, 1912);

Grammaire élémentaire de la langue serbe: Grammaire, exercices, textes, lexique, by Pierre de Lanux and Ujević (Paris: Delagrave, 1916);

Lelek sebra: Pjesme (Belgrade: S. B. Cvijanović, 1920);

Kolajna: Pjesme (Belgrade: S. B. Cvijanović, 1926);

Nedjela maloljetnih: Jedna podvrsta Moderne (Sarajevo: Mlada Bosna, 1931);

Dva glavna bogumila: Lav Tolstoj i Mahatma Gandi (Sarajevo: Večernja pošta, 1932);

Auto na korzu: Pjesme (Nikšić, Yugoslavia: Slobodna misao, 1932);

Ojadjeno zvono: Pjesme (Zagreb: Matica hrvatska, 1933);

Pesme (Belgrade: Srpska književna zadruga, 1937);

Ljudi za vratima gostionice (Zagreb: Društvo hrvatskih književnika, 1938);

Skalpel kaosa: Iskopine is sedre sadašnjice (Zagreb: Hrvatska književna naklada, 1938);

Rukovet (Zagreb: Zora, 1950);

Žedan kamen na studencu: Pjesme (Zagreb: Društvo književnika Hrvatske, 1954);

Mamurluci i pobješnjela krava (Zagreb: Lykos, 1956);

Mudre i lude djevice: Pjesničke proze (Sarajevo: Narodna prosvjeta, 1957);

Sabrana djela, 17 volumes (Zagreb: Znanje, 1963–1967).

Edition in English: *Libraries: A Fragment of an Ethical Autobiography,* translated by Antun Nizeteo and Marvin Tatum (New York: Croatian Academy of America, 1975).

Augustin ("Tin") Ujević

Most critics today agree that Augustin ("Tin") Ujević is one of the greatest modern South Slavic poets; indeed, he has been called the greatest Balkan poet since Homer. Ujević's work breathed new life, new energies, and new sensations into South Slavic poetry. One of the leading figures of South Slavic modernism, Ujević contributed to the new modern and cosmopolitan quality of South Slavic poetry and helped to erase its sense of belatedness in European culture. With the writing of Ujević and contemporaries such as Rastko Petrović and Miloš Crnjanski, South Slavic poetry reached unprecedented heights of creativity and sophistication.

Though Ujević's poetry often employed classical forms such as the sonnet, his sensibility was very modern. In his fusion of form and content he tried to achieve a new modern mode of expression going beyond his classical models. Ujević was often regarded as a *poet maudit* (damned poet) by his contemporaries, but this reputation may have arisen partially from his determination to break new poetic ground. He was an exceptionally educated intellectual; his mind was open and ready to receive, absorb, and re-create the world around him. His oeuvre includes works whose characteristics are both classical and modern. In his poetry Ujević succeeds in expressing his own private pains, dreams, rebellions and acceptances, loves, and sufferings. At the same time, his poetry transcends the domain of the personal and strives for relevance to a wide variety of readers. His language conveys the existence of another, poetic world in which the superb, magical music of words reigns.

Ujević was born on 5 July 1891 in Vrgorac, near Imotski. He was the third of five children of Ivan Ujević, a teacher, and Jerolima (née Livačić-Markusović) from Milna, Brač. Ujević's parents were serious, strict people who showed little warmth and affection to their children. Ujević's biographers have often explained his lifelong search for love and affection by this deficiency from his early childhood. From 1896 to 1899 Ujević attended the first three grades of elementary school in Imotski. There he was taught by his father, a stern and critical taskmaster who set rigorous standards for his son. In 1899 the family moved to Makarska, where Ujević finished the fourth grade and the first two grades of middle school. From his earliest childhood Ujević had developed a love for the coastal mountains of Velebit and Biokovo and for the Adriatic Sea, two settings that remained important throughout his poetry.

In 1902 Ujević continued his education in a Catholic high school in Split that was designed to prepare its students for the priesthood. Friends from that time remember him as an awkward, sensitive, impractical, and wary youth who loved books and learning. He was extremely poor, and his intense awareness of this poverty only increased his difficulties in dealing with his fellow students. He eventually gained a scholarship that alleviated his poverty to a certain extent, but he was a sensitive, introverted child who did not react well either to the strict rules of his parents or to the regimentation of his clerical education. He had already developed an aversion to authority, which remained anathema to him throughout his life. While at the high school he became fiercely anticlerical and struggled with his parents to renounce his vocation. He succeeded in 1907, though he was allowed to remain in school

until his graduation, with the highest marks, in 1909. He lost his scholarship and returned to extreme poverty, but Ujević never regretted his decision.

At that time he was already writing poetry, though he kept his early literary efforts secret until he published his first sonnet, "Za novim vidicima" (Toward New Horizons) in the Zagreb journal *Mlada Hrvatska* (Young Croatia) shortly before leaving high school. Soon other poems followed, including "Sreć a sanje" (Happiness of a Dream), "Epigrami" (Epigrams), "Vjera u sebe" (Self-Reliance), "Sumnja" (Doubt), "Hrvatskim mučenicima" (To Croatian Martyrs), and "Beskućnik" (The Homeless One). These were mostly sonnets, novice efforts that showed a youthful longing for escape from reality, but they had already begun to display the lyricism and phonic richness that distinguishes his later work.

After graduation from high school Ujević went to Zagreb, where he enrolled at the Philosophical College to study Croatian language and literature, classical philology, philosophy, and aesthetics. There Ujević became a friend and a disciple of the great Croatian writer and poet Antun Gustav Matoš, who had recently returned from exile to Zagreb. Despite Ujević's vehement denials, critics have pointed out the strong influence that Matoš had on his disciple both in his poetic development and his political orientation and lifestyle. However, the friendship did not last long — they quarreled in 1911 — and Ujević stayed highly critical of Matoš long after Matoš's death in 1914. The young Ujević was also influenced by other poets, such as Silvije Strahimir Kranjčević, Paul Verlaine, Charles Baudelaire, Arthur Rimbaud, and Walt Whitman.

Ujević was burdened throughout his life with various fears — of height, death, sickness, humiliation, debilitation, women, love — and those fears often became themes in his poetry. He also became a fervent Croatian nationalist, partly under the influence of Matoš. However, Ujević was critical of the pro-Catholic and pro-Austrian tendencies of most nationalists in Croatia and soon became convinced that the only way the Croats could achieve their freedom was through unity with other South Slavic peoples, especially Serbs, into a new Yugoslav state. By 1909 Ujević was already heavily involved with the political situation and devoted much of his time to the political fight for Serbian-Croatian unity. In 1912 he interrupted his studies in Zagreb and left for Belgrade where he joined the secret organization Ujedinjenje ili smrt (Unification or Death). He wrote articles and gave speeches against the Austro-Hungarian domination of his homeland. In this year, in poems such as "Vječita romantika" (Eternal Romance) in the journal *Savremenik* (Contemporary) and "Agonija" (Agony) in *Misao* (Thought), he began the practice of signing his works as "Tin" rather than "Augustin."

During 1912–1913 Ujević became one of the most active and capable leaders of the Yugoslav nationalist movement in Croatia, and the Austro-Hungarian government persecuted him accordingly. He was arrested three times for his political activities. During one of the arrests he pointed out that his primary aim was to achieve "an independent Croatia as a Yugoslav republic." He was sentenced to exile from Zagreb and Slavonia for ten years. Some of this time he spent with his parents in Split, then in Dubrovnik, Šibenik, Zadar, and Rijeka. During this period he remained politically active. After his third arrest he decided to leave the country and go to Paris, where he arrived at the end of 1913. While Ujević was in Paris he sent articles to the journal *Sloboda* (Liberty) in Split. He also met Leon Trotsky and Anatoly Lunacharsky and became interested in the revolutionary movements in Russia. At that time Ujević's financial situation was extremely difficult. He supported himself by writing political articles and essays and by translating articles from Serbo-Croatian into French. With Pierre de Lanux he also published *Grammaire élémentaire de la langue serbe* (Basic Grammar of the Serbian Language, 1916).

Ujević was highly critical not only of the Austro-Hungarian rule in Croatia but also of the Croatian people who succumbed to that rule. He criticized the narrow-mindedness of the political and cultural life in Croatia; he attacked the people for their lack of pride, courage, energy, and creativity and for their acceptance of their inferior and slavelike position in the empire. To him the fight against Austro-Hungarian domination was the utmost priority of his life, and his poems from that period reflect this stand. They are mostly patriotic and social-revolutionary poems colored by his patriotism and belief in Pan-Slavism, and they are full of understanding and sympathy for the oppressed and the poor. In his poem "Rusija" (Russia), revolutionary Russia becomes a symbol of hope and betterment. His poem "Rotonda" – after the well-known Paris café Rotonda, where Slavic émigrés and revolutionaries used to gather – depicts exiled patriots full of revolutionary zeal.

In 1914 the anthology *Hrvatska mlada lirika* (Croatian Young Poetry) was published, which introduced a new generation of Croatian poets; one of

them was Tin Ujević. But at that time Ujević was more interested in the fight for freedom and the creation of an independent Yugoslavia. Eager to help embattled Serbia after the outbreak of World War I, Ujević, with some other young patriots, joined the French Foreign Legion. They were promised that they would be sent to fight in the Balkans, but soon they became disappointed with the war and concluded that France was more interested in furthering its own power than in liberating the Balkans. With the help of Croatian politician Frano Supilo, Ujević left the legion and joined the organization Jugoslavenski odbor (Yugoslav Committee) in Paris in order to spread its ideas in support of the creation of a Yugoslav state.

Meanwhile, Ujević was gradually becoming more and more disappointed with the real world of politics, with its intrigues, compromises, and shady deals. By 1916 his interest began to shift from political problems to literature. At this time he wrote his well-known poem "Svakidašnja jadikovka" (Everyday Lament), a brilliant lamentation on disappointment and disillusionment. His personal crisis deepened in 1917: he broke off with the politicians in the Jugoslavenski odbor after many disagreements, he became disappointed with the Serbian embassy as well, and he did not receive a scholarship from the Kingdom of Montenegro that he had expected. In addition, he had an emotional and sentimental crisis when he fell in love with a woman who did not or could not return his love. Slowly, Ujević changed from an elegant and striking young intellectual, politician, and artist into a disappointed and bitter bohemian disgusted at the world and interested only in his own inner life.

Although Ujević was actively engaged in politics, he was not a political person by nature: he was too emotional and too scrupulous and proud. His standards and expectations, both for himself and others, were impossibly high. When reality failed to match his unrealistic moral and ethical standards, he became highly disappointed and turned away from the world. By the end of the war the disillusioned Ujević was virtually indifferent to the subsequent creation of Yugoslavia. His personal crisis is reflected in the poems he wrote at that time, which focused more and more on his personal disappointments and disillusionment. Many of the poems written during this period were later published in the important collection *Lelek sebra* (A Serf's Lament, 1920). In 1919 Ujević returned to Zagreb, where he finished *Lelek sebra*. He also wrote and published extensively, especially in Zagreb's *Književni jug* (Literary South), *Savremenik,* and *Plamen* (Flame). The

Drawing of Ujević as an older man

next year he left for Belgrade. In November *Lelek sebra* and his translation of Gustave Flaubert's *Novembre* (1885) were published there.

Lelek sebra is the collection in which Ujević found his own artistic voice. He dedicated the book to the Serbian poet Sima Pandurović. In the collection Ujević follows the rules of traditional metrics, and all poems except "Svakidašnja jadikovka" are rhymed. Many of the poems are sonnets. In this book he powerfully expresses anger, bitterness, despair, and helplessness. Anxiety, horror, fear, and pain permeate the poems. He registers the horrors of war, personal disillusionment, and his intimate tragedies, and the poems are a testimony to his enormous suffering and pain.

Critics greeted the publication of *Lelek sebra* with enthusiasm, and he was immediately recognized as one of the finest Yugoslav poets. Despite the recognition and acclaim that this collection received, Ujević's deep personal malaise persisted. His rejection of society and all its demands was complete. He was leading a bohemian life – sleeping on park benches and drinking heavily in the pubs of Belgrade, where he became involved in numerous drunken altercations. He lived the life of an outcast by wearing rags, exhibiting strange behavior, and living in filth. Throughout the 1920s Ujević scandalized Belgrade's petite bourgeoisie. Nevertheless,

the bohemian and intellectual segments of that society, including many writers and critics, recognized the importance and greatness of Ujević's poetry. Also, Ujević retained a great personal charisma, transfixing his friends and the clientele of the pubs and cafés he frequented with his knowledge and eloquence.

In 1924 a group of Belgrade surrealists began to publish the modernist journal *Svedočanstva* (Testimonies), the first issue of which was dedicated to Ujević's poetry. Because of his numerous political quarrels and public insults to the king and queen of Yugoslavia, Ujević was banished from Belgrade to Croatia in 1925, causing a considerable outcry among the literary community in Belgrade. In response to Ujević's internal exile, his collection of poems *Kolajna* (Necklace) was published in Belgrade in 1926 after a six-year delay. It immediately received numerous positive reviews. The poems in this collection are written in traditional metrical forms; thirteen out of thirty-five are sonnets. The language of the poems is clear, beautiful, and musical; the metaphors are innovative, vivid, and intense. These poems are again expressions of extreme emotions and of the poet's "complete, icy loneliness." In his biography of Ujević, Mirko Žeželj suggests that this collection is Ujević's tribute to Lusila, the object of his unrequited love from his

Paris years. But Ujević, who had virtually no relationships with women in his real life, tends to represent them in his poetry in abstract terms ranging from revulsion toward women as images of evil to the Petrarchan adoration of women as ideals of beauty and goodness.

In 1926 Ujević also published two important essays, "Oroz pred Endimionom" and "Adonai," describing his theory of poetry as a spiritual and mystical communication between poet and reader and also emphasizing the importance of innovation in poetry. In these essays he describes the poet as a visionary leader in the mode of Friedrich Nietzsche's *Übermensch*.

He returned to Belgrade in 1927. Unable to find a job in which he could use his immense knowledge of literature, languages, history, and culture, he supported himself with odd jobs, such as working in a secondhand bookstore. Losing all faith in the value of any creative activities, he completely stopped writing. He spent his time in Belgrade's pubs conversing and drinking with his bohemian admirers and friends, but he remained fundamentally an introvert whose life was focused on his own inner world.

In 1929 Ujević left Belgrade, wandering from Sarajevo to Split to Brač and finally returning to Sarajevo, where he stayed from 1930 until 1937. At this time he again started to write prolifically. He published numerous essays, poems, autobiographical pieces, polemics, feuilletons, and criticism. His work of this period reflects his newfound energy and will for life. He was constantly burdened by financial difficulties and continued to lead a bohemian life, but he avoided the excesses of the Belgrade period.

During the 1930s Ujević wrote numerous critical essays about both foreign and Yugoslav writers. He was particularly interested in modern art, and he often wrote about its important predecessors. He also wrote about various social topics. At the same time, he intensely studied Asian culture, religion, and philosophy, publishing numerous essays on those subjects. Some critics argue that Ujević regained his peace of mind because of the beneficial influence of Asian wisdom.

The subjects of Ujević's essays tellingly display his vast knowledge and interests: they include Baudelaire, Rimbaud, Leo Tolstoy, Abraham Lincoln, Fyodor Dostoevsky, Sergei Esenin, André Gide, Desiderius Erasmus, Miguel de Cervantes, Bernard Shaw, Stendahl, Johann Wolfgang von Goethe, Joseph Conrad, Edgar Allan Poe, George Meredith, Lao-tzu, Pablo Picasso and cubism, Jean-

Baptiste-Camille Corot, Gustave Courbet, Frédéric Chopin, Mohandas Gandhi, Thomas Masaryk, acupuncture, surrealism, and politics. Ujević also often engaged in literary debates with writers such as Rade Drainac, Ljubomir Micić, Eli Finci, and Ivan Goran Kovačić during the 1930s. In these debates Ujević addressed the issue of literature and its position and function in a society as well as the issue of the moral integrity of writers and artists.

In 1931 Ujević published two important essays. In "Dva glavna bogumila – Lav Tolstoj i Mahatma Gandi" (Two Major Bogomils: Lev Tolstoy and Mahatma Gandhi; published in book form a year later) Ujević analyzed similarities among the Russian writer Tolstoy, the Indian leader Gandhi, and the Bogomils, a medieval Bosnian religious sect. The essay displays the wide scope of his knowledge of these subjects and is an excellent illustration of Ujević as a critical and original thinker. "Nedjela maloljetnih: Jedna podvrsta Moderne" (Mischief of the Young: A Subgenre of Modernism) is Ujević's radical criticism of contemporary writers who under the banner of modernism and avant-gardism irresponsibly champion spiritual laziness, incompetence, and ignorance. For Ujević these young artists lack talent and creativity. Instead of being truly avant-garde, they are trendy and superficial, even decadent and reactionary. His criticism was a shock to a generation of avant-garde artists who had looked up to him as their guru and who had idolized him. His criticism is a cogent, if most uncompromising, critique of his literary contemporaries.

In 1932 Ujević's third collection of poems, *Auto na korzu* (Auto on the Promenade), was published in Nikšić. This collection, informed by expressionism and surrealism, departs from the previous two collections in its form and spirit. In it Ujević attempts to depart from his earlier subject of the bitter and tragic disappointments of his life and to initiate a renaissance of his old, dead self. Many of the poems are written in free verse, but the language is rhythmic and powerful, and the feeling for the beautiful is strong. Their dominant tone is optimism; they are full of powerful visions, deep inspiration, and pure lyricism. The tone of the collection may best be expressed in the poem "Visoki jablani" (Tall Poplar Trees), where giant poplar trees serve as a powerful symbol of independence and of the beauty of poetry. The might of the poplars suggests the Promethean energy of poetry – its purity, dignity, and pride. A poet is a lone figure who contributes enormously to humanity, although poets are usually not understood by ignorant and base people. The poem is full of Dionysian energy and will. It describes the poetic ideal, which is often unattainable. However, the poet has come to terms with this unattainability and does not despair. On the contrary, he is exalted by the contemplation of his ideal and the guidance it provides.

In 1933 Ujević published his next collection, *Ojadjeno zvono* (Distressed Bell). This collection marked a new phase of hope and optimism in his work, though its poems reflect a wide range of feelings, from optimism to melancholy and sadness. Here Ujević continues to express a belief in the eternal purity of nature, but the poems show a political turn as well. They are informed by a visionary utopian socialism and show a newfound respect and sympathy for the common person.

In 1937 the collection *Pesme* (Poems) was published in Belgrade. The collection was generally well received and confirmed his high poetic reputation. However, Ujević's bohemian lifestyle had by this time begun to take its toll on his health; in 1937 he moved from Sarajevo to Split in search of quieter surroundings and a healthier climate.

In 1938 Ujević published two books of essays in Zagreb: *Ljudi za vratima gostionice* (People Behind the Doors of an Inn) and *Skalpel kaosa* (Scalpel of Chaos). Both books were acknowledged as important literary events and major contributions to the development of the essay genre in Yugoslavia. The books are yet another proof of Ujević's encyclopedic knowledge. His essays are philosophical and contemplative, though most critics emphasize their dominantly lyrical quality. Ujević was an unconventional thinker who focused upon his own perceptions of art and its position in his contemporary society and who elaborated upon his own impressions and reflections. His prose has been placed by some critics in the tradition of great essays by writers such as Michel de Montaigne and Blaise Pascal.

Ujević remained a wanderer through most of his life, continually moving to new locales in search of fresh inspiration. In 1940 he moved to Zagreb, where he remained until his death from cancer of the esophagus in 1955. There he obtained an editorial position in the Croatian democratic trade-union journal *Pravica* (Justice). During World War II he worked as a journalist and translator for Velebit, the information agency of the government of the newly independent state of Croatia. Once a fervent political activist, Ujević did not participate in politics during this period. He did not ascribe to the Fascist ideology of the Croatian government, but neither did he actively oppose it, and he remained an employee of Velebit throughout the war. As punishment for this employment, the new Communist government of postwar Yugoslavia banned Ujević from publishing until 1950; during this time he lived as a virtual beggar. In 1950 he resumed publishing as a literary translator. In 1950 he published *Rukovet* (Handful), a new collection of his earlier poems. In 1954 he published *Žedan kamen na studencu* (Thirsty Stone at the Fountain), his last collection of poems. All of the poems in this collection had been written and published between 1921 and 1943. The collection was well received both by critics and readers.

Ujević's work, spanning the period from before World War I to after World War II, encompasses the period of the birth of Yugoslav modernism. His essays and criticism made an important contribution to his contemporary intellectual climate. In his poetry he took important inspiration from the Croatian literary tradition, but he instilled this tradition with the spirit of European modernism and with his own individual style and vision. Ujević's enchantingly beautiful poetry became a touchstone of Yugoslav culture and set the standards for the new generation of Yugoslav poets who followed him.

Letters:

Sabrana djela, volume 14, edited by Dubravko Jelčić (Zagreb: Znanje, 1966).

Interviews:

Sabrana djela, volume 14, edited by Dubravko Jelčić (Zagreb: Znanje, 1966).

Bibliography:

Sabrana djela, volume 17, edited by Vladimir Popović (Zagreb: Znanje, 1967).

Biography:

Mirko Žeželj, *Veliki Tin* (Zagreb: Znanje, 1976).

References:

Dragomir Gajević, "Geneza političke misli Tina Ujevića," *Mogućnosti,* 32 (1985): 743–758;

Gajević, *Ogledi o Tinu Ujeviću* (Sarajevo: Oslobodjenje, 1988);

Gajević, "O Tinovim ishodištima: u povodu 90-godišnjice rodjenja," *Stvaranje,* 36 (1981): 1485–1494;

Gajević, *Tin Ujević u jugoslavenskoj književnoj kritici* (Zagreb: Grafički zavod Hrvatske, 1988);

Velibor Gligorić, "Mladi Ujević – borac i ideolog, književni kriticar i esejist," in his *U vihoru* (Belgrade: Nolit, 1975), pp. 184–203;

Dubravko Jelčić, ed., *Opojnost uma: Misli i pogledi Tina Ujevića* (Zagreb: August Cesarec, 1986);

Jelčić, *Približavanje sfingi: Diptih o Ujeviću – Esej i drama* (Zagreb: Znanje, 1979);

Vujadin Jokić, *Geneza stvaralaštva Tina Ujevića* (Belgrade: Obelisk, 1971);

Marko Kovačević, *Ujevićevo pjesničko i mistično iskustvo: Ujevićevo teorijsko shvaćanje pjesništva* (Zagreb: Kršćanska sadašnjost, 1982);

Antun Nizeteo, *Whitman in Croatia: Tin Ujevic and Walt Whitman* (Brooklyn: Czas, 1971);

Predrag Palavestra, "Ispovedna poezija Tina Ujevića," *Život,* 12 (1963): 13–22;

Vlatko Pavletić, *Tin Ujević* (Belgrade: Rad, 1966);

Pavletić, *Ujević u raju svoga pakla* (Zagreb: Liber, 1978);

Bruno Popović, "Jednodušni Ujević: Hodočašće k utopiji pjesništva," in his *Matoš i nakon njega* (Zagreb: Studentski centar sveučilišta, 1972);

Roberta Reeder, "'Where Does the Evening Come From' by Tin Ujević," *Southeastern Europe,* 9, nos. 1–2 (1982): 137–146;

Vladimir Rem, *Tinbez vina* (Osijek, Yugoslavia: Revija, 1980);

Isidora Sekulić "Poezija Augustina Ujevića," *Srpski književni glasnik,* 13 (1924): 111–119;

Ante Štamać, "Tin Ujević as a European Poet," in *Comparative Studies in Croatian Literature,* edited by Miroslav Beker (Zagreb: Zavod za znanost i književnosti Filozofskog fakulteta u Zagrebu), pp. 409–432;

Štamać, *Ujević* (Zagreb: Kolo, 1971);

Husein Tahmiščić, "Razgovor o pjesništvu Tina Ujevića," *Književnost,* 74 (1982): 936–949;

Šime Vučetić, *Tin Ujević i drugi* (Zagreb: August Cesarec, 1978);

Mirko Žeželj, "Prve Tinove godine na obalama sene," *Letopis Matice srpske,* 416 (1975): 409–433.

Papers:

Major holdings of Ujević's literary papers are at the Institut za književnost and Sveučilišna i nacionalna knjižnica in Zagreb.

Ivan Vazov

(27 June 1850 – 22 September 1921)

Kleo Protokhristova
University of Plovdiv

BOOKS: *Pryaporets i gusla. Stikhotvoreniya,* as Peychinovich (Bucharest: Bŭlgarsko tsentralno blagotvoritelno druzhestvo, 1876); republished as *Narodna i stara pesnopoyka* (Sofia: Pavle M. Lyutov, 1882); republished as *Pryaporets i gusla (1875–76)* (Sofia: Pechatnitsa Vŭlkov, 1895);

Tŭgite na Bŭlgariya. Stikhotvoreniya (Bucharest: Pech. Yosif Andrich, 1877);

Izbavlenie. Sŭvremenni stikhotvoreniya (Bucharest: Iliya Blŭskov i G. Tsonchov, 1878);

Vidul. Trakiyska idiliya (Sofia: Skoro-pechatnitsa na Yanko S. Kovachev, 1879);

Mayska kitka. Stikhotvoreniya (Plovdiv, Ruse & Salonika: Khrito G. Danov, 1880);

Gusla. Nai-novy liricheski i epicheski stikhotvoreniya. 1879–1881 (Plovdiv, Sofia & Ruse: Khrito G. Danov, 1881);

Mitrofan. Povest (Plovdiv: Pechatnitsa na D. V. Manchov, 1882);

Mikhalaki chorbadzhi, komediya v dve deystviya (Plovdiv, Svishtov & Salonika: D. V. Manchov, 1882);

Zagorka (Plovdiv: D. V. Manchov, 1883);

Ruska, drama v chetiri deystviya (Plovdiv, Svishtov & Salonika: D. V. Manchov, 1883);

Stikhotvoreniya za malki detsa (Plovdiv, Svishtov & Salonika: D. V. Manchov, 1883);

Polya i gori. Nova sbirka stikhotvoreniya (Plovdiv: D. V. Manchov, 1884);

Italiya. Liricheski stikhotvoreniya (Plovdiv: D. V. Manchov, 1884);

Podporuchik Vŭlko. Razkazi iz Srŭbsko-bŭlgarskata voyna (Plovdiv: Slavyanska knizharnitsa "Zora" na G. Tsakov, 1886);

Slivnitsa. Stikhotvoreniya po voynata ni sŭs sŭrbite prez 1885 (Plovdiv: D. V. Manchov, 1886);

Sŭchineniya. Povesti i razkazi, 3 volumes (Sofia: Iv. Daskalov i s-ie, 1891–1893);

V nedrata na Rodopite. Pŭtni belezhki i nablyudeniya (Sofia: Dŭrzhavna pechatnitsa, 1892; enlarged edition, Sofia: Khr. Olchevata knizharnitsa, 1904);

Ivan Vazov

Velikata Rilska pustinya. Pŭtni belezhki i vpechatleniya (Sofia: Dŭrzhavna pechatnitsa, 1892; enlarged edition, Sofia: Khr. Olchevata knizharnitsa, 1904);

Zvukove. Liricheski stikhotvoreniya (Sofia: Ivan P. Daskalov, 1893);

Poemi (Sofia: "Liberalni klub," 1893); revised and enlarged as *Poemi. 1879–1884* (Sofia: Olchevata knizharnitsa, 1904);

Draski i sharki (Ocherki iz stolichniya zhivot), volume 1 (Sofia: Iv. B. Kasŭrov, 1893);

Pod igoto. Roman iz zhivota na bŭlgarite v predvecherieto na Osvobozhdenieto (Sofia: T. F. Chipev, 1894; revised, 1910); translated by Edmund Gosse as *Under the Yoke* (London: Heinemann, 1894; revised, 1912); translated by Marguerite Alexieva and Theodora Atanassova as *Under the Yoke* (Sofia: Narodna Kultura, 1955);

Khŭshove. Drama v pet deystviya (Sofia: T. F. Chipev, pechatnitsa Progres, 1894; revised edition, Sofia: T. F. Chipev, 1899);

Draski i sharki (Ocherki iz stolichniya zhivot), volume 2 (Sofia: Pencho V. Spasov, 1895);

Nova zemya. Roman iz zhivota na bŭlgarite prez pŭrvite godini sled Osvobozhdenieto (Sofia: T. F. Chipev, 1896);

Skitnishki pesni. Vpechatleniya i useshtaniya v Malata i Golyama Stara planina (Sofia: Iv. B. Kasŭrov, 1899);

Vestnikar li? Komediya v edno deystvie (Sofia: P. M. Buzaytov, 1900);

Pod nasheto nebe. Novi stikhotvoreniya (Stara Zagora: Nadezhda, 1900);

Videno i chuto. Razkazi, spomeni, pŭteshestviya (Sofia: Khr. Olchevata knizharnitsa, 1901);

Pŭstŭr svyat. Razkazi, spomeni, draski, pŭtni vpechatleniya (Sofia: Khr. Olchev, 1902);

Kazalarskata tsaritsa. Roman (Sofia: Khr. Olchevata knizharnitsa, 1903);

Sluzhbogontsi (Stanco Kvasnikov na gosti u ministŭra). Komediya v dve deystviya (Sofia: Khr. Olchev, 1903);

Utro v Banki. Dobrodushni razkazi (Sofia: T. F. Chipev, 1905);

Ivan Aleksandŭr. Istoricheska povest iz zhivota na Tŭrnovskoto tsarstvo v sredata na XIV stoletie (Plovdiv: Biblioteka "Dukhovna probuda," P. Belovezhdov, 1907);

Svetoslav Terter. Roman iz bŭlgarskata istoriya v kraya na XIII vek (Sofia: T. F. Chipev, 1907);

Nora. Povest (Plovdiv: Biblioteka "Dukhovna probuda," N8, Petko Belovezhdov, 1908);

Borislav. Istoricheska drama v pet deystviya iz tsaruvaneto na Ivana Asena II (Sofia: T. F. Chipev, 1909);

Kŭm propast. Piesa v pet deystviya i edna kartina. Izvlechenie iz povestta "Ivan Aleksandŭr" (Sofia: Iv. G. Ignatov, 1910);

Legendi pri Tsarevets. Baladi i poemi (Sofia: Iv. G. Ignatov, 1910);

Pod igoto. Piesa v 10 dramaticheski kartini (Sofia: T. F. Chipev, 1911);

Ivaylo. Istoricheska drama v shest deystviya (Sofia: Al. Paskalev i s-ie, 1913);

Kazalarskata tsaritsa, drama v pet deystviya i edna kartina (Sofia: Al. Paskalev, 1913);

Pod grŭma na pobedite. Stikhotvoreniya, pisani prez Pŭrvata balkanska voyna (Sofia: Nar. osigur. d-vo Balkan, 1914);

Pesni za Makedoniya. 1913–1916 (Sofia: T. F. Chipev, 1916);

Novi ekove. Disonansi (Sofia: T. F. Chipev, 1917);

Yulska kitka (Kakvo pee planinata) Vpechatleniya i poeticheski navei pri Kostenetskiya vodopad, yuli 1917 g. (Sofia: Knigi na bŭlg. pisateli, 1917);

Lyuleka mi zamirisa, liricheski stikhotvoreniya (Sofia: "Slŭntse," Sbirka na bŭlgarski pisateli N2, 1919);

Ne shte zagine! Stikhotvoreniya. Pisani prez septemvriy-oktomvriy 1919 g. v Sofia (Sofia: Chipev, 1920);

V Iztochna Rumeliya. Spomeni (Sofia: Bŭlg. pechatnitsa, 1920);

Iz belezhnika na poeta (Otkŭsletsi ot prirodata i zhivota) (Sofia: Pobeda, 1920);

Poeticheska biografiya na Ivana Vazova do 20-godishnata mu vŭzrast, by Vazov and T. Gabrovski (Sofia: T. F. Chipev, 1920);

Lyubov i priroda. Stikhotvoreniya (Sofia: Chipev, 1921);

Neizdadeni proizvedeniya, edited by Man'o Stoyanov (Sofia: Bŭlgarski pisatel, 1968);

Editions and Collections: *Pŭlno sŭbranie na sŭchineniyata,* 8 volumes (Sofia: Paskalev, 1911–1918, unfinished);

Pŭlno sŭbranie na sŭchineniyata na Ivan Vazov, 28 volumes (Sofia: Paskalev, 1921–1922);

Sŭbrani sŭchineniya. Pŭlno izdanie pod redaktsiyata na M. Arnaudov, 22 volumes (Sofia: Khemus, 1942–1950);

Sŭbrani sŭchineniya, 20 volumes, edited by P. Dinekov and others (Sofia: Bŭlgarski pisatel, 1955–1957);

Sŭbrani sŭchineniya, 22 volumes, edited by M. Tsaneva and others (Sofia: Bŭlgarski pisatel, 1974–1979).

PLAY PRODUCTIONS: *Mikhalaki chorbadzhi, komediya v dve deystviya,* Ruse, local theater group, 11 November 1881;

Ruska, Plovdiv, Theatre Lyuksemburg, 1883;

Sluzhbogontsi, Sofia, Slavyanska Beseda, 1902;

Kŭm propast, Sofia, Naroden teatŭr, 29 November 1907;

Borislav, Sofia, Naroden teatŭr, 1 September 1909;

Pod igoto, Sofia, Naroden teatŭr, 16 October 1910;

Kazalarskata tsaritsa, Sofia, Naroden teatŭr, 10 November 1911;

Ivaylo, Sofia, Naroden teatŭr, 5 December 1913.

OTHER: *Bŭlgarska khristomatiya ili sbornik ot izbrani obraztsi ot vsichki rodove sŭchineniya, s prilozhenie na kratki zhizneopisaniya na nay-znamenitite pisateli, 2*

ПРѢПОРЕЦЪ И ГУСЛА

Стихотворения.

ОТЪ

ПЕЙЧИНА.

——

КНИЖКА I.

*Издава за въ ползата си Бѫлгарското Цен-
трално Благотворително Общество
въ Букурещъ.*

1876.

Title page for Vazov's first book of poetry, Pryaporets i gusla *(The Banner and the Lute), which he published under the pseudonym Peychinovich*

volumes, edited and translated by Vazov and Konstantin Velichkov (Plovdiv, Svishtov & Salonika: D. V. Lesingov, 1884);

Iz golemite poeti. Stikhotvorni prevodi, translated and edited by Vazov (Sofia: Biblioteka "Znanie," 1911).

For more than fifty years Ivan Vazov was the most prominent figure in Bulgarian literature after the liberation. He was a citizen-poet who considered the social mission of literature an organic part of the nation's life and fate. He wrote his most compelling works to glorify Bulgaria's national reawakening and to articulate the ideals of the past, lest they be forgotten by postliberation society. His view of the Bulgarian national character had an enormous impact on his people, and to this day his works remain an invaluable treasure of Bulgarian cultural history. Vazov is considered the patriarch of Bulgarian literature because he provided the highest standards for future generations of writers, who would seek in his verse a solution to their doubts and a confirmation of their ideas. Vazov was in fact the founder of all

the literary genres employed by modern Bulgarian literature. His wide-ranging works are a brilliant manifestation of his artistic creativity. Partly because of his love of his homeland, its freedom and its nature, and his ability to incorporate into his works Bulgaria's traditions, history, morality, and national spirit, Vazov has come to be regarded as Bulgaria's national poet.

Ivan Minchov Vazov was born on 27 June 1850 in Sopot, a small town at the foot of the Stara Planina Range. The whole sub-Balkan region played a crucial role in the Bulgarian national revolution. Vazov came from a family in which traditional values were highly regarded. His father, Mincho Vazov, was a merchant. An open-minded person, he combined a conservative, patriarchal spirit with sympathy for the Enlightenment and the national revival. Vazov's mother, Sŭba, was an intelligent, generous, and charming woman who supported her son's creative aspirations. Vazov was profoundly grateful to her all his life and dedicated to her memory some of his most deeply felt verse. Despite the austerity maintained by both parents, the family with its nine children lived in an atmosphere of warm affection.

From 1857 to 1865 Vazov attended the local school. As a student he voraciously read virtually everything that was published in Bulgaria at the time. At age fourteen he began composing poems. Most of these early attempts are concerned with historical themes. In 1865 he went to study in Kalofer, another sub-Balkan town, where Botio Petkov, Khristo Botev's father, taught. For a year Vazov studied Greek and assisted his teacher. In Kalofer, Vazov found a rich library filled with Russian and French books. This year had a significant impact on his intellectual and artistic growth. In 1866 he was sent to Plovdiv, where he enrolled in the fourth grade of the middle school run by Yoakim Gruev to study Greek and Turkish – the languages that would help him as a merchant, the profession chosen for him by his father. Vazov instead set about improving his French and was fascinated by the poetry of Victor Hugo, Alphonse-Marie-Louis de Lamartine, and Pierre-Jean de Béranger. When his father ordered him back to his native town to take over the merchant business, Vazov was reluctant to agree. He stayed in Plovdiv to be with Pelagia, the woman he loved. Married and ten years older than he, she inspired his early poems dedicated to the beauties of nature and to the experiences of love. Some of these poems later appeared in the collection *Mayska kitka* (A May Bouquet, 1880).

Although Vazov's mother encouraged his choice, his father was profoundly disappointed and insisted that his son take up a more prestigious profession. Thus in 1870 he sent him to an uncle who was a merchant in Oltenitsa, Romania, to become an assistant and learn the trade. Instead, Vazov spent his time studying the language and reading Romanian poetry while continuing to write his own verse. At this period the prevailing spirit in his verse was patriotic and instructive.

In 1872 Vazov published his first poems in *Periodichesko spisanie* (Periodical Journal), edited by Vasil Drumev, in Lyuben Karavelov's newspaper *Svoboda* (Freedom), and in the journals *Chitalishte* (The Reading Room) and *Otechestvo* (Fatherland). During the same period, which proved to be very important for his literary career, Vazov met Pencho Slaveykov and began to collaborate with Konstantin Velichkov, with whom he enjoyed a lifelong friendship. Exhausted by his uncle's permanent disapproval and almost penniless, he escaped to Braila, the center of the Bulgarian revolutionary emigration. He remained there for a couple of months, sharing the life of the Bulgarian exiles. This experience had a considerable effect on the young poet's personal development. In addition, he was strongly influenced by his encounters with Botev in Braila and Galats and became more involved with the patriotic and civic fervor of the times.

Back in Bulgaria, he taught for some time from 1872 to 1873 in Mustafa Pasha (now Svilengrad), where he shared his patriotic ideas with his students. Later he worked as a translator at the railway line constructed between Sofia and Kyustendil. There Vazov studied German and perfected his French. He greatly valued the opportunity to reflect upon the life of the Bulgarian peasantry with which he came into contact while working there. In 1875 he returned to his hometown and joined the local revolutionary committee. The growing revolutionary enthusiasm in his country and the influence of Botev's poetry on him led Vazov to write poems with a distinct revolutionary bias. After the failure of the April uprising in 1876 and its subsequent suppression, Vazov was forced to leave Bulgaria lest he be arrested. He went to Bucharest and entered the Central Bulgarian Charity Society, becoming its secretary.

While living in difficult and miserable conditions he composed and published his first book, *Pryaporets i gusla* (The Banner and the Lute, 1876), under the pen name Peychinovich. In 1877 he followed with a second collection of poems, titled *Tŭgite na Bŭlgariya* (The Griefs of Bulgaria), written under his real name. The first two collections represent the period of national revival on the eve of the April uprising. Although most of these poems fail to manifest the poetic perfection Vazov later attained, some match the best of his poetic output. In them Vazov expresses his confidence in his people's ability to win their liberty. A constant theme, which runs through his later works as well, is the hope for help from Russia. The struggles for national liberation remained the dominant theme in many of Vazov's works after 1878. Better mastered and emotionally controlled because of the distance in time and perspective, they express a deep understanding of the historical and moral values at play during this time. The collection of poems he wrote to express his feelings about the war of liberation was titled *Izbavlenie* (Deliverance, 1878).

During the Russian-Turkish war in 1877–1878 Vazov worked in Svishtov as a clerk for Gov. Nayden Gerov and later was sent on business to Ruse, where he remained for a year. The launching of his bureaucratic career gave Vazov an occupation that counterbalanced his literary activity for decades.

His next job, starting in March 1879, was in Berkovitsa, where he was nominated chairman of the regional court. A case from his practice there inspired the composition of the narrative poem "Gramada" (The Heap, 1880), an account of a conflict between a whole village and a *chorbadzhiya* (a rich landowner) first published in the journal *Bŭlgarska ilyustratsiya* (Bulgaria Illustrated). The title refers to a folk custom of throwing stones on a pile to symbolize the people's curse upon their oppressor. Some material from his experience in Berkovitsa later gave birth to the comic story "Mitrofan i Dormidolski" (1882), first published in his book *Mitrofan* (1882), which describes the quarrel between two old friends against the background of an aimless and vulgar provincial life.

Already famous, Vazov became the object of hostile attacks and slander in the press occasioned by envy and malice. The campaign against him resulted in Vazov's resignation. Rather than accept a transfer to Vidin, which he saw as a demotion, he retired and settled in Plovdiv, the capital of Eastern Rumelia. This period, beginning in October 1880, was one of the most fruitful for Vazov both socially and artistically. He took an active part in the political and cultural life of the region, was elected a deputy in the local parliament, worked as an editor and reviewer, and wrote some of his most significant works in addition to political journalism and literary criticism. A major activity during this period

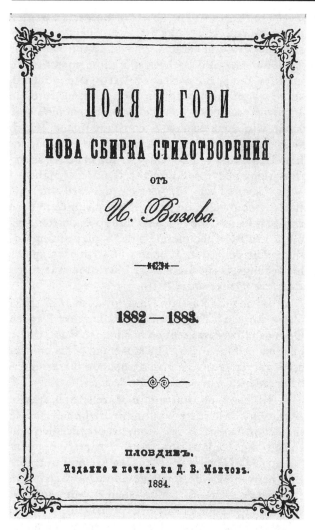

Title page for Vazov's Polya i gori *(Fields and Forests), which includes poems on love and nature*

was his editorship with Velichkov of the newspaper *Narodniy glas* (National Voice). In 1881 Vazov was nominated chairman of the Plovdiv literary society and became the editor in chief of the society's journal *Nauka* (Science), the first important literary periodical after the liberation. In 1885 he founded the literary journal *Zora* (Dawn). Together with his friend and coworker Velichkov he compiled the well-known *Bŭlgarska khristomatiya* (Bulgarian Reader, 1884), a two-volume set representing more than a hundred Bulgarian and foreign authors. In fulfilling this large-scale project the editors faced innumerable difficulties and had to do most of the work themselves.

Vazov's work from this period is surprisingly rich and diverse. He wrote in several different genres, creating the foundation for a new Bulgarian literature. During the years in Plovdiv he published

the verse collections *Mayska kitka, Gusla* (The Lute, 1881), and *Polya i gori* (Fields and Forests, 1884), which dealt predominantly with love and nature's beauties. Following a visit to Italy in 1884 his next book of poems appeared, titled *Italiya* (Italy, 1884). While in Plovdiv, Vazov also wrote a comedy, *Mikhalaki chorbadzhi* (1882), which inaugurated his theatrical career.

Some of the works that date from these years are masterpieces that became a significant part of Bulgarian classical literature. Among them are the poems "Bŭlgarskiy ezik" (Bulgarian Language), "Na svobodata" (To Liberty), "Ne se gasi tuy shto ne gasne" (You Cannot Extinguish What Never Fades) — all published in *Polya i gori* in 1884; "Novoto grobishte na Slivnitsa" (The New Cemetery at Slivnitsa; published in *Slivnitsa,* 1886); the short story "Ide li?" (Is He Coming?; published in *Sŭchineniya. Povesti i razkazi,* 1891); and the novellas "Nemili-nedragi" (Unloved and Unwanted, 1883) and "Chichovtsi" (Uncles, 1884).

"Nemili-nedragi" chronicles the life of Bulgarian revolutionary émigres in Romania. Although the work is largely autobiographical — the character Brŭchkov is obviously Vazov's double — it is less insistent on historical fact than on sympathy and respect for the anonymous heroes unrecognized by history, whom Vazov vividly depicts with a charming mixture of patriotic excitement, sentimentality, and mild humor.

In his comic novella "Chichovtsi" Vazov presents a gallery of portraits, most drawn from his memory. The world of these "uncles" was his childhood — petty, provincial, primitive, and backward, yet nevertheless attractive with its natural curiosity and buoyancy. The trivial events depicted in the narrative do not deprive the characters of their originality and color. On the contrary, it is precisely the pettiness of everyday life that serves as a background for their uniqueness. Paradoxically enough, the very triviality of the events most clearly reflects the general spirit of the time and people's hopes, feelings, and aspirations, which Vazov later depicted from yet another perspective in his novel *Pod igoto* (1894; translated as *Under the Yoke,* 1894, 1955).

Vazov's literary tour de force from this period is his cycle of poems "Epopeya na zabravenite" (The Epopee of the Forgotten), which he wrote between 1881 (five poems in *Gusla*) and 1884 (seven in *Polya i gori*). In it he creates an impressive panorama of the Bulgarian national revival. Each poem is a portrait of a particular hero: Paisiy Hilendarski, the author of *Istoriya slavenobolgarskaya* (A Slavic Bulgarian History, 1762), whose work is considered to have inaugurated the revival; Vasil Levski and Georgi Sava Rakovski, the remarkable figures of the national revolutionary movement; the apostles of the April uprising, Georgi Benkovski, Todor Kableshkov, and Panayot Volov; and finally the volunteers who fought in the decisive battle of the Russian-Turkish war of liberation at Shipka Pass in "Opŭlchentsite na Shipka" (Volunteers at Shipka). In these poetic tributes to the figures of the epoch, Vazov's enthusiasm and admiration diverged from the prevailing pragmatic views of the time, which were frequently devoid of ideals. The general mood of Vazov's works during the 1880s is disillusionment. His critical approach to the unheroic present was the background that gave the poet's admiration of the heroic past its real dimension. The heroes of the past were forgotten by many, and forgetfulness was one of the most widespread ideological conventions of the time – hence Vazov's title.

Along with the notion of forgetfulness, Vazov introduced another idea to the literature of this period, namely the sickness of the new generation. One of the poems that best illustrates this theme is "Linee nashto pokolenie" (Our Generation Languishes, 1883). Vazov felt that this sickness had its origins in the mercantile and egoistic attitude of the new Bulgarian society and in the lack of great ideals that could unite the nation. This mood, which prevails in poems such as "Pustota" (Desolation; published in the periodical *Navka,* 1881) and "Poet i vdŭkhnovenie" (Poet and Inspiration; published in *Gusla,* 1881) and became one of the dominant topics in his work after 1885, can be traced back to "Vekŭt" (The Age, 1876).

After the union of the two artificially divided parts of Bulgaria in 1885, Vazov remained in Plovdiv for some time. There he published two books in which he voiced his response to the Serbian-Bulgarian war: a collection of poems titled *Slivnitsa* and a book of short stories, *Podporuchik Vŭlko* (Lieutenant Vulko), both in 1886. That same year he was forced into exile by the political situation, under which the government began to persecute Russophiles. He went to Constantinople, where he remained for some months, and later settled in Odessa, Russia. Deeply missing his fatherland and absorbed in his nostalgia, he began writing *Pod igoto,* which was published after his return home in the first three volumes of the newly founded *Sbornik za narodni umotvoreniya, nauka i knizhnina* (Journal of Folklore, Scholarship, and Literature).

Pod igoto is undoubtedly Vazov's greatest achievement and has earned a place among the classics of Bulgarian literature. It represents a broad

picture of the April uprising, the events leading up to it, and its subsequent failure and suppression. The events are described through the effect they had on ordinary people's lives. The broad picture of the national revolutionary uprising serves as the background for a complicated plot, which revolves around the protagonist, Boycho Ognyanov. He appears in the opening scene of the novel after escaping from Turkish imprisonment and becomes the leading figure in the local revolutionary movement. The story of Ognyanov's social and political activities is interwoven with his love for the schoolteacher Rada Gospozhina. The personal intrigues in which most of the characters find themselves involved develop alongside the political events of the story, simultaneously reaching both climax and catastrophe. Although the story refers to certain historical events, the narrative is based on fictional dramatic conflicts. The novel, however, is successful in grasping the essence of the epoch; the magic of the reawakening manifested itself in everyday life, spanned virtually every strata of Bulgarian society, and was accomplished in every person's mind.

In 1889 Vazov settled in Sofia. The next year he founded the journal *Denitsa* (Daystar), which ran for only two years but managed to attract many of the significant authors of the time, among them Velichkov, Stoyan Mikhaylovski, and Slaveykov. In the following years Vazov produced prose works that were sharply critical of contemporary Bulgarian society, such as *Draski i sharki* (Scribbles and Patterns, 1893, 1895).

In depicting contemporary life Vazov preferred to work within the genre of the short story. During the last decade of the nineteenth century and the beginning of the twentieth century this genre dominated his literary output. In addition to *Draski i sharki* Vazov published the three volumes of *Sŭchineniya. Povesti i razkazi* (Novellas and Short Stories, 1891–1893), *Videno i chuto* (Things Seen and Heard, 1901), *Pŭstŭr svyat* (A Varicolored World, 1902), and *Utro v Banki* (Morning in Banki, 1905), which includes almost all of his short stories. Most of them describe the atmosphere of the 1890s. The stories can be divided into satirical works depicting the vices of contemporary society, such as "Kardashev na lov" (Kardashev Hunting; published in 1895 in *Draski i sharki*), "Epokha – kŭrmachka na veliki khora" (An Epoch, Breeder of Great People; published in 1890 in the periodical *Dennitsa*), and "Tŭmen geroy" (A Shady Hero); and another, much smaller group consisting of works that preserve the preliberation ideals, such as "Edna bŭlgarka" (A Bulgarian Woman), first published under a different title in the periodical *Bŭlgarska sbirka* in 1899. The story "Dyado Lotso gleda" (Old Lotso Looks Out), from his book *Videno i chuto,* shares the features of both groups in that it depicts an old blind man's enthusiasm and joy for Bulgaria's progress alongside the disillusionment of those who are able to see.

During this period Vazov also composed his best travel works: *V nedrata na Rodopite* (In Rhodopa's Recesses, 1892; enlarged, 1904) and *Velikata Rilska pustinya* (The Great Rila Wilderness, 1892; enlarged, 1904). Like his poetry, they are devoted to nature. Vazov was one of the first Bulgarian authors to glorify nature in his homeland. Facing its greatness and unattainability, he contemplated the issues of life, philosophical and social questions, ethics, and art.

In 1896 Vazov published the novel *Nova zemya* (New Land), written as a sequel to *Pod igoto;* several characters from the former appear in the latter. It depicts the final stage of the Bulgarian national liberation movement, the union of 1885. The dominant mood is disillusionment with the new social and political morals in contrast to the high ethos of the preliberation period. The protagonist, Nayden Stremski, moves from his sub-Balkan town to Plovdiv, the center of political and revolutionary activities that resulted in the union. The plot revolves around his political activity and love affairs and includes several subplots that detract from the novel's cohesiveness. Vazov's attempt to provide his readers with an in-depth picture of this epoch results in an overabundance of detail, which complicates an already elaborate plot structure. The novel was received with severe criticism and thought to be much inferior to *Pod igoto.* Despite its imperfections, *Nova zemya* probably has been undervalued as a literary work because of the tendency to compare it to Vazov's masterpiece.

After the publication of this novel Vazov found himself in a deep crisis. He intended never to write again. Partially out of his own painful uncertainty over what path to take, he accepted a position as minister of education in Konstantin Stoilov's government in 1897. This position proved to be a burden for the poet, and when the government resigned in January 1899 it came as a great relief for him. Withdrawing from public service to his house and to life in a small family circle, Vazov could return to his intellectual and artistic occupations. This event, however, marked the beginning of a new period in his artistic life that lasted until World War I. At this time Vazov developed a deep friendship with Ivan Shishmanov, out of which grew a remark-

able book of memoirs written by Shishmanov called *Ivan Vazov. Spomeni i dokumenti* (Ivan Vazov: Memoirs and Documents, 1930).

After his return to literary life Vazov published *Skitnishki pesni* (A Wanderer's Songs, 1899), followed by *Pod nasheto nebe* (Under Our Skies, 1900). The poems of these collections, which are predominantly patriotic in mood, reflect Vazov's preoccupation with historical themes during the first decade of the twentieth century. During this period Vazov also published his comedies *Vestnikar li?* (A Newspaper Man?, 1900) and *Sluzhbogontsi* (Position Seekers, 1903) and his major collections of short stories. In some of the works included in *Videno i chuto, Pŭstŭr svyat,* and *Utro v Banki,* Vazov employed the same tools he had in *Draski i sharki.* He wrote biting satire directed against those who strove for financial advantages and undeserved social positions, a subject that was also central to his comedies. In these collections Vazov also included memoirs, in which he expressed his love for the past and the great personalities he had once known, including Lyuben Karavelov, Stefan Stambolov, and his teachers. Finally, he produced sketches of nature and various places he had visited.

During the same period Vazov wrote the novel *Kazalarskata tsaritsa* (The Tsarina of Kazalar, 1903), an attempt to present Bulgarian society of the 1890s both in Sofia and in the country. The plot is organized around two parallel stories, that of the schoolteacher Tsonka, who is seduced and abandoned by her lover, and of her sister, Mila Khrusanova, whose love with Brankov is meant to serve as a positive role model. Although the novel was widely read, critics were unanimous in their disapproval of it. Subsequent critical response has suggested that they were accurate in their assessment.

Vazov's fascination with history found expression in his novel *Svetoslav Terter* (1907) and the novella *Ivan Aleksandŭr* (1907), as well as in his plays *Borislav* (1909) and *Ivaylo* (1913) and in his collection of ballads and narrative poems titled *Legendi pri Tsarevets* (Legends at Tsarevets, 1910). In *Svetoslav Terter* he revisited the events of the latter part of the thirteenth century in order to depict the struggles of the brave and ambitious boyar against Tartar rule. *Ivan Aleksandŭr* provides an account of the decade preceding the Turkish invasion. In depicting palace life and corruption in society, Vazov made clear the parallels with contemporary Bulgarian society.

Between 1907 and 1917 Vazov won recognition as a playwright. His most successful dramatic works are *Kŭm propast* (Toward the Precipice, 1910),

Borislav, and *Ivaylo,* which are landmarks in the development of Bulgarian drama. The most successful among his plays are adaptations from his narrative works. *Khŭshove* (Exiles, 1894; revised, 1899) is taken from "Nemili-nedragi," while *Kŭm propast* is an adaptation of *Ivan Aleksandŭr.* In the dramatic versions the author added new moral and political accents. A suggestive example is *Kŭm propast,* whose title is a metaphor for the irresponsible actions of the czar and the boyars, who led the state to the brink of collapse. The title also alludes to the contemporary political situation and personality of Czar Ferdinand, a fact that was grasped and decoded by the critics. This type of historical drama was in accord with the public's expectations during that time. For more than a decade Vazov was the most popular and outstanding playwright in Bulgaria; between 1907 and 1912 his plays were performed at the National Theater more than 150 times. No doubt his immense popularity encouraged him during that time to plan the publication of a complete edition of his works. The plan was partially carried out with the appearance of eight volumes (1911–1918).

During the wars beginning in 1912 Vazov wrote patriotic poems to encourage the soldiers at the front. His collection of verse *Pod grŭma na pobedite* (In the Thunder of Victories, 1914) represented the heroism of the ordinary Bulgarian soldier on the battlefield. Vazov's response to World War I was twofold. Although he was among those who opposed Bulgaria's involvement in the war as an ally of Germany, later, when faced with the reality of the war, he wrote some of his most enthusiastic patriotic poems in praise of the courage and the victories of the Bulgarian soldiers. In 1916 he published *Pesni za Makedoniya* (Songs of Macedonia), in which he rejoiced over the liberation of the Bulgarian territories.

The national catastrophe at the end of the war was an ordeal for Vazov, who had lived so long with the ideals and hopes of the newly born Bulgaria. Disappointed and bored with politics, he turned to the writing of lyric poetry. His books *Novi ekove* (New Echoes, 1917), *Yulska kitka* (A July Bouquet, 1917), and *Lyuleka mi zamirisa* (I Caught a Scent of Lilac, 1919) are verses of a personal nature. More and more the poet contemplated his own self and his poetry in an attempt to locate his own place and that of his verse within a larger historical perspective. His inborn vitality and interest in the world about him nevertheless helped him to retain an optimistic view of the future of his fatherland. In his last collection of verse, significantly titled *Ne shte*

zagine! (It Will Not Perish!, 1920), he expressed the indestructible faith that constituted his life.

In 1920 Vazov celebrated his seventieth birthday and his fiftieth anniversary as a writer. Both were observed on a national scale. He was the most beloved and respected Bulgarian author of his time. Fortunately, he had the opportunity to witness the outpourings of tribute and love from his people, for the following year he unexpectedly died on 22 September in Sofia of a heart attack; he was mourned by the whole country. His personality and his literary works gradually came to be valued not only as a part of the historical epoch to which he belonged, but as a symbol of all that was quintessentially Bulgarian.

Letters:

Pisma ot Iv. Vazov do E. Mars, edited by Todor Pavlov (Sofia: Narizdat, 1947);

Ivan Vazov. Nepublikuvani pisma, edited by Velichko Vŭlchev (Sofia: BAN, 1955);

Sŭbrani sŭchineniya, volumes 21 and 22 (Sofia: Bŭlgarski pisatel, 1979).

Interviews:

Ivan D. Shishmanov, *Ivan Vazov. Spomeni i dokumenti* (Sofia: BAN, 1930); enlarged as Shishmanov and Mikhail Arnaudov, *Ivan Vazov. Spomeni i dokumenti* (Sofia: Bŭlgarski pisatel, 1976).

Bibliography:

Velichko Vŭlchev, *Ivan Vazov, 1850–1921: Bio-bibliographia* (Sofia: Narodna biblioteka "Kiril i Metodiy," 1985).

Biographies:

Stoyan Romanski, ed., *Ivan Vazov: Zhivot i tvorshestvo* (Sofia: Pridvorna pechatnitsa, 1920);

Pierre Christoforov, *Ivan Vazov: La formation d'un écrivain bulgare, 1850–1921* (Paris: Droz, 1938);

Mikhail Arnaudov, *Ivan Vazov, zhivot i delo* (Sofia: Khemus, 1939);

Nikolay Liliev, ed., *Ivan Vazov. Sbornik ot spomeni, materiali i dokumenti* (Sofia: BAN, 1949);

Georgi Dimov, ed., *Ivan Vazov v spomenite na sŭvremennitsite si* (Sofia: Bŭlgarski pisatel, 1966);

Velichko Vŭlchev, *Ivan Vazov. Zhiznen i tvorcheski pŭt* (Sofia: BAN, 1968);

Milka Markovska, *Letopis za zhivota i tvorchestvoto na Ivan Vazov,* volume 1 (Sofia: Dŭrzh. izd-vo nauka i izkustvo, 1981).

References:

Mikhail Arnaudov, *Iz zhivota i poeziata na Ivan Vazov* (Sofia: BAN, 1958);

Iliya Boyadzhiev, *Epopeya na bŭlgarskiya zhivot* (Sofia: Narodna prosveta, 1989);

Stiliyan Chilingirov, ed., *Proslava na Ivana Vazova. Sbornik za tŭrzhestvata i chestvuvaniyata na narodniya ni poet po sluchay 50 godini ot negovata knizhovna deynost* (Sofia: "Gutenberg," 1921);

K. H. Derzhavin, *Ivan Vazov. Ocherk zhizni i tvorchestva* (Moscow & Leningrad: Akademiya nauk SSSR, 1951);

Georgi Dimov, *Ivan Vazov v Bŭlgarskata literaturna kritika* (Sofia: BAN, 1971);

Petŭr Dinekov, "Vazov – nash sŭvremennik," in his *Literaturna sŭdba i sŭvremennost* (Sofia: Nauka i izkustvo, 1972), pp. 240–251;

Dinekov, "Vazov v razvitieto na Bŭlgarskata literatura," in his *Literaturni obrazi* (Sofia: Narodna kultura, 1963), pp. 138–188;

Stefan Elevterov, "Povestite na Ivan Vazov," *Literaturna misŭl,* 22, no. 6 (1978): 59–79;

Ditmar Endler, "Za kŭsite razkazi v tvorchestvoto na Ivan Vazov," *Literaturna misŭl,* 4 (1971): 61–73;

Nikola Georgiev, "Ot Khilendar do Shipka ('Epopeya na zabravenite' i nravstveno – istoricheskite tsennosti na bŭlgarskoto natsionalno vŭzrazhdane)," *Literaturna misŭl,* 3 (1975): 13–32;

Simeon Hadzhikosev, "Kŭm poetikata na Vazovia razkaz," *Literaturna misŭl,* 9 (1983): 37–46;

Svetlozar Igov, "Patriarkhŭt," in his *Bŭlgariyo, za tebe pyakha!* (Sofia: Bŭlgarski pisatel, 1985), pp. 82–163;

Radosvet Kolarov, "Mezhdu mraka i svetlinata. Nablyudenya vŭrkhu poemata na Iv. Vazov 'Paisiy,' " *Literaturna misŭl,* 2 (1977): 85–100;

Iskra Panova, *Vazov, Elin Pelin, Yovkov: Maystori na razkaza* (Sofia: Bŭlgarski pisatel, 1975);

Todor Pavlov, N. Liliev, and S. Bozhkov, eds., *Ivan Vazov. Sbornik po sluchay 100 godishninata ot rozhdenieto mu* (Sofia: BAN, 1950);

Nikolay Raynov, *Vechnoto v nashata literatura. tom II. Ivan Vazov* (Sofia: S. Atanasov, 1941);

Milena Tsaneva, *Ivan Vazov v Plovdiv* (Sofia: Nauka i izkustvo, 1966);

Tsaneva, *Iz poetichniya svyat na Ivan Vazov: Literaturno kriticheski statii* (Sofia: Bŭlgarski pisatel, 1965);

Tsaneva, *Po stranitsite na "Pod igoto"* (Sofia: Bŭlgarski pisatel / Veliko Tŭrnovo: D. Naydenov, 1976);

Tsaneva, ed., *Bŭlgarskata kritika za Ivan Vazov* (Sofia: Bŭlgarski pisatel, 1988);

Tsaneva, ed., *Ivan Vazov. Kolokvium "Problemi na bŭlgarskata literatura"* (Sofia, 1983);

Tsaneva, ed., *Ivan Vazov: Sbornik materiali ot nauchnata sesiya po sluchay 125 godishninata ot rozhdenieto na pisatelya* (Plovdiv: Khr. G. Danov, 1976);

Aleksandŭr Yordanov, "Edin zabraven poeticheski dialog," *Septemvri,* 7 (1988): 213–223.

Ivo Vojnović
(9 October 1857 – 30 August 1929)

Thomas Eekman
University of California, Los Angeles

BOOKS: *Perom i olovkom,* as Sergije P. (Zagreb: Matica hrvatska, 1884);

Ksanta (Zagreb: Matica hrvatska, 1886); republished as *Stari grijesi* (Zagreb: Društvo hrvatskih književnika, 1919);

Psyche (Zagreb: Matica hrvatska, 1889);

Ekvinocij (Zagreb: Matica hrvatska, 1895); republished as *Ekvinocijo* (Belgrade: Srpska književna zadruga, 1905);

Dubrovačka trilogija (Zagreb: Matica hrvatska, 1903; Novi Sad: Matica srpska, 1909); *Suton* translated by Fanny S. Copeland as "The Dying Republic," *Slavonic Review* (1922–1923): 184–216; *Suton* translated by John Batistich and George R. Noyes as "The Twilight," *The Occident,* 84 (November 1924): 7–15; translated by Ada Broch as *A Trilogy of Dubrovnik* (Graz: Leyham, 1921); translated by Batistich and Noyes as *A Trilogy of Dubrovnik, Poet Lore,* 56, no. 2 (1951): 99–142; 56, no. 3 (1951): 195–218; 56, no. 4 (1951): 291–340;

Smrt majke Jugovića (Zagreb: Dionička tiskara, 1907);

Gospodja sa suncokretom, San mletačke noći, Triptyhon (Zagreb: Matica hrvatska, 1912);

Lazarevo vaskrsenje (Dubrovnik: Matica srpska, 1913); translated by Batistich and Noyes as "The Resurrection of Lazarus," *Poet Lore,* 37, no. 3 (1926): 317–395;

Jakobina (Zagreb: Matica hrvatska, 1914);

Djela, 3 volumes (Dubrovnik: J. Tošković, 1914–1922);

Akordi (Zagreb: Jug, 1917);

Imperatrix (Zagreb: Književni Jug, 1918);

Maškarate ispodl kuplja (Zagreb: Zabavna biblioteka, 1922);

Prolog nenapisane drame (Belgrade: Srpska književna zadruga, 1929);

Sabrana dela, 3 volumes (Belgrade: Geca Kon, 1939–1941).

PLAY PRODUCTIONS: *Psyche,* Zagreb, 1890;
Gundulićev san, Dubrovnik, 1893;

Ekvinocij, Zagreb, National Theater, 1895;
Smrt majke Jugovića, Belgrade, 1906;
Gospodja sa suncokretom, 1913.

Ivo Vojnović was born on 9 October 1857 in Dubrovnik, the old Ragusa on the Adriatic coast, and all his life he felt a strong attachment to this city, its history as an independent republic, and its patriciate, to which he and his brother Lujo claimed to belong, although they actually did not. The Vojnovićes were an old Serbian noble family, some of whose members moved to Russia, where they received the title of count. Vojnović's great-grandfather Djordje was, as a Russian major, involved in the Russian-French-Austrian conflict in the Adriatic (1802–1813) and settled in the region. His father, Konstantin (Kosto), lived in Dubrovnik and turned Catholic; in 1855 he married Maria Serragli, whose grandfather had settled in Dubrovnik from Italy and whose father was knighted by Austria. A year after his birth the family moved to Split, where his father opened a law office; he was an active publicist and politician. Besides his brother, who also became a writer, a publicist, and a diplomat and who left memoirs about Vojnović, Vojnović had two sisters, Katica and Gjene. He was especially close to his mother, whom he idolized. She taught him French, drawing, and painting. From Split the family often went to Dubrovnik, especially during the summer. He attended an Italian high school in Split; but in 1874 when he was seventeen, the family moved to Zagreb, where his father became a law professor at the newly opened university and later a member of the Croatian parliament. Vojnović studied law in Zagreb (1878–1880) and was then appointed as an assistant in law school.

During his student years he became a correspondent with *Narodni list* (People's Newspaper) in Zadar, where he regularly published notes and reviews dealing with cultural life in Zagreb. He contributed to other papers and had his first fiction, the novella *Geranium,* printed in installments in *Vijenac* (Wreath) in 1880.

This "romance of a spinster," as the subtitle reads, Vojnović's only work set in Split, was an instant success. The geranium is a metaphor of the barren, unsatisfactory existence of a good but unattractive poor girl. The narrative structure is rather complex; its style shows influences of some of the authors he had read and admired, including George Sand, Alexandre Dumas, Charles Dickens, Alessandro Manzoni, and August Šenoa. *Geranium* includes typical romantic elements, but Nikola Ivanišin has claimed that Croatian realism starts with it.

The symbolism of this early work is related to the spirit of the new school of symbolist poets and writers in France with whom Vojnović was familiar. He highly valued Edmond Rostand, Maurice Maeterlinck, Henrik Ibsen, Richard Wagner, and, somewhat later, Gabriele D'Annunzio. On the other hand, in his prose of the mid 1880s a certain influence of the French realists can be established, including Alphonse Daudet, Emile Zola, and especially Gustave Flaubert.

When the political situation in Croatia became tense and the Hungarian governor Khuen-Hédeváry took measures to quell the opposition, he exiled Vojnović, whom he considered a potential opponent, to the small town of Križevci. He spent five years there alone and unhappy, but he wrote the series of four short stories *Perom i olovkom* (With Pen and Pencil, 1884), the novella *Ksanta* (1886), and his first drama, *Psyche* (1889). In his prose he continued to cultivate a luxuriant, flamboyant style with an abundance of images, comparisons, metaphors, inversions, and other elegant stylistic features.

The first of the four stories in *Perom i olovkom,* "U magli" (In the Fog), is a sentimental narrative about a poor, blind organ-grinder in Zagreb whose young son has died. "Sirena" is a much more joyous work about three girls swimming in the blue Adriatic, their conversations, and their meeting with the old fisherman Pavo. An impressionistic picture of sun, sea, and youth, it includes memories of summers spent in Dubrovnik. "Rose Méry" has the subtitle "Bečka idila" (Viennese Idyll); the setting is Vienna, which he loved to visit. Rose Méry is a mysterious beauty in love with the impoverished young Count Marko Branski; after detailed descriptions of the ambience, the "idyll" ends in failure. The fourth story, "Čemu?" (Why?), subtitled "Prizori iz života" (Scenes from Life), is set in Rome and also centers around a mysterious, even somewhat demoniac, female character. Here a young Dubrovnik violinist falls in love with a renowned singer; but love interferes with art, and the artist commits suicide. The stories were well received; soon after their publication they appeared in German translation in the *Agramer Zeitung* (Agramer Newspaper), and "Sirena" was translated in a Paris magazine.

For Vojnović, according to his biographer Mirko Žeželj, women remained a longing, not a reality: he denied himself or was unable to have any passionate love. His fixation on his mother seems to be the main reason for his passive attitude toward women, but he claimed his total dedication to art as the primary cause.

Ksanta is an unfinished novel and Vojnović's last attempt at the genre. It was his first work of fiction published under his own name. In 1919 he revised it and published it as *Stari grijesi* (Old Sins). He envisioned this as the first part of a long novel, but apparently he lacked the perseverance to sit and concentrate on an extensive piece of work. The novel is about Pero Dubović, who jilts his fiancée when he becomes carried away with the Greek girl Ksanta. He marries her and plans to embark with her on a long sea voyage. The story is set in Dubrovnik, which is painted with all the lively details and bright colors his memory could conjure up. However, this descriptiveness – for example, the lengthy depiction of a storm – is detrimental to the plot development.

Psyche was finished in 1888. According to Žeželj, Josip Kulundzić characterized it as "a pseudo-symbolistic conversational comedy in three acts with a realistic dialogue." The ancient myth of Cupid and Psyche is the basis of the plot, the protagonist being in this case a Polish painter named Braniewski. He is painting Olga, with whom he falls in love; however, she is engaged to a wealthy prince. A character named Wanda also loves the painter but sacrifices herself and convinces the prince to renounce his engagement so Olga can marry Braniewski. The prince is willing to break off the engagement, and the happy couple is united. The play is distinguished by vivid dialogue, but the characters are insufficiently believable or psychologically deepened and there is too little action, so on the whole it is a rather weak play. It premiered in 1890 in Zagreb, and in 1892 it was performed in Graz, making it probably the first South Slavic play ever to be performed abroad.

From letters and diaries from this period in Križevci it is known that Vojnović had two love affairs; he supposedly portrayed his two sweethearts in the figures of Olga and Wanda. But whereas the play has a happy ending, his own affairs did not, and he was aware of his shortcomings. In his diary, according to Žeželj, he remarked, "My soul is a prisoner in a body to which it does not belong. That is the secret of my existence!" and "What kind of a monster is born in me! Prometheus in the shape of a gnome!" All he longed for was "the refined milieu of beauty and art – and the mother's breast: to sink my head in her lap, to close my eyes and to hear mother's heartbeat, saying to myself: this is heaven! That is the origin of my poetry and my force!"

In 1889 Vojnović was transferred, first to Bjelovar, then four months later to Zadar, an old city on the Adriatic coast, where he was employed in the governor's office. He was closer to Dubrovnik, and, keeping aloof from local politics, he made friends with some civil servants, intellectuals, Italians, and Austrian officers. After a year he was sent on a commission to Dubrovnik and stayed there for seven years, succeeding in obtaining a modest government post. In 1892 his parents joined him; his younger sister had married a Frenchman and lived in southern France.

On the occasion of the unveiling of a statue of the well-known seventeenth-century Dubrovnik poet Ivan Gundulić, Vojnović composed a lyrical drama, *Gundulićev san* (Gundulić's Dream), that was performed in 1893 with Lujo and Gjene, who came over from France, in the principal parts. The play, replete with Ragusan patriotism and pathos, was performed in Zagreb every year between 1897 and 1920, yet for a twentieth-century public this kind of Romantic theatricality is indigestible. The play includes an appeal for concord between the Serbs and Croats, who were locked in bitter conflicts at that time.

This is the period of another platonic love, probably the greatest and longest he experienced. He got to know Marie Rubricius in 1884; in 1891 she married a physician named Pugliesi. Apparently she also had an affection for Vojnović as a man of enormous culture who was extremely well read and had a rich inner life. Her death in 1914 shocked him; in response he wrote a series of poetic "Pisma onoj koja ode" (Letters to Her Who Left), published in 1923 in the periodical *Jugoslavenska njiva* (Yugoslav Field). She is immortalized in his play *Imperatrix* (1918).

From 1891 to 1901 he wrote a cycle of six sonnets titled "Lapadski soneti" (Sonnets from Lapad), set in the peninsula west of Dubrovnik. He had them all read by his father and brother, and he threw some out because Lujo did not like them. They were published in 1917 in *Akordi* (Accords) with a seventh sonnet, "Carmen." Later he produced eight more poems as well as several occasional verses. His poetry is marked by a melancholy lyricism, the use of symbols and attributes from the Adriatic, and partly the historical ambience in which the poems are situated, such as cypresses, olive trees, laurel and myrtle, a gale, sea, sun, rocks, *gospari* (lords), *knez* (overlords), tombs, and an old little church. The archaisms contribute to the suggestiveness of the poems. They are widely anthologized in Serbo-Croatian literature.

An attempt at dramatizing *Ksanta* evolved into the drama *Ekvinocij* (Equinox, 1895), the first of his series of noteworthy plays that are still performed. It was premiered in the Zagreb National Theater in 1895. It preserves some elements from *Ksanta:* the equinoctial thunderstorm and the young sea captain Pero, who becomes two characters: the sea captain Frano and the "rich man from America," the antagonist of the play, Niko Marinović. Surprisingly, this is not a society play: there is no *vlastela* (the old Dubrovnik nobility) as in his prose, poetry, and some of his other plays.

Scene from Vojnović's play Na taraci *(On the Terrace, 1902), part of his* Dubrovačka trilogija *(1903; translated as* A Trilogy of Dubrovnik, *1922, 1951)*

The cast consists of common Dubrovnik people: a bark worker, a shipyard worker, an apprentice, a priest, a grave digger, a blind man, an old sailor, a mailwoman, and several other women from the lower classes. He had earlier expressed the desire to write "a piece from the common people's life"; next to Wagner, there was also the influence of Pietro Mascagni's *Cavalleria rusticana* (1890), an opera in a democratic spirit with people's choirs. The main conflict of the drama originates in an old theme: a girl loves a man but is forced to marry someone else. In this case, the calculating and angry father is Frano, the lover the shipyard worker Ivo, the successful suitor the rich "American" Niko, who, to complicate matters, was Ivo's mother's lover before he left for America and, unknowingly, Ivo's father. When Ivo plans to kill his rival Niko, his mother Jele reveals to him that he is Niko's natural son. Obviously, Vojnović was alluding to the myth of Oedipus in his drama. This conflict coincides, in the third act, with a hurricane.

A second crisis is reached in the fourth act when Jele kills her former lover, the father of her son and his and her enemy, and then dies. The motif of the unbreakable bond between mother and son – the mother protecting him and revenging herself on his waylayer to ensure the son's happiness – is prominent in this realistic-symbolic drama full of strong passions and with gripping turning points. The only optimistic, sunnier element is found in Anica, Captain Frano's daughter, and Ivo, who finally leave for America, convinced that they will build a better future. The scene is similar to the situation of Anja and Trofimov, who escape from the oppressive atmosphere of Anton Chekhov's *The Cherry Orchard* (1904). Of course, there are influences, with Ibsen the most evident. The language of the play is saturated with local and Italian words and expressions. After the Zagreb premiere and the one in Belgrade some years later, critics found considerable fault with *Ekvinocij;* nevertheless, it was often performed, served as a libretto for three operas, and was made into the film *Nevjera* (Infidelity). Vojnović also translated it into Italian.

Next he wrote a one-act play, which he started in 1895 and completed in 1889–1890 on the Adriatic island of Brač, where he was sent to serve in the local administration. The initial title was "Sjene" (Shadows), but he changed it to *Suton* (Twilight; translated as "The Dying Republic," 1922–1923; translated as "The Twilight," 1924). In 1901 he finished another one-act play with the French title *Allons enfants* (Go, Citizens), and in 1902 a third one titled *Na taraci* (On the Terrace). These three short plays formed a triptych he called *Dubrovačka trilogija* (1903; translated as *A Trilogy of Dubrovnik,* 1921; translated as *A Trilogy of Dubrovnik,* 1951), and they are often performed and usually printed together. The title "Twilight" would be appropriate for the whole cycle, as the period of decay of old Dubrovnik is at the core of each drama. They are set during three periods in Dubrovnik's history: 1806 (*Allons enfants*), 1832 (*Suton*), and 1900 (*Na taraci*).

Allons enfants is set during the turbulent period of Ragusan history when the Napoleonic army conquered the Adriatic coast and entered the town, putting an end to centuries of independence and rule by the patrician class. The helpless patricians, such as Orsat and Lady Ane, are contrasted with the naive plebeians, such as the maid Lucija, who instinctively choose the side of the French. The reader is confronted with a decaying class tragically lacking any awareness of the seriousness of their situation and the historical juncture through which they live.

Suton deals with the further decline of the Dubrovnik aristocracy, only not as a massive phenomenon (in *Allons enfants* there are, besides the overlords, twenty gentlemen on stage) but symbolically within one family: a sixty-eight-year-old, impoverished aristocratic lady and her three daughters, of whom the youngest, Pavle, is being courted by a sea captain of plebeian birth, Lujo. After two dramatic encounters between the two, Pavle rejects him because her class counsciousness does not allow her to violate the exclusiveness of her family by a morganatic marriage. She decides to enter a nunnery and ostentatiously cuts her hair on stage. For the modern reader the situation and the mentality are somewhat hard to apprehend; however, Vojnović brings the protagonists of this short play to life, making even the sensitive, unhappy, but proud Pavle somehow believable. He avoids rhetorical pathos, even from the mouth of the rigid mother.

The third panel of the triptych is about the agony of the Ragusan patriciate in Vojnović's own time. The action takes place among fourteen young and old patricians on the wide, white terrace of Count Lukša's home just outside the town. Like in the play *Wesele* (The Wedding, 1901) of his Polish contemporary Stanisław Wyspianski, the protagonists appear on stage in pairs: first the village owner Lukša and the priest to whom he dictates his memoirs, then his older sister Mare and her young niece Ida, then the coquettish Baroness Lidija and her lover, Count Hans. But then Lidija brings a whole throng of merry singers, dancers, and musicians to the terrace, who rehearse an operetta. The whole company disappears, other figures appear, and the dialogue is fragmented and incoherent, exactly as in *Wesele*. What is different is the monologue by Count Lukša, an old, decrepit man who bemoans not only his own decline but that of his class and his city. But then he harshly forbids Vuko, a servant, to marry a maid because he does not earn enough money. Shortly after he finds out that Vuko is his illegitimate son, he calls him back and grants him permission to marry the girl. His last words, the final words of the trilogy, are "And now — let's go to bed."

Dubrovačka trilogija has been called the apogee of Vojnović's dramatic work. There was criticism as well: he was a sentimental-romantic author who constantly looked back at the past of one city and used patriotic rhetoric, decorative melodramatic effects, and a fashionable symbolism but lacked in great, new ideas and personalities.

After another stay in Zadar, in 1903 Vojnović was for the second time appointed as a district inspector to Brač, where his mother and older sister joined him. He held regular musical-literary soirees with guests from Split and Zadar, and he wrote his drama *Smrt majke Jugovića* (The Death of the Mother of the Jugovićes, 1907).

This time the inspiration came from the idea of South Slavic (Yugoslav) unity, with Serbia as the kernel of statehood for a future political organization. At the time this idea was gaining support in the various South Slavic areas. Vojnović based his drama on the generally known epic folk song relating how in 1389 the Serbian army under King Lazar was defeated by the Turks on the Kosovo plain. This traumatic event became an important Serbian national legend. A sweeping enthusiasm for this Yugoslav concept made many Croats forget the controversies and join the movement for unification.

Vojnović wrote his play in unrhymed verse in the style and decasyllabic meter of the folk song,

Ivo Vojnović

paraphrasing or sometimes taking over lines from well-known anonymous epic texts. He finished it in 1905, and the premiere took place in Belgrade in 1906; the Zagreb premiere followed in 1907. It was never reprinted in this form and not even staged later; no edition of Vojnović's complete works exists, and interest in the play waned, both for political reasons and because of its overstated symbolism and melodramatic nature.

He called his work "A Dramatic Lay in Three Cantos." The first canto or act bears the title "Daughters-in-Law," referring to the wives of the nine sons of Jug Bogdan who are waiting for the outcome of the battle. Their mother-in-law's voice is heard from the tower, where she stands watch. The daughters-in-law complain that she oppresses them and does not even allow them to cry. She then enters and drinks from Jug's goblet, brought by the main figure among the daughters, Andjelija, who, in Vojnović's version, is a native of Dubrovnik. In the second act, "The Specter," Andjelija's husband, Damjan, who ran from the battlefield, enters and reports the death of his father, Jug, and his eight brothers. His mother asks, "And the ninth?" She

calls him a sly fugitive and orders him to go back to Kosovo: "Blessed is he who dies for the honor!" The act is full of pathos. The third act is simply called "Kosovo." The battle is over, the mother enters, and the "Kosovo girl," known from the folk epic, tells her of Damjan's glorious death with Andjelija's name on his lips. In *Ekvinocij* a mother had sacrificed herself for the happiness of her son; here a mother sacrifices her son for the defense and the honor of the whole nation — a higher law had to be obeyed. Only after the defeat the human mother wakes up in her: she kisses Damjan's hand, which was cut off in the battle and brought to her, and dies of grief. Vojnović thus aimed at creating a figure of truly pathetic proportions, a heroine of classical tragedy who should be seen not just as the mother of her sons but of a whole nation, representing the Serbian ethos of *Vidovdan* (Saint Vid's day, the date of the battle).

After the Balkan War of 1912, when the Serbs defeated the Turkish army and claimed that "Kosovo was revenged," Vojnović wrote a fourth canto or act called "The Guslar" (folk singer). It is actually a monologue of the blind *guslar,* who then regains his sight and sees the Mother of the Jugovićes as the great Serbian martyr; it continues in the same high-pitched if not bombastic tone of the earlier acts. With the epilogue, or fourth canto, the play had a solemn, official performance in 1919 on Saint Vid's Day in Belgrade. This drama, and particularly the fourth canto, was strongly influenced by D'Annunzio's "Adriatic tragedy" *La Nave* (The Ship, 1907).

Vojnović's next play in this vein, *Lazarevo vaskrsenje* (1913, translated as "The Resurrection of Lazarus," 1926), was equally tendentious, pro-Serbian, and full of excessive floridity and a highflown oratorical and oracular style, for which he was chided by the critics, especially the Croat ones. Again there is a mother, who cannot save her son from fighting and dying in the Balkan War but who sacrifices herself for her grandchildren, who will become national avengers.

Along with this nationalistic play he produced a work of a very different character: the cosmopolitan *Gospodja sa suncokretom* (The Lady with the Sunflower, 1912), performed in 1913. The setting is a fashionable Venetian hotel with an array of wealthy and titled guests. The globe-trotter Malipiero arrives and is struck by the beautiful wife of a Russian count, Jekaterinskaja, who seems vaguely familiar to him. The second act is a flashback in which a Miss Mag and a young man enter a small London hotel room. Although she took him there, she does not surrender to him and leaves, locking him up in the room. He falls asleep, and when he wakes up he finds under his bed a corpse with a sunflower in its hand. He realizes the woman lured him into the room in order to incriminate him, and he flees after breaking the window. Then follows the third act, which is even more sensational; the action is based on a true event. Jekaterinskaja is enchanted by a fellow hotel guest, Goljukov, and intends to kill her husband. She confesses to Malipiero she had lured him into the hotel room in order to divert suspicion from herself: she had murdered her fiancé in order to marry the rich count. Malipiero realizes she has an eye on Goljukov now, and when she asks him for a sunflower, he understands what is going to happen. This is the day of a great festival in Venice; at the height of it, the news comes that Jekaterinskaja has thrown herself from her balcony into the sea. *Gospodja sa suncokretom* was received critically by the press: in particular, the corpse under the bed was mentioned as a sign of Vojnović's declining power as a dramatist.

In 1913–1914 he wrote his next drama, already started in 1907, *Imperatrix*. The most abstract-symbolic play he ever produced, it includes very few concrete and live features, although he and Lujo considered it his most perfect and profound work. However, as Vlatko Pavletić remarks, "Not everything is deep of which we do not see the bottom." The protagonist is the empress of a mystical "island of oblivion," her opponent the chancellor who aims at starting a war. They clash only in the fifth act: the preceding four are filled with verbose rhetoric. There are endless stage directions and inserted author's comments, which had become increasingly abundant in his dramatic works. Most of the play has no scenes, and it has never been performed, even though he repeatedly revised the text. He translated it into Italian.

In the meantime, he had left Brač and settled in Zagreb, but not of his own free will. As a result of his craving for grandeur, he lived far beyond his modest means and ran into huge debts. A scandal resulted in which he was even suspected of embezzlement. At fifty years old and without a pension, he was thrown out of his job. Fortunately, the Croatian National Theater in Zagreb appointed him as its theater manager in 1907. Now living in the Croatian capital, he had an interesting and stimulating position and was in day-to-day contact with the leading writers, dramatists, actors, and critics of his time. His post left him much free time, which he used to travel, sometimes staying for months in Dubrovnik, Belgrade, Paris, Italy, and other places.

However, it was not a quiet period of personal and family happiness. He soon discovered that Zagreb society was torn apart by sharp animosities and conflicts; he was disappointed in the general atmosphere. In 1911 the theater management freed him of all duties so he would be able to work on a new play (*Gospodja sa suncokretom*).

He never took up his duties again and became a professional writer. However, the outbreak of World War I turned out to be a catastrophe for him. He and his brother were arrested in Dubrovnik by the Austrian authorities as sworn adversaries of the Hapsburg state. He was interned in Šibenik for seventeen months, out of which he spent five in a hospital. He had suffered for some time from glaucoma; during his confinement, without any medical care, his condition deteriorated, and even after his release he was not allowed to see an eye specialist in Trieste. Consequently, he lost the sight in his left eye.

In May 1915 Vojnović was accomodated in a Zagreb hospital, where he spent almost four years. Here he wrote his unpublished "Hospital Diary." Although his internment was formally ended in 1916, he stayed in the hospital. In 1917 his sixtieth birthday was nationally celebrated. During the euphoria of 1918 due to the foreseeable end of the war and the fall of the Austro-Hungarian Empire, Vojnović, as a staunch champion of Serbian-Croatian brotherhood and Yugoslav unity, was elevated to the height of a national hero and martyr. In those days he was especially close to Ivo Andrić, who spent time in the same hospital.

In 1922 Vojnović finished his last play *Maškarate ispod kuplja* (Masquerade In the Attic). It was written for the most part during a prolonged stay in France, where he lived with his sick mother – she died in 1922 in Zagreb, a heavy blow to him – and sister Gjene in Nice, where he even functioned as a Yugoslav consul, and also with his brother in Paris. The play starts with a prologue in which the author once again introduces his old Dubrovnik in the mid nineteenth century and his two protagonists, the elderly, unmarried, aristocratic sisters Jele and Ane. The play unfolds in three hours, and in fact the three acts are called "hours." In the first, Jele and Ane go upstairs to see the young maid Anica, who is ill. It is carnival, and they dress up and mask for the bedridden girl: a whole bizarre, exuberant scene of dancing and merrymaking follows. The second hour is spent in the drawing room downstairs, where a crowd of ladies and girls enters dressed up in rococo style. Jele and Ane appear disguised as eighteenth-century Dubrovnik lords. Their nephew

Jero is dressed as a Pierrot and dances a gavotte with them. It is again a scene of wild carnival frenzy. The third hour is again set in the attic, where two older maids dress up for the sick Anica. Then the Pierrot-Jero enters, who is in love with her. A fantastic love scene in a mystical atmosphere follows. The clock strikes five, whereupon the live statue of Saint Vlah enters with the bronze men who every hour strike the bell with their hammers. Anica dies in the arms of Jero. Thus ends Vojnović's swan song in a mystical, elegiac, and at the same time elated mood: "How lucky she is!" are Ane's last words before the curtain falls. Anica, unlike her namesake in *Ekvinocij*, is not leaving with her beloved for a better future: she passes away, leaving only the two ladies and their maids behind in the house. But the grandeur of old Dubrovnik is once more brought to life in this play.

Ivo Vojnović's role in Croatian and Yugoslav literature was outstanding. He has rightfully been called a precursor of the *Moderna* movement of the early twentieth century, both with his prose, in which the expressive, picturesque element takes precedence over the plot, and his dramatic works, which elevated Croatian drama to a European level. He introduced new concepts, styles, and themes in the theater of his time, and several of his plays became extremely popular among the South Slavs as well as the Czechs: they were part of the modern repertoire in many European countries in the years shortly before and after World War I. His lapse into tendentious pro-Serbian plays and the sensational *Gospodja sa suncokretom* does not diminish his significance as an early modernist and an affectionate, fervent painter and resuscitator of the historical free city of Dubrovnik. He died in Belgrade on 30 August 1929.

Biography:
Mirko Žeželj, *Gospar Ivo* (Zagreb: Centar za informacije i publicitet, 1977).

References:
Milan Begović, "Conte Ivo," *Hrvatska revija*, 2 (1929): 561–569;

Frano Čale, "O romantičnom porijeklu 'subjektivno-lirskog' postupka u stilu Ive Vojnovića," *Umjetnost riječi*, 2 (1963);

Dubrovnik, special issue on Vojnović, nos. 3–4 (1957);

Branko Gavela, "Što mislim da znam i što ne znam o Ivu Vojnoviću," introduction to Vojnović's *Dubrovačka trilogija* (Belgrade: Nolit, 1963);

Branko Hećimović, "Zapisi o dramama Ive Vojnovića," in his *Trinaest hrvatskih dramatičara* (Zagreb: Znanje, 1976);

Nikola Ivanišin, "Drama i dramatika u Vojnovićevom stvaralaštvu do 1889 godine," *Split*, 8 (1962);

Alfred Jensen, "En sydslavisk dramatiker," in his *Fran Balkan* (Stockholm, 1917), pp. 82–97;

Raško V. Jovanović, *Ivo Vojnović* (Belgrade: Institut za književnost i umetnost, 1974);

Jovanović, "Ivo Vojnović na beogradskoj sceni," *Književnost*, 28 (1959): 157–174;

Ante Kadić, "Vojnović's *Trilogy* – The Decline of the Dubrovnik Nobility," in his *The Tradition of Freedom in Croatian Literature* (Bloomington, Ind.: Croatian Alliance, 1983), pp. 216–232;

Miroslav Krleža, "Ivo Vojnović," *Književna republika*, 1, no. 4 (1924): 146–152;

Marijan Matković, preface to Vojnović's *Pjesme, pripovijetke, drame* (Zagreb: Matica hrvatska – Zora, 1964), pp. 7–31;

Giovanni Maver, *Ivo Vojnović* (Rome: Istituto per L'Europa Orientale, 1924);

Vlatko Pavletić, *Drame Iva Vojnovića* (Zagreb: Školska knjiga, 1962);

Dragutin Prohaska, *O pjesniku slobode: Studije o književnom radu Ive Vojnovića povodom njegove šezdesetgodišnjice* (Osijek, Yugoslavia: Radoslav Bačić, 1918);

Savremenik, special issue on Vojnović, 6, no. 4 (1912);

Darko Suvin, "*Dubrovačka trilogija* Iva Vojnovića kao cjelina," *Forum*, 25 (1973): 753–795;

Suvin, "Uz genealogiju Iva Vojnovića," *Forum*, 20 (1970): 818–832;

Suvin, "Vojnović's Dramaturgy and Its European Context," *Canadian Review of Comparative Literature*, 2 (1975): 10–34;

Umberto Urbani, *Scrittori jugoslavi*, volume 1 (Trieste: Parnaso, 1927), pp. 137–155;

Arsen Venzelides, "The Plays of Ivo Vojnović," *Slavonic and East European Review*, 8 (1929): 368–374;

Lujo Vojnovic, "Spomeni o bratu," in Vojnović's *Sabrana dela*, volume 1 (Belgrade: Greca Kon, 1939).

Prežihov Voranc

(10 August 1893 – 18 February 1950)

Irma M. Ozbalt

BOOKS: *Povesti* (Ljubljana: Zadružna založba, 1925);
Požganica: Roman iz prevratnih dni (Ljubljana: Naša založba, 1939);
Doberdob: Vojni roman slovenskega naroda (Ljubljana: Naša založba, 1940);
Samorastniki: Koroške povesti (Ljubljana: Naša založba, 1940);
Jamnica: Roman soseske (Ljubljana: Slovenski knjižni zavod, 1945);
Od Kotelj do Belih vod (Ljubljana: Državna založba Slovenije, 1945);
Borba na tujih tleh (Ljubljana: Slovenski knjižni zavod, 1946);
Naši mejniki: Kratke storije iz minulih dni (Celje: Mohorjeva družba, 1946);
Solzice (Ljubljana: Mladinsa knjiga, 1949);
Kanjuh iz Zagate, edited by Ivan Skušek (Ljubljana: Slovenski knjižni zavod, 1952);
Lovro Kuhar – Prežihov Voranc: Zbrano delo, 12 volumes, edited by Drago Druškovič and Jože Koruza (Ljubljana: Državna založba Slovenije, 1962–1990);
Lovro Kuhar – Prežihov Voranc: Izbrana dela, 5 volumes, edited by Herman Vogel (Maribor: Založba Obzorja, 1981).

PLAY PRODUCTION: *Pernjakovi,* completed by Herbert Grün, Kranj, Prešernovo gledališče, 24 April 1951.

Prežihov Voranc is his nation's most outstanding representative of social – not socialist – realism, a style that prevailed in Slovene literature during the 1930s. His pen name is a combination of the geographic designation Prežihov vrh and a dialect form of his personal name.

Voranc was born Lovro Kuhar on 10 August 1893 in Kotlje, a village in southeast Carinthia. His father, Ivan, a tenant farmer and lumberjack, was a determined nationalist who instilled in his four sons a fierce pride in their Slovene heritage, which was in constant danger of being subsumed by neighboring German-speaking Austria. Their mother, Marjeta, cared less about the "Carinthian question," although she was a great source of local history, old beliefs, and myths. Her storytelling was Voranc's first source of literary inspiration.

Voranc had little formal education: he completed his compulsory schooling in the two-room school at Kotlje, where German was the predominant language of instruction. He supplemented his learning by voracious reading. His father subscribed to the annual series of books issued by Mohorjeva družba (Mohor's Society), a Catholic publishing house in Celovec (which Austria renamed Klagenfurt), and to the Celovec weekly *Mir* (Peace). Voranc also borrowed books from his teachers. He read – mostly while grazing cattle – Slovene authors as well as Russian novels in German translation. However, the most important stimulus in his early literary development was a humble monthly magazine, *Domači prijatelj* (Home Friend), which the Kuhars received free from a coffee dispatcher in Prague. Its editor, Zofka Kveder, a Slovene writer and feminist, published Voranc's first contribution, a story about a local drunk, "Petkov Cenc," in 1909. In the following years Voranc contributed to *Domači prijatelj* more than twenty sketches depicting the peasants and picturesque characters from his native mountains.

In 1911 Voranc was seized by wanderlust. He traveled first to Trieste and then to Gorica in search of work and adventure. He found little of either and ended up in Celovec. Unemployed, he spent the winter in the company of drifters. This experience provided him with new material for writing. He began writing starkly realistic portraits of social misfits around him. Some of the sketches were published in 1912 in a Socialist magazine, *Zarja,* as "Obrazi s ceste" (Faces from the Street). They were as influenced by Maksim Gorky as his earlier stories had been patterned on Slovene models.

In the spring of 1912 Voranc returned home, penniless but wiser. In the fall he managed to enroll in a five-month course in cooperative management in Ljubljana. There he approached the editor of *Ljubljanski Zvon* (Ljubljana Bell), the leading Slovene literary review, and offered him a short story set in the swampy fields surrounding Ljubljana, "Tadej pl. Spobijan." It was published in 1913.

In the spring of 1914 Voranc took another course in co-op management, this time in Vienna. The two courses, each lasting a few months, were the only education he received beyond his elementary schooling.

When World War I broke out he was drafted immediately. He spent two horrible years at different fronts. During that time he came to the conclusion that all wars were barbaric and senseless, but to fight in a war for the Austrians, who had oppressed Slovenes for so long, was insane. In 1916, therefore, he crossed over to the Italian side and then spent two years in prisoner-of-war camps, trying in vain to join the newly formed Yugoslav Legion. Having experienced the hard lot of the working-man firsthand, he was a willing listener and pupil of an Italian doctor – a Socialist – and of a Bosnian Marxist. These two men greatly influenced his philosophical and political orientation.

His experience in the trenches shook Voranc so deeply that he could not write about what he saw. He published only two war stories, both at the beginning of the war. In the first postwar decade he wrote five more, but his war novel *Doberdob* (1940) matured more than twenty years later.

In February 1919 Voranc returned to Kotlje without any prospects for his future. He spent the spring and summer working on his father's newly acquired fourteen-acre farm. In the fall he was hired as a clerk at the steelworks in nearby Guštanj. Following his beliefs, he immediately joined the Socialist Workers Party and became completely involved in its sociopolitical activities: during the Carinthian referendum, which split the region between Austria and Yugoslavia, he campaigned for Yugoslavia, helped persecuted leftists escape across the border, organized lectures, and directed plays. In 1924 he married Marija Sisernik, a peasant girl. They had two daughters.

In spite of his busy schedule during the 1920s, Voranc maintained contacts with his publishers and continued writing. He returned to his original source of inspiration, the peasant folk of his native village and valley. In 1921 he published, in *Ljubljanski Zvon,* the short story "Borba" (The Struggle), which depicted the life story of his father and included Voranc's childhood memories. The story already displayed the elements of his unique, mature style, which would propel him into the apex of his literary fame ten years later. In the 1920s, however, when expressionism and formal experimentation reigned supreme in Slovene literature, such a simple, realistic story evoked no critical response.

In 1925 Voranc assembled a collection of his writings and published them under the simple title *Povesti* (Stories). The book includes his stories about peasants and picturesque characters from his immediate surroundings. The stories were written in his early, simple style. Among them, however, was the balladlike "Vodnjak" (The Well), which later merited inclusion in his best-known collection, *Samorastniki* (The Self-Sown, 1940). Like "Borba," it was written in Voranc's powerful realistic style, depicting the tragic fate of a mountain farmer in dramatic, determined strokes. The critics did not notice it.

In 1930, to escape political prosecution and jail, Voranc escaped to Austria. He soon established connections with the International Red Aid Organization, which then supported and used him for nearly ten years. As an adviser and organizer of the farmers and farm laborers, he traveled on secret missions all over Europe under false names and passports, staying in Vienna, Berlin, Prague, Norway, Romania, and Bulgaria. In 1936–1937 he spent more than six months in Vienna prisons. His last stop was Paris, where he worked in a bookshop that was a clearinghouse for Slovene and Russian publications. He wrote and translated many political articles for distribution in Slovenia. He also looked after newly arrived Slovene political refugees. He was overworked and underpaid, yet he directed his Ljubljana publishers to send all payments for his work to his immediate family and to his debtors in Guštanj, where he had incurred some debts at the time of his sudden departure.

Poor, exhausted, and on the run, Voranc not only continued writing but created his best work during this time. He wrote travel essays on Carinthia and France, publishing mostly in *Sodobnost* (Our Time), a newly founded leftist review in Ljubljana. But political writings and travel reports were only his peripheral writings. In the 1930s he planned and partially executed his most ambitious work, which he published under his new pen name, Prežihov Voranc. He has been known as Prežihov Voranc, Prežih, or Voranc ever since.

In 1935 *Sodobnost* published his short story "Boj na požiralniku" (Struggle in the Swamps). It caused a sensation. Voranc was finally discovered by the Slovene literary elite, who had previously dismissed him as a self-taught Carinthian folk artist. He was recognized as a great new talent, a writer who had introduced a new style into Slovene literature. "Boj na požiralniku" is a small masterpiece describing the tragically hopeless fight of a peasant family against the swampy, collapsing land. It exhibits all the characteristics of Voranc's style: realistic events intermingle with lyrical descriptions of landscape; the characters are larger than life, their features outlined with dramatic, balladlike intensity; and the language is vivid, greatly enhanced by vocabulary and metaphors from the Carinthian dialect.

Between 1935 and 1939 *Sodobnost* published five more of Voranc's stories: "Jirs in Bavh" (Two Oxen), "Odpustki" (Indulgences), "Samorastniki" (The Self-Sown), "Prvi spopad" (The First Encounter), and "Pot na klop" (On the Bench). All deal with peasants eking out a living on the sloping fields of the Carinthian mountains. They are heavy-footed and rough-spoken, with a tremendous physical and mental capacity for suffering; yet their core is soft,

their appreciation of nature verging on humble worship. They are superstitious, ignorant, slow, and wicked, but they are also guileless, brave, noble, and faithful.

All of Voranc's stories in *Sodobnost* were heavily edited by Ferdo Kozak, to whose corrections of grammar and even vocabulary Voranc humbly submitted. In 1940 Kozak arranged for the publication of the stories in book form. The collection, *Samorastniki,* also included "Vodnjak" and "Ljubezen na odoru" (Passion in the Fields), a monumental novella about a tragic rural Venus and her lumberjack lover.

Critical assessments of *Samorastniki* were superlative, claiming Voranc as a first-class epic talent. His characters, critics said, are mighty in their precision, his descriptions of scenery are magnificent, and his language is powerful. One of the critics applied a new label in Slovene literature for Voranc's style: social realism. *Samorastniki* represents the peak of Voranc's achievement. The collection has been repeatedly reprinted, and some of its stories have been adapted for theater, film, and television.

During the 1930s Voranc also worked on his three novels. The only time he could totally devote to his art was the months in Vienna jails. Thus, the only novel he brought to conclusion and had published while living abroad was *Požganica* (The Burnt Mountain, 1939). Its topic is the 1919 Carinthian referendum, and the novel deals with sociopolitical upheavals in Voranc's native valley. It is a novel with a thesis, a chronicle of a community. It has no central hero; the carriers of events are the inhabitants of a village huddled under the lofty Požganica, its burning the symbol of their dashed hopes for national and social liberation.

Požganica earned Voranc the City of Ljubljana Literary Award. The critical reception of his first novel was generally positive. Although many critics considered parts of the narrative more political reporting than fiction, all emphasized that Voranc was a powerful writer who had introduced into Slovene literature a fresh, new style. However, the rightist critics attacked him for his political allegiances, totally ignoring the artistic value of *Požganica.*

At the end of 1939 Voranc returned to Slovenia from Paris. He brought his unfinished novels and dedicated most of his time in the underground to revising and finishing them. The reasons for his decision to return are not clear, especially since an eight-year prison term, received in absentia, still hung over his head. He lived incognito, constantly changing his abode, but in 1941, when Yu-

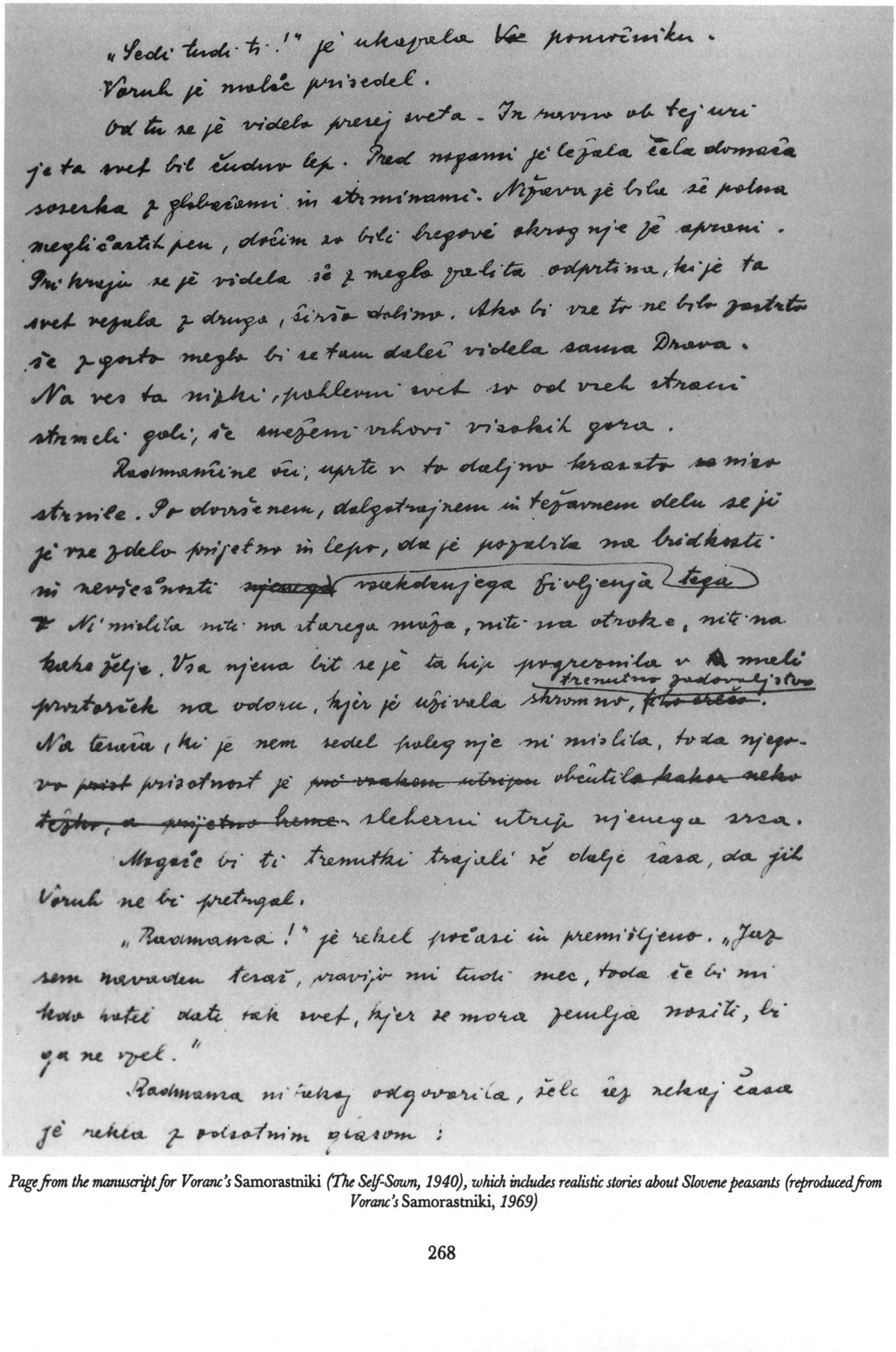

„Sedi tudi ti!" je ukazala ponirčniku.
Voruh je molče prisedel.
Od tu se je videla prerej sveta. In nevino ob tej uri je ta svet bil čudno lep. Pred nogami je ležala cela domača soseska z globečemi in strminami. Nižava je bila še polna meglic. .... pen, dočim so bili bregovi okrog nje že aprnemi. Pri kraju se je videla še z meglo zalita odprtina, ki je ta svet rezala z drugo, širšo dolino. Ako bi vse to ne bilo zastrto še z gosto meglo bi se tam dalež videla sama Drava. Na ves ta nizki, pohlevni svet so od vseh strani strmeli goli, še sneženi vrhovi visokih gora.
Radmanciine oči, uprte v to daljno krasoto, so mirno strmele. Po dovršenem, dolgotrajnem in težavnem delu se ji je vse zdelo prijetno in lepo, da je pozabila na bridkosti in nevšečnosti ~~njenega~~ vsakdanjega življenja ~~tega~~
Ni mislila niti na starega moža, niti na otroke, niti na kake želje. Vsa njena bit se je tačas pogreznila v mali prostorček na odoru, kjer je uživala skromno, trenutno zadovoljstvo ~~...~~.
Na Voruha, ki je nem sedel poleg nje ni mislila, toda njegovo ~~prisot~~ prisotnost je ~~pri vsakem utripu~~ občutila ~~kakor neko težko, a prijetno breme~~ sleherni utrip njenega srca.
Mogoče bi ti trenutki trajali še dalje časa, da jih Voruh ne bi pretrgal.
„Radmanca!" je rekel počasi in premišljeno. „Jaz sem navaden tesač, pravijo mi tudi mec, toda če bi mi kdo hotel dati tak svet, kjer se mora zemlja nositi, bi ga ne vzel."
Radmanca ni takoj odgovorila, šele čez nekaj časa je rekla z odsotnim glasom:

Page from the manuscript for Voranc's Samorastniki *(The Self-Sown, 1940), which includes realistic stories about Slovene peasants (reproduced from Voranc's* Samorastniki, *1969)* goslavia succumbed to the Germans and Italians, he finally settled in Ljubljana. He lived there until 1943, when he was arrested. He was sent to German concentration camps, first to Sachsenhausen, then Mathausen. He remained there until the end of the war.

Doberdob, named after its setting, was his war novel, the result of persistence and dedication. He had already written its first draft before 1930, but the Austrian police seized it. In the Vienna jails he rewrote the novel from memory, adding two more parts to it. This manuscript was also taken from him. He eventually got it back and started revising it in 1938, when the twentieth anniversary of the armistice revived his war memories. He anchored the characters within historical facts and deepened the novel's message: wars are unethical because they cripple humanity physically and psychologically.

Doberdob was finally published in 1940. The critics declared that it was a novel without a central hero and that it was mostly of documentary value. Some compared it unfavorably with his short fiction and *Požganica.*

Jamnica (1945) was Voranc's longest and most ambitious work. It represents the culmination and synthesis of all his "peasant fiction." He had been planning the novel for many years, but his early plans became more concretely focused during his stay in Norway in 1933, when he read Knut Hamsun's novel *Markens grode* (1917; translated as *The Growth of the Soil,* 1920), which he considered a falsified picture of peasant life not only in Norway but everywhere where people fertilize the soil with the sweat of their brows. His first reaction to Hamsun was *Samorastniki,* but *Jamnica* represents his final rebuttal of the Norwegian novelist.

He began writing *Jamnica* while still involved with *Doberdob,* but the bulk of the novel was written in a wine cellar in the Dolenjsko countryside in the summer of 1940. He kept enlarging and editing it until his return to Ljubljana. Instead of publishing it, however, he hid it, with some other manuscripts, at a friend's house, observing the so-called cultural silence declared by some Slovene artists for the duration of the war. In 1945 *Jamnica* was resurrected and published.

The hero of the novel is again a whole community, the village of Jamnica, which is caught in the political and economic crises between the two wars. Against a background of fields and forests, castles and churches, and farmhouses and shacks appears a group of unforgettable characters: farmers, lumberjacks, beggars, and half-wits, and here and there a teacher, a priest, or a Socialist agitator.

Their activities are not only determined by political changes but also conditioned by heritage, customs, and the whims of changing seasons. Voranc based every character on a real person. Communal events, such as weddings, parish feasts, political gatherings, and the harvest, are painted with the vivid colors of a folk artist who is himself part of the picture. *Jamnica* is composed as a string of episodes, each chapter a self-contained short story, a ballad, or a grotesque.

Voranc had put his very soul into *Jamnica* and was sensitive to any criticism of this novel, which sold out quickly but received a lukewarm response from reviewers. Literary historian Anton Slodnjak found the narrative a monumental work of a self-taught genius but criticized it for its descriptions of "moral excesses." Marxist critics faulted it for ideological omissions as well as for its structure. Voranc responded that his critics had missed the essence of *Jamnica,* judging it on the basis of preconceived ideas and literary theories.

While working on his novels, Voranc also continued writing travel essays. In 1940 and 1941 he published his impressions of Norway and Romania and began thinking of republishing all his travel writings in book form. During the war he prepared two collections, one comprising his articles on Carinthia, the other his essays on the countries he had visited during the 1930s. The manuscripts then waited in their hiding place, together with *Jamnica,* for his return from Germany.

Od Kotelj do Belih vod (From Kotlje to Bele vode, 1945) received generally favorable reviews. Some critics resented his didactic passages, some praised him as an excellent observer and judge, and some compared the collection with Maksim Gorky's *Na dne* (The Lower Depths, 1902), while some saw it as a combination of autobiography that reads like fiction, of discussions on social issues, of descriptions, and of lyrical musings.

The second collection, *Borba na tujih tleh* (Struggle on Foreign Soil, 1946) was reviewed briefly. Most critics believed that this type of prose was not meant to be creative. To them Voranc was here simply a reporter, a keen observer, or a traveler with a mission.

Voranc returned from the concentration camps a sick man. He lived only another five years, in and out of hospitals, seeking help for stomach problems, heart disease, and diabetes. He lived on a farm at his beloved Prežihov vrh. But although illness sapped his energy, he was active in local politics as an elected deputy to the federal house of representatives. He traveled to Belgrade and all over northern Slovenia, supervising the effectiveness of the Socialist reforms in agriculture and forestry and writing reports on his findings. His involvement in the community's political activities and projects, as well as his declining health, prevented him from carrying out numerous literary plans, although he continued writing until the end.

It is significant that Voranc remained loyal to Mohorjeva družba, the educator of his youth. He helped to reestablish this Catholic society in the new political environment, which ideologically was vastly removed from it. He served on its board as an in-house critic. In 1946 Mohorjeva družba even published a collection of his wartime stories, *Naši mejniki* (Our Frontiers). Voranc's political associates were displeased with his involvement in the society, and the critics decided that *Naši mejniki* was of more documentary than literary value. The book did not earn him that year's Prešeren Award, for which he had been hoping.

Among his unfinished projects Voranc left behind one act of a projected play, *Pernjakovi* (The Pernjak Family), which was later completed by Herbert Grün, and one masterful chapter of a planned historical novel, "Pristrah."

However, he did complete his magnificent swan song *Solzice* (Teardrops, 1949), a collection of short stories about peasant children, many of them autobiographical. *Solzice* is a mellow counterpart to *Samorastniki*. He had already written two of the stories during the war, but he wrote the rest at Prežihov vrh, surrounded by the bittersweet memories of his childhood. Each story is like an exquisite impressionistic painting saturated with vibrant colors, light, and shadow. The events are secondary; the emotions are intense and existential. The critics declared *Solzice* the dying author's finest book. It earned him three prestigious awards in the last year of his life.

Voranc died on 18 February 1950 in Maribor, where he had lived during the last few months of his life in order to be closer to the hospital.

Interviews:

Irma M. Ozbalt, "Pogovor v čebelnjaku," *Prosveta* (1, 8, 15 October 1986): 4;

Ivan Sivec, "Dolgo življenjsko potovanje za Lovrom in brez njega," *Delo* (25 January 1991): 5.

References:

Marja Boršnik, ed., *Prežihov zbornik* (Maribor: Založba Obzorja, 1957);

Jože Koruza, "O Prežihovem Vorancu in njegovih *Solzicah*," in Voranc's *Solzice* (Ljubljana: Mladinska knjiga, 1968), pp. 123–127;

Marjan Kramberger, "Problem kmetstva v Prežihovih novelah," in Voranc's *Samorastniki*, edited by Kramberger (Maribor: Založba Obzorja, 1969), pp. 225–289;

Lino Legiša, ed., *Zgodovina slovenskega slovstva*, volume 6 (Ljubljana: Slovenska Matica, 1968), pp. 393–399;

Irma M. Ozbalt, "Stubble Fields in Purple: Impressionism in Prežihov Voranc's Stories," *Slovene Studies*, 9, nos. 1–2 (1987): 165–172;

Anton Slodnjak, *Slovensko slovstvo* (Ljubljana: Mladinska knjiga, 1968), pp. 329–330, 422–428;

Josip Vidmar, *Obrazi* (Ljubljana: Državna založba Slovenije, 1980), pp. 346–360.

Papers:

Most of Voranc's papers are kept at his home at Prežihov vrh, Kotlje, in Carinthia, Slovenia. Some are housed in the reference library at Ravne na Koroškem, a sizable part in the National and University Library in Ljubljana, and a smaller portion in the University Library in Maribor.

Peyo Yavorov

(1 January 1878 – 17 October 1914)

Charles A. Moser
George Washington University

BOOKS: *Stikhotvoreniya* (Varna: Stefan Georgiev, 1901);

Stikhotvoreniya (Sofia: Khristo Olchev, 1903 [i.e. 1904]);

Gotse Delchev (Sofia: Khristo Olchev, 1904);

Bezsŭnitsi (Sofia: Spisanie Biblioteka, 1907);

Khaydushki kopneniya: Spomeni ot Makedoniya 1902–1903 (Sofia & Salonika: Ivan kh. Nikolov, 1909);

Podir senkite na oblatsite (Sofia: A. Paskalev, 1910);

V polite na Vitosha: Tragediya (Sofia: A. Paskalev, 1911);

Kogato grŭm udari, kak ekhoto zaglukhva (Sofia: A. Paskalev, 1912);

Sŭchineniya, 3 volumes (Sofia: A. Paskalev, 1924);

Sŭchineniya, 5 volumes, edited by Vladimir Vasilev (Sofia: Khemus, 1934–1936);

Sŭbrani sŭchineniya, 5 volumes, edited by Pencho Danchev (Sofia: Bŭlgarski pisatel, 1959–1960);

Sŭbrani sŭchineniya, 5 volumes (Sofia: Bŭlgarski pisatel, 1977–1979).

PLAY PRODUCTIONS: *V polite na Vitosha,* Sofia, National Theater, 1911;

Kogato grŭm udari, Sofia, National Theater, 1913.

Peyo Yavorov

Peyo Yavorov is generally considered one of the finest poetic talents of the turn of the century in Bulgaria. Although a prominent member of the *Misŭl* group, an intellectual circle of writers and thinkers gathered about Krŭstyo Krŭstev's journal *Misŭl* (Thought), he had little formal education – unlike Pencho Slaveykov, for example – and was not even especially interested in literature. Indeed, in his later years he once declared that he had "never cared for poetry." In addition, he displayed little self-discipline in his writing: he was preeminently a lyric poet who produced short pieces that he did not bother to rework. Despite all this, he had an innate poetic gift that was evident even in writings lacking in shape or organization.

Yavorov was born Peyo Kracholov on 1 January 1878, the year of his country's liberation, in the small town of Chirpan, located between Plovdiv and Stara Zagora. His family was relatively well-to-do, and he had seven brothers and sisters. He received his early education in his hometown and later in Plovdiv but eventually had to drop out of school because of his father's straitened financial circumstances and his own poor health.

The year 1894 was important for the young poet: his first poem, "Chirpan," appeared in a Plovdiv publication, and he found employment in Chirpan as an apprentice telegrapher. The following year he was promoted to telegrapher. Having some time on his hands, he began reading both Russian and Bulgarian literature. In the fall of 1895 he made his first visit to Sofia. Upon his return home he evinced a deep interest in Socialist thought: he did a great deal of reading on the topic and even organized a Socialist group. This dovetailed with his interest in the cause of Macedonian independence in its more radical formulations, a cause with which he later was closely associated.

While continuing to work as a telegrapher and moving about the country – first to Sliven, then to Straldzha, finally to Ankhialo – the young poet, who thought for a time of becoming an actor, read Heinrich Heine and the Russian author Semyon Nadson and wrote poems reflecting a thirst for social justice shaped by the populist movement in Russia. His first poem to appear in *Misŭl*, then the leading literary journal in Bulgaria, had a heavy Socialist coloration: "Na edin pesimist" (To a Pessimist, 1898). Here the poet admits that the Bulgarian people are seemingly enslaved and asleep but argues that their souls are very much alive, and if they are enlightened and encouraged, they will themselves find the path to a better future.

Kracholov published individual poems periodically in *Misŭl*, without attracting any particular attention until he sent the editorial office a longer poem, "Kaliopa" (Calliope), composed during his cultural isolation in Ankhialo. This work aroused the positive enthusiasm of the journal's editors: they published it in their first issue for the new century and contrived to have him transferred to Sofia. Slaveykov even became Kracholov's poetic godfather, christening him Yavorov, from the word for sycamore. Certainly the pen name was more euphonic than the poet's real name. His first book, *Stikhotvoreniya* (Poems), appeared in Varna in 1901.

During this period Yavorov was a relatively straightforward writer. In "Velikden" (Easter, 1900), dedicated to one of his brothers, Yavorov recalls his "happy, cherished childhood," with his parents, brothers, and sisters – although the poem ends on a pessimistic note as he confronts the "unknown road" of life with "no companion to give me his hand." If hints of his mature development are to be found in this conclusion, it is also true that his early poetry includes many notes of social protest. In one of his best-known poems, "Armentsi" (Armenians, 1900), inspired by groups of Armenian refugees he had seen arriving in Bulgaria in 1894 after Turkish massacres, he pays tribute to the remnants of this heroic nation, even though too many of the refugees

drown their grief in drink and melancholy song. The poem is structured about the alliterative parallel between *piya* (drink) and *peya* (sing).

Yavorov became a full-fledged member of the *Misŭl* group quite early. Krŭstev provided him attentive analyses regularly, and Slaveykov wrote an important introduction to the second edition of Yavorov's *Stikhotvoreniya*, which appeared in late 1903. (Yavorov had previously dedicated one of his lyric poems to Slaveykov.) But Yavorov was not content to be only a writer at this point: he felt the call of social conscience, now in the form of a dedication to the Macedonian cause. In 1901 he quit his job; after editing a newspaper for a brief time, in 1902 he went to Macedonia with Gotse Delchev, a leading radical Macedonian revolutionary. He returned to Sofia but in 1903 was off to Macedonia again. There, moving from place to place, he brought out twelve issues of a hectographed bulletin, *Svoboda ili smŭrt!* (Freedom or Death!), between February and April 1903. He was the major contributor to this publication, writing editorial articles and poems intended both to fill up space and to advance the revolutionary cause. However, by July 1903 he had returned to Sofia as his permanent home, though he continued to work for the Macedonian cause. For example, in 1904 he published a short biography of Delchev, who was killed in the revolutionary struggle in mid 1903.

Yavorov was soon established at the National Library in Sofia, which served as a haven for many writers and intellectuals at the time, and he became chief librarian in 1904. He had the opportunity to travel abroad a bit that summer, and in 1906 he was sent with official government backing to Paris, although he actually got only as far as Nancy. There he wrote most of the poems comprising his "Prozreniya" (Insights), published as part of *Bezsŭnitsi* (Insomnias, 1907). In October 1906 he sent from Nancy to Krŭstev a description of his soul, with distinctly modernist overtones:

My soul is like a balloon with a car filled with the entire population of a zoo – a ball striving upward with the horsepower of a Niagara Falls, while the car is heading downward with all the mulish power of the twentieth century. In my loneliness here I sense a slow ascent of the balloon – and dismay in the car. When I hit the ceiling of my apartment, I shall simply turn the car upside down.

The Bulgarian critic Malcho Nikolov has written that *Bezsŭnitsi* marked a turning point in Yavorov's art. Under the influence of the *Misŭl* group, he holds, Yavorov adhered to a philosophy of extreme individualism, and under the influence of Western literature he moved in the direction of symbolism, although the general hostility of the *Misŭl* group to symbolism insured that he would not become an outright symbolist himself. Nikolov also identifies the influence upon Yavorov of Friedrich Nietzsche in his denial of established absolutes, his disdain for the crowd, and his exaltation of the poet's personality; of Stanisaw Przybyszewski in his demonic ambitions and strivings and in his tendency to hyberbolize his personal feelings into universals; and of Maurice Maeterlinck in his emphasis upon humanity's helplessness and its inexplicable horror in the face of death.

"Pesen na pesenta mi" (Song of My Song), the first poem in *Bezsŭnitsi,* was a more specifically defined turning point in Yavorov's poetic development. In it he treats his own song erotically, personifying it as a woman (the word for song in Bulgarian is feminine): he speaks to his song as a lover might to his beloved. The poet spoke of this change as related to content more than form. Where before he had been precise and clear, he said, in "Pesen na pesenta mi" one finds "the skepticism of a desperate soul, painful self-analysis, unclear, mysterious visions, and a mystical mode of expression." In this instance Yavorov was an excellent critic of his own work, and the elements he mentions here were developed further in other lyrics of this period.

Thus, for example, in "Posveshtenie" (Dedication) the poet addresses *misŭl* (thought, also a feminine noun in Bulgarian) as a woman: "my comrade, my free thought." In "Mozhe bi" (Perhaps) the poet's soul (also feminine) is almost a persona of the piece. If he blurs the line between pure concepts and human beings, he does something analogous for himself and natural phenomena, as when in "Demon" he declares, "I am whirlwind and mist . . . I am sultriness and hoar-frost."

Terror in the face of death now emerges as an important element in Yavorov's writing, in the philosophical, autobiographical, but not especially original "Smŭrtta" (Death), which presents the poet's childhood in a different light from "Velikden":

Death – o dread specter! In my very earliest childhood
When I had departed from my mother's knee
But hardly knew the world, a nameless fear
Had been instilled in me . . . [.]

If the "unknown path" the poet saw earlier at the end of "Velikden" was merely disquieting, now he is virtually in despair over the road ahead:

I wander
without faith that I shall ever find

a way out of this forest
choked in mist.

In "Ugasna slŭntse" (Extinguished Sun) the persona exclaims, "And I lie there, powerless to cry out / In the cemetery silence of the night." Another poem displays the characteristic title "Samota" (Loneliness), a favorite theme of Bulgarian poets.

Another indication of symbolist influence upon Yavorov is his sometimes-excessive interest in alliteration and rhyme. "Blyan" (Dream), for example, suffers from too much emphasis on rhyme; "Dve khubavi ochi" (Two Beautiful Eyes), one of Yavorov's best-known love poems, is based upon inverted sound patterns.

The poem that concludes *Bezsŭnitsi,* however, combines the social concern of Yavorov's first period with the modernism, even decadence, of his second period in an unusual way. In "Shte doydesh ti" (You Will Come) the persona addresses the "long-awaited day," the "savior day" that he is sure will arrive. One could read this as a prediction of a political revolution, but if so, the revolution will have merely personal significance for the poet – and it will not even bring him joy:

You will come, O savior day.
And then, with tender sympathy –
A disembodied spirit – I shall weep alone
Over a cold corpse, my own.
You will come, O long-awaited day!

Bezsŭnitsi was not only a turning point in Yavorov's poetic career, but also its summit: although in 1910 he published a large collection with his most poetic title, *Podir senkite na oblatsite* (Following the Shadows of the Clouds), many of the poems included in it were from earlier collections, and the new ones were somehow crabbed and bitter. One of his best-known lines is "My soul is a groan. My soul is a cry" from "To Lora" (To Lora). In "Dve dushi" (Two Souls) he proclaims, "I do not live; I burn." In "Nedeyte ya razbuzhda" (Do Not Wake Her) he speaks of his soul as an "orphan homeless in the world," a soul that has "fallen asleep in the bosom of the night" and should not be awakened, for it may be dying. His tone in "Slavata na poeta" (The Poet's Glory) is sarcastic and embittered. All of this fits well with an extraordinary passage found in a letter by Yavorov to Krŭstev from August 1908:

Alas, I write, and everything I write ceases to be mine. And I often think that if I could tear from people's hands and memories everything I have given them, I should be the most happy of mortals. Jesus was a great symbolist poet. As he distributed the bread and wine, he would

Poster for Yavorov's play V polite na Vitosha *(In the Foothills of Vitosha, 1911)*

say to his disciples: "Eat, this is my flesh, – drink, this is my blood." Afterwards he wept, at Gethsemane and on Golgotha, as he gave the last remnant of himself to others.... So I must also be allowed an egotistical scream of supreme suffering as I am compelled by my poetic profession to distribute of myself to others ... [.]

This period of relative poetic infertility coincided with a time of instability in Yavorov's life. In 1908 he left the National Library to take up the Macedonian cause again, working with the newspaper *Ilinden* (named for a Macedonian uprising in 1903) and publishing *Khaydushki kopneniya* (Guerrilla Dreams, 1909), a memoir of his experiences with the Macedonian revolutionaries half a decade earlier. But since these activities were not enough to support his way of life, he accepted an invitation to become the dramaturge of the National Theater in August 1908, even though at that point he had never written a play.

Yavorov is now remembered in part as the author of two plays. The second and less important of the two is *Kogato grŭm udari* (When Lightning Strikes 1912; produced 1913), a drama written under the influence of Anton Chekhov, that details the destruction of a family after the gradual disclosure that a man's son is not his own but his best friend's. This was followed by a separately titled epilogue, *Kak ekhoto zaglukhva* (The Echo Fades Away), in which the original situation of the family is nearly duplicated in the succeeding generation.

Yavorov wrote his finest play, *V polite na Vitosha* (In the Foothills of Vitosha), taken from the name of a mountain that towers over Sofia, in 1910. In November of that year he told Krŭstev and Slaveykov that he had had to "liberate his soul" of this tragedy and that he had written every night for a week from 10 P.M. to 4 or 5 A.M. as if he were "living in some sort of nightmare." The play was published in 1911 and first staged later that year.

V polite na Vitosha turned out to be a powerful drama. Its central figure, Khristo Khristoforov, is a young, idealistic political leader in love with Mila Dragodanova, whose brother is at political odds with him. Khristoforov wants Bulgaria to develop its own cultural characteristics in order to justify its modest existence in the world: if it cannot do this, it would be better for it to be a part of Russia, part of a great world culture, he argues. But where Khristoforov dreams of abstract ideals, Mila is entirely wrapped up in him personally: at one point she tells him that, despite her dread of death, she would welcome it if Khristoforov were to die before her. Not surprisingly, she is also very jealous. The drama reaches a climax when her brother tries to compel her to marry another man and abandon Khristoforov. Mila runs out of the house and, whether intentionally or not, falls under a passing streetcar. Upon learning of this catastrophe, Khristoforov reaches her bedside before she expires. To give her courage to face death, he pulls out a pistol and shoots himself by her bedside so that she will not fear to follow him into the darkness. The entire scene is accompanied by thunder and lightning and is a bit overwrought by Western standards. However, it had its analogue in Yavorov's life.

At the time he composed *V polite na Vitosha* Yavorov had just passed through a personal love drama. The fourth member of the *Misŭl* circle, Petko Todorov, who is now remembered as the author of prose idylls written in poetic language, had a sister, Mina, with whom Yavorov was deeply in love for several years. When she died a sudden, tragically early death in Paris in June 1910, Yavorov was distraught. Writing *V polite na Vitosha* was for him a means of overcoming his grief. In March

1912, taking issue with an interpretation by his friend, critic Boyan Penev, Yavorov argued that, although there were obviously autobiographical elements in Khristoforov, in the final account any parallel between them failed because, he said, "I managed to live through my tragedy, whereas he takes his own life."

History soon proved him incorrect in this self-assessment. The tragedy began at the time of Mina Todorova's death when another beautiful young woman, Lora Karavelova, went to Paris to declare her love for Yavorov, for she realized that she had no chance with him as long as Mina was alive. Yavorov would not accept her advances at that time, but she was so persistent that eventually he gave in and married her, thinking he might not return from the first Balkan war, in which the small Balkan countries expelled most of the remnants of Turkish power from the peninsula. When he did come back, he found himself tied to an extremely jealous, possessive woman who berated him if he so much as looked at anyone else. On 30 November 1913 the couple went out for the evening. When they returned Lora began as usual to quarrel with him for flirting with other women, while he assured her she was being unreasonable. He then went into his study to go to bed. Lora entered the room, found the pistol he usually carried in his jacket, and after listening to a few further self-justifications from Yavorov suddenly shot herself in the heart in front of him. Yavorov wrote a suicide note and tried to follow suit but succeeded only in partially blinding himself. Later he went entirely blind.

Afterward, Yavorov's friends tried to brighten his spirits and to avert another suicide attempt, but in vain: he was determined to end his life. On 17 October 1914 he made certain that he would not fail: he first took poison, then shot himself.

On the whole Yavorov is a greater presence in modern Bulgarian culture than any other member of the *Misŭl* circle. His home, including the study where his 1913 tragedy took place, is preserved as a museum in the center of Sofia, and his work is a favorite subject of literary critics.

Bibliography:
Elena Furnadzhieva and others, *P. K. Yavorov 1878–1914: Bio-bibliografiya* (Sofia: Narodna Biblioteka "Kiril i Metodiy," 1978).

Biographies:
Pencho Slaveykov, P. K. Yavorov, P. Yu. Todorov v spomenite na sŭvremennitsite si (Sofia: Bŭlgarski pisatel, 1963);
Nikola Gaydarov, *Zhiteyskata drama na Yavorov: Pravni i psikhologicheski izsledvaniya* (Sofia: Bŭlgarska akademiya na naukite, 1979);
Ganka Naydenova-Stoilova, *P. K. Yavorov: Letopis za zhivota i tvorchestvoto mu* (Sofia: Bŭlgarska akademiya na naukite, 1986);
Milka Markovska, ed., *Spomeni za P. K. Yavorov* (Sofia: Universitetsko izdatelstvo, 1989).

References:
Mikhail Arnaudov, *Yavorov: Lichnost, tvorchestvo, sŭdba,* second edition (Sofia: Bŭlgarski pisatel, 1970);
Pencho Danchev, *Yavorov: Tvorcheski pŭt – Poetika* (Sofia: Bŭlgarski pisatel, 1978);
Ganka Naydenova-Stoilova, *P. K. Yavorov,* volume 1: *Istoriko-literaturno izsledvane* (Sofia: Nauka i izkustvo, 1957); volume 2: *Pŭtyut kum dramata* (Sofia: Nauka i izkustvo, 1962);
Georgi Tsanev, *Pŭtyut na Yavorov* (Sofia: Kamara na narodnata kultura, 1947).

Yordan Yovkov

(9 November 1880 – 15 October 1937)

Lyubomira Parpulova-Gribble
Ohio State University

BOOKS: *Razkazi,* 2 volumes (Sofia: Kniga, 1917, 1918);

Razkazi (Sofia: Shtab na deystvuvashtata armiya, 1917);

Zhetvaryat: Povest (Sofia: Obrazovanie, 1920; revised edition, Sofia: Khemus, 1930);

Posledna radost: Razkazi (Sofia: Khemus, 1926); republished as *Pesenta na koleletata* (Sofia: Khemus, 1933);

Staroplaninski legendi (Sofia: Khemus, 1927);

Vecheri v Antimovskiya khan (Sofia: Zh. Marinov, 1928);

Razkazi, 3 volumes (Sofia: Khemus, 1928, 1929, 1932);

Albena: Drama (Sofia: Khemus, 1930);

Milionerŭt: Komediya (Sofia: Khemus, 1930);

Boryana: Drama (Sofia: Khemus, 1932);

Chiflikŭt kray granitsata: Roman (Sofia: Khemus, 1934);

Zhensko sŭrtse: Razkazi (Sofia: Khemus, 1935);

Ako mozhekha da govoryat: Razkazi (Sofia: Khemus, 1936);

Obiknoven chovek: Drama (Sofia: Khemus, 1936);

Priklyucheniyata na Gorolomov: Roman (Sofia: Khemus, 1938);

Sŭbrani sŭchineniya, 7 volumes, edited by Angel Karaliychev and others (Sofia: Bŭlgarski pisatel, 1956);

Sŭbrani sŭchineniya, 6 volumes, edited by Simeon Sultanov (Sofia: Bŭlgarski pisatel, 1970–1973).

Editions in English: *The White Swallow and Other Short Stories,* translated by Milla Cholakova and Marko Minkov (Sofia: Ministry of Information and Arts, 1947);

Short Stories, edited by Mercia MacDermott, translated by Minkov and Marguerite Alexieva (Sofia: Foreign Languages Press, 1965 / New York: Vanous, 1965);

The Inn at Antimovo; and, Legends of Stara Planina, translated by John Burnip (Columbus, Ohio: Slavica, 1990).

Yordan Yovkov

Yordan Yovkov has the reputation, along with Elin Pelin, of being one of the two outstanding Bulgarian prose writers in the period between the world wars. Of the many attempts to characterize him, "visionary realist," "dreamer," and "bard of Dobruja" are the ones that best capture his distinctive features. Yovkov is called a visionary realist and a dreamer because in his works the realistic details are always refracted through the prism of his memories and dreams. Moreover, he staunchly guarded the sovereignty of his fictional world by declining all invitations to visit the places described in his works. The third characterization, bard of Dobruja, notes the most frequent setting in Yovkov's writings, the large plain in northeastern Bulgaria.

Yordan Stefanov Yovkov was born on 9 November 1880 in the village of Zheravna in the Sliven district. He was the fifth child of Stefan Yovkov and Pena Boychova. Yovkov's father, like most men from that village tucked high up in the Balkan range, spent about ten months a year in Dobruja. There he raised sheep at first and later bought a large farm in the village of Chifutkyoy (now named Yovkovo). Consequently, Yovkov's mother not only took care of her six children and the household for most of the year but also managed to turn the large amounts of wool sent by her husband into homespun material for sale. In 1897 the entire family moved to Chifutkyoy.

Yovkov finished school in his native village (1887–1893), studied for a year in the port city of Ruse (1893–1894), then after a year on his father's farm continued his education in Zheravna and in the town of Kotel (1895–1897), and, finally, completed high school in Sofia (1897–1900). He worked as a teacher in the village of Dolen Izvor (1900–1901) until he was drafted into the army and sent to the school for reserve officers in Knyazhevo, a village near Sofia. During his two years in the military (1902–1904) he tried his hand at poetry. His first published work is the poem "Pod tezhkiya krŭst" (Under the Heavy Cross, 1902), which appeared in the journal *Sŭznanie*. For nine more years Yovkov continued to write verse, but later he virtually disowned these poems by never including them in his collected works. After his military service he enrolled in the University of Sofia to study law but had to drop out because of lack of money.

In 1904 Yovkov returned to Dobruja and for eight years worked as a teacher in various villages. In 1912 he was drafted into the army because of the first Balkan war. During his stay in Dobruja, Yovkov published several short stories. Later, however, he considered them too weak to republish. "Ovcharova zhalba" (A Shepherd's Grief, 1910) was the only piece that, after substantial revisions, met the demanding criteria of the mature author; it was included in *Staroplaninski legendi* (Legends of Stara Planina, 1927). The subtitle of this early story, "Staroplaninska legenda" (A Legend of Stara Planina) – Stara planina is the Bulgarian name for the Balkan range – gave Yovkov the idea for the title of the entire collection. The Dobruja period was important for the author not because of the amount or the quality of the works he produced during that time, but because of the wealth of experiences it supplied for his mature works.

Yovkov won national recognition as a writer with his stories about the wars. During the Balkan Wars (1912–1913) he fought as an officer in Eastern Thrace and later in Macedonia. In 1913 he was wounded in the foot, and only the camaraderie of his soldiers, who carried him for four kilometers, saved him from becoming a prisoner of war.

After a short period of peace between August 1913 and September 1915, Yovkov was called again for military duty as Bulgaria entered World War I. He served at the front only until 10 July 1916. After that date he was assigned to the editorial staff of *Voenni izvestiya* (Military News) and transferred to Sofia. In the capital he joined a group of promising young writers that included the poet Nikolay Liliev, the prose writers Georgi Raychev and Konstantin Konstantinov, and several others. Yovkov still spent time at the front lines, but only as an observer. His stories appeared first in various periodicals, such as *Voenni izvestiya*, *Narod i armiya* (People and Army), *Demokraticheski pregled* (Democratic Review), *Sŭvremenna misŭl* (Contemporary Thought), *Otechestvo* (Fatherland), *Zlatorog* (Golden Horn), *Zora* (Dawn), and others. He republished most of them in his two-volume *Razkazi* (Short Stories, 1917, 1918). Part of them appeared in a single volume also called *Razkazi* (1917). The most extensive collection of war stories can be found in the three-volume edition of *Razkazi* (1928, 1929, 1932).

The war stories exhibit most of the main features of Yovkov's literary work. One is the tendency to view the individual works as parts of thematically and emotionally bound units or, as Bulgarian scholars call them, the first cycles of stories. This tendency first manifested itself in the first *Razkazi*, where stories are organized in several cycles, such as "Zemlyatsi" (Countrymen), "Kray Mesta" (Near the River Mesta), and "Beli rozi" (White Roses). This interest in larger narrative structures also produced the novelettes "Zemlyatsi" (published in *Demokraticheski pregled*, 1915) and *Posledna radost* (Last Joy, 1920). In "Balkan" (1915), the short story that made Yovkov a nationally recognized literary figure, one already finds several of the major themes and ideological concerns of his writings, including the themes of Dobruja, the border, and the unity between humanity and nature. This early work also has the typical Yovkovian structure of the plot that is not organized around a single main episode but unfolds as a series of relatively minor events.

For Yovkov the loss of Dobruja, which after the second Balkan war was taken by Romania, was a deeply personal drama. The border separated him from the place where he spent his youth, where his brothers and sister still lived, and where his parents

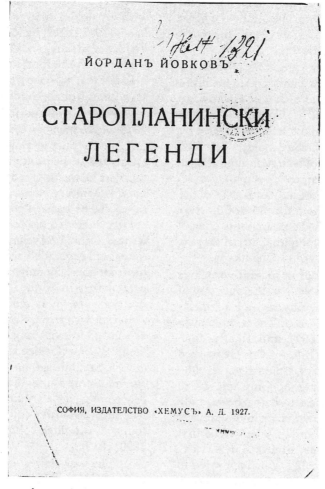

Title page for Yovkov's Staroplaninski legendi *(Legends of Stara Planina, 1927), about larger-than-life characters in a small village*

were buried (his mother died on the day the Romanian army occupied Chifutkyoy). Still, "Balkan" is far from advocating elementary nationalistic ideas. Rather, it explores the psychological impact of ethnic and political frontiers by juxtaposing the animal world and the world of people. The events take place in a Bulgarian village in southern Dobruja. The Bulgarian border guards leave the village and take with them their dogs, including Balkan, who is known for his devotion to his duties as a border guard and his hostility to anyone but the soldiers. The occupied village lives in a state of limbo waiting for the men to return from the front. Suddenly Balkan appears at the village square and raises hopes that the Bulgarian troops are coming back. Moved by his persistent patrolling of the nonexistent border, the peasants remain friends with Balkan even after these hopes have long disappeared. The innkeeper Kŭnyu, whom the dog had previously attacked, now becomes one of his best friends. As time goes by and the situation remains unchanged, the vil-

lagers and Balkan are overwhelmed by despair and anxiety. One evening the dog attacks two Romanian soldiers, but Kŭnyu manages to prevent him from doing any harm. This insignificant incident, however, has grave consequences. The soldiers arrest the innkeeper and detain the dog. The next day Kŭnyu, his face black and blue, returns home. When asked about Balkan, he says that a Romanian soldier told him that the dog refused to eat or drink and died tied up next to the food. Soon after that two soldiers of the night patrols are killed, and the people abandon the village in fear of repercussions.

Another story, "Svetata nosht" (Holy Night, 1917), raises once again the theme of the border. This time the border is the front line dividing the Bulgarian and Greek troops during World War I. Here the psychological probing acquires a religious dimension. The protagonist, a Bulgarian officer, watches the soldiers on both sides of the border celebrate the resurrection of Christ with chants and candles and listens to the recollections of a fellow officer who as a child believed that one Easter Eve he had witnessed the miracle of the Resurrection in the church of his native village. He also thinks of Chanyu, a soldier who constantly reads the gospel, hoping to understand Christ's commandments better, and of the feebleminded old man who on this Easter Eve risks his life crossing the border to see his two grandchildren. The fortifications on both sides of the front line, bristling with barbed wire and heavy artillery, stand as an absurd background to all these events. The implication is that, in spite of its inability to avoid wars at present, there is still hope that through its faith in Christ humanity might eventually free itself of this madness.

Yovkov does not deny that war has its moments of grandeur and special beauty. "Beliyat eskadron" (The White Squadron), for example, gives a masterful picture of the awesome beauty of a cavalry unit on white horses charging into battle. Yovkov can be also deeply impressed by individual acts of bravery and self-sacrifice. Usually such themes appear when the purpose of military action is to liberate the population from foreign oppression. But even then the writer does not abandon his humanistic rejection of war as a senseless act of destruction. With the same humanistic compassion he writes about the Bulgarian servicemen who died during the first Balkan war and about their enemies, the Turkish soldiers killed or captured during the same war. Love, pain, and nostalgia for one's homeland unite Bulgarians, Turks, Greeks, Russians, Germans, Romanians, and even Eski Arap, the old black man from the Sudan whom the Turkish landlord places with others of his countrymen to toil the swampy lands near the river Mesta. Military posturing and rhetoric are the two things that Yovkov definitely despises. The intensity of his disapproval varies from the friendly humor with which he draws Nikola in *Zemlyatsy* to the condescending ridicule toward the Romanian major in "Triumf" (Triumph), to the sarcastic treatment of the Bulgarian colonel in *Posledna radost*.

Posledna radost was first published in 1920 in *Zlatorog*, the most prestigious literary journal of the time, and republished in 1926 in a separate volume, *Posledna radost: Razkazi*, with several other stories, none of which are connected with the wars. Its main character, Lyutskan, is a somewhat ridiculous dreamer who makes a living as a flower vendor. His slightly drooping eyelids, fragile constitution, and black frock coat and bowler, together with his life story, which is a moving mixture of tragic and comic episodes, recall some of the best roles of Charlie Chaplin. Before the war Lyutskan carries his tray of flowers in some kind of ecstasy over their beauty. Hopelessly in love with the most beautiful girl in town, he is particularly sympathetic toward young lovers and uses the medieval symbolism of flowers to pass confidential messages. When the first Balkan war is declared, he enlists as a volunteer, attaches a large wooden cross to his hat, and goes to the front, believing that he will be fighting for a just cause in the battle between the cross and the crescent. The highest point of his otherwise dreadful war experience is the day when a beautiful girl gives him a white chrysanthemum. Sick and exhausted, Lyutskan carries it for days pinned on his uniform and breaks into tears when a soldier, embittered by the hardships of the campaign, stomps the wilted flower into the mud. Lyutskan's last joy is the sight of a white chamomile blooming near the spot where he has fallen, mortally wounded, during one of the most fierce battles of the war. He dies while reaching for it. After a cease-fire is signed, a colonel from a sanitary unit notices Lyutskan's body and remarks that his outstretched arms express a desire "once again to charge against the enemy." The contrast between the painful truth and the pompous propagandistic cliché in the final episode of *Posledna radost* makes it the most powerful antiwar piece in Bulgarian literature. The novelette marks the end of Yovkov's war stories and the beginning of his vintage works of the 1920s and 1930s.

The second edition of this volume appeared as *Pesenta na koleletata* (The Song of the Wheels, 1933), the title of one of the most exquisite stories of the mature Yovkov. The action of "Pesenta na koleletata" takes place in a Turkish village in prewar Dobruja. The blacksmith Sali Yashar has the special talent of assembling the iron parts of the carriages he makes in such a way that each one of them produces a different tune. He is one of the many elderly men typical of Yovkov's mature work who deeply appreciate the beauty of God's creation and believe that love is the most precious thing in human life. Sali Yashar wants to use part of his fortune for some traditional good deed, such as building a fountain, a bridge, or an inn. Several events, however, make him realize that the best good deed he could do is to make his singing carriages, because they bring joy to the people by announcing from far away that a loved one is coming home. His daughter, the charming Shakire, is one of the first images of beautiful women endowed with the special power to change the lives of men who inhabit Yovkov's works of the 1920s and 1930s.

Beauty, especially the beauty of women, is one of the major driving forces of his imaginary world. Critics consider the "cult of beauty" as one of the most characteristic features of Yovkov's writings.

Yovkov's funeral, 1937

Strangely, the man who as an author almost worshiped extraordinary women wanted a wife who would be content to be a devoted homemaker and mother. In 1918 Yovkov married Despina Koleva, a student at the University of Sofia who was fifteen years his junior and whose family lived in Dobrich (now Tolbukin), the largest city of southern Dobruja. In her memoirs she wrote that she was the kind of woman who was happy to live solely for and through her husband. Yovkov was extremely attached to his family and at times somewhat overprotective of his daughter Elka. Yet writing was always his main concern.

In 1918 he not only married but also made the final decision to devote himself to literature. He led a kind of double life. On the one hand he was a neatly dressed man who conscientiously fulfilled his duties as a press attaché and translator at the Bulgarian Legation in Bucharest (1920–1927), a member of the editorial board of the Sofia newspaper *La Bulgarie* (1927–1929), and an associate editor in the Sofia press department (1936–1937). On the other hand he was the almighty creator of a fictional universe in which he lived much more intensely than in the real world. For instance, this usually reserved

man was able to cry all night while writing "Balkan." In 1920 Yovkov developed serious stomach problems. During the resulting attacks he had excruciating pain, could not eat at all, and felt totally exhausted. In spite of this, however, he continued to write in bed. In order to comply with the doctor's orders for a rigorous diet and to save his energy for creative work, Yovkov had to reduce his social life to a minimum and avoided traveling. His illness made him even more withdrawn and at times more irritable. It also increased his worries about the welfare of his family. Over the years these stomach problems developed into a malignant tumor, which caused his death in 1937.

In contrast to his quiet and uneventful personal life, the last two decades of Yovkov's literary career are a real success story. In the 1920s he published the novelette *Zhetvaryat: Povest* (The Harvester, 1920, revised 1930) and three collections of short stories: *Posledna radost: Razkazi, Staroplaninski legendi,* and *Vecheri v Antimovskiya khan* (Evenings in the Inn at Antimovo, 1928). The novelette received mixed reviews, but the other three books were an instant success. In *Zhetvaryat* the action takes place in the same village, Lyulyakovo (The Lilacs) in which the events in "Balkan" were set. It depicts the life of the village in times of peace. The main idea of the work is that the attitude of the peasants toward their land and work is the foundation of their moral and spiritual values. The conflict between the wealthiest man in Lyulyakovo, Vŭlchan, and the poor peasant, Grozdan, is a dramatic clash of social and moral values resolved only when moral – including religious – concerns prevail over social ones. Thus, in an unexpected turn that irritated Marxist critics, a plot that begins as a typical class-struggle story ends with a Christian reconciliation following the principle of "love thy neighbor."

Staroplaninski legendi takes the reader to Zheravna. Yovkov goes back to the nineteenth century and creates ten stories about extraordinary love, bravery, treachery, and suffering. Each piece has an epigraph taken from a folk song, legend, or chronicle that sets the stage for the main conflict. The stories, however, are neither stylizations nor imitations. On the contrary, Yovkov is independent in both the style of the narrative and the development of the plot. The texts unfold in a manner that seems natural and effortless but that in fact is carefully orchestrated by the deliberately unobtrusive narrator. Masterfully painted landscapes and portraits lend depth to the events. The characters are larger-than-life, and the situations are intensely dramatic. In "Shibil" the gypsy outlaw Shibil falls in love with Rada, the beautiful daughter of the wealthiest Bulgarian in Zheruna, a local form of the name Zheravna, and comes down from his hideout in the Blue Rocks to marry her. Her father, with the Turkish authorities, organizes an ambush at the village square. After the first round of shooting Rada realizes what is happening and runs out trying to protect Shibil, but the second round of fire kills them both. In "Prez chumavoto" (In Time of Plague) the most powerful man in Zheruna, Khadzhi Dragan, plans a big wedding for his daughter, Tikha, at a time when everyone is terrified by rumors that the plague is raging in the nearby villages. The entire village gathers at the church to see the ceremony, but as it is about to start Velichko, Tikha's former fiancé, who has been away for three years, suddenly appears and collapses in front of the altar. Black spots, a sure sign of the plague, begin to cover his face. Everyone, including his mother, flees the church. The only person who remains is Tikha, who in a desperate attempt to comfort the dying man sits on the steps to the altar and places his head on her knees.

In *Vecheri v Antimovskiya khan* the romantic trend so pronounced in *Staroplaninski legendi* is still present, although some of its most obvious features have been omitted. Folk legends, chronicles, and the distant past give way to Yovkov's memories of village life in prewar Dobruja. The first story, "Dryamkata na Kalmuka" (Kalmuk Slumbers), written in 1921, introduces six more texts that are tightly knit together by common events and characters. Contemporary readers noted that the description of the inn in the fictional village of Antimovo gives a realistic picture of the inns throughout Dobruja during these years. Literary critics, however, suggest that the inn is also a metaphor connected with the road as a symbol of life.

All seven stories explore the various ways in which men respond to the charm of two remarkable women, the courageous and attractive innkeeper Sarandovitsa and her beautiful daughter Vasilka. The remaining nine stories are mostly unrelated. Among them are such finely crafted pieces as "Po zhitsata" (Along the Wire) and "Grekhŭt na Ivan Belin" (The Sin of Ivan Belin). "Po zhitsata," a story known to virtually every Bulgarian, uses the folk belief that the sight of a white swallow will cure any disease. The white swallow becomes a symbol of the eternal wavering between hope and despair in the hearts of suffering people. "Grekhŭt na Ivan Belin," a work selected to represent Bulgarian literature in the prestigious anthology *Die schönsten Erzählungen der Welt* (The Most Beautiful Stories in the World, 1956), is an impressive prelude to what became an important theme in Yovkov's writings during the 1930s: the issue of the unity between humanity and all other living creatures.

When Yovkov returned to Bulgaria in 1927, he already was a literary celebrity. His status as a leading author was officially recognized in 1929, when upon the recommendation of the Bulgarian Academy of Sciences he was awarded the Kiril and Metodiy prize for literature. He was a welcome contributor to the prestigious magazines *Zlatorog* and *Bŭlgarska misŭl* (Bulgarian Thought) and to the newspaper *Zora*. In spite of his reclusive character, Yovkov had a small circle of close friends, which included university professors, writers, and literary critics. They met frequently in the coffeehouses Bulgaria, Tsar Osvoboditel, and BIAD, which were known as gathering places of the Bulgarian artistic and cultural elite. His friends avoided sitting at Yovkov's table between 5 and 7 P.M. because this was his working time. He sat there with an unlit cigarette in his hand and a cup of linden tea in front of him and thought about his latest work. Even when among friends, Yovkov rarely talked. To use Charles

Moser's apt observation, "the spoken word was not his favorite medium."

The 1930s were a period of intensive experiments that broadened the scope of literary genres, narrative techniques, and thematic range in Yovkov's work. His first play, *Albena: Drama* (1930), was immediately staged by the National Theater, but the reviews were mostly negative. Contemporary critics grossly misjudged the play. In later years it was shown successfully both in the country and abroad, and it is now considered one of the classic Bulgarian dramas. In the process of transforming "Albena," a short story from *Vecheri v Antimovskiya khan,* into a play, Yovkov not only introduced new scenes and characters but also made some changes concerning the main character. In the story Albena is married to an unpleasant boor, the miller Kutsar. She falls in love with another man and helps him kill her husband. When the police arrest her, she does not give away the man she loves and takes the entire blame upon herself. As Albena is about to be taken to prison, the villagers, spellbound by her extraordinary beauty, forget their previous indignation and wish she could be saved. In the play Albena is not an immediate accomplice to the crime, but she is still guilty because her extramarital relationship was the motive for the murder. Albena is one of the few beautiful women in Yovkov's writings who is connected with evil and crime.

Extremely sensitive to negative reviews, Yovkov was deeply hurt by the critical response to his first play. He obviously decided to prove that he could be a successful playwright and quickly published two more works. *Milionerüt: Komediya* (The Millionaire, 1930) is a comedy of errors. It shows amazing changes in attitudes toward a young veterinarian after a rumor that a million leva had been deposited in his name in the local bank spreads around a small provincial town. The critical response to the play was split between strongly positive and completely negative evaluations. Yovkov's next drama, *Boryana* (1932), finally changed the tide and received predominantly positive reviews. Unlike Albena, the charming Boryana is a benevolent force who brightens the dark atmosphere in the extended family of her husband. The weakest of Yovkov's plays is the drama *Obiknoven chovek* (An Ordinary Man, 1936).

Chiflikut kray granitsata (The Farmstead at the Frontier, 1934) is Yovkov's first novel. It describes the gradual disintegration of a *chiflik* (rural estate) in Dobruja and of the old patriarchal way of life. As in *Vecheri v Antimovskiya khan,* the plot revolves around an extraordinary woman, Antitsa, the mistress of the estate, and her daughter Nona. Here, however, Antitsa is already dead and appears only in the memories of the characters. The novel is Yovkov's first work in which the personal lives of the characters are interwoven with recent political events, namely the Communist-organized uprising of 1923. Another new feature is the fact that the conflict is not resolved through spiritual reconciliation. Still, it is obvious that Yovkov does not accept violence as a way of solving social problems. Because of this position, the novel drew sharp criticism from the Communist camp.

The collection of short stories *Zhensko sürtse* (A Woman's Heart, 1935), in spite of its name, is not completely devoted to women. Rather, it deals with a variety of human emotions, such as love and jealousy, vengeance and forgiveness, and suffering and compassion. It includes several excellent pieces, such as "Zhensko sürtse," "Greshnitsa" (Sinner), "Serafim," and "Vülkadin govori s Boga" (Vülkadin Speaks to God).

Ako mozhekha da govoryat (If They Could Speak, 1936) was the last book published while Yovkov was alive. Since its individual stories are bound together by the same characters and the same setting, many critics feel that it is more a novel than a collection of stories. The work was praised as a new stage in the development of the author's manner of writing: the cause-and-effect motivation of the plot is replaced by the correspondence and contrast of relatively independent events, and the narrative is organized not around a central episode but around several semantically important metaphors. Half of the twenty-two stories in this collection have as main characters the animals on a large *chiflik* in Dobruja. The people connected with the farm belong to two categories: those who love and understand the animals and those who have severed their ties with nature. The people from the first category attract the reader with their integrity, physical beauty, and humaneness. The unity between humanity and nature, Yovkov implies, goes much deeper than what one could express with words.

His second true novel, *Priklyucheniyata na Gorolomov: Roman* (Gorolomov's Adventures, 1938), was published after his death. A curious blend of humorous and tragic misunderstandings, it invites comparisons with Miguel de Cervantes's *Don Quixote* (1605, 1615) and Nikolay Gogol's *Myortvye dushi* (Dead Souls, 1842) but has never attracted the attention of the broad reading audience.

After World War II the official attitude to Yovkov's works sharply changed. The Communist critics who had always been unhappy with his treatment of social problems and his respect for traditional moral values, including Christian ones, now gained an upper hand and denounced him as a "bourgeois" writer. In the 1960s, however, due to pressure from the general public and ideologically independent critics, the official evaluation began to change, and in the last two decades Yovkov has been praised again as one of the most talented Bulgarian authors. Speaking of the impact of Yovkov on the later development of Bulgarian literature, Edward Mozejko names Angel Karaliychev, Iliya Volen, Ivaylo Petrov, and Yordan Radichkov as writers who have benefited from his literary achievements. One might also add to this list such a major figure in modern Bulgarian fiction as Emiliyan Stanev. Yovkov's works have been frequently translated and published abroad, and several foreign authors and scholars have written about him.

Letters:

Grigor Vasilev, ed., *Yordan Yovkov: Spomeni i pisma* (Sofia: Knipegraf, 1940);

Despina Yovkova, *Yordan Yovkov: Spomeni, zapiski, pisma,* edited by Elka Yovkova and Petŭr Dinekov (Sofia: Nauka i izkustvo, 1987).

Interview:

Spiridon Kazandzhiev, *Sreshti i razgovori s Yordan Yovkov* (Sofia: Nauka i izkustvo, 1980).

Bibliography:

Petya Dyugmedzhieva and others, *Yordan Yovkov (1880–1937): Biobibliografski ukazatel* (Sofia: Narodna biblioteka "Kiril i Metodiy," 1980).

Biography:

Dimo Minev, *Yordan Yovkov: Dokumenti i svidetelstva za zhivota i tvorchestvoto mu* (Varna: BAN, 1947).

References:

Mikhail Arnaudov, ed., *Yordan Yovkov (1880–1937): Literaturen sbornik* (Sofia: Fakel, 1938);

Elena Dimitrova, "Yordan Yovkov," in *A Biobibliographical Handbook of Bulgarian Authors,* edited by Karen Black, translated by Predrag Matejic (Columbus, Ohio: Slavica, 1981), pp. 200–204;

Petŭr Dinekov, "Zhivotŭt i smŭrtta v tvorchestvoto na Yordan Yovkov," in his *Istoricheska sŭdba i sŭvremennost* (Sofia: Nauka i izkustvo, 1972), pp. 252–261;

Ivan Meshekov, *Yordan Yovkov: Romantik-realist* (Sofia: D. Gologanov, 1947);

Svetoslav Minkov, ed., *Yordan Yovkov (1880–1937): Spomeni, statii i belezhki za zhivota i tvorchestvoto mu* (Sofia: Khemus, 1937);

Charles Moser, "The Visionary Realism of Yordan Yovkov," *Slavic and East European Journal,* 11 (Spring 1967): 43–60;

Edward Mozejko, *Yordan Yovkov* (Columbus, Ohio: Slavica, 1983);

Iskra Panova, *Vazov, Elin Pelin, Yovkov: Maystori na razkaza* (Sofia: Nauka i izkustvo, 1967);

Simeon Sultanov, *Yovkov i negoviyat svyat: Literaturni etyudi* (Sofia: Bŭlgarski pisatel, 1968);

Georgi Tsanev, *Yordan Yovkov: Literaturno-kriticheski statii* (Sofia: Nauka i izkustvo, 1982);

Vladimir Vasilev, "Ot 1920 do dnes: Yordan Yovkov," *Zlatorog,* 14 (April 1933): 185–196.

Oton Župančič
(23 January 1878 – 11 June 1949)

Timothy Pogacar
Bowling Green State University

BOOKS: *Čaša opojnosti* (Ljubljana: Schwentner, 1899);

Pisanice (Ljubljana: Schwentner, 1900);

Čez plan (Ljubljana: Schwentner, 1904);

Samogovori (Ljubljana: Bamberg, 1908);

Lahkih nog naokrog (Ljubljana, 1913);

Sto ugank (Ljubljana: Omladina, 1915);

Ciciban in še kaj (Ljubljana: Omladina, 1915);

Mlada pota (Ljubljana: Omladina, 1920);

V zarje Vidove (Ljubljana: Schwentner, 1920);

Veronika Desniška (Ljubljana: Zvesna tiskarna in knjigarna, 1924);

Dela Otona Župančiča, 4 volumes, edited by Josip Vidmar (Ljubljana: Akademska založba, 1936–1938);

Zimzelen pod snegom (Ljubljana: Državna založba Slovenije, 1945).

Editions and Collections: *Izbrane pesmi,* edited by Janko Glazer (Ljubljana: Državna založba, 1948);

Izbrane pesmi Otona Župančiča, edited by Glazer (Ljubljana: Slovenski knjižni zavod, 1950);

Dela Otona Župančiča, 5 volumes, edited by Cene Vipotnik (Ljubljana: Cankarjeva založba, 1950);

Zbrano delo, volumes 1–3 edited by Dušan Pirjevec, volumes 4–11, edited by Joža Mahnič (Ljubljana: Državna založba, 1956–1989);

Izbrane pesmi, edited by Glazer (Ljubljana: Mladinska knjiga, 1963).

Translations in English: *A Selection of Poems,* edited by Janko Lavrin (Ljubljana: Državna založba, 1967);

"Duma," translated by Henry R. Cooper, Jr., *Slovene Studies,* 8, no. 2 (1986): 87–94.

Oton Župančič

Oton Župančič's origins on the periphery of the Slovene lands and his evolution into Slovenia's central literary figure after World War I parallel his country's road to statehood. The poet was not as politically active as his contemporary Ivan Cankar or the older Ivan Tavčar; neither was he a social critic like the poet Anton Aškerc. Yet his guiding theme, the sanctity of individual expression, perhaps resonated more deeply in his countrymen's imaginations than his fellow writers' overtly partisan ideas. Further, no Slovene writer has presented his or her culture's coming to terms with its European context as did Župančič, who was also an accomplished translator.

He was descended on his mother's side from the Malić family, which had probably resettled on the Kupa River, in the southernmost part of Slovenia that juts into Croatia near Karlovac, from the Lika area of western Croatia in the first quarter of the sixteenth century. Throughout most of that century this extremity of Slovenia, known as Bela Krajina, was subject to Turkish raids that forced the Malić family north. Župančič's early poetry displayed South Slavic motifs, and he remained more sympathetic than most Slovene writers to the neighboring Slavic cultures.

Ana Malić, the oldest daughter of a merchant, married a young trader from Dolenjske Toplice named Franc Župančič in 1876 and bore Oton Župančič on 23 January 1878 in her hometown of Vinica. By 1880 the couple had become proprietors of a tavern and store in Dragatuš, north of Vinica on the way to the main city of Črnomelj. Župančič began school in Dragatuš in 1883. Economic conditions in this part of Slovenia were poor because it remained exclusively dependent on agriculture while the population expanded. Some of the heaviest immigration to North America of all the Slovene regions came from Bela Krajina, a fact that no doubt helped form Župančič's thinking on Slovene national problems. His poetry includes regional folk motifs and linguistic traits.

After Župančič completed two years of school, in 1886 his father took him to the city of Novo Mesto in southern Carniola, where he studied two more years before qualifying to enter the high school. The ten-year-old Župančič received good marks despite the fact that German was the language of instruction and he had had difficulties with the local Slovene dialect his first year in Novo Mesto. Three years later he moved with his parents and his younger brother and sister to Ljubljana and transferred to the high school there, thus gradually coming to know four Slovene dialects, an important factor in the development of his linguistic talent. Debts, legal troubles, and generally poor business conditions had ended the Župančič family's twelve-year stay in Dragatuš.

Župančič helped in his father's new tavern on Saint Peter's (now Trubar Street) in a working-class section of Ljubljana. From 1892 to 1896 he attended the senior high school. Latin, Greek, German, and Slovene – in that order – were the languages studied. The faculty included true scholars, including the well-known lexicographer Maks Pleteršnik. From 1893 to 1896 the young Župančič belonged to a secret young Catholic club of liberal inclination and visited the cultural leader and priest Janez Evangelist Krek, who helped him publish his first children's poems, "Vrtec" and "Angelček," in the Catholic journal *Dom in svet* (Home and World). Other early poems appeared in *Zadruga* (Cooperative) and the leading literary journal, *Ljubljanski zvon* (Ljubljana Bell), all under pseudonyms. In 1896 Župančič completed high school and went to Vienna to study geography and history.

The poet's early years in Ljubljana were important in two respects. He associated with a group of young writers, three of whom – Ivan Cankar, Dragotin Kette, and Josip Murn – later became identified with Župančič as the leading Slovene modernists. Also during this time, Slovene critics debated the value of European literary trends such as naturalism, modernism, and decadence, gradually sorting out literary and moral criteria and providing the basis for the reception of turn-of-the-century Slovene modernist poetry. Thus Župančič was probably prepared for firsthand experience of recent literary trends in Vienna, as well as his introduction to reading Charles Baudelaire, Richard Dehmel, Friedrich Nietzsche, and Paul Verlaine. Literary historian Janko Kos asserts that Župančič was then and remained a poet open to primarily formal literary influences; however, regarding such defining concepts as self-contained art and absolute subjectivism, Župančič was not a modernist poet.

Ample evidence of Župančič's exposure to modernist poetry is found in his first published collection, *Čaša opojnosti* (A Cup of Intoxication, 1899). The sixty-nine mostly brief poems in the volume convey the ecstasy of love and pain at its loss; rapturous enjoyment of beauty, especially in the lyrical self; and an exaltation of the individual and dissatisfaction with the world around him. The book displays variations of poetic orchestration attesting to the young Slovene modernists' creed of individual freedom. If, as they believed, art is the peak of individual expression, poetic forms should reflect the diversity of outlooks and sensations.

One of the exemplary poems in *Čaša opojnosti* addresses the poet's inner self, symbolized as a flower:

You my mysterious blossom, flower of paradise,
I searched for you,
I passed by and looked upon you
and I began to quake.
And my heart contemplated
your hidden power,
and my heart sensed
the night become light.
And in my soul bloomed
uncounted treasures,
all my being longed
for you, for you,
my mysterious blossom, flower of paradise . . .
Oh, I am rich –
help, help me to raise
my soul's treasure!

The rhymes in the original are simple, the parallelisms and rhythm being more important to achieving the emotional effect. Only the symbolic flower stands apart in the rhyme scheme and in the inner setting of the poet's heart (soul and being), which it represents and from whence it arises. The lyric voices the poet's love of his spiritual beauty and plentitude, but the final lines indicate that the poem anticipates rather than celebrates true creativity.

Love poems predominate in *Čaša opojnosti*. Župančič's great love at this time, and for the entire decade, was the Ljubljana teacher Berta Vajdič, who is called Albertina in the poems; however, the melancholy, retrospective tone of the poems predicts the friendship's unsuccessful conclusion. Early in 1901 Župančič returned to Ljubljana having completed some of his exams but without a diploma. Once again he was with his friends Cankar and Murn. In 1899 Kette had died in the former sugar mill on the Ljubljanica River, which was well-known as a dwelling of young artists and laborers. Murn's premature death there in June 1901 was a blow to Župančič. He memorialized his deceased friend in one of the central poems of his next collection, *Čez plan* (Across the Plain, 1904). Its motifs of light and dark, flight and distance, as well as the themes of pride and freedom, link the dead poet with Župančič's own poetic self-image in other works. In the poem he creates and describes auditory impressions, a technique already found in *Čaša opojnosti*. The closing poem of the book, "Ptič Samoživ" (The Phoenix), describes the poet confronting his isolation and gathering the prophetic courage to answer his call, or the call of "his proud eyes."

Župančič's observations of nature in his first two books are best characterized as impressionistic. Temporal elements, the existential relationship between observer and concrete objects, and movement are some of their defining characteristics. The poem "Prišla si" (You've Come) from the earlier collection combines the motifs of distance, eyes, and song in a different arrangement that shows Župančič's impressionistic technique of emphasizing the fleeting nature of human experience:

You've come ... thus comes a golden cloud
upon the evening sky:
the traveler but reined his step
and his eye but caught the marvel,
when dark shrouded it in black veils.

You've come ... thus comes the maidens' song
from the distance to quiet oak groves:
the traveler halts ... it's silent again ... the echo
still ensnared midst the trunks of gaping copses,
and in the rustling of the woods the song is drowned.

You've come ... and I looked in your eyes,
listened to your ringing voice –
you've gone ... the traveler closed his eyes
and dreamed of the cloud's golden color,
and dreamed of a song that will never die out ...

The blending of eroticism and inspiration typical of Župančič's first collection is continued in *Čez plan*. For instance "Vihar" (The Tempest) unites the sensual experience of beauty with an exaltation of power in nature and in the male lover.

The Josip Murn cycle and the closing poems devoted to poetic power circumscribe the main body of love poems. *Čez plan* contains almost sixty texts written between 1899 and early 1903 and evinces Župančič's personal growth, increased awareness of sociopolitical reality, and a more imposing presence of his lyrical self. Perhaps the best-known poem from *Čez plan* was written and received as a protest against what Župančič's generation perceived as the dominant Liberal party's cynical use of Francè Prešeren's heritage and against the literary establishment in general. Each of the three parts of "Pesem mladine" (Song of Youth) begins with the image of God leading young Slovenes, compared to the Israelites, in the form of a flame. Župančič criticizes backwardness and oppression in sweeping terms, concluding with a call to the future, which he declares to be the only just way to honor the poet, understood as both the iconic Prešeren and contemporary artists. Župančič helped build and exploited the Prešeren myth in much less glowing terms in the caustic lyric "Daj, drug, zapoj" (Lend, Friend, Your Song): Prešeren's pagan hero Črtomir from the epic *Krst pri Savici* (1836; translated as "The Baptism on the Savica," 1985) becomes in Župančič's poem an antihero who succumbs to the imperative of Christianization because of his impotence. If Prešeren's hero seems to compromise for the cultural survival of his nation, Župančič's Črtomir – "our hero," he calls him – is reduced to a symbol of impotence and a victim of imperial forces. This poem in particular anticipates the less triumphant tone of his next collection.

The artist's prophetic image in *Čez plan* is the result of Župančič's intense individualism and new-found expression of will. From this time on he frequently refers to the poet as the center of the universe. Years later he expressed this central tenet to writer and critic Izidor Cankar: "Poetry is a sort of path to oneself and to man, a sort of vital movement towards things and the middle of all things, a drawing near to the center. . . . At such times I feel there is nothing around me but a sort of power and radiation all about." This view was not only an artistic concept, but in another sense it was justified by Župančič's rapid maturation into his role as the nation's leading poet. Beside *Čaša opojnosti* and *Čez plan* he had published his first collection of children's verses, *Pisanice* (Painted Easter Eggs, 1900), and a one-act play titled "Noč na verne duše" (All Souls Eve, 1904), which appeared in *Ljubljanski zvon,* and he had translated William Shakespeare's *Julius Caesar* (1599).

Župančič's private life had not yet stabilized. He had been employed in an uncle's business in Vienna for a time and earned some income from publishing, yet he still remained largely dependent on his struggling parents. From the fall of 1901 until early 1903 he served in the infantry in Gradec. These were difficult months. He was almost penniless, and barracks life was taxing. His younger sister by eight years died in 1902, and he was unable to attend the funeral. That year he began the satiric poem "Jerala," which he continued writing into the 1920s but left unfinished. The first part deals with the poet's lot; a second chapter is about social conditions in Bela Krajina. Župančič intended to lead his narrator throughout Slovenia in what was a reflection of his longing for home.

Since he did not return from Vienna with a diploma, Župančič was ineligible for a permanent teaching position when he was decommissioned, but he worked one semester in the classical high school and gave Slovene language instruction privately during 1903. In 1904 his father lost his tavern, and the family was forced to move several times within Ljubljana during the next two years since his father was employed in the civil service, first in Kočevje in the south and then in Ljubljana. His parents lived modestly their entire lives.

During the next several years the poet learned about other European societies firsthand. He traveled to Paris, where he lived with friends for several months in 1905, then was back in Ljubljana in 1906, a year in which he continued publishing poetry in the leading journals *Ljubljanski zvon* and *Slovan.* In Paris Župančič read Henri Bergson, Emile Verhaeren, and Walt Whitman, attended lectures, and became acquainted with contemporary French art. In the fall of 1907, on the recommendation of a friend, he obtained an attractive tutoring job at Duke Waldburg's home in Württemberg. All of these experiences proved beneficial to his writing as his most celebrated collection, *Samogovori* (Monologues), was prepared for press in 1908. In order to obtain a better price Župančič abandoned his Slovene publisher, who had printed Kette and Murn's posthumous collections, and gave the book

Title page for Župančič's first collection of poems, which were influenced by Slovene modernism

to a German publisher. Unfortunately, the year 1908 saw political unrest in Slovenia, culminating in the shooting of Slovene demonstrators and a boycott of all German-owned businesses in September. For this reason, not only did conservative critics pan *Samogovori* as expected, but others were critical or ignored it. This was the first of several occasions in his lifetime that Župančič had to cope with the public's misunderstanding, which he usually did by retreating into silence.

The poems in *Samogovori* revolve around the oppositions between the ideal and real, body and soul, and reason and intuition. The first of five cycles is made up, for the most part, of melancholy love poems. Occasional verses follow. The third and fourth cycles contain philosophical poems that make liberal use of religious symbols. The longer poems "Z vlakom" (By Train) and "Duma" (translated as "Duma," 1986) complete the book.

Župančič incorporates the new oppositions in his love poems; for example, in "Umetnik in ženska" (The Artist and the Woman) the female presence mollifies the poet's doubt and conflict with reality, which arise from his extreme individualism and – in contrast to *Čez plan* – lack of confidence. A more optimistic resolution of life's contradictory claims on the individual is found in "Prebujenje" (Awakening). The world's temporal, spatial, and ascriptive inadequacies, epitomized in the constant vying of sea and sky on the horizon, are overcome by belief in the ideal. The first and last stanzas of the seventy-one-line poem provide a nocturnal setting that conveys a sense of universality while suggesting a sleeping state from which the poet's heart wakes. Indeed, night shades predominate in *Samogovori*. The heart represents, as from his earliest poetry, the poetic self, here bewildered by the surrounding silence. The contradictions with which the poet wrestles produce varying moods from poem to poem.

The most vigorous verses in *Samogovori* are the ninety lines of "Z vlakom" in part five. The poem binds nocturnal imagery and geographic elements for the purpose of expanding the poet's native realm or homeland, which he addresses directly: "With me, you stars, with me, you mountains! / Spread, expand, my native realm, / foam forth like the sea / to the limitless horizon, / my home!" The actual setting is the poet's departure from Ljubljana by train into the "demonic night." Despite his supplication to his native land to abide with him, in the closing lines a foreign dawn greets the poet incognito.

The Whitmanesque character of "Z vlakom" is attenuated in Župančič's longest complete work of poetry, "Duma," which also employs free verse. The title, free form, and content resemble the Ukrainian lyrical epic form of the fifteenth to seventeenth centuries adopted by nineteenth-century poets. But, as in his handling of Prešeren's epic, Župančič draws the reader's attention to the modern context, in particular its urban and industrial aspect. The first part of "Duma" features a female voice that praises the idyllic beauty of the Slovene countryside, followed by a longer description of the foreign, modern world by a male voice. The male voice argues the value of foreign ideas and progress, as does the speaker in part 3, who also alludes to his homeland's failings and the tragedy of emigrants. In six concluding stanzas the poet returns to the question of locating his homeland spatially, then ends by comparing his heart to an oyster and his searchings to pain that produces a pearl.

The juxtaposition in these stanzas of Mount Triglav, symbolic of Slovenia, and the Karavankan Alps with industrial images encapsulates the tension between the first two parts of the poem. In part 3 the poet had used doves and migrating swallows in depicting his home in Bela Krajina, then substituted the comparison of his young poetic self with a dove in search of home for that of an eagle seeking the homeland. The doves in the former comparison were dazed in flight above the burning house; Slovenia's emigrants in the conclusion are charmed. The woman in the first part has a "pearl white laugh," which resonates in the work's culminating stanza. By interweaving such images the poet supports the unity of the poem, the four-part structure of which suggests idealism. Though the core national problem is seen in its modern context, the imagery and motivation harken back to Župančič's essentially romantic roots, especially as regards his view of the Slovene people. His most pronouncedly patriotic poems were written in the last years of World War I and were motivated by the situation in the Italian borderlands and the Slovenes' relations with other nations within the crumbling empire.

In 1909, in debt and on poor terms with Vajdič and his friends, Župančič left Slovenia. He went to Vienna, where he completed some of his exams, then taught in Württemberg again. Returning to Ljubljana at the end of 1910, he was crushed to learn of Vajdič's marriage. He began a poor existence in rented rooms – occasionally staying with his parents, who had moved into the center of the city again – until taking up quarters with Cankar on a hill, Rožnik, outside Ljubljana. While staying with Cankar, he became a regular visitor of the Kesslers, a family that he had probably met in 1908 and that was involved in the pro-Yugoslav movement. Župančič eventually married Ani Kessler, thirteen years younger, on 22 September 1913. In the meantime, his fortunes improved as he served as dramaturge in the Ljubljana Drama Society in 1911, translated Charles Dickens's *Oliver Twist* (1838) in 1911, and became city archivist in early 1913, for which he received several months of training in Prague. His sons Marko and Andrej were born in 1914 and 1916. In 1916 the family moved to Dalmatin street, where they lived until the end of World War II. A daughter, Jasna, was born in 1923.

Župančič understood children well and was a devoted family man. His first collection of poetry was actually the children's book *Pisanice*. Another, *Lahkih nog naokrog* (Quick Feet All About), appeared in 1913. In 1915 the poet and publisher Ivan Zorman brought out two more collections, *Sto ugank* (A Hundred Riddles) and *Ciciban in še kaj* (Ciciban and

Something More). Župančič's poetry for children became progressively more concerned with the physical world, paralleling his other collections, and richer in fantasy. It remains among the best children's poetry in Slovene.

With his settling into family life and Slovenia's preliminary step toward nationhood within the newly created Yugoslavia, Župančič's original work decreased. These private and public factors were not direct causes of a decline in the poet's output; rather, they point to the close of the modernist period in Slovene literature, marked in part by Cankar's death in 1918, and also a waning of the poet's erotic and spiritual impulses that inspired his greatest poetry. Selected works were published in *Mlada pota* (New Paths, 1920), and his poetry written from the outset of World War I was collected in *V zarje Vidove* (The Dawn of Vid's Day, 1920). The latter book primarily includes poems occasioned by events during and immediately after the war but also some love and confessional poems, including the well-known "Vihar," an impressionistic view of the harmony inherent in contrasting phenomena. Another poem conceived at the Kessler family's house on Lake Bled, "Slap" (The Waterfall), extrapolates from the unity of two young lovers to that of all people and times through the symbol of the constantly flowing water. This poem is a prime example of Župančič's appreciation of Bergson's concept of universal creative energy.

While impressionistic technique persists in *V zarje Vidove* and varying stress patterns already seen in *Čez plan* continue, there is also a tendency toward more proselike language and expressionist formulations. Župančič had indeed employed all of the formal techniques that had revolutionized Slovene poetry during those three decades. His energy during the 1920s, however, was applied to translating and to his work as dramaturge and secretary of the National Theater in Ljubljana. Among his major accomplishments in translation during the decade were Shakespeare's *As You Like It* (1599), *A Comedy of Errors* (1594), *Macbeth* (1606), *The Merchant of Venice* (1596-1598), *A Midsummer Night's Dream* (1595 or 1596), *Othello* (1602-1604), and *The Taming of the Shrew* (circa 1592); Friedrich von Schiller's *Maria Stuart* (1800); and works by G. K. Chesterton, Gustave Flaubert, and Pedro Calderón de la Barca. In the 1930s and 1940s he translated Shakespeare's *Hamlet* (1601), *Romeo and Juliet* (1595), and *The Tempest* (1611); Molière's *Tartuffe* (1664); and Hugo von Hofmannsthal's *Jedermann* (Everyman, 1912). In particular, Župančič's renderings of Shakespeare were a major contribution to Slovene letters and theater (he translated eighteen works of Shakespeare in all), although close scrutiny of his work shows that it left room for improvement by later translators. Shakespeare's influence can be seen in Župančič's second and last complete drama, the five-act tragedy in blank verse *Veronika Desniška* (1924). Set in the early fifteenth century in the court of the ambitious counts of Celje, its portrayal of political motivation conquering love was received as a reflection upon Yugoslav state building. However, the play's strengths are its individual scenes and poetic language rather than the overall dramatic effect, which is hampered by ambiguous characterization and static movement.

Župančič was not happy with his position in the theater, which improved when he became managing director in 1929, nor was he especially pleased with the recognitions he received on his ten-year anniversaries and from various international associations such as P.E.N. when he was not inspired to write poetry. He found relief in vacations on Lake Bled, where he also did some translating. The tension between his lyrical self and the Slovene question came to a head in 1932 with the publication of his essay "Adamič in slovenstvo" (Adamic and the Slovenes) concerning the American writer Louis Adamic's visit. Župančič's observation that Adamic had forfeited little in abandoning Slovene as a teenager and becoming an American writer caused a storm of controversy in the Slovene intellectual community, which was threatened by Yugoslav cultural centralism. The essay caused trouble for *Ljubljanski zvon* and resulted in Župančič's retreat from further public pronouncements on the subject. In his rather naive impressions of Slovenia, Adamic names Župančič once, preferring the epithet "Slovenia's foremost living poet" to make the point of how Slovenes value literature:

In 1928, as I was told some time after my homecoming, Slovenia's foremost living poet – Oton Župančich – celebrated his fiftieth anniversary, and on that occasion, which was a special holiday for the entire province, nearly one hundred delegations from all parts of the country called on him. Most of them were peasant delegations, some from remote mountain villages and counties. All of them brought him gifts. Women came with exquisite national handwork. Some presented him with bags of potatoes, hams, sausages, and other peasant products. Nearly all of them brought him money appropriated by their respective county or village councils. Singing societies came from country districts to sing under his window. Student quartettes from Lublyana schools sang his poems set to music.

Ironically, while Adamic basked in the overwhelming attention given him from the moment he disembarked in Trieste and found the attention substantiated in this story about Župančič, the poet was experiencing a trying dry spell in his writing.

He attempted to end the drought in retreat near the southwestern mountain of Snežnik. There he wrote about forty poems collectively titled "Med ostrnicami" (Amid the Haystacks), inspired by the surrounding countryside in the spirit of then-widespread regional literature. Seventeen of them appeared in *Ljubljanski zvon* in 1934, some of the remainder in his last book, *Zimzelen pod snegom* (The Snowbound Evergreen, 1945). Poems composed during World War II, many of them didactic, predominate in Župančič's final book. Although he clearly supported the Communist Partisans, the authorities did not dare arrest him. They did, however, arrest his family members, including his daughter and son Marko, in 1942. His son Andrej fought with the Partisans. Župančič was more optimistic about Slovene prospects after the second of two world wars. He spoke at the official ceremony at Ljubljana University when the new government was installed on 9 May 1945, saying in part, "Proud joy fills my heart. After a difficult and long period administrative power has passed into unsoiled, clean hands that are eager to work for our future, for a new order and justice in our homeland and throughout the world." He left the theater after the war. The last years of his life were devoted to work on Slovene linguistics in the Academy of Sciences.

Župančič, with Prešeren and Cankar, is among the leading Slovene writers of the last two centuries. Župančič's keen perception of the political threats to Slovene culture during his lifetime, coupled with national and international literary recognition, assured his public standing. Yet his most enduring contribution to Slovene letters is his credo of individual liberty, conceived of in harmony with his nation but also with the modern world.

Interview:

Izidor Cankar, *Obiski* (Ljubljana: Nova založba, 1920).

Biographies:

Evgen Lovšin, *Rod in mladost Otona Župančiča* (Ljubljana: Mladinska knjiga, 1975);

Josip Vidmar, *Oton Župančič* (Ljubljana: Partizanska knjiga, 1978).

Bibliographies:

Alfonz Gspan, *Letopis Slovenske akademije znanosti in umetnosti,* volume 3 (Ljubljana: SAZU, 1950), pp. 235–254;

Caricature of Župančič by H. Smrekar

Janko Moder, "Bibliografija prevodov Otona Župančiča," in *Oton Župančič v prevodih,* edited by Kajetan Gantar, Frane Jerman, and Moder (Koper, Yugoslavia: Lipa, 1979), pp. 135–147.

References:

Louis Adamic, *The Native's Return: An American Immigrant Visits Yugoslavia and Discovers His Old Country* (New York: Harper, 1934);

France Bernik, ed., *Oton Župančič: Simpozij 1978* (Ljubljana: Slovenska matica, 1979);

Bernik, "Slovenska moderna v 'horizontu pričakovanja,' " *Slavistična revija,* 39 (1991): 439–453;

Matej Bor and others, "Oton Župančič v gledališču," *Dokumenti Slovenskega gledališkega muzeja,* 14, no. 31 (1978): 2–65;

Andrej Capuder, "Bergson in Župančič po Samogovorih," *Primerjalna književnost,* 7, no. 1 (1984): 13–22;

Henry R. Cooper, Jr., "Župančič and Whitman," *Southeastern Europe,* 9 (1982): 147–159;

Arturo Cronia, *Ottone Župančič* (Rome: Istituto per l'Europa orientale, 1928);

Kajetan Gantar, Frane Jerman, and Janko Moder, eds., *Oton Župančič v prevodih* (Koper: Lipa, 1979);

Velemir Gjurin, "Semantic Inaccuracies in Three Slovene Translations of *King Lear,*" *Acta Neophilologica,* 9 (1976): 59–83;

Alfonz Gspan, "Iz časov moderne: Po Župančičevih pismih Ivan Prijatelju iz 1907–1910," *Sodobnost,* 11, nos. 8–10 (1963): 779–798, 897–903;

Marko Juvan, *Imaginarij Kersta v Slovenski literaturi* (Ljubljana: Literatura, 1990), pp. 150–156;

Joža Mahnič, "Oton Župančič in Louis Adamič," *Zbornik Občne Grosuplje,* 13 (1984): 85–98;

Mahnič, "Župančičevo delo za gledališče," *Dokumenti Slovenskega gledališkega in Filmskega Muzeja,* 17, nos. 36–37 (1981): 7–34;

Mahnič, "Župančič kot prevajalec," *Jezik in slovstvo,* 26 (1981): 175–177;

Boris Paternu, "Slovene Modernism: Župančič, Kosovel, Kocbek," *Cross Currents,* 7 (1988): 321–336;

Dušan Pirjevec, "O liriki slovenske moderne," *Naša sodobnost,* 3, nos. 3–4 (1955): 238–264;

Pirjevec, "Oton Župančič in Ivan Cankar," *Slavistična revija,* 12, nos. 1–4 (1959–1960): 83–87;

Dmitrij Rupel, "Oton Župančič, 1878–1978," *Sodobnost,* 26 (1978): 89–111;

M. I. Ryžova, "Russkaia poèzija v slovenskikh perevodakh Otona Župančiča," *Russkaia literatura,* 20, no. 3 (1977): 157–168;

Anton Slodnjak, *Obrazi in dela slovenskega slovstva: od začetka do osvoboditve* (Ljubljana: Mladinska knjiga, 1975), pp. 239–253;

Lucien Tesnière, *Oton Joupantchitch, poète slovène: L'Homme et l'oeuvre* (Paris: Les Belles-lettres, 1931);

Josip Vidmar, *Oton Župančič: Kritična portretna študija* (Ljubljana: Hram, 1935);

Franc Zadravec, *Elementi slovenske moderne književnosti* (Murska Sobota: Pomurska založba, 1980), pp. 117–161;

Zadravec, "Oton Župančič in Louis Adamič," in *Louis Adamič: Simpozij,* edited by Janez Stanonik (Ljubljana: Univerza v Ljubljani, 1981), pp. 101–111;

Zadravec, *Zgodovina slovenskega slovstva,* volume 5 (Maribor: Obzorja, 1970), pp. 52–59;

Zadravec, ed., *Obdobje simbolizma v slovenskem jeziku, književnosti in kulture* (Ljubljana: Filozofska fakulteta, 1983), pp. 239–284, 309–332.

Checklist of Further Readings

Barac, Antun. *A History of Yugoslav Literature.* Ann Arbor: Michigan Slavic Publications, 1973.

Barac. *Hrvatska književnost od Preporoda do stvaranja Jugoslavije.* 2 volumes. Zagreb: JAZU, 1954–1960.

Bogdanović, Dimitrije. *Istorija stare srpske književnosti.* Belgrade: Srpska književna zadruga, 1980.

Bogišić, Rafo. *O hrvatskim starim pjesnicima.* Zagreb: Matica hrvatska, 1968.

Bŭlgarska akademiya na naukite, Sofia, Institut za literatura. *Istoriya na bŭlgarskata literatura.* 4 volumes. Sofia: Bŭlgarska akademiya na naukite, 1962–1976.

Cronia, Arturo. *Storia della letteratura Serbo-Croata.* Milan: Nuova accademia editrice, 1956.

Deretić, Jovan. *Istorija srpske književnosti.* Belgrade: Nolit, 1983.

Deretić. *Srpski roman 1800–1950.* Belgrade: Nolit, 1981.

Dinekov, Petŭr. *Problemi na starata bŭlgarskata literatura.* Sofia: Bŭlgarski pisatel, 1989.

Dinekov. *Vŭzrozhdenski pisateli.* Sofia: Nauka i izkustvo, 1962.

Eekman, Thomas. *Thirty Years of Yugoslav Literature (1945–1975).* Ann Arbor: Michigan Slavic Publications, 1978.

Ekspresionizam i hrvatska književnost. Zagreb: Kritika, 1969.

Holton, Milne, and Vasa D. Mihailovich, eds. *Serbian Poetry from the Beginnings to the Present.* New Haven: Yale Center for International and Area Studies, 1988.

Igov, Svetlozar. *Istoriia na bŭlgarskata literatura (1878–1944).* Sofia: Bŭlgarska akademiya na naukite, 1990.

Kadić, Ante. *Contemporary Croatian Literature.* The Hague: Mouton, 1960.

Kadić. *Contemporary Serbian Literature.* The Hague: Mouton, 1964.

Kadić. *From Croatian Renaissance to Yugoslav Socialism.* The Hague: Mouton, 1969.

Kapidžić-Osmanagić, Hanifa. *Srpski nadrealizam i njegovi odnosi sa francuskim nadrealizmom.* Sarajevo: Svjetlost, 1966.

Kašanin, Milan. *Srpska književnost u srednjem veku.* Belgrade: Prosveta, 1975.

Kermauner, Taras. *Dileme sodobnega slovenskega pesništva.* Ljubljana: Cankarjeva založba, 1971.

Koblar, F. *Dvajset let slovenske drame.* Ljubljana: Slovenska matica, 1964.

Koljević, Svetozar. *The Epic in the Making.* Oxford: Clarendon Press, 1980.

Kombol, Mihovil. *Povijest hrvatske književnosti do narodnog preporoda.* Zagreb: Matica hrvatska, 1945.

Koneski, Blaže. *Makedonska književnost.* Belgrade: Srpska književna zadruga, 1961.

Koneski and others, eds. *Kniga za Kliment Ohridski.* Skopje: Kočo Racin, 1966.

Košutić, Vladeta P. *Parnasovci i simbolisti u Srba.* Belgrade: SANU, 1967.

Lasić, Stanko. *Sukob na književnoj ljevici 1928–1952.* Zagreb: Liber, 1970.

Legiša, Lino, ed. *Zgodovina slovenskega slovstva.* 7 volumes. Ljubljana: Slovenska matica, 1956–1971.

Leovac, Slavko. *Helenska tradicija i srpska književnost XX veka.* Sarajevo: Veselin Masleša, 1963.

Likova, Rozaliya. *Istoriya na bŭlgarskata literatura: Poeti na 20-te godini.* Sofia: Nauka i izkustvo, 1979.

Lord, Albert B. *The Singer of Tales.* Cambridge, Mass.: Harvard University Press, 1960.

Lukić, Sveta. *Contemporary Yugoslav Literature.* Urbana: University of Illinois Press, 1972.

Manning, Clarence A., and Roman Smal-Stocki. *The History of Modern Bulgarian Literature.* New York: Bookman, 1960.

Matejić, Mateja, and Karen Black, eds. *A Biobibliographical Handbook of Bulgarian Authors.* Columbus, Ohio: Slavica, 1981.

Maver, Giovanni. *Letteratura Slovena.* Milan, 1960.

Mihailovich and Matejić. *A Comprehensive Bibliography of Yugoslav Literature in English 1593–1980.* Columbus, Ohio: Slavica, 1984; First Supplement 1981–1985 (1988); Second Supplement 1986–1990 (1992).

Moser, Charles A. *A History of Bulgarian Literature 865–1944.* The Hague: Mouton, 1972.

Palavestra, Predrag. *Istorija moderne srpske književnosti.* Belgrade: Srpska književna zadruga, 1986.

Pavić, Milorad. *Istorija srpske književnosti baroknog doba (XVII–XVIII vek).* Belgrade: Nolit, 1970.

Pavić. *Istorija srpske književnosti klasicizma i predromantizma: Klasicizam.* Belgrade: Nolit, 1979.

Pavletić, Vlatko. *Panorama hrvatske književnosti XX stoljeća.* Zagreb: Stvarnost, 1965.

Pavlović, Dragoljub. *Iz naše stare književnosti.* Sarajevo: Svjetlost, 1964.

Peleš, Gajo. *Poetika suvremenog jugoslavenskog romana 1945–1961.* Zagreb: Naprijed, 1966.

Penev, Boyan. *Istoriya na novata bŭlgarska literatura.* 4 volumes. Sofia: Bŭlgarski pisatel, 1976–1978.

Popović, Miodrag. *Istorija srpske književnosti: Romantizam.* 3 volumes. Belgrade: Nolit, 1968–1972.

Radojičić, Djordje Sp. *Tvorci i dela stare srpske književnosti.* Titograd: Grafički zavod, 1963.

Rechnik na bŭlgarskata literatura. 3 volumes. Sofia: Bŭlgarska akademiya na naukite, 1976–1982.

Šicel, Miroslav. *Pregled novije hrvatske književnosti.* Zagreb: Matica hrvatska, 1966.

Skerlić, Jovan. *Istorija nove srpske književnosti.* Belgrade: Kolarčeva zadužbina, 1914.

Slavov, Atanas. *The "Thaw" in Bulgarian Literature.* Boulder: East European Monographs, 1981.

Slodnjak, Anton. *Geschichte der slovenischen Literatur.* Berlin: De Gruyter, 1958.

Slodnjak. *Slovensko slovstvo.* Ljubljana: Mladinska knjiga, 1968.

Stanoyevitch, Milivoy. *Early Yugoslav Literature 1100–1800.* New York: Columbia University Press, 1922.

Subotić, Dragutin. *Yugoslav Popular Ballads: Their Origin and Development.* Cambridge: Cambridge University Press, 1932.

Torbarina, Josip. *Italian Influence on the Poets of the Ragusan Republic.* London: William & Norgate, 1931.

Vaupotić, Miroslav. *Hrvatska suvremena književnost/Contemporary Croatian Literature.* Zagreb: Croatian P.E.N. Club Center, 1966.

Vitošević, Dragiša. *Srpsko pesništvo 1900–1914.* 2 volumes. Belgrade: Vuk Karadžić, 1975.

Zadravec, Franc, and Jože Pogačnik, eds. *Zgodovina slovenskega slovstva.* 8 volumes. Maribor, Yugoslavia: Založba Obzorja, 1968–1972.

Živković, Dragiša. *Evropski okviri srpske književnosti.* 3 volumes. Belgrade: Prosveta, 1970–1983.

Translations of Primary Works into English

Alexieva, Marguerite, Petco Drenkoff, and Sider Florin, trans. *In the Fields: Bulgarian Short Stories.* Sofia: Narodna kultura, 1957.

Bartók, Béla, and Albert B. Lord, eds. *Serbo-Croatian Folk Songs and Instrumental Pieces from the Milman Parry Collection,* volume 1 of *Yugoslav Folk Music.* Albany: State University of New York Press, 1978.

Bonifačić, Antun, ed. *The Anthology of Croat Verse 1450–1950.* Chicago, 1981.

Bowring, John, ed. and trans. *Narodne srpske pjesme / Servian Popular Poetry.* London: Privately printed, 1827.

Butler, Thomas, ed. and trans. *Monumenta Serbocroatica: A Bilingual Anthology of Serbian and Croatian Texts from the Twelfth to the Nineteenth Century.* Ann Arbor: Michigan Slavic Publications, 1980.

Ćurčija-Prodanović, Nada, ed. and trans. *Heroes of Serbia.* London: Oxford University Press, 1964.

Ćurčija-Prodanović, ed. and trans. *Yugoslav Folk Tales.* New York: Oxford University Press, 1957.

Cvetanovska, Danica, Irma Rosenfeld, and William Rosenfeld, trans. *The Moon and the Well: Macedonian Folk Tales.* New York: Grienfield Review Press, 1988.

Danchev, Pencho, ed., Marguerite Alexieva, trans. *Bulgarian Short Stories.* Sofia: Foreign Languages Press, 1960.

Davies, Ellen Chivers, ed. *Tales of Serbian Life.* London: Harrap, 1919.

Djordjević, Mihailo, ed. and trans. *Anthology of Serbian Poetry: The Golden Age.* New York: Philosophical Library, 1984.

Filipič, France, ed., Janko Lavrin, trans. *Some Other Land.* Maribor, Yugoslavia: Založba Obzorja, 1965.

Goy, E. D., ed. and trans. *Zelen bor / A Green Pine: An Anthology of Love Poems from the Oral Poetry of Serbia, Bosnia and Herzegovina.* Belgrade: Prosveta/Vukova zadužbina, 1990.

Grant, Geoffrey, ed. *Told in Serbia: Fifteen Peasant Tales.* London: Roberts, 1928.

Holton, Milne, and Vasa D. Mihailovich, eds. *Serbian Poetry from the Beginnings to the Present.* New Haven: Yale Center for International and Area Studies, 1988.

Kijuk, Predrag R. Dragić, ed. *Medieval and Renaissance Serbian Poetry.* Belgrade: Relations, 1987.

Kirilov, Nikolai, and Frank Kirk, eds. *Introduction to Modern Bulgarian Literature: An Anthology of Short Stories.* New York: Twayne, 1969.

Koljević, Svetozar, ed. and trans. *Yugoslav Short Stories.* London: Oxford University Press, 1966.

Lavrin, ed. *An Anthology of Modern Yugoslav Poetry.* London: Calder, 1962.

Lenski, Branko, ed. *Death of a Simple Giant, and Other Modern Yugoslav Stories.* New York: Vanguard, 1965.

Lockhart, John Gibson, ed. *Translations from the Servian Minstrelsy to Which Are Added Some Specimens of Anglo-Norman Romances.* London, 1826.

Low, D. H., ed. *The Ballads of Marko Kraljević.* Cambridge: Cambridge University Press, 1922.

Mackenzie, G. Muir, and A. P. Irby, eds. *Marko, the King's Son, Hero of the Serbs.* New York: McBride, 1932.

Matejić, Mateja, and Dragan Milivojević, eds. *An Anthology of Medieval Serbian Literature in English.* Columbus, Ohio: Slavica, 1978.

Matthews, William, and Anton Slodnjak, eds. *The Parnassus of a Small Nation: An Anthology of Slovene Lyrics.* London: Calder, 1957.

Matthias, John, and Vladeta Vučković, eds. and trans. *The Battle of Kosovo.* Athens: Ohio University Press–Swallow Press, 1987.

Meredith, Owen, ed. *Serbski Pesme; or National Songs of Serbia.* London: Chapman-Hall, 1861.

Mihailovich, ed. *White Stones and Fir Trees: An Anthology of Contemporary Slavic Literature.* Rutherford, N.J.: Fairleigh Dickinson University Press, 1977.

Mijatovich, Chedo, ed. *Servia and the Servians.* London: Pitman, 1908.

Mijatovich, Elodie Lawton, ed. and trans. *Kossovo: An Attempt to Bring Serbian National Songs about the Fall of the Serbian Empire at the Battle of Kossovo into One Poem.* London: Isbister, 1881.

Mijatovich, ed. *Serbian Fairy Tales.* London: Heinemann, 1917.

Mijatovich, ed. *Serbian Folk-Lore: Popular Tales.* London: Isbister, 1874.

Mikasinovich, Branko, Milivojević, and Mihailovich, eds. *Introduction to Yugoslav Literature: An Anthology of Fiction and Poetry.* New York: Twayne, 1973.

Miletich, John, ed. and trans. *The Bugarštica: A Bilingual Anthology of the Earliest Extant South Slav Folk Narrative Song.* Urbana: University of Illinois Press, 1990.

Morison, Walter Angus, ed. *The Revolt of the Serbs against the Turks: Translations from the Serbian National Ballads.* Cambridge: Cambridge University Press, 1942.

Mrkich, Dan, ed. and trans. *Kosovo: The Song of the Serbs.* Ottawa: Commoners' Publishing Society, 1989.

Muegge, Maximilian A., ed. *Serbian Folk Songs, Fairy Tales and Proverbs.* London: Drane, 1916.

Noyes, George Rapall, and Leonard Bacon, eds. *Heroic Ballads of Servia.* Boston: Sherman-French, 1913.

Parry, Milman, Albert Bates Lord, and David E. Bynum, eds. *Serbo-Croatian Heroic Songs,* 5 volumes. Cambridge, Mass.: Harvard University Press & Serbian Academy of Science, 1953–1979.

Pennington, Anne, and Peter Levy, eds. and trans. *Marko the Prince: Serbo-Croat Heroic Songs.* London: Duckworth, 1983.

Petrovitch, Woislav M., ed. *Hero Tales and Legends of the Serbians.* London: Harrap, 1914.

Pinto, Vivian, ed. *Bulgarian Prose and Verse*. London: University of London Press, 1957.

Popović, Pavle, ed. and trans. *Jugo-Slav Stories*. New York: Duffield, 1921.

Pridham, Radost, and Jean Norris, eds. and trans. *The Peach Thief and Other Bulgarian Stories*. N.p.: Casell, 1963.

Riggs, E., ed. *Popular Bulgarian Songs and Proverbs*. New York, 1863–1864.

Rootham, Helen, ed. *Kossovo: Heroic Songs of the Serbs*. Oxford: Blackwell, 1920.

Selver, Paul, ed. *Anthology of Modern Slavonic Literature in Prose and Verse*. New York: Dutton, 1919.

Stanojevich, Beatrice Stevenson, ed. *An Anthology of Yugoslav Poetry: Serbian Lyrics*. Boston: Badger, 1920.

Stipčević, Augustin, ed. *An Anthology of Yugoslav Short Stories*. New Delhi: Indian Council for Cultural Relations, 1969.

Tammer, Zora P., and Anthony Tammer, eds. and trans. *Macedonian Folk Songs*. Vallejo, Cal.: Privately printed, 1981.

Tempest, Peter, ed. *Anthology of Bulgarian Poetry*. Sofia: Sofia Press, 1980.

Traerup, Birthe, ed. *East Macedonian Folk Songs: Contemporary Traditional Material from Maleševo, Pijanec and Razlog*. Copenhagen: Akademisk Forlag, 1970.

Underwood, Edna, ed. and trans. *The Slav Anthology*. Portland, Oreg.: Mosher Press, 1931.

Wiles, James William, ed. *Serbian Songs and Poems: Chords of the Yugoslav Harp*. London: Allen & Unwin, 1917.

Zimmerman Devrnja, Zora, ed. *Serbian Folk Poetry: Ancient Legends, Romantic Songs*. Columbus, Ohio: Kosovo, 1986.

Zorman, Ivan, ed. and trans. *Slovene (Jugoslav) Poetry*. Cleveland, 1928.

Chronology of Important Events, Authors, and Works

third–sixth centuries	Slav migration to Balkan Peninsula
679	Subjugating the Slavs, original Bulgars Slavicized by ninth century
eighth–ninth centuries	Slovene independent state
eighth century–1102	Croatian independence
850	First Serbian state
ninth century	South Slavs convert to Christianity; first Bulgarian written documents
tenth century	First Slovene written documents
eleventh century	First Croatian and Serbian written documents
1175–1235	Saint Sava, founder of Serbian church, education, and literature; beginning of Serbian ascendance under Nemanjić dynasty
1389	Battle of Kosovo; Serb loss of independence
1459	Last Serbian state conquered by Turks
1521	Marko Marulić, *Judita*
1550	Marin Držić, *Dundo Maroje*
1568	Petar Hektorović, *Ribanje i ribarsko prigovaranje*
1637	Ivan Gundulić, *Osman*
1690	Great Serbian migration to Vojvodina
1783	Dositej Obradović, *Život i priključenija*
1804	First Serbian uprising
1814	First Serbian grammar and first collection of folk poetry published by Vuk Stefanović Karadžić
1815	Second Serbian uprising; Serbian liberation
1828	Illyrian movement born in Croatia
1834	Francè Prešeren, *Sonetni venec*
1845	Petar Petrović Njegoš, *Luča mikrokozma*
1846	Ivan Mažuranić, *Smrt Smail-Age Čengića*
1847	Njegoš, *Gorski vijenac*
1877	August Šenoa, *Seljačka buna*
1878	Berlin Congress; liberation of Bulgaria
1893	Ivan Vazov, *Pod igoto*
1899	Ivan Cankar, *Vinjete*

1908	Annexation of Bosnia by Austria-Hungary; Jovan Dučić, *Pesme*
1912	First Balkan war against Turks
1913	Second Balkan war between Serbia and Bulgaria
1914–1918	World War I; Serbia occupied by Central Powers
1918	Creation of first Yugoslavia; Slovenia and Croatia independent but within a unified South Slav state
1932	Miroslav Krleža, *Povratak Filipa Latinovicza*
1934	King Alexander assassinated in Paris
1941	Conquered by Germany, Yugoslavia abolished; newly created Independent State of Croatia committing genocide against Serbs; beginning of the resistance against the occupation
1943	Yugoslavia re-created under Marshal Tito
1945	Yugoslavia together again; all South Slavs ruled by Communists; Macedonia in its own republic for first time, leading to flowering of literature; Ivo Andrić, *Na Drini ćuprija, Travnička hronika,* and *Gospodjica*
1948	Yugoslavian split with Soviet Union
1961	Nobel Prize in literature for Ivo Andrić
1980	Tito's death
1989	Bulgaria free from communism
1992	Yugoslavia split up again; independence for Slovenia, Croatia, Bosnia-Herzegovina, and Macedonia; civil war in Bosnia

Contributors

Michael Biggins..*University of Washington*
Michele Bulatovic..*University of Louisville*
Henry R. Cooper, Jr. ....*Indiana University*
Dasha Čulić Nisula ....*Western Michigan University*
Ljerka Debush..*Harvard University*
Thomas Eekman.......................................*University of California, Los Angeles*
Ellen Elias-Bursać..*Cambridge, Massachusetts*
Radmila J. Gorup ....*Columbia University*
E. D. Goy ....*Cambridge University*
E. Celia Hawkesworth..*University of London*
Dubravka Juraga..*University of Arkansas*
Ante Kadić ....*Indiana University*
Maria B. Malby..*East Carolina University*
Vasa D. Mihailovich ....*University of North Carolina at Chapel Hill*
Vladimir Miličić...*Western Washington University*
Nicholas Moravcevich ....*University of Illinois at Chicago*
Charles A. Moser ....*George Washington University*
Irma M. Ozbalt ....*Montreal, Quebec*
Lyubomira Parpulova-Gribble ....*Ohio State University*
Timothy Pogacar..*Bowling Green State University*
Kleo Protokhristova...*University of Plovdiv*
Graham W. Reid ....*University of Skopje*
Peter Scherber ....*University of Göttingen*
Cynthia Simmons ....*Boston College*
Biljana Sljivic-Simsic ....*University of Illinois at Chicago*
George Vid Tomashevich...................*State University of New York — College at Buffalo*

Cumulative Index

Dictionary of Literary Biography, Volumes 1-148
Dictionary of Literary Biography Yearbook, 1980-1993
Dictionary of Literary Biography Documentary Series, Volumes 1-11

Cumulative Index

DLB before number: *Dictionary of Literary Biography*, Volumes 1-148
Y before number: *Dictionary of Literary Biography Yearbook*, 1980-1993
DS before number: *Dictionary of Literary Biography Documentary Series*, Volumes 1-11

A

Abbey Press DLB-49

The Abbey Theatre and Irish Drama,
1900-1945 ....DLB-10

Abbot, Willis J. 1863-1934 ....DLB-29

Abbott, Jacob 1803-1879 ....DLB-1

Abbott, Lee K. 1947- DLB-130

Abbott, Lyman 1835-1922 ....DLB-79

Abbott, Robert S. 1868-1940 ....DLB-29, 91

Abelard, Peter circa 1079-1142 .....DLB-115

Abelard-Schuman DLB-46

Abell, Arunah S. 1806-1888 ....DLB-43

Abercrombie, Lascelles 1881-1938 ...DLB-19

Aberdeen University Press
Limited DLB-106

Abish, Walter 1931- DLB-130

Abrahams, Peter 1919- DLB-117

Abrams, M. H. 1912- DLB-67

Abrogans circa 790-800 ....DLB-148

Abse, Dannie 1923- DLB-27

Academy Chicago Publishers DLB-46

Accrocca, Elio Filippo 1923- DLB-128

Ace Books DLB-46

Achebe, Chinua 1930- DLB-117

Achtenberg, Herbert 1938- DLB-124

Ackerman, Diane 1948- DLB-120

Acorn, Milton 1923-1986 ....DLB-53

Acosta, Oscar Zeta 1935?- DLB-82

Actors Theatre of Louisville DLB-7

Adair, James 1709?-1783? DLB-30

Adam, Graeme Mercer 1839-1912 ...DLB-99

Adame, Leonard 1947- DLB-82

Adamic, Louis 1898-1951 ....DLB-9

Adams, Alice 1926- Y-86

Adams, Brooks 1848-1927 ....DLB-47

Adams, Charles Francis, Jr.
1835-1915 .... DLB-47

Adams, Douglas 1952- Y-83

Adams, Franklin P. 1881-1960 ...... DLB-29

Adams, Henry 1838-1918 .... DLB-12, 47

Adams, Herbert Baxter 1850-1901 ... DLB-47

Adams, J. S. and C.
[publishing house] DLB-49

Adams, James Truslow 1878-1949 ... DLB-17

Adams, John 1735-1826 .... DLB-31

Adams, John Quincy 1767-1848 ..... DLB-37

Adams, Léonie 1899-1988 .... DLB-48

Adams, Levi 1802-1832 .... DLB-99

Adams, Samuel 1722-1803 ...... DLB-31, 43

Adams, William Taylor 1822-1897 .. DLB-42

Adamson, Sir John 1867-1950 ...... DLB-98

Adcock, Arthur St. John
1864-1930 .... DLB-135

Adcock, Betty 1938- DLB-105

Adcock, Betty, Certain Gifts DLB-105

Adcock, Fleur 1934- DLB-40

Addison, Joseph 1672-1719 .... DLB-101

Ade, George 1866-1944 .... DLB-11, 25

Adeler, Max (see Clark, Charles Heber)

Adonias Filho 1915-1990 .... DLB-145

Advance Publishing Company DLB-49

AE 1867-1935 .... DLB-19

Ælfric circa 955-circa 1010 .... DLB-146

Aesthetic Poetry (1873), by
Walter Pater DLB-35

After Dinner Opera Company Y-92

Afro-American Literary Critics:
An Introduction DLB-33

Agassiz, Jean Louis Rodolphe
1807-1873 .... DLB-1

Agee, James 1909-1955 .... DLB-2, 26

The Agee Legacy: A Conference at
the University of Tennessee
at Knoxville Y-89

Aguilera Malta, Demetrio
1909-1981 ....DLB-145

Ai 1947- DLB-120

Aichinger, Ilse 1921- DLB-85

Aidoo, Ama Ata 1942- DLB-117

Aiken, Conrad 1889-1973 ....DLB-9, 45, 102

Aikin, Lucy 1781-1864 ....DLB-144

Ainsworth, William Harrison
1805-1882 ....DLB-21

Aitken, Robert [publishing house] ...DLB-49

Akenside, Mark 1721-1770 ....DLB-109

Akins, Zoë 1886-1958 ....DLB-26

Alabaster, William 1568-1640 ......DLB-132

Alain-Fournier 1886-1914 ....DLB-65

Alarcón, Francisco X. 1954- DLB-122

Alba, Nanina 1915-1968 ....DLB-41

Albee, Edward 1928- DLB-7

Albert the Great circa 1200-1280 ...DLB-115

Alberti, Rafael 1902- DLB-108

Alcott, Amos Bronson 1799-1888 .....DLB-1

Alcott, Louisa May
1832-1888 ....DLB-1, 42, 79

Alcott, William Andrus 1798-1859 ....DLB-1

Alcuin circa 732-804 ....DLB-148

Alden, Henry Mills 1836-1919 ......DLB-79

Alden, Isabella 1841-1930 ....DLB-42

Alden, John B. [publishing house] DLB-49

Alden, Beardsley and Company DLB-49

Aldington, Richard
1892-1962 .... DLB-20, 36, 100

Aldis, Dorothy 1896-1966 ....DLB-22

Aldiss, Brian W. 1925- DLB-14

Aldrich, Thomas Bailey
1836-1907 .... DLB-42, 71, 74, 79

Alegría, Ciro 1909-1967 ....DLB-113

Alegría, Claribel 1924- DLB-145

Aleixandre, Vicente 1898-1984 .....DLB-108

Aleramo, Sibilla 1876-1960 ....DLB-114

B

C

G

O

Cumulative Index

Y

Z